Cultures of Empire

Cultures of Empire

Colonizers in Britain and the Empire in the Nineteenth and Twentieth Centuries

A READER

EDITED BY CATHERINE HALL

ROUTLEDGE

NEW YORK

First published in the USA in 2000 by Routledge Inc.
29 West 35th Street, New York, NY 10001-2299, USA
http://www.routledge-ny.com

Routledge edition published by special arrangement with Manchester University Press, Oxford Road, Manchester M13 9NR, UK

Library of Congress Cataloging-in-Publication Data applied for

ISBN 0-415-92906-7 *hardback*
     0-415-92907-5 *paperback*

Typeset in Caslon and Frutiger Condensed
by Koinonia Ltd, Manchester
Printed in Great Britain
by Bookcraft (Bath) Ltd, Midsomer Norton

Contents

PART III THE EMPIRE AND ITS OTHERS 'AWAY'

PART IV LEGACIES OF EMPIRE

List of illustrations

Plates

Maps

Acknowledgements

This reader comes out of my teaching at the University of Essex and University College London over the last few years and I thank the students who have worked with me on imperial and postcolonial questions. The choice of articles was very difficult, and thanks to Antoinette Burton, David Glover, Joanna de Groot, Peter Hulme, Cora Kaplan, Keith McClelland, Clare Midgley and Jane Rendall for discussing it with me. Stuart Hall, Gail Lewis and Bill Schwarz all gave me comments on the introduction: especial thanks to them. The staff at Manchester University Press were most helpful. The editor and publishers wish to thank the following for permission to use copyright material: M. Jacqui Alexander, for 'Not just (any) body can be a citizen: the politics of law, sexuality and postcoloniality in Trinidad and Tobago and the Bahamas', *Feminist Review*, 48 (1994), pp. 5–23, by permission of the author; John Barrell, for 'Death on the Nile: fantasy and the literature of tourism, 1840–60', *Essays in Criticism*, 41:2 (1991), pp. 99–127, by permission of Oxford University Press; Antoinette Burton, for 'Who needs the nation? Interrogating "British" history', *Journal of Historical Sociology*, 10:3 (1997), pp. 227–48, by permission of Blackwell Publishers; Luke Gibbons, for 'Race against time: racial discourse and Irish history', from *Neocolonialism*, ed. Robert J. C. Young, *Oxford Literary Review*, 13:1–2 (1991), pp. 95–117, copyright © 1991 *Oxford Literary Review*, by permission of the *Oxford Literary Review*; Joanna de Groot, for '"Sex" and "race": the construction of language and image in the nineteenth century', in Susan Mendus and Jane Rendall, eds, *Sexuality and Subordination: Interdisciplinary Studies of Gender in the Nineteenth Century*, Routledge (1989), pp. 89–129, by permission of the author; Patricia Hayes, for '"Cocky" Hahn and the "Black Venus": the making of a Native Commissioner in South West Africa, 1915–46', *Gender and History*, 8:3 (1996), pp. 364–92, by permission of Blackwell Publishers; Janaki Nair, for 'Uncovering the *zenana*: visions of Indian womanhood in Englishwomen's writings, 1813–1940', *Journal of Women's History*, 9:4 (1998), pp. 104–30, by permission of Indiana University Press; Gyan Prakash, for 'Subaltern

Studies as postcolonial criticism', *American Historical Review*, 99 (1994), pp. 1475–90, by permission of the American Historical Association; Sonya O. Rose, for 'Sex, citizenship and the nation in World War II Britain', *American Historical Review*, 103:4 (1998), pp. 1247–76, by permission of the American Historical Association; Nancy Leys Stepan, for 'Race, gender, science and citizenship', *Gender and History*, 10:1 (1998), pp. 25–52, by permission of Blackwell Publishers; Ann Laura Stoler, for 'Cultivating bourgeois bodies and racial selves', in Ann Laura Stoler, *Race and the Education of Desire: Foucault's 'History of Sexuality' and the colonial Order of Things*, pp. 98–136, copyright © 1996 Duke University Press, by permission of Duke University Press; Nicholas Thomas, for 'Colonial conversions: difference, hierarchy and history in early twentieth-century evangelical propaganda', *Comparative Studies in Society and History*, 34 (1992), pp. 366–95, by permission of Cambridge University Press; Elizabeth Vibert, for 'Real men hunt buffalo: masculinity, race and class in British fur traders' narratives', *Gender and History*, 8:1 (1996), pp. 4–21, by permission of Blackwell Publishers; Kathleen Wilson, for 'Citizenship, empire and modernity in the English provinces, *c.* 1720–90', *Eighteenth Century Studies*, 29:1 (1995), pp. 69–96, copyright © 1995 American Society for Eighteenth Century Studies, by permission of the Johns Hopkins University Press. Every effort has been made to trace the copyright holders but if any have been inadvertently overlooked the publishers will be pleased to make the necessary arrangement at the first opportunity.

1

Introduction:
thinking the postcolonial,
thinking the empire

CATHERINE HALL

Europe is literally the creation of the Third World. (Frantz Fanon)

J. R. Seeley was an imperial thinker and the founding father of British imperial history. He brought the empire into historiography and devised a philosophy of history appropriate to writing about empire. Introducing his argument about the significance of empire for the late nineteenth-century nation, he drew attention to 'the simple obvious fact of the extension of the English name into other countries of the globe, the foundation of Greater Britain'. This 'simple obvious fact' had been neglected: he saw it as his task to make the English rethink nation and empire. In his widely read series of lectures published in 1883 as *The Expansion of England* he commented on the indifference with which empire was viewed and noted with dismay, 'nor have we even now ceased to think of ourselves as simply a race inhabiting an island off the northern coast of the continent of Europe'. His concern was to challenge that insular thinking and encourage an imperial frame of mind. For Seeley, Regius Professor of History at Oxford, the empire meant the colonies of settlement – Australia, New Zealand, the West Indies, Canada and South Africa. Like the Liberal politician Charles Dilke before him, his interest focused on those areas which were truly colonies, the offshoots of the mother country, Greater Britain. For Seeley these territories were 'in the main … one nation' and should not be thought of as outside England, and for him England was the nation. The dominance of 'Englishmen' meant that smaller racial groups such as the Celts or the Maoris could be comfortably assimilated 'without marring the ethnological unity of the whole'. India was another matter entirely, for the 250 million Indians were 'of alien race and religion, and are bound to us only by the tie of conquest'.[1] The *Dictionary of National Biography*, that custodian of the national culture, remarked in its notice on Seeley that:

> the book was eagerly taken up by a very large public: it drew attention, at an opportune moment, to a great subject; it substituted imperial for provincial

interests; and it contributed perhaps more than any other single utterance to the change of feelings respecting the relations between Great Britain and her colonies which marks the end of the nineteenth century.[2]

Late nineteenth-century popular imperialism, in other words, owed much to Seeley, and imperial history was to become intimately associated with his name.

Seeley's focus on the name, England, the race, Englishmen, and the nation, which is also an empire, provides a rich starting point for an investigation of the new questions which have informed the work represented in this reader.[3] For rethinking imperial history in postcolonial times requires reconnecting race, nation and empire: Seeley knew they were intimately connected. The English – and for him it was the English rather than the British – took their name to 'empty' parts of the globe which they settled and made 'English throughout'. The scale of this expansion meant that in the eighteenth century, to his mind, 'the history of England is not in England but in America and Asia'. Yet he was concerned that in the 1880s the significance of this Greater Britain was not appreciated: having lost its first empire in the 1770s, England was in danger of losing another at a moment when the United States was expanding in the west and Russia in the east. Moreover, England was losing it because the English had not fully realized they were an imperial race. It was essential that the deep bonds between England and her global territories should be recognized: nation and empire were not separate, they were one and the same. And expansion 'was necessary to the national life'.[4]

Seeley was exploring these arguments before the moment of high imperialism in the late nineteenth century, and before nationalisms and anti-colonialisms became a significant threat to the stability of empire. But his considerations are pertinent to our thinking now. In the time after empire, when expansion, defined by Seeley as essential to the national life, is finished, and new nations have replaced old colonies, how do race and nation look? If the nation is no longer an empire, what is it? If the English have not succeeded in making Britain, let alone the empire, 'English throughout', what are the effects? If Englishness is no longer a hegemonic identity, defining the national characteristics of all those who claim belonging in Britain, then what does it mean to be British? When the fantasy of 'ethnological unity' – one people, one nation – can no longer be maintained, what kind of nation is left? When Jamaicans, Barbadians and Trinidadians, Indians, Pakistanis and Bangladeshis, Sri Lankans, Nigerians and others from the erstwhile empire are an established presence in Britain, no longer imperial subjects at a distance but British citizens at home, what difference does that make to 'our island story'? When the Scots and the Welsh have devolved government, how does England look, and what is its relation to Britain? As the European Union moves towards federalism, what does national sovereignty mean? Globalization, the power of multinational corporations, ecological patterns which pay no attention to national boundaries, movements of population on an unprecedented scale – all these developments place the centrality of the nation as a sovereign power in question. It is these issues, issues of identity and belonging, which have underpinned the new interest in nation and empire, culture and colonialism, among the historians, anthropologists and cultural critics whose work is represented in this book.

While the British have a particular set of questions which disrupt and trouble older histories of progress and civilization, of national homogeneity and self-determination, these questions of identity and belonging cross the globe, never in quite the same ways but with significant lines of connection.[5] Histories which are built around nations and nationalisms no longer seem entirely adequate to some, and histories have become hotly contested terrains. Empires, forgotten in the wake of decolonization as an embarassment and source of guilt, re-emerge as it becomes clear that neo-colonialism is alive and well, and that imperial histories are playing a part in postcolonial politics. Some Australians, no longer at ease with their history as a white dominion, thinking of abandoning the monarchy in favour of a republic and looking to Asia rather than the West for their future, have rediscovered Aboriginality and their own history as colonizers.[6] Indian nationalist historiography, a response to colonialism, has been substantively critiqued, and the nation is no longer celebrated as *the* answer to all social, economic and political problems.[7] Irish nationalist historiography has been subjected to extensive revision, and nationalism is no longer seen as the be-all and end-all of Irish history.[8] Canadians are rethinking internal and external colonialisms in the wake of separatisms and the mobilization of First Peoples.[9] Americans in the United States are rediscovering the 'racing' of their nation and the complex histories of inclusion and exclusion upon which the American dream has been constructed.[10] New times, the time of globalization and migration, the time of supranational states and small nations, the time of ethnic confict and racial belonging, all these require new forms of analysis and understanding and new histories to help us grasp the past in the present. Seeley's categories – race, nation and empire – remain central to reconfiguring those histories in postcolonial times.

'Postcolonial', the term which at its most commonsensical denotes 'after colonialism', is a contentious term. While it is widely recognized that the colonial system which dominated the nineteenth and early twentieth centuries has been dismantled, it is clear that neo-colonialism, informal economic domination by, for example, the United States, continues to flourish. Is it, therefore, misleading to use the term 'postcolonial'? The ending of the great empires of Western Europe, however, marks a very distinct moment in world history, and the term 'postcolonial' can, as Peter Hulme suggests, be used descriptively, to signify the aftermath of those world systems.[11] This is not to suggest that all societies which were colonized were colonized in the same ways, nor that all postcolonial societies are postcolonial in the same ways, but that the term draws attention to the systems of colonialism and the relations between colonizer and colonized which operated.[12] Postcolonial forms of analysis serve to highlight the centrality of colonial relations to patterns of global politics and power in the early modern and modern worlds. But, as Ali Rattansi argues, the term 'postcolonialism' signifies both a historical periodization and a particular form of theorization and analysis.[13] That historical periodization

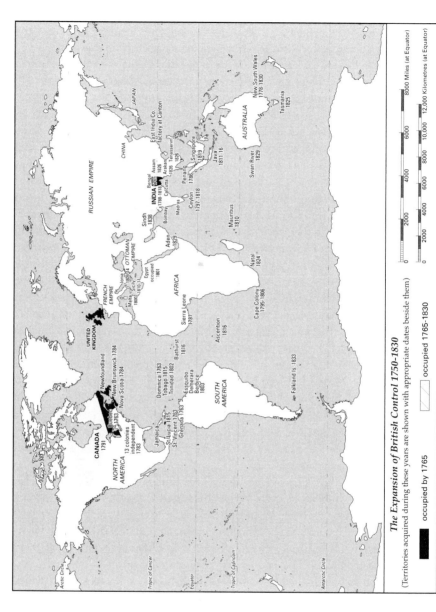

Figure 1.1 The expansion of British control, 1750–1830

has to be understood broadly: it spans the American revolution of the 1770s, the Latin American anti-colonial struggles of the late eighteenth and nineteenth centuries, and the twentieth-century dismantling of the great Western empires.

In the contemporary struggles against colonialism it had been assumed that the overthrow of colonial systems and the establishment of full self-government for those who had been colonized would mean a break with all that had gone before. By the late 1970s and 1980s, however, it had begun to be apparent that decoloniz-ation must tackle forms of representation as well as political and economic systems. Colonialism was about material exploitation and a political structure which depended on the rule of the colonizers over the colonized – but it was also about something more. 'Postcoloniality', as David Scott observes, 'has been concerned principally with the decolonization of representation: the decolonization of the West's theory of the non-West'.[14] The particular form of intellectual enquiry that is postcolonial is a form of enquiry focused on the relations between colonizer and colonized, on the mutuality of those relations, on, as the Martiniquan theorist Frantz Fanon put it, turning the usual common sense upside down: 'Europe is literally the creation of the Third World.'[15] Colonialism made both colonizers and colonized, and postcolonial forms of analysis attempt to understand that process.

The critic Simon Gikandi argues that the postcolonial moment may be understood as the moment of transition, the time when it has become clear that decolonization has not resulted in total freedom. At this point, he suggests, 'the foundational histories of both the metropolis and the decolonized nation, and the categories that defined them, would begin to unravel in unexpected ways'.[16] Some of that unravelling is reflected in this volume.

The British Empire

The British Empire provides the central focus of the volume. From the sixteenth century British expansion proceeded steadily, and the empire was the product of the new world systems built in the aftermath of the 'discoveries' – world systems which were rooted in colonial growth. Colonialism, the creation of colonies and their exploitation in systematized ways, deriving from the Latin term *colonia*, meaning a settlement of Roman citizens in a newly conquered territory, is often used interchangeably with imperialism. I use 'colonialism' to describe the European pattern of exploration and 'discovery', of settlement, of dominance over geograph-ically separate 'others', which resulted in the uneven development of forms of capital-ism across the world and the destruction and/or transformation of other forms of social organization and life.[17] I use 'imperialism' to refer to the late nineteenth/early twentieth century moment when European empires reached their formal apogee.

The expansion of the British Empire from the sixteenth century was interrupted by the War of American Independence and a significant loss of territory and influence, with a consequent diminution of enthusiasm on the part of the British for colonial adventures. By the Napoleonic Wars, however, Britain was

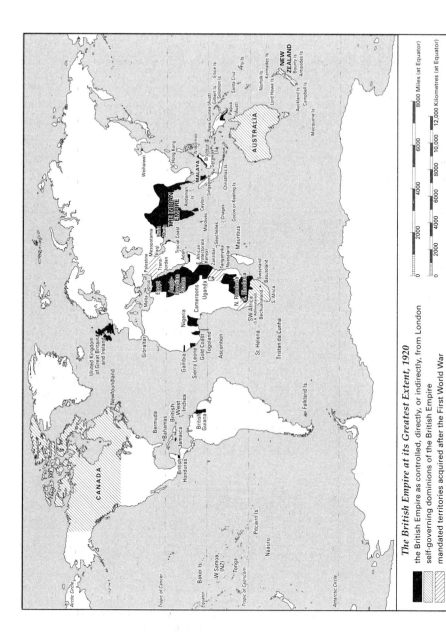

The British Empire at its Greatest Extent, 1920

■ the British Empire as controlled, directly, or indirectly, from London

self-governing dominions of the British Empire

▨ mandated territories acquired after the First World War

Figure 1.2 The British Empire at its greatest extent, 1920

recovering such interest and by 1820, having made considerable territorial gains, Britain ruled 26 per cent of the world's total population.[18] That empire was differentiated: from colonies of settlement such as Australia, New Zealand and Canada to the protectorates and dependencies – some tiny, such as the Ionian Islands, others vast, like India – in which a small group of colonial officials ruled an indigenous population. By the mid-nineteenth century the white settler colonies were achieving representative self-government in domestic matters while the dependencies were firmly bound into the control of the Crown and the Colonial Office. Such a neat demarcation, however, fails to represent the differences in systems of colonial rule across the empire. As Bernard Porter puts it in relation to the mid-nineteenth century:

> There was no single language covering the whole empire, no one religion, no one code of laws. In their forms of government the disparities between colonies were immense: between the Gold Coast of Africa, for example, ruled despotically by British officials, and Canada, with self-government in everything except her foreign policy, and here London's control was only hazily defined. In between, Nigeria was ruled by a commercial company, the states of Australia by their own prime ministers, Sierra Leone by a governor, Sarawak by a hereditary English rajah, Somaliland by a commissioner responsible to India, Egypt by a consul-general who in theory only 'advised' a native Egyptian cabinet, Ascension Island by a captain, as if it were a ship…. There was no kind of overall logic …[19]

But the variety of forms of rule *was* underpinned by a logic of rule – colonial governmentality, what Partha Chatterjee calls 'the rule of colonial difference'. This was the rule that distinguished the colonizers from the colonized, that was predicated on the power of the metropole over its subject peoples.[20]

Seeley believed that the dominance of the Manchester school in the mid-nineteenth century, with its insistence on the primacy of free trade, reflected lack of interest in the empire, a lack of interest which urgently needed rectifying. This became the orthodoxy in imperial historiography until a new interest in the 'imperialism of free trade' in the 1950s, and the revelation that the 'informal empire' had continued to grow in the mid-Victorian years. This 'informal empire' increased and multiplied, a process associated with the expansion of Britain's world market.[21] Between 1840 and 1860 the value of Britain's trade with the world had tripled.[22] British manufacturers exported their goods to the rest of the world on British ships and railways, backed by British insurance and banking services. The British depended on 'the rest of the world' to supply raw materials and foodstuffs. The economic dependence was mutual but the power relation unequal. The 'imperialism of free trade' could easily turn into more formal control, as in West Africa or Malaya, for example. By the late nineteenth century, as the fear of threats to British interests multiplied, particularly from Germany, Russia and the United States, formal interventions and annexations, the creation of protectorates and 'spheres of influence', increased. As Seeley had argued, England must expand, and in the 1880s the formal empire grew.

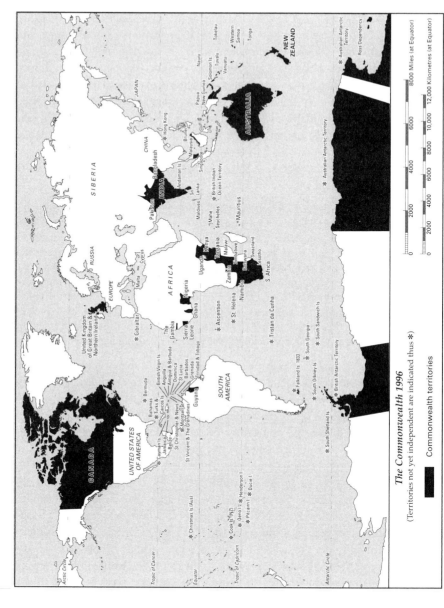

Figure 1.3 The Commonwealth, 1996

Between 1880 and 1914, as Eric Hobsbawm notes, most of the world outside Europe and the Americas was formally partitioned into territories controlled by the major European states, the United States and Japan. Africa and the Pacific were effectively divided up. Between 1876 and 1915 about a quarter of the globe's surface was distributed or redistributed into colonies. Britain increased its territories by about 4 million square miles: perhaps a third of the world was dominated by the British, both economically and culturally. It was in this period that imperialism first became part of a widespread political vocabulary. As J. A. Hobson, himself a key theorist of imperialism, argued, the word 'was on everybody's lips … and used to denote the most powerful movement in the current politics of the Western world'. It was Lenin who codified thinking about the relation between capitalist development and imperialism. He suggested that the new imperialism of the late nineteenth century had economic roots in a specific phase of capitalism which was leading to the territorial carve-up of the world among the great capitalist powers. It was the rivalries between these powers which were to lead to the First World War. For Hobsbawm, the imperialism of this period was indeed 'new'. Its association with the competition between rival industrial capitalist countries and their increasing intervention in economic affairs, its links with the development of large corporations and the shift to a period when the peripheral part of the global economy became increasingly significant were all new.[23]

The high expansionist imperialism of the late nineteenth century, when Joseph Chamberlain hoped that the colonies would secure national prosperity and wealth for all at home and Rhodes dreamed of a white Central and South Africa, faded. The war in South Africa clarified the difficulties associated with territorial expansion, and the founding of South Africa in 1910 marked a significant break. The First World War brought questions of nationalism and anti-colonialism more to the surface, especially in India, Ireland and the Middle East. Britain's interests remained firmly identified with the empire in the 1920s and 1930s. Indeed, the period after 1918 saw the extension of effective colonial government as well as white settlement in Central and East Africa. Post-1945 the colonial order fell to pieces and was replaced, in theory at least, by a 'world of nations' and, in the British context, a Commonwealth of nations.[24] In the period between 1955 and 1975 the so-called Bandung era marked the call from the movement of non-aligned countries whose representatives met at the Bandung conference for a new international economic order. In this period the 'Third World', as it was named, became the site of intense debate about the possibility of a non-capitalist route to socialism. The 1980s and 1990s saw the collapse of the Soviet bloc and the triumph of economic neo-liberalism and neo-colonialism.

The articles in this volume focus for the most part on the period from the early nineteenth century to 1945. They deal with the metropolis, with sites of informal empire and formal empire. Their geographical range is from the 'Middle East' to the Solomon Islands, from that most particular 'metropolitan colony',[25] Ireland, to a colony of white settlement, Canada; from India, brought directly under the Crown in 1858, to the mandated territory of South West Africa, under the control of South Africa, still itself at that point a semi-colony. This variety across metropolitan and colonial sites in terms of both time and place highlights the dangers of thinking of empire as one thing, or assuming forms of rule which work in any straightforward way across it. At the same time, however, there is an assumption of connections across the empire which link its histories in ways worth reflecting upon.

Several of the essays here also problematize assumed temporalities of empire and modernity, questioning notions of before and after colonialism. Kathleen Wilson, following Paul Gilroy's suggestion that modernity 'might be thought to begin in the constitutive relationships with outsiders that both found and temper a self-conscious sense of Western civilisation',[26] argues that a chronology which distinguishes sharply between the first empire, pre- the War of American Independence, and the second is disrupted if we take on the significance of the processes of inclusion and exclusion which characterize the modern nation and empire. Forms of national belonging emerged in the eighteenth century, she argues, which shaped the way in which nationality was understood until the twentieth. Nancy Stepan's preoccupation with ideas of embodiment in relation to citizenship emphasizes the significance of forms of knowledge and understanding established in the nineteenth century to questions of political rights today. Similarly M. Jacqui Alexander focuses on the importance of legacies of empire for the postcolonial nation and state. All three are preoccupied with the continuities between times understood as colonial and those which are not.

Culture

If the empire provides the site of analysis, it is the cultures of empire which are the particular focus of this book, for to decolonize representation means to decolonize the cultures through which those systems of representation were produced. Culture, as Raymond Williams remarked:

> is one of the two or three most complicated words in the English language … This is so partly because of its intricate historical development, in several European languages, but mainly because it has now come to be used for important concepts in several distinct intellectual disciplines and in several distinct and incompatible systems of thought.

Williams argues that the *earliest* meaning of 'culture' can be found in the fifteenth century, when the word was used to refer to the tending of crops or looking after animals.

A *second* meaning developed in the early sixteenth century when culture became associated with the culture of the mind, the idea that only some people were cultured and they were likely to be upper-class. This meaning also became linked with 'the arts', the general state of civilization. Culture is music, literature, painting, sculpture, etc. In the twentieth century this meaning has been extended to include popular culture, the culture of the working classes, often associated with the mass media. 'High culture' is often seen as in tension with 'popular culture'.

A *third* definition of culture stems from the Enlightenment and was linked with the Enlightenment view that all societies would pass through stages of development and that Europe would play the central role, setting universal human standards because it stood at the apex of civilization.

The German philosopher Herder critiqued the notion of a superior European culture and argued that it was necessary to think about cultures in the plural. This provided a basis for a *fourth* definition – *cultures* – meaning the distinct ways of life, shared values and meanings common to different groups and periods. This is sometimes described as the anthropological definition of culture.[27]

Robert Young has argued in a critique of Williams that the concept of culture itself is intertwined with conceptions of racial difference. Culture, he argues, was interconnected from its beginnings with race. The term 'culture' was always a way of giving meaning and value to sameness and difference, distinguishing between culture and nature, culture and civilization, culture and anarchy. 'Culture was invented for difference.' But that history was intimately associated with racial thinking. Tracing the connections between developing notions of culture, race and civilization in post-Enlightenment Europe, he argues:

> Culture has always marked cultural difference by producing the other; it has always been comparative, and racism has always been an integral part of it … Race has always been culturally constructed. Culture has always been racially constructed.[28]

Young, in other words, suggests that culture is always imbricated with race. The implication is that it is an unusable term for postcolonial analysts. This suggests that there may be a way of characterizing what is distinctive about particular forms of life without difference. But the problem with this is that difference, which is constitutive of meaning, is not always racialized. Difference is not the same as racism.

A *fifth* definition has developed, associated with what has come to be called the 'cultural turn' in both the humanities and the social sciences. Work in cultural studies particularly has emphasized the importance of meaning to the definition of culture. As Stuart Hall argues, culture is not so much about a set of things, novels, paintings or television programmes, as about a process, a set of practices. Culture is associated primarily with the production and exchange of meanings, how we make sense of the world. But it is not simply about ideas in the head, it is also about how those ideas organize and regulate social and institutional worlds. Meanings are constructed in languages, and languages work through representation. They use signs and symbols to stand for or represent ideas and feelings in ways that allow others to decode and interpret them. Meaning is constructed through language, and language is therefore crucial to culture. 'It is through culture and language that the production and circulation of meaning take place.'[29]

Semiotic approaches to language – the study of signs, associated particularly with the work of Saussure and Barthes – have been significant in this 'cultural turn'. The focus on language is taken further in Foucault's understanding of discourse and how discourses work culturally. For Foucault discourses are tied not only to languages but to practices, institutions and power: discourses include institutional practices and technologies of power. Hall defines it in this way:

> The discursive approach … examines not only how language and representation produce meaning, but how the knowledge which a particular discourse produces connects with power, regulates conduct, makes up or constructs identities and subjectivities, and defines the way certain things are represented, thought about, practised and studied. The emphasis in the *discursive* approach is always on the historical specificity of a particular form or 'regime of representation': not on 'language' as a general concern, but on specific *languages* or meanings, and how they are deployed at particular times, in particular places. It points us towards greater historical specificity – the way representational practices operate in concrete historical situations, in actual practice.[30]

Historians and cultural critics concerned with understanding colonialism as a culture have made discursive analysis a central tool, and the authors in this volume tend to work with this discursive meaning of culture.

Cultures of empire

The influence of Frantz Fanon has been pervasive in post/colonial studies – nowhere more so than in his recognition that colonialism made both colonizers and colonized. Born in Martinique in 1925, Fanon fled to France from Vichy-occupied Martinique to fight with the Resistance. In the metropole he discovered that, far from being recognized as an equal citizen of France, he was black. In a traumatic encounter with a white child he saw himself as black, an object, fixed by the look of the child into his negritude. He studied medicine and then psychiatry; his first book, *Black Skin, White Masks*, was his thesis. Citing his compatriot Cesaire, he wrote, 'I am talking of millions of men who have been skilfully injected with fear, inferiority complexes, trepidation, servility, despair, abasement.' His question, turning Freud's interrogation of the meanings of femininity around, was: what does a black man want? His proposition: 'the black is not a man'. His first demand: that the black man must be liberated from himself. 'What I want to do is to help the black man to free himself of the arsenal of complexes that has been developed by the colonial environment.' Colonizers assumed that black men had no culture, no civilization, no long historical past. In learning their masters' language they took on a world and a culture – a culture which fixed them as essentially inferior. Drawing on his clinical experience and his self-knowledge, he explored the 'epidermal-ization' of inferiority, how the meanings of blackness were taken inside the self by the colonized, both inscribed on the skin and internalized in the psyche. Lack of self-esteem, deep inner insecurity, obsessive feelings of exclusion, no sense of place, 'I am the other,' characterized what it was to be black. The black man recognized himself as a 'nigger', knew a 'crushing objecthood', knew his blackness only in relation to the white man. The 'corporeal schema', the hierarchy of skin colour, was also 'a historico-racial schema' – colonialism. Above all, the black man was fixed in the white man's eye, fixed by the inscription of race on his skin, fixed by the look which spoke of 'tom-toms, cannibalism, intellectual deficiency, fetishism, racial defects, slave ships …'.[31]

But Fanon did not dissect only the psyche of the colonized. In his work as a psychiatrist in Algeria and Tunisia, treating victims from both sides of the conflict over decolonization, he studied the torturers as well as the tortured. Settlers had to become colonizers: had to learn how to define and manage the new world they were encountering and creating. Whether as missionaries, colonial officials, bounty hunters, planters, doctors or military men, they were in the business of creating new societies, wrenching what they had found into something different. As Sartre noted in his introduction to Fanon's *The Wretched of the Earth*, first published in France in 1961, a book which was to become essential reading for those engaged in struggles over decolonization, 'the European has been able to become a man only through creating slaves and monsters'. Europeans made history and made themselves through becoming colonizers. The process of decolonization necessarily meant that Europeans were being decolonized too: 'the settler which is in every one of us is being savagely rooted out'. For Fanon decolonization was inevitably a violent phenomenon, for it meant 'the replacing of a certain "species" of men by another species of men'. This involved the 'veritable creation of new men … the "thing" which has been colonized becomes man' and the colonizer in his or her turn had to become different. To Fanon's mind the world which the settlers created was a Manichean world. 'The settler paints the native as a sort of quintessence of evil.' 'Natives' could become fully human only by violently expelling their colonizers both from their land and from their own psyche. The settlers meanwhile were the heroes of their stories, the champions of a modern world, expunging savagery and barbarism, as they constructed it, in the name of civilization and freedom.

> The settler makes history; his life is an epoch, an Odyssey. He is the absolute beginning: 'This land was created by us.' 'If we leave all is lost and we go back to the Middle Ages.' Over against him torpid creatures, wasted by fevers, obsessed by ancestral customs, form an almost inorganic background for the innovating dynamism of colonial mercantilism. The settler makes history and is conscious of making it. And because he constantly refers to the history of his mother country he clearly indicates that he himself is the extension of that mother country. Thus the history which he writes is not the history of the country which he plunders but the history of his own nation in regard to all that she skims off, all that she violates and starves.

Europe, he concluded, 'is literally the creation of the Third World'. Without that 'Third World', without colonialism, there was no Europe.[32]

This analysis of the figure of the colonizer was written in 1963 but Europeans were not ready for some time to take on these insights. Decolonization brought with it a long silence on the part of the former colonial powers on questions of empire. It was a new political conjuncture, the recognition that decolonization was by no means complete and the movement of once colonized people into the metropoles, that made it possible to open up these questions. Indeed, it was a Palestinian living in the United States, Edward Said, whose work articulated a set of arguments and preoccupations and signalled a breakthrough. The publication of Said's *Orientalism* marked a turning point, for it became the iconic text which linked culture with colonialism.[33] Numerous studies have now rehearsed Said's major arguments and the problems which his work did not address.[34] But the book was a catalyst, inspiring the development of a significant new field of study, variously named, according to the predilections of its practitioners, colonial or postcolonial studies.

(Post)colonial studies are concerned with the analysis of colonial discourse (meaning 'the variety of textual forms in which the West produced and codified knowledge about non-metropolitan areas and cultures, especially those under colonial control'[35]) and colonial cultures. Said's critical argument was that 'European culture was able to manage – and even produce – the Orient politically, sociologically, militarily, ideologically, scientifically and imaginatively during the post-Enlightenment period.'[36] That management was a discursive production, through the discourse of orientalism which made 'the Orient' an object of knowledge and an object of power. Said argued that these forms of cultural power, organized through academic disciplines such as history, anthropology and philology, were as significant in the maintenance of colonial rule as the political, economic and military policies which had dominated academic study. Said drew on Foucault's notion of discourse to examine the Western European constructions of those who lived in the Middle East, and the ways in which orientalist discourse became, in Foucault's terminology, a regime of truth. He linked this with Gramsci's notion of hegemony, or the winning of consent by the rulers to their rule. Truth resided in the power of writers and academics to tell tales of the Orient which claimed successfully to represent it. Those representations depended on a set of binary oppositions between Europeans and orientals which always worked to the detriment of the latter. Yet the othering of orientals also rested on fantasied notions of their sexuality which made them objects of Western desire. The work of orientalist discourse, whether in museums, Colonial Offices, the academy or popular fiction, was to secure the binaries between West and East. This could be done only by constant discursive work, fixing and refixing the boundaries between Western rationality and oriental irrationality, Western industry and oriental laziness, Western self-control and the oriental lack of it.

Said's focus on the European (predominantly French and British) construction of the Orient was complemented in *Culture and Imperialism* with his account of the importance of narrative in the formation of imperial and anti-imperial attitudes. Taking on the criticism that *Orientalism* had not dealt with the response of the colonized to Western imperialism which resulted in struggles over decolonization, the book looked at the place of fiction in the construction of the structures of feeling of both colonizer and colonized:

> Stories are at the heart of what explorers and novelists say about strange regions of the world; they also became the method colonised people use to assert their own identity and the existence of their own history ... The power to narrate, or to block other narratives from forming and emerging, is very important to culture and imperialism, and constitutes one of the main connections between them.

In the novels, histories and travel writings that proliferated, he suggested, the Western eye and Western consciousness were always represented as the principal authority. His method was to focus on individual works and read them as productive of the imagined relation between culture and empire.[37]

'Throughout the exchange between Europeans and their "others" that began systematically half a millennium ago,' wrote Said, 'the one idea that has scarcely varied is that there is an "us" and a "them", each quite settled, clear, unassailably self-evident.'[38] Such certainty about the divisions between 'us' and 'them' has been undermined as the focus has turned to the ambivalence of colonial discourse, a shift associated especially with the work of Homi Bhabha. His emphasis is on the different meanings which are always present in colonial representation. These make the entry of other knowledges possible and potentially undermine colonial authority.[39] At the same time a focus on the shifting nature of these divisions and the ways in which they were constantly cross-cut by divisions of sexuality and of gender has come from feminist historians and critics who have explored the gendering of orientalisms (see Chapters 2 and 10 in this volume).[40] Said's conviction that 'there was very little domestic resistance to these empires', his certainty that 'there was virtual unanimity that subject races should be ruled' and his desire to identify a 'consolidated vision' of empire all need careful historical investigation.[41] 'The West' was not as homogeneous as Said imagined, and empire was constantly debated and discussed in the nineteenth century, just as questions of race and nation are matters of heady political debate today. But the central questions his work gives rise to were how imperial cultures were formed, how ideas of empire were imaginatively shaped, how novels constructed 'home' and 'away', how they produced an imperial structure of feeling (the term is Raymond Williams's): these issues remain vital. Said's contribution was to link culture inexorably with colonialism – a link which has been taken up in different ways by many scholars.

The anthropologist Nicholas Dirks goes so far as to argue that culture, which he defines in the anthropological sense as 'the congeries of values, beliefs, practices, and discourses that have come to carry the force of nature', was a colonial formation, colonialism a cultural formation. Colonialism, he suggests:

> was itself a cultural project of control. Colonial knowledge both enabled colonial conquest and was produced by it; in certain important ways culture was what colonialism was all about. Cultural forms in newly classified 'traditional' societies were reconstructed and transformed by and through colonial technologies of conquest and rule, which created new categories and oppositions between

colonizers and colonized, European and Asian, modern and traditional, West and East, even male and female.[42]

Colonialism, of course, was not a unified phenomenon. There were the colonialisms associated with the different European empires, and the different forms of colonialism which operated within the British Empire. On each of those sites different groups of colonizers engaged in different colonial projects. Travellers, merchants, traders, soldiers and sailors, farmers, prostitutes, teachers, officials and missionaries – all were engaged in colonial relations with their own particular dynamics. The antagonisms between different conceptions of what colonizers should do were often sharp: how should particular groups behave in relation to the 'natives', what should their connections with the colonial authorities be? How did missionaries, colonial officials and the plantocracy, for example, coexist in the early nineteenth-century Caribbean? A book such as Emilia da Costa's *Crowns of Glory, Tears of Blood*, an investigation of the slave rebellion of 1823, indicates how close the world pictures of even such sworn enemies as the plantocracy and the missionaries in Demerara in the 1820s were.[43] Clearly an urgent task for scholars now is to trace these different colonial cultures and investigate the threads of connection between them. As Nicholas Thomas urges:

> only localized theories and historically specific accounts can provide much insight into the varied articulations of colonizing and counter-colonial representations and practices ... colonialism can only be traced through its plural and particularized expressions ...[44]

In his own detailed ethnographic work he is at pains to move away from the representation of colonial discourse as global and transhistorical and focus on the differences between competing forms of colonialism (see Chapter 13 of this volume).

The focus of this book is on the cultures of the colonizers, not those of the colonized. How did colonialism make Europeans? How did travellers, or missionaries, or colonial officials become colonizers? How was colonialism lived domestically, at home in the metropole? What were the cultures of empire?

Difference

New ways of theorizing difference are central to the task of writing new imperial histories. Difference should be understood in this context, as Himani Bannerji argues, in terms of the 'social relations of power and ruling, not as what people intrinsically *are*, but what they are ascribed as in the context of domination'.[45] Differences, whether of race, ethnicity or gender, are always socially constituted, and they always have a dimension of power. Questions of difference became a central preoccupation from the 1980s, associated in part with the politics of race and sexual liberation which undermined the assumption that class was the privileged form of social differentiation requiring attention, in part with new theoretical approaches which drew on linguistic and psychoanalytical forms of knowledge. For the Swiss linguist Saussure, whose work has been crucial to new understandings of language, meaning depended on difference: meaning was relational, fixed only through opposition. We know what black is because we know what white is. The French philosopher Derrida was to take this argument further, arguing that binary oppositions, man–woman, black–white, are rarely neutral and always express relations of power. Bakhtin, another theorist of language, had a rather different emphasis. He focused on the ways in which meanings were constructed between speakers, the fundamentally dialogic character of all interactions, and the impossibility of finally determining how meanings were received. Hence the possibility of struggle over meanings, as, for example, Bhabha posits in relation to the ambivalence of colonial discourse. Freud also contributed to debates over difference, since for him sexual difference was fundamental to the constitution of the self and to sexual identity.[46] The approaches to difference derived from these theorists have all been utilized in writing on the postcolonial. All would share the view that language is constitutive of difference rather than reflective of it.

For historians class provided the central category of historical analysis until the 1960s but the advent of feminism, of new theories of language, and of new understandings of racial difference has transformed the ways it is possible to think about how societies work, what forms of power operate within them. From the late 1960s feminists began to try and make sense of the unequal relations between men and women in the workplace and at home, to grasp why it was that women were paid less than men, had less status, less political agency, less power and carried domestic and reproductive responsibilities. The category of gender emerged as the analytical tool which, like class, could help to explain the inequalities and differences between men and women: gender organized the divisions between men and women, demarcated where men and women could operate. Much of the work of feminist historians in the 1970s and 1980s focused on the different worlds of men and women, the 'separate spheres' which defined their relative places in new ways in the late eighteenth century. This culture of 'separate spheres' has been seen as crucial to the development of specifically bourgeois societies such as Britain and the United States. It was these boundaries which marked off what women could do and which feminists from the 1850s worked so hard to redefine.[47]

Joan Scott was able to take this argument forward when, utilizing Foucault, she turned attention to the ways in which gender, meaning 'the social creation of ideas about women and men', bodies of knowledge about the differences between the sexes, were discursively constituted. Gender, she argued, is both a constitutive element of social relations based on perceived differences between the sexes and a primary way of signifying relations of power. There were no fixed or essential meanings of masculinity or femininity, only discursive practices which articulated and organized particular sets of relations through the workings of knowledge and power, always in historically specific ways. Scott's work was particularly helpful in illuminating the ways in which gender operated as a category of difference, constructing meaning even when it was apparently not there. (This links with the practice of 'reading against the grain' which was to be articulated by subaltern historians.) Thus, for example, Scott took the iconic text of social and cultural history, E. P. Thompson's *The Making of the English Working Class*, and elaborated the ways in which Thompson's assumptions about masculinity and femininity structured his understanding of class. Class appears to be gender-neutral in his text but the form of class consciousness which he depicted – rational, secular and universalist – was a masculine form yet is represented as natural. Scott illustrates how Thompson endorsed particular movements and offered negative contrasts to them: so, for example, his archetypical radical figure of the 1790s is the thinking, articulate, literate Paine, who is set against the mad, hysterical, irrational woman Joanna Southcott. Paine's particular form of masculine class consciousness is legitimated as class consciousness *tout court*.[48] In a later essay on the category 'experience', a category which was crucial to Thompson's understanding of class consciousness, Scott argued that 'experience' is a category which historians need to stop taking for granted. Rather, we need to understand the ways in which both experience and identity are historically constructed categories, discursively produced. 'Experience', she argues,

> is at once always already an interpretation *and* is in need of interpretation. What counts as experience is neither self-evident nor straightforward; it is always contested, always therefore political. The study of experience, therefore, must call into question its originary status in historical explanation. This will happen when historians take as their project *not* the reproduction and transmission of knowledge said to be arrived at through experience, but the analysis of the production of that knowledge itself. Such an analysis would constitute a genuinely non-foundational history, one which retains its explanatory power and its interest in change but does not stand on or reproduce naturalized categories.[49]

For historians seriously to rethink the category class was a tall order: it had provided the conceptual building block of labour and social history. The debates over the implications of poststructuralism, a form of analysis that foregrounds relationality between social categories and their meanings and how subjects are constructed in and through a variety of cultural and social practices, seriously divided professional historians in the late 1980s and early 1990s and weakened social history as a form of enquiry. Gareth Stedman Jones's article on the language and politics of Chartism argued for more attention to the political language which the Chartists themselves used. Such attention, he proposed, revealed that class divisions were organized linguistically rather than by relation to the means of production. Since then historians such as Patrick Joyce, James Vernon and Dror Wahrman have been concerned to challenge the dominance of class as *the* primary category of historical explanation, the 'motor of history' in Marx's terminology, to investigate the salience of other forms of identification and belonging such as 'the people' or 'the nation', and to trace the ways in which class itself was an effect rather than a cause. Thus, to quote Wahrman on the making of the 1832 Reform Act, usually interpreted as the sign and symbol of middle-class power:

It was not so much the rising 'middle class' that was the crucial factor in bringing about the Reform Act of 1832, as it was the Reform Bill of 1832 that was the crucial factor in cementing the invention of the ever rising 'middle class'. [50]

Similar arguments about race, challenging the notion of any fixed or essential differences, arguing that race was a discursive category, and recognizing the need for non-foundational or post-foundational histories which do not take those categories as given, were emerging at the same time. From the time of the 'discoveries', the increasing contacts between peoples meant for Europeans a preoccupation with difference. It was the colonial encounters which produced a new category, race, a term the meanings of which have always been contested and challenged. The Enlightenment inaugurated a debate about racial types and natural scientists began to make human races an object of study, labouring to produce a schema out of the immense varieties of human life. On the one hand were those who operated within a Christian universalism which assumed that all peoples were the descendants of Adam and Eve and that the differences between peoples could be explained by the differences of culture and climate. On the other were those who focused on the notion of permanent physical differences which were inherited and which distinguished groups or races of people one from another. Nineteenth and twentieth-century racial thinking has been shaped by these arguments between an emphasis on cultural distinctions between peoples and insistence on the immutable character of racial difference. In the wake of the impact of Darwinian evolutionary thinking, classificatory racial schemes which involved hierarchies from 'savagery' to 'civilization', with white Anglo-Saxons at the apex, became common. Exclusion, from political or social rights, for example, could be justified by reference to these differences.[51] Joanna de Groot (in Chapter 2) investigates the construction of 'sex' and 'race' as categories and explores the ways in which nineteenth-century discourses of sexual identity and difference drew upon and contributed to discourses of ethnic and racial identity and difference: these analagous languages drew on under- standings of both domination and subordination.[52] As Nancy Stepan notes, the scientific theorizing which was so strategic to understanding human variation depended heavily on an analogy linking race to gender:

> Once 'woman' had been shown to be indeed analogous to lower races by the new science of anthropometry and had become, in essence, a racialized category, the traits and qualities special to woman could in turn be used in an analogical understanding of lower races. The analogies now had the weight of empirical reality and scientific theory.[53]

As with sexual difference the particular problematic of thinking about race has been the associations with natural difference. Despite a great deal of research by scientists which demonstrates that the physical and biological differences between groups defined as races are insignificant, racisms are still widespread and as James Donald and Ali Rattansi argue, people continue to act as if race is a fixed objective category.[54] In the nineteenth century the measurement of the skull and the brain was supposed to carry the answers to racial classification: in the twentieth, skin colour and hair, in particular, have carried the idea of fixed racial types.

But, if we think race does exist, why does it acquire different meanings at different historical moments? 'Like gender and class,' as Evelyn Brooks Higginbotham puts it, 'race must be seen as a social construction predicated upon the recognition of difference and signifying the simultaneous distinguishing and positioning of groups vis-a-vis one another'.[55] Then the historical questions become 'How are races discursively constructed and particular groups racialized?' 'Since "race" does not have fixed meanings, what meanings does it carry, and when?' Out of this new way of conceptualizing race, as a way of constituting difference between one group and another, rather than reflecting existing differences – a process that is always inflected with power – has come preoccupation with otherness, with racialized identities, with whiteness as well as blackness. For blackness is not a given, not a self born with skin colour; rather it was created, as in the context of political struggle in the 1960s and 1970s. As Stuart Hall argues:

> The fact is 'black' has never been just there either. It has always been an unstable identity, psychically, culturally and politically. It, too, is a narrative, a story, a history. Something constructed, told, spoken, not simply found.[56]

This new focus on *difference*, the differences between men and women, between black and white, between middle-class and working-class, has come to dominate much of the work being done in imperial history. The time of empire was the time when anatomies of difference were being elaborated: it was the work of culture. These oppositions, constituted through processes of differentiation which positioned men and women, colonizers and colonized, as if such divisions were natural, were constantly in the making, in conflicts of power. For as Cooper and Stoler argue, the most basic tension of empire was that 'the otherness of colonised persons was neither inherent nor stable; his or her difference had to be defined and maintained'. This meant that 'a grammar of difference was continuously and vigilantly crafted as people in colonies refashioned and contested European claims to superiority'.[57] The construction of this 'grammar of difference' was the cultural work of both colonizers and colonized.

Histories

As Himani Bannerji has noted, 'the writing of history is not a transparent affair'. Nor, she adds, is it innocent.[58] Imperial history is no exception. Seeley was clear that the English public needed to be educated – they were to be educated in the truth of imperial relations. The early histories of empire have been seen by some critics as little more than 'an adjunct of empire' and Clare Midgley has pointed to close links between imperial history and the practice of imperial rule:

> with academics themselves acting as advisers on imperial policy and administration, providing education for future members of the Colonial Service, and

fostering the development of imperial pressure groups such as the Imperial Federation League and the Round Table.[59]

As yet, however, we have no substantive study of the development of history as a discipline in its relation to empire: undoubtedly that history will prove to be complex and variegated, for historians have had and continue to have serious differences on matters imperial.[60] In 1984 David Fieldhouse reflected on the problems which imperial historians faced when confronted with the end of empire. What were they to do once decolonization had destroyed the notion of 'imperial destiny' and national histories were being produced in erstwhile colonies? He recommended a focus on both colony and metropole but this was out of key with the focus on the nation which was characteristic of the 1980s, and was in itself in part associated with the loss of empire.[61] One response to the problem of imperial history in post-imperial times came from what might be dubbed the Manchester school of imperial history. Inspired by the ideas, energy and enthusiasm of John MacKenzie, a group of studies have been published by Manchester University Press which explore the ways in which imperialism permeated British popular and elite culture through the nineteenth and twentieth centuries: from children's books to theatrical productions, from hunting and sport to propaganda, from sexuality to soldiers, from travel writing to fiction. For the most part, though with significant exceptions, this work has been done within the traditions of British social history and has been sceptical of new theoretical approaches.[62]

Another response has come from scholars influenced by postcolonial and feminist theory. They have been exploring a range of topics: from the impact of the empire on the metropole to the construction of identities across those boundaries; from the gendering of nationalisms and nations to the gendering of colonial space; from the specificities of contests within colonies to the ways in which such contests can disrupt the established periodicities of metropolitan histories; from the histories of particular colonial projects to the representations of the colonized. Feminist historians and critics have been in the forefront of this effort to construct new imperial histories, because of their particular interest in the links between differences, the ways in which inequalities of power have crossed gender and race, sexuality and class. Their work is to deconstruct those binaries and see how, why and where they were established.[63] Anne McClintock, for example, in *Imperial Leather*, explores the relations between imperialism, domesticity, sexuality and capitalist development and argues that the categories of race, class and gender came into existence in relation to each other. Utilizing feminist, Marxist and psycho-analytical approaches, she suggests that the prosperity of the European bourgeoisie, with their particular forms of domesticity and sexuality, was connected in the most intimate ways with colonialism. Not only was the conquest of the sexuality and labour power of colonized women central to 'progress' but as domestic space was racialized 'at home', colonial space was in turn domesticated.[64]

Ann Laura Stoler also engages with questions about the bourgeois self. In her dialogue with Foucault, *Race and the Education of Desire*, she utilizes a new reading of some of Foucault's unpublished work to theorize the relation between discourses of sexuality and race and the construction of what Fanon had called the 'colonial order of things'. That colonial order was a cultural order in which subjects were constituted, selves made. Stoler, drawing on her extensive research in the Dutch East Indies, explores the ways in which Foucault's insights into the construction of the bourgeois self can be utilized in a wider imperial context to reveal 'the work of racial thinking in the making of European bourgeois identity'. For the making of the colonizer took place in both the metropole and the colonies. In mapping the features of what she defines as a 'colonial bourgeois order' she suggests that the Dutch, the British and the French 'each defined their unique civilities through a language of difference that drew on images of racial purity and sexual virtue'. Racial configurations were central to the processes of identifying marginal members of the body politic and constructing a politics of exclusion[65] (see Chapter 4). Or, to take another instance, Mrinalini Sinha explores the making of the colonizer and the colonized, the constitution and reconstitution of the 'manly Englishman' and the 'effeminate Bengali' in the Britain and India of the 1880s and 1890s, demonstrating how these identities were coded and recoded in both the metropole and the colony in the context of particular debates and struggles.[66]

A focus on the particularity of the work of the colonizer, in different projects of empire, at different sites and different times, characterizes some of the historical work which has been done and which is reproduced in this volume. In Chapter 12 Elizabeth Vibert looks at the narratives of fur traders in the North American Plateau in the early nineteenth century. She investigates the ways in which the traders constructed their own masculinities both in relation to 'home' and through their encounter with Indian buffalo hunters, lauded for their physical prowess and manliness yet denigrated as inferior. Patricia Hayes's lens in Chapter 14 is on northern Namibia a century later, ruled by South Africa when that country was only semi-independent from Britain. Here is one of those instances where colonizers were also colonized, constituting ambivalent identities and reminding us of the limitations of thinking with the binary colonizer/colonized, the cross-cuttings which interrupt simple identifications. Australian historians have been particularly interested in those white settlers who were both colonizers and colonized, who depended on the seizure of land from Aboriginal peoples and on the exploitation of their labour yet at the very same time struggled to establish their rights in relation to the mother country.[67] 'Cocky' Hahn, Native Commissioner in Ovamboland, exercised his power both physically and through the production and dissemination of ethnographic knowledge about the Ovambo, not least through his photography. While Vibert and Hayes both focus on the masculine colonizer, Janaki Nair looks in Chapter 10 at Englishwomen writing about Indian woman-hood. She reflects on the ways in which they represented Indian women, the particularities of the meanings they gave to the *zenana*, and how in the process they empowered themselves.

In 1938, in his inspirational history of the Haitian revolution, *The Black Jacobins*,

C. L. R. James argued for the intimate connections between metropole and colony. The French Revolution was in part brought about by the demands of the financial bourgeoisie whose fortunes had been made by Caribbean slavery and the Santo Domingo revolution was inspired by the politics of Paris. In his account, cause and effect linked so-called metropole and periphery, challenging the assumption that historical causality always runs from the centre to the colony, and that metropolitan domestic politics were unrelated to those of the colonies.[68] This argument, largely neglected by historians, has been rediscovered in the postcolonial moment. 'Colonialism was less a process that began in the European metropole and expanded outward,' argues Dirks, 'than it was a moment when new encounters within the world facilitated the formation of categories of metropole and colony in the first place.'[69] Metropole and colony, as Cooper and Stoler put it, must be treated in the same analytical frame.[70] Such a frame necessitates a revisioning of 'nation', another theme of this volume. In Chapter 7 Kathleen Wilson investigates the ways in which different imaginings of empire were central to particular visions of nationhood and national belonging in eighteenth-century England.[71] Antoinette Burton argues, in Chapter 6, that we need to question the particular ways of focusing on the nation which for so long characterized British history writing, and the persistent conviction that home and empire were separate spheres. This emphasis on linkages and connections, patterns of dependence and interdependence, the recognition that nations do not have fully autonomous histories, remain significant in new ways in the time after empire. In Chapter 15, on the postcolonial state in the Bahamas, M. Jacqui Alexander notes that country's dependence on international processes of political economy in the time after colonialism, and the ways in which its government claims to represent the nation, in the process constructing links between citizenship, masculinity and heterosexuality.

Since nations, as we now understand, are always in process, always being constructed, moments of definition such as war, or significant changes in the nature of citizenship, can be investigated in terms of the ideas of the nation and national belonging which were in operation at the time.[72] But nations cannot be understood outside of empire, as authors explore in different ways in this book. Sonya Rose (Chapter 11) investigates ideas about citizenship, sexuality and nation in Second World War Britain, when black American GIs, representatives of a lost colony, were figured as a particular masculine threat to English femininity. The juxtaposition of nation and empire clarifies boundaries of belonging. Who is inside and who is outside? Who is a citizen and who is a subject? Ann Stoler reflects in Chapter 4 on the connections between bourgeois selves and the politics of exclusion, whether on class, race or sexual lines. As she and Frederick Cooper argue:

> The colonies of France, England and the Netherlands … did more than reflect the bounded universality of metropolitan political culture: they constituted an imaginary and physical space in which the inclusions and exclusions built into the notions of citizen, sovereignty and participation were worked out.[73]

While political theorists have focused on the ways in which classical liberalism excluded women or those who were not white, Nancy Stepan insists in Chapter 3 on the importance of notions of embodiment in discussions of citizenship. Both racial science and the science of gender were used to justify a system in which bodily difference equalled differences in rights and entitlements; the facts of difference, skin colour or bodily parts were seen as explaining and legitimating forms of citizenship.[74]

If Fanon, Said and other postcolonial and feminist critics have offered one set of inspirations for these new imperial histories, another has come from the Indian historians gathered around the production of *Subaltern Studies*. This began from a critique of Indian nationalist historiography as well as the Cambridge school of colonialist history, and the recognition that Indian histories, heavily influenced by Marxism, were failing to represent the subaltern. The term came from Gramsci, utilized in his effort to understand the success of fascism in Italy and the central importance of the peasantry in the failure of a revolutionary politics. An analysis which depended on classical Marxism was not enough, and Gramsci turned to questions of dominance and subordination. As Gyan Prakash argues in his account of this intellectual development (Chapter 5) the early studies of this group led by Ranajit Guha paid much attention to the work of cultural historians such as Thompson and the significance of 'history from below'. Guha's own research, however, pushed him in the direction of engagement with colonial discourse, a development which was taken up by Partha Chatterjee and others. Subalternity, they began to argue, operated in the dominant discourse, and it was only by 'reading against the grain', reading for the silences and absences in colonial texts, that subaltern voices could be heard. This opened up the debate initiated by Gayatri Chakravorty Spivak as to whether the subaltern could speak. Was it possible to recover the agency of those whose words and actions were represented only by others?[75] Historians will need to push at the limits of historical knowledge, to work at turning the contradictions, ambivalences and gaps in the sources we have into rewritten histories. Such histories Prakash characterizes as 'post-foundational', post-foundational in the sense that there are no givens, no foundations, no classes, no nations, no binaries except as they were discursively created. India was made only through colonial discourse, as was Britain.[76] Europe, as Fanon reminds us, was 'literally the creation of the Third World'.

Interdisciplinarity

The work on colonial cultures has come from literature, anthropology and history, the history of medicine and psychiatry, geography, art history and cultural studies, political theory and philosophy, for colonialism operated across the field of culture. For settlers to possess the lands which they fondly constructed as 'vacant' they needed to map them, to name them in their own language, to describe and define them, to anatomize the land and its fruits, for themselves and the mother country, to classify their inhabitants, to differentiate them from other 'natives', to fictionalize them, to represent them visually, to civilize and cure them. They needed cartographers, botanists, artists and writers as well as soldiers to support their enterprise, and sailors to ensure their traffic across the seas.[77] As Ruth Roach Pierson notes, the period of European expansion and the Enlightenment quest for encyclopaedic knowledge were part of the same project:

> Hand-in-hand with European conquerors, explorers, slave traders, merchants, missionaries, and imperial and colonial administrators, European cartographers, botanists, biologists, and budding anthropologists fanned out over the globe, returning home with the booty that fuelled the mania for classification and categorization.[78]

The scientists of empire, men like Sir Roderick Murchison, geologist and key figure in the Royal Geographical Society in the nineteenth century, were critical to the project of overseas exploration and imperial development.[79] These were, of course, heavily gendered activities, as an example from mid-nineteenth-century England reminds us. While Darwin developed his theory of evolution on the *Beagle* and his cousin Francis Galton his science of eugenics, one of their aunts in Birmingham utilized her skills of classification in the house and garden, painting labels for pots and pans, garden tools and the plants in her flower beds.[80]

Colonialism was itself heavily implicated in the development of disciplines. 'It was through discovery,' as Nicholas Dirks argues, that:

> the siting, surveying, mapping, naming, and ultimately possessing – of new regions that science itself could open new territories of conquest: cartography, geography, botany and anthropology were all colonial enterprises.[81]

Anthropology – the science of man – was perhaps the most intimately associated with the colonial project, engaged as it was in the practical work of colonialism, utilizing the colonial theatre as a laboratory from which to develop schemes of classification of peoples. Bernard Cohn suggests that historians and anthropologists are particularly close in the work they do, for they 'have a common subject matter, "otherness"; one field constructs and studies "otherness" in space, the other in time'. While historians have tended to follow national histories, he argues, anthropologists have followed empires. His plea for an anthropological history, with its focus on the construction of cultures through representation, is a powerful statement of the links between the disciplines:

> In the historical situation of colonialism, both white rulers and indigenous peoples were constantly involved in representing to each other what they were doing. Whites everywhere came into other people's worlds with models and logics, means of representation, forms of knowledge and action, with which they adapted to the construction of new environments, peopled by new 'others'. By the same token those 'others' had to restructure their worlds to encompass the fact of white domination and their powerlessness ... the European colonialist and the indigene are united in one analytic field.[82]

And so, one might add, are the historian and the anthropologist. The fruits of one joint venture can be seen in the collection edited by Frederick Cooper, historian of South Africa, and Ann Stoler, anthropologist and historian of the Dutch East Indies, *Tensions of Empire*, which represents the work of cultural critics and political theorists as well as anthropologists and historians.

Anthropologists have been in the forefront of the analysis of different aspects of colonial cultures: from the work on missionaries and their colonial encounters (see Thomas in Chapter 13) to the significance of rituals of colonial power.[83] Mary Louise Pratt's work on travel writing, *Imperial Eyes*, has been influential in shaping what is by now a considerable body of writing on this topic. Pratt takes the mid-eighteenth century as the starting point for her account of the ways in which travel writing produced the rest of the world for Europe. One of Europe's proudest instruments of expansion, she argues, was the scientific expedition, which utilized new forms of natural history to bring the 'new world' into patterns of European order whilst occluding the competition, exploitation and violence which were taking place. The attempt to periodize different moments of Europan expansion and the particular modes of representation associated with them, alongside the concepts which she developed of the 'contact zone' – the social space in which cultures meet and clash in relations of dominance and subordination – and 'transculturation' – the ways in which European constructions of subordinate others have been shaped by those others – has proved very useful.[84]

As Simon Gikandi notes, 'the trope of travel generates narratives that are acutely concerned with self-realization in the spaces of the other'.[85] It is this which has made travel writing such a productive site for the analysis of both colonizer and colonized. Again the work is interdisciplinary: whilst Pratt started as an anthropologist but has done extensive work on textual analysis, Gikandi is a critic and Billie Melman is a historian who turned to travel writing.[86] Similarly James Clifford, whose first anthropological study was on missionaries, has turned increasingly to critical theory and has done extensive work on cultural translation – looking at museums, for example, as significant sites of colonial encounters.[87]

The writing on travel which is represented in this volume is by a literary and cultural critic, John Barrell. As he argues in Chapter 8, writers were crucial to the project of creating an imperial frame of mind for the audience at home. 'It should not be possible,' as Spivak commented, 'to read nineteenth-century British literature without remembering that imperialism, understood as England's social mission, was a crucial part of the cultural representation of England to the English.'[88] Print culture, as Anderson argued so famously, was central to the creation of an imagined nation.[89] Reading was vital to the domestic culture of empire and travel writing may have played a particular part. Travel narratives, Margaret Hunt argues, helped to 'change racism from a rather unsystematic … medley of popular beliefs into an elaborately worked out taxonomy that embraced the entire globe'.[90] Said, as we have seen, argues that the novel is a particularly rich site for exploring this structure of feeling in the British Empire, and much of the best work on the cultures of colonialism has come from literature.[91] Textual analysis can provide rich insights into particular cultural logics, particular constructions of self and other, particular fantasies and projections, the ways in which a historically specific form of racism operates in a piece of writing. Luke Gibbons (see Chapter 9) explores the meanings of Irishness, that colonized identity which was both inside and outside Britain, through a variety of textual readings. The Irish were colonized yet they were white. This lack of clear racial markers meant that colonial discourse had to work differently, with a different cultural logic from that which relied on the black–white distinction. Chapter 9 makes an important contribution to the debate over the racialization of the Irish.[92] Other cultural critics have mobilized a range of disciplinary and theoretical skills, from cultural studies to psychoanalyis and feminist theory, to analyse particular imperial identities.[93]

Nicholas Thomas comments that if literature has put colonialism into culture, historians and anthropologists have put culture into colonialism.[94] No discipline, it must be clear, can do the work of analysing colonial cultures on their own. Yet the different disciplines retain an interest in particular questions, questions which are worth holding on to. For literary and visual historians, textual analysis will remain at the centre of their investigation. For historians an interest in change over time, in causality and determination, in what happened where and when and why remain central. *Cultures of Empire* explores these questions.

Notes

1 J. R. Seeley, *The Expansion of England* (London: Macmillan, 1883), 1899 edition, pp. 10, 59, 13. Seeley included the West Indies in his Greater Britain, seeing white settlement there as its key characteristic. As yet, he argued, there was no national sentiment and no community of feeling across the islands (p. 57); Charles Wentworth Dilke, *Greater Britain: A Record of Travel in English-speaking Countries during 1866 and 1867* (London: Macmillan, 1867), 1869 edition.

2 Sidney Lee (ed.), *Dictionary of National Biography* LI (1897), p. 192.

3 Historians interested in re-examining imperial history in the 1990s have been quick to see the significance of Seeley. See Bill Schwarz's introduction to his edited collection, *The Expansion of England: Race, Ethnicity and Cultural History* (London, Routledge, 1996); Antoinette Burton, 'Rules of Thumb: British History and "Imperial Culture" in Nineteenth and Twentieth-century Britain', *Women's History Review*, 3:4 (1994), 483–500; Clare Midgley's introduction to her edited collection *Gender and Imperialism* (Manchester: Manchester University Press, 1998).

4 Seeley, *The Expansion of England*, pp. 55, 10, 19.

5 On Britain see, for example, Tom Nairn, *The Break-up of Britain* (London: Verso, 1977); Paul Gilroy, *There ain't no Black in the Union Jack* (London: Routledge, 1987), and *Small Acts: Thoughts on the Politics of Black Cultures* (London: Serpents Tail, 1993); Jonathan Rutherford (ed.), *Identity* (London: Lawrence & Wishart, 1990), see particularly the essays by Stuart Hall and Kobena Mercer; 'History, the Nation and the Schools', *History Workshop Journal*, 29 (spring 1990), 92–133, and 30 (autumn 1990), 75–12; Raphael Samuel, *Island Stories: Unravelling Britain* (London: Verso, 1998).

6 See, for example, the work of Henry Reynolds, e.g. *Frontier: Aborigines, Settlers and Land* (Sydney: Allen & Unwin, 1987); Patricia Grimshaw, Marilyn Lake, Ann McGrath and Marian Quartly, *Creating a Nation, 1788–1990* (Melbourne: McPhee Gribble, 1994). For

critical discussion of new history writing see Ann Curthoys, 'Feminism, Citizenship and National Identity', *Feminist Review*, 44 (summer 1993), 19–38, and 'Identity Crisis: Colonialism, Nation and Gender in Australian History', *Gender and History*, 5:2 (1993), 165–76.

7 See, for example, Ranajit Guha, *Elementary Aspects of Peasant Insurgency in Colonial India* (Delhi: Oxford University Press, 1983); R. Guha and G. C. Spivak (eds), *Selected Subaltern Studies* (New York: Oxford University Press, 1988).

8 See, for example, the work of R. F. Foster, e.g. *Modern Ireland, 1600–1972* (Harmondsworth: Penguin, 1988); D. G. Boyce and Alan O'Day (eds), *The Making of Modern Irish History: Revisionism and the Revisionist Controversy* (London: Routledge, 1996).

9 See, for example, Ruth Roach Pierson, 'International Trends in Women's History and Feminism: Colonization and Canadian Women's History', *Journal of Women's History*, 4:2 (fall 1992), 134–56.

10 See, for example, Toni Morrison, *Playing in the Dark: Whiteness and the Literary Imagination* (Cambridge MA: Harvard University Press, 1992); Carroll Smith-Rosenberg, 'Captured Subjects/Savage Others: Violently engendering the New American', *Gender and History*, 5:2 (summer 1993), 177–95.

11 Peter Hulme, 'Including America', *Ariel*, 26:1 (1995), 117–23.

12 Stuart Hall, 'When was "the Post-colonial"? Thinking at the Limit', in Iain Chambers and Lidia Curti (eds), *The Post-colonial Question: Common Skies, Divided Horizons* (London: Routledge, 1996). For critiques of the term 'postcolonial' see Anne McClintock, *Imperial Leather: Race, Gender and Sexuality in the Colonial Context* (London: Routledge, 1995), especially pp. 1–17; Frederick Cooper and Ann Laura Stoler, 'Between Metropole and Colony: Rethinking a Research Agenda', in their edited collection *Tensions of Empire: Colonial Cultures in a Bourgeois World* (Berkeley CA: University of California Press, 1997), particularly p. 33.

13 Ali Rattansi, 'Postcolonialism and its Discontents', *Economy and Society* 26:4 (November 1997), 480–500.

14 David Scott, *Refashioning Futures: Criticism after Postcoloniality* (Princeton NJ: Princeton University Press, 1999), p. 12.

15 Frantz Fanon, *The Wretched of the Earth* (Harmondsworth: Penguin edition, 1967), p. 81.

16 Simon Gikandi, *Maps of Englishness: Writing Identity in the Culture of Colonialism* (New York: Columbia University Press, 1996), p. 17.

17 For two classic accounts of this development see Sidney W. Mintz, *Sweetness and Power: The Place of Sugar in Modern History* (New York: Viking, 1985); Eric R. Wolf, *Europe and the People without History* (Berkeley CA: University of California Press, 1982).

18 C. A. Bayly, *Imperial Meridian: The British Empire and the World* (London: Longman, 1989), p. 3.

19 Bernard Porter, *The Lion's Share: A Short History of British Imperialism, 1850–1995*, third edition (London: Longman, 1996), pp. 1–2. For another very readable and informative short history see Denis Judd, *Empire: the British Imperial Experience from 1765 to the Present* (London: Harper Collins, 1996).

20 Partha Chatterjee, *The Nation and its Fragments: Colonial and Post-colonial Histories* (Princeton NJ: Princeton University Press, 1993), p. 10.

21 J. A. Gallagher and R. E. Robinson, 'The Imperialism of Free Trade', *Economic History Review*, second series, 6 (1953), 1–15; Bernard Semmel, *The Rise of Free Trade Imperialism* (Cambridge: Cambridge University Press, 1970); P. J. Cain and A. G. Hopkins, *British Imperialism: Innovation and Expansion, 1688–1914* (third edition, London: Longman, 1993); C. C. Eldridge (ed.), *British Imperialism in the Nineteenth Century* (London: Macmillan, 1984).

22 B. R. Mitchell and P. Deane, *Abstract of British Historical Statistics* (Cambridge: Cambridge University Press, 1962), p. 283, quoted in Porter, *The Lion's Share*, p. 4.

23 This paragraph relies heavily on E. J. Hobsbawm, *The Age of Empire, 1875–1914* (London: Weidenfeld & Nicolson, 1987), pp. 56–83. Hobson is quoted on p. 60.

24 John Darwin, *Britain and Decolonisation: The Retreat from Empire in the Post-war World* (Basingstoke: Macmillan, 1988), p. 4.

25 The phrase is Roy Foster's: *Paddy and Mr. Punch: Connections in Irish and English History* (Harmondsworth: Penguin, 1995), p. 86.

26 Paul Gilroy, *The Black Atlantic: Modernity and Double Consciousness* (London: Verso, 1993), p. 17.

27 Raymond Williams, *Keywords* (London: Fontana, 1983), p. 87. These definitions also draw heavily on Robert Bocock, 'The Cultural Formations of Modern Society', in Stuart Hall and Bram Gieben (eds), *Formations of Modernity* (Cambridge: Polity Press, in association with Blackwell and the Open University, 1992), pp. 230–4.

28 Robert J. C. Young, *Colonial Desire: Hybridity in Theory, Culture and Race* (London: Routledge, 1995), pp. 49, 54.

29 Stuart Hall, introduction to his edited volume, *Representation: Cultural Representations and Signifying Practices* (London: Sage, in association with the Open University, 1997), pp. 1–7.

30 *Ibid.*, p. 7.

31 Frantz Fanon, *Black Skin, White Masks* (London: Pluto Press, 1952), 1986 edition, pp. 10, 13, 30, 76, 109–10, 112, 116.

32 Fanon, *The Wretched of the Earth*, introduction by Jean-Paul Sartre, pp. 21–3, 'Concerning Violence', pp. 27, 39–40, 81.

33 Edward W. Said, *Orientalism* (London: Routledge, 1978).

34 See, for example, Patrick Williams and Laura Chrisman (eds), *Colonial Discourse and Postcolonial Theory: A Reader* (Hemel Hempstead: Harvester, 1994).

35 The definition is that of Williams and Chrisman, *Colonial Discourse and Postcolonial Theory*, p. 5.

36 Said, *Orientalism*, p. 3.

37 Edward W. Said, *Culture and Imperialism* (London: Chatto & Windus, 1993), p. xiii.

38 *Ibid.*, p. xxviii.

39 Homi K. Bhabha, *The Location of Culture* (London: Routledge, 1994).

40 For work on the gendered nature of colonial discourse see, for example, Sara Mills, *Discourses of Difference: An Analysis of Women's Travel Writing and Colonialism* (London: Routledge, 1991); Billie Melman, *Women's Orients: English Women in the Middle East, 1718–1918* (Basingstoke: Macmillan, 1992); Lisa Lowe, *Critical Terrains: French and British Orientalisms* (Ithaca NY: Cornell University Press, 1991); Reina Lewis, *Gendering Orientalism: Race, Femininity and Representation* (London: Routledge, 1996); Anne McClintock, *Imperial Leather*; Inderpal Grewal, *Home and Harem: Nation, Gender, Empire and the Cultures of Travel* (Durham NC: Duke University Press, 1996).

41 Said, *Culture and Imperialism*, pp. 10, 62, 77.

42 Nicholas B. Dirks (ed.), *Colonialism and Culture* (Ann Arbor MI: University of Michigan Press, 1992), pp. 2–3.

43 Emilia Viotti da Costa, *Crowns of Glory, Tears of Blood: The Demerara Slave Rebellion of 1823* (New York: Oxford University Press, 1994).

44 Nicholas Thomas, *Colonialism's Culture: Anthropology, Travel, Government* (Cambridge: Polity Press, 1994), pp. ix, x.

45 Himani Bannerji, 'Politics and the Writing of History', in Ruth Roach Pierson and Nupur Chaudhuri with the assistance of Beth McAulay, *Nation, Empire, Colony: Historicizing Gender and Race* (Bloomington IN: Indiana University Press, 1998), p. 287.

46 For an introduction to some of these issues see Stuart Hall, 'The Spectacle of the "Other"' in his edited volume *Representation*; Michèle Barrett, 'The Concept of "Difference"' in the collection of her essays, *Imagination in Theory: Essays on Writing and Culture* (Cambridge: Polity Press, 1999); Avtar Brah, 'Difference, Diversity, Differentiation', in *Cartographies of Diaspora: Contesting Identities* (London: Routledge, 1996), pp. 95–127.

47 See, for example, Leonore Davidoff and Catherine Hall, *Family Fortunes: Men and Women of the English Middle Class, 1780–1850* (London: Hutchinson, 1987). For discussion of 'separate spheres' see Linda Kerber, 'Separate Spheres, Female Worlds, Woman's Place: the Rhetoric of Women's History', *Journal of American History*, 75:1 (1988), 9–39; Nancy Hewitt, 'Beyond

the Search for Sisterhood: American Women's History in the 1980s', *Social History*, 10 (1985), 299–321; Amanda Vickery, 'Historiographical Review. Golden Age to Separate Spheres? A Review of the Categories and Chronology of English Women's History', *Historical Journal*, 36 (1993), 383–414; Jane Lewis, 'Separate Spheres: Threat or Promise?', *Journal of British Studies*, 30:1 (1991), 105–15. For an autobiographical account of the shifts in feminist history see Catherine Hall, 'Feminism and Feminist History', in *White, Male and Middle Class: Explorations in Feminism and History* (Cambridge: Polity Press, 1992), pp. 1–40.

48 Joan Wallach Scott, *Gender and the Politics of History* (New York: Columbia University Press, 1988), pp. 42–5, 68–92.

49 Joan W. Scott, "Experience", in Judith Butler and Joan Wallach Scott (eds), *Feminists Theorize the Political* (New York: Routledge, 1992), p. 37.

50 Dror Wahrman, 'Virtual Representation: Parliamentary Reporting and Languages of Class in the 1790s', *Past and Present*, 136 (1992), 113; see also his *Imagining the Middle Class: The Political Representation of Class in Britain, c. 1780–1840* (Cambridge: Cambridge University Press, 1995); Gareth Stedman Jones, *Languages of Class: Studies in English Working-class History, 1832–1982* (Cambridge: Cambridge University Press, 1983); Patrick Joyce, *Democratic Subjects: The Self and the Social in Nineteenth-century England* (Cambridge: Cambridge University Press, 1994); James Vernon, *Politics and the People: A Study in English Political Culture, c. 1815–67* (Cambridge: Cambridge University Press, 1993). For a longer discussion of the impact of these debates on political history see Catherine Hall, Keith McClelland and Jane Rendall, *Defining the Victorian Nation: Class, Race, Gender and the Reform Act of 1867* (Cambridge: Cambridge University Press, 2000).

51 On the development of racial thinking see, for example, George W. Stocking Jr, *Race, Culture and Evolution: Essays in the History of Anthropology* (Chicago IL: University of Chicago Press, 1968); Philip D. Curtin, *The Image of Africa: British Ideas and Action, 1780–1850* (Madison WI: University of Wisconsin Press, 1964), 2 vols; Michael Banton, *The Idea of Race* (London: Tavistock, 1977) and *Racial Theories* (Cambridge: Cambridge University Press, 1987); Nancy Stepan *The Idea of Race in Science: Great Britain, 1800–1960* (London: Macmillan, 1982); David Theo Goldberg (ed.), *Anatomy of Racism* (Minneapolis MN: University of Minnesota Press, 1990).

52 The work of Sander Gilman has been important to the understanding of links between race and sex. See, for example, 'Black Bodies, White Bodies: towards an Iconography of Female Sexuality in late Nineteenth-century Art, Medicine and Literature', in James Donald and Ali Rattansi (eds), *'Race', Culture and Difference* (London: Sage, 1992), pp. 171–97.

53 Nancy Leys Stepan, 'Race and Gender: the Role of Analogy in Science', in Goldberg, *Anatomy of Racism*, p. 43.

54 Donald and Rattansi, *'Race', Culture and Difference*, pp. 1–4.

55 Evelyn Brooks Higginbotham, 'African-American Women's History and the Metalanguage of Race', *Signs*, 17 (1992), 251–374, p. 253.

56 Stuart Hall, 'Minimal Selves', in *Identity* (London: Institute of Contemporary Arts, 1997) 6, p. 45. On whiteness see, for example, Vron Ware, *Beyond the Pale: White Women, Racism and History* (London: Verso, 1992); David Roediger, *The Wages of Whiteness: Race and the Making of the American Working Class* (London: Verso, 1992); Virginia R. Dominguez, *White by Definition: Social Classification in Creole Louisiana* (New Brunswick NJ: Rutgers University Press, 1986).

57 Cooper and Stoler, *Tensions of Empire*, pp. 3–4, 7.

58 Himani Bannerji, 'Politics and the Writing of History', in Pierson *et al.*, *Nation, Empire, Colony*, p. 290.

59 Dane Kennedy, 'Imperial History and Post-colonial Theory', *Journal of Imperial and Commonwealth History*, 24:3 (September 1996), 345–63; Clare Midgley, 'Introduction' to her edited collection *Gender and Imperialism*, p. 3.

60 For a fascinating study of one historian see Billie Melman, 'Under the Western Historian's Eyes: Eileen Power and the early Feminist Encounter with Colonialism', *History Workshop Journal*, 42 (autumn 1996), 147–68.

61 David Fieldhouse, 'Can Humpty-Dumpty be put together again? Imperial History in the 1980s', *Journal of Imperial and Commonwealth History*, 12:2 (January 1984), 9–23.

62 See, for example, John M. MacKenzie, *Propaganda and Empire: The Manipulation of British Public Opinion, 1880–1960* (Manchester: Manchester University Press, 1984); (ed.), *Imperialism and Popular Culture* (Manchester: Manchester University Press, 1986); (ed.), *Popular Imperialism and the Military, 1850–1950* (Manchester: Manchester University Press, 1992).

63 It is impossible to give a full bibliography of this work, though a considerable amount of it is referenced in this volume. For some other key texts see: K. Sangari and S. Vaid (eds), *Recasting Women: Essays in Indian Colonial History* (New Brunswick NJ: Rutgers University Press, 1990); Nupur Chaudhuri and Margaret Strobel (eds), Western Women and Imperialism: Complicity and Resistance (Bloomington IN: Indiana University Press, 1992); Kumari Jayawardena, *The White Woman's other Burden: Western Women and South Asia during British Rule* (London: Routledge, 1995); Moira Ferguson, *Subject to Others: British Women Writers and Colonial Slavery, 1670–1834* (London: Routledge, 1992); Clare Midgley, *Women against Slavery: The British Campaigns, 1780–1870* (London: Routledge, 1992); Antoinette Burton, *Burdens of History: British Feminists, Indian Women and Imperial Culture* (Chapel Hill NC: University of North Carolina Press, 1994) and *At the Heart of the Empire: Indians and the Colonial Encounter in late Victorian Britain* (Berkeley CA: University of California Press, 1998); Pamela Scully, *Liberating the Family? Gender and British Slave Emancipation in the Rural Western Cape, South Africa, 1823–53* (Oxford: James Currey, 1997); *Gender, Nationalisms and National Identities*, special issue of *Gender and History*, 5:2 (summer 1993); Ida Berg, Karen Hagemann and Catherine Hall (eds), *Gendered Nations: Nationalism and gender order in the long nineteenth century* (Oxford: Berg, 2000); Susan Thorne, *Congregational Missions and the Making of an Imperial Culture in Nineteenth-century England* (Stanford CA: Stanford University Press, 1999); Madhavi Kale, *Fragments of Empire: Capital, Slavery and Indian Indentured Labor Migration in the British Caribbean* (Philadelphia PA: University of Pennsylvania Press, 1999).

64 McClintock, *Imperial Leather*, especially p. 36.

65 Ann Laura Stoler, *Race and the Education of Desire: Foucault's 'History of Sexuality' and the Colonial Order of Things* (Durham NC: Duke University Press, 1995), pp. 5, 10. See also her essays: 'Rethinking Colonial Categories: European Communities and the Boundaries of Rule', *Comparative Studies in Society and History*, 13:1 (1989), 134–61; 'Carnal Knowledge and Imperial Power: Gender, Race and Morality in Colonial Asia', in Joan W. Scott (ed.), *Feminism and History* (Oxford: Oxford University Press, 1996), 209–66; 'Sexual Affronts and Racial Frontiers: European Identities and the Cultural Politics of Exclusion in Colonial Southeast Asia', in Cooper and Stoler, *Tensions of Empire*, 198–237.

66 Mrinalini Sinha, *Colonial Masculinity: The 'Manly Englishman' and the 'Effeminate Bengali' in the late Nineteenth Century* (Manchester: Manchester University Press, 1995).

67 See, for example, Marilyn Lake, 'Colonised and Colonising: the White Australian Feminist Subject', *Women's History Review*, 2:3 (1993), 377–86; Patricia Grimshaw, 'Maori Agriculturalists and Aboriginal Hunter-Gatherers: Women and Colonial Displacement in Nineteenth-century Aotearoa/New Zealand and Southeastern Australia', in Pierson *et al.* (eds), *Nation, Empire, Colony*, pp 21–40; Gyan Prakash (ed.), *After Colonialism: Imperial Histories and Postcolonial Displacements* (Princeton NJ: Princeton University Press, 1995).

68 C. L. R. James, *The Black Jacobins: Toussaint l'Ouverture and the San Domingo Revolution* (second edition, New York: Vintage, 1963).

69 Dirks, *Colonialism and Culture*, p. 6.

70 Cooper and Stoler, *Tensions of Empire*, p. 4.

71 See also her full-length study, Kathleen Wilson, *The Sense of the People: Politics, Culture and Imperialism in England, 1715–85* (Cambridge: Cambridge University Press, 1998). Wilson provides a very different account from that of Linda Colley in *Britons: Forging the Nation, 1707–1837* (New Haven CT: Yale University Press, 1992). However, Colley's neglect of empire in *Britons* shifts in her later 'Britishness and Otherness: an Argument', *Journal of British Studies*, 31 (October 1992), 309–29.

72 For an exploration of the making of nationhood and national belonging at decisive moments
    in British history see Hall *et al.*, *Defining the Victorian Nation*, and Catherine Hall, 'The Rule
    of Difference', in Blom *et al.*, *Gendered Nations*. There is a well established literature on the
    African and South Asian presence in Britain, as, for example, Peter Fryer, *Staying Power:
    The History of Black People in Britain* (London, Pluto Press, 1984); Rozina Visram, *Ayahs,
    Lascars and Princes: The Story of Indians in Britain, 1700–1947* (London, Pluto Press, 1986).
    More recently historians have been concerned to rethink national histories through racial
    and ethnic questions. See, for example, David Feldman, *Englishmen and Jews: Social
    Relations and Political Culture* (London: Yale University Press, 1994); Laura Tabili, *'We ask
    for British justice': Workers and Racial Differentiation in late Imperial Britain* (Ithaca NY:
    Cornell University Press, 1994).
73 Cooper and Stoler, *Tensions of Empire*, p. 3.
74 On the limits of liberalism see, for example, Carole Pateman, *The Sexual Contract* (Stanford
    CA: Stanford University Press, 1988); Uday S. Mehta, 'Liberal Strategies of Exclusion', in
    Cooper and Stoler, *Tensions of Empire*, pp. 59–86.
75 Guha and Spivak (eds), *Selected Subaltern Studies;* Partha Chatterjee, *Nationalist Thought and
    the Colonial World: A Derivative Discourse* (London: Zed Press, 1986) and *The Nation and its
    Fragments;* Dipesh Chakrabarty, 'Postcoloniality and the Artifice of History: who Speaks for
    "Indian" Pasts?', *Representations*, 37 (1992), 1–26; G. C. Spivak, 'Can the Subaltern speak?', in
    C. Nelson and L. Grossberg (eds), *Marxism and the Interpretation of Culture* (London:
    Macmillan, 1988), pp. 271–313; Lata Mani, *Contentious Traditions: The Debate on Sati in
    Colonial India* (Berkeley CA: University of California Press, 1998).
76 Gyan Prakash, 'Writing post-Orientalist Histories of the Third World: Perspectives from
    Indian Historiography', *Comparative Studies in Society and History*, 32 (1990), 383–408; see
    also Prakash, *After Colonialism*, which focuses on attempting to move beyond the colonizer-
    colonized binary and work with notions of liminality and hybridity. For a debate about the
    relative merits of Marxism and poststructuralism for Indian historiography see R. O'Hanlon
    and D. Washbrook's response to Prakash, 'After Orientalism: Culture, Criticism, and
    Politics in the Third World', *Comparative Studies in Society and History*, 34 (1992), 141–67;
    Prakash, 'Can the "subaltern" ride? A Reply to O'Hanlon and Washbrook', *Comparative
    Studies in Society and History*, 34 (1992), 168–84.
77 This book does not include the work of art historians, which has been very significant in new
    imperial histories. See, for example, Annie E. Coombes, *Reinventing Africa* (London: Yale
    University Press, 1994).
78 Pierson *et al.*, *Nation, Empire, Colony*, p. 3.
79 Robert A. Stafford, *Scientist of Empire: Sir Roderick Murchison: Scientific Exploration and
    Victorian Imperialism* (Cambridge: Cambridge University Press, 1989). This book does not
    include the new and important work in geography. For an introduction to some of those
    questions see, for example, Felix Driver, 'Geography's Empire: Histories of Geographical
    Knowledge', *Environment and Planning* D: *Society and Space*, 10 (1992), 23–40.
80 Davidoff and Hall, *Family Fortunes*, p. 312.
81 Dirks, *Colonialism and Culture*, p. 6.
82 Bernard S. Cohn, 'History and Anthropology: the State of Play', in *An Anthropologist among
    the Historians* (Oxford: Oxford University Press, 1996), pp. 19, 44.
83 See, for example, Jean and John Comaroff, *Of Revelation and Revolution: Christianity,
    Colonialism and Consciousness in South Africa* I (Chicago IL: University of Chicago Press,
    1991); Bernard Cohn, 'Representing Authority in Victorian India', in *An Anthropologist
    among the Historians*.
84 Mary Louise Pratt, *Imperial Eyes: Travel Writing and Transculturation* (New York:
    Routledge, 1992).
85 Gikandi, *Maps of Englishness*, p. 8.
86 Melman, *Women's Orients*.
87 James Clifford, *Person and Myth: Maurice Leenhardt in the Melanesian World* (Berkeley CA:
    University of California Press, 1982); with George Marcus (eds), *Writing Culture: The Poetics*

and Politics of Ethnography (Berkeley CA: University of California Press, 1986); *Routes: Travel and Translation in the late Twentieth Century* (Cambridge MA: Harvard University Press, 1997).

88 Gayatri Chakravorty Spivak, 'Three Women's Texts and a Critique of Imperialism', *Critical Inquiry*, 12 (autumn 1985), 243–61.

89 Benedict Anderson, *Imagined Communities: Reflections on the Origin and Spread of Nationalism* (London: Verso, 1983).

90 Margaret Hunt, 'Racism, Imperialism and the Traveller's Gaze in Eighteenth Century England', *Journal of British Studies*, 32:4 (1993), 333–57.

91 See, for example, Peter Hulme, *Colonial Encounters: Europe and the Native Caribbean, 1492–1797* (London: Methuen, 1986); Patrick Brantlinger, *Rule of Darkness: British Literature and Imperialism, 1830–1914* (Ithaca NY: Cornell University Press, 1988); Gauri Viswanathan, *Masks of Conquest* (New York: Columbia University Press, 1989); Sara Suleri, *The Rhetoric of English India* (Chicago IL: University of Chicago Press, 1992); Jenny Sharpe, *Allegories of Empire* (Minneapolis MN: University of Minnesota Press, 1993); Nancy L. Paxton, *Writing under the Raj: Gender, 'Race' and Rape in the British Colonial Imagination, 1830–1947* (New Brunswick NJ: Rutgers University Press, 1999).

92 See, for example, Sheridan Gilley, 'English Attitudes to the Irish in England, 1780–1900', in C. Holmes (ed.), *Immigrants and Minorities in British Society* (London: Allen & Unwin, 1978), pp. 81–110; R. F. Foster, *Paddy and Mr Punch;* Mary J. Hickman, *Religion, Class and Identity: The State, the Catholic Church and the Education of the Irish in Britain* (Aldershot: Avebury, 1995).

93 See, for example, Graham Dawson, *Soldier Heroes: British Adventure, Empire and the Imagining of Masculinities* (London: Routledge, 1994).

94 Thomas, *Colonialism's Culture*, p. 18.

PART I
Using theory

2

'Sex' and 'race': the construction of language and image in the nineteenth century

JOANNA DE GROOT

They cannot represent themselves: they must *be* represented. (Karl Marx, *The Eighteenth Brumaire of Louis Bonaparte*)

Both racism and sexism belong to the same discursive universe. (A. Brittan and M. Maynard, *Sexism, Racism and Oppression*)

Sexuality is recognized as a crucial issue in the history of Western societies in the nineteenth century, just as it is recognized that subordination is a central theme in the history of women during that period; yet there remain substantial gaps in analysis and areas of confusion in the historical work which deals with these questions. As the Introduction to this volume observes, it is no longer adequate to treat the history of sexuality in nineteenth-century Europe solely in terms of control, hypocrisy, and repression; similarly, the framework of women's history has extended beyond exclusive concern with female subordination to explore the many and diverse forms of subversion, accommodation, and resistance which women developed in order to deal with their situation. This contribution to our examination of themes of sexuality and subordination will seek both to clarify some confusions and to illuminate new areas of discussion opened up in the historiography of the last decade. It will argue that nineteenth-century representations and discourses of sexual identity and difference drew upon and contributed to comparable discourses and representations of ethnic, 'racial', and cultural identity and difference.

This 'cultural' approach is offered not as an alternative to material analysis but rather as an essential component of the history of a social whole within which both elements interact. It takes the view that perceptions and definitions of women's identities and roles emerged from and in turn influenced the material circumstances of their lives. These circumstances underwent radical change during the nineteenth century with the growth of new forms of production, of family life and residence, and of new forces of market relations and international interconnections. Such changes were experienced by women of all kinds, from wage-workers in northern English textile districts to Egyptian peasant women, and from Afro-American slave women to housewives in the residential suburbs of Birmingham. Their experiences can be analysed from a materialistic and structural perspective through the study of paid employment, child rearing, and consumption, or of urban development and household organization, as well as the shifting forms of legal and political authority. However, both productive and reproductive relations, like political systems, have a social and personal character which requires the historian to give attention to the language, feelings, values, and meanings which are part of such systems and relations. It is within this framework that an analysis of the construction of 'sex' and 'race' in which experience, image, and discourse interact is now offered.

I should like to clarify the treatment of the history of 'sex' and 'race' adopted in this chapter by making some general points about how women's experience will be observed and analysed. First, it can be observed that women's situation as women, and the rules or values applied to that situation, evolved not in isolation but as part of the material and cultural history of both feminine and masculine genders, and the development of boundaries and/or interactions between them. While in no way questioning the central importance of studying women's histories in their own right, I would argue that such histories need to be situated in relation to the history of gender relations and masculine histories. Second, one notes that, just as women's experience develops in relation to the other side of the gender divide, so on that female side of the divide there are important distinctions of class and culture which interact with gender-specific aspects of women's lives. Thus, while I would argue that ethnic or class divisions should undoubtedly be approached from a gendered point of view, so too gender questions and female specificity need to be seen in relation to these other divisions, and to the interactions of gender, class, and ethnic aspects of women's experience.

Studies of how gender boundaries were drawn in Europe during the nineteenth century have frequently discussed possible connections between the differences and power relations between men and women and those based on class.[1] There have also been numerous studies of the ways in which westerners (actually Western men of the dominant classes) redrew the social, cultural, and political boundaries between themselves and people in other societies, although the interaction of this process with the evolution of class and gender divisions is less often explored. This chapter seeks to make connections between the expression of gender and of cultural/ethnic difference (both verbal and visual) which may complement the more extensive existing treatment of gender–class questions. It will argue that there are not only similarities but structural connections between the treatment of women and of non-Europeans in the language, experience, and imaginations of Western men. The structural link is constructed around the theme of domination/subordination central both to nineteenth-century masculine identity and to the Western sense of superiority. It will be explored through *cultural* forms – art, travel literature, media imagery – but linked to the *material* aspects of male–female relations and European hegemony in the world at large in the post-Napoleonic era.

In Western Europe during the nineteenth century one can observe the reshaping and intensifying of a range of social boundaries and differences. On the one hand this process involved the emergence of clearer distinctions between female and male, worker and employer, and between different ethnic or cultural groups; on the other hand it required closer, more compelling interactions and interdependence between 'sexes', 'classes', or 'races'. In gender terms this meant sharper male–female distinctions within families but also close mutual economic and personal reliance, a paradox manifest in struggles around the 'family wage', women's rights, and the cult of domesticity. In class terms it involved growing divisions and commercialization in production, and conflicts over the control and exploitation of workers, but also new forms of involvement and interdependence at work which sustained the system. In international terms the growth of a world system based on European economic, political, and cultural dominance generated increased involvement of westerners with non-westerners alongside greater stress on Western superiority, success, and self-confidence as opposed to difficulties, defeats, and doubts in other societies.

The emergence of new relations and perceptions of class, race, and gender was a matter not so much of total change as of the development of new additions, forms, and directions for existing beliefs and practices. Established political patterns, religious traditions, or social customs and values interacted with new scientific ideas, divisions of labour and status, or forms of political action, as is evident in the history of class conflicts, of feminist or anti-feminist movements, and of controversies over race and empire during the period. Moreover, we may note that sharpening theories of gender, race, and class distinction were not merely accidental or academic developments, but rather clear political, pragmatic, and personal responses to attacks on those distinctions by those who found them injurious. 'Class' protest over economic and political subjection, feminist opposition to subordination and to the gender-blindness of both liberal individualism and radical collectivism and populism, and challenges to slavery and imperialism all produced increasingly developed responses both of actual discrimination and of intellectual justifications for discrimination, whether on grounds of race, gender, or class.[2]

The political and cultural activity of the period provides evidence not only of how various groups *responded* to difference or functionally defended sex, race, and class interests, but also of how they *constructed* themselves within and against such differences. The concepts of 'Self' and 'Other' or of 'us' and 'them' which are frequently invoked to explain the *separation* of masculine and feminine, or civilized and savage, or occidental and oriental in nineteenth-century perceptions of the world need also to include the sense of the symbiotic *connections* joining each apparently opposed pair. Such connections did not, of course, belie the fundamental *inequalities* embedded in the developing characteristics and relations of gender, race, and class. The discussion which follows will explore all three of these aspects of the experience, perception, and representation of gender and ethnic difference; I shall consider how concepts of 'sex' and 'race' were founded on increasingly strongly drawn distinctions; I shall discuss the ways in which these concepts also involved interaction, reciprocity, and mutual need; finally I shall see how these apparently contradictory elements existed within a framework of relations of domination and subordination.

Whereas the theories and practices related to 'class' distinctions and relationships were founded on the new 'sciences' of political economy and social investigation, theories and practices related to 'race' and 'sex' drew on biological, anthropological, and medical scholarship, often grounding themselves in part on observable and 'inescapable' physical aspects of difference. The inequalities inherent in male–female relationships and Western hegemony in the world in the nineteenth century involved elements of personal intimacy and cultural encounter very different from the experiences and perceptions which constructed the history of 'class' in that period. For these reasons, and others that will emerge in the course of discussion, it is the parallels and interactions between the images and languages of 'sex' and 'race' that evolved during the nineteenth century which will be the focus of this chapter. The material upon which the discussion will be based is drawn from verbal and visual depictions of societies in the Middle East,[3] and in particular of women in those societies. Such material was initially offered to elites in England and France in the form of highly successful 'orientalist' genres of literature, painting, and travel writing, but reached a wider audience through reproduction in popular and accessible media forms (journals, cartoons, novels, lithographic reproduction). It finally entered twentieth-century 'mass culture' via photographic and cinema versions of themes and images originally elaborated in the early nineteenth century.

It was during this period that the development of increasingly explicit and elaborated arguments for the crucial importance of gender and ethnic differences took place. Religious and moral arguments for the distinctive roles of women as mothers and helpmates, and of men as providers and heads of households, and opinions about the moral, intellectual, and psychological differences between the sexes, were extended and reinforced in new ways. As shown elsewhere in this volume, medical 'science' was invoked to reconstruct concepts of female identity around women's biological cycles and reproductive functions, 'proving' their inadequacy and categorizing any who would not accept biology as destiny as 'diseased' or 'abnormal'.[4] This scientific addition to conventional wisdom about women converged with middle-class concern to distinguish the female/domestic sphere from the male/public sphere, and to argue that separation of these spheres was essential to the maintenance of virtue, progress, and stability. It also converged with lower-class concerns about deskilling and competition in the labour market, and about the material and personal insecurity of families experiencing changes in production, urban and demographic growth and mobility, and sharp fluctuations in incomes and employment. For (male) middle-class opinion-makers or entre-preneurs, as for (male) working-class critics of the new political economy and 'old corruption', the family was reified as a guarantee of moral and material progress and order, but simultaneously defined in terms of sexual division and subordination.[5]

Such views were not, of course, unchallenged, and indeed, as has been mentioned, they developed in part through engagement with opposed opinions and arguments. There was debate and disagreement among workers and political activists, as among middle-class intellectuals and reformers, as to women's fitness for or right to education, political involvement, paid employment, or citizenship; there were similar disagreements over the respective roles of biological and social influences on women's abilities, over the significance of domesticity, and over marriage and the nuclear family.[6] It was the process of confrontation with critiques of women's subordination, and establishment of a hegemonic view of gender roles, relations, and boundaries, which gave force and shape to evolving concepts of femininity in which morality, science, and convention intertwined.

Significant parallels to the emergence of this gender discourse can be found in the changing views of cultural and physical differences between human groups during the same period. Here too there were by the late eighteenth century established opinions on these matters, combining religious traditions and philosophical ideas on the 'chain of being', human nature, and history with new theories and techniques of classification in natural and social science. In our period this was expanded, altered, and elaborated by the use of a rapidly growing body of empirical and descriptive material produced by European visitors to non-European societies, but also by the development of the 'scientific' disciplines of biology, ethnology, and anthropology. These were based on measurement and classification but equally importantly on the construction of systematic theories about the differences and inequalities between various types of humans. Increasing stress on physical characteristics (skull or brain size, bodily form and structure) and on biological heredity, itself a 'scientific' recasting of older ideas on the importance of blood descent, redirected and reinforced social and cultural arguments about non-European societies expressed by writers like James Mill on India and Volney on the Middle East.[7] What became a widely accepted picture of the 'savage', 'decadent', 'uncivilized', i.e. *inferior*, character of African, Indian, Aboriginal, or Middle Eastern societies was based not just on prejudice or convention but on systematic comparisons, empirical detail, and developed theoretical argument.

Thus the images, values, and stereotypes used to define both femininity and non-European cultures and people combined the newly prestigious insights and techniques of science with older cultural myths and traditions. Just as the skull and brain size of Negroes or Eskimos was part of the evidence for their cultural and social inferiority, so the size of women's brains was brought into the argument about their capacity for education. When James Macgrigor Allen lectured on female invalidism and its link to menstruation, he did so at the Anthropological Society of London, and the lecture was published in the *Anthropological Review* of 1865.[8] Science and expertise seem to converge on both women and non-European here, and indeed this is merely one example of a whole new set of structures within which 'knowledge' and 'understanding' of these groups were established by European males. The founding of learned societies, journals, and academic institutions for medicine, anthropology, geography, and linguistic studies brought the study of human characteristics, differences, or cultures firmly into the sphere of science, rationality, and professional expertise. As will be shown, this is by no means the only or even the most powerful source of images of 'sex' or 'race', but it certainly constituted *one* of the most authoritative and influential ways of grounding the 'Otherness' of femininity or ethnic identity in 'real' knowledge wielded by prestigious professionals (doctors, academics, 'experts').

Not only did the power of definition and prescription in matters of gender and race come into the hands of similar 'experts' in each case, but also the arguments which constructed and justified the subordination of female or non-European persons in both cases followed comparable lines. Three prominent elements are worth noting. First, differences between women and men, or between one 'race' and another, were considered to be *essential*, that is to say differences of 'nature' (a significant term) or kind, not of specific or transient detail. Basic biology, whether in the form of reproductive functions, intelligence, physical attributes, or genetic heritage, was made central to definitions of gender or ethnic identity, using the powerful language and 'evidence' of science as described above. 'Femininity' or 'negritude' or 'oriental' characteristics were conceived of as inborn or given features with which 'nature' endowed people – 'nature' now carrying a new forceful meaning of the (scientifically understood) 'real' world, as well as the older meaning of someone's true and proper place or role in the world.[9] This, of course, allowed any woman or 'race' who resisted conformity to the norms thus established to be defined as *not* normal or natural, while also allowing the argument that if 'natives' or women were not fitted *by nature* for civic rights or education there was little point in offering such benefits to them. If gender and race were conceived as *essential*, 'naturally' fixed categories, then they could not be affected by *contingent* factors, whether history, social change, or demands for reform.

Second, the fixed 'natural' and essentialist definitions of gender and race were also based on an assumption of inequality between genders and races. The physical and cultural differences between women and men, or between different groups of humans, which had been observed by linguists, anthropologists, historians, or medical and social investigators, were placed along a spectrum, one end of which was more highly valued than the other. Not for nothing was the Comte de Gobineau's famous study of racial issues entitled *Essay on the Inequality of Human Races*. Discussions on femininity or ethnic character were frequently presented in terms of the ways in which women or particular ethnic groups deviated from, or lacked, or failed to achieve the qualities, attainments, or indeed the potential considered 'normal' for European males of the dominant classes. Here is the philosopher and philologist Ernest Renan comparing 'Semitic' with 'Indo-European'[10] characteristics:

in all things the Semitic race appears ... *an incomplete race* by virtue of its simplicity. The race – if I dare use the analogy – is to the Indo-European family what a pencil sketch is to painting; it *lacks* that variety, that amplitude, that abundance of life which is the condition of perfectibility. Like those individuals who possess so little fecundity that, after a gracious childhood, they *attain only the most mediocre virility*, the Semitic nations ... *have never been able to achieve true maturity*. (my italics)[11]

It is interesting to note the intertwining of gender metaphors (fecundity, virility) with the assertions of the inequality of Semite and Indo-European, an inequality founded on the inability of the former to improve or mature as the latter can. Similar perceptions of the inadequacy, inequality, and incapacity of women as compared to men can be seen in the comments of a pseudonymous writer of the 1860s:

> The reasoning powers are more perfect in [man] than in [woman]. The creative powers belong almost exclusively to him ... it was impossible for her ever completely to know or to realize the tempest of passions which sway the soul of an Othello or a Faust.[12]

As will be seen, there were also perceptions of gender or race difference which stressed complementarity if not equality, but it is hard to ignore the force of the conviction that by their very nature women and non-Europeans could not or would not attain the cultural, political, or social achievements of white males.

Two images of inferiority evolved to evoke both that conviction and the intimacy of gender relations and race relations in the family in colonial systems and in sexual encounters. Powerful and old-established images of the parent–child relationship on the one hand, and the master–servant relationship on the other, provided models and metaphors blending the unquestioned subordination, physical closeness, and servicing of personal needs involved in the role both of women towards men and of 'natives' to imperial superiors. In both cases men valued natives or women according to their obedience, devotion and ability to serve and nurture. In her study of the relationship between Hannah Cullwick and Arthur Munby, Davidoff has shown that a powerful combination of male–female, master–servant, and even black slave–white owner images drew on common elements of loyalty, intimacy, and hard physical work which contributed both to their everyday activity and to highly charged erotic fantasy.[13] Similarly, among the most positive depictions of non-Europeans in the travel books, social comment, and fiction of empire and exploration were the 'loyal servants' (or soldiers) – Arab, African, Indian – who were shown as simultaneously personally close and properly obedient to dominant European males. In such depictions, service and devotion might even extend to a willingness to sacrifice life for their imperial superiors (Gunga Din), or of women to do the same in bearing or protecting children, favourite themes in popular art and literature.[14]

Women and natives might also be portrayed and treated as children in need of the protection and care of male/imperial authority by virtue of their weaknesses, innocence, and inadequacy. The use of a parental concept of authority combined a sense of care and involvement with the subordinate sex or race as well as power and control over them, and as such was equally appropriate for the definition of the power of men over women or of dominant over subordinate races. 'Treat them as children; make them do what we know is for their benefit,' robustly advised one 'China hand' in 1860 as British entrepreneurial and strategic interests tried to push into Chinese markets: he was echoed in numerous other uses of the 'child' metaphor for Africans, Tibetans, Tahitians, or the Indians of Kipling's work, uses which can also be paralleled by comparable images of femininity ranging from Dickens's child-women to Burke's ideal of 'infantine' female beauty and Carlyle's addressing a girl child as 'little woman'.[15] Indeed, Davidoff and Hall comment that the 'young, dependent, almost child-like wife was portrayed as the ideal in fiction, etchings, songs and poetry'.[16]

The third stage in the argument developed precisely the points about power which begin to emerge in the images described above. It can be seen that these analyses and images of 'difference' and 'inequality' of sexes and races contributed to the view that it was necessary, justifiable, and proper that the superior sex/race control the inferior, that the weaker sex/race accept the authority of the stronger. It was frequently argued that, since Indian or African societies could be shown ('scientifically'!) to be unable to produce acceptable forms of government, religion, or law, it was appropriate (and beneficial) for Europeans to provide what they lacked and could never achieve for themselves. Scholarly and popular histories of British rule in India depicted it as an act of salvage from the violence, corruption, and instability of the regimes that preceded it, which were vividly described. A Frenchman like Lamartine could characterize the people he saw on his visit to the provinces of the Ottoman Empire as 'nations without territory, *patrie*, rights, laws or security … waiting anxiously for the shelter' of European occupation.[17] Such themes were taken up by Western missionaries wishing to rescue the benighted heathen, by political economists and reformers planning the 'improvement' of backward economic and social systems, and by entrepreneurs anxious to open up the world to modern, progressive, commercial market forces.

In a similar way, men argued that women's nurturing, domestic, spiritual talents, their mental and physical frailty, and their inability to act successfully in the public spheres of economic life, politics, or high culture should be protected by male political, legal, and social authority. Since, because of their physical and mental nature, women lacked the stability or assertiveness to compete effectively or take responsibility without damaging their 'essential' femininity, they needed men to play the role of 'sturdy tree' to which their 'vine' could cling (a metaphor found not only in Charlotte Brontë's *Jane Eyre* but in popular sermons and poems collected in middle-class families[18]). Trade-unionists like Broadhurst, advocating the exclusion of women from competition in the labour market, and writers like Ruskin, defining men as 'givers of laws' protecting women from temptation and danger, contributed to the arguments against female access to higher education, paid work, and political or trade-union rights. Others contributed to similar controversies over the rights of 'natives' and colonial subjects, and in each case examples of 'naturally'/'normally' unreliable or irrational behaviour were given as evidence that women or 'natives' were by nature unfit for public life and achievement in work, politics, or creative activity. Moreover, it could be argued that the 'natural' virtues and qualities which Western males 'discovered' and valued in women were best protected from damage by excluding them from those public spheres. Thus the circle was closed, as dominant males, having constructed definitions and descriptions of the female or non-Western 'Other', could resist challenges or alternatives to their views, not in the interests of male power, but in defence of the 'true' identity and needs of those Others whom Western men had discovered and needed.

This account of new perceptions of ethnic and gender identity developing in nineteenth-century Europe has by no means dealt with all the facets, complexities, and contradictions within such a major area of European culture. While not fully discussed here, other historical work has shown how the role of religion in both idealizing and restricting the 'female sphere', the ambiguities in male attitudes to the very Western 'civilization' of which they were the makers and bearers at home and abroad, and the conflicting views of 'nature', 'culture', 'reason', or 'emotion' were all significant for the history of sexuality and ethnicity.[19] Two important points emerge from the discussion so far and now need to be emphasized: first, in examining concepts of 'sex' and 'race' we are dealing with the terrain of male power; second, such power should be understood not just as a practical function but also as a process of defining the self and others. Explanations and justifications of male advantage and authority over women, or of Western superiority to non-westerners, were deployed quite specifically against feminists and anti-imperialists, but to argue that this was the purpose of the images and arguments involved would be a mistake. We shall need to go beyond any merely functionalist account of them as tools for the creation and maintenance of Western male power over or against women and non-Europeans.

The images of Otherness and subordination which will now be examined further in the particular setting of 'orientalism' need to be understood as ways for men to explore and deal with *their own* identity and place in the world as sexual beings, as artists and intellectuals, as imperial rulers, and as wielders of knowledge, skill, and power. The concepts of 'sex' and 'race' which came into use in European culture, elite and popular, did not just make the control of women or natives easier, but also expressed the conflicts, desires, and anxieties which were part of the lived relationships between sexes and races, the *realities* of sexuality and imperial power. The fact that these areas of experience were dealt with through fiction, through artistic fantasy and imaginative constructions of the female and non-Western Other in travel literature, popular journals, and high theory, should not mislead us about the sharp personal and practical importance of the images concerned. This point will be pursued and amplified in the discussion of orientalist art and writing, which will also stress that this material illustrates not merely similarity but actual symbiotic intermingling of the racial and sexual themes which concerned its creators. As male writers, artists, and journalists in England and France constructed their versions of gender difference, they drew on a repertoire of images, ideas, and information about alien societies and cultures. As they constructed their concepts of societies and cultures in the Middle East and North Africa, they drew on a body of language and opinion about sexuality and sexual difference. The outcome, it will be argued, was a sexualization of Western definitions of these non-Western societies, and an exoticization of definitions of sexuality in European culture.

First, however, it will be useful to establish the circumstances in which orientalist art and literature developed. From the later eighteenth century, growing British and French commercial and strategic interests in the Middle East led to diplomatic, commercial, and military intervention in Egypt. Algeria, and Syria/ Lebanon as well as the Ottoman court, while trade and communication with the eastern Mediterranean and North Africa increased similarly. Politically, European powers confronted the issues posed for them by movements for 'national' autonomy and for government reform and centralization in the Ottoman Empire.[20] Economically, new opportunities for Europeans were provided by the demand for their manufactures and technology in the Middle East, the emergence of cotton production in Egypt for the Western market, and the interest of Middle Eastern rulers in attracting European financial support and investment.[21] This expansion of material involvements was paralleled by growing cultural and intellectual interest on the part of the British and French (and German) writers, artists, travellers, and scholars. Some took practical advantage of improved opportunities to visit the Middle East, collect linguistic, historical, ethnographic, and archaeological evidence for study, or to depict their experiences in books or pictures. The publication of the work of the scholars who accompanied Napoleon's expedition to Egypt began an era of European investigation, accumulation, and transmission of material about the Middle East, and of extensive use of Middle Eastern themes by artists and writers. Observations, translations, and interpretations of author/travellers like Edward Lane or Richard Burton, and imaginative flights by Goethe, Hugo, or Byron and other Romantics, added new dimensions to the established conventions (reaching back to the Crusades) about what now became known as the Orient.[22]

Perhaps one of the most important features to note in the orientalist art and writing of our period was the absence of clear distinctions or boundaries between observed and imagined reality. Travellers to the Middle East drew not just on their actual observations, but on concepts, images, and quotations taken from fellow French or British writers, to describe and explain their experiences. Artists repeatedly reworked sketches and rearranged artefacts brought back from North Africa, Turkey, or Egypt to create their own pictures of 'oriental' scenes and people in French or British studios, or drew on European literary sources to inspire such pictures. Thus Gérard de Nerval's *Journey to the Orient* incorporated unacknowledged material from Lane's *Manners and Customs of the Modern Egyptians*, while Gautier and Lamartine, arriving in Smyrna or Istanbul or Cairo, drew on phrases or images from Chateaubriand or Victor Hugo to convey their reactions.[23] Painters like Ingres could construct pictures of odalisques and 'Turkish baths' from Lady Mary Wortley Montague's travel letters, and it was Byron's work that inspired the 'oriental' picture of *The Death of Sardanapalus* produced by Delacroix before ever he visited the Middle East.[24] Others like Jean-Léon Gérôme and John Frederick Lewis did indeed make use of objects and sketches from life acquired during extended stays in Egypt and Turkey, blending them with Parisian model girls and judicious rearrangements to produce their personal versions of harem or street scenes. While it is to some extent true that between the 1820s and 1870s there was a shift from depictions of a romantically imagined Orient by Hugo or Ingres to a realistically detailed Orient as portrayed by Gérôme or Doughty, it is the *interweaving* of imagination and observation to create complex images and explanations which was more characteristic of orientalism.[25]

When Lamartine described his 1833 journey to the Orient as 'a great episode in my interior life', as much the product of his reading and theorizing as of actual travel, he conveyed exactly the blend of observed and constructed experience so important to travellers and writers.[26] Similar features emerge from the debate over the accuracy of accounts of the Arabian explorer Palgrave, Nerval's use of a friend's experience with a slave girl as part of his own experience of life in Egypt, and indeed the whole structure of his *Journey to the Orient*, with its combination of storytelling *à la Arabian Nights* and autobiographical travel narrative.[27] A similar synthesis can be seen in the presence of Western female models in orientalist settings, posed among 'genuine' details of architecture, décor, and objects from the Middle East. Sometimes the tensions and disappointments arising from the encounter between orientalist imaginings and actual experience were themselves an important theme, a source of romantic sadness such as Nerval described, regretting that Egypt was 'driven out of my imagination, now that I have sadly placed it in my memory'.[28] Flaubert too found that observing realities in Egypt produced a sense of barrenness and loss:

> what we lack is the intrinsic principle, the soul of the thing, the very idea of the subject. We take notes, we make journeys: emptiness! emptiness! We became scholars, archaeologists, historians, doctors, cobblers, people of taste. What is the good of all that? Where is the heart, the verve, the sap?[29]

However, his Egyptian experience and his orientalist imaginings also came together in a complex whole, as he explained in a letter to his mother:

> You ask me whether the Orient is up to what I imagined it to be. Yes, it is; and more than that, it extends far beyond the narrow idea I had of it. I have found, clearly delineated, everything that was hazy in my mind. Facts have taken the place of suppositions – so excellently so that it is often as though I were suddenly coming upon old forgotten dreams.[30]

However, there is another significance in Lamartine's comment on oriental travel as an episode in *interior* life. If on the one hand the emergence of orientalist writing and art in the nineteenth century was the product of external circumstances favouring contact with and interest in the Middle East, on the other hand the work that came out of the encounter of westerners with the Middle East contributed to their *self-development*. The depiction of the Orient involved the self-discovery of the writer or artist as well as voyages of discovery to the Orient, and the construction of this Orient through fiction, art, and scholarship involved also the construction of the identities and careers of those who produced such work. At a mundane level the production of orientalist material could be the key to success and reputation; John Frederick Lewis's achievement as president of the Watercolour Society and Royal Academy exhibitor was founded on orientalist work; the fame of Richard Burton began with his adventures on the pilgrimage to Mecca and was later consolidated by his version of *The Thousand and One Nights*; many more writers and artists earned a living from orientalist material, whether it was the salon success of Gérôme or the anonymous illustrators of periodicals, travel books, or Jules Verne novels. In a more complex and personal sense the experience of oriental travel and the encounter with orientalist ideas might be part of the emergence of creative talent, as Steegmuller argues was the case for Flaubert.[31] The Orient, said Lamartine, is the 'fatherland of my imagination', expressing both the sense in which it is something which he invents, but also the sense in which it provided a creative personal opportunity for him as a writer and theorist.[32]

In general, scholars have discussed the contribution of orientalist experience and work to the self-development and self-discovery of writers and artists primarily in just those terms. However, this approach is less than adequate if it ignores the fact that these writers, travellers, and artists were defined by their masculinity, their class, and their European culture. They dealt with Middle Eastern societies as males from professional, gentry, or middle-class backgrounds in Britain or France, formed by and connected to the gender, class, and cultural structures of their own societies, and influenced by the emerging views of race, gender, and class already examined. The 'Otherness' which was central to westerners' concepts of the Orient – it was what they were not – is expressed in terms which are both racial/cultural and profoundly sexual, both elements combining to define a terrain – the Orient – for control, power, and domination. It is therefore worth exploring the verbal and visual terms in which the Orient was presented in order to reveal features already identified as being characteristic of gender and race discourses generally.

Perhaps the more obvious approach focuses on the use of women and of gender and sexual themes and concepts to depict and define 'the Orient'. Oriental societies were frequently characterized by reference to the way in which women were treated, by descriptions of the laws and customs affecting women, by references to polygamy, veiling, and the seclusion of women, or by fascinated anecdotes of harems, dancing-girls, and sexual encounters. All these provided powerful evidence for the 'Otherness' of the Orient, whether it took the form of Edward Lane's self-consciously learned ethnographic descriptions, or the famous encounters of Flaubert and Nerval with prostitutes and slave girls, which became powerful literary *tours de force*.[33] Moreover, whether the treatment of these subjects was voyeuristic and indulgent, or judgemental and moralizing, it also contributed to the emergence of the most widely accepted stereotypes of the Orient as corrupt and decadent, uniting sexual licence with violent cruelty. Victor Hugo's poetic cycle *Les Orientales* (1829) and Delacroix's *Death of Sardanapalus* (1827) portrayed luxury, cruelty, and sexuality in ways which allowed the audience both to enjoy and to judge the oriental images before them. Pierre Jourda sums up the exotic Orient of the 1820s and 1830s as 'blood, voluptuousness, and death', themes which were alive and well a century later in films like *The Sheik* and *Lawrence of Arabia*, and in a product as recent as a television film of 1987 entitled *Harem* (!).[34]

However, the sexualizing of race, culture, and society in the Orient was a matter not just of colourful reportage of exotic stereotypes, but of persuasive definitions and symbols. Since European commentators endowed the Orient they had created with qualities with which men of the period also endowed females, they came on occasion to characterize the Orient as essentially or generally 'feminine'. The use of the phrase 'mysterious Orient', like 'mysterious female', indicated that both were seen as hard for Western men to understand; references to the irrationality and emotional extremes to which 'orientals' were inclined carried the implied comparison with similar tendencies attributed to women. More generally the Orient, like women, is discussed by Western men in terms of its actual or potential susceptibility and need for their control and authority, whether that was Lamartine's vision of the 'European right to power' in the east, or Burton's bold assertion that 'Egypt is a treasure to be won … the most tempting prize that the East holds out'. Feminine images of nature and landscape, common in a European context, also appear in oriental travel literature, as when Flaubert describes the pleasure of swimming in the Red Sea 'as though I were lying on a thousand liquid breasts', or when Thomas Moore talks of the 'light of Eve' over 'Syria's land of roses'.[35] Above all, women were presented as the *means* for imagining or finding out about the Orient. In the romantic travel literature it is the sight of veiled women which tells the voyager that he is in the Orient, just as their presence on the eastward voyage poses the first challenge to understanding.[36] They are the image of what the 'Other' actually is, their veils and harems the symbol of that 'Other', just as in visual terms they are one of the commonest subjects of orientalist painting, both exotic and 'realist'.

The fact that the 'Otherness' and subordination of the Orient were reinforced through the use of the gender connection and female subject matter itself requires discussion, and its implications further examination. In particular we should look at how women represented an Other which was not merely different and subordinate, but also desirable, intimate, and necessary to men. It follows that to introduce a feminine element into the construction of the 'oriental' was therefore to introduce notions of the *attraction* and *close connection* of the oriental for the Western male. Indeed, the encounters and representations by travellers and artists with oriental women did precisely suggest that desire and personal contact were part and parcel of their reaction to the oriental experience as a whole. More than many alien cultures, those in the Middle East were seen by westerners as part of Europe's past and heritage, and both radical Saint-Simonians and conservative Catholics like Chateaubriand imagined it in that way, using feminized language and images to reinforce that sense of familial intimacy. A highly sexual version of male–female intimacy was provided by the prostitute episodes in Flaubert, the story of Nerval's 'Zeynab', and the numerous women displayed in harem, bath, or bedroom settings who populate so much orientalist art.

By producing such material, ranging from the explicit reminiscent writings of Flaubert to the parade of sexological scholarship in Burton's *Thousand and One Nights*, or the popularized semi-pornographic products of the period, several messages are conveyed. These products not only made the 'oriental' into the sexually desirable, but also made the desirable Other more so precisely because She was oriental (as no doubt Rider Haggard realized!). European men could not only revel in the (real or imagined) purchase or possession of Egyptian or Algerian women as sexual partners, as models for their paintings, even as slaves, but could also have their enjoyment reinforced by the 'alien' character of the women concerned. The cultural gaps, the limited ability to communicate, the 'exotic' dress, or undress, or squalor that are evoked in these situations actually helped Europeans to construct the experience itself in their writing, pictures, and theories. In doing so they not only gratified male power and male desire but had also to confront that desire, and even give voice to the ambiguities and anxieties involved in the erotic and the intimate, and in male need itself. If it was shown that the female/oriental was desired as well as dominated or despised, if need was admitted as well as superiority, then the nature of male power and desire becomes very complex. That complexity is expressed in the multiple voices and images of orientalist writing and painting, as has been shown by Harper in the case of Nerval and of Lane.[37]

From this it follows that, while the Orient came to be explored and characterized through images of gender and sexuality, it is equally important that the 'oriental' became an image through which gender and sexuality in turn could be defined within European culture. The popularity of terms like 'seraglio figure', 'Turkish beauties' (meaning female buttocks), and 'Asiatic ideas' (meaning sexual desire) in the discourse of male British writers on sex and male responses to femininity brings the oriental theme back to Europe, giving a significant new dimension to discourses of sexuality there.[38] The very market for orientalizing erotica and sexual imagery suggests that both masculinity and femininity were constructed by such means. Princess Pauline Bonaparte's refusal to hang Ingres's painting *The Turkish Bath* in her rooms can be seen not as prudery but as rejection of the male fantasies of desire and domination which the painting represents and gratifies, and which degrade, subordinate, and exploit women. The picture offers the viewer a room full of nude females displayed in a variety of attitudes expressing sensual abandon and availability in an 'oriental' setting. It invites a *male* gaze to enjoy the stimulus of their sexualized nudity, the voyeuristic thrill of observing a private female scene (and even some suggested lesbian loveplay), and the vicarious pleasure of identification with the Turkish delights of the harem. Princess Pauline's refusal of such an invitation should not be dismissively categorized as prudish.[39] There is an echo of her problem in Louise Colet's attempt to come to terms with her lover Flaubert's involvement (personal and literary) with the Egyptian woman Kucuk Hanem, an involvement recounted by him with sexually explicit and intellectually imaginative detail.[40] While Flaubert dismissed both Louise and Kucuk Hanem with male artistic confidence, it is clear that this episode in his Egyptian voyage was both an exercise in male sexual gratification and also the occasion for a complex and confused encounter with his own sexuality and his ambitions as a writer within the oriental setting.

For these endlessly reproduced male fantasies of harems and dancing-girls, of gratification through domination, and of intimacy with subordinates, represented not only the indulgence of male desire and power, but also one of the few means of dealing with the contradictions of masculinity and male needs as they developed at this period. The very existence of needs (personal, sexual, emotional) in men for which they sought satisfaction from women itself raised questions about the nature and limits of male domination. Male power, enshrined in law and custom, gave men sexual advantages over women, but it did not eliminate the reality of desire, attraction and bonding between men and women. To this contradiction should be added others posed by the separation of spheres and different gender identities in this period. While masculinity was becoming based on the distinctions between the male sphere of power, authority, reason, and public activity and the female sphere of nurture, service, emotion, and domestic activity, it also involved not only the right but the desire for access by men to the 'female' sphere. New forms of male socialization, whether through the working-class discipline of the labour process, or the middle-class discipline of schooling, sought to get young males to restrain or control emotion, weakness, and self-indulgence in order to earn a living, rule the empire, or gain authority in home, business, or state.[41] Hard work (mental or physical) and self-discipline involved a control of the self which in turn allowed men to control others (their women and children, their subjects, their employees).

However, in the process of attaining such control, men did not so much eliminate emotional and personal needs as transfer responsibility for them to women, whose caring, nurturing, feeling role was to satisfy them. The paradox was that this transfer embodied both the male power which made it happen, and the *loss* of power to understand and deal with the world of emotion, personal expression, and intimacy. It was this world which could be repossessed through male fantasies of the female, who stood not only for the Other which they had created, but for aspects of their selves which they did not wish to lose.

As has been often observed, it was the Romantic vision and its products which helped the European middle classes of the period to deal with the contradictions inherent in the change and disruption caused by the very economic processes of which their own progress was a part, but which also entailed squalor, loss, and insecurity. This vision might draw on images of the rural and the natural, on the idealization of domesticity as the haven 'where Womanhood waited and from which Manhood ventured abroad to work, to war, *and to the Empire*' (my italics), and on constructions of the medieval and the exotic as imaginary spheres where the conflicts of reason and emotion, of desire and duty, and of competition and harmony could be resolved.[42] In this context the feminized image of the sensual oriental (like those of natural/primitive Africans, spiritual Indians, or chivalrous medieval knights) enabled European men to handle the ambiguities in their situation. It was, of course, a function of their power that they could make, use and impose such images to protect sexual and racial privileges, manage their contradictions, and consolidate their dominance.

It is not surprising, therefore, that images of oriental sexuality were a feature not only of Western relations with the Middle East but also of discussions of male–female relationships in Europe. When Charlotte Brontë's heroine Jane Eyre is sparring over her relationship with her lover, the harem metaphor appears to illustrate the problems of women's autonomy and equality in love. He claims to value her more than a 'whole seraglio'; she refuses her allotted role in the fantasy, but pursues it by sketching out how she will enter his harem to subvert it. She has already seen his 'sultan's' smile and earlier watched him dress up convincingly as 'the model of an Eastern emir' since he has 'Paynim features'.[43] What at one level is play-acting at another raises questions of male despotism and sexual licence which are in fact central problems in Jane's relationship to Mr Rochester. Nor was this the only occasion when Brontë used oriental motifs to illuminate contradictions in westerners' sexuality. In *Villette* her use of episodes concerning a portrait of Cleopatra (clearly drawn from orientalist art of the period), and a stage perform-ance about the Eastern queen Vashti, to develop the internal struggles of her heroine over emotional/sexual need and female autonomy is equally striking.[44] The fact that these are all situations involving make-believe, performance, disguise, and artistic invention heighten rather than weaken their role as conscious dramatiz-ations of problems that cannot easily be presented at the level of 'realism'.

One could multiply examples of both casual and extended use of oriental references, images, and motifs as part of the 'common wisdom' as to what (Western) male sexuality and female identity are actually about. In Tennyson's *Princess* and *Fatima*, in Byron's Haidee in *Don Juan*, in Trollope's *Unprotected Female at the Pyramids*, such usages give an exotic, sometimes superior and critical, sometimes fascinated and yearning, dimension to love stories, to explorations of gender in male artists and female heroes, and to public interest in poetic/fictional resolutions to their own anxieties on those questions. Flaubert returned repeatedly to his oriental material to provide a source of fantasy (and comment) for the sexuality of Emma Bovary or Frédéric Moreau, as well as for full-scale orientalist fictions in *Salammbô* and *Hérodias*. Another tourist in Cairo, Thackeray, fleshed out the picture of aristocratic decadence in *Vanity Fair* with a staged harem charade at Lord Steyne's house. Thus the fantasy that 'appealed to an instinct of possession and domination as well as of mere pleasure' in European males also entered the mainstream of middle-class culture, becoming an accepted part of the discussion of sexuality, as influential when trivialized as when elaborately presented.[45] By the 1880s, not only could a major literary figure like Flaubert benefit from access to orientalist material, but the material had also inspired a whole range of popular genre writing of which the novels of Pierre Loti are still remembered, not to mention providing a stock of metaphors, clichés, and references casually and frequently used in Western art and writings to this day.

Of course, the power of orientalist imaginings was available for audiences as well as authors. Through writing and painting, others could share in the harem femininity created by Gérôme or Lewis, or the sexual explorations of the Orient undertaken by Flaubert or Nerval, and extensive reproduction and imitation of their works widened the audience, and hence the participation in these imaginings. Their power rested on the combination of 'realistic' detail and 'Romantic' invention of which orientalist work was composed. It is the sweat and smell of Kucuk Hanem as well as Flaubert's 'story' about her which make our encounter with her memorable; it is the vivid portrayal of Egyptian architecture, Turkish carpets, Syrian tilework as well as of the delights of imaginary female availability and desirability which makes Gérôme's odalisques so attractive. Through these safely seductive and exotic scenarios, Western middle-class men could recover enjoyment of a sexuality which had become problematic in their own homes, just as some did through involvement with working-class women, a parallel which Flaubert realized when commenting on his recollections of Parisian brothels while in bed with Kucuk Hanem.[46] Through the familiar form of (commercialized) sexual contact, such men could deal with the demands posed by their encounters with other societies, just as they used the equally familiar structures of military hierarchy and domestic service for similar purposes. Personal and sexual contact mediated cultural Otherness, just as culturally exotic formats mediated sexual Otherness. The conflicts, desires, and anxieties within the sexual or cultural involvements between Western males and the subordinate Other could be expressed and perhaps contained, however precariously, within oriental images, stories, or travels. Nature and feeling, both now controlled in a very real sense by science and reason to an extent hitherto unknown in human history, could be allowed back into men's lives in forms and conditions established by them.

It is not surprising, therefore, that sexual and ethnic relations were often expressed in terms of power and domination. The term 'penetrate', used by explorers travelling in unfamiliar territory, by imperialists describing conquests, or by voyeurs speculating on what lay behind veils and harem doors, is, of course, a forcefully male sexual metaphor as well. When Lamartine and other travel writers speak of penetrating the seraglio, or the orientalist Hogarth (who combined archaeology with intelligence work for the British government) entitled his history of Western exploration *The Penetration of Arabia*, they evoked an image of male aggression both sexual and imperial.[47] The depiction of women in harem or bath scenes accompanied by guards, or Negro attendants, or even on occasion their male masters, ties their sexual attraction closely to possession, control, and subordination. In fact the apparent parallel between the submission of Middle Eastern societies to Western economic, cultural, and political influence, and the subordination of women to male needs and authority, actually converges in a single image of sexualized imperial power or imperial masculine power.

The blending of conquest and enjoyment, of power and pleasure, of desire and domination, became part both of the lived experience of travel, conquest, and authority, and of the imaginative world of writing and painting of the Western men who created the Orient as well as ruling and exploiting it. These complex themes have been analysed through the written record of explorers, novelists, imperial officials, and scholars, notably by Said, but some of the most powerful depictions of sex/race images were contributed by the visual arts. These visualizations of 'sex' and 'race' are a central feature of the developing European consciousness of those matters during the nineteenth century. The salon art which developed in Paris from the 1840s onward was paralleled in the work of British, Italian, Central European, and Spanish orientalist artists from the era of Romanticism to that of post-impressionism. Lithographs and etchings spread the images beyond the limited audience of collectors, dealers, and patrons to a larger public who could see them in illustrated travel books, in periodicals like the *Magasin Pittoresque* and *Le Tour du monde* and their British and German counterparts, and in orientalizing illustrations of fiction like Jules Verne's *Michel Strogoff*, let alone the *Arabian Nights*.[48]

Equally striking is the demonstration of the actual material power of artists to control and indeed manufacture the images which they offered to the public. Fantasy pictures of harems and dancing-girls were composed from objects *purchased* by the artists for their studies, from sketches *taken home* from travel and regularly reworked, and from female models *paid for* and arranged in the settings chosen by the artists. These might be European women earning a living by working as models in the studios of Paris, London, Rome, or Vienna, or they might be Turkish, North African, or Egyptian women from lower classes or religious minorities more willing to allow themselves to be portrayed by Western artists. In either case they were socially marginal, sexually powerless, and vulnerable, and regarded by westerners and Middle Eastern societies as inferior, morally suspect, even virtual prostitutes. Their faces and bodies were labelled Circassian or Greek (supposedly light-skinned groups), their naked pallor contrasted with the skin colour of other Negro or Indian models posing as slaves or attendants, or with the richly robed guards and masters of the harem; *they* remain anonymous (unlike portraits of their sisters in the privileged classes), transformed into the 'odalisque' or 'the *almeh*' (dancer), or into Cleopatras, Scheherazades, or a dozen other heroines of Western imaginings, from the 'Zuleika', 'Leila', and 'Haidee' of Byron to Nerval's 'Queen of Sheba' or Oscar Wilde's 'Salome'. They 'become' whoever artists want them to be, yet they were actually flesh-and-blood women whose lives were no less real for being hidden from history. It was the social, gender, and colonial power of Western men which made such subordination and concealment possible.

As can be seen, there were close links between the visual and the verbal forms of the sexual-exotic images under discussion. At one level it was a case of literature and painting inspiring one another: the poetic Orient of Byron stimulated Delacroix, Corot, and others; Hugo's *Orientales* and the exotic travel literature of the mid-century did as much to shape the orientalist art of Ingres, Lewis, and Gérôme as did their own studies of female models and Middle Eastern scenes; publication of Western versions of the *Arabian Nights* provided opportunities for orientalist illustration, as did the proliferation of travel books; the celebrated artist Eugène Fromentin produced major travel books about North Africa as well as influential paintings of its scenery and people; Lane's descriptions and drawings of Cairo reappear in the paintings of Gérôme and Deutsch, and in turn Gérôme's 1861 work *The Prisoner* (set on the Nile) inspired one of José-Maria de Heredia's sonnets; similarly, some 1830s rendering of an oriental female provided material for Brontë's 'Cleopatra' in *Villette*, while travellers to Egypt, Morocco, or Turkey took with them recollections of orientalist pictures which shaped their written accounts of their travels as much as the actual experience.[49] Whether one considers the 'literary' quality of orientalist painting, linked as it was to orientalist poetry, travel writing, and fiction, or the strong 'visual' elements in the literary depiction of harems, odalisques, etc., it is clear that the sexual and exotic elements in the Western concept of the Orient rested on both, and the language of glamour, power, and desire is manifest in either form.

Thus, when Harriet Martineau satirized Bulwer-Lytton 'on a sofa, sparkling and languishing, among a set of female votaries – he and they dizened out, perfumed and presenting *the nearest picture to a seraglio* to be seen on British ground – only the indifference or hauteur of the *lord of the harem* being absent' (my italics), or when J. S. Mill noted that 'men desire to have, in the woman most nearly connected with them, not a forced slave, but a willing one, not a slave merely, but a favourite', they were using images which readers could both visualize and understand.[50] That such images were used by liberal 'pro-women' writers like Martineau and Mill testifies to the depth of their absorption into the consciousness of the dominant culture, shaping even 'enlightened' critiques of that culture. Mill's clear perception of the ambiguous nature of male power – 'men do not want solely the obedience of women, they want their sentiments' – does not belie the fact that he uses an accepted discourse of gender and domination with its exotic and colonial overtones.[51] Like Jane Eyre dealing with Rochester's 'seraglio' discourse, Martineau and Mill may dislike or challenge the oriental image, but they do not deny it.

Such cultural observations would have little more than curiosity value, were they not bound up with real material, legal, and political subordination and discrimination which gave Western men power over gender, class, and ethnic 'inferiors'. Slavery, sexual discrimination, and imperialism did actually exist in the nineteenth century, so that references to 'votaries' or 'favourite slaves' cannot be set aside as mere colourful language, but rather should be seen as comments on the *real* subordination of women and non-westerners, made sharper by the introduction of the 'exotic' motif into the Victorian milieu.

Jane Eyre ends not with the 'happy ever after' of the marriage celebrated at the opening of the final chapter, but with an account of the missionary St John Rivers 'labouring for his race' in India, glorified as a stern 'warrior' and 'indefatigable pioneer', with the 'ambition of a *master* spirit'.[52] It would seem that the affirmation of male achievement (and sacrifice) is given pride of place over the 'feminine' goals of marital and domestic happiness. Perhaps this authorial choice tells us something about the world as perceived and experienced by Charlotte Brontë in the 1840s; it certainly provides readers with a poignant picture of the imperial male/male imperialist. Forty years later Kipling's *The Man Who Would Be King* similarly makes male sacrifice (of women and drink) central to the realization of the ambition to rule expressed in the 'contract' drawn up by the two would-be kingdom winners and to their downfall.[53] Self-control, sexuality, imperial power, and male integrity are evoked in two otherwise very different fictions. Manliness and empire confirmed one another, guaranteed one another, enhanced one another, whether in the practical disciplines of commerce and government or in the escape zones of writing, travel, and art. It is for this reason that the history of orientalism and its contribution to new perceptions and practices of 'race' and 'sex' relations is worth the attention which it has been given here. On the principle of 'knowing the enemy', let Kipling have the last word: he was the author of the famous cliché 'East is East and West is West and never the twain shall meet'– a classic formulation of Otherness; however, the end of the verse which opens with that line and stands at both the beginning and the end of one of his 'ballads' merits fuller attention as a far more revealing evocation of the deep mutuality of sex/race images and consciousness:

> There is neither East nor West, nor Border nor breed nor birth
> When two strong men stand face to face, tho' they come
> from the ends of the earth.[54]

Notes

This chapter is extracted from a longer piece, which includes a detailed discussion of a number of visual images of race and gender. This detailed analysis is integral to the development of the full argument of the essay. The original version is in Susan Mendus and Jane Rendall (eds), *Sexuality and Subordination* (London, Routledge, 1989) pp. 89–128.

1 See L. Davidoff, 'Class and gender in Victorian England: the diaries of Arthur J. Munby and Hannah Cullwick', *Feminist Studies*, 5, 1979, reprinted in J. Newton, M. Ryan, and J. Walkowitz (eds), *Sex and Class in Women's History*, London, Routledge & Kegan Paul, 1983, from which subsequent references are taken; see also S. Alexander, 'Women, class and sexual difference in the 1830s and 1840s: some reflections on the writing of feminist history', *History Workshop Journal*, 17, 1984.

2 This and some of the subsequent discussion are drawn from a variety of sources, the most relevant of which are J. Rendall, *The Origins of Modern Feminism: Women in Britain, France*

and the USA 1780–1860, London, Macmillan, 1985; L. Davidoff and C. Hall, *Family Fortunes: Men and Women of the English Middle Class 1780–1850*, London, Hutchinson, 1987; N. Stepan, *The Idea of Race in Science: Great Britain 1800–60*, London, Macmillan, 1982; C. Bolt, *Victorian Attitudes to Race*, London, Routledge & Kegan Paul, 1971; E. Said, *Orientalism*, London, Routledge & Kegan Paul, 1978; V. Kiernan, *The Lords of Human Kind*, Harmondsworth, Penguin, 1972; R. Meek, *Social Science and the Ignoble Savage*, Cambridge, Cambridge University Press, 1976. For the development of dominant ideas in response to challenge, see J. Swindells, *Victorian Writing and Working Women*, Cambridge, Polity, 1985; J. Burstyn, *Victorian Education and the Ideal of Womanhood*, London, Croom Helm, 1978; F. Hutchins, *The Illusion of Permanence*, Princeton NJ, Princeton University Press, 1967 (chs 4, 7–9); R. Austin and W. Smith, 'Images of Africa and slave trade abolition: the transition to an imperialist ideology', *African Historical Studies*, 1969; Said, *Orientalism*, 31–49, 195–7, 220–5.

3 This misleading term is retained without comment, since it is a familiar, though ethnocentric, name applied to societies around the eastern Mediterranean and coast of North Africa by western commentators.

4 See Anne Digby's contribution to this volume; Burstyn, *Victorian Education*, chs 4, 5; L. Duffin, 'Prisoners of progress: women and evolution', in S. Delamont and L. Duffin (eds), *The Nineteenth Century Woman: Her Cultural and Physical World*, London, Croom Helm, 1978; C. Dyhouse, 'Social Darwinist ideas and the development of women's education in England 1800–1929', *History of Education*, 3, 1977.

5 See B. Taylor, '"The men are as bad as their masters": socialism, feminism and sexual antagonism in the London tailoring trade', *Feminist Studies*, 5,1979; Alexander, 'Women, class and sexual difference', S. Lewenhak, *Women and Trades Unions*, London, Benn, 1977, chs 2–4; C. Cockburn, *Brothers: Male Dominance and Technological Change*, London, Pluto, 1983, ch. l.

6 See Taylor, '"The men"', and Lewenhak, *Women and Trades Unions*, 39–40, 73, 88–91, for evidence of trade-union support for women, more fully analysed in S. Boston, *Women Workers and the Trade Union Movement*, London, Lawrence & Wishart, 1987, chs 1, 2. Other debates can be followed in K. Millet, 'The debate over women: Ruskin v. Mill', in M. Vicinus (ed.), *Suffer and be Still: Women in the Victorian Age*, London, Methuen, 1980; Rendall, *The Origins of Modern Feminism*, 74–101, 208–15; C. Moses, 'Saint-Simonian men/ Saint-Simonian women: the transformation of feminist thought in 1830s France', *Journal of Modern History*, 54, 1982; B. Taylor, *Eve and the New Jerusalem: Socialism and Feminism in the Nineteenth Century*, London, Virago, 1983, 32–8, 53–4, 68–70, 183–92.

7 J. Mill, *History of India*, London, 1819, book 2, 'Of the Hindus'; Comte de Volney, *Voyage en Egypte et en Syrie*, Paris, 1787.

8 Quoted by E. Showalter, 'Victorian women and menstruation', in Vicinus, *Suffer and be Still*, 40, referring to *Anthropological Review*, 7, 1869, 98–109. There are other examples of discussions on women appearing in anthropological journals, e.g. W. Distant, 'On the mental difference between the sexes', *Journal of the Royal Anthropological Society*, 4, 1875, 78–87, and E. Wallington, 'The physical and intellectual capacities of Woman equal to those of Man', *Anthropologia*, 1874, 552–65.

9 The shift in the connotations of the concept 'nature' from the philosophical to the scientific/ empirical came about through the work of Enlightenment theorists and the development of 'physical' sciences (chemistry, geology, physics, zoology), which in turn provided models for the 'human' sciences (anthropology, medicine, sociology).

10 The categories 'Semitic' and 'Indo-European' originally described groupings of related languages but by the mid-nineteenth century had also become accepted terms for the people (= races?) who spoke them.

11 Said, *Orientalism*, 149, citing E. Renan, *Œuvres complètes*, Paris, Flammarion, 1947–61, vol. 8, 156.

12 *Christian Observer*, 64, 1865, 547 ('The education of women'), cited in Burstyn, *Victorian Education*, 73.

13 Davidoff, 'Class and gender', 24–7, 40–1, 46–8.

14 The poem 'Gunga Din' appeared in R. Kipling's *Barrack-Room Ballads*, London, 1892; and Kipling's 'Her Majesty's Servants', in *The Jungle Book*, London, 1894, is a classic depiction of the links between service, empire, and military sacrifice, links publicly expressed in Queen/ Empress Victoria's display of her Sikh soldier-servants. The emotive depiction of mothers dead in childbirth or sacrificing life for children was a staple of middle-class novels and popular fiction in the nineteenth century.

15 Captain S. Osborn, *The Past and Future of British Relations in China*, Edinburgh, 1860, 15; on Tibet, see the comment in Kiernan, *The Lords of Human Kind*, 180; on Africa, see J. H. Speke, *Journal of the Discovery of the Source of the Nile*, London, 1863, 14 ('a grown child'), or David Livingstone, quoted in J. I. McNair, *Livingstone the Liberator*, London, Collins, 1940, 99 ('they are mere children'). Dickens's Dora and Little Dorrit are well-known child/woman images, interestingly placed in context in P. Rose, *Parallel Lives*, Harmondsworth, Penguin, 1985, 143–93, which also tells the story of Carlyle and the little girl on p. 257; Burke's ideas of infantine beauty are discussed in Davidoff and Hall, *Family Fortunes*, 28. See also Ruskin's comment on 'majestic childishness' as central to female 'loveliness' in 'Of Queens' Gardens', in *Sesame and Lilies*, London, 1865.

16 Davidoff and Hall, *Family Fortunes*, 323.

17 Alphonse de Lamartine, *Voyage en Orient*, Paris, 1835–87, vol. 2, 533.

18 C. Brontë, *Jane Eyre*, London, 1847, Harmondsworth, Penguin, 1966, 469; Davidoff and Hall draw attention to the tree/vine metaphor in *Family Fortunes*, 325, 397, quoting popular poems of 1828 and the 1830s.

19 A very full discussion of the role of religion in the definition of gender roles in the nineteenth century can be found in Rendall, *The Origins of Modern Feminism*, ch. 3, and Davidoff and Hall, *Family Fortunes*, chs 2, 7–9. Ambiguities in male attitudes to femininity are examined in C. Christ, 'Victorian masculinity and the "angel in the house"', in M. Vicinus (ed.), *A Widening Sphere: Changing Roles of Victorian Women*, Bloomington IN, Indiana University Press, 1977, and M. Harper, 'Recovering the Other: women and the Orient in writings of early nineteenth century France', *Critical Matrix*, 1, 1985. Many studies of imperial and racial thought draw attention to the fact that the authors of such ideas were aware of both the inferiority *and* the attractions of the primitive, the wilderness, the exotic, and the natural.

20 See M. Anderson, *The Eastern Question*, London, Macmillan, 1966, or S. Shaw, *The Ottoman Empire*, 2 vols, Cambridge, Cambridge University Press, 1976–77.

21 The best up-to-date survey is R. Owen, *The Middle East and the World Economy 1800–1914*, London, Macmillan, 1981.

22 The Napoleonic *Description de l'Egypte* appeared between 1809 and 1828, Edward Lane's *Account of the Manners and Customs of the Modern Egyptians* in 1836, and Richard Burton's *A Pilgrimage to al-Medinah and Mecca* in 1856. The orientalizing poetry of Goethe (*West-östlicher Diwan*) and Hugo (*Les Orientales*) appeared in 1819 and 1829 respectively. Byron's *The Giaour* and *The Bride of Abydos* appeared in 1813, *The Corsair* in 1814, *Don Juan* in 1819–24, and *Sardanapalus* in 1821. Successful translation/versions of the *Thousand and One Nights and a Night/Arabian Nights* were produced by Lane in the 1840s and Burton in the 1880s. See Said, *Orientalism*, 116–21.

23 See Said, *Orientalism*, 176–7, 179–81; P. Jourda, *L'Exotisme dans la littérature française depuis Chateaubriand*, 2 vols, Paris, Boivin, 1938, 1956, vol. 2, 37–47, shows how different travellers echoed one another.

24 Delacroix's painting, *The Death of Sardanapalus*, inspired by a play of Byron's on the tale of a despot defeated in war destroying his whole household prior to his own death, appeared in 1827, and he had already painted an odalisque in 1825–28; his only visit to the Orient was to Algiers and Morocco in 1832.

25 The move from 'Romanticism' to 'realism' is discussed in P. Jullian, *The Orientalists*, Oxford, Phaidon, 1977, 28, 56–74, and M. Stevens (ed.), *The Orientalists*, London, Royal Academy, 1984, 15–24. The blend of observation and imagination is discussed in Said, *Orientalism*, ch. l, pts II, III, ch. 2, pts I, III, IV; and also Harper, 'Recovering the Other', 9–10.

26 Lamartine, *Voyage en Orient*, vol. 1, 10; Said, *Orientalism*, 177–9.

27 G. de Nerval, *Journey to the Orient*, trans. N. Glass, London, M. Haag, 1984, was originally published in 1851, the journey having taken place in 1843; for the 'borrowing' from his friend's and Lane's experiences, see the introduction, p. 16; and Said, *Orientalism*, 176–7, 181. For an analysis of the use of 'storytelling' in Nerval, see Harper, 'Recovering the Other', 15–24.

28 On Palgrave, see P. Brent, *Far Arabia: Explorers of the Myth*, London, Quartet, 1979, 120–32; Nerval to Théophile Gautier (also a traveller to the Orient) in *Œuvres*, ed. A. Béguin and J. Richer, Paris, Gallimard, 1960, vol. 1, 933.

29 *Flaubert in Egypt*, trans. and ed. F. Steegmuller, London, M. Haag, 1983, is a selection of Flaubert's notes and correspondence during a visit to Egypt in 1849–50 with a friend, Maxime du Camp, some of whose notes and recollections are also included; the quotation is on pp. 198–9.

30 Ibid., 75.

31 Ibid., 11–17, 221–2.

32 Lamartine, *Voyage en Orient*, vol. 1, 179.

33 Nerval's fictional relationship with the slave 'Zeynab' forms 'Part One' of the *Journey*; the disturbing accounts of Flaubert's pursuit of prostitutes can be found in *Flaubert in Egypt*, 39–40, 43–50, 69–70, 76, 110–11, 113–22, 128–31, 153, 157–8, 192, 215, 219–21.

34 Jourda, *L'Exotisme*, vol. 1, 184: 'voilà tout l'Orient romantique; du sang, de la volupté et de la mort'.

35 R. Burton, *A Personal Narrative of a Pilgrimage to al-Medinah and Mecca*, ed. I. Burton, London, G. Bell & Sons, 1913, vol. 1, 112, 114; T. Moore, *Lalla Rookh: An Oriental Romance*, London, numerous editions in the 1820s.

36 Jourda, *L'Exotisme*, vol. 2, 37–8, 42–4, drawing on Lamartine, Gautier, Flaubert, and du Camp.

37 Harper, 'Recovering the Other', 13–14, 15–23.

38 P. Fryer, *Mrs Grundy: Studies in Victorian Prudery*, London, Transworld/Corgi, 1965, 40, 273; C. Ryskamp and F. Pottle (eds), *Boswell: The Ominous Years*, London, Heinemann 1963, 65, 293–4.

39 For a discussion of the painting (which defends Ingres's work as healthily masculine – *sic!* – and pure), see W. Pach, *Ingres*, New York, Harker Art Books, 1973, 131–6; see also N. Schlenoff, *Ingres: ses sources littéraires*, Paris, Presses Universitaires de France, 1956, 281–4.

40 *Flaubert in Egypt*, 113–19, 129–30, 219–21, where Steegmuller seems to identify with Flaubert rather than with what is pejoratively described as Colet's 'jealousy'.

41 Davidoff and Hall, *Family Fortunes*, 22, 25–8; see also L. Davidoff, J. L'Esperance and H. Newby, 'Landscape with figures', in J. Mitchell and A. Oakley (eds), *The Rights and Wrongs of Women*, Harmondsworth, Penguin, 1976; Christ, 'Victorian masculinity', and Harper, 'Recovering the Other', 4–10, are also evocative of ambiguities in gender and male desire.

42 Davidoff and Hall, *Family Fortunes*, 28; Kiernan, *The Lords of Human Kind*, 132, 136; Said, *Orientalism*, 182–3, 184–91, 194–7; H. Ridley, *Images of Imperial Rule*, London, Croom Helm, 1983, 14–30, chs 3, 4, 6; see also Karen Hodder in Susan Mendus and Jane Rendall, *Sexuality and Subordination* (London, Routledge, 1989), and M. Girouard, *The Return to Camelot: Chivalry and the English Gentleman*, New Haven CT, and London, Yale University Press, 1981.

43 Brontë, *Jane Eyre*, 297–8, 212–13.

44 C. Brontë, *Villette* (1853), Harmondsworth, Penguin, 1979, 275–7, 338–42.

45 W. Thackeray, *Vanity Fair*, ch. 51; Kiernan, *The Lords of Human Kind*, 140.

46 *Flaubert in Egypt*, 130.

47 Lamartine, *Voyage en Orient*, vol. 2, 159; D. Hogarth, *The Penetration of Arabia: A Record of the Development of Western Knowledge Concerning the Arabian Peninsula*, 1904.

48 Mathias Sandor used orientalist subjects to illustrate Verne, according to Jullian, *The Orientalists*, 112–13, which also illustrates an 1840 *Arabian Nights* (110).

49 Jullian, *The Orientalists*, Fromentin's works are *Un Eté dans la Sahara*, Paris, 1856, and *Une Année dans le Sahel*, Paris, 1858. For the role of Byron, see Jullian, *The Orientalists*, 47 (*Sardanapalus*), 114 (Corot's *Haidée*); for appropriations of Lane's material, see G. Ackerman,

Jean-Léon Gérôme (catalogue), Dayton OH, Dayton Art Institute, 1972, 16–17; M. Verrier (ed.), *The Orientalists*, London, Academy Edition, 1979, plates 12 (Gérôme) and 40 (Deutsch). Compare with E. Lane, *Manners and Customs of the Modern Egyptians* (1836), New York, Dover, 1973, 314, 316, 317.

50 H. Martineau, *Autobiography* (1877), ed. G. Weiner, London, Virago, 1973, vol. l, 350–1; J. S. Mill, *The Subjection of Women* (1869), Everyman, London, Dent, 1970, 232.

51 J. S. Mill, *The Subjection of Women*, 232.

52 Brontë, *Jane Eyre*, 474–7.

53 R. Kipling, *The Man Who Would Be King*, first published in a collection of stories in the Indian Railway Library series, called *The Phantom Rickshaw*, in December 1888. It was reprinted in England in 1890 and 1892. I have used the World's Classics edition, *The Man Who Would Be King and Other Stories*, ed. L. Cornell, Oxford, Oxford University Press, 1987. The eponymous story is on pp. 244–79. The 'Contrack' is described on p. 254.

54 The lines are from 'The Ballad of East and West', dated 1889, first published in Britain in *Barrack-Room Ballads* (1892), 75–83 (also available in *Rudyard Kipling's Verse: Definitive Edition*, London, Hodder & Stoughton, 1960, 234–8). The lines used here occur in the opening and closing verses, which 'frame' the poetic tale of an encounter between an officer of the (British) Indian Army and a chieftain of the North West Frontier in which manly gallantry (officer/gentleman style) transcends the confrontation of the 'native' with imperial military power.

3

Race, gender, science and citizenship

NANCY LEYS STEPAN

This chapter makes an argument by way of two stories. In effect, I use gender to think about the science of race, and vice versa, and both to think about science and citizenship. My aim is to draw on recent scholarship to provide a framework for the history of science, medicine and the racial/sexual body. I say 'a' framework, since there are many frameworks available. The chapter is argued rather abstractly, since there is no space for historical detail and nuance; but its deepest meaning and intent are historical, as I hope I shall be able to show.

The more immediate motivation for organizing my ideas in the way I do here derives from my experience of working between 1994 and 1996 in Eastern Europe, where matters that concern all of us come into especially sharp focus: ethnic conflict and nationalism; fortress Europe, human migration, and new immigration controls; more generally, that is, the question of citizenship and who can claim it in a polity. I have also been reflecting, as we all must, on our contemporary sciences: reproductive technologies, virtual reality, the Human Genome Project – and their social meanings. It is with these issues in mind – the issues of the ambiguities and power of concepts such as citizenship, nature, and science in the Western tradition – that my chapter wishes to engage.

The point of departure for my argument is gender and *citizenship*, and concerns a problem that has been identified as critical to contemporary gender studies, namely the difficulties of achieving women's full citizenship rights. In the countries of Eastern Europe, the so-called transitions to democracy have brought in their train increased inequalities between men and women, politically, economically and socially. The opening up of the spaces of civil and political society in the post-1989 years, spaces considered so central to political democracy, almost paradoxically creates new *kinds* of gender inequalities.[1] The inequality of citizenship in democracy is confirmed when we look to Western Europe and the United States, where even in the most established democracies (where women have long had the vote and other formal political rights), women are significantly under-represented in the political sphere – in national legislatures or other governing bodies, for instance. In the economic sphere, women consistently earn less than men even when in the same kinds of work, while in the social, familial, and sexual areas of life, women in general do not have the same degree of autonomy of the self (e.g. bodily autonomy) that most men enjoy.

Scholars such as Joan Scott, Ann Snitow, and Anne Phillips (to name only some of the best-known) have all grappled with the dilemma of women's citizenship in modern democracies. In her most recent book, *Only Paradoxes to Offer*, Scott writes about the wearisome *repetition* that afflicts the women's movement in France, and the demands women make for equality and rights; women seem, she says, to be for ever returning to the same point, to be constantly stumbling over the same issue – the issue of the same and the different in relation to equality. Women continually evoke first the irrelevance, and next the relevance, of their sex difference.[2] They find they have to make both arguments at one and the same time; no sooner do women deny that they are different from men because of their sex, and protest against their political and other exclusions, than they find themselves calling on the very difference (they are not the same as men, they have special needs) that they want to eliminate.

Scott maintains that women cannot choose between these two positions; this is the paradox that lies at the heart of women's citizenship. She shows the persistence of this paradox in French feminism, from the time of the French Revolution to 1944, when French women were finally granted the vote. In her words, feminists 'refused to be women in the terms their society dictated, and at the same time they spoke in the name of those women'.[3] And in her view, citizenship in French Republicanism has always been gendered in this paradoxical fashion, and has shaped the varieties of feminism and the intractability of women's demands to this day.

Ann Snitow, in her marvellous 'Gender Diary', explores the iteration of the same paradox – equality versus difference – in the very different legal, cultural, and constitutional setting of the United States, especially as it has marked her own life during the second wave of feminism, starting in the mid-1960s and extending to the present day. She remarks that 'this tension – between needing to act as a woman and needing an identity not over-determined by our gender – is as old as Western feminism … [Today] the divide is more urgent and central a part of feminism than ever before'. It is a divide that appears between those who insist that women have a commonality, their womanhood, without which there can be no feminist movement, and those who insist that the unity of womanhood is a fiction and that women are divided by every conceivable kind of difference – class, ethnic, geographic, religious, family, fertility experience and so on. It separates so-called 'motherists' from other kinds of feminists, cultural feminists from postmodernists; it is a divide that also reappears *within* each of these approaches.[4] This divide at the heart of women's demand for quality is profound, and shapes deeply how women make their case for full citizenship and rights.[5] As a paradox, it is not uniquely American, or French.[6]

Yet, as Ann Snitow and others remark, this tension between difference and sameness is not a transcendental, universal phenomenon, produced by the timeless features of womanhood, but is the result of *a specific history, or more correctly, two or three or more histories*, of the last 250 years or so.[7]

One of these specific histories is about liberal individualism and it is this history that has drawn most attention from feminist scholars. Starting in the seventeenth century, and culminating in the writings of the new social contract philosophers of the eighteenth century, a new concept of the political individual was formulated – an abstract and innovative concept, an apparent oxymoron – the imagined *universal individual* who was the bearer of equal political rights. The genius of this concept, which opened the door to the modern polis, was that it defined, at least theoretically, an individual being who could be imagined so stripped of individual substantiation and specification (his unique self), that he could stand for every man. Unmarked by the myriad specificities (e.g. of wealth, rank, education, age, sex) that make each person unique, one could imagine an abstract, non-specific individual who expressed a common psyche and political humanity. This Kantian notion of the abstract, empty subject could be used to establish the theoretical grounds for moral autonomy and democracy.

But, as many scholars have argued, the universal individual, the bearer of rights, who seemed to be everyone and no particular one, turned out on closer inspection to have some special characteristics of gender, sexuality and ethnicity. The universal individual was male and European.[8] Now this is an old saw – an old criticism – of liberalism, made most forcibly in political philosophy by Carole Pateman.[9] What we might call the transcendental 'emptiness' of rights discourse was a logical possibility but a historical illusion; the individual of liberal theory was (and still largely is) actually masculine, a sexual identity which is disguised by the claims of liberalism to be neutral and universal. Since the male is understood implicitly to be the norm of the universal individual, women's difference from men becomes a problem, a deviation, a challenge to the neutrality of the universal. Against the theoretical universality and neutrality of individual rights, affirmative actions (or positive discrimination) on behalf of (some) women somehow looks suspect, because they seem to privilege the 'difference' of sex.[10] On the other hand, to claim to be the same as men often backfires against women, because some women – not all, not all the time – are different from (some) men.[11]

Scott, Pateman and others trace the paradox of gender, then, to the very origins of liberal theory and the modern liberal state.[12] They argue that the difficulties women face in achieving full citizenship, the feeling that women are stuck circling around and around the dilemmas of the same/different/equality/ inequality, without surcease, are not of women's own making, but a symptom of something else – namely a tension within the heart of liberal theory itself. The abstract citizen is conceived of as male, and this forces women either to make the case for being a man, thereby suppressing our particular needs, or to insist we are 'not-men', thereby emphasizing our special or different rights.[13]

This now long-standing argument about liberal individualism and gender resonates with other urgent, and sometimes acrimonious, debates taking place today about citizenship, rights and inequality: about universalism versus particularism, individual rights versus group rights, and multiculturalism in relation to race or ethnic differences – debates, that is, about the value or otherwise of the Enlightenment, and whether liberalism can be recuperated for the modern world.[14] All universalisms, it has been said, result from the elevation of a particularism to universal status, so that the act of universal inclusion is always at the same time an act of exclusion. The universal liberal theory was also defined, historically, in racial/ethnic terms as well as sexual; the universal subject of rights was Western, European, civilized, as opposed to non-Western, non-European, barbaric. These norms of ethnicity were disguised, once again, by the language of universality (until recently, whiteness was effaced as a race, it was the universal).[15] Those making the argument for racial equality were trapped in much the same disputes concerning the same/different/equality/inequality that have marked the history of feminism. The reason I begin with a gender analysis is because it points economically to the repetition and intractability of the same and the different in modern Western philosophy; gender, we might say, is especially disruptive of the homogeneous subject.

Yet despite the limitations of liberal citizenship, it remains a powerful political and intellectual framework for demands for political liberty and rights. There is a case to be made for the universalism of rights, for making universalism live up to its name.[16] Yet this has proved extremely difficult to do. The question is why? Is sexism basic to the very creation of liberalism and the identity of the Western political subject? Do the universalistic terms and transcendence of material particularity associated with liberalism nonetheless set the 'bounds of sex (and race)'?[17]

In analysing these questions, I want to go beyond the arguments made by Pateman, Scott, Snitow and others, with their focus on the history of liberal political theory, to look at another critical history (or set of critical histories) connected to the paradoxes of modern citizenship. This is the history of the naturalized body – of the construction of races and genders as natural, biologically grounded entities, entities which render their members lesser or even non-individuals. It is my argument that the historical counterpart to the *disembodiment* of the individual citizen of modernity – an individual imagined stripped of all substantiation – was the *ontologizing via embodiment* of sex and racial difference, a rendering of groups as distinct in their biology and differentiated from an implicit white, male norm. By being embodied as qualitatively different in their substantial natures – by creating group identities in difference – communities of individuals were placed outside the liberal universe of freedom, equality and rights. In effect, a theory of politics and rights was transformed into an argument about nature; equality under liberalism was taken to be a matter not of ethics, but of anatomy.

The appeal to nature in deciding what was a moral and political issue was fatal to rights, and has haunted the discussion of rights since the Enlightenment. At times, the discussion has turned back from the discourse of bodies to the discourse of politics; even so, I would argue, the political question of liberal rights and universalism always occurs in a subtle exchange with that of anatomy (using the term here for a shorthand for all the natural and medical sciences involved, *qua* sciences, in determining the natural traits of human variation). In this chapter, I trace the shift from politics to nature and back in the area of race and rights. I conclude that, given the close connection and interpenetration of the two discourses, a science of similarity and difference can never be a reliable guide to questions of rights and liberal freedoms. This is true even when, as is the case in the general consensus that emerged after World War II, science seems to support an anti-racist view of human variation – to show that 'races don't exist' in any scientifically meaningful sense. The consequences of this conclusion for our understanding of science and the gendered body are addressed in the second half of the chapter.

As I have said, the brilliant conception of the individual who was at one and the same time a unique self, yet who could be imagined as stripped of his uniqueness, to be thought of as a generic universal, allowed the formulation of the political principle of democracy – that all individuals, regardless of their unique characteristics, possessed universal political and other rights. But not every individual could position herself as this supposedly abstract individual unmarked by unique specificities. Instead she was positioned as a substantiated representative of a larger group, type, race or gender. And it was the characteristics of the type – the very features of the difference – that, it was claimed, debarred her from the right to full citizenship. Thus some differences (small differences within the white male population) could be theoretically stripped away and discounted in relation to rights; but other differences could not be so discounted.[18] If, the argument went, bodily similarity to an implicit or explicit norm of bodilyness, the white male type, existed, then political similarity in rights followed; if bodily difference existed, then political difference in rights followed. The reality of the differences embodied in the human species turned a political/ethical argument about individual rights into a biological argument about group difference – a move made repeatedly throughout the nineteenth and twentieth centuries.[19]

My point, then, is that the history of embodiment must be seen as part of the story of citizenship and its limits; and that it is no accident that 'race' and 'sex', in their modern, primarily naturalized or biological meaning, emerged in the eighteenth century, when the new political concept of the individual self and the individual bearer of rights was being articulated.[20] The politics of empire and colonialism were other sources of new reflections on, and scientific studies of, embodied difference,[21] the politics of women and their rights another. It is here, of course, that the history of science and medicine comes into the story. The search for measurable signs of difference, both externally visible (e.g. colour of skin, texture and quality of hair, shape of nose or skull), and those hidden from direct sight within the body, signs which could act as reliable guides to human difference, was the work of anatomists, physiologists, anthropologists and physicians. Starting with the founders of modern biology and anthropology – such as Linnaeus, Buffon, Blumenbach – scientists began to apply to human beings a zoological concept of species and varieties. The 'human' (or *humaine*) became transformed through scientific investigation into 'the human species' and its zoological variations.[22] By the middle of the nineteenth century, a dense web of ideas, practices and measurements was employed to establish the natural facts of human variation, facts increasingly understood not as a continuum of traits and characteristics linking all members in a common human family, but of dichotomies and categorical distinctions. Phrenology, physical anthropology, anatomy, clinical medicine, social statistics and evolutionary biology were all at different historical periods drawn into the tasks of sorting out the differences separating human populations in racial and sexual terms, and weighing the meaning of such differences for social reform and social policies.[23]

Many historians have commented on the deep commitment to the importance of embodiment and of the embodied type in modern Western thought. In scientific practice, the elusiveness of the type has been a constant problem to scientists; they confronted the multiple factors of migration, interbreeding, environmental influence and human history that 'confused' the supposed racial elements in populations. The anthropologist was presented not with static types, but instead with a bewildering number of differences and similarities. No individual might in fact be found to possess all the attributes of the type, so that choosing the individual to represent the type always involved subjective judgements and exclusions. As the scientist William Ripley said in 1899: 'Never is the perfect type in view, while it is always possible.'[25] But no matter the ambiguities and contradictions in the usage of the term 'race'; science was a powerful, authenticating instrument of reason and objective truth, and the truth discovered was that, by nature, human beings formed a hierarchy of races and sexes which were not equal in the traits required for civilization.

It is not my intention to review here the long and complicated histories of the racial and sexual sciences, and their intersections. I only wish to make the following two points. First, many historians have pointed out that the sciences of human difference cannot and should not be dismissed lightly as something belonging thankfully to the past and therefore of interest mainly to antiquarians. They were the work of the best scientists of the day and were at the centre, not the margins, of science. Evolutionary biology, modern genetics, bacteriology, sciences which still provide the framework for the sciences of biology and medicine today, were all closely tied to racial (and sexual) sciences. Racialism was thus part of the very modernity of science. (Moreover, it is possible to argue that race is still critical to much of the contemporary social sciences which supposedly replaced the old biology of race, a point to which I return later in the chapter.)

Second, the assumptions made by scientists – that human groups formed distinct biological types, and that biological differences were the ultimate foundation or source of social differences and inequalities between groups in society – were extremely widely shared well into the twentieth century in science and everyday life. They were normative. Increasingly, science provided the ontological grounding for political arguments about the differential treatment of human groups. It also set the terms of the general debate about rights. Critics of the claims made in racial/sexual science (often the people most stigmatized by the sciences of their day) found themselves stuck in the terms of the same and the different, *as though the facts of difference would answer questions about rights.*

But if the science of racial difference is part of the story of liberal individualism and its limitations from the late eighteenth century until well into the twentieth, we must remember that scientific racism was eventually contested from within that same liberal framework. Nature, that is, was rejected as the grounds of right. Before turning to why and how this happened, however, I would like to indicate briefly some new historical questions that the citizenship–nature framework raises.[26] New methods in history (e.g. social constructionism, the new historicism, deconstruction); new kinds of sources (e.g. literary, legal, but especially the visual); new areas of enquiry (e.g. colonial and imperial); new kinds of questions (e.g. about the history of the emergence of race categories and classifications in specific historical/political contexts; about the politics of race hybridization, about when and why its scientific study becomes urgent; about gender in relation to race mixing; about racial acclimatization and adaptation; about the history of urban and other spaces in relation to race) – all have contributed to expanding our understanding of the relations between race, gender and the history of science and medicine.[27] Feminist scholarship has been especially important in exploring the interconnections between sexuality and race. From such a diverse and broad set of enquiries, I have space to comment on only a few. The ones I have chosen follow from the overall framework of my argument.

First, what *model* of science and causality are we using? Science, it is clear, does not simply step in to provide an answer to the question of *how* to exclude certain groups or explain social and other inequalities; the relations of science and medicine to social, political and economic life are surely not that simple. Rather, we should think in terms of the *many histories* that were linked to the shifts we see in the scientific and medical study of human variation, especially in the crucial period of transition to industrialization and modern colonialism between roughly 1770 and 1870. These histories would include the history of work and the new divisions of labour; the history of slavery and abolition; the history of the emergence of new definitions of the public and the private, in relation to class and gender; the history of religion and secularization; the histories of class politics and changes in political economy. As Thomas Laqueur rightly remarks in his study of sexual science, these other histories did not cause the new racialized (and sexualised) body to come into existence; rather, he suggests, the remaking of the human body was implicated in all these developments.[28]

Now that we have some understanding of the specific histories of phrenology and neurology, evolutionary biology, and genetics in relation to race and gender in different national and historical settings, a focus on the interrelated histories of the body, scientific epistemology, work, religion and the social sphere seems called for. Here, then, is a space for detailed historical enquiries.

My second question is precisely about one such history, the history of *scientific autonomy*. How has it been established? By what institutional processes? What constitutes modern scientific epistemology? These issues are important because it was the autonomy of scientific knowledge, and its particular epistemological standing, that gave authority to scientific claims about the facts of nature and natural difference. In the nineteenth century science became 'the dominant mode of cognition of industrial society' and was increasingly conceptualized as 'a sharply edged, value-neutral apolitical, non-theological, empirical and objective form of knowledge unlike any other'.[29] This conceptualization was not simply the natural outcome of the unproblematic study of nature, but a social outcome of a process (or many processes) whereby science acquired new epistemological status in new institutions and through new scientific practices. The authority of science was tied not only to industrialization, but to the politics of class, the closing of the ranks of bourgeois society in the face of challenges from the working class, especially in the 1830s and 1840s, and to the politics also of race and gender. The process of boundary-setting between science and non-science was contested at many points, since it meant the delegitimation of many areas of knowledge and their redefinition as pseudo-science or 'outside' science.[30] Science as a form of knowledge separated itself from other ways of knowing; in the process, the dichotomies between the pure and the impure, the rational and the irrational, the objective and the subjective, the hard and the soft, the male and the female, were given epistemo-logical and material (organizational) form. Such polarities, and the institutional boundaries that created and maintained them, were not, I repeat, the inevitable outcomes of a nature merely discovered and described but were produced out of active institutional work, and the successful uses of political and cultural resources to achieve these ends.

It is not the specific *content* of scientific claims about the human body that is the issue here – these were certainly extremely varied, often contradictory, and were shaped by their many different disciplinary frameworks and political locations. It is rather the rhetoric of science, the processes of inclusion and exclusion of themes and fields, and the evolution of claims about scientific method and reasoning that I am asking about. Institutional studies, such as Morrell and Thackray's of the British Association for the Advancement of Science, between its founding in 1832 and the 1870s, which is concerned with the rhetoric and politics by which the BAAS established itself as a source of scientific authority in mid-nineteenth-century Britain, are rare; they are all the more important in the area of human sciences, since statements about the nature of human beings made by scientists acquire political weight precisely because of their supposed non-political character.

Though this has been said by many scholars, I think we must see the emergence of our modern scientific epistemology as a historically contingent process requiring study in relation to scientific studies of bodily variation, and not merely a 'given' of the growth of modern science. It is precisely in the interplay between epistemology and scientific racism and sexism that the interest lies. The organizations, professional societies and institutions of anthropology, ethnology, social statistics and medicine are all settings where questions about how the authority of knowledge was secured, and its neutrality, could be examined. Studies of medical institutions and societies would repay special attention, since medicine was extremely important to the study of natural differences and the shaping of racial and sexual categories – whether in bacteriology, genetics and eugenics, physiology, or clinical fields such as disease resistance and acclimatization. These questions about the historical development of the authority of knowledge-claims would also put the history of laboratory medicine, medical experimentation and medical technology in a new relation to the history of race and sex.

Very closely connected to the history of scientific authority in general is the specific instance of scientific writing as a new cultural genre. How did styles of scientific writing contribute to the development of epistemological authority? I am thinking here especially of the short scientific article, which began in mid-century to replace the more discursively open, varied, metaphorically porous, and literary forms of scientific exposition of earlier decades. As Markus has shown in a brilliant analysis, the short, depersonalized empirical paper that is the hallmark of science today served (and still serves) normative functions, and through its form (its non-authorial voice, its requirement for a peculiarly prepared or competent scientific readership, its facticity) successfully satisfies the requirements of science for constant innovation and accumulation of knowledge.[31] The neutral style of the scientific text also disguises the political structure of scientific knowledge, by presenting nature as an empirical world existing independently of human beings, and revealed by the specific methods (empirical, technical, experimental) of the disinterested scientist. Hermeneutically, that is, science achieves autonomy from social life through this cultural innovation.

Third, and along the same lines, how did *nature* and *naturalization* change as scientific authority changed? As Lorraine Daston remarks, nature, like scientific authority, has a history, and so do the tactics of naturalization.[32] She shows, for example, how the meaning of 'nature' in eighteenth-century discussions of the 'nature of women's intellect' shifted from connoting plenitude, perfection and harmony to mean limit, indifference to human concerns, neutrality and inexora-bility. By the early nineteenth century, nature was coming to stand for facticity, inevitability, necessity; for a descriptive reality which was, like science itself, independent of human passions and desires. As Daston says, appeal to *this* nature was often to remind people of the impossibility of change in the social places assigned to human groups in society; nature was a question of unchanging matter which was not open to moral will and human goals. These shifts in the meaning of nature had important effects on how race and sex differences were understood and argued about.[33]

Fourth and lastly, how, and in what terms and languages, were the claims made by scientists and physicians about natural difference and inequality *challenged*? Though natural facts are always social facts, imbued with the values of the society in which they are produced, and unstable in their social meanings, nonetheless, resistance to social claims made in the name of neutral science and inexorable nature had increasingly, from the mid-nineteenth century on, to be made in the languages and terms of science to which the resisters often stood in a problematical and marginalized position. (The exclusion of groups negatively stereotyped by the sciences was part of the process of the construction of the sciences of difference and inequality, a result of the scientific expectation that the so-called lower races, and women in general, served mainly as objects of study, but not as scientific truth-seekers themselves.)

In the circumstances, social groups confronting a 'purely factual' science, whose message was apparently ever more negative about themselves, tried to resist the process of naturalization associated with science; they tried, that is, to refuse to separate the moral issues of rights and justice from scientific ones. But, as time passed, the professionalization of science made such tactics less effective. By mid-century, strategies of resistance to scientific racism and sexism were increasingly structured by the discourse of neutral science itself. Science's conceptual categories, rhetorical styles, and methodologies were adopted by those categorized as different and unequal. Thus African-Americans produced texts of blackness, pictures of anthropological heads, cranial measurements and scientific tables of racial health and illness. Jewish scientists, who were particularly drawn to use scientific representations of self and race, because of their greater access to scientific education and commitment to the norms of science, turned to evolution, hereditarianism, genetics, and even eugenics, to describe the facts of themselves and to reinterpret, and refute, the claims of inferiority made against them.[34] The use of science to dismantle the claims of science involved the authors in complex processes of transformation of the meaning of scientific facts; it opens up for discussion what I have referred to as the 'politics of scientific interpretation'.[35] Any analysis of the critical responses to scientific racism in the nineteenth and twentieth centuries must acknowledge how the need to meet science on its own terms limits the nature of the response, without foreclosing completely the possibility of new narratives of identity.

The echoing, parodying, and employment of scientific ideas and figures in *fiction* – the arena of fantasy and imagination according to the epistemologies of science and non-science – can also be usefully explored as a site of what Cora Kaplan calls a 'textual politics of resistance' to the dominant claims about racial, sexual and other differences.[36] Her own work, like that of Mary Poovey, Gillian Beer and others, demonstrates the strong influence of anthropological, ethnological, evolutionary, hereditary and medical ideas about the human species in English literature of the 1840s to 1860s.[37] Since the field of racial and sexual science is never monolithic or univocal, but on the contrary heterogeneous, and fuelled by contradictory impulses, so are the resisting discourses that echo, comment on and modify them. Much of the historical work of analysis of the struggles against stereotypes in the natural and medical sciences remains to be done. Women's efforts to appropriate scientific and medical arguments for their own purposes are especially important, because of their exclusion from science, such exclusion itself being part of the construction of the sciences as a masculine field of neutral and objective knowledge.

I return from this brief discussion of some of the new questions raised by the citizenship/nature framework, to my main argument. As is well known, the race paradigm in science was eventually contested from within the same liberal framework that had lived so long with 'natural difference and inequality'. The pendulum swung back towards universalism (to the unity of the species, to a shared humanity, to rights; a universalism with its own exclusions). After the Second World War, a new consensus emerged in science that 'races don't exist'. Race was replaced by the population, the cline (and now the genome). The word 'race' lost its legitimacy in science, and an effort was made to substitute the phrase 'ethnic group' (e.g. in the UNESCO Statement on Race drawn up by scientists in 1950, and again in 1952). The idea that races formed closed, static biological units which determine human behaviours or entire cultures was given up; biology gave ground to sociology – to the new 'race relations'. Race as a concept was severed from its secure roots in biology. New definitions of what was to count as 'human' in the 'human species' emerged, in a liberal moment of anti-racism.

The new sociology of race and ethnicity (a term of even more recent vintage) was fraught with incoherences and difficulties, to which I will come. But first, why did the old paradigm break down? In part, the very scientific methods that produced races led to an undermining of the concept of race. As more and more measurements of human skulls, noses, colour of skin, hair, ear shapes and brain parts were made, scientists found it more and more difficult to agree on *what* the basic racial units of human societies were. The epistemological uncertainty of race as a biological category was evidenced by the inconsistencies and disagreements in the racial classifications scientists proposed. Categorical biological divisions were not easy to stabilize; no sooner, for example, had a particular segment of the European population been divided into Nordic, Alpine and Mediterranean types than further measurements showed overlapping between the types, compelling scientists to make subdivisions, and yet further subdivisions, in their classifications; the logic of human variation and the logic of racial mapping were ultimately opposed, so that the racial categories risked dissolving and merging into each other.[38] Within physical anthropology, indeed, there was by the early twentieth century a 'hopeless mistrust of anthropological measurement'.[39]

But if science itself helped destabilize racial science, the larger world of politics in which science and medicine operated played the decisive role. *The political made the natural, and the political undid the natural.* It is usual to date the collapse of the morphological, anatomical and genetic (eugenical) sciences of race to the Second

World War, and the heinous crime of the systematic extermination of Jews (and Gypsies) carried out at least in part in the name of the sciences of race inferiority. Even before World War II, the race concept was being challenged by scientists. The appearance of the word 'racism', which first came into use in the 1930s, already suggests a critique of the still widely held assumption in science that people could be fitted neatly into racial boxes differing in body and mental/moral worth.

Though there is not space here to sketch the slow, hesitant, piecemeal and incomplete ways in which the biological concept of race was undermined, it is worth remarking that much of the change was fuelled by the entry into science (especially in the UK and the United States, where the chief critiques were made) of individuals from groups who were situated at some distance from the mainstream scientific culture of the times, and were themselves the targets of the racial/ sexual science of difference and inequality of their day – were themselves stereotyped in the languages of biology (e.g. Jews). On the importance of the political to science it is also interesting to note that very often assumptions about race were challenged and reversed without any new scientific information being added to the pool of knowledge. So, for example, although Mendelian genetics generated new information which was seen as falsifying many of the claims of earlier racialists, scientists also changed their minds about such things as the supposed evil effects of human hybridization, without the addition of any new scientific data. The political valence of race changed, for political reasons.[40]

Of course, racism did not disappear because scientists no longer provided the biological-ontological grounding for racial thinking (post-World War II South African apartheid is an obvious case).[41] With race and ethnicity we are dealing with political definitions of the self and others which depend on social relations of inequality, not scientific argument, for their continued currency. Even if some scientists claim to prefer to avoid it, 'race' is nonetheless a commonly used term in politics and the law; it underlies and undergirds, whether explicitly or implicitly, contemporary debates on citizenship, nationality, and immigration; and is used regularly in affirmative action policies – is used, that is, to exclude and to include.[42] The US census is a good example of the political relevance, inconsistency and power of race categories; today, Cambodians and Laotians are lobbying the government to change their classification from Pacific Americans to Asians; some African-Americans are claiming a new 'mixed race' identity for the offspring of black and white parents. The difficulty of deciding who will qualify for this racial designation brings us back to the extraordinary debates about fractions of 'colouredness' that preoccupied the census-makers early in the twentieth century, when four out of the eight categories employed in the census referred to fractions of blackness.[43]

Any examination of race usually shows it to be mired in these kinds of confusions. The undercutting of the old certainties of racial science turned the issue of human inequality back to the realm where it started – the realm of the political, the economic, and the social. The factors that create group identities, that increase hostility between groups, that make people think in terms of 'us' and 'them' are extremely varied and complicated, and our new terminologies do not always add clarification. 'Ethnicity' is not the same kind of thing everywhere, and the term 'ethnic' is often only a convenient (and in my view not always very useful) shorthand for extremely diverse political, social and economic groups and phenomena. Generally speaking, it is used to escape from the biological connotations of race, in an effort to take the biology out of the concept, in keeping with the anti-race consensus in science; but the inconsistencies in its usage parallel the inconsistencies of the term 'race' itself. The same can be said for many uses of 'cultural difference', which, like ethnicity or 'ethnic difference', is used to avoid the biological connotations of race; yet, again, much of what is meant when the phrase is used was in the past expressed by the term 'race'. Indeed, the literary critic Walter Benn Michaels maintains that *every* effort to come up with an anti-essentialist account of cultural identity fails – is either banal (because a 'cultural identity' is just what people are presently doing), or relies ultimately on a genealogical (descent or racial) definition.[45] At the same time, of course, the scientific denial of the reality of race – the claim that 'races don't exist' – flies in the face of political experience and can cause anger on the part of groups who know the weight of discrimination in their own lives; as an oppositional strategy, claiming a racial identity will often make sense. People are thus positioned within the framework of the same/different, equality/inequality, with which this chapter began.[46]

Moreover, a cautionary word is in order here. For if there is a lesson to be drawn from this history of science, race and liberalism, it is that science is always a social product and tends to reflect in general terms the political and social values of its times. This is especially evident in the human – all too human – sciences of ourselves. Racial science was born in late eighteenth-century Europe, and came to prominence in the nineteenth century, in a period of nation-building and nationalism, conflict and differentiation, and reflected the values of national homogeneity, exclusion and social differentiation. It was challenged only after a murderous world war of destruction against selected human populations made the science of race morally repugnant and politically unacceptable.

Today, however, the post-war consensus of the Cold War is unravelling. Is it possible that the post-war scientific consensus about race will unravel also?[47] In this regard it is interesting to note that, even at the height of the *anti-racist* consensus in science in the 1980s, 50 per cent of the biological anthropologists working in graduate university departments in the United States still claimed that race was a meaningful concept in human biology.[48] In the thermidorian climate in which we now live, is it conceivable that new scientific knowledge could be given political interpretations that are harmful to groups? If so, the comfort that science offers the anti-racist may be less than complete. The extraordinary attention given in the United States to Herrnstein and Murray's book, *The Bell Curve: Intelligence and Class Structure in American Life* (1994), which argues that class (and by implication, race) inequalities are due to inherited differences in intelligence, suggests a move in this direction.[49] Of greater importance, because of the greater credentials of the science involved, is the Human Genome Diversity Project (part of the Human Genome Project), which aims to map the genetic traits that characterize selected small groups or tribes. The project has been promoted by liberals such as the geneticist Cavalli-Sforza, because he believes the results will help combat racism, by demonstrating that important genetic traits in human beings vary less between groups than within them. Yet the project has also been resisted (especially by the indigenous peoples from whom the DNA samples are to be taken) precisely because it raises the spectre of distinguishing groups by genetic traits, in a way that could turn out to be to a group's disadvantage.[50] So, will science prove human difference or human similarity?

Or is this the wrong question? For what this brief history of the rise and (perhaps temporary) decline of racial science suggests is that science is not a reliable guide to issues of human morality and politics. This point was made over a hundred years ago, and brilliantly, by the black abolitionist Frederick Douglass in a little-known address on anthropology. In an argument that could hardly be bettered today, Douglass first reviewed for an audience of African-American college students what was known of the science of human racial differences. He refuted the claims of the race scientists of his day, challenging their logic, their data, and their conclusions concerning the supposed gulf separating the white and black groups. He argued that, anatomically and craniologically, the similarities between African-Americans and other Americans far outweighed their differences, that the human species was one, and that the African-American could therefore claim full membership in the human species.

But at the end of his address, Douglass made a crucial move from the discourse of anatomy to the discourse of ethics, politics and rights. 'What', he asked, if the case [of anatomical similarity] is not made out? Does it follow that the Negro should be held in contempt?' He answered his own question with a resounding 'No', because the title to freedom and liberty was not a question of science, of natural similarity or difference, but one of rights and morality.[51] Douglass thereby asked a question that would virtually disappear from science and politics from that time to this: what difference does difference make to human rights? The silence of both science and politics on this matter after the mid-nineteenth century suggests the power of science to occupy the terrain formerly held by religious, political and ethical discourse, and to disguise the political projects that helped constitute the scientific field.[52]

This is not an argument that science has nothing to offer in the area of human variation, or to deny the many gains we have made in understanding human variation. Science is a productive form of knowledge which allows us to manipulate the material world for good or ill. It is to argue, however, that the social meanings or conclusions we derive from nature are not the predictable outcomes of the inherent content or logic of science; that nature, or the science that as a human practice produces it, does not escape the value conflicts existing in its social surroundings. Inferences from nature are therefore not merely extrapolated, but are themselves always a matter of values and interpretation – are, that is, socially constructed. At issue here is the complicated circle of meanings which tie the natural to the political.

And what about gender? My argument is that gender difference acquired a new kind of embodiment and new forms of naturalization in specific ways, starting in the eighteenth century; and that this history of the ontological grounding of sex in women's bodies is as critical to the paradox of women's citizenship as is the history of liberalism itself. But unlike the story of racial science, where the relation of the natural to the political has been at least questioned periodically, the science of gender rarely (or only very recently) receives sustained analysis of its simplicities and inconsistencies. No cataclysmic struggle, like a world war, served to undermine sexual science. We have daily evidence in newspaper stories that people believe that, for women, biology is still destiny. Indeed, so deeply is woman's bodily difference to man's written into political theory and social life that a science of sex difference has been extremely difficult to challenge. Women who do so are suspect, because their critiques are taken to represent a form of special pleading. And anyway, why should it be challenged? Do not women, after all, insist that their biology is indeed different from men's? Do not women themselves contribute to the study of sex differences in animals and humans? Surely only objective and neutral science is the issue here?

The difficulty for most women themselves, as well as men, is that the idea of a fundamental biological basis for the distinctions between the sexes – that there is a biological female sex and a biological male sex, and that social life is or should be organized differently for each sex – seems so commonsensically true that it is almost impossible to denaturalize. Yet it is women who largely bear the burden of being biological; it is our reproduction, our hormones, our brains, that seem to be the problem. It is we who are 'the sex', not men. This biology is deeply woven into the fabric of our law, politics and social life.

It was because of the imposed burden of being defined biologically by sex, in ways that reduce women's individuality (for not all women are by any means alike, even in the seemingly most 'basic' characteristics, such as reproduction), that the English word 'gender' (which has no equivalent in most other languages) was introduced into feminist studies in the 1970s. Linda Nicholson points out in a recent article, however, that since its introduction, the word 'gender' has been used in two rather different senses, one more innovative than the other.[53] Originally, and therefore in its first meaning, 'gender' was used to refer to everything about women and men that was not biological sex; it meant social roles, femininity and masculinity, and was contrasted with biological sex (rather as 'ethnicity' and 'culture' were used to refer to group identities in non-biological terms).[54] Gender was used to argue that the known facts of biology were not enough to explain why women were denied the vote so long, were treated as legal minors on a par with children, or were excluded from certain kinds of work. Gender in this sense drew attention away from biology, to the social world where masculinity, femininity, heterosexuality, homosexuality are defined and given their social meanings. The move from sex to gender opened the door to a wide range of studies – historical, literary, psychoanalytic – concerning the various ways in which the masculine and the feminine are defined in relation each other in different historical periods. At the same time, however, this use of 'gender' left the biology of sex differences to one side, in unproblematic fashion. Nicholson suggests that today many feminists, even those of a social constructionist persuasion, continue to think of the biological distinctions between the sexes as providing the ultimate, if distant, grounding for male and female identity, an identity that is transcultural. She calls this idea 'biological foundationalism'.[55]

But a second use of 'gender' is much more innovative; it problematizes the gender/sex connection, by arguing that the body itself, the supposed bearer of sex, is always a social construction (or interpretation) so that gender is always part of our definition of sex, and vice versa.[56] Scholars, that is, mean to indicate by the term 'gender' that the biological differences between men and women are not, as they are often taken to be, just 'givens' of nature discovered by the neutral and observing eye of the scientist, but complicated social constructions connected to larger historical developments, social practices and institutions. Joan Scott expressed this more powerful and innovative understanding of gender in the following way:

> gender is the social organization of sexual difference. But this does not mean that gender effects or implements fixed and natural physical differences between men and women; rather gender is the knowledge that establishes meanings for bodily difference … We cannot see sexual differences except as a function of our knowledge of the body and that knowledge is not 'pure', cannot be isolated from its implications in a broad range of discursive contexts.[57]

If you like, everything one wants to say about sex already has in it a claim about gender, and vice versa; there is a constant circulation between culture and nature, so that anatomical and physiological facts of our bodies are embedded in signifying practices and institutional routines.

This is not to deny the existence of bodily differences, as some feminists do, nor is it to glorify differences, as other feminists also do. It is rather to argue that our bodies are gendered by and through a science of the body that cannot be separated from other discourses and political practices. The sexed body, like the racialized body, is a product of history; to extract it from history cannot be done.

With this emphasis on the intertwined contexts and connections between sex and gender, and above all with a focus on the *historically specific emergence of particular models of biological gender*, what elements of this story about sexual science are now available to us? It must be said that, so natural and familiar does a two-sex anatomical model of sexualities seem to us, uncovering its historical and discursive history has proved much more difficult than uncovering the history of racial science. In my view, sexual science *could* only be given a history after the second wave of feminism developed.

In the last few years, many new historical studies of sexual science have appeared, as well as investigations into its complex interweavings with racial science.[58] For my purposes here, Thomas Laqueur's work is perhaps the most provocative, in making the case that the sexual/gender difference became embodied in new ways in the eighteenth century. In a radical yet subtle analysis, Laqueur traces the shift that took place in Western anatomical and medical views of sexual difference in the eighteenth century, when, he argues, a classical 'one-sex' model of the human body (a model, that is, which posited that men and women had the same bodily plan and anatomies, though women's bodies were less hot and less perfect than men's and their genitalia were found within the body rather than without), was replaced with a 'two-sex' model (in which women's bodies were understood to be radically different from men's). The belief we have that men and women are unlike in their sex, are bipolar and complementary opposites, is shown, in this analysis, to be a fairly recent invention of modernity.[59]

The earlier, almost counter-intuitive one-sex model of the human body (a model that lasted from Greek antiquity to the mid-eighteenth century) did not by any means signify that men and women, being very alike in their bodily parts and processes, were treated as, or thought of as, equals. But before the Enlightenment, what counted in the distinction between men and women was social gender, not biology. As Laqueur argues, the patriarchal values which placed fathers over daughters, brothers over sisters, and husbands over wives, were not assignable to, or explained by reference to, fundamental differences in the sexual anatomies of the male and the female, as they are in our own times. Rather, 'the boundaries between male and female [in the classical and medieval period] are primarily political; rhetorical rather than biological claims regarding sexual difference and sexual desire are primary'. Indeed, given that men and women were thought of as being very similar in their bodily anatomies, it was believed that a man could at times lactate, or a girl turn into a boy. Given the likenesses, too, a differentiated body could not serve as the 'real' or ultimate reference point for understanding the differences between men and women socially, economically or culturally (religion, convention and custom served then as the courts of authority). In effect, before the Enlightenment, 'sex (or the body) must be understood as the epiphenomenon, while gender, what we would take to be a cultural category, was primary or "real"'.[60] Gender difference was established, not on the ontological, natural differences of bodies, but in the realm of the political and cultural.

But in the eighteenth century, this understanding of human sexuality and the body changed. From 1800 on, the biologically sexed bodies of the male and the female were understood to be radically unlike, and these differences taken to be the cause or origin of the different qualities (sexual, emotional, rational), and political, legal and social places, of men and women in society. Even if Laqueur overstates his thesis, his insistence that complementary, embodied gender difference emerged as a central aspect of biology and politics in the eighteenth century is convincing.[61] Not only did scientists come to emphasize marked differences in reproductive anatomy and function between women and men, but eventually almost every part of a woman's body, properly studied, was shown to express an essential femaleness that differentiated it from man's essential maleness.[62] From this point on, ontologically speaking, woman *was* her bodily difference from man; and since man's body, though marked by its own biological and sexual character, was taken to be the biological/political norm, woman's bodily difference became the deviation from the norm. It was also the ultimate reference point (as it still is today) for explaining why women as a group have not achieved social equality with men. Thus was born the paradox of modern women's citizenship: the need to insist on the irrelevance of bodily difference and its relevance at one and the same time.[63]

Now one might argue that our modern understanding of the biological differences between men and women did not exist before the Enlightenment because science had not developed far enough, or lacked adequate means (e.g. good enough microscopes) to get human anatomy and physiology right. But Laqueur undermines this interpretation by showing that the shift to our modern 'two-sex' model did not depend on, or coincide with, the emergence of new discoveries about reproductive physiology; nothing new was learned about, say, ovulation, for scientists to begin to represent the male and female genitalia, and sexuality, as radically different from each other. All anatomies are abstractions of very complicated realities, and the new anatomies were products of the social understanding of sexual difference. The shift in anatomical understanding was connected to many other political, intellectual and other shifts as old social relations changed, religious authority waned, and the places of women and men in the new political society were contested.

I have argued in this chapter that the discursive histories of politics and the discursive histories of the human body have to be connected if we are to understand women's need to argue for and against the importance of their bodily difference at one and the same time. In a brilliant section of his book, called 'The Politics and Biology of Two Sexes', Laqueur makes precisely this connection; he argues that 'The universalistic claims made for human liberty and equality during the Enlightenment did not inherently exclude the female half of humanity. Nature had to be searched if men were to justify their dominance of the public sphere, whose distinction from the private would increasingly come to be figured in terms of sexual difference.'[64] As he, Fraisse and other historians have demonstrated, the battle for women's rights was fought over the issue of women's bodies during the French Revolution; it gave birth to a worry about the role of women in the new political contract (famously or infamously displayed in the writings of Rousseau), and also to the creation of new 'political boundaries that engendered sexual boundaries to match'.[65] Biology entered to demonstrate and represent women's physical, mental and emotional non-suitability for the new civil and political liberties and rights that were in the process of being defined.

Though Condorcet maintained it was ridiculous to exclude women from political rights because of biology, exclaiming, 'Why should individuals exposed to pregnancy and other passing indispositions be unable to exercise rights which no one has dreamed of withholding from persons who have the gout or catch cold quickly?' his was a minority position. From 1800 on, the idea of the sexed body was endlessly elaborated in the sciences – in phrenology (and later neurology), reproductive physiology, evolutionary biology, craniology – and used to explain why it was that women's demands for education and political rights could not be met.

Laqueur's argument is twofold: first, that the sexed body is a historical product, a representation, and not the unproblematic foundation of social gender, and second, that science, though it can be a powerful instrument of knowledge about the human body (no one denies that we can and do know more about the human body today than in the past), was and is not in itself the key to female liberation. The work of other scholars on sexual embodiment in the late eighteenth century and nineteenth century confirms our sense that the stable biological body of sex that seems to lie as the ultimate foundation of differentiations in the social world, is a specific historical product.

Where, then, does my argument about race, gender, science and citizenship leave me? First, we note the great difficulty women in particular have had in escaping from biological foundationalism. Indeed, a marked tendency among many feminists today is to insist on 'difference', not because they are practising a pernicious form of biopolitics, as the philosopher Agnes Heller has claimed, but because the world of politics is still deeply governed by biological definitions that damage their citizenship.[66] As long as biological sex is made relevant to politics and rights, women will have to embrace the paradox of biological sameness and difference.[67]

But if we can recognize the historicity of our biological models of sex and gender, we can begin the task of rethinking our categories of 'woman', 'women', 'man', 'men'. These categories are not unitary but only appear to be. Different women have multiple characteristics; as Nicholson says, any particular individual belongs to multiply defined 'families' of characteristics; she enters or leaves these groups of families in the course of a lifetime. This comment speaks to the issue of the relation of any individual to a group. Any individual belongs to several groups, to both advantaged and disadvantaged ones. Thus, though most women may need or want time off from paid labour during pregnancy, or after childbirth, not all women wish or are able to conceive, and not all women who give birth wish (or are in a position) to devote all their energies to child-rearing. The old models of sexuality are changing (we even have third and fourth sexualities now). As Nicholson argues, actual women, not 'women' as an abstract concept, 'are part of a map of intersecting similarities and differences. Within such a map, the body does not disappear, but rather becomes a historically specific variable whose meaning and importance are recognized as potentially different in different historical contexts'.[68]

Such an understanding of gender would place it, with race, where it should be, in the place of the political. Gender exclusions are fundamentally political exclusions, which may (or may not) include reference to actual (or presumed) biological factors. Any conception of rights and citizenship, it seems to me, must be able to absorb the specificities of individuals and groups; a politics of 'rights for women' would not disappear but neither would it freeze around pre-given or static definitions of what woman is, or women are.

This is not – I emphasize *not* – to argue that biology is irrelevant to human experience or that the sexual characteristics of individual women and men do not have consequences – after all, to discuss abortion as though it were *not* occurring in a woman's body would be strange indeed. Nor is it to deny that science can, and has, contributed much knowledge that is useful to women. The feminist project in this regard is twofold – to demonstrate the lack of coherence in many representations of women's nature, *and* to use science to get an accurate picture of actual, specific women's realities. A group of women may share certain biological characteristics (e.g. the risk of genetic disease, the experience of lactation, or pregnancy) which could provide an appropriate basis for devising social and economic policies for individuals or groups (genetic screening, facilities for breast feeding, paid leave from work).

The aim of the analysis here is different – it is to avoid reducing complex populations to simple dichotomous groupings or seeing the world only by and through such groupings, and above all, it is to separate the argument about rights from any simple view of the natural. Recognizing the interlaced histories of politics and biology – that there is never going to be a nature out there that can resolve, once and for all, the meaning of our sexual differences, that this is the wrong question to ask – we can ask different questions. What made certain kinds of sciences of gender and race possible? What have been the governing metaphors of difference? How have political meanings already been written into sex and sexualities, so that there is no going to a neutral ground of natural facts to answer questions of meaning? Why have we been so preoccupied by sex and/or racial differences? Asking these kinds of historical and political questions will allow us to acquire a deeper understanding of the significance of body differences to our political histories, and, in the long run, to construct a more adequate and inclusionary model of citizenship and rights.

Notes

From *Gender and History*, 10:1 (April 1998), 26–52.

1 Barbara Einhorn, 'Ironies of History: Citizenship Issues in the New Market Economies of East Central Europe', in *Women and Market Societies: Crisis and Opportunity*, ed. B. Einhorn and Eileen Janes Yeo (Edward Elgar, Aldershot, 1995), pp. 217–33; and Peggy Watson, 'Eastern Europe's Silent Revolution: Gender', *Sociology*, 27 (1993), pp. 471–87, and 'The Rise of Masculinism in Eastern Europe', *New Left Review* (1993), pp. 71–82.

2 Joan W. Scott, *Only Paradoxes to Offer: French Feminists and the Rights of Man* (Harvard University Press, Cambridge MA and London, 1996), especially ch. 1. See also her 'Universalism and the History of Feminism', *Differences: A Journal of Feminist Cultural Studies*, 7 (1995), pp. 1–14. The entire issue of the journal is devoted to universalism in politics and history.

3 Scott, *Only Paradoxes to Offer*, p. 11.
4 Ann Snitow, 'A Gender Diary', in *Conflicts in Feminism*, ed. Marianne Hirsch and Evelyn
   Fox Keller (Routledge, New York and London, 1990), pp. 9–43.
5 Maternity leave versus parental leave is a classic example.
6 I have not sketched out this paradox in order to choose sides between postmodernists and
   anti-postmodernists in feminism. Though Scott bases her analysis on a deconstructive
   reading of texts, the same cannot be said of Pateman and others. My point here is that the
   conflict between essentialism and anti-essentialism is not resolvable as such within the terms
   available to us. Any anti-essentialist move always depends on an essentialism.
7 See especially Denise Riley, *'Am I that Name? Feminism and the Category of 'Women' in History*
   (Macmillan, Basingstoke, 1988).
8 Scott's argument is more subtle than this. She explores the tension between one notion of
   the individual – the abstract universal – and another, the individuated unique self. Terms like
   'self' and 'individual' are ambiguous in their meanings. The sexual difference of women from
   men secured men's individuality in the second sense. See Scott, *Only Paradoxes to Offer*, pp.
   5–9.
9 Carole Pateman, *The Sexual Contract* (Polity Press, Cambridge, 1988) and *The Disorder of
   Women: Democracy, Feminism and Political Theory* (Polity Press, Cambridge, 1989). Her
   argument is that we need to pay attention to the fraternal contract implicit in 'Liberté,
   Egalité et Fraternité', since the new civil/social contract entailed a sexual contract disbarring
   women from political rights and political individualism. The critique has been made in many
   different registers and forms by scholars of very different political viewpoints; the
   conclusions drawn from the critique – in relation to universalism, liberalism and difference –
   are equally varied.
10 Zillah R. Eisenstein, *The Color of Gender: Reimagining Democracy* (University of California
   Press, Berkeley CA and London, 1994), p. 3.
11 As Elizabeth Colwill remarks, 'the gendered boundaries of republican and liberal theory' are
   subjects of heated debate; moreover, the new male individual, and notions of masculinity and
   sexuality, were not without their own tensions and uncertainties. See Colwill, 'Women's
   Empire and the Sovereignty of Man in *La Décade Philosophique*, 1794–1807', *Eighteenth-
   Century Studies*, 29 (1996), pp. 265–89.
12 An especially fine and nuanced account of the centrality of gender and science to the
   Enlightenment and the French Revolution, an account based on close textual readings of
   legal, philosophical, literary, religious and scientific works, is Genevieve Fraisse's *Reason's
   Muse: Sexual Difference and the Birth of Democracy* (University of Chicago Press, Chicago and
   London, 1994).
13 Which is why feminism is emerging now in Eastern Europe. Only with the introduction of
   liberal democracy does gender difference acquire political salience. On this point, see Peggy
   Watson, 'The Rise of Masculinism in Eastern Europe'.
14 This literature is too large to cite here. But see Tzvetan Todorov, *On Human Diversity:
   Nationalism, Racism and Exoticism in French Thought* (Harvard University Press, Cambridge
   MA, 1993) for a broad-ranging philosophical discussion and enquiry; or Kenan Malik's more
   popular *The Meaning of Race: Race, History and Culture in Western Society* (Macmillan,
   Basingstoke, 1996). A powerful argument in support of group rights (anathema in the classic
   liberal tradition) is given by the political philosopher Joseph Raz in *The Morality of Freedom*
   (Oxford University Press, New York, 1988), pp. 250–5, and Will Kymlicka, *Multicultural
   Citizenship: A Liberal Theory of Minority Rights* (Clarendon Press, Oxford, 1995). Kymlicka
   has the additional virtue of addressing the issues of women in relation to group rights.
15 Recent studies which make racial whiteness their focus include David R. Roediger, *The
   Wages of Whiteness: Race and the Making of the American Working Class* (Verso, London, 1991),
   Theodore W. Allen, *The Invention of the White Race* (Verso, London, 1994), and Noel
   Ignatieff, *How the Irish Became White* (Routledge, New York and London, 1995).
16 See especially the important efforts to rethink women's citizenship within a democratic
   framework by Anne Phillips; her *Engendering Democracy* (Polity Press, Cambridge, 1991) and

The Politics of Presence (Clarendon Press, Oxford, 1995) are especially valuable in dealing with women in ways that recognize women's needs without locking women into fixed and trans-historical identities. For a succinct statement of the universalism/difference issue, see her 'Universal Pretensions in Political Thought', in *Destabilizing Theory: Contemporary Feminist Debates*, ed. Michèle Barrett and Anne Phillips (Polity Press, Cambridge, 1992), pp. 10–30. For a spirited defence of universalism, especially for women and feminist theory, see Martha C. Nussbaum, 'Human Capabilities, Female Human Beings', in *Women, Culture, and Development: A Study of Human Capabilities*, ed. Nussbaum and Jonathan Glover (Clarendon Press, Oxford, 1995), pp. 61–104, and the response from Susan Wolf, pp. 105–15.

17 From the title of the book *The Bounds of Race: Perspectives on Hegemony and Resistance*, ed. Dominick LaCapra (Cornell University Press, Ithaca NY, New York and London, 1991).

18 Among European men, property qualifications determined who could vote and who not – determined political rights in this limited sense of rights. This is not to say that at times the poor (men and women) have not been seen as 'races apart' in their bodily difference from a middle-class bodily norm. Indeed, one could argue that the preoccupation with the scientific measurement of bodily differences between groups in Europe in the nineteenth century was a translation of class into the languages of racial difference. Certainly brachycephaly and dolicocephaly can be interpreted in this fashion.

19 This is a point discussed in Nancy Leys Stepan and Sander L. Gilman, 'Appropriating the Idioms of Science: The Rejection of Scientific Racism', in *The Bounds of Race*, pp. 72–103.

20 Race is a sexualized category and vice versa; yet how to analyse the mutual constitution of bodily differences remains one of the most vexed topics in contemporary gender and racial studies. Historically, scientists often drew gross analogies between males of 'lower' and females of 'higher' races, though the groups compared occupied very different places in society and experienced very different kinds of inequality. Initially, in the eighteenth century, lower races tended to be studied in relation to 'the human species' and sex differences within the European race; but by the nineteenth century, gender and sexuality were an intricate part of the scientific discourse on human races. On these points, see Nancy Leys Stepan, 'Race and Gender: The Role of Analogy in Science', *Isis*, 77 (June 1986), pp. 261–77; Londa Schiebinger, *'Nature's Body': Sexual Politics and the Making of Modern Science* (Pandora, London, 1994), especially ch. 5, and Sander L. Gilman, 'Black Bodies, White Bodies: Toward an Iconography of Female Sexuality in Late Nineteenth-Century Art and Literature', in *'Race', Writing and Difference*, ed. Henry Louis Gates, Jr (University of Chicago Press, Chicago IL, 1986), pp. 223–61.

21 See, for example, Sean Quinlan, 'Colonial Encounters: Colonial Bodies, Hygiene and Abolitionist Politics in Eighteenth-Century France', *History Workshop Journal*, 42 (1996), pp. 107–25.

22 For a very useful study of the emergence of our modern usage of the term race (e.g., for Hume, race meant 'real differences embedded in nature'), see Nicholas Hudson, 'From "Nation" to "Race": The Origin of Racial Classification in Eighteenth Century Thought', *Eighteenth-Century Studies*, 29 (1996), pp. 247–64. Hudson is especially interesting on the way 'race' as a concept separated from that of 'nation' in the eighteenth century, only to reunite with nation once 'race' had acquired its biological/zoological definition; thus by the mid-nineteenth century racial embodiment was connected to nationalism.

23 The new conceptions of nature, race and gender were hardly monolithic; for example, 'lower' races were childlike, or bestially ferocious; European women were by nature sexually passive, or potentially dangerously erotic. But whatever the characterization, their natures were taken as proof that European women's proper sphere was domestic and private, not public and political; the nature or anatomy of so-called lower races relegated them to backwardness and the need for tutelage, etc.

24 On embodiment in Western Christianity, see Caroline Bynum, *Fragmentation and Redemption: Essays on Gender and the Human Body* (Zone Books, New York, 1991), and *The Resurrection of the Body in Western Christianity, 200–1336* (Columbia University Press, New York, 1995).

25 Quoted in Nancy Stepan, *The Idea of Race in Science: Great Britain, 1800–1960* (Macmillan, Basingstoke, 1982), p. 94.

26 The study of the body is now very much in fashion (though its materiality often seems to disappear into textuality and words). For a review and critique of 'body studies' see Roy Porter, 'History of the Body', in *New Perspectives on Historical Writing*, ed. Peter Burke (Polity Press, Cambridge, 1991), pp. 203–32.

7 Note the appearance of new journals, for example, *Social Identities.*

28 Thomas Laqueur, *Making Sex: Body and Gender from the Greeks to Freud* (Harvard University Press, Cambridge MA and London, 1990).

29 The four points discussed in this section of the article are based on and are an extension of, remarks found in Stepan and Gilman, 'Appropriating the Idioms of Science'. The quotation is from Jack Morrell and Arnold Thackray, *Gentlemen of Science: Early Years of the British Association for the Advancement of Science* (Oxford University Press, London and New York, 1981), p. 32.

30 For instance, Morrell and Thackray show in their study of the BAAS, practitioners in fields of enquiry ruled unscientific were excluded from the association and therefore representation within science. Areas fraught with moral and political controversies kept a place within the boundaries of science only when purged of those concerns, as scientists adopted the neutral, empirical language by then seen as defining science itself.

31 Gyorgy Markus, 'Why Is There No Hermeneutics of the Natural Sciences? Some Preliminary Theses', *Science in Context*, 1 (1987), pp. 5–51.

32 Lorraine Daston, 'The Naturalized Female Intellect', *Science in Context*, 5 (1992), pp. 209–35.

33 One reason for the long persistence of belief in Lamarckian forms of inheritance lay, no doubt, in the permeability of the boundaries posited between hereditary material and the social world; social reform thus could have long-term, hereditary effects. Nonetheless, Lamarckianism was also compatible with conservative policies; the meaning of heredity is always a matter of interpretation. Latin American eugenics provides a good example of the varieties of social Lamarckianism; see Nancy Leys Stepan, *'The Hour of Eugenics': Race, Gender and Nation in Latin America* (Cornell University Press, Ithaca NY, 1996).

34 See especially John M. Efron, *Defenders of the Race: Jewish Doctors and Race Science in Fin-de-Siècle Europe* (Yale University Press, New Haven CT, 1994); Sander L. Gilman, *Freud, Race, and Gender* (Princeton University Press, Princeton NJ, 1993) and his *The Case of Sigmund Freud: Medicine and Identity at the Fin de Siècle* (Johns Hopkins University Press, Baltimore MD, 1993).

35 Stepan, *'The Hour of Eugenics'*, ch. 7.

36 Cora Kaplan, '"A Heterogeneous Thing": Female Childhood and the Rise of Racial Thinking in Victorian Britain', in *Human, All Too Human*, ed. with an introduction by Diana Fuss (Routledge, New York and London, 1996), p. 172.

37 Mary Poovey, *Uneven Developments: The Ideological Work of Gender in Mid-Victorian England* (University of Chicago Press, Chicago IL, 1988); Gillian Beer, *Darwin's Plots: Evolutionary Narrative in Darwin, George Eliot, and Nineteenth-Century Fiction* (Routledge & Kegan Paul, London, 1983).

38 On these changes, see Stepan, *The Idea of Race in Science*, chs 6 and 7; Elazar Barkan, *The Retreat of Scientific Racism: Changing Concepts of Race in Britain and the United States Between the World Wars* (Cambridge University Press, Cambridge, 1992); and Stephen Jay Gould, 'Why We Should Not Name Human Races – A Biological View', in his *Ever Since Darwin: Reflections in Natural History* (W. W. Norton, New York, 1977), ch. 29.

39 Charles Myers, 'The Future of Anthropometry', *Journal of the Royal Anthropological Institute*, 33 (1903), pp. 36–40.

40 William B. Provine, 'Genetics and the Biology of Race Crossing', *Science*, 182 (23 November 1973), pp. 790–96.

41 Saul Dubow, in his book *Scientific Racism in Modern South Africa* (Cambridge University Press, Cambridge, 1995), gives a thorough account of science, race and the making of apartheid policies after World War II.

42 On the uses of race in post-war British politics, see Robert Miles, *Racism After 'Race Relations'* (Routledge, London and New York, 1993), especially ch. 6.

43 On these contemporary struggles over race classifications in the United States see Lawrence Wright, 'Annals of Politics: One Drop of Blood', *New Yorker* (25 July 1994), pp. 46–55. On the importance of skin colour to racial classifications in the United States, and the role of the Census in creating distinctions within blackness, and later in creating pan-ethnic identities (e.g. Asians), as well as the general confusions that surround the Census categories, see Sharon M. Lee, 'Racial Classification in the US Census: 1890–1990', *Ethnic and Racial Studies*, 16 (January 1993), pp. 75–94. For a critical look at the new 'biracial' category favoured by some groups in the United States, see Lewis R. Gordon, 'Specificities: Cultures of American Identity: Critical "Mixed Race"?', *Social Identities*, 1 (1995), pp. 381–95.

44 Paul Gilroy, 'One Nation Under a Groove: The Cultural Politics of "Race" and Racism in Britain', in *Anatomy of Racism*, ed. David T. Goldberg (University of Minnesota Press, Minneapolis MN, 1990), pp. 263–82, and his *'There Ain't No Black in the Union Jack': The Cultural Politics of Race and Nation* (Hutchinson, London, 1987).

45 See the debate in *Critical Inquiry*: Walter Benn Michaels, 'Race Into Culture: A Critical Genealogy of Cultural Identity', *Critical Inquiry*, 18 (1992), pp. 655–85; Daniel Boyarin and Jonathan Boyarin, 'Diaspora: Generation and the Ground of Jewish Identity', *Critical Inquiry*, 19 (1993), pp. 693–727; Avery Gordon and Christopher Newfield, 'Critical Response: White Philosophy', *Critical Inquiry*, 20 (1994), pp. 737–57; and Walter Benn Michaels, 'Critical Response: The No-Drop Rule', *Critical Inquiry*, 20 (1994), pp. 758–67.

46 See the dispute over race and black identity between Kwame Anthony Appiah and Houston Baker, in Appiah, 'The Uncompleted Argument: Du Bois and the Illusion of Race', and Baker, 'Caliban's Triple Play', in *'Race', Writing, and Difference*, pp. 21–37 and 381–95. An interesting modern response to the persistent use of biological criteria to differentiate whiteness and blackness in American populations is the claim by Afro-American nationalists to biological superiority, based on the supposed biological advantages conferred by melanin.

47 This is the argument of Marek Kohn's *The Race Gallery: The Return of Racial Science* (Jonathan Cape, London, 1995).

48 Leonard Lieberman, Blaine W. Stevenson, and Larry T. Reynolds, 'Race and Anthropology: A Core Concept Without Consensus', *Anthropology and Education Quarterly*, 20 (1989), pp. 67–73.

49 Richard J. Herrnstein and Charles Murray, *The Bell Curve: Intelligence and Class Structure in American Life* (Free Press, New York, 1994). For reviews and critiques, see *The Bell Curve Wars: Race, Intelligence and the Future of America*, ed. Steven Fraser (Basic Books, New York, 1995), among several similar publications.

50 The geneticist Steve Jones, in his book *In the Blood: God, Genes and Destiny* (Flamingo, London, 1996), which was tied to his very successful television series in Britain with the same title, is very astute about the confusions and contradictions surrounding notions of genetic ancestry and group identity; he concludes that the biological differences between groups are small, yet admits that the debate about race, class and biology, however confusing and uncertain the evidence, will not go away. And his own language of genes, destiny and his casual use of racial identities (Jews, Indians) certainly indicate the easy slippage from technical genetic language to common-day everyday language. Along these same lines, see Dorothy Nelkin, 'The Politics of Predisposition: The Social Meaning of Predictive Biology', in *Biopolitics: The Politics of the Body, Race and Nature*, ed. Agnes Heller and Sonja Puntscher Riekmann (Avebury, Aldershot, 1996), pp. 133–43. Donna Haraway, in a recent paper, evaluates the redefinition of what it is to be human that is inscribed within the new molecular genetics and the Genome Project. She also has interesting things to say about the universal norms implicit in the 'family of man' model of humanity (especially in relation to sex and sexuality) that emerged as the anti-racist answer to racism in science after World War II. Though accepting the anti-racist intent of scientists after the war, she remains sceptical of universalisms, and fears that despite the shift in paradigms from race to the

population to genome, too much remains the same about race and difference even in self-consciously anti-racist practices. The main thrust of her argument is to find a definition of what it is to be human that does not depend on models of genealogy, reproduction, kinship and family. See her article 'Universal Donors in a Vampire Culture: It's All in the Family: Biological Kinship Categories in the Twentieth Century US', in *Uncommon Ground: Toward Reinventing Nature*, ed. William Cronon (W. W. Norton, New York and London, 1995), pp. 321–66.

51 Frederick Douglass, 'The Claims of the Negro Ethnologically Considered', in *The Life and Writings of Frederick Douglass*, ed. Philip S. Foner (Rochester University Press, Rochester NY, 1975), vol. 2, pp. 289–309.

52 Quoted in Stepan and Gilman, 'Appropriating the Idioms of Science', p. 81.

53 Linda Nicholson, 'Interpreting Gender', *Signs*, 20 (1994), pp. 79–105.

54 Verena Stolcke, in 'Is Sex to Gender as Race is to Ethnicity?', in *Gendered Anthropology*, ed. Teresa del Valle (Routledge, London, 1993), pp. 17–37, tries to draw parallels and distinctions between gender and ethnicity as terms from an anthropological point of view.

55 Nicholson, 'Interpreting Gender', p. 82.

56 This is the definition I gave in my book, *'The Hour of Eugenics'*, p.12.

57 Joan Scott, *Gender and the Politics of History* (Columbia University Press, New York, 1989), p. 2.

58 See especially Londa Schiebinger's *The Mind Has No Sex? Women in the Origins of Science* (Harvard University Press, Cambridge MA and London, 1989), and her *Nature's Body*; and Ornella Moscucci, *The Science of Woman: Gynaecology and Gender in England, 1800–1929* (Cambridge University Press, Cambridge, 1990), among others.

59 Thomas Laqueur, 'Orgasm, Generation, and the Politics of Reproductive Biology', in *The Making of the Modern Body: Sexuality and Society in the Nineteenth Century*, ed. Catherine Gallagher and Thomas Laqueur (University of California Press, Berkeley, Los Angeles and London, 1987), pp. 1–41, and his *Making Sex*.

60 Laqueur, *Making Sex*, p. 8.

61 For instance, there is evidence to suggest that the older model of women as 'lesser men' persisted well into the nineteenth century. In addition, some of Laqueur's comments in his introduction almost seem to undercut his own, constructionist interpretation of the body and its meanings.

62 Laqueur is particularly interesting about how the traditional view of woman as the especially fleshly, passionate sex (for whom orgasm was essential for conception) was replaced by the idea of woman as the 'passionless' sex for whom orgasm was unnecessary for reproduction. See Laqueur, *Making Sex*, p. 9.

63 The new universal woman constructed by science involved its own exclusions and suppressions of difference; the universal was white, middle-class and European, a norm against which other women were measured as deviations.

64 Laqueur, *Making Sex*, pp. 194–207, quote from p. 194.

65 Laqueur, *Making Sex*, p. 194.

66 See Agnes Heller, 'Has Biopolitics Changed the Concept of the Political? Some Further Thoughts About the Political', in *Biopolitics*, pp. 3–15. She takes the Hegelian/Arendtian view that the sphere of the political is ideally the sphere beyond and above body and that any effort to place the body in politics is to demean politics. Thus, according to Heller, feminists who seek women's political identity in the woman's body are equivalent to Hitler's racists. This is to ignore the non-neutrality of the universal space of the political and the way that embodiment has, historically, been central to the argument about political disembodiment and gender.

67 The persistence of the claim by scientists that there are two kinds of capacities, a male and female one, is an interesting phenomenon in the modern world; see Ann Fausto-Sterling's demolition of many contemporary scientific claims about sex differences, in her book *Myths of Gender: Biological Theories about Women and Men* (Basic Books, New York, 1985), a demolition which she bases on the failure of the scientists involved to meet normal standards of scientific evidence and method (thus her analysis rests within the use–abuse model of

science). Nussbaum points out that most scientific assertions of difference between the sexes refer to a statistical claim about some specialized human capability; basic capabilities thus remain untouched. Moreover, if the claim is statistical, it tells nothing about how an individual should be treated. See Nussbaum, *Women, Culture and Development*, p. 100.

68 Nicholson, 'Interpreting Gender', p. 101.

4

Cultivating bourgeois bodies and racial selves

ANN LAURA STOLER

The emphasis on the body should undoubtedly be linked to the process of growth and establishment of bourgeois hegemony; not, however, because of the market value assumed by labor capacity, but because of what the 'cultivation' of its own body could represent politically, economically, and historically for the present and the future of the bourgeoisie. Its dominance was in part dependent on that cultivation ... (Foucault, *History of Sexuality* 125)

In the two preceding chapters, I closely followed Foucault's treatments of modern racism in *The History of Sexuality* and the lectures, as he traced its emergence through a discourse of sexuality, normalizing power, and the technologies of the biopolitical state. In *The History of Sexuality*, modern racism is a late effect in the biohistory of bourgeois hegemony; in the lectures that genealogy is more nuanced, more complicated, and in some ways more blurred. There, a discourse of races (if not modern racism itself) antedates nineteenth-century social taxonomies, appearing not as a result of bourgeois orderings, but as constitutive of them. It is to this shift in analytic weight and to incumbent colonial implications that I turn here. I want to suggest that by drawing on Foucault's deeper genealogy of racial discourse in the lectures, we can re-examine his history of bourgeois sexuality to enrich that account in ways more consonant with what we are beginning to understand about the work of race and the place of empire in the making of Europe's bourgeois world.

Thus, I want to keep two sorts of issues in focus: how we can use Foucault to think about a specific range of colonial issues, and, in turn, what these colonial contexts afford us for rethinking how European bourgeois culture recounted the distinctions of its sexuality. Two themes of the lectures are of interest here: one is Foucault's attention to racism as part of a state's 'indispensable' defence of society against itself. This resonant and recurrent theme in the racial discourses of colony and metropole was critical to how European colonial communities expressed the 'defence' of its privileged members. I look here at how the regulatory mechanisms of the colonial state were directed not only at the colonized, but as forcefully at 'internal enemies' within the heterogeneous population that comprised the category of Europeans themselves. What is compelling in Foucault's analysis is less its novelty than its anticipation and confirmation of some of the very directions that studies of nationalism and colonialism are now taking.

On the other hand, Foucault by no means prefigured nor anticipated all these new directions. While he insisted on the primacy of a discourse on social war within Europe's eighteenth-century borders, giving only marginal attention to France's simultaneous colonial ventures that were under way, students of colonialism have made tentative efforts to sort out that connection. Lisa Lowe, for example, has drawn on eighteenth-century French travel literature to show how that literature became 'the means through which internal domestic challenges to social order could be figured and emplotted as foreign challenges'.[1] While Foucault plotted the rise of modern racism out of these domestic tensions, Lowe, like Ben Anderson, turns that same observation of noble and popular attacks on monarchical sovereignty to a different end to show how critical this early period of colonial expansion was in 'registering and regulating' Europe's domestic conflicts. If empire already figured in the class politics of eighteenth-century Europe, as Lowe, Pratt and others suggest, then surely it becomes harder to imagine a nineteenth-century bourgeois order that excludes empire from it.[2]

Still, other insights of Foucault's, particularly his identification of a nineteenth-century shift in the tactic of power away from discipline to a 'technology of security', dovetail with new directions in colonial studies in important ways. Key to this 'technology of security' – like biopower more generally – was its joining of the governing of a population to new interventions in the governing of the self. While this form of power emerged around 1800 (as signalled in *Discipline and Punish*), in the course of the nineteenth century it comes to legitimate increasing intervention in the ethics of conduct, geared to the management of 'how to live'. In the late colonial order, such interventions operated on European colonials in gendered forms that were class-specific and racially coded. Management and knowledge of home environments, child-rearing practices, and sexual arrangements of European colonials were based on the notion that the domestic domain harboured potential threats both to the 'defence of society' and to the future 'security' of the (European) population and the (colonial) state.

In short, these colonial variants confirm some of Foucault's claims, but not others. I want to focus not on the *affirmation* of bourgeois bodies as Foucault does in *The History of Sexuality*, but on the uncertainties and porous boundaries that surrounded them. I am concerned with the ways in which racial discourse reverberated between metropole and colony to secure the tenuous distinctions of bourgeois rule; how in this 'management of [bourgeois] life', middle-class distinctions were made not only in contrast to a European-based working class, but through a racialized notion of civility that brought the colonial convergence of – and conflict between – class and racial membership in sharp relief. My starting point is not the hegemony of imperial systems of control, but their precarious vulnerabilities.

While convinced that an understanding of the relationship between bourgeois biopower and colonial taxonomies entails tracing discourses on morality and sexuality through empire and back to the making of the interior frontiers of European nation-states, I only suggest some of those trajectories here. This task demands a reassessment of the anthropology of empire as well as of Foucault's selective Europe-bound genealogies. As a first step, I treat bourgeois sexuality and racialized sexuality not as distinct kinds, as does JanMohamed, but as dependent constructs in a unified field. Not least, my account confirms those challenges levelled at a European historiographic tradition in which the 'age of empire' and this 'century of bourgeois liberalism' have been bracketed more often than treated as parts of a whole.[3] In drawing on this emergent scholarship that attempts to span metropolitan and colonial social histories, I pursue those questions we are just beginning to ask, and suggest why we have not asked them until now.[4]

Rethinking colonialism as a bourgeois project

> It is beyond the fifty degree longitude that one starts to become conscious of what it means to be European.[5]

It may be the case that Foucault's work speaks less to the making of colonized subjects than to how European colonials constructed themselves, that his insights address, as Gayatri Spivak notes, more the 'constitution of the colonizer'.[6] Despite her allusion to Foucault's possible applicability to the normalizing contexts in which European colonials lived, Spivak never pursues this particular venture, dismissing it as a dangerous project. But even if we were to apply Foucault's story of the making of bourgeois distinctions to the ruling technologies of colonizing agents, that story and our treatment of it come up against some serious problems. Some are Foucault's, and some our own.

Much of the anthropology of colonialism, as I have argued for some time, has taken the categories of 'colonizer' and 'colonized' as givens, rather than as constructions that need to be explained.[7] Scholars have focused more on colonizers' accounts of indigenous colonized societies than on how Europeans imagined themselves in the colonies and cultivated their distinctions from those to be ruled. In short, there may be so few colonial readings of *The History of Sexuality* because questions of what constituted European identities in the colonies and the problematic political semantics of 'whiteness' have only recently come squarely within the scope of our analysis.[8]

The ellipses deriving from that constricted vision are more than apparent now as students of African, Asian, and Latin American colonial contexts have come to dismantle the received notion of colonialism as a unified bourgeois project. We have boldly and deftly undone its hegemonic conceits in some domains, but still skirt others. We know more than ever about the legitimating rhetoric of European civility and its gendered construals, but less about the class tensions that competing notions of 'civility' engendered.[9] We are just beginning to identify how bourgeois sensibilities have been coded by race and, in turn, how finer scales measuring cultural competency and 'suitability' often replaced explicit racial criteria to define access to privilege in imperial ventures.[10]

We still need to turn away from a founding premise. Colonialism was not a secure bourgeois project. It was not only about the importation of middle-class sensibilities to the colonies, but about the *making* of them. This is not to suggest that middle-class European prescriptions were invented out of whole cloth in the outposts of empire and only then brought home. I want to underscore another observation: that the philanthropic moralizing mission that defined bourgeois culture in the nineteenth century cast a wide imperial net; that the distinctions defining bourgeois sexuality were played out against not only the bodies of an immoral European working class and native Other, but against those of destitute whites in the colonies and in dubious contrast to an ambiguous population of mixed-blood origin. If we accept that 'whiteness' was part of the moral rearmament of bourgeois society, then we need to investigate the nature of that contingent relationship between European racial and class anxieties in the colonies and bourgeois cultivations of self in England, Holland, and France.

This issue of 'contingency' is not easy to unpack in part because scholars have taken such different phenomena as evidence and have relied on such varied sources. The very range of questions we have started to pose reflect that breadth of approach and perspective. Should evidence of that contingency be the submerged presence of racially charged colonial images in the European bourgeois novel or the studied absence of them?[11] Were European bourgeois norms developed in contrast to a phantom colonized Other, and can we talk about common European bourgeois imaginings of empire at all? Was it the experience of empire that produced these linkages, as Malleret's quote above suggests, or was it the metropolitan imaginings of what that experience was? Were the racial politics of colonialism the dominant backdrop against which European bourgeois sexuality was defined or did the eroticization of the exotic play more indirectly into how Dutch, French, and British middle classes garnered their moral authority over metropolitan working classes, using representations culled from colonial contexts to define themselves?[12] Or was the language of class itself racialized in such a way that to subscribe to bourgeois respectability entailed dispositions and sentiments coded by race? Finally, if this relationship between the affirmation of bourgeois hegemony and colonial practices was contingent, should we assume that the latter was necessary to the former's 'cultivation' or merely supportive of it?

This chapter broaches some of these questions more fully than others, but they should all be kept in mind. I pose them here to underscore how much recent efforts to identify these tensions of empire remain dependent on different assessments of what those connections were. Even a partial untangling should allow us a more analytically and historically nuanced story of what part colonialism has played in the construction of Europe's bourgeois order and some minimal agreement about what we might take to be a substantiation of it. In that effort, I turn first to the class tensions around racial membership in the Indies and then back to the work of race in fixing bourgeois distinctions in Europe itself.

Colonial oxymorons: on bourgeois civility and racial categories

If there is anything shared among historians about the nature of French, Dutch, and British colonial communities in the nineteenth century, it is the assumed fact that they were largely peopled by what Ben Anderson has called a 'bourgeois aristocracy'; those of petty bourgeois and bourgeois origins, who saw their privileges and profits as racially bestowed.[13] But this picture of European colonial communities is deeply flawed and not only for certain missionary groups, as Thomas Beidelman, John Comaroff and Catherine Hall have so rightly pointed out.[14] In the nineteenth-century Indies, it is impossible to talk about a European bourgeois order that was not racially problematic at the outset.

What is striking is both how self-evident *and* tentative the joinings of middle-class respectabilities and membership in European colonial communities actually were. If colonial enterprises were such secure bourgeois ventures, then why were European colonials so often viewed disparagingly from the metropole as *parvenus*, cultural incompetents, morally suspect, and indeed 'fictive' Europeans, somehow distinct from the real thing? While many historians would agree that colonized European-educated intellectuals and those of mixed racial origin were seen as 'white but not quite', this was also true of a large segment of those classified as 'fully' European.[15] If colonialism was indeed a class-levelling project that produced a clear consensus about European superiority – a consoling narrative that novels, newspapers, and official documents were wont to rehearse – we are still left to explain the pervasive anxiety about white degeneration in the colonies, the insistent policing of those Europeans who fell from middle-class grace, the vast compendium of health manuals and housekeeping guides that threatened ill-health, ruin, and even death, if certain moral prescriptions and modes of conduct were not met.

The question is whether those who made up these European colonial communities in fact saw themselves as part of a firmly entrenched ruling class, and if so on what basis? Eric Hobsbawm's definition of Europe's nineteenth-century bourgeoisie offers a useful contrast:

> [It was] … a body of persons of power and influence, independent of the power and influence of traditional birth and status. To belong to it a man had to be 'someone'; a person who counted as an individual, because of his wealth, his capacity to command other men, or otherwise to influence them.[16]

Some European colonial men would have numbered themselves within that class but not others. Some may have characterized themselves as having 'power and influence' over the native population, but not over other Europeans. Still others, as George Orwell's subdistrict officer in 'Shooting an Elephant' attests, were only too well aware of their dubious command over 'the natives', and their limited mastery over themselves.[17] While the colonial right to command was allegedly independent of 'traditional birth and status', the rosters of high government officials in India and the Indies suggest otherwise. In the nineteenth century, these positions were increasingly delimited to those who could afford to send their sons to law school in Leiden or to an Oxbridge public school, to those of the 'cultivated classes', and to those of 'full-blooded' Dutch or British birth. If 'everyone [European] in India was, more or less, somebody' as the British novelist Maud Diver professed in 1916, how do we explain the sustained presence of a subterranean colonial discourse that anxiously debated who was truly European and whether those who were both poor and white should be included among them?[18] *Contra* Diver's claim, we know from a range of colonial contexts that class distinctions within these European colonial communities were not increasingly attenuated but sharpened over time, lending credence to Robert Hughes's contention for another colonial context that 'the question of class was all-pervasive and pathological'.[19]

In fact, it is not clear how many 'Europeans' in the colonies ever enjoyed the privileges of belonging to a 'bourgeois aristocracy' at all.[20] This is not to suggest that there was not a large segment of the European population that made up a social and economic elite. Those of the Indies' stolid *burgerstand* (middle-class/bourgeois citizenry) recruited from Holland included plantation and trading company management, upper-level civil servants, professional personnel in the fields of education, health, and agriculture. But while colonial sources bespeak a European colonial elite comprised of those from 'good' families, birth in the Indies could exclude well-heeled creole families from membership. In 1856, W. Ritter observed:

> We count as European all those with white faces, who are not born in the Indies, all Dutch, English, French, Germans ... even North Americans. Our readers will repeat: A European is a European and will remain so wherever he finds himself ... We know him well. But you are greatly mistaken, Readers, for a European ... in the Indies is an entirely different being than in his country ... There, he identifies himself so much with all that surrounds him that he no longer can be considered as a European, at least for the duration of his stay in the Indies, but rather as belonging to a specific caste of the Indische population ... whose morals, customs and habits are certainly worthy of close examination.[21]

While Ritter's exclusion of all those born in the Indies from the category 'European' was unusual, it belies an anxiety that was much more widely shared: that even for the European-born, the Indies was transformative of cultural essence, social disposition, and personhood itself. His Lamarckian distinction was rarely so explicitly expressed; namely, that 'Europeanness' was not a fixed attribute, but one altered by environment, class-contingent, and not secured by birth.[22] Thus the Dutch doctor Kohlbrugge would write fifty years later that Europeans born and bred in the Indies lived in surroundings that stripped them of their European sensibilities to such an extent that they 'could easily ... metamorphize into Javanese'.[23] What is at issue here is not a shared conviction of the fixity of European identity but the protean nature of it. In both cases, as we shall see, what sustained racial membership was a middle-class morality, nationalist sentiments, bourgeois sensibilities, normalized sexuality, and a carefully circumscribed 'milieu' in school and home.

Ritter counted three major divisions among Europeans in the Indies – the military, civil servants and merchants – for whom the lines of class distinction [were] 'not clearly drawn'. By his account, the Indies had no 'so-called lower [European] classes'.[24] But such lower classes did exist and in increasing numbers throughout the nineteenth century as a burgeoning archive of government investigations on the problem of destitute Europeans in the Indies can attest. For the category 'European' also included an ill-defined population of poor whites, subaltern soldiers, minor clerks, abandoned children of European men and Asian women, as well as creole Europeans whose economic and social circumstances made their ties to metropolitan bourgeois civilities often tenuous at best.[25] At later moments it was to include Japanese, Africans and Chinese.[26] Being 'European' was supposed to be self-evident but was also a quality that only the qualified were equipped to define.

Complicated local folk taxonomies registered these internal distinctions. Thus, the term *indischen menschen* might refer, as did Ritter, to those hybrid offspring of Dutch men and native women 'whose blood was not unmixed European', but it could also connote those with lasting ties in the Indies, marking cultural and not biological affiliations. Creole whites born in the Indies were distinguished from those who were not. Those who came from and returned to Holland when their contracts expired (*trekkers*) were distinguished from those for whom the Indies were a permanent residence for generations (*blijvers*). 'Pure-blooded' (*zuiver*) Dutch were distinguished from those *mestizen*, 'Indo-European', *métis*, of mixed-blood origin.

But perhaps the most telling term in this racial grammar was that which prevailed throughout the nineteenth century for those who were white but impoverished, and usually, but not always, of mixed-blood origin. Firmly dissociated from the European-born, the term *inlandsche kinderen* neither referred to 'natives' nor 'children' as a literal translation might lead us to expect. It identified an ambiguous, hybrid population of those who were neither native nor endowed with the class background nor cultural accoutrements that could count them as truly European and fit to rule (accounting perhaps for Ritter's categorical exclusion of them). In the 1860s, some officials estimated thousands of such impoverished whites in the Indies; by the turn of the century, others calculated as many as sixty thousand.[27]

The enormous administrative energy levelled at the destitute living conditions of the *inlandsche kinderen* and proposals for their amelioration joined the policing of individuals with the defence of Dutch rule in specific ways. It was this group that confused the equation of whiteness and middle-class sensibilities in a discourse that legitimated the state's interventions in how all Europeans raised their children and managed their domestic and sexual arrangements. The discourse on destitute and degenerate whites whose 'Dutchness' was suspect underscored what could happen to European colonials who did not know 'how to live'. Debates about the moral degradation of the *inlandsche kinderen* did more than produce narratives about maternal vigilance, child rearing, and appropriate milieu. It prompted new institutional initiatives and government policies that made claims to racial superiority *dependent* on middle-class respectability for the entire European population. It made linguistic competence in Dutch the marker of cultural 'suitability' for European middle-class norms. It implicitly tied the quality of maternal sentiment and parental care to racial affiliation and nationality.

Architects of colonial policy worked off a set of contradictory premises. If the legitimation of European privilege and profit rested on a social taxonomy that equated Europeanness and bourgeois civilities, were those legally classified Europeans who fell short of these economic and cultural standards to be pulled back into these communities or banished from them? Was being poor and white politically untenable, a veritable colonial oxymoron? Were the unacknowledged children of European men and their native concubines to be reclaimed and redeemed by the state as Dutch, French, and British citizens or categorically barred?

These questions of racial identity and class distinction pervaded the colonial discourses in the Dutch East Indies, French Indochina, British Malaya, and India in the nineteenth and early twentieth centuries at different moments but in patterned ways. Mixed bloods were seen as one problem, poor whites as another, but in practice these persons were often treated as indistinguishable, one and the same. In each of these contexts, it called into question the very criteria by which Europeanness could be identified, how citizenship would be accorded and nationality assigned. In the Indies, the problem of 'European pauperism', debated and scrutinized in government commissions throughout the late second half of the nineteenth century, was about indigent whites and their mixed-blood progeny, mixed-blood European men and their native wives whose life styles indicated not always a failed effort to live up to the standards of bourgeois civility but sometimes an outright rejection of them.[28]

But subaltern and economically marginal whites were not the only challenge to the taxonomic colonial state. The equation of middle-class dispositions and European membership was threatened by creole Europeans as well, not by those impoverished but as strongly by the well-heeled and well-to-do. Thus, it was this group of respectable 'city fathers' of creole origin who petitioned the Dutch authorities in 1848 for the establishment of equivalent schools of higher education in the Indies and protested policies requiring their sons be sent for training to Holland to meet civil service entry requirements. It was their children who conversed more easily in Malay than Dutch, whose fatherland was more the Indies than the Netherlands, who were feared to see themselves as 'world citizens', not faithful partisans of continued Dutch rule.[29]

It is striking, for example, that in the 1850s Indo-Europeans born in the Indies were barred from posts in the civil service that would put them in direct contact with the native population at precisely the time when new administrative attention was focused on the inadequate training in native languages displayed by the Indies' colonial civil servants. At issue was obviously not whether civil servants knew local languages, but how those languages were learned and used and whether that knowledge was appropriately classified and controlled. While enormous funds were dispensed on teaching Javanese at the Delft Academy in Holland to students with a proper 'Dutch rearing', those *inlandsche kinderen* who already knew Javanese or Malay but lacked the proprieties and cultural knowledge that a Dutch rearing provided, were categorically barred. What was being taught to future officers in the colonial civil service at Delft was not only language but a more general set of disciplines that included distancing postures of comportment and imperious forms of address to inferiors that were crucial to appropriate language use.[30] Given the emphasis placed on 'character' and conduct, the sustained attention of the colonial state to the importance of home environments is not surprising. The increasing attention given to a moral 'upbringing' (*opvoeding*) as a prerequisite for the proper use of a formal education (*onderwijs*) turned on a basic assumption: that it was in the domestic domain, not the public sphere, where essential dispositions of manliness, bourgeois morality, and racial attribute could be dangerously undone or securely made.

While we could read these debates on the 'so-called *inlandsche kinderen*' and the philanthropic moralizing impulses directed toward them as discourses prompted by threats to white prestige, these discourses spoke to other concerns as well. The 'civilizing mission' of the nineteenth century was a bourgeois impulse directed not only at the colonized, as often assumed, but at recalcitrant and ambiguous partici-pants in imperial culture at home and abroad.[31] But these bourgeois initiatives were as strongly directed at 'reform of themselves'.[32] As a new generation of Dutch social historians now argue, the 'civilizing offensive' was not only about the 'poor and their needs, but the rich and their motives'.[33] In Indies perspective, the validity of these observations is well borne out. To abide by *burgerlijk* values was crucial to the racial rhetoric of rule, but that rhetoric often diverged from the messier realities of culturally hybrid urban wards where persons of varied class origin, in a range of domestic and sexual arrangements, lived side by side – where the moral high ground of middle-class prescripts was seen as under threat in how the 'European village population' (*Europeesche kampongbevolking*) lived – on colonial ground.[34] The charged discourse on the sexual precocity of Indies youth was not only a discourse about native contamination but about the education of bourgeois desire, about alienations of affection in the homes of the most stolid *burgerlijk* colonial families themselves. As Nancy Armstrong has so convincingly argued for eighteenth and nineteenth-century Britain, 'programs for cultivating the heart … constituted a new and more effective method of policing' those who were to embody 'the triumph of middle-class culture'.[35]

Taking our cue from Armstrong's contention that British conduct books and novels during this period antedated the bourgeois way of life they represented, we might read the colonial guides to European survival in the tropics in a similar light: as prescriptive texts of how a *burgerlijk* colonial life style was supposed to look, not *a posteriori* affirmations or distillations of what colonial ventures had secured and already become. These were not reflections of a commonly shared knowledge, but creative sites of a new kind of knowledge that tied personal conduct to racial survival, child neglect to racial degeneracy, the ill management of servants to disastrous consequences for the character of rule. They register how much a lack of self-discipline was a risk to the body politic. But, most importantly, in prescribing the medical and moral care of adult and children's bodies, the requirements for a *gezellig* (cosy) and well protected European home, and the attributes of a 'modern white mother' whose native servants were kept in check, they tied bourgeois domesticity to *European* identities and thus racial orderings to bourgeois rule.

Recasting Foucault's frame, this micro-management of domestic life might be seen less as an affirmation of bourgeois hegemony than as a contested and transgressive site of it. For if one definition of the nineteenth-century middle class in Europe was its 'servant-holding status', in the Indies (as in Europe) it was precisely those who served the needs of the *middenstand* who were viewed as subversive contagions in those carefully managed colonial homes. It is only as historians have turned to these other domains of imperial culture where the meanings of 'whiteness' were far less veiled that the 'vigour' of European bodies shows itself as precariously secured through these racialized prescriptions and practices.

Our blind spots in colonial studies derive from certain assumptions, Foucault's from others. His story of what sexuality meant to the eighteenth-century bourgeoisie refutes an account that explains the management of sexuality in any class relational terms, i.e. as a strategy to harness the energies of the working class. For Foucault, the technologies of sex were first designed to affirm the bourgeois self. He writes:

> The primary concern was not the repression of the sex of the classes to be exploited, but rather the body, vigour, longevity, progeniture, and descent of the classes that 'ruled'. This was the purpose for which the deployment of sexuality was first established, as a new distribution of pleasures, discourses, truths, and powers; *it has to be seen as the self-affirmation of one class rather than the enslavement of another*, a defence, a protection, a strengthening, and an exaltation that were *eventually extended to others* – at the cost of different transformations – as a means of social control and political subjugation … What was formed was a political ordering of life, *not through an enslavement of others*, but through an affirmation of self … it provided itself with a body to be cared for, protected, cultivated, and preserved from the many dangers and contacts, to be isolated from others so that it would retain its differential value; and this, by equipping itself with – among other resources – a technology of sex. (*History of Sexuality* 123; my emphasis)

Here sexuality is about middle-class affirmation, not working-class exploitation; the term 'enslavement' is used only in its metaphorical sense. Foucault's economy of sex produces power, truths, and pleasures. It contrasts the sort of repressive model of sex implied in an analysis of political economy where the energies expended on sex are viewed as detractions from the energies expended on work and where labour power is exchanged. But in substituting an economy of sex for an economy of labour does Foucault let the discourse of bourgeois sexuality stand in for the sociology of it? Even if we were to accept his bourgeois emphasis, we cannot help but notice the awkward syntax that absents key actors from his account. For even within his frame, these bourgeois bodies were never in fact isolated, but defined by intimate relationships and daily contacts of a special kind.

We are just beginning to explore some of the quotidian ways in which European bourgeois bodies were produced in practices, but these were never contingent on the will to self-affirmation alone. The cultivation of the European bourgeois self in the colonies, that 'body to be cared for, protected, cultivated, and preserved from the many dangers and contacts ...' required other bodies that would perform those nurturing services, provide the leisure for such self-absorbed administerings and self-bolstering acts. It was a gendered body and a *dependent* one, on an intimate set of exploitative sexual and service relations between European men and native women, between European women and native men, shaped by the sexual politics of class and race. Those native women who served as concubines, servants, nursemaids and wives in European colonial households not only defined what distinguished bourgeois life: they threatened that 'differential value' of adult and children's bourgeois bodies they were there to protect and affirm. Others did so as well. Young European women of modest rural means who served as governesses to European colonial children were part of that 'large supporting cast of houseboys, grooms, gardeners, cooks, amahs, maids, [and] washerwomen' whose tendings invaded these well guarded homes.[36] This 'cast of characters' were not only there as ritual objects, symbolically affirming the hierarchies of Dutch authority; through them Europeans could conjure a typology of natives that legitimated the structured subordinations of rule.

The self-affirmation of white, middle-class colonials thus embodied a set of fundamental tensions between a culture of whiteness that cordoned itself off from the native world and a set of domestic arrangements and class distinctions among Europeans that produced cultural hybridities and sympathies that repeatedly transgressed these distinctions. The family, as Foucault warns us, should not be seen as a haven from the sexualities of a dangerous outside world, but as the site of their production. Colonial authorities knew it only too well. They were obsessed with moral, sexual, and racial affronts to European identity in *Indische* households, but also in 'full-blooded' Dutch homes. Housekeeping guides, medical manuals, and pedagogic journals produced in the nineteenth-century Indies and the Netherlands reiterated such dangers in many forms. Nor should it be surprising that this barrage of advice on contamination intensifies as germ theory develops and biomedicine begins its triumphs.[37]

These prescriptive texts repeatedly urged that mixed-blood children in poor white households needed to be salvaged from the 'damaging domestic milieu', severed from their native mothers and social environments. As late as the 1930s, the Indies civil service and police were congratulating themselves for 'isolating' the daughters of European men and Javanese women from the 'fatal, disastrous surroundings' and nefarious influences to which they were subject when 'abandoned' to their mothers' village homes.[38] European children of the well-to-do were equally at risk of degeneration, of 'metamorphosing into Javanese', if the proper habitus was not assured and certain social protocols were not met; if they played in the streets with Indo-European children, if they attended Indies schools that could not instil a proper Dutch 'spirit', and most perniciously, if they enjoyed too much indulgence from their native nursemaids, and in general had too much intimacy with and knowledge of things Javanese. I have explored these quotidian technologies of self-affirmation elsewhere.[39] Here, however, there are several distinctive features in this making of a bourgeois habitus in the colonies that I want to underscore.

First of all, Foucault assumes a middle-class culture sure of what it needed to defend and sure of how to do it. It is not clear this was the case in Europe or in the United States; in the colonies it was certainly not.[40] These strategies of identity-making and self-affirmation were unstable and in flux. European identities in the colonies were affirmed by a cultural repertoire of competences and sexual prescriptions that altered with the strategies for profit and the stability of rule. Thus, concubinage was still seen to uphold a European middle-class standard in the 1880s, but seen to undermine it two decades later.[41] Adoptions of Javanese dress by European-born Dutch colonials were only permissible at leisure, as other more hard-and-fast cultural distinctions between European and native were drawn. Early nineteenth-century warnings against the performance of manual labour for whites in the tropics were reassessed by its end, when the Indies-born Netherlanders became associated with indulgent and ostentatious lifestyles, contrasting the work ethic prescribed for the self-disciplined European-born Dutch. In short, while the vocabulary of European moral superiority was constant, that was neither true of the criteria used to measure that superiority nor of the specific sub-population of 'Europeans' deemed morally worthy of inclusion in that select category.

Moreover, the logic that made being *echte* Dutch contingent on being middle-class frequently came up against the changing demands of the Indies' economy. As new demands for skilled technical labour emerged in the nineteenth century, the *inlandsche kinderen* were promoted as suitable candidates to fill such positions in naval shipyards, arms ateliers, and the expanding plantation industry. Various proposals designed to provide 'scientific' as well as 'practical' training to the Indies' European underclass were quickly defeated: others were never tried. Efforts, as early as 1835, to train Indies-born children of European descent to become 'an industrious *burgerstand*' met with little success, prompting officials twenty years later to question whether they should be 'made into a self-supporting *burgerlijk* class or a skilled working class differentiated from the natives'.[42] By 1874 some authorities considered the notion of creating an independent *middenstand* a 'total fiasco', on the argument that the *inlandsche kinderen* lacked both the 'inclination' and the 'suitability' for manual work of any kind, even skilled artisanal labour. In a revised vision, the state's task was reconceived as one that would turn them not into 'imitation' or 'defective Europeans' but into 'perfected natives'.[43]

At the heart of these debates were competing visions of what constituted a European 'critical mass', and whether the 'quality' and 'character', of European residents was less important than the sheer quantity of them; whether the rash passions of subaltern soldiers and other lower-class men could reflect the nineteenth-century image of the 'stolid and dispassionate' (*bezagigd*) Dutch nation and not undermine the moral tenets of Dutch rule.[44] Thus it was not only the mixed-blood *inlandsche kinderen* whose moral and intellectual attributes were under attack. Some observers in fact claimed that those workers imported directly from Holland were so utterly dissipated, so lacking in 'vitality' (*levenskracht*) and zest for work (*werklust*) that the notion of making them into a *burgerklasse* was absurd.[45] Others claimed that the problem in the Indies was of a different order. As J. van de Waal put it in 1916:

> The descendants of Europeans who are 'unfit' for European nationality because of a lack of intellectual development and a high moral conscience and who were brought up in pure native, and largely immoral, surroundings form a troubling part of society in the Indies that does not show itself, as in Europe, in reckless anarchism or dissolute bestiality but that works in secret, nearly invisibly as a corroding cancer gnawing at the sexual strength (*steunkracht*) of our society.[46]

Note here that this 'biopolitical' discourse targets internal dangers and excesses within the Dutch polity, weak biological links within its ranks and not external, native contaminations.

Europeanness was not only class-specific but gender-coded. A European man could live with or marry an Asian woman without necessarily losing rank, but this was never true of a European woman who might make a similar choice to live or marry a non-European. Thus, in the legal debates on mixed marriage in 1887, a European woman who married a native man was dismissively accorded native legal status on the grounds that her very choice of sexual and conjugal partner showed that she had 'already sunk so deep socially and morally that it does not result in ruin … [but rather] serves to consolidate her situation'.[47] Foucault was undoubtedly right that the affirmation of the body was 'one of the primordial forms of class consciousness', but bourgeois 'class bodies' defined their 'healthy sexuality' with a consciousness of civilities and social hygiene always measured in racial terms (*History of Sexuality* 126). Sexual promiscuity or restraint were not abstract characteristics attached to any persons who exhibited those behaviours, but as often *post hoc* interpretations contingent on the racialized class and gender categories to which individuals were already assigned.[48] Being a less well-to-do woman *and* of mixed descent coded a range of social relations as erotically driven, sensually charged, and sexually precocious by definition. Such assessments valorized that bourgeois health was *pur sang* and European, governed by a logic in which moderation showed self-mastery and 'productive sexuality' defined what was morally acceptable and what would improve the race.

Questions about the shifting, visual signs of middle-class rearing were indices of what was invisible and harder to test – namely, what defined the essence of being European and whether creole and mestizen affinities for things Javanese were a threat to it. Thus the Indies 1884 law that specified the requirements for acquiring European equivalent status listed 'complete suitability for European society' and/or indisputable evidence that the concerned party was 'brought up in European surroundings as a European'.[49] Although Dutch language use, attire, schooling, and church membership matched *burgerlijk* values to European status, that was rarely enough. As van de Waal observed, children clothed in modest frocks and shoes when attending the government schools enjoyed such a short-lived and insufficient education that these efforts at 'Europeanism' were of little avail; 'native dishes as always were awaiting them' when they returned to their village homes.[50] The powerful force of 'environment' in this discourse slipped back and forth between two principal referents: the geography of the tropics and the architecture of sensibilities cultivated in the home. In constantly posing the question as to whether natives and *inlandsche kinderen* could be transformed, social reformers in metropole and colony could not help but ask the same question of themselves. But their answers were not the same. A basic disquieting asymmetry underwrote their racial grammar: for while an Indo child could not be shorn of its native sensibilities because of the 'native blood that flowed in its veins', that logic – as we have seen and *contra* the stories colonial elites sometimes told themselves – did not work the other way round.

Bourgois insecurities, racial selves and the 'stolid' Dutch nation

These colonial contexts make it clear that bourgeois culture was in question on its social and geographic outposts, among those working out its changing standards. But there is also good evidence that it was not securely hegemonic even at its ostensible core.[51] Although Dutch historians have long held that Dutch national character was clarified and fixed in the Golden Age of the seventeenth century, recent scholarship casts increasing doubt on that claim. Even Simon Schama, who otherwise insists that 'the essential traits of Dutch nationhood' endured major shifts in its governing institutions', concedes that the Dutch 'conventional self-image' in the early nineteenth century underwent fundamental change.[52] With convincing argument, the Dutch historian Siep Stuurman notes that although the nineteenth century commonly has been referred to as the 'century of the middle-class citizenry' (*burgerij*), that was only a partial truth.[53] His study of nineteenth-century liberalism contends that the '*burgers* who at this time were not called the middle classes without reason' had to wage a 'continuous and tenacious struggle to acquire a dominant position next to the old ruling elite'.[54] During the first half of the nineteenth century (from the French interregnum of 1795–1813 through the establishment of the Dutch monarchy and rise of constitutional democracy in 1848), there is little indication that state institutions were in the bourgeoisie's control.[55] By Stuurman's account, bourgeois hegemony in the Netherlands emerges at the end of the nineteenth century, not at its beginning. Liberalism was not the product of 'a bourgeoisie that already dominated state and society', but one whose power was in the making.[56] In a related vein, the Dutch historian, Ali de Regt, argues that the mid-nineteenth century 'civilizing offensive' that targeted the immoral living conditions of the working class as its object of reform was designed less to 'uplift' the latter than to distinguish a burger class whose boundaries of privileges were not clearly drawn.[57]

These rethinkings of Dutch social history raise issues that go beyond domestic politics alone. If *burgerlijk* identity was less self-evident than many Dutch historians have claimed, then the sustained efforts to define who could belong to the *burgerstand* and who was really Dutch in the nineteenth-century Indies may take on a different valence. They may signal more than the reactions of a beleaguered colonial minority in a vast sea of colonized as often assumed, but rather a dynamic – even productive – tension between the making of Dutch bourgeois identity at home in the Netherlands and abroad.

Whether the Indies were central to the construction of nineteenth-century Dutch bourgeois culture is still difficult to affirm, given the compartmentalization of Dutch historiography. Ritter's observation in 1856 that 'the Indies is nowhere less known than in the country to which it belongs', may no longer be true, but the discrete treatment of the social history of the Indies and the Netherlands remains true today.[58] The question itself places these Indies-based debates about what it meant to be Dutch, *burgerlijk*, and sexually moral in a different light. These were sites where the moral authority of bourgeois values was played out, where the tension between desire and decorum, opulence and thrift was in uneasy display. The Indies discourse about Dutch bourgeois virtues infused the vocabulary of social reform and nationalist priorities with racial meaning.

This is not to suggest that these debates about 'moral milieu' had their originary moment in colonial settings. Numerous studies of the late eighteenth century show that new directives for education and the domestic environment of children represented pointed attacks by a *burgerlijke middenklasse* on the social hierarchies of France and the Netherlands' *ancien régimes*, that such reforms were part of the identity formation of the middle class itself.[59] The Dutch campaign for popular education was framed as a reform of an 'orderless', morally corrupt society, where 'ignorance, immorality, and savagery' were the enemies of the natural order. Reform rested on the instilment of 'personal self-discipline' as well as collective moral control.[60]

But the nineteenth-century discourse, in which these internal enemies were identified and targeted, circulated in a racially inflected imperial field.

Metropolitan debates over the critical importance of well guided mothercare (*moederzorg*) for the alleviation of poverty, in the Indies fixated on whether mixed-blood and creole women specifically could provide the sort of *moederzorg* that would obviate assistance from the state (*staatszorg*). Similarly, European debates about whether men should be held responsible for their illegitimate children, in the Indies took on an explicitly racialized form: there, the question was whether European men should be charged with the care of their mixed-blood offspring and whether this would lead to an unhealthy expansion of a population of 'fabricated Europeans'.[61] Such parallel debates situate the moral contortions of Dutch colonials as part of the inherent contradictions within the liberal rhetoric of nineteenth-century bourgeois culture, rather than as marginal embellishments of it.

We have ample evidence that representations of racial ambiguity served to define the parameters of Dutch colonial communities in important ways. Racialized others of mixed-blood and creole origin and the suspect sexual moralities, ostentatious lifestyles, and cultural hybrid affiliations attributed to them were productive of a discourse on who was appropriate to rule. But this traffic in charged representations may have reflected deeper concerns still; not only the vulnerabilities of Dutch hegemony in the colonies, but uncertainties about what constituted the inclusionary distinctions of bourgeois culture in the Netherlands where the very term *burgerlijk* could ambiguously refer to that which was at once exclusively middle-class and that which was much more inclusively identified with the 'civic', the 'civil', the 'citizen'.[62]

Curiously, that tangled field that encompasses the cultivation of bourgeois bodies and the cultivation of *homo Europaeus* is one that few Dutch social historians have sought to entertain. While Stuurman and others have rightly noted how the Protestant nineteenth-century *burgerij* rewrote the past in their own image, using the myth of a Calvinist nation of 'civilized morals' (*beschaafde zeden*) to programme the future, their attention has focused more on the warped accounts of domestic social history than on the systematic and sustained omission of the East Indies from it.

Take the case of nineteenth-century Dutch liberalism and the history of social reform. The coincidence of dates that mark the *burgerlijk* 'civilizing mission' in the Netherlands and the Indies is striking. By virtually all accounts, 1848 marked the emergence of a liberal parliamentary state, identified with philanthropic bourgeois interventions to uplift the home environments of the domestic working class.[63] In the very same year, racial dualism in the Dutch East Indies was 'legally anchored' in explicit terms.[64] One could argue that there is nothing incompatible about this. As Stuurman notes, although Dutch 'liberals' spoke for the nation and the people, no pretence of universal representation was really implied: the 'democratic element' of the mid-nineteenth century was confined to the virtuous and industrious middle class alone.[65] Citizenship (*burgerrecht*) categorically excluded 'all women, minors, mad persons, beggars, prisoners, the dishonoured … and all persons who did not have full use of their freedom, their minds, or their possessions'.[66] While those excluded from citizenship in the Netherlands made up the population that was the object of state intervention, in the Indies race structured the parameters of dependence and excluded many of those same categories not only from citizenship, but even from assistance and/or the opportunity to benefit from social reform.

Simultaneous with the enormous expansion of juvenile reformatories, orphanages, and agrarian colonies that targeted Holland's urban poor were a concomitant set of similar Indies institutions that repeatedly faltered on whether their potential recipients should include the illegitimate children of mixed-blood origin. Even those supporters of expanded European orphanages in the Indies never forgot to distinguish the mixed-blood children of lower-class Dutch soldiers from the orphans of deceased civilians who had, in their lifetime been well-to-do. Similarly the debates over poor relief, widows' pensions, and improved medical care were implemented in ways that excluded not only those classed as 'native' but those Europeans of suspect origin, either because they were deemed culturally 'nativized' and lived in a fashion that required no such benefits or because some were seen as natives in disguise – only 'fictive' Europeans. State reforms to set up public schools for 'all Europeans and their legal equivalents' in the mid-nineteenth century promptly designated special schools (*armenscholen*, literally schools for the poor) for the children of subaltern whites, for those abandoned to the streets, for those destitute and of 'mixed' origin.[67] Even some of the practitioners of these policies were sometimes the same. Johannes van de Bosch, who founded the Maatschappij van Weldadigheid (Benevolent Society) in the Netherlands in 1818, was the same van de Bosch who, as the Indies' Governor General some years later, introduced the oppressive cultivation system on Java that liberals in Holland were soon to attack. It was also he who argued that the *inlandsche kinderen* were the colonial state's responsibility and its alone.[68]

The Frobel kindergarten movement that swept through Germany, England, Holland, and France in the mid-nineteenth century, that quintessential laboratory of liberal experiment, in the Indies was heralded not only as a hothouse for nurturing Dutch middle-class sensibilities of morality, self-discipline and thrift, but as a strategic method of removing [European] children from the immoral clutches of native nursemaids, native playmates and, most importantly, native mothers.[69] One might be tempted to argue that reformist gestures in the colonies produced these exclusionary, racialized reactions from a more conservative constituency. But this was not the case. These were proposals crafted by the most ardent social reformers whose visions were racially specific, highly class conscious, and exclusionary by definition.

Even such critically persuasive historians as Stuurman, who argues that 'liberal-burgerlijke culture' was in the making in the nineteenth-century Netherlands, makes only passing reference to the Indies context where the exclusionary principles of liberalism were in such sharp relief. Ali de Regt's observation that the civilizing offensive in the Netherlands was never aimed at embourgeoisment resonates in the Indies in virtually every field of social reform. Plans to set up artisanal and industrial schools for impoverished whites and those of mixed origin foundered on whether such a population could and should be shaped into an 'industrious *burgerstand*' or not.[70] In debunking the myth of the 'stolid' Dutch nation as the culture of a 'self-sufficient middle-class', Stuurman prompts us to ask just those questions that Dutch historians have not sought to pose, questions about the relationship between bourgeois projects and imperial ventures that are being asked by students of colonialism for Germany, the United States, Britain, and France.[71] While this relationship was certainly tighter and more explicit in some places than in others, we cannot begin to contrast them unless we sort out whether national variations of emphasis and absence in historiography reflect national variations in lived history as well.

Discourses of race/languages of class

One might argue that racialized notions of the bourgeois self were idiosyncratic to the colonies and applicable there alone. But a repertoire of racial and imperial metaphors were deployed to clarify class distinctions in Europe at a very early date. While social historians generally have assumed that racial logics drew on the ready-made cultural disparagements honed to distinguish between middle-class virtues and the immorality of the poor, as well as between the 'undeserving' and the 'respectable' poor among themselves, it may well be that such social etymologies make just as much sense reversed. The racial lexicon of empire and the sexualized images of it, in some cases, may have provided for a European language of class as often as the other way around. In a study of race and politics in Jamaica and Britain, Tom Holt cautiously notes that 'this language of class [may have] provided a vocabulary for thinking about race, or vice-versa. It hardly matters; what is important is the symmetry of the discourse …'[72] For my reading of Foucault, however, these racial etymologies of the language of class matter very much. They place the making of racial discourse, and a discourse on slavery in particular, as formative in the making of a middle-class identity rather than as a late nineteenth-century addition to it.

Certainly, Foucault's contention that the language of class grew out of the discourse of races would support such a claim. From Montaigne to Mayhew to Balzac, in Britain, the Netherlands, and France, imperial images of the colonized native American, African, and Asian as eroticized savage or barbarian saturated the discourses of class. In an intriguing analysis similar to Foucault's, Hayden White argues that the 'race fetishism' surrounding the eighteenth-century notion of the 'noble savage' was 'soon transformed … into another, and more virulent form: the fetishism of class'.[73] But, unlike for Foucault, the template is not only an earlier racial discourse directed at internal enemies within Europe, but one prompted by imperial expansion. White writes:

> Like the 'wild men' of the New World, the 'dangerous classes' of the Old World
> define the limitations of the general notion of 'humanity' which informed and

justified the Europeans' spoliation of any human group standing in the way of their expansion, and their need to destroy that which they could not consume.[74]

The opening chapter of Eugen Weber's *Peasants into Frenchmen*, entitled 'A Country of Savages', is emblematic of the confused ways in which these social categories were seen to converge. Quoting a mid-nineteenth-century Parisian traveller in rural Burgundy who opines that 'You don't need to go to America to see savages,' Weber argues that the theme of the French peasant as the 'hardly civilized', rural savage 'of another race' was axiomatic in a discourse that 'sometimes compared them unfavourably with other colonized peoples in North Africa and the New World'.[75] Nor do we have to wait for the nineteenth century to find those convergences between class and racial disparagements sharply drawn. The *abbé* Sieyes, that late eighteenth-century Frenchman so renowned for his egalitarian treatise that redefined the French nation in terms of its Third Estate, produced other visions of a just society that reveal profound contradictions in his argument.[76] Although Sieyes professed an identity between participation in work and citizenship, in a pre-revolutionary note he invoked the notion of a hierarchy of races, and a definition of citizens that would exclude the real producers and include only the 'heads of production' who 'would be the whites'. Sieyes's language of class and nation drew on a racial lexicon as well.

Edmund Morgan notes for seventeenth-century Britain that the poor were 'the vile and brutish part of mankind … in the eyes of unpoor Englishmen, [they] bore many of the marks of an alien race'.[77] Certainly this was true of British images of the Irish, who as early as the seventeenth century were seen as 'racially distinct'.[78] Strong parallels were made between the immoral lives of the British underclass, Irish peasants, and 'primitive Africans' by the eighteenth century, crescendoing in the early nineteenth century when the 'influx of Irish amounted to an urban invasion'.[79] *Punch* ran articles in the mid-nineteenth century suggesting that the Irish were 'the missing link between the gorilla and the Negro'.[80]

Thus for the nineteenth century the case is stronger still. Reformers such as Mayhew pursued their projects with a moral authority that rested on comparing the moral degradation of the British urban poor with 'many savage tribes' (1851: 43). Such colonial historians as Victor Kiernan were well aware of the connection:

> In innumerable ways his [the European gentleman's] attitude to his own 'lower orders' was identical with that of Europe to the 'lesser breeds'. Discontented native in the colonies, labour agitator in the mills, were the same serpent in alternate disguise. Much of the talk about the barbarism or darkness of the outer world, which it was Europe's mission to rout, was a transmuted fear of the masses at home.[81]

Jean and John Comaroff note that efforts to shore up British bourgeois domesticity drew on resonant parallels between the 'dangerous classes' at home and abroad, a 'coupling [of] the pauper and the primitive in a common destiny', in ways that implicated African domesticity in the making of modern English society.[82] Susan

Thorne, in a study of missionary imperialism, argues that racial metaphors were pervasive in the religious discourse that shaped the language of class in early industrial England.[83] Edward Said synthesizes another strand of that story by looking at the canonical texts of British fiction in which colonial landscapes provided the backdrop against which British middle-class culture was set in relief. Catherine Hall explores the pervasive presence of a racialized Other in the repertoire of visual, verbal, and written images that set off the distinctions of bourgeois sensibilities and the virtues of the bourgeois home.[84] As Eric Hobsbawm once put it, 'the bourgeois was, if not a different species, then at least the member of a superior race, a higher stage in human evolution, distinct from the lower orders who remained in the historical or cultural equivalent of childhood or adolescence. From master to master race was thus only a short step.'[85]

There is something strikingly similar in most of these accounts; namely, that the invocation of race is interpreted as a rhetorical political strategy. Race serves as a charged metaphor with allegorical weight. It emphasizes the deep differences between working-class and bourgeois culture, naturalizing the inherent strengths or weaknesses that these collectivities allegedly shared. In short, as Elaine Showalter notes, 'metaphors of race were … used to describe class relationships'.[86] But is metaphor and allegory all that this relationship is about? I think not. For it assumes first of all that 'class' and 'race' occupied distinct spaces in the folk social taxonomies of Europe, that they were discursively and practically discrete social categories. We might question whether this was the case, particularly for the eighteenth century, when notions of 'race' and 'class' had both looser and richer meanings and when the hardened distinctions inherited from the nineteenth century were not yet so clearly drawn.[87]

The point is an important one because if these were indeed not only 'symmetrical discourses' as Tom Holt has argued but at once overlapping and interchangeable ones, then some notion of race must figure much more organically in the making of bourgeois distinctions than we have assumed.[88] Such an argument would not rest on the assumption that the social categories of 'race' and 'class' were always substitutable or that the meanings of 'race' in the seventeenth, eighteenth, and nineteenth centuries were the same. Nor would Foucault's reverse genealogy in which the language of class always emerges out of an earlier discourse of race necessarily be the case. On the contrary, both 'race' and 'class' in their early usage marked a more fluid environmentally conditioned Lamarckian set of somatic differences, differences in ways of being and living, differences in psychological and moral essence – differences in human kind. When Douglas Lorimer argues that 'English racism … rested upon established attitudes toward distinctions of class', and that mid-Victorians 'perceived race relations abroad in the light of class relations at home', his own evidence belies a more fluid semantic field.[89] For he also writes that the white London poor were considered 'a race' apart, that servants were also not a 'distinct class but … a separate race'.[90] Those features that confirmed the Irish as a separate race – 'chronic self-indulgence, indolence and laxity of purpose' were invoked to distinguish the urban and rural labouring classes throughout Europe, both mixed-bloods and subaltern whites throughout the colonies. It captured in one sustained image internal threats to the health and well-being of a social body where those deemed a threat lacked an ethics of 'how to live' and thus the ability to govern themselves. When Mayhew wrote that 'hearth and rootedness', those 'sacred symbols to all civilized races' (*London Labour* 1851: 43), were lacking in London's poor, he was not only claiming that the unmanaged mobility of society's subalterns was a threat to colonial and metropolitan authority. He was identifying what was distinctively part of the bourgeoisie's conception of itself: one that embraced property ownership, rootedness, and an orderly family life as attributes that at once distinguished the middle class and explained why they were inherently and socially superior.

While Foucault may be right that the discourse of races was immanent in the language of class, I would still question his limited tracing of its varied meanings. If racial discourse is polyvalent, as he would argue, it also has multiple etymologies. In its varied nineteenth-century forms, it came loaded with a barrage of colonial representations of savagery, licentiousness, and basic truths about human nature that joined early visions of the 'others' of empire with the 'others' within Europe itself.

Nowhere is this colonial imprint clearer than in how bourgeois bodies were evinced to be sexually distinctive and in how their self-cultivation was conceived. Sharon Tiffany and Kathleen Adams argue that the sexual model of the promiscuous working-class woman in nineteenth-century, industrializing England construed her as a 'primitive relic of an earlier evolutionary period', a myth of the 'wild woman' who stood in contrast to 'the moral model of … middle-class sexual restraint and civility'.[91] Sander Gilman similarly shows how the iconography of prostitutes in nineteenth-century France was modelled on the 'lascivious sexuality' and exaggerated genital physiogomy of Hottentot women of South Africa, on depictions that naturalized and *explained* the pathological, unrestrained, atavistic, and diseased bodies of both.[92] In both cases, bourgeois bodies were both race and class-specific, based on distinctions of quality and human kind.

Of course, they were also heavily gendered. If there is any discourse that joins the triumph of rational bourgeois man in colony and metropole, it is that which collapsed non-Europeans and women into an undifferentiated field, one in which passion and not reason reigned.[93] Empire provided the fertile terrain on which bourgeois notions of manliness and virility could be honed and put to patriotic test. Passion was unseemly, but compassion was as well. As Hugh Ridley has argued, it was in the colonies that 'indifference to suffering was a sign of national strength, an essential condition of manhood, proving, as the French colonial novelist Henry Daguerches writes, 'the strength of my blood and the strength of my race'.[94]

But colonial conditions also highlighted conflicting interpretations of manliness and its vulnerabilities. If George Hardy's warning in 1926 that 'a man remains a man as long as he remains under the watchful gaze of a woman of his race' was held to be a truth, then an enormous number of European men would have had little claim to a secure European manhood at all.[95] In the Indies, more than half of the European male population were cohabiting out of wedlock with native women in the late nineteenth century. Among subaltern soldiers, concubinage was the 'necessary evil' that would ward off venereal disease and, more importantly, homosexuality within the lower ranks.[96]

Hardy's warning underscores that good reason and 'character' – that common euphemism for class breeding – were not all that imperial security was about. It required managed passions, self-discipline over unruly drives and the education of sentiment and desire as well. As Tom Holt argues, the liberal democratic presumption that all men shared certain inherent traits and values also assumed that 'the boon of freedom – the right to govern oneself – should be granted only to those who had assimilated certain internal controls. For liberals and conservatives alike, work-discipline was both the source and the test of [it].'[97] In the case of those descendants of Europeans labelled *inlandsche kinderen*, this axiom was precisely what classified them as 'children of the Indies', not Europeans. They allegedly lacked the 'inclination' to skilled work, the 'suitability' for it, the self-discipline, sexual morals, and economic independence that would count them among a citizenry fit to rule. But whether it was their 'class location' or racial attributes that were maligned is difficult to tell, for here was a scrambled social category that made the distinctions between racial and class discriminations blurred and problematic.

To see the struggle of classes as economic and 'the natural fight of races' as biological (as Hannah Arendt and others do) may be not only misleading and ahistorical but anachronistic. For if Foucault's biohistory of the discourses of race and class is correct, that both emerged out of an earlier binary conception of the social body as part of the defence of society against itself, out of a shared vision of a deeper biologized 'internal enemy' within, then racism emerges not as the ideological reaction of those threatened by the universalistic principles of the modern liberal state, but as a foundational fiction within it. This is precisely where recent studies of liberalism and nationalism have taken us. We could look specifically to those who have attempted to explain the racialized 'interior frontiers' that nationalisms create, not as excesses of a nationalism out of hand, but as social divisions crucial to the exclusionary principles of nation-states.

Sexuality, race, and the bourgeois politics of exclusion

Empire figured in the bourgeois politics of liberalism and nationalism in ways we have only begun to explore. Uday Mehta makes the strong case that eighteenth-century liberalism, that quintessential inclusionary philosophy of the European bourgeoisie, had written into it a politics of exclusion based on race. The most basic universalistic notions of 'human nature' and 'individual liberty', elaborated by Locke and Mill, rested on combined notions of breeding and the learning of 'naturalized' habits that set off those who exhibited such a 'nature' and could exercise such liberty from the racially inferior – and in their cases – South Asian colonized world.[98] David Goldberg makes a similar argument, more generally:

> the primary principles of our moral tradition – virtue, sin, autonomy, and equality, utility and rights – are delimited in various ways by the concept of race … liberalism's commitment to principles of universality is practically sustained only by the reinvented and rationalized exclusions of racial particularity.[99]

Edmund Morgan has argued that racism was 'an essential ingredient of a republican ideology' devoted to equality and liberty and that racism in colonial Virginia was crucial to disciplining the poor.[100] Etienne Balibar not only makes the stronger claim, that universalistic principles were used to 'cover and implement racist policies', but reminds us how many historians and philosophers have argued that the very concept of universalism was gendered – as Carole Pateman has shown – and racially inflected.[101]

If liberalism was implicitly exclusionary, most nineteenth-century national-isms were explicitly so by definition. Throughout Europe, the nationalizing of education designated radically different learning strategies and environments for the middle-classes versus the 'undeserving poor'. Dutch liberal proposals for an extension of the franchise specified the exclusion of 'all men who had been on poor relief at any time during the three years prior to elections'.[102] Citizenship in a national polity, as feminist historians have demonstrated, made the rights of women and children solely dependent on their sexual and conjugal contracts with men. Women were seen as crucial to civil society not as participatory citizens in the public sphere, but as those who would ensure that marriage, sexual morality, and family provided the natural foundations for civil life.[103] Many have argued that women's rights were restricted by the argument that motherhood was a 'national service'.[104] It was also a heavily racialized one; as much as a rhetoric of a master race in peril forced middle-class women in Britain to accept limits put on their civil rights, this same rhetoric of racial superiority served British women in India, American women in the Philippines, and Dutch women in the Indies, all of whom sought new ways to clarify their selfhood and assert their independence.[105]

While these discourses around citizenship and national identity were centred on the constituents of European polities, the very principles of national belonging implicated race in many of these distinctions. The charged debate in the late nineteenth century on nationality and citizenship rights for women prompted by the emigration of thousands of women overseas devolved into one about their needed protection against 'white slavery' on the argument that European women would never 'willingly submit to sexual commerce with foreign, racially varied men'.[106] Dutch debates over the citizenship rights of European women in mixed marriages in the Indies were less concerned with the civil status of women than with another consequence: the conferral of Dutch citizenship on their native husbands and mixed-blood sons. It was the clarity of racial membership, among other things, that jurists and policy-makers had in mind.

In this age of empire, the question of who would be a 'subject' and who a 'citizen' converged on the sexual politics of race. Whether a child was born out of prostitution, concubinage, cohabitation, or marriage and whether that child was acknowledged by a European father partially sealed his or her fate. It is not coincidental that the same colonial lawyers who wrote the Indies mixed-marriage laws were those with a strong voice in the changing Dutch nationality laws of the same period. French and Dutch authorities strongly debated whether *métis* and *Indos* displayed inherent dispositions that were more native than European and whether education could deeply transform them.

Concern for such ambiguously positioned interstitial groups in the national body preoccupied colonial authorities, but also resonated from colony to core. In a study of French antisemitism, Stephen Wilson argues that late nineteenth-century nationalist (and antisemitic) rhetoric in France was 'modelled' on the violent cultural racism against Jews who straddled the colonial divide in French Algeria decades earlier.[107] The naturalization of Algerian Jews under the Crémieux decree of 1870 that preceded the Dreyfus affair heightened anxieties in the metropole that Jews were an internal enemy, morally, and sexually distinct from those who were of 'pure French blood'.[108] This is not to argue that European antisemitism derived from colonial tensions across the board, but rather that the dangers of cultural and racial hybridity were deeply embedded in popular and scientific discourses whose cast of characters could include subversive Indo-Europeans at one moment and perverse Jews at another.

Discourses of sexuality, racial thinking, and rhetorics of nationalism have several things in common. All hinge on visual markers of distinction that profess to – but only poorly – index the internal traits, psychological dispositions, and moral essence on which these theories of difference and social membership are based. The strength and weakness of such social taxonomies are that they are malleable, their criteria opaque and ill-defined.[109] Balibar touches on those anxieties when he notes 'that the "false" are too visible, will never guarantee that the true are visible enough'.[110] The German philosopher Fichte saw eighteenth-century German society as based on 'invisible ties', a moral attitude, and 'interior frontiers' that bounded both the nation and the constitution of individual subjects within it.[111] In the nineteenth century, nationalist discourses about who was *echte* Dutch or 'truly French' were replete with such ambiguous evaluations of breeding, cultivation, and moral essence. In the Dutch East Indies, it was no longer *jus soli* (right of birth) and *jus sanguinis* (right of descent) that could provide the criteria of nationality, but rather what the colonial lawyer Nederburgh defined in 1898, echoing Fichte, as shared 'morals, culture, and perceptions, feelings that unite us without one being able to say what they are'.[112]

This quest to define moral predicates and invisible essences tied the bourgeois discourses of sexuality, racism, and certain kinds of nationalism in fundamental ways. Each hinged on the state's moral authority to defend the social body against degeneration and abnormality. As George Mosse has argued for nineteenth-century Germany, nationalism was animated by notions of bourgeois respectability and a 'moral terror' that rigidly defined what was deviant sex and what was not.[113] Nationalist discourse staked out those sexual practices that were nation-building and race-affirming, marking 'unproductive eroticism, as Doris Sommer has so well shown, 'not only [as] immoral, [but as] unpatriotic'.[114]

In such a frame, the discourse of middle-class respectability was double-billed, playing several roles. Bourgeois women in colony and metropole were cast as the custodians of morality, of their vulnerable men, and of the national character. Parenting, and motherhood specifically, were a class obligation and a duty of empire.[115] In short, the cultivation of bourgeois sensibilities was inextricable from the nationalist and racial underpinnings of them. Whether Foucault assumed these links or underestimated their importance is unclear. In volume 1, he simply referred to the 'Hitlerite politics of sex' as an 'insignificant practice' (p. 150). But Nazism's politics of sex and reproduction were not insignificant by any stretch of the imagination. Feminist historians have shown how significant cults of manliness, motherhood, homoeroticism, and misogyny were to the racial politics of Nazi rule.[116] In Foucault's lectures, where one might expect such connections to be elaborated, they are not. It is normalization that drives racism. The proliferation of sexualities and racisms that Nazi nationalism underwrote is not part of that account.

Feminist critics have long criticized Foucault's concern with sexuality and not gender, his lack of attention to differential access to power eclipsed by a focus on diffused power relations throughout the social body at large.[117] But the problem may be broader still. By not engaging the significance of the nineteenth-century discourses of nation and empire and the gender-specific nature of them, the cultivation of the bourgeois self and its sexual deployments remain rooted in Europe and *inside* the bourgeois nation, rather than constitutive of it. Foucault may have alluded to the metonymic quality of the bourgeois body for the nation, but left us to show that its cultivation and unique sexuality were nourished by a wider colonial world of Manichean distinctions: by Irish, 'Mediterranean', Jewish, and non-European Others who provided the referential contrasts for it.

By marginalizing the link between nationalism and desire in both his genealogy of racism and his history of sexuality, Foucault eclipses a key discursive site where subjugated bodies were made and subjects formed. The technologies of sexuality that concerned Foucault were productive of power in specific ways that targeted disciplined sentiment as much as normalized sexuality in the governing of oneself. The knot that bound subversion to perversion could only be undone if people themselves believed in the sexual codes of the moralizing state, if personal affect and sentiments could be harnessed to national projects and priorities for racial regeneration.[118] Doing so was no easy task. It first required identifying where disaffections were produced, where children's 'instincts' were schooled, how early, and by whom. It required distinguishing those contaminations of the social environment from those reproduced in the intimate confines of bourgeois homes.

Notes

From Ann Laura Stoler, *Race and the Education of Desire: Foucault's 'History of Sexuality' and the Colonial Order of Things* (Duke University Press, Durham NC and London 1995).

1   Lisa Lowe, *Critical Terrains: French and British Orientalisms* (Ithaca NY: Cornell University Press, 1991) 54.
2   *Ibid.*; Benedict Anderson, *Imagined Communities: Reflections on the Origin and Spread of Nationalism* (London: Verso, 1987); Mary Louise Pratt, *Imperial Eyes: Travel Writing and Transculturation* (London: Routledge 1992).
3   For one of the earlier and still definitive statements on this connection see Eric Stokes, *The English Utilitarians and India* (Oxford: Clarendon Press,1959) and, of course James Mill himself, *The History of British India*, sixth edition, 6 vols. (London: James Madden, 1858). For one specific effort to draw these linkages for the late nineteenth century, see David Johnson, 'Aspects of a Liberal Education: Late Nineteenth-Century Attitudes to Race, from Cambridge to the Cape Colony', *History Workshop Journal* 36 (1993): 162–82. Also see Javed Maheed, *Ungoverned Imaginings: James Mill's The History of British India and Orientalism* (Oxford: Clarendon Press, 1992), who argues that the colonies were more than a 'testing ground' for bourgeois liberal philosophy but the means through which European society 'fashioned a critique of itself' (128). Also see Linda Colley ('Britishness and Otherness: an Argument', *Journal of British Studies* 331, October 1992: 309–29) who argues that for nineteenth-century Britons 'empire did serve as a powerful distraction and cause in common' (325).
4   On the problematic bracketing of national from imperial history in Britain and a well-argued plea for a rethinking of it, see Shula Marks, 'History, the Nation and Empire: Sniping from the Periphery', *History Workshop Journal* 29 (1990): 111–19.
5   Louis Malleret, *L'Exotisme indochinois dans la littérature française* (Paris: Larose, 1936) 51.
6   The quote in full reads: 'what remains useful in Foucault is the mechanics of disciplinarization and institutionalization, the constitution, as it were, of the colonizer. Foucault does not relate it to any version, early or late, proto- or post-, of imperialism. They are of great usefulness to intellectuals concerned with the decay of the West. Their seduction for them, and fearfulness for us, is that they might allow the complicity of the investigating subject (male or female professional) to disguise itself in transparency' (*Marxism and the Interpretation of Culture* 294).
7   See my 'Rethinking Colonial Categories: European Communities and the Boundaries of Rule', *Comparative Studies in Society and History* 31:1 (January 1989): 134–61.
8   On the variable meanings of 'whiteness' see, for example, my *Carnal Knowledge and Imperial Power* (Berkeley CA: University of California Press, forthcoming); Catherine Hall's 'Gender and Ethnicity in the 1830s and 1840s', in *White, Male and Middle-Class: Explorations in Feminism and History* (London: Polity Press, 1992) 205–53.
9   For recent work on the gendered tensions of colonial projects, in addition to works already cited, see: Nupur Chaudhuri and Margaret Strobel, eds, *Western Women and Imperialism: Complicity and Resistance* (Bloomington IN: Indiana University Press, 1992); Claudia Knapman, *White Women in Fiji, 1835–1930: The Ruin of Empire?* (Boston MA: Allen & Unwin, 1986); Patricia Grimshaw, *Paths of Duty: American Missionary Wives in Nineteenth-Century Hawaii* (Honolulu: University of Hawaii Press, 1989); Nancy Paxton, 'Mobilizing Chivalry: Rape in British Novels about the Indian Uprising of 1857', *Victorian Studies* (fall 1992): 5–13; Frances Gouda, 'The Gendered Rhetoric of Colonialism and Anti-colonialism in Twentieth Century Indonesia', *Indonesia* 55 (April 1993): 1–22. For a critique of some of this literature see Margaret Jolly, 'Colonizing Women: The Maternal Body and Empire', *Feminism and the Politics of Difference*, ed. Sneja Gunew and Anna Yeatman (Boulder CO: Westview Press, 1993).
10 On the substitution of a discourse of cultural competence for an explicitly racial discourse see my 'Sexual Affronts and Racial Frontiers…', *Comparative Studies in Society and History* 34, 3 (July 1992): 514–51.

11 On the processes of imperialism consolidating within that 'sanitized' realm of Europe's 'unchanging intellectual monuments' in education, literature, and the visual and musical arts, see Edward Said, *Culture and Imperialism* (New York: Knopf, 1993). Fredric Jameson argues that imperialism did more than leave 'palpable traces on the *content* of metropolitan literary works' but on how modernism resolved the fact that there was always necessarily 'something missing' and outside metropolitan experience in an imperial world. ('Modernism and Imperialism', *Nationalism, Colonialism and Literature*, Minneapolis MN: University of Minnesota Press, 1990: 44, 51).

12 See Sharon Tiffany and Kathleen Adams, *Wild Woman: Inquiry into the Anthropology of an Idea* (Cambridge MA: Schenkman, 1985).

13 At least one plausible accounting for this perspective is that it was extrapolated, as Victor Kiernan does, from 'the run of officials' who populated the British civil service in India. Thus Kiernan writes: '[they] belong to the type of the *gentleman* who was evolving in Victorian England. An amalgam of the less flighty qualities of the nobility with the more stodgy of middle-class virtues, he had a special relevance to the empire, and indeed was partly called into existence by its requirements, made to measure for it by England's extraordinary public-school education.' (*The Lords of Human Kind*, London: Weidenfeld & Nicolson, 1969, 37.) But even in India, this knighted bourgeoisie was not in the majority. David Arnold calculated that 'nearly half the European population [living in India by the end of the nineteenth century] could be called poor whites' (104). 'European Orphans and Vagrants in India in the Nineteenth Century', *Journal of Imperial and Commonwealth History* 7:2 (January 1979): 104–27. Also see Hugh Ridley's detailed and subtle analysis of the myth of an 'aristocratic democracy' of whites in German, French, and British colonies in *Images of Imperial Rule* (London: St Martin's Press, 1983), especially 124–45.

14 See John Comaroff, 'Images of Empire, Contests of Conscience: Models of Colonial Domination in South Africa', *American Ethnologist* 16:4 (1989): 661–85, that demonstrates the colonial effects of a Nonconformist missionary movement in Africa whose members 'were caught uneasily between a displaced peasantry, an expanding proletariat and the lower reaches of the rising British bourgeoisie' (663). Also see T. O. Beidelman, *Colonial Evangelism* (Bloomington IN: Indiana University Press 1982).

15 Homi Bhabha's provocative analysis of a difference that is 'almost the same but not quite' ('Of Mimicry and Man: The Ambivalence of Colonial Discourse', in *The Location of Culture*, London: Routledge, 1994, has spawned a profusion of studies that examine the inherent ambivalence of specific colonial institutions that at once incorporated and distinguished colonized populations without collapsing the critical difference between ruler and ruled. My point is that this sort of colonial ambivalence was also a national one, directed at a much broader population whose class differences literally coloured their perceived and proper racial membership as designated by colonial authorities.

16 Eric Hobsbawm, *The Age of Capital: 1845–1878* (New York: Scribner, 1975) 244.

17 See Michael Taussig's 'Culture of Terror – Space of Death', *Comparative Studies in Society and History* 26 (1984): 467–97, and my 'In Cold Blood: Hierarchies of Credibility and the Politics of Colonial Narratives', *Representations* 37 (winter 1992): 151–89 that both broach the 'epistemic murk', the incomplete sorts of knowledge, and the terror of rumor through which many colonial officials operated.

18 Divers quoted in Hugh Ridley, *Images of Imperial Rule* (London: St Martin's Press, 1983) 129.

19 George Woodcock, *The British in the Far East* (New York: Atheneum, 1969) 163; Robert Hughes, *The Fatal Shore* (New York: Knopf, 1987) 323.

20 Benedict Anderson, *Imagined Communities* (London: Verso, 1983).

21 W. L. Ritter, *De Europeanen in Nederlandsche Indie* (Leyden: Sythoff, 1856) 6.

22 These categories were further complicated by the fact that the Indies was never wholly a Dutch-populated colony and certainly not from its beginning when many of its European inhabitants spoke no Dutch, were unfamiliar with Dutch cultural conventions, and were not Dutch by birth. In the seventeenth century, Portuguese served as the lingua franca 'on the streets, in the markets, in church and in the households where European men kept Asian

mistresses'. Jean Taylor, *The Social World of Batavia* (Madison WI: University of Wisconsin Press, 1983) 18–19. In the nineteenth and twentieth centuries, the colonial enclave was an international community made up of temporary and permanent expatriates who used Malay more easily than Dutch and many of whom had never been to Holland.

23 J. Kohlbrugge. 'Het Indische kind en zijne karaktervorming', *Blikken in het zielenleven van den Javaan en zijner overheerschers* (Leiden: Brill, 1907).

24 Ritter, *De Europeanen* 30.

25 See Charles van Onselen, 'Race and Class in the South African Countryside: Cultural Osmosis and Social Relations in the Sharecropping Economy of the South-Western Transvaal, 1900–1950', *American Historical Review* 95 (1990): 99–123, who argues for a more complex view of South African racial history that challenges prevailing assumptions about the homogeneity of race relations by attending to the divergent alliances and interests of a broader class spectrum of subaltern whites.

26 A. Van Marle, 'De group der Europeanen in Nederlands-Indie', *Indonesia* 5:2 (1952): 77–121; 5:3 (1952): 314–41; 5:5 (1952): 481–507.

27 Algemeen Rijksarchief, Verbaal 9 July 1860. Governor General's summary report to the Minister of Colonies concerning the establishment of a technical/craft school in Surabaya; J. H. F. van de Wall, 'Het Indoisme', *De Reflector* 39 (1916): 953.

28 This point is detailed in ch. 5 of *Carnal Knowledge and Imperial Power* (Berkeley: University of California Press, forthcoming).

29 On the fact that a 'European upbringing' was considered 'necessary to cultivate love for the fatherland and to strengthen the ties binding the colony to the motherland' see Algemeen Rijksarchief, Kol. 1848 geheim, No. 493 and the additional reports cited therein where this discourse on subversion, national security and upbringing is explicitly expressed.

30 See Fasseur, who, while not taking note of this paradox, does provide evidence of the rationales for barring *inlandse kinderen* and the simultaneous emphasis placed on native language acquisition in the Indies colonial civil service (*De Indologen* 112–29).

31 Hans Rigart, 'Moraliseringoffensief in Nederland in de periode 1850–1880', *Vijf Eeuwen van Gezinsleven*, ed. H. Peeters *et al.* (Nijmegen: SUN, 1986) 194–208.

32 Stuurman (1993) 360.

33 Ali de Regt, *Arbeidersgezinnen en beschavingsarbeid* [Working-class families and the civilizing mission] (Boom: Amsterdam, 1984) 151.

34 On the living conditions of village-based Europeans as compared to the housing of the poor in Amsterdam see H. C. H. Gunning, 'Het Woningvraagstuk', *Koloniale Studien* 2 (1918): 109–26.

35 Nancy Armstrong, *Desire and Domestic Fiction: A Political History of the Novel* (London: Oxford University Press, 1987) 15.

36 Anderson, *Imagined Communities* 137.

37 This is not to suggest that biomedicine, and germ theory in particular, were merely colonial ideologies, but rather to understand how the technologies of colonial rule and the construction of certain kinds of scientific knowledge were, as Jean and John Comaroff convincingly argue, 'cut from the same cultural cloth'. 'Medicine, Colonialism and the Black Body', *Ethnography and the Historical Imagination* (Boulder CO: Westview Press, 1992) 216. Also see Paul Rabinow's perceptive discussion of the central roles that the 'concept of milieu in biology and *conditions de vie* or *modes de vie* in geography' played at this time. *French Modern* (Cambridge MA: MIT Press, 1989) 126–67.

38 C. T. Bertling, 'De zorg voor het adatlooze kind', *Koloniale Studien* 15 (1931): 790–844.

39 See my 'Sexual Affronts and Racial Frontiers: European Identities and the Cultural Politics of Exclusion in Colonial Southeast Asia', *Comparative Studies in Society and History* 34:2 (1992): 514–51, and 'A Sentimental Education …' in *Fantasizing the Feminine*, ed. L. Sears, Durham NC: Duke University Press, 1995.

40 On the emergent bourgeoisie's efforts to 'impose order on the chaos that surrounded them' in the United States see Carroll Smith-Rosenberg, *Disorderly Conduct: Visions of Gender in Victorian America* (New York: Oxford, 1985), especially 86–87. Also see Dorinda Outram's

discussion of Alan Cobban and François Furet's similar chancterizations of the French revolutionary period and its aftermath as a 'competition for legitimacy among various sections of the French middle class through the appropriation of a validating political discourse and its embodiment' in *The Body and the French Revolution: Sex, Class and Political Culture* (New Haven CT: Yale University Press, 1989) 29.

41 See my 'Carnal Knowledge and Imperial Power' (1991) for a discussion of the different timings of this shift in British Malaya and the Dutch East Indies.

42 Algemeen Rijksarchief, Considerations and advice of the directors of the naval establishment and factory in Soerabaja, 24 November 1858.

43 Algemeen Rijksarchief, KV 18 March 1874, 47. Also see *Het Pauperisme onder de Europeanen in Nederlandsch-Indie. Deerde Gedeelte. Kleine Landbouw* (Batavia: Landsdrukkerij, 1901).

44 On a similar note Hugh Ridley makes the point that a racial difference in British India was predicated on the notion that 'sentiment' was 'a European experience' while 'sheer passion' was Indian (*Images of Imperial Rule*, New York: St Martin's Press, 1983, 74).

45 Algemeen Rijksarchief, Verbaal 9 July 1860, 13, 24 November 1958.

46 Van de Waal, 'Het Indoisme', 953.

47 Taco Henny, *Verslag van het Verhandelde in de Bijeenkomsten der Nederlandsch-Indische Juristen-Vereeniging* (Batavia, 1887) 39.

48 In a process similar to that described by Ian Hacking in 'The Looping Effects of Human Kinds', Fyssen Foundation Conference, Paris, 7–11 January 1993.

49 W. F. Prins, 'De Bevolkingsgroepen in het Nederlandsch-Indische Recht', *Koloniale Studien* 17 (1933): 677.

50 Van de Waal, 'Het Indoisme', 953.

51 For a succinct review of the debate on the hegemony *v.* the 'failure' of the British middle class to 'stamp its authority on the whole social order' see Janet Wolff and John Seed, eds, *The Culture of Capital: Art, Power, and the Nineteenth Century Middle Class* (New York: St Martin's Press, 1988), especially 1–44. My argument is not contingent upon proving the existence of bourgeois hegemony in the nineteenth century but, if anything, on its opposite – on its precarious ascendancy and its deployment of a biopolitical technology of power in which racial discourse played a pivotal role.

52 Simon Schama, *Patriots and Liberators: Revolution in the Netherlands, 1780–1813* (New York: Vintage, 1977).

53 Siep Stuurman, *Wacht op onze daden: Het liberalisme en de vernieuwing van de Nederlandse Staat* (Amsterdam: Bert Bakker, 1992) 14. Dictionary definitions of the term *burgerij* differ markedly. In some its first meaning is 'commoners', in others 'citizenry', and in others the 'middle class'. On the different uses of the term *burgerlijk* and its similarities and differences with the term 'bourgeois' in Dutch historiography and national politics see Henk te Velde's 'How High Did the Dutch Fly? Remarks on Stereotypes of Burger Mentality', in *Images of the Nation: Different Meanings of Dutchness, 1870–1940*, ed. A. Galema, B. Henkes, and H. te Velde (Amsterdam: Rodopi, 1993) 59–80.

54 Stuurman, *Wacht op onze daden* 14.

55 In addition to those cited above see Jart Lenders, *De Burgers en de Volksschool: Culturele en mentale achtergronden van een onderwijshervorming. Nederland 1780–1850* (The Hague: SUN, 1988) 31. On the political struggles leading up to the establishment of the Dutch monarchy and the restoration of the House of Orange in 1813 see Simon Schama's magisterial account in *Patriots and Liberators: Revolution in the Netherlands 1780–1813* (New York: Random House, 1977). On the importance of the year 1813 to the subsequent development of a specifically Dutch form of liberalism see C. H. E. de Wit, *De strijd tussen Aristocratie and Democratie in Nederland, 1780–1848* (Heerlen: Winants, 1965).

56 Stuurman, *Wacht op onze daden* 14.

57 Ali de Regt, *Arbeidersgezinnen*, 246–7. Others have interpreted the '*burgerlijk* civilizing offensive' as the direct expression of a 'deep angst' about paupers, a disciplining gesture in which the valorization of 'virtue' (*deugdzame*) would denote the forces of popular discontent. See Hans Righart, 'Moraliseringsoffensief in Nederland in de periode 1850–1880',

Vijf Eeuwen gezinsleven, ed. H. Peeters *et al.* (Nijmegen: SUN, 1986) 205, and Bernard Kruithof, 'De deugdzame natie: het burgerlijk beschavingsoffensief van de Maatschappij tot Nut van 't Algemeen tussen 1784 en 1860', *Symposion* II:I (1980): 22–37.

58 Ritter, *De Europeanen* 17.

59 See Lenders, *De Burger en de Volksschool* 21, 52.

60 *Ibid.*, 63.

61 Cf. Selma Sevenhuijsen's nuanced discussion of the contradictions around the discourse on paternal responsibility and women's rights in the Netherlands (*De orde van het vaderschap*, Amsterdam: Stichting Beheer IISG, 1987).

62 For an effort to explore the contingency between colonial racism and its metropolitan variant in a later period, see Willem Wenheim's 'Netherlands Indies Colonial Racism and Dutch Home Racism' in Jan Breman, ed., *Imperial Monkey Business: Racial Supremacy in Social Darwinist Theory and Colonial Practice* (Amsterdam: Vrige Universiteit Press, 1990) 71–88.

63 Ali de Regt, 'Arbeiders, burgers and boeren: gezinsleven in de negentiende eeuw', *Familie, Huwelijk en Gezin in West-Europa*, ed. Ton Swaan (Boom: Open Universiteit, 1993) 193–218. Also see Frances Gouda's well documented comparative study of the nineteenth-century discourses on poverty, pauperism, and state-sponsored welfare in the Netherlands and France (*Poverty and Political Culture*, Lanham MD: Rowman & Littlefield, 1995).

64 C. Fasseur, 'Connerstone and Stumbling Block: Racial Classification and the Late Colonial State in Indonesia', in *The Late Colonial State in Indonesia: Political and Economic Foundations of the Netherlands Indies, 1880–1942*, ed. Robert Cribb (Leiden: KITLV, 1994) 31–56.

65 Stuurman, *Wacht op onze daden* 134.

66 Quoted in *ibid.*, 120.

67 See Izaak Johannes Brugmans, *Gescheidenis van het Onderwijs in Nederlandsch-Indie* (Groningen: J. B. Wolters, 1938), who notes that in 1875 many of the children attending an *armenschool* in Soerbaja ('even of parents who were pure European') came to school in a 'neglected state, shabbily clothed, timid, speaking and understanding nothing but Malay even at the age of eleven or twelve' (269). Note that the term 'mixed' is virtually always racially inflected but discursively labelled in national terms. I have rarely seen it used to refer, for example, to children of 'mixed' French and Dutch origin. It is most commonly used only for children of 'mixed' *racial* descent, African fathers and Asian mothers, European and Chinese, etc.

68 See Gouda, *Poverty and Political Culture*, 115–16.

69 See Ann Tylor Allen, 'Gardens of Children, Gardens of God: Kindergartens and Daycare Centers in Nineteenth Century Germany', *Journal of Social History* 19 (1986): 433–50, and Michael Shapiro, *Child's Garden: The Kindergarten Movement from Froebel to Dewey* (University Park: Pennsylvania State University Press, 1983). In the Indies, the first nursery school, set up in Batavia in 1850, was designed to keep children from the ages of two to seven 'out of the harmful environment of native servants' (Brugmans, *Gescheidenis* 276). See my 'A Sentimental Education: European Children and Native Servants in the Netherlands Indies', in *Fantasizing the Feminine in Indonesia*, ed. Laurie J. Sears (Durham NC: Duke University Press, 1996), where I discuss the Dutch colonial administration's interest in European nurseries at much more length.

70 Algemeen Onderwijs Verslag 1846–49, 55, quoted in Brugmans, *Gescheidenis* 87.

71 Stuurman, *Wacht op onze daden* 23, 25. I have in mind a growing field of interdisciplinary scholarship that includes the recent work of Catherine Hall (in her collected essays entitled *White, Male and Middle-Class*). See the contributions of Lora Wildenthal and Susan Thorne in Frederick Cooper and Ann Laura Stoler, eds, *Tensions of Empire: Colonial Cultures in a Bourgeois World*, forthcoming. A new generation of dissertations on these subjects includes Laura Bear on Anglo-Indians, railways and modernity, Elizabeth Beuttner on British children and colonial South Asia, John Stiles on culture and citizenship in France and Martinique, and Laurent Dubois on questions of race and citizenship in the Antilles during the French revolution. See Chris Schmidt-Nowara, 'Hispano-Antillean Antislavery: Race, Labor and Nation in Spain, Cuba, and Puerto Rico, 1833–1886', dissertation, University of

Michigan, 1995. All the above are, or have been, doctoral students in history and/or anthropology at the University of Michigan.

72 Tom Holt, *The Problem of Freedom* (Baltimore MD: Johns Hopkins University Press, 1992) 308.

73 See Haydn White's analysis of the entanglements of class and racial categories in 'The Noble Savage Theme as Fetish', in *The Tropics of Discourse: Essays in Cultural Criticism* (Baltimore MD: Johns Hopkins University Press, 1978) 183–96. Drawing on Louis Chevalier's *Laboring Classes and Dangerous Classes in Paris during the First Half of the Nineteenth Century*, he, like Foucault, finds the nineteenth-century language of class rooted in an earlier discourse of race and also in the *bourgeoisie*'s efforts to undermine 'the nobility's claim to a special human status' (194).

74 White, 'The Noble Savage' 193.

75 Eugen Weber, *Peasants into Frenchmen* (Stanford CA: Stanford University Press, 1976) 3, 6, 7.

76 See William Sewell, *A Rhetoric of Bourgeois Revolution: The Abbé Sieyes and 'What is the Third Estate'?* (Durham NC: Duke University Press, 1994).

77 Edmund Morgan, *American Slavery, American Freedom* (New York: Norton, 1975) 325–6.

78 Richard Lebow, *White Britain and Black Ireland* (Philadelphia: Institute for the Study of Human Issues, 1976) 41.

79 See Lebow, *White Britain*, and Lynn Hollen Lees, *Exiles of Erin: Irish Migrants in Victorian London* (Ithaca NY: Cornell University Press, 1979) 15.

80 Quoted in Lebow, *White Britain* 40.

81 Kiernan, *The Lords of Human Kind* 316.

82 Jean and John Comaroff, 'Home-made Hegemony: Modernity, Domesticity, and Colonialism in South Africa', in *African Encounters with Domesticity*, ed. Karen Hansen (New Brunswick NJ: Rutgers University Press, 1992) 37–74.

83 Susan Thorne, 'The Conversion of England and the Conversion of the World Inseparable: Missionary Imperialism and the Language of Class, 1750–1850', in *Tensions of Empire: Colonial Cultures in a Bourgeois World*, ed. Frederick Cooper and Ann Laura Stoler, forthcoming.

84 See Hall, *White, Male and Middle-Class*, especially ch. 9, 205–53.

85 Hobsbawm, *Age of Capital* 247–8.

86 Elaine Showalter, *Sexual Anarchy: Gender and Culture at the Fin-de-Siècle* (London: Penguin, 1990) 5.

87 On the changing meanings of 'class' see Raymond Williams, *Keywords* (London: Croom Helm, 1976) 51–8.

88 On the 'interchangeability' of class and racial discrimination see Hugh Ridley, *Images of Imperial Rule* (London: St Martin's Press, 1983) 140.

89 Douglas Lorimer, *Colour, Class and the Victorians* (Leicester: Leicester University Press, 1978) 93.

90 *Ibid.* 105.

91 Tiffany and Adams, *The Wild Women* 12–17.

92 Sander Gilman, 'Black Bodies, White Bodies', in *Race, Writing and Difference*, ed. Henry L. Gates, Jr (Chicago: University of Chicago Press, 1986). For a discussion of empire as one of the domains in which European middle-class 'conflicts of reason and emotion, of desire and duty, and of competition and harmony could be resolved' see Joanna de Groot's '"Sex" and "Race": the Construction of Language and Image in the Nineteenth Century', in *Sexuality and Subordination*, ed. Susan Mendus and Jane Rendall (London: Routledge, 1989) 108.

93 See Jean and John Comaroff's identification of this shackling of women and non-Europeans to their sexual natures in *Of Revelation and Revolution* (Chicago: University of Chicago Press, 1991), especially 105–8. For an excellent more general discussion see Nancy Leys Stepan's 'Race and Gender: The Role of Analogy in Science', in *The Anatomy of Racism*, ed. David Goldberg (Minneapolis MN: University of Minnesota Press, 1990).

94 Ridley, *Images of Imperial Rule* 142.

95 George Hardy, quoted in C. Chivas-Baron, *La Femme française aux colonies* (Paris: Larose, 1929) 103.

96 See Hanneke Ming, 'Barracks-Concubinage in the Indies, 1887–1920', *Indonesia* 35 (1983): 65–93. The absent presence of the dangers of homosexuality in these debates is striking. What is more, in the Dutch archives, the threat of homosexual desire among stolid Dutch agents of empire, of the colonial *middenstand*, is rarely if ever mentioned. When homosexuality is broached, it is always in the form of a *deflected* discourse, one about sodomizing Chinese plantation coolies, about degenerate subaltern European soldiers, never about respectable Dutch men. My silence on this issue and the prominent place I give to heterosexuality reflects my long term and failed efforts to identify any sources that do more than assume or obliquely allude to this 'evil', thereby making the other 'lesser' evils of concubinage and prostitution acceptable. Hyam seems to have come up with many more accusations if not explicit accounts. As such, my colonial treatment of Foucault's fourth 'strategic unity', constituting the 'perverse adult', is only minimally explored. Ronald Hyam, *Empire and Sexuality: The British Experience* (Manchester: Manchester University Press, 1990).

97 Holt, *Problem of Freedom* 308.

98 Uday Mehta, 'Liberal Strategies of Exclusion', *Politics and Society* 184 (1990): 427–54.

99 David Goldberg, *Racist Culture: Philosophy and the Politics of Meaning* (Oxford: Blackwell, 1995) 39.

100 Morgan, *American Slavery, American Freedom* 386.

101 Etienne Balibar, *Masses, Classes, Ideas* (London: Routledge, 1994) 195; Carol Pateman, *The Sexual Contract* (Stanford CA: Stanford University Press, 1988).

102 Siep Stuurman, 'John Bright and Samuel van Houten: Radical Liberalism and the Working Classes in Britain and the Netherlands, 1860–1880', *History of European Ideas* II (1989): 595.

103 Pateman, *The Sexual Contract* 177.

104 See the articles in Seth Koven and Sonya Michel, eds., *Mothers of a New World: Maternalist Politics and the Origins of Welfare States* (London: Routledge, 1993) and in Gisela Bock and Pat Thane, eds, *Maternity and Gender Policies: Women and the Rise of the European Welfare States 1880s–1950s* (London: Routledge, 1991). Two important pieces not included in the above are Susan Pedersen, 'Gender, Welfare, and Citizenship in Britain during the Great War', *American Historical Review* 95:4 (1990): 983–1006, and Nancy Fraser and Linda Gordon's 'Key Words of the Welfare State', *Signs* 19 (1994): 309–36.

105 See Rosemary George, 'Homes in the Empire, Empires in the Home', *Cultural Critique* (winter 1993–94): 95–127, and Vincente Rafael's careful attention to the 'phantasmagoria of domesticity' for American women in the Philippines and at 'home' ('Colonial Domesticity: White Women and United States Rule in the Philippines', unpublished manuscript). For the Indies see Gouda, 'The Gendered Rhetoric'. For a telling tale of the ways in which women in England deployed campaigns for indigenous women's rights to their own ends see Susan Pederson 'National Bodies, Unspeakable Acts: The Sexual Politics of Colonial Policymaking', *Journal of Modern History* 95:4 (1990): 983–1006.

106 This issue of white slavery comes up in a wide range of colonial contexts. See Donna J. Guy, '"White Slavery", Citizenship and Nationality in Argentina', *Nationalisms and Sexualities*, ed. Andrew Parker, Mary Russo, Doris Sommer and Patricia Yaeger (New York: Routledge) 203, and Cecile Swaisland, *Servants and Gentlewomen to the Golden Land: The Emigration of Single Women from Britain to Southern Africa, 1820–1939* (Oxford: University of Natal Press, 1993), especially 24–5. An earlier racial inflection on the need for national and cross-national regulation of prostitution focused on the fact that in the late nineteenth century the alleged traffic in women was organized by New York and Johannesburg-based Jewish men. See van Onselen, 'Prostitutes and Proletarians, 1886–1914', in *Studies in the Social and Economic History of the Witwatersrand*, I: *New Babylon* (New York: Longman, 1982) 109–11, 137, 138.

107 Stephen Wilson, *Ideology and Experience: Antisemitism in France at the Time of the Dreyfus Affair* (London: Associated University Presses, 1982); see especially ch. 9 and 12.

108 Elizabeth Friedman, *Colonialism and After: An Algerian Jewish Community* (South Hadley MA.: Bergin & Garvey, 1988) 25.

109 As Michael Banton notes for the case of nineteenth-century racial typologies: 'the notion of type was a convenient one because it was not tied to any particular classificatory *level* in zoology, so that it was easy to refer to the physical types characteristic of particular nations, to "types of cranial conformation", or to say that a skull "approximates to the Negro type" without having to establish just what that type was' (*The Idea of Race* 31).

110 Etienne Balibar, 'The Paradoxes of Universality', in *Anatomy of Racism*, ed. David Goldberg (Minneapolis MN: University of Minnesota Press, 1990) 285.

111 Quoted in Etienne Balibar, 'Fichte and the Internal Border: On *Addresses to the German Nation*', in *Masses, Classes, Ideas* 61–87.

112 J. A. Nederburgh, *Wet en Adat* (Batavia: Kloff, 1898) 87–8.

113 George Mosse, *Nationalism and Sexuality* (Madison WI: University of Wisconsin Press, 1985).

114 Doris Sommer, 'Irresistible Romance: the Foundational Fictions of Latin America', in *Nation and Narration*, ed. Homi Bhabha (London: Routledge, 1990) 87.

115 Anna Davin, 'Motherhood and Imperialism', *History Workshop* 5 (1978): 9–57.

116 Mosse, *Nationalism and Sexuality*; Klaus Theleweit, *Male Fantasies* (Minneapolis MN: University of Minnesota Press, 1989); Claudia Koontz, *Mothers in the Fatherland* (New York: St Martin's Press, 1987).

117 See, for example, Biddy Martin, 'Feminism, Criticism and Foucault', *New German Critique* 27 (fall 1987): 3–30; Judith Newton, 'History as Usual: Feminism and the New Historicism', *Cultural Critique* (spring 1988): 87–121. Other efforts to explore the productive tension between Foucault and feminism include Caroline Ramazanoglu, ed., *Up against Foucault* (London: Routledge, 1993) and a less inspired effort, Jana Sawicki, *Disciplining Foucault: Feminism, Power and the Body* (London: Routledge, 1991), and Lois McNay, *Foucault Feminism* (Boston MA: Northeast University Press, 192). None of the above deals directly with Foucault's historical arguments or engages his formulation of those 'four strategic unities' in which women are absent but figure so strongly.

118 Two dazzling works on this subject include Lauren Berlant's discussion of the 'harnessing of affect to political life through the production of a national fantasy' in *The Anatomy of a National Fantasy: Hawthorne, Utopia and Everyday Life* (Chicago IL: University of Chicago Press, 1991) 5, and Doris Sommer's masterly analysis of how bourgeois goals of nationhood co-ordinated 'sense and sensibility, productivity and passion' in Latin American novels in *Foundational Fictions: The National Romances of Latin America* (Berkeley CA: University of California Press, 1991) 14. Also see my 'A Sentimental Education' in *Fantasizing the Feminine*, 1996.

5

Subaltern Studies
as postcolonial criticism

GYAN PRAKASH

To note the ferment created by Subaltern Studies in disciplines as diverse as history, anthropology, and literature is to recognize the force of recent postcolonial criticism. This criticism has compelled a radical rethinking of knowledge and social identities authored and authorized by colonialism and Western domination. Of course, colonialism and its legacies have faced challenges before. One has only to think of nationalist rebellions against imperialist domination and Marxism's unrelenting critiques of capitalism and colonialism. But neither nationalism nor Marxism broke free from Eurocentric discourses.[1] As nationalism reversed Orientalist thought, and attributed agency and history to the subjected nation, it staked a claim to the order of Reason and Progress instituted by colonialism. When Marxists turned the spotlight on colonial exploitation, their criticism was framed by a historicist scheme that universalized Europe's historical experience. The emergent postcolonial critique, by contrast, seeks to undo the Eurocentrism produced by the institution of the West's trajectory, its appropriation of the other as History. It does so, however, with the acute realization that its own critical apparatus does not enjoy a panoptic distance from colonial history but exists as an aftermath, as an after – after being worked over by colonialism.[2] Criticism formed as an aftermath acknowledges that it inhabits the structures of Western domination that it seeks to undo. In this sense, postcolonial criticism is deliberately interdisciplinary, arising in the interstices of disciplines of power/knowledge that it critiques. This is what Homi Bhabha calls an in-between, hybrid position of practice and negotiation, or what Gayatri Chakravorty Spivak terms catachresis: 'reversing, displacing, and seizing the apparatus of value-coding'.[3]

The dissemination of Subaltern Studies, beginning in 1982 as an intervention in South Asian historiography and developing into a vigorous postcolonial critique, must be placed in such a complex, catachrestic reworking of knowledge. The challenge it poses to the existing historical scholarship has been felt not only in South Asian studies but also in the historiography of other regions and in disciplines other than history. The term 'subaltern' now appears with growing frequency in studies on Africa, Latin America, and Europe, and subalternist analysis has become a recognizable mode of critical scholarship in history, literature, and anthropology.

The formation of Subaltern Studies as an intervention in South Asian historiography occurred in the wake of the growing crisis of the Indian state in the 1970s. The dominance of the nation-state, cobbled together through compromises and coercion during the nationalist struggle against British rule, became precarious as its programme of capitalist modernity sharpened social and political inequalities and conflicts. Faced with the outbreak of powerful movements of different ideological hues that challenged its claim to represent the people, the state resorted increasingly to repression to preserve its dominance. But repression was not the only means adopted. The state combined coercive measures with the power of patronage and money, on the one hand, and the appeal of populist slogans and programmes, on the other, to make a fresh bid for its legitimacy. These measures, pioneered by the Indira Gandhi government, secured the dominance of the state but corroded the authority of its institutions. The key components of the modern nation-state – political parties, the electoral process, parliamentary bodies, the bureaucracy, law, and the ideology of development – survived, but their claim to represent the culture and politics of the masses suffered crippling blows.

In the field of historical scholarship, the perilous position of the nation-state in the 1970s became evident in the increasingly embattled nationalist historiography. Attacked relentlessly by the 'Cambridge school', which represented India's colonial history as nothing but a chronicle of competition among its elites, nationalism's fabric of legitimacy was torn apart.[4] This school exposed the nationalist hagiography, but its elite-based analysis turned the common people into dupes of their superiors. Marxists contested both nationalist historiography and the 'Cambridge school' interpretation, but their mode-of-production narratives merged imperceptibly with the nation-state's ideology of modernity and progress. This congruence meant that, while championing the history of the oppressed classes and their emancipation through modern progress, the Marxists found it difficult to deal with the hold of 'backward' ideologies of caste and religion. Unable to take into account the oppressed's 'lived experience' of religion and social customs, Marxist accounts of peasant rebellions either overlooked the religious idiom of the rebels or viewed it as a mere form and a stage in the development of revolutionary consciousness. Thus, although Marxist historians produced impressive and pioneering studies, their claim to represent the history of the masses remained debatable.

Subaltern Studies plunged into this historiographical contest over the representation of the culture and politics of the people. Accusing colonialist, nationalist, and Marxist interpretations of robbing the common people of their agency, it announced a new approach to restore history to the subordinated. Started by an editorial collective consisting of six scholars of South Asia spread across Britain,

India, and Australia, Subaltern Studies were inspired by Ranijit Guha. A distinguished historian whose most notable previous work was *A Rule of Property for Bengal* (1963), Guha edited the first six *Subaltern Studies* volumes.[5] After he relinquished the editorship, *Subaltern Studies* was published by a rotating two-member editorial team drawn from the collective. Guha continues, however, to publish in *Subaltern Studies*, now under an expanded and reconstituted editorial collective.

The establishment of *Subaltern Studies* was aimed to promote, as the preface by Guha to the first volume declared, the study and discussion of subalternist themes in South Asian studies.[6] The term 'subaltern', drawn from Antonio Gramsci's writings, refers to subordination in terms of class, caste, gender, race, language, and culture and was used to signify the centrality of dominant/ dominated relationships in history. Guha suggested that while Subaltern Studies would not ignore the dominant, because the subalterns are always subject to their activity, its aim was to 'rectify the elitist bias characteristic of much research and academic work' in South Asian studies.[7] The act of rectification sprang from the conviction that the elites had exercised dominance, not hegemony, in Gramsci's sense, over the subalterns. A reflection of this belief was Guha's argument that the subalterns had acted in history '*on their own*, that is, *independently of the elite*'; their politics constituted 'an *autonomous* domain, for it neither originated from elite politics nor did its existence depend on the latter'.[8]

While the focus on subordination has remained central to Subaltern Studies the conception of subalternity has witnessed shifts and varied uses. Individual contributors to the volumes have also differed, not surprisingly, in their orientation. A shift in interests, focus, and theoretical grounds is also evident through the eight volumes of essays produced so far and several monographs by individual subaltern-ists.[9] Yet what has remained consistent is the effort to rethink history from the perspective of the subaltern.

How the adoption of the subaltern's perspective aimed to undo the 'spurious primacy assigned to them [the elites]' was not entirely clear in the first volume. The essays, ranging from agrarian history to the analysis of the relationship between peasants and nationalists, represented excellent though not novel scholarship. Although all the contributions attempted to highlight the lives and the historical presence of subaltern classes, neither the thorough and insightful research in social and economic history nor the critique of the Indian nationalist appropriation of peasant movements was new; Marxist historians, in particular, had done both.[10] It was with the second volume that the novelty and insurgency of Subaltern Studies became clear.

The second volume made forthright claims about the subaltern subject and set about demonstrating how the agency of the subaltern in history had been denied by elite perspectives anchored in colonialist, nationalist, and/or Marxist narratives. Arguing that these narratives had sought to represent the subaltern's consciousness

and activity according to schemes that encoded elite dominance, Guha asserted
that historiography had dealt with 'the peasant rebel merely as an empirical person
or member of a class, but not as an entity whose will and reason constituted the
praxis called rebellion'.[11] Historians were apt to depict peasant rebellions as spontaneous eruptions that 'break out like thunderstorms, heave like earthquakes,
spread like wildfire'; alternatively, they attributed rebellions as a reflex action to
economic and political oppression. 'Either way insurgency is regarded as *external* to
the peasant's consciousness and Cause is made to stand in as a phantom surrogate
for Reason, the logic of consciousness.'[12]

How did historiography develop this blind spot? Guha asked. In answering
this question, his 'Prose of Counter-insurgency' offers a methodological *tour de force*
and a perceptive reading of the historical writings on peasant insurgency in colonial
India. Describing these writings as counter-insurgent texts, Guha begins by
distinguishing three types of discourses – primary, secondary, and tertiary. These
differ from one another in terms of the order of their appearance in time and the
degree of their acknowledged or unacknowledged identification with the official
point of view. Analysing each in turn, Guha shows the presence, transformation,
and redistribution of a 'counter-insurgent code'. This code, present in the
immediate accounts of insurgency produced by officials (primary discourse), is
processed into another time and narrative by official reports and memoirs (secondary
discourse) and is then incorporated and redistributed by historians who have no
official affiliation and are farthest removed from the time of the event (tertiary
discourse). The 'code of pacification', written into the 'raw' data of primary texts
and the narratives of secondary discourses, survives, and it shapes the tertiary
discourse of historians when they fail to read in it the presence of the excluded
other, the insurgent. Consequently, while historians produce accounts that differ
from secondary discourses, their tertiary discourse also ends up appropriating the
insurgent. Consider, for example, the treatment of peasant rebellions. When
colonial officials, using on-the-spot accounts containing 'the code of pacification',
blamed wicked landlords and wily moneylenders for the occurrence of these events,
they used causality as a counter-insurgent instrument: to identify the cause of the
revolt was a step in the direction of control over it and constituted a denial of the
insurgent's agency. In nationalist historiography, this denial took a different form,
as British rule, rather than local oppression, became the cause of revolts and turned
peasant rebellions into nationalist struggles. Radical historians, too, ended up
incorporating the counter-insurgent code of the secondary discourse as they
explained peasant revolts in relation to a revolutionary continuum leading to
socialism. Each tertiary account failed to step outside the counter-insurgent
paradigm, Guha argues, by refusing to acknowledge the subjectivity and agency of
the insurgent.[13]

Clearly, the project to restore the insurgent's agency involved, as Rosalind
O'Hanlon pointed out in a thoughtful review essay, the notion of the 'recovery of
the subject'.[14] Thus, while reading records against their grain, these scholars have

sought to uncover the subaltern's myths, cults, ideologies, and revolts that colonial and nationalist elites sought to appropriate and that conventional historiography has laid waste by the deadly weapon of cause and effect. Ranajit Guha's *Elementary Aspects of Peasant Insurgency in Colonial India* (1983) is a powerful example of scholarship that seeks to recover the peasant from elite projects and positivist historiography. In this wide-ranging study, full of brilliant insights and methodological innovation, Guha returns to nineteenth-century peasant insurrections in colonial India. Reading colonial records and historiographical representations with an uncanny eye, he offers a fascinating account of the peasant's insurgent consciousness, rumours, mythic visions, religiosity, and bonds of community. From Guha's account, the subaltern emerges with forms of sociality and political community at odds with nation and class, defying the models of rationality and social action that conventional historiography uses. Guha argues persuasively that such models are elitist in so far as they deny the subaltern's autonomous consciousness and that they are drawn from colonial and liberal-nationalist projects of appropriating the subaltern.

It is true that the effort to retrieve the autonomy of the subaltern subject resembled the 'history from below' approach developed by social history in the West. But the subalternist search for a humanist subject-agent frequently ended up with the discovery of the failure of subaltern agency: the moment of rebellion always contained within it the moment of failure. The desire to recover the subaltern's autonomy was repeatedly frustrated because subalternity, by definition, signified the impossibility of autonomy: subaltern rebellions only offered fleeting moments of defiance, 'a night-time of love', not 'a lifetime of love'.[15] While these scholars failed to recognize fully that the subalterns' resistance did not simply oppose power but was also constituted by it, their own work showed this to be the case. Further complicating the urge to recover the subject was the fact that, unlike British and US social history, Subaltern Studies drew on anti-humanist structuralist and poststructuralist writings. Ranajit Guha's deft readings of colonial records, in particular, drew explicitly from Ferdinand de Sassure, Claude Lévi-Strauss, Roman Jakobson, Roland Barthes, and Michel Foucault. Partly, the reliance on such theorists and the emphasis on 'textual' readings arose from, as Dipesh Chakrabarty points out, the absence of workers' diaries and other such sources available to British historians.[16] Indian peasants had left no sources, no documents from which their own 'voice' could be retrieved. But the emphasis on 'readings' of texts and the recourse to theorists such as Foucault, whose writings cast a shroud of doubt over the idea of the autonomous subject, contained an awareness that the colonial subaltern was not just a form of 'general' subalternity. While the operation of power relations in colonial and metropolitan theatres had parallels, the conditions of subalternity were also irreducibly different. Subaltern Studies, therefore, could not just be the Indian version of the 'history from below' approach; it had to conceive the subaltern differently and write different histories.

This difference has grown in subsequent *Subaltern Studies* volumes as the desire to recover the subaltern subject became increasingly entangled in the analysis of how subalternity was constituted by dominant discourses. Of course, the tension between the recovery of the subaltern as a subject outside the elite discourse and the analysis of subalternity as an effect of discursive systems was present from the very beginning.[17] It also continues to characterize Subaltern Studies scholarship today. Recent volumes, however, pay greater attention to developing the emergence of subalternity as a discursive effect without abandoning the notion of the subaltern as a subject and agent. This perspective, amplified since *Subaltern Studies III*, identifies subalternity as a position of critique, as a recalcitrant difference that arises not outside but inside elite discourses to exert pressure on forces and forms that subordinate it.

The attention paid to discourse in locating the process and effects of subordination can be seen in Partha Chatterjee's influential *Nationalist Thought and the Colonial World* (1986). A study of how Indian nationalism achieved dominance, this book traces critical shifts in nationalist thought, leading to a 'passive revolution' – a concept that he draws from Gramsci to interpret the achievement of Indian independence in 1947 as a mass revolution that appropriated the agency of the common people. In interpreting the shifts in nationalist thought, Chatterjee stresses the pressure exerted on the dominant discourse by the problem of representing the masses. The nationalists dealt with this problem by marginalizing certain forms of mass action and expression that ran counter to the modernity-driven goals that they derived from the colonial discourse. Such a strategy secures elite dominance but not hegemony over subaltern culture and politics. His recent *The Nation and its Fragments* (1993) returns once again to this theme of appropriation of subalternity, sketching how the nation was first imagined in the cultural domain and then readied for political contest by an elite that 'normalized' various subaltern aspirations for community and agency in the drive to create a modern nation-state.

Investigating the process of 'normalization' means a complex and deep engagement with elite and canonical texts. This, of course, is not new to Subaltern Studies. Earlier essays, most notably Guha's 'Prose of Counter-insurgency', engaged and interrogated elite writings with enviable skill and imagination. But these analyses of elite texts sought to establish the presence of the subalterns as subjects of their own history. The engagement with elite themes and writings, by contrast, emphasizes the analysis of the operation of dominance as it confronted, constituted, and subordinated certain forms of culture and politics. This approach is visible in the treatment of the writings of authoritative political figures such as Mahatma Gandhi and Jawaharlal Nehru and in the analyses of the activities of the Indian National Congress – the dominant nationalist party. These strive to outline how elite nationalism rewrote history and how its rewriting was directed at both contesting colonial rule and protecting its flanks from the subalterns.[18] Another theme explored with a similar aim is the intertwined functioning of colonialism, nationalism, and 'communalism' in the partition of British India into India and

Pakistan – a theme that has taken on added importance with the recent resurgence of Hindu supremacists and outbreaks of Hindu–Muslim riots.[19]

The importance of such topics is self-evident, but the real significance of the shift to the analysis of discourses is the reformulation of the notion of the subaltern. It is tempting to characterize this shift as an abandonment of the search for subaltern groups in favour of the discovery of discourses and texts. But this would be inaccurate. Although some scholars have rejected the positivistic retrieval of the subalterns, the notion of the subalterns' radical heterogeneity with, though not autonomy from, the dominant remains crucial. It is true, however, that scholars locate this heterogeneity in discourses woven into the fabric of dominant structures and manifesting itself in the very operation of power. In other words, subalterns and subalternity do not disappear into discourse but appear in its interstices, subordinated by structures over which they exert pressure. Thus Shahid Amin shows that Indian nationalists in 1921–22, confronted with the millennial and deeply subversive language of peasant politics, were quick to claim peasant actions as their own and Gandhian. Unable to acknowledge the peasants' insurgent appropriation of Gandhi, Indian nationalists represented it in the stereotypical saint–devotee relationship.[20] Amin develops this point further in his innovative monograph on the peasant violence in 1922 that resulted in the death of several policemen and led Gandhi to suspend the non-co-operation campaign against British rule. Returning to this emotive date in Indian nationalist history, Amin shows that this violent event, 'criminalized' in the colonial judicial discourse, was 'nationalized' by the elite nationalists, first by an 'obligatory amnesia' and then by selective remembrance and reappropriation.[21] To take another example, Gyanendra Pandey suggests that the discourse of the Indian nation-state, which had to imagine India as a national community, could not recognize community (religious, cultural, social, and local) as a political form; thus it pitted nationalism (termed good because it 'stood above' difference) against communalism (termed evil because it did not 'rise above' difference).[22]

Such re-examinations of South Asian history do not invoke 'real' subalterns, prior to discourse, in framing their critique. Placing subalterns in the labyrinth of discourse, they cannot claim an unmediated access to their reality. The actual subalterns and subalternity emerge between the folds of the discourse, in its silences and blindness, and in its overdetermined pronouncements. Interpreting the 1922 peasant violence, Amin identifies the subaltern presence as an effect in the discourse. This effect manifests itself in a telling dilemma the nationalists faced. On the one hand, they could not endorse peasant violence as nationalist activity, but, on the other, they had to acknowledge the peasant 'criminals' as part of the nation. They sought to resolve this dilemma by admitting the event in the narrative of the nation while denying it agency: the peasants were shown to act the way they did because they were provoked, or because they were insufficiently trained in the methods of non-violence.

Subalternity thus emerges in the paradoxes of the functioning of power, in the functioning of the dominant discourse as it represents and domesticates peasant agency as a spontaneous and 'pre-political' response to colonial violence. No longer does it appear outside the elite discourse as a separate domain, embodied in a figure endowed with a will that the dominant suppress and overpower but do not constitute. Instead, it refers to that impossible thought, figure, or action without which the dominant discourse cannot exist and which is acknowledged in its subterfuges and stereotypes.

This portrait of subalternity is certainly different from the image of the autonomous subject, and it has emerged in the confrontation with the systematic fragmentation of the record of subalternity. Such records register both the necessary failure of subalterns to come into their own and the pressure they exerted on discursive systems that, in turn, provoked their suppression and fragmentation. The representation of this discontinuous mode of subalternity demands a strategy that recognizes both the emergence and displacement of subaltern agency in dominant discourses. It is by adopting such a strategy that the Subaltern Studies scholars have redeployed and redefined the concept of the subaltern, enhancing, not diminishing, its recalcitrance.

The Subaltern Studies relocation of subalternity in the operation of dominant discourses leads it necessarily to the critique of the modern West. For if the marginalization of 'other' sources of knowledge and agency occurred in the functioning of colonialism and its derivative, nationalism, then the weapon of critique must turn against Europe and the modes of knowledge it instituted. It is in this context that there emerges a certain convergence between Subaltern Studies and postcolonial critiques originating in literary and cultural studies. To cite only one example, not only did Edward Said's *Orientalism* provide the grounds for Partha Chatterjee's critique of Indian nationalism, Said also wrote an appreciative foreword to a collection of Subaltern Studies essays.[23] It is important to recognize that the critique of the West is not confined to the colonial record of exploitation and profiteering but extends to the disciplinary knowledge and procedures it authorized – above all, the discipline of history.

Dipesh Chakrabarty offers a forceful critique of the academic discipline of history as a theoretical category laden with power. Finding premature the celebration of Subaltern Studies as a case of successful decolonization of knowledge, Chakrabarty writes that,

> insofar as the academic discourse of history – that is, 'history' as a discourse produced at the institutional site of the university – is concerned, 'Europe' remains the sovereign, theoretical subject of all histories, including the ones we call 'Indian', 'Chinese', 'Kenyan', and so on. There is a peculiar way in which all these other histories tend to become variations on a master narrative that could be called 'the history of Europe'. In this sense, 'Indian' history itself is in a position of subalternity; one can only articulate subaltern subject positions in the name of this history.[24]

The place of Europe as a silent referent works in many ways. First, there is the matter of 'asymmetric ignorance': non-Westerners must read 'great' Western historians (E. P. Thompson or Emmanuel Le Roy Ladurie or Carlo Ginzburg) to produce the good histories, while the Western scholars are not expected to know non-Western works. Indeed, non-Western scholars are recognized for their innovation and imagination when they put into practice genres of enquiry developed for European history; a 'total history' of China, the history of *mentalité* in Mexico, the making of the working class in India are likely to be applauded as fine studies.

Even more important, Chakrabarty suggests, is the installation of Europe as the theoretical subject of all histories. This universalization of Europe works through the representation of histories as History; even 'Marx's methodological/ epistemological statements have not always successfully resisted historicist readings'.[25] Chakrabarty's study of jute workers in Bengal runs up against precisely the same Eurocentrism that undergirds Marx's analysis of capital and class struggle.[26] In his study, Chakrabarty finds that deeply hierarchical notions of caste and religion, drawn from India's traditions, animated working-class organization and politics in Bengal. This posed a problem for Marxist historiography. If India's traditions lacked the 'Liberty Tree' that had nourished, according to E. P. Thompson, the consciousness of the English working class, were Indian workers condemned to 'low classness'? The alternative was to envision that, sooner or later, the Indian working class would reach the desired state of emancipatory consciousness. This vision, of course, assumes the universality of such notions as the rights of 'free-born Englishmen' and 'equality before the law', and it posits that 'workers all over the world, irrespective of their specific cultural pasts, *experience* "capitalist production" in the same way'.[27] This possibility can only arise if it is assumed that there is a universal subject endowed with an emancipatory narrative. Such an assumption, Chakrabarty suggests, is present in Marx's analysis, which, while carefully contrasting the proletariat from the citizen, falls back nonetheless on Enlightenment notions of freedom and democracy to define the emancipatory narrative. As a result, the jute workers, who resisted the bourgeois ideals of equality before the law with their hierarchical vision of a pre-capitalist community, are condemned to 'backwardness' in Marxist accounts. Furthermore, it allows the nation-state to step on to the stage as the instrument of liberal transformation of the hierarchy-ridden masses.

It is not surprising, therefore, that themes of historical transition occupy a prominent place in the writing of non-Western histories. Historians ask if these societies achieved a successful transition to development, modernization, and capitalism and frequently answer in the negative. A sense of failure overwhelms the representation of the history of these societies. So much so that even contestatory projects, including Subaltern Studies, Chakrabarty acknowledges, write of non-Western histories in terms of failed transitions. Such images of aborted transitions reinforce the subalternity of non-Western histories and the dominance of Europe as History.[28]

The dominance of Europe as history not only subalternizes non-Western societies but also serves the aims of their nation-states. Indeed, Subaltern Studies developed its critique of history in the course of its examination of Indian nationalism and the nation-state. Guha's reconstruction of the language of peasant politics in his *Elementary Aspects of Peasant Insurgence in Colonial India* is premised on the argument that nationalist historiography engaged in a systematic appropriation of peasants in the service of elite nationalism. Chatterjee's work contains an extended analysis of Jawaharlal Nehru's *Discovery of India*, a foundational nationalist text, showing the use of History, Reason, and Progress in the normalization of peasant 'irrationality'.[29] The inescapable conclusion from such analyses is that 'history', authorized by European imperialism and the Indian nation-state, functions as a discipline, empowering certain forms of knowledge while disempowering others.

If history functions as a discipline that renders certain forms of thought and action 'irrational' and subaltern, then should not the critique extend to the techniques and procedures it utilizes? Addressing this question, Chakrabarty turns to 'one of the most elementary rules of evidence in academic history-writing: that your sources must be verifiable'.[30] Pointing out that this rule assumes the existence of a 'public sphere', which public archives and history writing are expected to reproduce, he suggests that the canons of historical research cannot help but live a problematic life in societies such as India. The idea of 'public life' and 'free access to information' must contend with the fact that knowledge is privileged and 'belongs and circulates in the numerous and particularistic networks of kinship, community, gendered spaces, [and] ageing structures'. If this is the case, then, Chakrabarty asks, how can we assume the universality of the canons of history writing. 'Whose universals are they?'[31]

It is important to note that 'Europe' or 'the West' in Subaltern Studies refers to an imaginary though powerful entity created by a historical process that authorized it as the home of Reason, Progress, and Modernity. To undo the authority of such an entity, distributed and universalized by imperialism and nationalism, requires, in Chakrabarty's words, the 'provincialization of Europe'. But neither nativism nor cultural relativism animates this project of provincializing Europe; there are no calls for reversing the Europe/India hierarchy and no attempts to represent India through an 'Indian', not Western, perspective. Instead, the recognition that the 'third-world historian is condemned to knowing "Europe" as the original home of the "modern", whereas the "European" historian does not share a comparable predicament with regard to the pasts of the majority of human kind' serves as the condition for a deconstructive rethinking of history.[32] Such a strategy seeks to find in the functioning of history as a discipline (in Foucault's sense) the source for another history.

This move is a familiar one for postcolonial criticism and should not be confused with approaches that insist simply on the social construction of knowledge and identities. It delves into the history of colonialism not only to document its record of domination but also to identify its failures, silences, and impasses; not only to chronicle the career of dominant discourses but to track those (subaltern) positions that could not be properly recognized and named, only 'normalized'. The aim of such a strategy is not to unmask dominant discourses but to explore their fault lines in order to provide different accounts, to describe histories revealed in the cracks of the colonial archaeology of knowledge.[33]

This perspective draws on critiques of binary oppositions that, as Frederick Cooper notes,[34] historians of former empires look upon with suspicion. It is true, as Cooper points out, that binary oppositions conceal intertwined histories and engagements across dichotomies, but the critique must go further. Oppositions such as East/West and colonizer/colonized are suspect not only because they distort the history of engagements but also because they edit, suppress, and marginalize everything that upsets founding values. It is in this respect that Jacques Derrida's strategy to undo the implacable oppositions of Western dominance is of some relevance.

> Metaphysics – the white mythology which reassembles and reflects the culture of the West: the white man takes his own mythology, Indo-European mythology, his own *logos*, that is, the *mythos* of his idiom, for the universal form that he must still wish to call Reason … White mythology – metaphysics has erased within itself the fabulous scene that has produced it, the scene that nevertheless remains active and stirring, inscribed in white ink, an invisible design covered over in the palimpsest.[35]

If the production of white mythology has nevertheless left 'an invisible design covered over in the palimpsest', Derrida suggest that the structure of signification, of 'difference', can be rearticulated differently than that which produced the West as Reason. Further, the source of the rearticulation of structures that produce foundational myths (History as the march of Man, of Reason, Progress) lies inside, not outside, their ambivalent functioning. From this point of view, critical work seeks its basis not without but within the fissures of dominant structures. Or, as Gayatri Chakravorty Spivak puts it, the deconstructive philosophical position (or postcolonial criticism) consists in saying an 'impossible "no" to a structure which one critiques, yet inhabits intimately'.[36]

The potential of this deconstructive position has been explored effectively in the readings of the archival documents on the abolition of *sati*, the Hindu widow sacrifice in the early nineteenth century. The historian encounters these records, as I have suggested elsewhere, as evidence of the contests between the British 'civilizing mission' and Hindu heathenism, between modernity and tradition, and as a story of the beginning of the emancipation of Hindu women and about the birth of modern India.[37] This is so because, Lata Mani shows, the very existence of these documents has a history that entails the use of women as the site for both the colonial and the indigenous male elite's constructions of authoritative Hindu traditions.[38] The questions asked of accumulated sources on *sati* – whether or not the burning of widows was sanctioned by Hindu codes, did women go willingly to the funeral pyre, on what grounds could the immolation of women be abolished – come to us marked by their early nineteenth-century history. The historian's confrontation today with sources on *sati*, therefore, cannot escape the echo of that previous rendezvous. In repeating that encounter, how does the historian today not replicate the early nineteenth-century staging of the issue as a contest between tradition and modernity, between the slavery of women and efforts toward their emancipation, between barbaric Hindu practices and the British 'civilizing mission'? Mani tackles this dilemma by examining how such questions were asked and with what consequences. She shows that the opposing arguments assumed the authority of the law-giving scriptural tradition as the origin of Hindu customs: both those who supported and those who opposed *sati* sought the authority of textual origins for their beliefs. In other words, the nineteenth-century debate fabricated the authority of texts as Hinduism without acknowledging its work of authorization; indigenous patriarchy and colonial power colluded in constructing the origins for and against *sati* while concealing their collusion. Consequently, as Spivak states starkly, the debate left no room for the widow's enunciatory position. Caught in the contest over whether traditions did or did not sanction *sati* and over whether or not the widow self-immolated willingly, the colonized subaltern woman disappeared: she was literally extinguished for her dead husband in the indigenous patriarchal discourse, or offered the choice to speak in the voice of a sovereign individual authenticated by colonialism.[39] The problem here is not one of sources (the absence of the woman's testimony) but of the staging of the debate: it left no position from which the widow could speak.

The silencing of subaltern women, Spivak argues, marks the limit of historical knowledge.[40] It is impossible to retrieve the woman's voice when she was not given a subject-position from which to speak. This argument appears to run counter to the historiographical convention of retrieval to recover the histories of the trad-itionally ignored – women, workers, peasants, and minorities. Spivak's point, how-ever, is not that such retrieval should not be undertaken but that the very project of recovery depends on the historical erasure of the subaltern 'voice'. The possibility of retrieval, therefore, is also a sign of its impossibility. Recognition of the aporetic condition of the subaltern's silence is necessary in order to subject the intervention of the historian-critic to persistent interrogation, to prevent the refraction of 'what might have been the absolutely Other into a domesticated Other'.[41]

These directions of postcolonial criticism make it an ambivalent practice, perched between traditional historiography and its failures, within the folds of dominant discourses and seeking to rearticulate their pregnant silence – sketching 'an invisible design covered over in the palimpsest'. This should not be mistaken for the postmodern pastiche, although the present currency of concepts such as decentred subjects and parodic texts may provide a receptive and appropriative frame for postcolonial criticism. Postcolonial criticism seizes on discourse's silences and aporetic moments neither to celebrate the polyphony of native voices nor to privilege multiplicity. Rather, its point is that the *functioning* of colonial power was heterogeneous with its founding oppositions. The 'native' was at once an other and entirely knowable; the Hindu widow was a silenced subaltern who was nonetheless sought as a sovereign subject asked to declare whether or not her immolation was voluntary. Clearly, colonial discourses operated as the structure of *writing*, with the structure of their enunciation remaining heterogeneous with the binary oppositions they instituted.

This perspective on history and the position within it that the postcolonial critic occupies keeps an eye on both the conditions of historical knowledge and the possibility of its reinscription. It is precisely this double vision that allows Shahid Amin to use the limits of historical knowledge for its reinscription. His monograph on the 1922 peasant violence in Chauri Chaura is at once scrupulously 'local' and 'general'. It offers a 'thick description' of a local event set on a larger stage by nationalism and historiographical practice. Amin seizes on this general (national) staging of the local not only to show that the Indian nation emerged in its narration but also to mark the tension between the two as the point at which the subaltern memory of 1922 can enter history. This memory, recalled for the author during his fieldwork, is not invoked either to present a more 'complete' account of the event or to recover the subaltern. In fact, treating gaps, contradictions, and ambivalences as constitutive, necessary components of the nationalist narrative, Amin inserts memory as a device that both dislocates and reinscribes the historical record. The result is not an archaeology of nationalism that yields lifeless layers of suppressed evidence and episodes. Instead, we get a stage on which several different but interrelated dramas are performed, jostling for attention and prominence; the curtain is abruptly drawn on some, and often the voices of the peasant actors can only be heard in the din of the other, more powerful, voices.

To read Amin's work in this way shows, I hope, that his deconstructive strategy does not 'flatten' the tension that has existed, as Florencia Mallon notes correctly,[42] in this scholarship from the very beginning. To be sure, Amin's account is not animated by the urge to recover the subaltern as an autonomous subject. But he places his enquiry in the tension between nationalism's claim to know the peasant and its representation of the subalterns as the 'criminals' of Chauri Chaura. The subaltern remains a recalcitrant presence in discourse, at once part of the nation and outside it. Amin traffics between these two positions, demonstrating that subaltern insurgency left its mark, however disfigured, on the discourse – 'an invisible design covered over in the palimpsest'.

Neither Amin's retelling of the 1922 event nor Chakrabarty's project of 'provincializing Europe' can be separated from postcolonial critiques of disciplines, including the discipline of history. Thus, even as Subaltern Studies has shifted from its original goal of recovering the subaltern autonomy, the subaltern has emerged as a position from which the discipline of history can be rethought. This rethinking does not entail the rejection of the discipline and its procedures of research. Far from it. As Chakrabarty writes, 'it is not possible to simply walk out of the deep collusion between "history" and the modernizing narrative(s)'.[43] Nor is it possible to abandon historical research so long as it is pursued as an academic discipline in universities and functions to universalize capitalism and the nation-state. There is no alternative but to inhabit the discipline, delve into archives, and push at the limits of historical knowledge to turn its contradictions, ambivalences, and gaps into grounds for its rewriting.

If Subaltern Studies' powerful intervention in South Asian historiography has turned into a sharp critique of the discipline of history, this is because South Asia is not an isolated arena but is woven into the web of historical discourse centred, as Chakrabarty argues, in the modern West. Through the long histories of colonialism and nationalism, the discourse of modernity, capitalism, and citizenship has acquired a strong though peculiar presence in the history of the region. The institutions of higher education in South Asia, relatively large and thriving, have functioned since the mid-nineteenth century in relation to the metropolitan academy, including centres for South Asian studies in the West. For all these reasons, India's historical scholarship has been uniquely placed to both experience and formulate searching critiques of metropolitan discourses even as its object remains the field of South Asia. To its credit, Subaltern Studies turned South Asia's entanglement with the modern West as the basis for rendering its intervention in South Asian history into a critique of discourses authorized by Western domination.

Subaltern Studies has arrived at its critique by engaging both Marxism and poststructuralism. But the nature of these engagements is complex. If the influence of Gramsci's Marxism is palpable in the concept of the subaltern and in treatments of such themes as hegemony and dominance, Marxism is also subjected to the poststructuralist critique of European humanism. It should be noted, however, as Spivak points out, that while 'there is an affinity between the imperialist subject and the subject of humanism', the European critique of humanism does not provide the primary motive force for the Subaltern Studies project.[44] Thus, even as this project utilizes Foucault's genealogical analysis to unravel the discourse of modernity, it relies on the subaltern as the vantage point of critique. The recalcitrant presence of the subaltern, marking the limits of the dominant discourse and the disciplines of representation, enables Subaltern Studies to identify the European provenance of Marx's account of capital, to disclose Enlightenment thought as the unthought of his analysis. It is outside Europe, in subaltern locations, that Marx's emancipatory narrative is disclosed as a *telos* deeply implicated in a discourse that was once part of colonialism and now serves to legitimate the nation-state.[45] Such a critical and complex engagement with Marxism and poststructuralism, deriving its force from the concept of the subaltern, defines the Subaltern Studies project.

Clearly, Subaltern Studies obtains its force as postcolonial criticism from a catachrestic combination of Marxism, poststructuralism, Gramsci and Foucault, the modern West and India, archival research and textual criticism. As this project is translated into other regions and disciplines, the discrepant histories of colonialism, capitalism, and subalternity in different areas will have to be recognized. It is up to the scholars of these fields, including Europeanists, to determine how to use Subaltern Studies' insights on subalternity and its critique of the colonial genealogy of the discourse of modernity. But it is worth bearing in mind that Subaltern Studies itself is an act of translation. Representing a negotiation between South Asian historiography and the discipline of history centred in the West, its insights can be neither limited to South Asia nor globalized. Trafficking between the two, and originating as an ambivalent colonial aftermath, Subaltern Studies demands that its own translation also occur between the lines.

Notes

From the *American Historical Review*, 99 (1994), 1475–90. I am grateful to Frederick Cooper and Florencia Mallon for their comments and suggestions. Although I have not followed their advice in every instance, their careful and critical readings were helpful in rethinking and rewriting the chapter.

1   In calling these accounts Eurocentric, I do not mean that they followed the lead of Western authors and thinkers. Eurocentricity here refers to the historicism that projected the West as History.

2   Elsewhere, I elaborate and offer examples of this notion of the postcolonial. See my 'Introduction: After Colonialism', in Gyan Prakash, *After Colonialism: Imperial Histories and Postcolonial Displacements* (Princeton NJ, 1995). Gayatri Chakravorty Spivak speaks of postcoloniality in similar terms. 'We are always *after* the empire of reason, our claims to it always short of adequate.' Spivak, 'Poststructuralism, Marginality, Postcoloniality and Value', in *Literary Theory Today*, ed. Peter Collier and Helga Geyer-Ryan (London, 1990), 228. While literary theorists have been prominent in forcing postcolonial criticism on to the scholarly agenda, it is by no means confined to them: the work of Subaltern Studies historians must be considered an important part of the postcolonial critique. For other examples of historians' contribution to this criticism, see *Colonialism and Culture*, ed. Nicholas B. Dirks (Ann Arbor MI, 1992); *Confronting Historical Paradigms: Peasants, Labor, and the Capitalist World System in Africa and Latin America*, ed. Frederick Cooper, Allen F. Isaacman, Florencia E. Mallon, William Roseberry, and Steve J. Stern (Madison WI, 1993); Gyan Prakash, *Bonded Histories: Genealogies of Labor Servitude in Colonial India* (Cambridge, 1990): and Vicente L. Rafael, *Contracting Colonialism: Translation and Christian Conversion in Tagalog Society under Early Spanish Rule* (Ithaca NY, 1988). The essays by Frederick Cooper and Florencia Mallon in the issue of the *American Historical Review* in which this chapter first appeared also mention a number of historical works that have contributed to the current postcolonial criticism.

3   Homi K. Bhabha, *The Location of Culture* (London, 1994), 22–6; Spivak, 'Poststructuralism, Marginality, Postcoloniality and Value', 228.

4   The classic statement of the 'Cambridge school' is to be found in Anil Seal's study *The Emergence of Indian Nationalism: Competition and Collaboration in the Later Nineteenth Century* (Cambridge, 1968), which contended that Indian nationalism was produced by the educated elites in their competition for the 'loaves and fishes' of office. This was modified in *Locality, Province and Nation: Essays on Indian Politics, 1870–1940*, ed. J. Gallagher, G. Jognson, and Anil Seal (Cambridge, 1973), which advanced the view that nationalism emerged from the involvement of local and regional elites in colonial institutions. As the official institutions reached down to the locality and the province the elites reached up to the central level to secure their local and regional dominance, finding nationalism a useful instrument for the articulation of their interests.

5 Ranajit Guha, *A Rule of Property for Bengal* (Paris, 1963). I should also mention his important article 'Neel Darpan: The Image of a Peasant Revolt in a Liberal Mirror', *Journal of Peasant Studies*, 2 (1974): 1–46, which anticipates his fuller critique of elite historiography.

6 Ranajit Guha, *Subaltern Studies* I (Delhi, 1982), vii.

7 Guha, *Subaltern Studies I*, vii.

8 Ranajit Guha, 'On Some Aspects of the Historiography of Colonial India', *Subaltern Studies I*, 3–4.

9 *Subaltern Studies I–VI*, ed. Ranajit Guha (Delhi, 1982–89); *VII*, ed. Gyanendra Pandey and Partha Chatterjee (Delhi, 1992); *VIII*, ed. David Arnold and David Hardiman (Delhi, 1993); Ranajit Guha, *Elementary Aspects of Peasant Insurgency in Colonial India* (Delhi, 1983); Partha Chatterjee, *Nationalist Thought and the Colonial World: A Derivative Discourse?* (London, 1986); and Chatterjee, *The Nation and its Fragments: Colonial and Postcolonial Histories* (Princeton NJ, 1993); Dipesh Chakrabarty, *Rethinking Working-Class History: Bengal 1890–1940* (Princeton NJ, 1989); David Hardiman, *The Coming of the Devi: Adivasi Assertion in Western India* (Delhi, 1987); and Gyanendra Pandey, *The Construction of Communalism in Colonial North India* (Delhi, 1990).

10 See, for example, Majid Siddiqi, *Agrarian Unrest in North India: The United Provinces, 1918–22* (Delhi, 1978); and Jairus Banaji, 'Capitalist Domination and Small Peasantry: Deccan Districts in the Late Nineteenth Century', *Economic and Political Weekly*, 12:33 (1977): 1375–44.

11 Ranajit Guha, 'The Prose of Counter-insurgency', *Subaltern Studies II* (Delhi, 1983), 2.

12 *Ibid.*, 2–3.

13 *Ibid.*, 26–33.

14 Rosalind O'Hanlon, 'Recovering the Subject: Subaltern Studies and Histories of Resistance in Colonial South Asia', *Modern Asian Studies*, 22 (1988): 189–224.

15 Veena Das, 'Subaltern as Perspective', *Subaltern Studies VI* (Delhi, 1989), 315.

16 Dipesh Chakrabarty, 'Trafficking in History and Theory: Subaltern Studies', *Beyond the Disciplines: The New Humanities*, ed. K. K. Ruthven (Canberra, 1992), 102.

17 Gayatri Chakravorty Spivak's essay in *Subaltern Studies IV* pointed out this tension. 'Subaltern Studies: Deconstructing Historiography', *Subaltern Studies IV* (Delhi, 1985), 337–8.

18 Fine examples in this respect are Shahid Amin's 'Gandhi as Mahatma: Gorakhpur District, Eastern UP, 1921–2', *Subaltern Studies III* (Delhi, 1984), 1–61: and 'Approver's Testimony, Judicial Discourse: The Case of Chauri Chaura', *Subaltern Studies V* (Delhi, 1987) 166–202.

19 See Pandey, *Construction of Communalism*; and 'In Defense of the Fragment: Writing about Hindu–Muslim Riots in India Today', *Representations*, 37 (winter 1992): 27–55.

20 Amin, 'Gandhi as Mahatma', 2–7.

21 See Pandey's forthcoming *Event, Metaphor, Memory: Chauri Chaura 1922–1992* (Berkeley CA, 1995).

22 See Pandey, *Construction of Communalism*, 235–43, 254–61.

23 Chatterjee, *Nationalist Thought and the Colonial World*, 36–9; Edward Said, 'Foreword', *Selected Subaltern Studies*, ed. Ranajit Guha and Gayatri Chakravorty Spivak (New York, 1988), v–x.

24 Dipesh Chakrabarty, 'Postcoloniality and the Artifice of History: Who Speaks for "Indian" Pasts?' *Representations*, 37 (winter 1992): 1.

25 Chakrabarty, 'Postcoloniality and the Artifice of History', 4.

26 See Chakrabarty, *Rethinking Working-Class History*.

27 *Ibid.*, 223.

28 Chakrabarty, 'Postcoloniality and the Artifice of History', 4–5. In this essay, Chakrabarty includes the initial orientation of Subaltern Studies toward the question of transition, as reflected in Guha's programmatic statements in 'On Some Aspects of the Historiography of Colonial India' and Chakrabarty's own *Rethinking Working-Class History*.

29 Jawaharlal Nehru, *Discovery of India* (New York, 1946); Chatterjee, *Nationalist Thought and the Colonial World*.

30 Chakrabarty, 'Trafficking in History and Theory', 106.

31 *Ibid.*, 107.

32 Chakrabarty, 'Postcoloniality and the Artifice', 106.

33 See, in this connection, Homi K. Bhabha, 'Of Mimicry and Man: The Ambivalence of Colonial Discourse', in Bhabha, *Location of Culture*, 85–92.

34 In his essay in the 'forum' of the *American Historical Review* in which this chapter first appeared.

35 Jacques Derrida, *Margins of Philosophy*, trans. Alan Bass (Chicago, 1982), 213.

36 Gayatri Chakravorty Spivak, 'The Making of Americans, the Teaching of English, the Future of Colonial Studies', *New Literary History*, 21 (1990): 28.

37 This discussion of *sati* draws heavily on my 'Postcolonial Criticism and Indian Historiography', *Social Text*. 31–2 (1992): 11.

38 Lata Mani, 'Contentious Traditions: The Debate on Sati in Colonial India', *Cultural Critique*, 7 (fall 1987): 119–56.

39 Gayatri Chakravorty Spivak, 'Can the Subaltern Speak?' in *Marxism and the Interpretation of Culture*, ed. Cary Nelson and Lawrence Grossberg (Urbana IL, 1988), 271–313, especially 299–307.

40 For more on this argument about the colonized woman caught between indigenous patriarchy and the politics of archival production, see Gayatri Chakrabarty Spivak, 'The Rani of Sirmur: An Essay in Reading the Archives', *History and Theory*, 24 (1985): 247–72.

41 Gayatri Chakravorty Spivak, 'Three Women's Texts and a Critique of Imperialism', *Critical Inquiry*, 12 (1985): 253.

42 In her article in the same issue of the *American Historical Review* as that in which this chapter first appeared.

43 Chakrabarty, 'Postcoloniality and the Artifice of History', 19.

44 Spivak, 'Subaltern Studies: Deconstructing Historiography', 337.

45 Chakrabarty, *Rethinking Working-Class History*, 224–9.

6

Who needs the nation?
Interrogating 'British' history

ANTOINETTE BURTON

In his 1964 essay 'Origins of the Present Crisis', Perry Anderson argued that British colonialism had made 'a lasting imprint' on English life because of the historically imperial basis of mercantile capitalism. As interlocutors of capitalism from J. A. Hobson to E. P. Thompson have done (on those rare occasions when they have addressed the impact of empire on domestic English culture at all), Anderson focused his attention on the working classes – who, he argued, were 'undeniably deflected from undistracted engagement with the class exploiting them. This was the real – negative – achievement of social-imperialism', according to Anderson. 'It created a powerful "national" framework which in normal periods insensibly mitigated social contradictions and at moments of crisis transcended them.'[1]

Although Anderson touched but briefly on empire, he was rare among his left academic contemporaries in suggesting that Britain's colonial enterprises had a constitutive effect on working-class and indeed on English life as a whole in the modern period – despite the fact that the expropriation of colonial rent and resources was, historically, one of the two major pillars of primary capital accumulation in the West.[2] Eric Williams's 1944 *Capitalism and Slavery* had posited both empirical and ideological connections between the plantocratic practices of empire and domestic British politics and society, though its impact outside of Caribbean history or slavery/emancipation studies was arguably limited for decades.[3] It is tempting to stop here and talk about the relative invisibility of empire in British Marxist analyses, at least in the 1960s and 1970s. Eric Hobsbawm's *Industry and Empire* (1968) is an important exception, though it does not deal with the cultural or even political ramifications of empire for 'domestic' culture and society. The consequences of historical amnesia in British historiographical traditions have been variously explored by Gauri Viswanathan's critique of Raymond Williams, E. P. Thompson's remarkable monograph *Alien Homage*, and the introduction to Catherine Hall's *White, Male and Middle Class* – all of which grapple with the ramifications of such wilful blindness in different ways and for different ends.[4] What I want to focus on here is Anderson's observation about the 'national' framework created through the appropriation of imperial discourses and politics by elites and populists because it signals, I think, a nostalgia for the nation which is often articulated even and perhaps especially by ostensible critics of empire. For Anderson, as for others interested in the relationship of imperial culture to British history, what was regrettable about empire was in many respects enabling for the nation – in so far as the fact of colonialism provided what, in Anderson's own estimation, was the very grounds for 'national culture'. In light of Anderson's 1967 essay, 'Components of the National Culture' – which argues that Britain produced no 'overall account of itself' because a classical sociology originating 'at home' failed to emerge – what empire achieved for the nation is hardly insignificant. Taken together Anderson's two essays imply that it was colonialism which provided the opportunity for Britons of all classes to conceive of the nation and to experience themselves as members of a 'national culture'.[5]

Such an observation runs the risk of seeming almost pedestrian, especially given the burgeoning of work in the last ten years on the imperial dimensions of Victorian, and to a lesser degree twentieth-century British, society. As a participant in and critic of these developments, I want to register my unease at some of the conservative effects of this remapping of Britishness, historically conceived. I want to suggest that among the subjects being implicitly and perhaps unconsciously conserved in current debates is the nation and its integrity, in part because there is nothing inherently destabilizing to the nation in critical attention to empire as a constitutive part of 'British' history and society – either in Anderson's time or now. Moreover, I want to argue here that one tendency in current responses to 'imperial studies' is to shore up the nation and reconstitute its centrality, even as the legitimacy of Great Britain's national boundaries are apparently under question. What is at stake in these debates is not just the nation *per se*, but the territorialized domains of the social versus the cultural and, with them, the complicity of history-writing itself in narratives of the 'national' citizen-subject as well. And despite traditional British historians' almost pathological fear of contamination by literary studies via the linguistic turn, it is actually anthropology and the 'ethnographic' turn which place the sovereignty of British history at risk.[6]

It would require a herculean effort in 1996 to gainsay Edward Said's claim that 'we are at a point in our work when we can no longer ignore empires and the imperial context in our studies'.[7] As Peter Hulme has pointed out, the enduring purchase of Said's work - its 'irritative process of critique' – lies in its insistence that what is at risk from attention to orientalism is the integrity of the European 'heartland' itself, because 'the principal motifs and tropes of ... European cultural tradition, far from being self-generated, were the product of constant, intricate, but mostly unacknowledged traffic with the non-European world'.[8]

Recent scholarship in British history has documented the traces of empire that were everywhere to be found 'at home' before World War I – in spaces as diverse as the Boy Scouts, Bovril advertisements, and biscuit tins: in productions as varied as novels, feminist pamphlets, and music halls; and in cartographies as particular as Oxbridge, London, and the Franco-British Exhibition.[9] And either because they were part of permanent communities with long histories and traditions in the British Isles, or because they were travellers or temporary residents in various metropoles and regions throughout the United Kingdom, a variety of colonial 'Others' circulated at the very heart of the British Empire before the twentieth century. They were, as Gretchen Gerzina has noted, a 'continual and very English presence' from the Elizabethan settlement onward.[10] If there is little consensus about the significance of empire's impact on Britain's domestic cultural formations, primary evidence of its constitutive role nonetheless abounds, and scholars of the Georgian, Victorian and Edwardian periods are at work to re-map Greater Britain as an imperial landscape using a variety of evidentiary bases and techniques.[11] Empire was, in short, not just a phenomenon 'out there', but a fundamental part of English culture and national identity at home, where 'the fact of empire was registered not only in political debate … but entered the social fabric, the intellectual discourse and the life of the imagination'.[12]

If these claims would seem to make good historical sense, they have met with an opposition so determined that it would be easy to imagine that they pose some kind of threat to national security. While it is undoubtedly true that there are important recent voices – Catherine Hall, Bill Schwarz, Laura Tabili and Mrinalini Sinha among them – taking issue with the siege mentality of British history, I have chosen to focus here on the battlements, and more specifically, on how and through what kinds of referents they have been drawn and defended. Studies which seek to rematerialize the presence of non-white Britons in the United Kingdom before 1945 have attracted the most censure, in part because, as Paul Gilroy has argued with regard to the emergence of black history in Britain, they are perceived as 'an illegitimate intrusion into a vision of authentic national life that, prior to their arrival, was as stable and peaceful as it was ethnically undifferentiated'.[13] Accusations by a British government Minister in 1995 that the elevation of historical figures like Olaudah Equiano and Mary Seacole to the status of British heroes constituted a 'betrayal' of true British history and 'national identity' certainly testify to the political contests that representation has the power to set in motion.[14] But attention to empire's influences at home has provoked a response even when the topics are commodities and aesthetics, ideologies and politics, rather than an 'alien' presence. Whether by a calm, cool refutation of claims about empire's centrality (as exhibited by Peter Marshall's essay in the *Times Literary Supplement*, 'No Fatal Impact?') or via the impassioned denunciations of Said (articulated in John MacKenzie's monograph, *Orientalism: History, Theory and the Arts*), those in charge of safeguarding Britain's national heritage, from Whitehall to the senior common room, have raised the standard in defence of the nation's impenetrability to outside forces. Although a number of scholars are beginning to track empire's constitutive impact on metropolitan society as the starting point for new critical geographies of British imperial culture, empire cannot be viewed as having made

Britain 'what it was' for Professor Marshall because it was so centrifugal and uneven – and by implication, perhaps, untraceable – in its impact.[15] This kind of response worries me because it seems to echo J. R. Seeley's infamous quip that the British Empire was acquired in 'a fit of absence of mind' (a phrase later amended to 'a fit of absence of wives' by Ronald Hyam). John MacKenzie's role in this debate is perhaps the most puzzling and intriguing, since his now twenty-plus volume series, Studies in Imperialism, has arguably advanced our understanding of the myriad ways in which empire was, to quote his 1984 monograph, 'a core ideology' of national culture.[16]

Clearly the persistent conviction that home and empire were separate spheres cannot be dismissed as just any other fiction.[17] Because history-writing is one terrain upon which political battles are fought out, the quest currently being undertaken by historians and literary critics to recast the nation as an imperialized space – a political territory which could not, and still cannot, escape the imprint of empire – is an important political project. It strikes at the heart of Britain's long ideological attachment to the narratives of the Island Story, of splendid isolation, and of European exceptionalism. It materializes the traffic of colonial goods, ideas and people across metropolitan borders and indeed throws into question the very Victorian distinctions between Home and Away that defined the imagined geography of empire in the nineteenth century – helping to challenge the equally Victorian conviction that 'England possesses an unbroken history of cultural homogeneity and territorial integrity'.[18] And yet what it potentially leaves intact is the sanctity of the nation itself as the right and proper subject of history. It runs the risk, in other words, of remaking Britain (itself a falsely homogeneous whole) as the centripetal origin of empire, rather than insisting on the interdependence, the 'uneven development', as Mrinalini Sinha calls it, of national/imperial formations in any given historical moment.[19] And – perhaps most significantly – it leaves untouched the conviction that 'national' history can be tracked through a linear chronological development (with empire added in) rather than as 'a set of relations that are constantly being made and remade, contested and refigured, [and] that nonetheless produce among their contemporaneous witnesses the conviction of historical *difference*'.[20] Anne McClintock, in *Imperial Leather*, for example, tends to see empire and nation precisely as *two*, and in a sequential relationship at that: for example, 'as domestic space became racialized', to quote from *Imperial Leather*, 'colonial space became domesticated'. Here not only is the binary reinstantiated, not only is the 'nation' represented as a privileged and cohesive subject, but empire follows nation in a fairly conventional linearity.[21] The fact that this relationship is a classically *imperial* concept of nation–empire relations should be our first clue to the limits of its critical usefulness (not to mention its historically specific constructedness). Rather than emerging as an unstable subject-in-the-making, the nation is in danger of functioning as a pretext for postmodern narrative in the same way it functioned as the foundation for post-Enlightenment historicism. Such a coincidence implicates them both, though differently, in the metanarrative(s) of

Western imperial discourse, where the nation has historically served as the sovereign ontological subject.[22]

Despite the veritable explosion of work in the field, few have been willing to embrace or even engage the notion of deracinated, mobile subjects posed by Paul Gilroy's *Black Atlantic* (a text that has been woefully under-engaged by British historians, at any rate). Britain – and England within it – tends to remain the fixed referent, the *a priori* body upon which empire is inscribed. Even when it is shown to be remade by colonialism and its subjects, 'the nation' often stands as the mirror to which imperial identities are reflected *back*.[23] This is perhaps because not many historians are willing to fully countenance the notion that the nation is not only *not* antecedent to empire, but that as both a symbolic and a material site the nation – as Judith Butler has argued for identity and Joan Scott for gender and experience – has no originary moment, no fixity outside of the various discourses of which it is itself an effect. And so, to paraphrase Anna Marie Smith, the fiction of a pre-existing England is left largely unchallenged.[24] Rarely is the starting point of the newly imperialized British history the 'precarious vulnerability' of imperial systems, as Ann Stoler has strenuously argued for the Dutch East Indies context.[25] Indeed, the very concept of Britain, and of England within it, seems to have a 'fantasy structure' that is more resilient and more resistant to its own displacement than almost any other 'national' imaginary today.[26] Even the naming of Britain as an imperial space – a manoeuvre which challenges the colonial *status quo* by implying that 'home' was not hermetically sealed from the colonies – potentially works to naturalize the distinctions between 'home' and 'empire', when it seems clear that the nineteenth century is one particular historical moment during which such discursive categories were being affirmed (if not invented) and circulated as evidence of 'modernity' and civilization in the first place. Perhaps this is a question of emphasis. In the case of McClintock, at any rate, I think the emphasis is not placed carefully enough.

One of the many queries that follow from such observations is this: if the fixity of nation is in fact being conserved in some new imperial studies projects, why has opposition to them been so fierce? I think this is a matter for discussion and debate. For my part, I believe that the terms upon which such critiques are articulated – both in print and in public – reveal a lot about the stakes involved. John MacKenzie, for example, takes Said and all those have who ever footnoted him to task because their work is not sufficiently historical. Here 'History' (capital H) is a convenient stick with which to berate the un- or underdisciplined and the great 'unwashed' – literary critics, yes, but feminists and postmodern sympathizers as well.[27] Rarely is the disciplinary power of history so blatantly on display – though other examples may be gleaned through a perusal of the pages of the book review section of the *American Historical Review* for the past decade, where the 'Real History' stick is routinely used to discipline authors of postmodern or cultural studies works, especially those interested in 'discourse' or textual analysis.[28] It might be argued that this is evidence that traditionalists are fighting a losing battle, since the book review is not a particularly effective or enduring site of protest.[29] And yet it also suggests that the re-fashioning of Britain's conceptual borders and, indeed, of British history's 'mission' itself, is by no means a *fait accompli*. Clearly, one of the purposes of a discipline is to discipline. The necessity of disciplinary action may seem especially urgent in an historical moment like this one when disciplinary boundaries are said to be dissolving – and their perceived dissolution is producing what Judith Allen aptly calls historically unprecedented 'spatial anxieties' as well.[30] The impulse to discipline may also be an indication of how invested some professionals in Britain and the United States are in the historicist (and, implicitly, empiricist) models which are at least partly responsible for their material and political hegemony, historically if not also today.[31] But an equally powerful purpose of 'disciplinary action' is also, surely, to enculturate – a project historically bound up with the mission to produce 'a certain sort of cosmopolitan liberal subject' among educated citizens and, especially, among university students. If disciplinarity is in fact a kind of cultural artefact, historians' attempts to patrol their own shifting boundaries may be read as an historically intelligible fear that literary studies and cultural studies more generally are in the process of stealing 'culture' itself.[32]

I want to be clear here that I am not unappreciative of Said's limits, oversights, or glosses, and that I find the materialist critique of *Orientalism* articulated by Mrinalini Sinha, Benita Parry and others to be helpful guides to a more politically engaged, rigorously historical approach to texts and contexts. Nor would I deny that the emergence of 'a new, multivocal historical discourse' may serve in part 'to hide stasis or even further segregation at the level of social relations'.[33] But I do think that recourse to arguments about the truest, 'most historically' historical method like those invoked by MacKenzie runs parallel to the desire for a return to the truest, purest nation – one not entirely untouched but certainly not centrally defined by empire, its institutional practices and its political legacies. 'Why the need for nation?' – a question posed, significantly, by the contemporary black British cultural critic, Kobena Mercer – is not, therefore, a rhetorical question.[34] Those who need it tend to require that their historical subjects be national at heart – not only fixed by borders but equally unfragmented and coherent, as stable as the rational post-Enlightenment subjects which postcolonial studies, feminist theory and postmodernism together have revealed as a kind of self-interested, if historically intelligible, modernist Western fantasy. Nostalgia for and attachment to the nation are thus connected with regret for the passage of that historical moment when the subjects of history were as yet uncontaminated by the critical apparatus set in motion by decolonization, the women's and other social movements and the gradual, if glacial, democratization of the Western academy over the past quarter of a century.[35] As historians of American women in the 1950s have argued, one historically engaged response to such nostalgia is to remind its advocates that, the power of her image notwithstanding, there never was a June Cleaver – or, rather, that she was a fiction, the invention of a cultural moment which has continued to displace and obscure the material conditions under which such iconography (like that of the nation) emerged.[36] This is not to say that we should disregard the historical 'fact' of nation, but rather to suggest that in our attempt to understand its historical significance, we need to pay more attention to the question of who needs it, who manufactures the 'need' for it, and whose interests it serves. In this sense, my initial interrogatory, 'Who needs the nation?' might profitably be imagined as a question of 'Who can afford to be sanguine about (or oblivious to) needing the nation?' – thus guaranteeing that social class, material dispossession and political disenfranchisement will inform historical narratives about imperial culture.[37] If, as Homi Bhabha claims, 'the Western metropole must confront its postcolonial history ... as an indigenous or native narrative internal to its national identity', then this kind of refiguration requires us to ask how – that is, through what kinds of practices – is it possible to practise 'British' history so that it does not continue to act as a colonial form of knowledge?[38]

The fact that arguments about the boundaries of the nation and the integrity of the citizen-subject are increasingly advanced by *social* historians who are simultaneously enmeshed in debates about the merits of *cultural* history/studies is surely significant. The coincidence of debates about empire with debates about the legitimacy of both culture as an object of historical enquiry and the tools used to unpack it (i.e. deconstruction) suggests that History, the Nation, and the category of the Social are being recuperated as endangered species in need of protection from a variety of 'others'. Susan Pederson constructed just such an identity of interests when she asserted that practitioners of history are, have been, and always will be interested in 'political outcomes' and as a result, the kinds of textual analyses performed by feminists and others in the field of gender and cultural history are not finally useful to Historians (capital H).[39] A similar kind of argument, offered as a lament in the context of an essay basically sympathetic to new narrative forms in history-writing, was articulated by Dorothy Ross, who claimed that cultural history's contributions are limited because it cannot address what for her represents historians' 'real' concern: change over time.[40] Nor is this debate limited to the West, as animated discussion of the way subaltern studies have been corrupted into 'bhadralok' and 'Bankim' studies in India testifies.[41] On offer in cultural history, of course, is the promise of new possibilities for 'the political narrative', through a set of analytical techniques that juxtaposes social history's commitment to history from the bottom up with a commitment to history from the side in, if you will – this is the turn to the ethnographic to which I alluded at the start, where the ethnographic allows for a vertical rather than an exclusively horizontal vision.[42] Projects concerned with public representation, material culture and historical memory – like Raphael Samuel's *Theatres of Memory*, James Vernon's *Politics and the People*, Judith Walkowitz's *City of Dreadful Delight*, Patrick Joyce's *Democratic Subjects* or Laura Mayhall's work on the Suffragette Fellowship – are good examples of how insights drawn from anthropology can give historical thickness to cultural forms and reshape our notion of the domains of the political, the social and the cultural – as well as challenge our convictions about their separability – in the process.[43] They also interrogate the convention that change over long periods of time is the 'real' interest of historians by emphasizing the local and the quotidian (two characteristics of ethnographic work). Despite the fact that it remains largely bounded by traditional conceptions of the nation, hardly touching on imperial culture at all, the success of this kind of scholarship is due in part to the fact that its authors do not insist that one historical technique must displace another, or even that one technique for recovering the past is more properly historical than the other. With the possible exception of Joyce, these authors do not operate as if the Whig interpretation of progressive evolution – and extinction – really obtained.[44] In fact, crucial to their approach is a critique of the very self-fulfilling, liberal narrative of progress that gave rise to, and continues to sustain, the idea of the autonomous, originary nation to begin with. In this sense, in the British context at least, such work threatens the sovereignty of a nation whose very sanctity is, historically and culturally, bound up with Victorian notions of progress, mission, and historical destiny – the very hallmarks of nineteenth-century imperial ideology itself – because it questions claims about the primacy of temporality that are at the heart of modern historical narrative practices.

As Elizabeth Ermarth has so persuasively argued, these claims appear to be so commonsensical that they continue to masquerade as 'a condition of nature' rather than as 'a convention and a collective act of faith' – not just among historians, but throughout Western culture as well.[45] Britain is not, therefore, an exceptional case – though, as a French observer has remarked, 'no country [is] more consistently bent upon differing from others' than Britain, and England within it.[46] The tenacity of the nation in debates about remaking British history signals an historically and culturally specific kind of attachment to the project of linear progress – even as it dramatizes how imperial traditions have shaped that investment and, finally, how tenuous the stability of 'national' culture really is. That these debates occur while a post-Thatcher Tory government tries to negotiate a place in the postcolonial European Union indicates how crucial it is to see imperial and Continental histories as equally implicated in the uneven development of 'British' history and society.[47] I hasten to add that the aim of such multiperspectival practices is not identical with liberal multicultural inclusion, which can tend to reinscribe identities in the process of politicizing them. Nor is its end 'a more cosmopolitan and sophisticated parochialism' – unless it is a less geographically fixed and, by implication, a less permanently realized version than the kind of parochialism to which we have become accustomed.[48] The kinds of new practices that are being resisted help to make this kind of imaginary possible by unmasking the fictionality of conventional historical narrative and exposing the fictions of an apparently insular 'British' culture – by insisting, in other words, that narratives of the nation (like all stories) are never 'found' in nature but are always construed by historians for implicit and explicit political purposes and in discrete historical circumstances.[49] And yet this remains the intriguing and unsettling paradox of the 'new' imperial history and studies: for the work of unmasking, however valuable, can and often still does leave the nation in pride of place, rather than staging it as precarious, unmoored and in the end, finally unrealizable.

It would be fair to say that the model of a performative, rather than a prescriptive, nation is one that has scarcely been explored in any national history.[50] Following Carlo Ginzburg and Emmanuel Le Roy Ladurie in the 1970s, there seemed to be a moment when some European historians were willing to recognize the historical precariousness of nation-state formation. But a monograph like Eugen Weber's *Peasants into Frenchmen* (1976) looks now like a kind of one-off production, rather than the beginning of a revisionist trend which took the artificiality of national categories and the coercive power of their normalizing regimes as its point of departure. In the English case, Philip Corrigan and Derek Sayer's *The Great Arch* (1985) – subtitled, significantly, 'English state formation as *cultural* revolution' – posited the state itself as a cultural effect in a series of essays which, in retrospect, look not just way ahead of their time, but like a model still waiting to be fully utilized, at least by British historians.[51] The combination of historical analysis and politically engaged scepticism about the naturalness of the modern state which their book enacts represents a model to which we might profitably return, not least because of its emphasis on the state, and with it the nation, as something *always* in the process of *becoming*. Or, to use language that draws as much on Bernard S. Cohn as it does on Greg Dening and Judith Butler, they managed to stage the state as an historically pliable ideal always being performed through repetitive and ritualized acts, but never fully achieved.[52] Here I want to note that historians of the early modern and early Victorian periods have been more interested in exploring how the nation was as such 'forged', a phenomenon that suggests how much work is yet to be done to subject the later nineteenth-century state to scrutiny in order to understand that it too was by no means a *fait accompli* but was also always in the making.[53] Yet it is equally important to underscore that the burden of representing fragmentation, diaspora and community-making as operations of nation-building would seem to have fallen disproportionately on ex-colonies and postcolonial nations, the United States included. Significantly, when national history is challenged there, it tends to be by those interested in the anti-citizens of modernity – slaves, African-American freed men and women, white suffragists, Native Americans and, most recently, gays and lesbians – many of whom are said to inhabit, *à la* George Chauncey's *Gay New York*, a kind of anti-national subculture, *even* (and perhaps especially) when they aspire to national belonging.[54] Not incidentally, this unequal burden is one of the lingering effects of the kind of asymmetry that is foundational to colonialism and its cultural productions. At the same time, concern about the disciplinary regimes imposed by history is articulated rarely enough, even as interdisciplinary work abounds and threatens, in quite concrete and salutary ways, to remake epistemologies at the heart of the liberal tradition – especially where 'discipline' works in opposition to the 'playfulness' of subjects when they end up exceeding conventional boundaries. Clearly the politics of who or what is the subject of a 'national' history begs the question of how such a subject becomes nationalized, as well as what kind of disciplinary action such a process requires.

I am not sure that I would go as far as Catherine Hall does in calling for Britain to be conceptualized as a 'post-nation' – one that is not ethnically pure but 'inclusive and culturally diverse'.[55] This is not because there is something inherently destabilizing to civil society in going 'beyond the nation', as Partha Chatterjee fears,[56] but rather because I am keenly aware of the persistent operations of 'the citizenship machinery' deployed by the contemporary transnational state (as I'm sure Hall is as well). Nor would I like to suggest that critics of national history are always or completely impervious to the romance of nation-building that seems to haunt all of the modern disciplines. Historians of women, of blacks and of other 'others' have often sought inclusion for their subjects in the narrative of the nation-state – trying to make them, in W. E. B. Dubois's wonderfully ambivalent phrase, 'the ward[s] of the nation'.[57] Even Ruth Behar and Deborah Gordon, the feminist anthropologists who edited *Women Writing Culture*, ground their attempt to remake the discipline in the hope that the new feminist anthropology will have 'no exiles'.[58] It is admittedly possible to read their call as an attempt to frustrate traditional structures of the nation-state – to argue that no one should have to be an exile in the sense of being prohibited from a place.[59] And yet even this generous reading tends to obscure the question of why critics of the regulatory power of their own discipline seek to reformulate it as some kind of idealized nation – that is, one with no exiles. Who writes – who even sees – the histories of subjects exiled from the 'national body', those refugees (deliberate or otherwise) from national history and its disciplinary regimes, especially before the twentieth century?[60] Feminist historiography, which works at the boundaries of a variety of disciplines, as well as at the intersection of the academy and the community, should be one site for this kind of interrogatory work. But as Ien Ang has observed, feminism, no less than the discipline of history, 'must stop conceiving itself as a nation, a "natural" political destination for all women, no matter how multicultural'.[61] Indeed, the rhetorics of destination, of arrival and of home itself have provided 'sentimental story lines' not just for women's national imaginaries, but for nation-states operating via transnational capital as well.[62] What we need is conceptual work that turns 'on a pivot' rather than on the axis of inside/outside – an image which suggests not just a balancing act but the kind of counter-clockwise historicizing manoeuvre such 'subjects' require in an era when national histories, unlike the pivot, seem unwilling or unable to budge.[63]

Why social history and cultural studies must necessarily do battle is, frankly, a puzzlement – except that this is an age when resources are scarce, when all histories can evidently lay claim with equal success to the notion that they are embattled, and when the Social Darwinist presumptions of the social science disciplines still apparently have some appeal for those who would have the strong triumph over the weak. Read in this context, Sherry Ortner's piece on 'Theory in Anthropology since the 1960s' – where she traces the clearly national divisions between American attachment to explanatory frameworks that privilege culture, versus British insistence on 'society' as the crucial analytical component – suggests that the contest for

British history may well be about who should be permitted to write it, and from what ideological perspectives.[64] Clearly this is an age-old battle with historically specific meanings which tell us as much about the political economy of the Western academy as they do about the crisis of Britishness, culturally speaking. The brouhaha in Britain over Roger Louis (an American) being chosen as the editor of the new *Oxford History of the British Empire* is one more indication of how easily these (again highly naturalized) nationalistic lines can be drawn in the sand.[65] And yet if we revisit Stuart Hall's equally compelling account of the rise of cultural studies paradigms in Britain, we see that the tensions between culture and the social as analytical premises are not merely lineaments of national difference, but have long and fraught legacies not just inside modern disciplinary practices like history-writing or anthropology, but at the heart of interdisciplinary products as well.[66] The fact that the category of 'culture' has traditionally been used to legitimate imagined communities either on the move or outside the West (as a substitute for nation-ness, if you will) may in part explain why metropolitan historians are loathe to see that category applied to the centre. In many ways, using culture rather than the nation or even the social as a primary historical tool means exoticizing the grand narratives of British history and defamiliarizing the naturalness of its ideological corollary, imperial greatness. Indeed, given its historic relationship to colonialism,[67] the analytic of culture may threaten to de-naturalize, if not to corrupt, the apparent coherence and purity of nation-ness of an always already fragmented and multicultural entity like the 'United Kingdom'– though cultural studies of the Celtic fringe in opposition to Englishness have not proved much more successful than colonial histories in challenging the presumptive originality of 'Britain' and, with it, 'England' as the heart of the empire, except perhaps to revive the 'four nations' impulse in domestic British historiography. This is an exception which is often as frustrating as it is interesting, in so far as it represents more of an additive than a reconstitutive position with regard to the construction of ideas about nation and national cultures.[68]

That social history is characterized as the strong, and cultural history as the weak 'historical' approach, bears some scrutiny. And the fact that the struggle between the social and the cultural is being played out on the terrain of empire should command our attention no less actively than the flowering of production on empire and imperial culture itself. Although the struggle is often framed as a Manichean battle between the empiricists and the deconstructionists – those who believe in coherent nations, subjects, and histories versus those who don't – this is a red herring designed to throw us off the scent of other compelling issues. Chief among these is the fact that modern history-writing (and not just in the West) has historically been a 'narrative contract' with the territorially bounded nation-state.[69] Prising the nation from that contract is nothing less than a struggle to reorganize and reconstitute the spatial bases of power.[70] Few can escape the struggle over geography, and British history in an age of postcoloniality is no exception. If narratives of geography are at stake in narratives of history[71] then undoing the narrative contract may mean displacing nation-states like Britain from centre stage. It may call for an analytic frame which recognizes that 'the imperium at the heart of the nation-state' was 'not an entity *sui generis*'.[72] It may even require a cultural map which is 'all border' as well – especially since the nation itself has historically served as 'the ideological alibi of the territorial state'.[73] This work involves more than just challenging the parameters of 'British' history or studies. It means unmasking the complicity of history-writing in patrolling the borders of national identity as well.

Casting the project of an unstable 'British' history may well end up letting the nation in through the back door, though such is not my intention. Such a result may in the last analysis be a testimony to how difficult it is to escape the grasp of national investigative frameworks even when one attempts a highly self-conscious and, hopefully, principled critique of the allure of nation-ness for 'British' historians. Admittedly in this chapter I offer more of a diagnosis than a prognosis, in part because I think that the question 'Who needs the nation?' still rings hollow for many. The extent to which we will succeed in displacing the nation from centre stage depends in the end on our willingness to take seriously the ramifications of the claim that a nation is never fully realized, but always in-the-making – and to interrogate the ways in which our own narrative strategies may help fetishize one of history's most common explanatory frameworks, if not its most seductive investigative modality. This is, hopefully, a practice worth imagining: for it suggests that one does not have to give up on history in order to interrogate the narrative strategies of its practitioners or to fight for (and about) its unstable meanings.

Notes

From the *Journal of Historical Sociology*, 10:3 (September 1997), 227–48. This chapter owes much to Bernard S. Cohn, for whose generosity of mind and spirit I have long been grateful. A number of friendly critics – including Nadja Durbach, Rob Gregg, David Goodman. Ian Fletcher. Madhavi Kale, Dane Kennedy, Philippa Levine, Laura Mayhall, Maura O'Connor, Fiona Paisley, Doug Peers, Minnie Sinha, Susan Thorne and Angela Woollacott – have helped to strengthen my arguments, for which I of course bear the final responsibility. Herman Bennett's long-term investment in this piece has made all the difference. I am equally indebted to Peter Marshall's energetic engagements. And finally, I greatly appreciate the feedback I received at presentations for the Australian Historical Association (Melbourne, 1996) and the Workshop on State Formation in Comparative Historical and Cultural Perspectives (Oxford, 1997), especially from Ann Curthoys, Philip Corrigan, Marilyn Lake, Vinay Lai, Derek Sayer, and Sudipta Sen.

1   Perry Anderson, 'Origins of the Present Crisis' (1964) and 'Components of the National Culture' (1967), reprinted in *English Questions* (London: Verso, 1992), pp. 15–47, 48–104.

2   Irfan Habib, 'Capitalism in History', *Social Scientist*, 23:7–9 (July–September 1995), 15–31.

3   Reprinted Chapel Hill NC: University of North Carolina Press (1994). See especially Colin Palmer's introduction, where he unearths the critical response to the manuscript before it was accepted for publication, followed by its review history (pp. xi–xxii). Perry Anderson does not cite Williams, though his argument in 'Origins of the Present Crisis' echoes much of what Williams had meticulously advanced in *Capitalism and Slavery*. Thomas C. Holt's *The Problem of Freedom: Race, Labor and Politics in Jamaica and Britain, 1832–1938* (Baltimore MD: Johns Hopkins University Press, 1992) is also relevant.

4   Gauri Viswanathan, 'Raymond Williams and British Colonialism', *Yale Journal of Criticism*,

4:2 (1991), 47–67; E. P. Thompson, *Alien Homage: Edward Thompson and Rabindranath Tagore* (Delhi: Oxford University Press, 1993); Catherine Hall, *White, Male and Middle Class: Explorations in Feminism and History* (London: Routledge, 1992); Harish Trivedi, *Colonial Transactions: English Literature and India* (New York: St Martin's Press, 1995). See also Robert Gregg and Madhavi Kale, 'The Empire and Mr Thompson: the Making of Indian Princes and the English Working Class', *Economic and Political Weekly* (forthcoming).

5 In this sense it was petty-bourgeois as well, though Anderson does not take this up explicitly. See his 'Components of the national culture', in *English Questions*, pp. 52, 103. For an instructive colonial take on the question of 'national' culture which was contemporaneous with Anderson's (but to which he does not allude, even in the 1990s reprint) see Frantz Fanon, 'On National Culture', in *The Wretched of the Earth* (Penguin edition, Harmondsworth, 1967). This chapter is also reprinted in Patrick Williams and Laura Chrisman (eds), *Colonial Discourse and Post-colonial Theory: A Reader* (New York: Columbia University Press, 1994), pp. 3–52. For evidence of the continued search for explanations about why Britain failed to produce a 'native' sociology see Jose Harris, 'Platonism, positivism and progressivism: aspects of British sociological thought in the early twentieth century', in Eugenio F. Biagini (ed.), *Citizenship and Community: Liberals, Radicals and Collective Identities in the British Isles, 1865–1931* (Cambridge: Cambridge University Press, 1996), pp. 343–60.

6 For a response to the literary turn which engages this phenomenon see Dane Kennedy, 'Imperial History and Postcolonial Theory', *Journal of Imperial and Commonwealth History*, 24:3 (September 1996), 345–63. The fact that the linguistic turn and the ethnographic turn are related is often overlooked: for a discussion of their historical connections see Sara Maza, 'Stories in History: Cultural Narratives in recent Works in European history', *American Historical Review*, 101:5 (December 1996), 1497 ff.

7 Edward Said, *Culture and Imperialism* (New York: Vintage Books, 1993).

8 Peter Hulme, 'Subversive Archipelagoes: Colonial Discourse and the Break-up of Continental Theory', *Dispositio*, 14:36–8 (1989), 1–23.

9 John M. MacKenzie's editorship of the Studies in Imperialism series is responsible for much of the wealth of historical material now available on the impact of empire on domestic British culture. See, for example, his *Propaganda and Empire: The Manipulation of British Public Opinion, 1880–1960* (Manchester: Manchester University Press, 1984) and (ed.) *Imperialism and Popular Culture* (Manchester: Manchester University Press, 1986). Other relevant monographs include Jenny Sharpe, *Allegories of Empire: The Figure of Woman in the Colonial Text* (Minneapolis MN: University of Minnesota Press, 1993); Firdous Azim, *The Colonial Rise of the Novel* (London: Routledge, 1993); Hall, *White, Male and Middle Class*; Vron Ware, *Beyond the Pale: White Women, Racism and History* (London: Verso, 1992); Antoinette Burton, *Burdens of History: British Feminists, Indian Women, and Imperial Culture, 1865–1915* (Chapel Hill NC: University of North Carolina Press, 1994); Annie E. Coombes, *Reinventing Africa: Museums, Imperial Culture, and Popular Imagination* (New Haven CT: Yale University Press, 1994); Mrinalini Sinha, *Colonial Masculinity: The 'Manly Englishman' and the 'Effeminate Bengali' in the late Nineteenth Century* (Manchester: Manchester University Press, 1995); Anne McClintock, *Imperial Leather: Race, Gender and Sexuality in the Colonial Contest* (New York: Routledge, 1995).

10 Gretchen Gerzina, *Black London: Life before Emancipation* (New Brunswick NJ: Rutgers University Press, 1995); Barnor Hesse, 'Black to Front and Black again', in Michael Keith and Steve Pile (eds), *Place and the Politics of Identity* (London: Routledge, 1993), pp. 162–82; Peter Fryer, *Staying Power: The History of Black People in Britain* (London: Pluto Press, 1987); Rozina Visram, *Ayahs, Lascars and Princes* (London: Pluto Press, 1986); Colin Holmes, *John Bull's Island: Immigration and British Society, 1871–1971* (London: Macmillan, 1988); Antoinette Burton, *At the Heart of the Empire: Indians and the Colonial Encounter in late Victorian Britain* (Berkeley CA: University of California Press, 1997).

11 John M. MacKenzie, *Orientalism: History, Theory and the Arts* (Manchester: Manchester University Press, 1995); P. J. Marshall, 'No fatal Impact? The Elusive History of Imperial

Britain', *Times Literary Supplement*, 12 March 1993, pp. 8–10.

12 Benita Parry, 'Overlapping Territories and Intertwined Histories: Edward Said's Postcolonial Cosmopolitanism', in Michael Sprinker (ed.), *Edward Said: A Critical Reader* (Oxford: Blackwell, 1993), pp. 19–47.

13 Paul Gilroy, *The Black Atlantic: Modernity and Double Consciousness* (Cambridge MA: Harvard University Press, 1993).

14 Olaudah Equiano was a slave from Benin who purchased his freedom in 1766 and wrote his life story (*The Interesting Narrative of the Life of Olaudah Equiano*) in 1789. Mary Seacole was a Jamaican nurse who served in the Crimean War and wrote an account of it (*The Wonderful Adventures of Mrs Seacole in many Lands*). See Paul Edwards and David Dabydeen (eds), *Black Writers in Britain, 1760–1890* (Edinburgh: Edinburgh University Press, 1991). For newspaper coverage of the Major government's response to their inclusion in British history texts see 'The "Betrayal" of Britain's History', *Daily Telegraph*, 19 September 1995; 'Heroic Virtues' and 'History fit for (Politically Correct) Heroes', *Sunday Telegraph*, 24 September 1995. I am grateful to Audrey Matkins for these references.

15 See Bill Schwarz (ed.), *The Expansion of England: Race, Ethnicity and Cultural History* (New York: Routledge, 1996); Catherine Hall, 'Histories, Empires and the Post-colonial Moment', in Ian Chambers and Lidia Curti (eds), *The Post-colonial Question: Common Skies, Divided Horizons* (New York: Routledge, 1996), pp. 65–77; P. J. Marshall, *The Cambridge Illustrated History of the British Empire* (Cambridge: Cambridge University Press, 1996). Professor Marshall agrees with two of the *O.E.D.*'s definitions of 'constitutive' as (1) 'having the power of constituting; constructive' and (2) 'that which goes to make up; constituent, component' but cannot agree with its third: 'that which makes a thing what it is'. (Private correspondence, 15 September 1996.)

16 MacKenzie, *Propaganda and Empire*.

17 I am grateful to Catherine Hall for pressing this point in conversation. See also her *White, Male and Middle Class*, p. 1, and her 'Rethinking Imperial Histories: the Reform Act of 1867', *New Left Review*, 208 (1994), pp. 3–29.

18 Ruth H. Lindborg, 'The "Asiatic" and the Boundaries of Victorian Englishness', *Victorian Studies* (spring 1994), pp. 381–404.

19 Sinha, *Colonial Masculinity*. For one example of how this false homogenization works to obscure the role of the Celtic fringe in empire see Dipesh Chakrabarty's discussion of how crucial Dundee was in the history of the jute mills of Calcutta (*Rethinking Working Class History*, Princeton NJ: Princeton University Press, 1989, ch. 2).

20 Kathleen Wilson, 'Citizenship, Empire and Modernity in the English Provinces, *c.* 1720–90', *Eighteenth Century Studies*, 29:1, 69–96.

21 I am aided in these observations by Prasenjit Duara's *Rescuing History from the Nation: Questioning Narratives of Modern China* (Chicago IL: University of Chicago Press, 1995).

22 See Elizabeth D. Ermarth, *Sequel to History: Postmodernism and the Crisis of Representational Time* (Princeton NJ: Princeton University Press, 1992), pp. 18, 21. She is not concerned with the imperial contexts of modern Western discourses but her characterizations of historical convention are extremely useful nonetheless.

23 I am aided in this observation by Kim F. Hall's reading of Richard Hakluyt in *Things of Darkness: Economies of Race and Gender in early modern England* (Ithaca NY: Cornell University Press, 1995), p. 48.

24 Anna Marie Smith, *New Right Discourse on Race and Sexuality* (Cambridge: Cambridge University Press, 1995); Judith Butler, 'Contingent Foundations', in Judith Butler and Joan Scott (eds), *Feminists theorize the Political* (New York: Routledge, 1992), pp. 3–21; Joan Scott, 'Experience', in *ibid.*, pp. 22–40.

25 Ann Stoler, *Race and the Education of Desire* (Durham NC: Duke University Press, 1995); Ann Stoler and Frederick Cooper, 'Introduction. Tensions of Empire: Colonial Control and Visions of Rule', *American Ethnologist*, 16 (1989), 609–21.

26 Renata Salecl, 'The Fantasy Structure of Nationalist Discourse', *Praxis International*, 13:3 (October 1993), 213–23.

27 MacKenzie, *Orientalism*.

28 See, for example, Harold Perkin's review of Jose Harris's *Private Lives, Public Spirit: A Social History of Britain, 1870–1914* in the *American Historical Review*, 100:1 (February 1995), p. 164, and Bruce Kinzer's review of James Vernon's *Politics and the People: A Study in English Political Culture*, c. *1815–67* in *American Historical Review*, 100:3 (June 1995), 900.

29 Gilroy's *Black Atlantic* has been held up in a review essay by Frederick Cooper as an example of a 'transcontinental' study that requires proper historical work to fill in its 'gaps'. See Cooper, 'Race, Ideology, and the Perils of Comparative History', *American Historical Review*, 101:4 (October 1996), 1129.

30 Judith A. Allen, 'Feminist Critiques of Western Knowledges: Spatial Anxieties in a Provisional Phase?' in K. K. Ruthven, *Beyond the Disciplines: The New Humanities*, Canberra ACT: Papers from the Australian Academy of the Humanities Symposium (1992), pp. 57–77.

31 Ermarth, *Sequel to History*.

32 Arjun Appadurai, 'Diversity and Disciplinarity as Cultural Artefacts', in Cary Nelson and Dilip Parameshwar Gaonkar (eds), *Disciplinarity and Dissent in Cultural Studies* (New York: Routledge, 1996), pp. 23–36.

33 Kate Brown, 'The Eclipse of History: Japanese America and a Treasure Chest of Forgetting', *Public Culture*, 9 (1996), 69–92.

34 Kobena Mercer, *Welcome to the Jungle: New Positions in Black Cultural Studies* (New York: Routledge, 1994).

35 Joyce Appleby, Lynn Hunt and Margaret Jacobs, *Telling the Truth about History* (New York: Norton, 1994).

36 The post-war television mom famous in the United States. Joanne Meyerowitz (ed.), *Not June Cleaver: Women and Gender in Post-war America* (Philadelphia PA: Temple University Press, 1994).

37 Although the exiles I have in mind in this particular formulation (and in this chapter in general) are people of colour and ex-colonial migrants in Britain, it must also be said that working-class men and women have a differently ambiguous though equally painful relationship to the nation and its ideological apparatus, the State. As Carolyn Steedman writes so poignantly in her autobiography *Landscape for a good Woman* (New Brunswick NJ: Rutgers University Press, 1987), 'I think I would be a very different person now if orange juice and milk and dinners at school hadn't told me, in a covert way, that I had a right to exist, was worth something' (p. 122). I am grateful to Nadja Durbach for this citation and for how it compelled me to refigure the question of 'who needs the nation?'.

38 Homi K. Bhabha, 'Life at the Border: Hybrid Identities of the Present', *New Perspectives Quarterly*, 14:1 (winter 1997), 30–1; Bernard S. Cohn, *Colonialism and its Forms of Knowledge: The British in India* (Princeton NJ: Princeton University Press, 1996).

39 Susan Pederson, keynote address on gender and imperial history at the Anglo-American conference, London, summer 1995.

40 Dorothy Ross, 'Grand Narrative in American Historical Writing', *American Historical Review*, 110:3 (June 1995), pp. 651–77.

41 Ramachandra Guha, 'Subaltern and Bhadralok Studies', *Economic and Political Weekly*, 19 August 1995, pp. 2057–8; Anita Chakravarty, 'Writing History', *ibid.*, 23 December 1995, p. 3320; Ramachandra Guha, 'Beyond Bhadralok and Bankim Studies', *ibid.*, 24 February 1996, pp. 495–6.

42 I am aided in this conceptualization by Greg Dening, 'P905.A512 x 100: an Ethnographic Essay', *American Historical Review*, 100:3 (June 1995), 864.

43 Raphael Samuel, *Theatres of Memory* (London: Verso, 1994); James Vernon, *Politics and the People: A Study in English Political Culture*, c. *1815–67* (Cambridge: Cambridge University Press, 1993); Judith Walkowitz, *City of Dreadful Delight: Narratives of Sexual Danger in late Victorian London* (Chicago IL: University of Chicago Press, 1992); Patrick Joyce, *Democratic Subjects: The Self and the Social in the Nineteenth Century* (Cambridge: Cambridge University Press, 1994); Laura Mayhall, 'Creating the "Suffragette Spirit": British Feminism and the Historical Imagination', *Women's History Review*, 4:3 (1995), 319–44.

44 Geoff Eley and Keith Nield, 'Starting over: the Present, the Postmodern and the Moment of Social History', *Social History*, 20 (1995), 355–64.

45 Ermarth, *Sequel to History*.

46 David Lowenthal, 'Identity, Heritage and History', in John R. Gillis (ed.), *Commemorations: The Politics of National Identity* (Princeton NJ: Princeton University Press, 1994), pp. 41–73.

47 I am grateful to Maura O'Connor for urging me to appreciate this point and for sharing her paper 'Imagining National Boundaries in the Nineteenth Century: English Travellers, Diplomats and the Making of Italy', presented at the North American Conference of British Studies, Chicago IL, 1996,

48 David Goodman, *Gold Seeking: Victoria and California in the 1850s* (Sydney: Allen & Unwin, 1994).

49 Ann Curthoys and John Docker, 'Is History Fiction?' *UTS Review: Cultural Studies and new Writing*, 2:2 (May 1996), 12–37.

50 Herman Bennett's *Strategic Conjugality: Race, Ethnicity and Creolization in the Making of Colonial Mexico's African Diaspora*, which posits the performative model, is a particularly promising exception.

51 Philip Corrigan and Derek Sayer, *The Great Arch: English State Formation as Cultural Revolution* (Oxford: Blackwell, 1985).

52 Greg Dening, 'The Theatricality of History Making and the Paradoxes of Acting' in *Performances* (Chicago IL: University of Chicago Press, 1996), pp. 103–27; Judith Butler, *Gender Trouble* (New York: Routledge, 1990); Bernard S. Cohn, 'Representing Authority in Victorian India', in Eric Hobsbawm and Terence Ranger (eds), *The Invention of Tradition* (Cambridge: Cambridge University Press, 1983), pp. 165–209.

53 C. A. Bayly, *Imperial Meridian: The British Empire and the World, 1780–1830* (London: Longman, 1989); Linda Colley, *Britons: Forging the Nation, 1707–1837* (New Haven CT: Yale University Press, 1992). This is especially challenging, I think, in the light of how powerful late Victorian rhetoric about the long history of the English nation state was in the wake of more recent Italian and German unification, not to mention the challenges posed by Irish Home Rule and the Indian National Congress.

54 George Chauncey, *Gay New York: Gender, Urban Culture, and the Making of the Gay Male World, 1880–1940* (New York: Basic Books, 1994).

55 Catherine Hall, 'Histories, Empires and the Post-colonial Moment', in Iain Chambers and Lidia Curti (eds), *The Post-colonial Question: Common Skies, Divided Horizons* (London: Routledge, 1996), pp. 65–77. See also M. Jacqui Alexander and Chandra Talpade Mohanty (eds), *Feminist Genealogies, Colonial Legacies, Democratic Futures* (New York: Routledge, 1997).

56 Partha Chatterjee, 'Beyond the Nation? Or within?' *Economic and Political Weekly*, 4–11 January 1997, 30–4.

57 W. E. B. Dubois, *The Souls of Black Folk* (Penguin edition, New York, 1989).

58 Ruth Behar and Deborah Gordon (eds), *Women writing Culture* (Berkeley CA: University of California Press, 1995).

59 Thanks to Darlene Hantzis for suggesting this possibility to me.

60 Madhavi Kale, 'Projecting Identities: Empire and Iindentured Labor Migration from India to Trinidad and British Guiana, 1836–85', in Peter van der Veer (ed.), *Nation and Migration: The Politics of Space in the South Asian Diaspora* (Philadelphia PA: University of Pennsylvania Press, 1994), pp. 73–92; Lisa H. Malki, *Purity and Exile: Violence, Memory and National Cosmology among the Hutu Refugees in Tanzania* (Chicago IL: University of Chicago Press, 1995); Smadar Lavie and Ted Swedenburg (eds), *Displacement, Diaspora and Geographies of Identity* (Durham NC: Duke University Press, 1996).

61 Ien Ang, 'I'm a feminist, but … "Other" Women and Postnational Feminism', in Barbara Caine and Rosemary Pringle (eds), *Transitions: New Australian Feminisms* (New York: St Martin's Press, 1995), pp. 57–73; Adele Murdolo, 'Warmth and Unity? Historicizing Racism in the Australian Women's Movement', *Feminist Review*, 52 (spring 1996), 69–86.

62 Rosemary Marangoly George, *The Politics of Home: Postcolonial Relocations and Twentieth*

Century Fiction (Cambridge: Cambridge University Press, 1996); Aiwha Ong, 'On the Edges of Empires: Flexible Citizenship among Chinese in Diaspora', *Positions*, 1:3 (1993), 745–78; Vincente Rafael, 'Overseas Filipinos and other ghostly Presences in the Nation-state', paper presented at the Seminar for Global Studies in Culture Power and History, Johns Hopkins University, Baltimore MD, October 1996.

63 Earl Lewis, 'Turning on a Pivot: Writing African-Americans into a History of overlapping Diasporas', *American Historical Review*, 100:3 (June 1995), 765–87.

64 Sherry B. Ortner, 'Theory in anthropology since the 1960s', in Nicholas B. Dirks, Geoff Eley and Sherry B. Ortner (eds), *Culture, Power, History: A Reader in Contemporary Social Theory* (Princeton NJ: Princeton University Press, 1984), pp. 372–411.

65 Mrinalini Sinha, '*Historia nervosa*, or, Who's afraid of Colonial-discourse Analysis?' *Journal of Victorian Culture*, 2:1 (1997).

66 Stuart Hall, 'Cultural Studies: two Paradigms', in Nicholas B. Dirks, Geoff Eley and Sherry B. Ortner (eds), *Culture, Power, History: A Reader in Contemporary Social Theory* (Princeton NJ: Princeton University Press, 1980), pp. 520–38.

67 Nicholas B. Dirks, *Colonialism and Culture* (Ann Arbor MI: University of Michigan Press, 1992).

68 Hugh Kearney, *The British Isles: A History of Four Nations* (Cambridge: Cambridge University Press, 1989); Keith Jeffery (ed.), *An Irish Empire? Aspects of Ireland and the British Empire* (Manchester: Manchester University Press, 1996).

69 Sudipta Kaviraj, 'The Imaginary Institution of India', in Partha Chatterjee and Gyanendra Pandey (eds), *Subaltern Studies VII: Writings on South Asian History and Society* (Delhi: Oxford University Press, 1993), pp. 1–39.

70 David Harvey, *The Condition of Postmodernity* (Oxford: Blackwell, 1990).

71 Robert Carr, 'Crossing the First World/Third World Divide: Testimonial, transnational Feminisms, and the Postmodern Condition', in Inderpal Grewal and Caren Caplan (eds), *Scattered Hegemonies: Postmodernity and Transnational Feminist Practices* (Minneapolis MN: University of Minnesota Press, 1994), pp. 153–72.

72 Carol Breckenridge, 'The Aesthetics and Politics of Colonial Collecting: India at World Fairs', *Comparative Studies in Society and History*, 31 (spring 1989), 195–216.

73 Carole Boyce Davies, *Black Women, Writing and Identity: Migratory Subjects* (London: Routledge, 1994); Arjun Appadurai, 'The Heart of Whiteness', *Callaloo*, 16:4 (1993), 796–807.

PART II

The empire and its others
'at home'

7

Citizenship, empire, and modernity in the English provinces, c. 1720–90

KATHLEEN WILSON

Now, by our country, considered in itself, we shall (I conceive) most rationally understand, not barely a certain tract of land, which makes up the external appearance of it; but chiefly, the collective body of its inhabitants, with their public and joint interests. (Rev. George Fothergill, 1758)

In faith, my friend, the present time is rather *comique* – Ireland almost in as true a state of rebellion as America – Admirals quarrelling in the West-Indies – and at home Admirals that do not chuse to fight – The British Empire mouldering away in the West, annihilated in the North – ... and England fast asleep ... – for my part, it's nothing to me, as I am only a lodger, and hardly that. (Ignatius Sancho, 1779)

Historicism contents itself with establishing a causal connection between various moments in history. But no fact that is a cause is for that very reason historical. It became historical posthumously, as it were, through events that may be separated from it by thousands of years. A historian who takes this as his point of departure stops telling the sequence of events like the bead of a rosary. Instead, he grasps the constellation which his own era has formed with a definite earlier one. (Walter Benjamin, 1940)[1]

Modernity and its discontents

The debates over 'modernity' that have reverberated in European cultural theory and history since World War II have not unduly troubled most historians of eighteenth-century Britain. Suspicious of any species of 'Whig' (that is, linear) history and confident that Continental theorizing bears little relevance to their enquiries, British historians have been content to fight less epochal battles over the appropriate characterization of their period. Hence whether England was an 'aristocratic' or 'bourgeois' society, an *'ancien régime'* or a 'commercialized' polity, marked predominantly by paternalism and deference or restiveness and resistance are the issues that have traditionally occupied many historians' attention.[2] Although such dichotomous readings have often been more geared towards advancing academic careers than productive debate, the status of eighteenth-century England as a progenitor of modernity is rarely taken seriously within the disciplinary wooden walls of Hanoverian history.

Certainly there is cause for scepticism about the historical returns of investigations into the location and meanings of modernity, not least since the term is twisted and turned to serve a variety of scholarly constituencies. Among more positivistic social scientists and historians, for example, modernity has been conceived as the story of 'modernization' – that is, of those objective, ineluctably unfolding processes that are believed to have generated the structures and texture of 'modern' life: urbanization, industrialization, democratization; bureaucracy, scienticism and technology.[3] Although heuristically useful in sketching in some fundamental shifts in Western culture, the 'modernity as modernization' perspective is a conceptual dead end for historians less interested in structural determinacy than in the specific meanings, ambiguities, and significance of a period's configurations. For this latter group, other historical and cultural critics have engaged more fruitfully with the notion of modernity as an unfolding set of relationships – cognitive, social, and intellectual as well as economic and technological – which, however valued or construed, are seen as producing the modern self and its expectations of perfection or progress. For Marshall Berman and Jürgen Habermas, to name but two, the promise of a modernity begun by the eighteenth-century 'Enlightenment project', embellished by nineteenth-century thinkers from Hegel and Baudelaire to Marx and Stendhal and betrayed by the savagery and genocide of the mid-twentieth century, has yet to be fulfilled.[4] Probably more fecund still has been the re-theorizing of modernity among the so-called 'postmodernists' – a disparate group of critics whose perceived unity rests on their intellectual debts to various French post-structuralisms as well as their shared belief in the discontinuity of the late twentieth-century present with the 'modern' period that came before it – who have located in the discursive and institutional matrices of power and resistance shaping late eighteenth-century European societies the genealogies of their own ages' discontents and transfigurations.[5] Their enquiries have replaced the stable and knowing 'bourgeois' subject beloved of the master narratives of Western modernity with the fractured, decentred, and destabilized subject of postmodernism, whose agency is both invented and undermined by the exterior and internalized forms of power that produced her.

Clearly, the investigation and analysis of 'modernity' and its historical operations have born rich scholarly fruit as well as some conceptual vacuities, and it is a rash (not to say naive) historian who would dismiss all efforts to interrogate and theorize modernity as ahistorical, dangerous, or irrelevant. For modernity need not be seen as *one* particular moment, whose 'origins' and characteristics can be identified with certainty and mapped on to a specific temporality between the sixteenth and twentieth centuries. Rather, given that each of these periods is modern and even 'postmodern' in relation to those before it, 'modernity', the latest point on the continuum of historical change, should be understood as an emphatically historical condition that can only be recovered, in Walter Benjamin's resonant phrase, in 'time filled by the presence of the now'.[6] Modernity in this sense is not one moment or age, but a set of relations that are constantly being made and unmade, contested and reconfigured, that nonetheless produce among their contemporaneous witnesses the conviction of historical *difference*. Such a conceptualization opens up whole new grounds for theorizing and understanding our histories without denying the specificity of a period's configurations or reducing the eighteenth century to the status of the great primordial swamp of a more 'modern' world.

This chapter will propose that such a reading of modernity can greatly enrich our understanding of English culture and politics in the Georgian decades. It is indebted to a number of recent studies that have challenged dominant narratives and periodizations of Western history by stressing the complexity, heterogeneity, and hybridity of modernity at the moments of its various historical articulations. From this perspective, modernity refers to the cultural practices and represent-ations that produced certain kinds of subjects and objects of knowledge, upheld widely shared notions of space and time, or facilitated the formation of cultural identities that resulted in pluralities and contradictions as well as unities and coherences. As various scholars have argued, the discontinuous and plural nature of the eighteenth-century experience – marked as closely by slavery as liberty, racial, class and gender exclusions as universality, and fractured and 'double' as unitary identities – requires nothing less than a modification of the boundaries by which 'modernity' and 'postmodernity' are demarcated and understood.[7] This chapter wishes to contribute to this projected rethinking of modernity by focusing on some of the forms of English identity and belonging produced by the British nation-state in the age of its first empire. For not only did the ideological legacies of eighteenth-century war, state, and empire-building shape the ways in which nationality was understood for two centuries or more to come; they also made possible the naturalization of certain kinds of identities – social, sexual, political, racial, and national – whose traces refuse to disappear.[8] In the continual reinventions of 'the nation' – always a constructed, mythic and contested rather than stable or self-evident unit of meaning and coherence – and the ideological significations of its activities at home and abroad may be found a place where, in Paul Gilroy's phrase, a modernity begins in the 'constitutive relationships with outsiders that both found and temper a self-conscious sense of western civilization'.[9]

Whose imagined community? Citizenship in a national imaginary

In an influential formulation, Benedict Anderson has theorized that the 'print-capitalism' of the eighteenth century produced one of the founding practices of modernity, namely the ability and propensity to imagine the 'community' of the nation. The commodified production of print in books, novels, and especially newspapers, Anderson argues, made possible the dissemination of a national consciousness, not only by stabilizing a vernacular language but also, and most importantly, by organizing distant and proximate events according to a calendrical simultaneity – of 'empty, homogeneous time' – that enabled their readers to co-ordinate social time and space, and thus to think relations to others across countries and continents.[10] Anderson has been rightly criticized for his unitary notion of the 'nation' and its unproblematic transpositioning to the colonial and postcolonial worlds.[11] But his attention to the newspaper press in constructing forms of national belonging is salutary, not least because it reminds historians of the inseparability of any society's historical 'reality' from its forms of cultural representation. 'The "lived reality" of national identity,' John Towlinson has noted, 'is a reality lived in representations – not in direct communal solidarity.'[12] In this respect, the news-paper press, a strategic part of the print culture of eighteenth-century England that encompassed both the spread of the artefacts of the press and the institutions and forms of sociability that subsidized it, was clearly of great importance in dissem-inating particularized interpretations of the state, nation, and polity. In conjunction with a range of other printed materials that were read in similar ways and social settings in towns throughout the kingdom, the newspaper press was instrumental in structuring national and political consciousness, binding ordinary men and women throughout the localities in particular ways to the processes of state and empire building.

Provincial newspapers, 244 of which sprouted up in fifty-five different towns over the century, offer one intriguing example of the operations of a 'national' political imaginary as constructed and supported in the press. The importance of provincial urban life to negotiating the stability of the Hanoverian state at home and abroad has long been underplayed in accounts of the national becoming.[13] Yet, catering to provincial urban publics whose interests in the processes of state were galvanized by decades of war and imperial expansion, provincial newspapers coaxed and confirmed their readers' involvement in national and international affairs in ways that gave form to contemporary conceptualizations of power and market relations, at home and abroad. For example, the newspapers of commercial and trading centres such as Newcastle, Norwich, Liverpool, Birmingham, and Bristol in the middle decades of the century produced in their structure and content a mercantilist world view in which trade and the accumulation of wealth appeared as the highest national and individual good. The progress of wars in Europe, America, Africa, and Asia, the coming and going of merchant and slaving ships and the lists of the contents of their laden bottoms – prices, stocks and bullion values – and advertisements for luxury goods culled from mercantile and military adventures abroad were consistent features of newspapers in the outports.[14]

In addition to an obsession with the movable products of empire and commerce, newspapers and provincial periodicals also evinced a widespread fascination with the mechanics of colonial acquisition and possession. By the 1740s and 1750s, provincial papers frequently included sections on 'American affairs' or 'British Plantations' that provided current news on politics and trade, while periodicals crowded their pages with the histories and settlement patterns of individual colonies and beautifully produced maps of British and rival European colonial territories. Such texts did more than literally and figuratively map imperial aspirations and accumulationist desire; they also organized time and space in ways that welded the national and imperial interest, while effacing the crueller aspects of empire, colonialism and 'trade' (the horrors of the Middle passage or the brutalities of plantation slavery, for example) and the subjectivities of the growing numbers of peoples under British rule.[15] Instead, the newspaper and periodical press produced a commercial, sanitized, and 'patriotic' vision of the British Empire and its apparent destiny of spreading profits throughout the nation while disseminating British goods, rights, and liberties across the globe.[16] 'Leonard Herd's African Coffee-house' in Liverpool, which boasted of its 'genteel accommodation' and current subscriptions to ten London and provincial newspapers and *Votes of the House of Common*s in the *Liverpool General Advertiser*, participated in this conjunction of empire, trade, politics, and male sociability at the heart of much of urban print culture.[17]

Other items in the papers integrated the imperial project and Britain's performance and standing abroad with the prosperity, *mores*, and class hierarchies of everyday life at home. Local and national politics, court gossip, the notable *rites de passage* of the local gentry and bourgeoisie, philanthropic and economic initiatives, and the 'quaint' customs or 'insensible' behaviours of the common people: such content endowed readers with the power of possession (*our* colonies, ships, MPs and gentry) and with the sense of entitlement to be on the right side of the vast social and cultural chasms between those who profited from the processes of imperial expansion and those who did not. In these and other ways, newspapers chronicled the bids of the urban commercial and middling classes to social authority and sketched out the structures of economic, political, and discursive power in the society, of market relations and forms of social, political, and sexual commerce, within England, Britain, and abroad. Above all, they made manifest the impact of state actions and politics on daily life and regional and national prosperity and standing, and allowed individuals to participate imaginatively as well as materially in the processes of domestic and imperial government.

Newspapers were thus central instruments in the social production of inform-ation: representing and verifying local experience and refracting world events into socially meaningful categories and hierarchies of importance, they helped produce, in Anderson's felicitous phrase, an 'imagined community' of producers, distri-butors, and consumers on both sides of the Atlantic who shared an avid interest in the fate of the 'empire of goods' that linked them together in prosperity and adver-sity.[18] However, the ascription of 'imagined community' to the world of goods and information constructed by newspapers begs a number of questions, not least, whose community? Who was imagining it? And what was it imagined to consist of? Clearly newspapers (or other forms of print) did not produce homogeneous cultural identities, but a highly mediated 'national' belonging that was constructed through and in tandem with other (local, regional, social) identities. Nevertheless, as the above analysis suggests, we can discern the social, gender, and racial contours of the national community constructed by the newspaper and periodical press. It was imagined to consist of free, flourishing, and largely, though not exclusively, white male British subjects within the locality, nation, and empire; its boundaries were defined and guarded by gender, race, productivity and profits. Hence despite the participation in the processes of state and imperial expansion by other citizens in the metropolis and provincial towns – women, slave and free Africans, Jews, servants, Catholics, labourers, and so on – who worked in urban economies as victuallers, retailers, craftsmen, carriers and peddlers, supported the state through taxes or otherwise played roles in financing, transporting, distributing, manufacturing or consuming the artefacts of colonial and international commerce, their status as a part of the public appealed to in the newspaper press was usually implicit at best, extrapolated through the claims to status of the male middling sorts or their betters.[19] The accessible, homogenized national identity cultivated by newspapers was in fact a delimiting one that recapitulated the self-representations of the urban upper and middle classes, and especially their male, white, and English members.[20]

Further, if we extend the metaphor of 'imagined community' to include the *political* imaginary, that is, to partisan representations of the state and its relations with individuals and localities, we can see how the conventional political biases of the provincial press could operate to deepen the identification between citizenship and the male upper and middle classes. G. A. Cranfield pointed out the marked propensity of provincial printers to capitalize on predominant hostility to successive court Whig Ministries by reproducing the parliamentary opposition's point of view.[21] By consistently printing essays and letters from the main opposition tracts, pamphlets, and journals, provincial papers like the *Norwich Gazette*, *Farley's Bristol Journal*, the *Gloucester Journal*, *Salisbury Journal*, *Newcastle Courant*, and *York Courant* adopted fairly hostile criteria for judging the state and its leaders that played a large role in shaping attitudes to metropolitan hegemony, the activities of the oligarchs and the abuses to which, it was alleged, the constitution was repeatedly subject at their hands. Equally important, through its representations of the state the opposition press in London and the localities also constructed the identity of the citizens positioned outside its confines. For example, in the contexts of Britain's imperial rivalries, continual wars, and Ministers who seemed disinclined to adopt an aggressively expansionist foreign policy, the frequent charges of corruption and 'effeminacy' levelled against the state by opposition writers inscribed their readers as activist, virtuous, masculine political subjects. It was only 'the people' (a deliberately ambiguous designation in the hands of most opposition journalists), inspired by a 'manly, rational love of liberty', who were capable of serving as guardians of the public trust. In this way, the oppositionist reading of politics retailed in the newspaper and periodical press produced definitions of patriotism and political subjectivity that were quite at odds with those proffered by ministerial advocates.[22]

'Every subject not only has the right, but is in duty bound, to enquire into the publick measures pursued,' one writer asserted, 'because by such enquiry he may discover that some of the publick measures tend towards overturning the liberties of his country; and by making such a discovery in time, and acting strenuously ... he may disappoint their effect.'[23] This activist conception of citizenship proclaimed the *duty* of the subject to monitor and canvass the state to ensure the accountability of those in power. As such it lay at the heart of oppositionist patriotic imperatives, based on 'the original Power of the People' to resist illegitimate power upon which scores of writers from Bolingbroke to John Cartwright insisted. Yet how was such an ideal to be enacted? Over the course of the century supporters offered a variety of answers to this question that differed according to the issues and agendas at hand, ranging from participating in instruction and petitioning movements, voting for members of Parliament, and engaging in political demonstrations or festivals to remonstrating the throne or setting up alternative conventions to speak the sense of the People.[24] Yet one of the perennial and pre-eminent ways the 'manly, rational love of liberty' could be demonstrated was in the public sphere of surveillance and opinion constructed by the press. Against government supporters' claims that 'inquiries into the corruptions and mismanagements of those in the administration, properly and solely belong to ... Parliament', opposition journalists continually asserted the people's right to monitor the state through the mechanisms of spectatorship provided by a free press. As one pamphleteer argued in 1740, since '[t]he People of Britain in general have an undubitable Right to Canvass publick affairs, to express their sentiments freely, and to declare their sense of any grievances under which they labour',

> ... treating political subjects freely in print, and thereby submitting them to the view and censure of the Nation in general, is so far from being dangerous that it is really conducive to the Publick Peace. By this means, all Degrees of People, who have leisure and abilities, and a turn to this sort of reading, acquire rational ideas of liberty and submission, of the rights of the Church, and of the power of the State, and of their duties as subjects, and of what they may justly claim as *Free men*.[26]

In this argument, literacy becomes the test of citizenship and the instrument of political subjectivity itself, and through print culture both the subject's right to monitor the state and his potential for citizen activism were fulfilled. Clearly, the political press recast politics into spectatorial, critical activities, capable of being exercised privately; but more appropriately enacted within the sphere of public society itself. The alehouse, tavern, newsroom, coffee house and club, as well as the counting house, shipyard and shop, made 'the people' temporarily visible, but print made it permanent, allowing it to exist through a 'steady, solid simultaneity through time' as Anderson has noted.[26] At the same time, through the role of spectator the political subject was delimited in class, gender and racial terms as 'independent', sovereign, and masculine – a critical, objective, manly, and hence white male subject, immune to the emoluments of power, whose contrast to the allegedly corrupt, irrational or, effeminate aristocratic state could not be more marked.[27]

Such particularized 'national imaginings' encouraged by the newspaper and political press were reinforced elsewhere in the culture of urban life, where a range of pursuits and practices, whether undertaken in the name of politics, science, art, 'useful knowledge', or civic improvement, could continually reinscribe the extra-legal definition of citizens as independent, male heads of households capable of defining and protecting the national interest. Indeed, the 'urban renaissance' itself, that much celebrated and masterfully described phenomenon of provincial urban renewal over the century, provided contexts for social and political action that enabled the middle classes to negotiate the status and authority of established elites in ways that privileged their claims for political recognition and status. Predicated largely on British economic expansion and prosperity, especially the growing importance of England's colonial and foreign trade in the provincial economy,[28] the urban renaissance could also bolster the masculinist patriotism espoused by opposition spokespersons and bellicose merchants alike.[29]

To be sure, the initiatives undertaken to improve public amenities and communications, expand leisure facilities, rebuild churches, or found hospitals were dependent upon the willingness and ability of a wide range of residents, men and women, artisans and merchants, shopkeepers and patricians, to associate and subscribe money and time in order to refashion and regulate their physical and cultural environments. And arenas of polite culture such as assembly rooms, tea rooms, and pleasure gardens promoted the cultivation of 'heterosocial manners' that afforded upper and middle-class women a valued status as arbiters of sociability and decorum.[30] Yet the institutions of the urban renaissance also advanced definitions of subjectivity that supported the prerogatives of middle and upper-class men. Voluntary hospitals for the sick poor, for example, those quintessentially mercantilist enterprises dedicated to expanding productivity by remodelling the poor, combined that ubiquitous method of capital mobilization, the subscription, and wide and heterogeneous community support with more delimiting rules of participation and voting that accorded with the gender and financial contribution of the subscriber.[31] Assembly rooms and theatres, built through the contributions of the wealthiest members of their communities, also did less than is usually supposed to disrupt dominant social and gender hierarchies. For example, the use of provincial assembly rooms was strictly regulated, with the formations of minuets and dances as well as the arrival and departures of carriages organized according to social rank and position.[32] Theatres brought together a more volatile cross-section of the public but were nonetheless stridently defended as bulwarks of the national character and fomenters of those manly, civilized, and patriotic manners necessary to English success abroad and stability at home. Indeed, in both rationale and performance, theatre frequently drew upon and exaggerated the masculinist cultural identities circulating elsewhere in the public sphere in a self-conscious effort to socialize audiences into the *mores* of gender and national differentiation.[33]

The proliferation of clubs and societies, one of the most celebrated and distinctive aspects of provincial urban culture in the eighteenth century, was perhaps most successful in authorizing particularized definitions of citizenship.

Whether devoted to philosophical enquiry, politics, or competitive gardening, most provincial clubs provided homosocial enclaves of conviviality, sociability, and discipline that, among their many manifest and latent functions, endowed their predominantly male memberships with the identity of decision-making subjects capable of associating for the public good.[34] Certainly associational life *per se* was not a male preserve. As the politics of trade and empire and the issues raised by state expansion worked to galvanize political consciousness and patriotism in new directions, merchants, traders and shopkeepers, journeymen and servants, and men and women initiated political activities on their own or joined national campaigns.[35] But the *signification* of such participatory patriotism was strictly narrowed by the demands and exigencies of politics and international military conflict. Decades of war had tended to bolster a militaristic, masculinist version of the national identity that privileged the claims of the white, trading and commercial classes to political status while excluding a range of 'effeminate' others who threatened their supposedly distinctive goals: not only the French or francophilic, but also the aristocratic, the foppish, the irrational, the dependent and the timid.[36] For example, in the virulent national political debates over the nature of the aristocratic leadership and the national character that resounded in the 1740s through 1760s, 'effeminacy' denoted a degenerate moral, political and social state that opposed and subverted the vaunted 'manly' characteristics – courage, aggression, martial valour, discipline and strength – constituting patriotic virtue. Its denigration intersected with other efforts to eradicate behaviours and practices (sexual and consumer as well as political) that blurred gender lines or otherwise threatened masculinity and force in the political and cultural realms. An effeminate nation was 'a Nation which *resembles Women*', John Brown asserted in his influential *Estimate of the Manners and Principles of the Times*, devoid of courage, liberty, principle and endurance, opposed to public-spiritedness and martial valour, and destined for international ignominy and derision.[37] As a diagnosis of national political ills, Brown's assessment was to have a recurring, if contested, longevity; as a marker of what was desirable and necessary in the nation's leaders and citizenry, this masculinist version of the national character became common currency in wartime, asserted and circulated in parades, dramatic tableaux, painting, periodicals, sermons and street theatre, artefacts and design as well as in the press.[38]

Not surprisingly, then, the expanding fiscal-military state forged and defined through war produced in political culture definitions of patriotism and the national character that represented its operations at home and abroad through the axes of class, gender and race, recuperating simultaneously an anti-conquest, humanitarian version of military acquisition and an aggressive, if compassionate, masculinity, potency and power. The social heterogeneity of subscribers to patriotic societies actually worked to uphold this composite as the primary instrument of the nation's survival and greatness: men and women, aristocrats and servants joining together to promote that 'manly, rational patriotism' and martial spirit without which the nation's security, self-sufficiency and destiny would crumble.[39]

The aftermath of war and massive imperial expansion saw these identities renewed and reworked by other means. The political and debating clubs of the Wilkite period, for example, not only articulated an overtly radicalized vision of the polity, but also an ideal of citizenship that recovered androcentric patriotism for new purposes. Wilkite journalism, street theatre, prints and plays retailed to a wide audience the ideology of independence and ideals of resistance and 'manly patriotism' that made explicit a hostility to intrusions of the feminine as well as effeminate in the political sphere. Defining as the true patriot one who would resist, at considerable personal cost, the illegitimate powers that threatened to overtake the polity, the model of manly patriotism defined and solicited a particular version of masculinity to be put at the call of the nation that marginalized and opposed non-resisting and hence 'effeminate' others. Hence the acerbic attacks of Wilkite journalists on 'Scottish' and aristocraric pollutions of the body politic, on 'sodomitical' peers and incestuous women behind the scenes exerting 'secret influence' at court, and on a 'Jacobitical', effeminate prince served a number of political purposes that included both privileging the claims of middle-class Englishmen to the prerogatives of political subjectivity and closing down the range of gender identities available to political subjects.[40]

A constitutive part of this milieu, Wilkite clubs embellished a long-standing belief of Masonic and pseudo-Masonic societies that women and 'effeminate' men were potential sources of contamination that would undermine the rationality and fraternity of their project.[41] They were also complicit with the rakish, heterosexist libertinism with which Wilkite radicalism was associated. Wilkes's pornographic *Essay on Women*, his flamboyant sexual escapades (including alleged participation in orgies as a member of the notorious Medmenham Monks, a 'Hell-Fire Club') combined with his attacks on such alleged evidences of aristocratic effeminacy as sodomy,[42] legitimated and mobilized a quite explicit sexual, as well as political, libertarianism among its supporters, from Sylas Neville to political revellers in the provinces.[43] Wilkes was 'free from cock to wig', in the words of a humble (male) admirer; while the voting qualification for the Wilkite club members that attended the mock election at Garrat was 'having enjoyed a woman in the open air within the district'.[44] Although the connection of the libertine version of masculine virility to radical politics did not go unchallenged, and women were participants in Wilkite festival and polemics, at the very least the multiply determined constructions of Wilkite radicalism drove home the point that political subjects and sexual subjects were one and the same.[45]

Hence, Wilkite clubs of the period, such as the Revolution Club in Newport, Isle of Wight, which annually commemorated 'the duty and honour of resisting Stuart Tyrants', the Patriotic Society in Leeds, formed to mark the day of Wilkes's enlargement from prison, and the African and American Club in Whitehaven, devoted, with no apparent awareness of contradiction, to promoting the slave trade abroad and the liberties of the subject at home, all equally aimed at a reconstruction capable of shaping notions of the national interest to their advantage and reconfiguring the terms of social exchange and political power. But they were also instrumental in establishing this broader symbolic valuation of gender identities, upholding a homosocial, heterosexual and predominantly masculine ethos of conviviality and politics that staked out both physically and ideologically a male domain within the socially mixed and potentially transgressive spaces of urban society.[46] Like print culture and other sites where extra-legal definitions of citizenship could be enacted or maintained, club life not only imbricated empire, state expansion and local and national prosperity in ways that multiply constituted the national; it also constructed the identity of the citizen, the nature of the state and the contours of the political nation in social, racial and gendered terms.

(Second class) citizens and (non) nationals

To restate the argument so far, the politically constructed national imaginings of urban life, and particularly the efforts to enact a 'national', rational political public to which the state was held to be accountable, also led to stridently gendered and exclusionary notions of political subjectivity that played central roles in consolidating oppositional categories of the domestic and public spheres. Yet the larger contexts and culture supporting and influenced by the expanding fiscal-military state and its actions at home and abroad also created spaces and sites for a wider range of groups to claim or imagine a status as citizens despite oligarchy and ethnic, class, and gender inequalities. To take the most obvious example, despite their legal status as dependants and the masculinist nature of much nationalistic political discourse, women frequently acted like political subjects within the commercialized world of extraparliamentary politics. Women made up 30 per cent of the patrons at circulating libraries in the country and accounted for between one-third and one-fifth of the membership at various book clubs that have left adequate records; they were avid newspaper readers and patrons of such institutions of politics and print culture as inns and taverns.[47] Further, numbers of women worked in London and provincial towns as writers, printers, engravers, newspaper publishers, newsagents, stationers, and booksellers as well as innkeepers and victuallers; as writers they engaged in polemical political debates from the consequences of the Glorious Revolution to the immorality of slavery.[48] Beginning in the 1730s, the development of the market for political artefacts increased the range of things women could buy (and sell) to express their political affiliations. Women in provincial towns wore appropriately coloured cockades and silks to assemblies and balls to signal their political affiliations, presided over politically correct teatables whose cloths commemorated the defeat of the excise Bill, or sold ballads, garlands or snuff that honoured the opposition hero Admiral Vernon.[49] Women were also participants in riots, demonstrations, chairings, and processions; spectators at the ceremonials of state and nation, from anniversary day celebrations to military reviews; avid attenders at the theatre and at debating societies; subscribers to philanthropic and patriotic societies; activists on the 'home front' during war and invasion scares; and occasionally the targets of vigorous propagandizing. Even the government itself interpellated women as political subjects by prosecuting them for seditious or treasonable words.⁵⁰

Clearly, long before the 1790s, the commercialized nature of English politics and culture provided middle-class women with wider opportunities to act like political subjects and appropriate the mantel of citizenship for themselves; the injunctions to 'manly rationality' could not be bounded by biological sex and were a source of identity for women as well as men.⁵¹ Nevertheless, the social acceptance and valuation of women's forays into politics were variable, dependent upon class and political context as well as those fluctuating variables that connived at suspending or amplifying the conventional misogyny of English political writers.⁵² Aristocratic women's influence at court, on the canvass, or behind the scenes was largely accepted; indeed, they played a crucial role in establishing, through marriage, sociability and friendships, the social and familial networks which brokered the high political world. An appropriately modest degree of political interest by bourgeois women was also tolerated, but lower-class women's political activism was denounced as evidence of their degraded natures.⁵³ Above all, national crises or emergencies were liable to make intrusions of the feminine into the political sphere a focus of intense male anxiety; and war both intensified the strident masculinism of patriotic discourse and effaced the extra efforts women made on the 'home front' that war simultaneously demanded.⁵⁴

As we have seen, the patriotisms legitimating or authorized by the fiscal-military nation-state depended upon a marginalization or subordination of the feminine in their notions of the national character. Certainly they did not prevent women from identifying with the imperatives of citizenship, but they did devalue or obscure women's contributions to national affairs and naturalized their exclusion from formal politics. Joseph Addison set a pattern in 1716 when he both urged right-minded women to support the Hanoverian Succession and then satirized their propensity to 'judge for themselves; look into the State of the Nation with their own Eyes, and be no longer led Blindfold by a Male Legislature'.⁵⁵ This double bind for women, being simultaneously urged to promote love of country and yet constrained by their lack of legal and political status and injunctions to domesticity, stimulated a great deal of the proto-feminist commentary of the day and was ultimately addressed in the ideas of republican motherhood. Equally important, however, this contradiction also confirmed women's status within contemporary political culture as split or incomplete subjects, whose capacities and resources at the service of the fiscal-military state were limited by their supposed biological and emotional otherness.⁵⁶ Free, sensible, tasteful, clean, sympathetic and decorous, but also domestic, luxurious, sensual and dependent, English women could serve as emblems or tokens of national superiority and civilization, or help purify the morally dubious public sphere through their influence. But they could not be independent political subjects, only auxiliary ones, whose ultimate role was to authorize masculine prerogatives and authority. Contemporary representations of the national character and citizenship trenchantly foregrounded these convergences and tensions between the symbolic feminine and the empirical positions of women, stimulating resistance and debate certainly but also partially structuring women's experience and desire. Hence Elizabeth Robinson Montagu, a highly articulate and integral player in the political gossip networks of the day, fantasized about being the consort of the 'conquering hero' (and pathologically violent) Cortez.[57]

Women's contingent and subordinate position within the imagined community of the nation was in some ways paralleled by, though in no way homologous to, that of marginalized ethnic and religious groups within the English polity. By the eighteenth century, England had acquired a reputation for providing refuge for groups persecuted elsewhere in Europe (Huguenots, Walloons, Gypsies, Sephardic Jews, for example); it was also a 'mother country' for colonial immigrants, both old and new (Irish, Scots, Americans, and West Indians), and a destination for others brought in through the privileges and exigencies of slavery and colonial trade (Africans, East Indians, Chinese).[58] The first European diaspora wrought by colonialism, commerce and exploration, in other words, wrought another, partly involuntary diasporic population living in the English metropole. Some of these immigrants and their children became almost permanent members of poor and disadvantaged communities in the capital and outports; others thrived in partially or wholly assimilated artisan, craft or mercantile occupations. The difficulties of 'forging a nation' in the face of such irreducible and inevitable internal difference has been recently summarized by Linda Colley, who has stressed its considerable successes by the years of the Napoleonic wars.[59] Nevertheless, the crises of the period produced by war, invasion and rebellion could confound the efforts to construct and maintain a unifying national identity. In particular, the presence and resistances of those whose Englishness or Britishness could not be taken as self-evident demonstrated that the continual reinventions of the nation and of the terms of national belonging could not be capacious or elastic enough to accommodate all of 'the others' within. Catholics, Jews, foreign Protestants, Irish, Scots, and Africans were among the groups targeted for denigration, harassment, physical segregation, or forced exile during the various political crises of the century.[60] As such, even if their members could act like citizens in the public sphere of association, voice opinions, and promote their own versions of the public interest, their membership in the nation was tentative and unstable, revealing the fictive nature of a 'national identity'.

To take one example, the 'black' population of England, comprised mostly of Africans and West Indians (though including a small contingent of South and East Asians), numbered between 15,000 and 20,000 by the 1770s, concentrated in London and those outports having extensive dealings with Africa and the planta-tion colonies.[61] Although Africans had been present in England since Elizabethan times, Britain's subsequent rise to dominance in the slave trade and changes in the laws meant that from the 1720s until the abolition of the slave trade in 1807 they arrived in greater numbers, in all conditions – as slaves, servants, refugees and stowaways, sailors and artisans, students and princes – and from all over the world. Despite endemic prejudices and pervasive economic hardships, their members came to occupy a variety of subject positions within English society. Probably the majority arrived as slaves and lived by custom as servants; if they gained their freedom while in the country, they had to live under the shadow of possible recapture and sale.[62] Free blacks worked as servants and sailors (by the 1790s one-quarter of the British navy was composed of Africans); as shopkeepers, artisans and labourers; as laundrymaids, seamstresses and children's nurses; or as peddlers, street musicians, players with travelling fairs, and pugilists; still others fell into begging or crime. Those with a specific skill or trade usually came in at the bottom of the hierarchy of labour that included the Irish and Jews as well as the mass of 'English' labouring poor.[63] English attitudes towards Africans and people of African descent were varied and variable, and among the labouring classes in particular relations between black and white Britons could be cordial and close. Nevertheless, Ukawsaw Gronniosaw, arriving in England as an adult after having been kidnapped into slavery and then held in bondage as a domestic servant in New York, illustrates the struggles that could beset an African immigrant who attempted to gain a livelihood in what he had been brought up to believe was a 'holy' land. Working as a navvy, carpenter and twisterer in London, Colchester and Norwich, he, his English wife (who was a weaver), and three children fell continually into those economic difficulties common to the insecure life of the labouring poor, but exacerbated in their case by racism. The hostility of the 'inferior people' in Norwich, in Gronniosaw's words, was such that resentful labourers resorted to working under price in order to starve the family out of town. 'Such is our situation at present,' Gronniosaw wrote in 1770 from Kidderminster. 'As Pilgrims, and very poor Pilgrims, we are travelling through many difficulties.'[64]

Gronniosaw's appropriation of the language of *Pilgrim's Progress*, that most Protestant and English of religious tracts, to make his own claim to subject status in a country hostile to such 'outsider's' claims points to another avenue of contestation and survival for former slaves in England, namely Christianity and especially Anglican Protestantism. Despite several court rulings to the contrary, it was widely believed that baptism would make slaves free, and slaves in England were eager to take advantage of this extra-legal loophole; indeed, the majority became Anglican communicants. Although their religious beliefs were probably genuine, and baptism or conversion were far from fail-safe methods of procuring freedom, the use of the privileged religion as a road out of bondage ironically gave Africans a leverage within English society that other persecuted or disadvantaged groups, such as Jews and Catholics, could not access. It 'gets the mob on their [i.e. the ex-slaves'] side', John Fielding reported, 'and makes it not only difficult, but dangerous, … to recover possession of them.'[65] The 'confessional state', that bulwark of the establishment, and Anglican Protestantism, the cornerstone of the national identity and a marker of the 'civilized' in the popular consciousness, thus became avenues through which Africans could make their tormented journeys in the

English mind from slave to humanity, or at least live as other English people and claim their rights in the national community. These claims to citizenship were extremely important in promoting the abolitionist cause.[66]

Sociability, politics and propaganda – all activities carried out in the public sphere of eighteenth-century urban life – also provided opportunities for non-white English citizens to promote their own versions of the public interest. The African-English community in London was large and close-knit, and a black variant of English urban culture upheld customs of civility that succoured its participants and took the edge off their sense of ethnic isolation. Taverns, assemblies and clubs dominated by black Britons were noted in London in the 1760s; and wealthier individuals attended the theatre and pleasure gardens.[67] Further, roused by slave revolts in the colonies and spurring the efforts of abolitionists like Granville Sharp and Thomas Day, a politicized black community galvanized the abolitionist movement beginning in the late 1760s; indeed, African-English writers played a major role in its growing popularity out of doors.[68] Their participation in print culture was multiply significant. As Henry Louis Gates Jr has argued, blacks and other people of colour were believed to be largely outside the community of reason in the eighteenth century, and 'reason' – rationality, objectivity, logic – was an instrument of delimiting citizenship as well as a commodity to be used in exchange for admission to 'humanity'. Hence Phillis Wheatley, domestic slave of a Boston merchant, who visited London in 1772 and charmed aristocratic bluestocking circles with her ardent anti-slavery poetry and spirit; Ignatius Sancho, butler to the Duke of Montagu, grocer, friend of Garrick, and admirer of Sterne, whose posthumously published letters garnered 600 initial subscribers and a number of editions; Olaudah Equiano, Igbo, ex-slave, mariner, explorer, writer and radical activist; and Ottabah Cugoano, a Fante kidnapped into slavery at age thirteen who in 1787 penned one of the most influential abolitionist tracts of the period, all joined Gronniosaw as Africans who simultaneously 'proved' their humanity and indicted European hierarchies of civilization by their writings.[69] Their prose and verse, in fact and content, also pluralized the universal and gave proof of its multiple embodiments, a strategy which aided other groups who were 'other' to the white, English male bourgeois subjects that political discourse valorized to stake their own claims for recognition.[70]

Nevertheless, the place of Africans and 'people of colour' (an eighteenth-century phrase) in the national imaginary was fraught and uncertain. In the newspaper debates that accompanied the Sierra Leone repatriation project in 1786–87 – a moment marked by economic crisis and high anxiety over an influx of black immigrants in the aftermath of the American war – toleration and the long-standing secular racism of the plantocracy and its supporters in England contended, while the contingent nature of black claims to national standing and the ambivalences of 'Englishness' itself were made richly apparent. The project to 'export' numbers of poor blacks from London to begin their own colony on the African coast, in an area first considered and then rejected as a potential penal colony, was hatched in May 1786.[71] Yet between October 1786, when the navy commissioned ships to carry the pioneers, and April 1787, when they finally left England, a number of circumstances had intervened to quell the initial enthusiasm for the project among the London African community and its leaders. Five hundred men, women, and children had boarded the *Atlantis* and the *Belisarius* (the name of the latter a spectacular if unintended irony)[72] by late October, yet as the departure was delayed, numbers began to perish with cold and sickness in an unsavoury imitation of a slave ship expedition. Other enlistees, unsettled by rumours about the British government's intentions and their own safety once they arrived in Africa, began to leave or refused to join the ships. Cugoano summarized their case some time later, arguing, 'Can it be readily conceived that government would establish a free colony for them nearly on the spot, while it supports its forts and garrisons, to ensnare, merchandize, and to carry others into captivity and slavery?' The *Morning Herald*, a liberal, abolitionist newspaper agreed, asserting that, in opting out, these blacks had shown their English predilections, 'prefer[ing] liberty with poverty' to being 'transported to a military government, like the white Felons to New Norfolk'. 'Would it not be dangerous innovation in this land of liberty,' an editorial pronounced, 'to suffer the exclusion of our fellow creatures from the rights of mankind, on account of difference of complexion?'[73]

Other reactions were less supportive. One writer to the *Public Advertiser* claimed that the Africans' distrust of the government showed how little they comprehended the English constitution and character: 'national honour' would prevent any circumvention of Parliament's commitment to protect their liberty. The *Morning Post* ignored the libertarian issues altogether, drawing instead on plantocratic fears of miscegenation and contamination in order to condemn the Africans' refusal to leave. Sarcastically referring to these 'dark-coloured patriots', it quoted the late Mr Dunning on the likelihood of London taking on 'the appearance of an Ethiopian colony' if the black population was not reduced and immigration stopped.[74] Equally hostile writers drew upon stereotypes that were also used to denigrate other disadvantaged or diasporic populations within: blacks were 'naturally indolent' and had to be forced to work (charges also levelled against the Irish); 'exporting' them would lower the crime rate (the same argument was used in favour of restraining the 'importation' of the Irish and Jews); and reducing their numbers would stave off the inevitable emasculation of English men that Africans' alleged sexual prowess and lasciviousness effected (a recurrent, fetishistic fantasy about racialized others that was also wielded against Irishmen, South Sea Islanders, and visiting Cherokee Indian warriors).[75] As the *London Chronicle* had put it twenty years before, 'there can be no just plea for [black Britons] being put on an equal footing with *natives whose birthright, as members of the community, entitles them to superior dues*'.[76] Blacks and 'people of colour' may have been human in this national imaginary, but they certainly were not English, and 'English' in these contexts served less as a universally recognized symbol or set of attributes than as a 'sign of difference', in Homi Bhabba's words, which could never be naturalized.[77]

As such, Africans living in England clearly experienced the fractured and hybrid identities that in part constituted, and were constituted by, the diasporic experience and the crucibles of nation-state and colonialism. Equiano, whose many occupations included ship's steward under Admiral Boscawen during the Seven Years War, sailor in a merchant ship, participant in Captain Constantine Phipps's expedition to the Arctic, and political organizer in abolitionist and corresponding society politics, adopted in his writings simultaneously the subjectivity of the quintessential English bourgeois (traveller, scientist, trader, explorer, Protestant) and that of an African, a 'Son of Africa' (the name of a group of black abolitionists in London), a former slave and a working-class, radical citizen. He was, in his words, 'almost an Englishman', and 'part of the poor, oppressed, needy and much degraded negroes' – an incompatibility that seemed irreducible. The multiplying 'double consciousness" of a diasporic modernity, to use W. E. B. Du Bois's phrase, permeated his political and autobiographical self-representations.[78] Equally palpable were the dislocation and alienation felt by Ignatius Sancho. Born on a slave ship and brought up in an English household before entering the Duke of Montagu's service, Sancho, with his aristocratic *penchants* for gambling, womanizing and polite entertainments, was once pointed to by scholars as a case study in successful assimilation. Yet in his private letters Sancho expressed a profound sense of isolation and unbelonging that national crises like the American war or the Gordon Riots only exaggerated. Reviewing the disasters that accompanied the former in 1779, he wrote that these national tribulations were 'nothing to me, as I am only a lodger, and hardly that' – a displaced African, not a black Englishman, as Folarin Shyllon has noted.[79]

In sum, although the sites that enabled or encouraged national imaginings could enact the gulfs between the public and the private, men and women, slaves and freemen, or 'the people' and the rabble, they also inevitably created spaces for participation, engagement and contestation by those outside the privileged halves of these oppositions. Such interventions, at the very least, gave embodied proof of the pluralities of the universals of citizenship, humanity and patriotism and contested the unitary deployments of the central tenets of libertarian discourse in the period. On the other hand, the place of England's peoples marked as 'other' in the imagined communities of the nation was contingent and incomplete at best, denigrated and despised at worst, and always the product of contestation and resistance.

Fractured desires: empire, citizenship, and nation

Finally, empire itself, its imagined forms and seemingly limitless possibilities, brought into sharp relief the difficulties of attempted national imaginings in ways that suggest both the fatal attractions and irreconcilable tensions between empire and nation. Benedict Anderson has argued that the nation was imagined as a 'community' because 'regardless of the actual inequality and exploitation that may prevail in each, the nation is always conceived as a deep horizontal comradeship'.[80] Yet empire and colonies, the knowledge, possession and processes of which were integral in constituting the British nation and English national identity in the eighteenth century, constantly demonstrated the contradictions and fissures produced by such attempted 'national' imaginings. Certainly England's imperial project at times provided a slate upon which a united national polity could be inscribed that overlaid the social and political tensions within the domestic polity.[81] But if the discourses of nationality sought to construct homogeneities within the territorial boundaries of the nation-state, they also sought to identify and assert *difference*, and those differences, however artificial and tenuous, not only distinguished the nation from other nations but also divided the citizens within its own boundaries. Empire confounded and completed this project in interesting and complex ways.

As we have seen, the English devotion to empire lay as much in its role as a bulwark and emblem of English superiority and benevolence as in its profitability, yet, especially as constituted in oppositionist patriotism, empire was imagined to create a far-reaching and inclusive *British* polity that preserved the most valued components of the national identity. In the 1730s and 1740s, such imaginings, galvanized and focused on the opposition hero Admiral Edward Vernon, who defeated the Spanish at Porto Bello in 1739, supported the spectacular vision of empire as an extensive, homogeneous polity bounded only by rights, liberties, and duties, and guided by manly and virtuous leaders. Clearly this belief was both rose-coloured and self-serving, mystifying or obscuring the brutal, exploitative, and violent processes of colonization and slavery and glossing over the differences between the various forms of British imperial dominance in the New World (and Old). Nevertheless, it was immensely attractive to domestic publics, who seemed fervently to subscribe to its view of the essentially fair-minded, just and paternalistic nature of British, as opposed to French or Spanish, empire, and the former's ability to 'tame the fierce and polish the most savage', civilizing the world through commerce and trade.[82] Through Vernon, empire was refracted back to his supporters as the ultimate patriotic project, diffusing wealth among the domestic population, protecting English freedoms (including the freedom of trade and navigation) from the threats of foreign powers and rapacious Ministries, and extending the birthrights of Englishmen throughout the world.

Over the next decade, a Jacobite rebellion and inconclusive war with France did little to satisfy these exalted hopes and much to promote a sense of national malaise and fears about the national character and leadership. By the 1750s, French encroachments on the American colonies and the loss of Minorca in 1756 amplified existing anxieties about the emasculation and degeneracy of the British body politic that seemed to be emanating from above. Empire was now represented as the antidote to aristocratic 'cultural treason' and effeteness, the bulwark and proving ground of the true national character and (middle-class) potency and virtue. The ultimately spectacular string of British victories and conquests in 1758–62 both soothed and reconstituted national masculinity and power, while also celebrating the war and the newly extended British Empire for saving the world from French tyranny, Spanish cruelty, and Amerindian barbarity alike.[83] 'Britain will never want a Race of Men ... who choose Dangers in defence of Their Country before an inglorious safety, an honourable Death before the unmanly pleasures of a useless and effeminate life,' was how a Newcastle clergyman summed up the situation in late 1759; while the Protestant Dissenting Deputies congratulated George III for inaugurating a new era of British imperial ascendancy and expansion, 'diffusing freedom and science, political order and Christian Knowledge through those extensive regions which are now sunk in superstitious barbarism ... and imparting even to the most uncultivated of our species, the happiness of *Britons*.'[84]

The homogenizing, 'patriotic' vision of empire produced for many citizens by the century's most successful war was soon shattered. The Peace of Paris brought to the fore a long-suppressed unease at the enormity of British possessions, their racial and religious diversity, the domestic divisions they mirrored and reproduced, and the authoritarian techniques used to govern them. Playwrights, political journalists, and parliamentarians alike began to condemn the Asian Indian empire's polluting impact, now designated as a conduit of 'luxury, effeminacy and profligacy' to those at home. The East India Company and its conquests on the subcontinent were a particular source of concern, especially when the parliamentary inquiry leading to the Regulating Act of 1773 made public Robert Clive's misadventures in Bengal and the extent of the huge personal fortune he had amassed.[85] West Indian debacles also underscored the unsavoury aspects of an empire of conquest. British attempts in the late 1760s to expatriate or exterminate the Caribbs on the island of St Vincent in order to appropriate their lands produced a particularly gruesome and bloody war on the island that forced English observers to confront, and decry, the realities of conquest and question the long-vaunted moral superiority of British imperialism over its European competitors. 'The honour of the British nation is at stake,' Alderman Barlow Trecothick exclaimed in a parliamentary debate on the propriety of the Ministry's sending troops to quell the Caribbs' resistance; 'a scene of iniquity and cruelty is transacting ... on the defenceless natives ... against [whom] you are exercising the barbarities of the Spaniards against the Mexicans.'[86] The Pacific explorations of Captain James Cook and his crews in the same period, widely publicized and celebrated at home, also increased, for the moment, domestic sympathy for indigenous peoples and mobilized sentiment against the use of force and conquest in the 'civilizing' process. Not surprisingly, the abolitionist movement had its roots in this period, when colonial examples, African resistance within England, and the Somerset case of 1772 forced the English public to acknowledge the brutal ways in which English rights were denied to other Britons throughout the empire, as well as to recognize the growing importance of slavery in the British and American economies.[87]

Significantly, the American war brought these ambivalences about empire to a head, while also underlining the tenuousness of long-held beliefs about the morality, virtue, and libertarianism of the imperial project. British commentators had long insisted that Britain's virtue as an imperial nation lay in not seeking conquest, but having conquest thrust upon her: colonial acquisition in the Seven Years War was thus continually justified as a *defence* against French aggression. The policies of the Pelhams and Chatham had done less to undercut these views than those of George III and his Ministers, who enacted measures which seriously confounded them. The Quebec Act, the 'Coercive Acts' and the entire, massive war effort aimed at coercing or murdering Protestant English people living in America indicated the loss of a virtuous empire, once 'as much renowned for the virtues of justice and humanity as for the splendour of its arms', as the Middlesex electors lamented in their address for reconciliation with America in 1775.[88]

Most importantly, the period of the American war forced into the English national consciousness the contradictions, inequities and atrocities perpetuated in the name of national identity and obscured by the fire and fury of imperial expansion. For it provided irrefutable evidence that the British Empire was comprised not just of free British subjects but also of large numbers of alien peoples, incorporated into the empire by conquest, not consent, and sustained, in Peter Marshall's words, 'by the deployment of British troops across the world in a way that was to last until the 1960s'.[89] As such, some English people who lived through the war and its aftermath believed themselves to be at a momentous historical crossroads, when the England that had orchestrated British imperial ascendancy seemed to be in danger of precipitous collapse, and the components of the national identity and the nation's role in the world had been unintentionally reconfigured. At the very least, this disjunctive moment gave many English people pause, forcing a confrontation between their history and their future, a moment intimated by Edward Gibbon's magisterial jeremiad on Roman decline and reworked by scores of commentators thereafter. 'A foolish or effeminate Prince, surrounded by a venal Senate … was not born to retain dominions acquired by republican wisdom, and republican valour; nor could a People, which had lost all pretensions to govern itself, long expect to rule over others,' was one radical writer's take on Gibbon's history that was meant to explain both the nature and singularity of the current crisis.[90] Imperial dismemberment, military defeat, the penetration of 'national' boundaries by the immigration of racialized others whose claims to belonging seemed tenuous at best – all brought into collision, and not for the last time, a present and a past 'charged with the time of the now', a self-confrontation that undermined national confidence and underlined both the historical specificity of the present moment in the national becoming and the possibilities for rethinking its future character.[91]

'Are we not compelled to … value what we hold most dear, next to our own salvation,' one dismayed observer inveighed in the midst of the American crisis, 'as we value our rights as Englishmen, our existence as a nation, and the safety and dignity of the British Empire?'[92] Yet, carried out as a right of Englishmen and in the name of English liberties, empire could not secure those rights for Britons, who within the context of a heterogeneous empire were not all created equal. A range of people living within and without the metropole were 'others', although not interchangeable ones, to the fair-minded, masculine English subject that the imperial project valorized, and were part of the amalgam which empire's gendered, commercial, and aggressive vision of the national identity sought to subordinate, at home and abroad. Within Britain itself, from the perspectives of the metropole, the Welsh and, more gradually, the Scots become naturalized as 'British', the Irish, Jews, Africans, and Asians perhaps never do; beyond the British isles, the claim of peoples of different races and cultures to British rights and liberties was even more remote and contingent, and 'Britishness' was conferred or denied not only in relation to the numbers of white British settlers in residence but also to the degree of acceptance by colonial peoples of English hegemony and the legitimacy of British rule.

Of course, colonized groups could destabilize the identities of Britishness formulated in the days of imperial glory and subvert their hegemonic deployment. The American colonists appropriated the 'rights of Englishmen' to reject Englishness and to continue to deny those rights to indigenous and slave populations, an effort that both 'heritage' and 'race' worked to make relatively successful. The beleaguered Caribbs were described by the British planters who desired their land as 'idle, ignorant and savage people', exalted by their defenders as exhibiting not only the rights but the temperament of Englishmen – 'Fighting for liberty, and every English heart must applaud them'; but they themselves feared they would be made slaves by their new British governors, to the apparent shock and dismay of liberal observers in England.[93] The period of the first British Empire thus consolidated a national identity, forged in over two centuries of imperial adventures and national and colonial expansion, that could not be readily naturalized, producing colonial subjects who were 'savages' or 'almost like Englishmen' but could never be English themselves.[94] The various hierarchical visions of the domestic polity were recognizably if irregularly mapped on to the imperial one, and the incompatibility of the rights of English people and those of Britons laid bare – the first must always take priority over the second, and national belonging kept within strict territorial, cultural, and increasingly, racial bounds. As a constitutive moment in the 'modern' national becoming, the traces still linger, and still confound.

Notes

From *Eighteenth-century Studies*, 29:1 (1995), 69–96. For comments on an earlier draft of this chapter, I would like to thank Ira Livingston, Nikhil Singh and especially Nicholas Mirzoeff.

1 The epigraphs are from: *The Duty, Objects and Offices of the Love of Country*, Restoration Day sermon: *Letters of the Late Ignatius Sancho, an African* (London, fifth edition, 1803), 213–14, quoted in Folarin Shyllon, *Black People in Britain* (London: Oxford University Press, 1977), 193; and Walter Benjamin, *Illuminations*, ed. Hannah Arendt (New York: Schochen Books, 1968), 263.

2 The 'commercialization' thesis has been most enthusiastically documented by J. H. Plumb and his students; see Plumb, *The Commercialisation of Leisure in Eighteenth Century England*

(Reading: University of Reading Press, 1973); Neil McKendrick, John Brewer and J. H. Plumb, *The Birth of a Consumer Society: The Commercialisation of Eighteenth Century England* (London: Hutchinson, 1982); John Brewer, *Party Ideology and Popular Politics at the Accession of George III* (Cambridge: Cambridge University Press, 1976); Roy Porter, *English Society in the Eighteenth Century* (London: Penguin, 1982); see also Paul Langford, *A Polite and Commercial People: England 1727–1783* (Oxford: Oxford University Press, 1989). Edward Thompson and his followers have countered with the more dyadic, neo-Marxist model of patrician hegemony and plebeian resistance: E. P. Thompson, 'Eighteenth Century English Society: Class Struggle without Class?' *Social History* 3 (1978): 123–65, and *Customs in Common: Studies in Traditional Popular Culture* (New York: New Press, 1991); and Douglas Hay, Peter Linebaugh, John G. Rule, E. P. Thompson and Cal Winslow, *Albion's Fatal Tree: Crime and Society in Eighteenth Century England* (New York: Pantheon Books, 1975); Thompson's hostility to 'French' theory is on display in *The Poverty of Theory and Other Essays* (London: Merlin Press, 1978). J. C. D. Clark has done most to advance the argument that England was an 'ancien régime' marked by aristocratic dominance, paternalism and deference (while also excoriating 'Whig' history and imported theory alike): see Clark, *English Society 1688–1832* (Cambridge: Cambridge University Press, 1985); *Revolution and Rebellion: State and Society in England in the Seventeenth and Eighteenth Centuries* (Cambridge: Cambridge University Press, 1986). For debates over Clark's position, see, e.g., Joanna Innes, 'Jonathan Clark, Social History and England's "Ancien regime"', *Past and Present*, No. 115 (1987): 165–200; and the essays in *Albion*, 21 (1989): 361–474.

3 See W. W. Rostow, *The Stages of Economic Growth* (Cambridge: Cambridge University Press, 1960); I. Wallerstein, *The Modern World System* (New York: Academic Press, 1974); Richard Brown, *Modernization: The Transformation of American Life 1600–1865* (New York: Hill & Wang, 1976); Paul Johnson, *The Birth of the Modern World 1815–30* (New York: Harper Collins, 1991). Sociologists such as Emile Durkheim, *The Division of Labor in Society*, trans. George Simpson (New York: Free Press of Glencoe, second edition, 1964) and Max Weber, *The Protestant Ethic and the Spirit of Capitalism*, trans. Talcott Parsons (London: Allen & Unwin, second edition, 1976), who stressed the costs and ambiguities as well as benefits of modernization, provide more interesting sociological ruminations on modernity. For the critique of 'modernization theory', see Andrew Webster, *Introduction to the Sociology of Development* (Basingstoke: Macmillan, 1984) and John Tomlinson, *Cultural Imperialism: A Critical Introduction* (Baltimore: Johns Hopkins University Press, 1991), chs 3 and 5.

4 Jürgen Habermas, 'Modernity: An Incomplete Project', in Hal Foster, ed., *Postmodern Culture* (London: Pluto Press, 1983), 3–15, and *The Structural Transformation of the Public Sphere* trans. Thomas Burber and Frederick Lawrence (Cambridge MA: Harvard University Press, 1989); Marshall Berman, *'All that is Solid Melts into Air': The Experience of Modernity* (New York: Verso, 1982), and *The Politics of Authenticity: Radical Individualism and the Emergence of Modern Society* (New York: Atheneum, 1970). Historians of France have been more favourably impressed by the potential of these readings of Enlightenment and modernity than have their English counterparts, and especially by Habermas's characterization of the eighteenth-century emergence of the 'public sphere': see, e.g., Lynn Hunt, *Politics, Culture and Class in the French Revolution* (Berkeley CA and Los Angeles: University of California Press, 1984) and Hunt, ed., *The Invention of Pornography: Obscenity and the Origins of Modernity 1500–1800* (New York: Zone Books, 1993); Thomas Crow, *Painters and Public Life in Eighteenth Century Paris* (New Haven CT: Yale University Press, 1985); Joan Landes, *Women and the Public Sphere in the Age of the French Revolution* (Ithaca NY: Cornell University Press, 1988); Roger Chartier, *The Cultural Origins of the French Revolution* (Durham NC: Duke University Press, 1991); Sarah Maza, *Private Lives and Public Affairs: The Causes Célèbres of Prerevolutionary France* (Berkeley CA and Los Angeles: University of California Press, 1993): and Dena Goodman, *The Republic of Letters: A Cultural History of the French Enlightenment* (Ithaca: Cornell University Press, 1994). Exceptions among historians writing on England include Geoff Eley, 'Rethinking the Political: Social History and Political Culture in Eighteenth and Nineteenth Century Britain', *Archiv für*

Socialgeschichte 21 (1981): 427–56; Lawrence Klein, *Shaftesbury and the Culture of Politeness* (Cambridge: Cambridge University Press, 1994), and the forthcoming work of John Brewer on English culture. The classic pessimist reading of the modernity inaugurated by the Enlightenment is Theodore Adorno and Max Horkheimer, *Dialectic of Enlightenment* (New York: Seabury Press, 1977).

5 Michel Foucault, *Discipline and Punish: the Birth of the Prison* trans. Roger Sheridan (New York: Vintage, 1971), and *The History of Sexuality* trans. Robert Hurley (New York: Pantheon, 1978); Jacques Derrida, *Of Grammatology* trans. Gayatri Chakravorty Spivak (Baltimore MD: Johns Hopkins University Press, 1976) and *Writing and Difference* trans. Alan Bates (Chicago: University of Chicago Press, 1987); Frederick Jameson, *The Political Unconscious: Narrative as a Socially Symbolic Act* (Ithaca NY: Cornell University Press. 1981); and Umberto Eco, *Travels in Hyperreality* trans. William Weaver (San Diego CA: Harcourt Brace Jovanovich, 1986). Thanks to Nick Mirzoeff for the latter reference.

6 Benjamin, *Illuminations*, 263.

7 Such as C. L. R. James, *The Black Jacobins* (New York: Vintage, second edition rev., 1989); Henry Louis Gates, Jr., ed., *'Race,' Writing and Difference* (Chicago: University of Chicago Press, 1985); Alice Jardine, *Gynesis: Configurations of Women and Modernity* (Ithaca NY: Cornell University Press, 1985); Trinh T. Min-ha, *Woman, Native, Other* (Bloomington IN: Indiana University Press, 1985); Paul Gilroy, *The Black Atlantic: Modernity and Double Consciousness* (Cambridge MA: Harvard University Press, 1993); Homi Bhabha, *The Location of Culture* (London: Routledge, 1994); Nicholas Mirzoeff, *Silent Poetry: Deafness, Sign and Visual Culture in Modern France 1700–1920* (Princeton NJ: Princeton University Press, 1995); and Felicity Nussbaum, 'The Politics of Difference', *Eighteenth Century Studies*, 23 (1990): 375–86. See also such journals as *Public Culture: Bulletin of the Project for Transnational Cultural Studies, Diaspora* and *Eighteenth Century Studies*, special issue, 'African-American Culture in the Eighteenth Century', ed. Rose Zimbardo, 27 (1994).

8 For the structure and efficiency of the British 'fiscal-military' state, see John Brewer, *The Sinews of Power: War, Money and the English State 1688–1783* (London: Unwin Hyman, 1989). For an extended discussion of its ideological significance, see my *The Sense of the People: Politics, Culture and Imperialism in England, 1715–85* (Cambridge: Cambridge University Press, 1995); 'The Good, the Bad and the Impotent: Imperialism and the Politics of Identity in Georgian Britain', in John Brewer and Ann Bermingham, eds, *The Culture of Consumption in Early Modern Europe* (London: Routledge, 1995) and *Staging the Nation: Theatre, Culture and Modernity in the English Provinces, 1720–1820* (in progress). For a differently conceived, if complementary view, see Linda Colley, *Britons: Forging the Nation, 1707–1827* (New Haven: Yale University Press, 1992).

9 *Black Atlantic*, 17. The notion of 'nationess' articulated here contests the more absolutist view put forth by Liah Greenfeld in her influential study, *Nationalism: Five Roads to Modernity* (Cambridge MA: Harvard University Press, 1992). See also Eric Hobshawm, *Nations and Nationalism since 1780: Programme, Myth, Reality* (Cambridge: Cambridge University Press, 1990).

10 Benedict Anderson, *Imagined Communities: Reflections on the Origins and Spread of Nationalism* (London: Verso, 1983), 16; this summary of Anderson's position is indebted to Tomlinson, *Cultural Imperialism*, 81–2.

11 The best critique is that by Partha Chatterjee, *The Nation and its Fragments: Colonial and Postcolonial Histories* (Princeton NJ: Princeton University Press, 1993). As I implicitly argue below, Anderson's model of the relationship between newspapers and nation-ness works better for the metropole than for creole society.

12 Tomlinson, *Cultural Imperialism*, 83–4. That is, the viability of an imagined community of the nation depends upon the ability of its members to '[project] individual existence into the weft of a collective narrative' constructed through traditions 'lived as the trace of an immemorial past (even when they have been fabricated and inculcated in the recent past)': Etienne Balibar, 'The Nation Form: History and Ideology', in E. Balibar and I. Wallerstein, *Race, Nation, Class: Ambiguous Identities* (London: Verso, 1991), 93. Thanks to Nikhil Singh for this reference.

13 The dominance of metropolitan cultural, economic and political forms in 'national' culture is assumed or argued in a number of otherwise excellent studies, among them Gerald Newman, *The Rise of English Nationalism: A Cultural History 1740–1830* (New York: St Martin's Press, 1987); Nancy Armstrong, *Desire and Domestic Fiction: A Political History of the Novel* (New York: Oxford University Press, 1987); John Feather, *The Provincial Book Trade in Eighteenth Century England* (Cambridge: Cambridge University Press, 1986) and the studies of 'commercialization' (see note 2). Recent fruitful work focusing on provincial life includes Jonathan Barry, 'The Cultural Life of Bristol, 1640–1775' (D.Phil. thesis, Oxford, 1985); Perer Borsay, *The English Urban Renaissance: Culture and Society in the Provincial Town, 1660–1770* (Oxford: Clarendon Press, 1989); Perer Clark, ed., *The Transformation of English Provincial Towns, 1600–1800* (London: Hutchinson, 1984); John Money, *Experience and Identity: Birmingham and the West Midlands, 1760–1800* (Manchester: Manchester University Press, 1977); Roy Porter, 'Science, Provincial Culture, and Public Opinion in Enlightenment England', *British Journal for Eighteenth-Century Studies* 3 (1980): 20–46; James Raven, *Judging New Wealth: Popular Publishing and Responses to Commerce in England 1750–1800* (Oxford: Clarendon Press, 1992); and Wilson, *Sense of the People, passim*.

14 Kathleen Wilson, 'Empire of Virtue: The Imperial Project and Hanoverian Culture', in Lawrence Stone, ed., *An Imperial Nation at War* (London: Routledge, 1994), 131–5.

15 Such representations were contested, of course, if not undermined, by the growth of abolitionist literature beginning in the 1760s, some of which was excerpted in periodicals and magazines.

16 See, e.g., *Newcastle Journal,* 27 January, 9 June, 1750; *Newcastle General Magazine,* 8 (1755), 7–15, 241–4, 405–9; *Liverpool General Advertiser,* 17, 24 November, 8, 15 December 1769; 15 June, 6, 27 July, 3 August, 1770; *Lancashire Magazine,* 1 (1763), 11–12. See also Margaret Hunt, 'Racism, Imperialism and the Traveller's Gaze in Eighteenth Century England', *Journal of British Studies* 32 (1993): 333–57.

17 *Liverpool General Advertiser,* 27 July 1770.

18 *Imagined Communities,* 51–63, 62–3; T. H. Breen, 'An Empire of Goods: the Anglicanization of Colonial America, 1690–1776', *Journal of British Studies* 25 (1986): 467–99.

19 See Wilson, *Sense of the People,* chs 1–5; Brewer, *Sinews of Power,* ch. 4; Shyllon, *Black People in Britain,* chs 2–5; James Walvin, *Black and White: The Negro and English Society 1555–1945* (London: Penguin, 1973), chs 4–5; Todd M. Endelman, *The Jews of Georgian England, 1714–1830* (Philadelphia PA: Jewish Publications Society of America, 1979), chs 1, 5; M. D. George, *London Life in the Eighteenth Century* (London: Penguin, 1966), ch. 3. Middle-class women's presence as economic actors and readers was made apparent largely through advertisements, for example.

20 Although such an inscribing of subjectivity was not uncontested, it was also bolstered by other related genres, such as travel writing: see Mary Louise Pratt, *Imperial Eyes: Travel Writing and Transculturation* (London: Routledge, 1992).

21 *The Development of the Provincial Newspaper, 1700–60* (Cambridge: Cambridge University Press, 1962).

22 Ministers tended to endorse an essentially non-resisting, passive version of political subjectivity and patriotism that located political legitimacy and authority solely within a Parliament whose sovereignty was absolute and in a Ministry which protected Parliament from domestic and foreign threats. See John Kenyon, *Revolution Principles* (Cambridge: Cambridge University Press, 1977); Reed Browning, *Political and Constitutional Ideas of the Court Whigs* (Baton Rouge LA: Louisiana State University Press, 1982); Kathleen Wilson, 'A Dissident Legacy: the Glorious Revolution and Eighteenth Century Popular Politics', in J. R. Jones, ed., *Liberty Secured? Britain Before and After 1688* (Stanford CA: Stanford University Press, 1992), 299–326; and Wilson, *Sense of the People,* chs 2 and 5.

23 *London Magazine,* 7 (1738), 241.

24 For recent investigations into the forms and meanings of extraparliamentary political activity in the eighteenth century, see Wilson, *Sense of the People, passim*; James Bradley, *Religion, Revolution and English Radicalism* (Cambridge: Cambridge University Press, 1990); Paul

Monod, *Jacobitism and the English People, 1688–1788* (Cambridge: Cambridge University Press, 1989); and Nicholas Rogers, *Whigs and Cities: Popular Politics in the Age of Walpole and Pitt* (Oxford: Clarendon Press, 1989).

25 Abel Boyer, *Political State of Great Britain*, 38 vols (1711–29), XXIII, 166; anon., *The Liveryman, or, Plain Thoughts on Public Affairs* (London, 1740), 2, 9. See also *The Monitor*, 9 August 1755.

26 Anderson, *Imagined Communities*, 52.

27 Women and 'inferior' races, from Africans to Highland Scots, as well the English lower classes were frequently identified in cultural and political discourse with the symbolic feminine, that is, as dependent, irrational and subordinate: see, e.g., Sander Gilman, 'Black Bodies, White Bodies', in Gates, Jr. *'Race', Writing and Difference*, 225–35; Vivien Jones, *Women in the Eighteenth Century* (London: Routledge, 1990), 101–24; Nancy Leys Stepan, 'Race and Gender: the Role of Analogy in Science', *Isis* 77 (1986): 261–77; Richard Popkin, Medicine, Racism, Anti-Semitism: A Dimension of Enlightenment Thought', in G. S. Rousseau, *The Languages of Psyche: Mind and Body in Enlightenment Thought* (Berkeley and Los Angeles CA: University of California Press, 1990), 405–42; Londa Schiebinger, 'The Anatomy of Difference: Race and Sex in Eighteenth Century Science', *Eighteenth Century Studies* 23 (1990): 387–405.

28 Borsay, *English Urban Renaissance*; Brewer, *Sinews of Power*, 184–5; E. A. Wrigley, 'Urban Growth and Agricultural Change: England and the Continent in the Early Modern Period', in R. I. Rotberg and T. K. Rabb, eds, *Population History: From the Traditional to the Modern World* (Cambridge: Cambridge University Press, 1986), 123–68; P. K. O'Brien and S. L. Engerman, 'Exports and the Growth of the British Economy from the Glorious Revolution to the Peace of Amiens', in B. Solow and S. L. Engerman, eds, *Slavery and the Rise of the Atlantic System* (Cambridge: Cambridge University Press, 1991), 177–209.

29 'Masculinist' in this context thus describes values and practices which are meant to uphold 'masculine' authority, attributes or hierarchy – it is unrelated to the question of women's presence or absence or to their contributions to its construction. This is important to stress, given its recent misinterpretation: as in Margaret Jacob, 'The Mental Landscape of the Public Sphere: a European Perspective', *Eighteenth Century Studies* 28 (1994): 98–9 and n. 13.

30 G. J. Barker-Benfield, *The Culture of Sensibility: Sex and Society in Eighteenth Century Britain* (Chicago IL: University of Chicago Press, 1992), xxvi; Lawrence Klein, 'Gender, Conversation and the Public Sphere', in Judith Still and Michael Worton, eds, *Textuality and Sexuality* (Manchester: Manchester University Press, 1993), 100–15.

31 Wilson, *Sense of the People*, ch. 1. Most hospitals' managements were in the hands of male subscribers of at least two guineas per year, each of whom had the right to recommend patients and vote; although women made up between 10 and 20 per cent of annual hospital contributors, they could vote and sometimes recommend patients only by proxy.

32 C. W. Chalklin, 'Capital Expenditure on Building for Cultural Purposes in Provincial England, 1730–1800', *Business History* 22 (1980): 51–70; Gateshead Public Library, Cotesworth MSS, 'Meeting of Subscribers for building New Assembly Rooms in Newcastle', 1774; Northumberland Record Office, Blackett (Maften) MSS, ZBL 228, *Rules for Regulating the Assemblies in Newcastle upon Tyne* [Newcastle, 1776]. The more liberatory pleasures and dangers of the masquerade described by Terry Castle were infrequently afforded in most non-spa provincial towns: *Masqerade and Civilization* (Stanford CA: Stanford University Press, 1986).

33 Wilson, 'Empire of Virtue', 136–43; Michael Dobson, *The Making of the National Poet: Shakespeare. Adaptation and Authorship, 1660–1769* (Oxford: Clarendon Press), especially 146–64; Theophilus Cibber, *Two Dissertations on the Theatres* (London, 1756), appendix.

34 See John Brewer, 'Clubs and Commercialization', in McKendrick *et al.*, *Birth of a Consumer Society*.

35 *Sense of the People*, chs 1 and 3; Kathleen Wilson, 'Empire, Trade and Popular Politics in Mid-Hanoverian Britain: the Case of Admiral Vernon', *Past and Present* 121 (1988): 74–109; Colley, *Britons*, 85–96.

36 This contentious claim is substantiated at length in my *Sense of the People*, chs 3–5; the reader is referred there for detailed references. For a contending view, see Colley, *Britons, passim*.

37 John Brown, *An Estimate of the Manners and Principles of the Times*, 2 vols (London, 1757), II, 40; see also I, 66–7, 78–82, 181–2; John Barrell, *The Battle of Pandora and the Division of Knowledge* (London: Macmillan, 1992); Randolph Trumbach, 'Sex, Gender and Sexual Identity in Modern Culture: Male Sodomy and Female Prostitution in Enlightenment London', *Journal of the History of Sexuality* 2 (1991): 186–203; Barker-Benfield, *Culture of Sensibility*, 37–153; Kristina Straub, *Sexual Suspects: Eighteenth Century Players and Sexual Ideology* (Princeton NJ: Princeton University Press, 1992); Robert Fahrner, 'A Reassessment of Garrick's *The Male Coquette; or, Seventeen-Hundred Fifty-Seven* as Veiled Discourse', *Eighteenth Century Life* 17 (1993): 1–13.

38 Wilson, *Sense of the People*, chs 3 and 5; *The Death of the late General Wolfe at the Siege of Quebec*, Manchester Central Library, Playbills, Marsden Street Theatre, 17 August 1763; *Salisbury Journal*, 22, 29 September 1761; *Newcastle Journal*, 23 June, 15 September, 27 October 1759; *Farley's Bristol Journal*, 7 June 1778; and *Norfolk Chronicle*, 18 July 1778.

39 [Jonas Hanway], *A Letter from a Member of the Marine Society, shewing the Usefulness and Utility of its Design* (London, 1756), 4, 12; *An Account of the Society for the Encouragement of British Troops in Germany and North America* (London, 1760). For anti-conquest narratives, see Pratt, *Imperial Eyes*.

40 For a fuller explication of this argument, see Wilson, *Sense of the People*, ch. 4. *Biographical History of Patriots* (London, 1770), advertised in *Liverpool General Advertiser*, 6 July 1770; *North Briton*, 23 April 1763 (No. 45), 3 July 1762 ff; John Brewer, 'The Misfortunes of Lord Bute', *Historical Journal*, 16 (1973), 7–30; *Salisbury Journal*, 14 April 1766.

41 For the Masonic clubs, see Margaret Jacob, *The Radical Enlightenment: Pantheists, Freemasons and Republicans* (London: Allen & Unwin, 1981) 206–8; and in France, Goodman, *Republic of Letters*, 233–80. Women were allowed to join the more progressive Wilkite debating societies in the West Midlands, but this seems to have been fairly exceptional: see Money, *Experience and Identity*, 112. In the event, it is not the empirical presence or absence of women that is at issue here, but the place of the symbolic feminine in the political imaginary of Wilkite radicalism.

42 Such as the attacks on Lord George Sackville Germain, called a 'buggering hero' by Wilkes and Churchill, which twinned his homosexuality with cowardice: *Interesting Letters Selected from the Political and Patriotic Correspondence of Messrs. Wilkes, Horn, Beckford and Junius* (London, 1769), 35–6; Piers Mackesy, *The Coward of Minden: the Affair of Lord George Sackville* (London: Allen Lane, 1979), especially 254–6. For the backlash against sodomy in this period, see Lawrence Stone, *Family, Sex and Marriage in England, 1500–1800* (New York: Harper & Row 1977), 541–2; Randolph Trumbach, 'Sodomy Transformed: Aristocratic Libertinage, Public Reputation and the Gender Revolution of the Eighteenth Century', *Journal of Homosexuality* 19 (1990), 160–1.

43 Adrian Hamilton, *The Infamous Essay on Women* (London: André Deutsch, 1972); George Rudé, *Wilkes and Liberty* (New York: Oxford University Press, 1969), ch. 1; Horace Walpole, *Memoirs of George III*, 4 vols (London, 1845), IV, 156–7 n; J. E. Ross, ed., *Radical Adventurer: the Diaries of Robert Morris, 1772–74* (Bath: Adams & Dart, 1971), 9–12, 23–6, 34–6; *The Diary of Sylas Neville*, ed. Basil Cozens-Hardy (Cambridge: Cambridge Univ, Press, 1958) 39–40, 160–1.

44 Raymond Postgate, *That Devil Wilkes* (New York: Vanguard Press, 1930), 140–5; Rudé, *Wilkes and Liberty*, 85–9; quotations from Richard Sennett, *The Fall of Public Man* (New York: Knopf, 1977), 103, and John Brewer, 'Theatre and Counter-theatre in Georgian Politics', *Radical History Review* 22 (1979–90): 8.

45 For the denigration of such discrepances between public and private virtue as Wilkes exhibited, see Leonore Davidoff and Catherine Hall, *Family Fortunes: Men and Women of the English Middle-Class* (Chicago IL: University of Chicago Press, 1987), 108–18; Barker-Benfield, *Culture of Sensibility*, chs 3–4. For women participants, see Wilson, *Sense of the People*, 32–3, 366–8; for the antagonism between contractarian politics and women's presence in the political sphere, see *ibid.*, ch. 4; Carol Pateman, *The Sexual Contract* (Stanford CA:

Stanford University Press, 1988), 1–16. The penalities for women's over-identification with the prerogatives of 'manly patriotism' were illustrated by the life of Catherine Macaulay; see Bridget Hill, *The Republican Virago: the Life and Times of Catherine Macaulay* (Oxford: Clarendon Press, 1992).

46 For the contending masculinities and femininities at play in eighteenth-century urban society, see Michael Kimmel, 'The Contemporary "Crisis" of Masculinity in Historical Perspective', in Harry Brod, ed., *The Making of Masculinities: The New Men's Studies* (Boston MA: Allen & Unwin, 1987), 121–53; Randolph Trumbach, 'London's Sapphists: From Three Sexes to Four Genders in the Making of Modern Culture', in *Body Guards: The Cultural Politics of Gender Ambiguity*, ed. Julia Epstein and Kristina Straub (London: Routledge, 1991, 112–41); and Castle, *Masquerade and Civilization*.

47 Paul Kaufman, *Libraries and their Uses* (London: Library Association, 1969), 222–4; British Library, Arderon MSS, Add. MS 27, 966, ff. 241b–42; Peter Clark, *The English Alehouse: A Social History* (London: Longman, 1983), 225.

48 Joseph Addison, *The Freeholder*, ed. James Leheny (Oxford: Clarendon Press, 1979), 1982; *The Correspondence of Sir James Clavering*, ed. H. T. Dickinson (Surtees Society, CLXXVIII, 1967), 70–5; [Eliza Haywood], *The Female Spectator* (London, 1744–45); Rachel J. Weil, 'Sexual Ideology and Political Propaganda in England, 1680–1714' (Ph.D. dissertation, Princeton University, 1991); Michael Harris, *London Newspapers in the Age of Walpole* (Cranbury NJ: Associated University Presses, 1987), 38–40; R. M. Wiles, *Freshest Advices: Early Provincial Newspapers* (Canton OH: Ohio State University Press, 1965), 269–302; Moira Ferguson, *Subject to Others: British Women Writers and Colonial Slavery, 1670–1834* (London: Routledge, 1992); Mary R. Mahl and Helene Koon, eds, *The Female Spectator: English Women Writers before 1800* (Bloomington IN: Indiana University Press, 1977).

49 *Newcastle Chronicle*, 11 April 1766; *Norwich Gazette*, 9 February 1733, 3 January, 19 December 1741; Huntington Library, Montagu MSS, Mo 245–6.

50 Frank O'Gorman, *Voters, Patrons and Parties* (Oxford: Clarendon Press, 1990), 93–4; Monod, *Jacobitism*, 190–218, 250; Thompson, *Customs in Common*, 306–61; *Newcastle Chronicle*, 19 March 1768; Donna Andrew, ed., *London Debating Societies, 1776–1799* (London Record Society Publications 30, 1993), viii–ix; Clare Midgley, *Women against Slavery: The British Campaigns 1780–1870* (London: Routledge, 1992), 15–25; *Female Spectator* II, 135–68; *Norwich Gazette*, 16 November 1745; *Bonner and Middleton's Bristol Journal*, 10 January 1778; *Freeholder*, 181–4.

51 Wilson, *Sense of the People*, chs 1, 3–5; for the 1790s, see Linda Colley, *Britons*, ch. 6; for the injunction to 'manliness' for women in feminist discourse, see Catherine Macaulay, *Letters on Education* (London, 1790), letters 22 and 24; and Mary Wollstonecraft, *Vindication of the Rights of Woman* (London, 1792), 80–1, 206–7. The long-hallowed link in Western culture between women's rights and commercial capitalism has been most recently argued by Barker-Benfield, *Culture of Sensibility*, especially chs 4 and 5; for an idealized view of its consequences, see Jacob, 'Mental Landscape of the Public Sphere', 95–113.

52 Political writers of all stripes, from 'civic humanists' to court Whigs and Tories, identified legitimate political activity with men and the symbolic masculine and subversion, rebellion, supineness and corruption with 'feminine' influences: J. G. A. Pocock, *Virtue, Commerce and History* (Cambridge: Cambridge University Press, 1985); Browning, *Ideas of the Court Whigs*; Barker-Benfield, *Culture of Sensibility*, 116–19; *The History of the Westminster Election* (London, 1785), 102–5, 227–8, 248; *The Female Parliament* (London, 1754); *The Female Patriot* (London, 1779). The *salonnières'* role in knowledge production in France was a cause of grave concern to Hume, among others, who thought it greatly exceeded woman's place: Goodman, *Republic of Letters*, 124.

53 Georgiana Hill, *Women in English Life*, 2 vols (London: R. Bentley & Sons, 1896), I, 2–20; *Georgiana: Extracts from the Correspondence of Georgiana, Duchess of Devonshire*, ed. Earl of Bessborough (London: Murray, 1955), 15–16, 25–35, 78–80; Gateshead Public Library, Ellison MSS, A54/11, 15 March 1739; *Freeholder*, 182, 52–4, 73–4, 205.

54 For women's participation in the war effort, see Wilson, *Sense of the People*, ch. 3; for its

effacement, see [Richard Baldwin], *An Impartial and Succinct History of the Origin and Progress of the Present War*, first published in instalments in the *London Magazine*, vols 28–9 (1759–60 ff). By the 1790s, the acknowledgment of women's contribution became a crucial part of loyalist political culture: Colley, *Britons*, 238–48.

55 *Freeholder*, 182; see also 52–4, 73–4, 205.

56 As Carol Pateman has noted, that women were held by virtually all political theorists to be incapable of men's ultimate political obligation – to give up their lives in defence of the state – is part of the notion of (sexual) difference that governed and circumscribed the terms of their inclusion in civil society and continues to bedevil their place there: *The Disorder of Women* (Stanford CA: Stanford University Press, 1989), 4–14. For additional reflections on the historical connections between 'woman', women and disorder in eighteenth-century political thought, see Linda M. Zerilli, *Signifying Woman: Culture and Chaos in Rousseau, Burke and Mill* (Ithaca NY: Cornell University Press, 1994).

57 Montagu MS MO 1384, 6 August 1758. For an insightful theoretical treatment of the tensions between 'woman as representation' and 'women as historical beings', see Teresa de Lauretis, *Technologies of Gender: Essays on Theory, Film and Fiction* (Bloomington and Indianapolis IN: Indiana University Press, 1987); for the signification of women's bodies in political iconography in the eighteenth century, see my 'Britannia into Battle. Empire, Citizenship and the Gendered Body Politic' (forthcoming).

58 John Geipel, *The Europeans: An Ethnohistorical Survey* (London: Longman, 1969), 163–5; V. G. Kiernan, 'Britons Old and New', in Colin Holmes, ed., *Immigrants and Minorities in British Society* (London: Allen & Unwin, 1978), 23–43; Edelman, *Jews of Georgian England*, ch. 4; Walvin, *Black and White*, ch. 4; Wilson, *Sense of the People*, ch. 6; John Steegmann, *The Rule of Taste from George I to George IV* (London: Macmillan, 1936), 39; Virginia Berridge, 'East End Opium Dens and Narcotic Use in Britain', *London Journal* 4 (1978): n. 3.

59 Colley, *Britons, passim.*

60 English Catholics were objects of penal laws throughout the century, kept under house arrest during the Jacobite rebellions of 1715 and 1745, and the animus of rioters in 1780; Irish Catholics were targets of popular and official animosity at various junctures, such as in 1736, 1745 and 1780; Jews and foreign Protestants were harassed during the furor over the naturalization Bills of 1751 and 1753 and the objects of exclusionary civic bye-laws; Scots were segregated and kept from apprenticeships in several northern towns; and Africans were not only attacked, harassed and kidnapped, but some were also rounded up for 'repatriation' in 1786–87.

61 Those outports included not only Bristol and Liverpool, but also Chester, Dartmouth, Exeter, Glasgow, Lancaster, Plymouth, Portsmouth, Preston, and Whitehaven. David Brion Davis, *The Problem of Slavery in Western Culture* (Ithaca NY: Cornell University Press, 1966); Nigel Tattersfield, *The Forgotten Trade. Comprising the Log of the Daniel and Henry of 1700 and Accounts of the Slave Trade from the Minor Ports of England, 1698–1725* (London: Jonathan Cape, 1991); Walvin, *Black and White*, 31–79; Peter Fryer, *Staying Power: The History of Black People in Britain* (London: Pluto Press, 1984), 58–64; Philip Morgan, 'British Encounters with Africans and African-Americans c. 1600–1780', in Bernard Bailyn and Philip Morgan, eds, *Strangers within the Realm: Cultural Margins of the First British Empire* (Chapel Hill NC: University of North Carolina Press, 1991), 157–219.

62 Eighteenth-century Britain was a slave-owning, if not slave, society, and slavery was confirmed as legal by court after court in the name of property rights. The Somerset case of 1772, which rendered illegal slaves' forcible removal from England, increased the freedom of black servants but was ignored or evaded by West Indian planters, who tried to have it overturned by Act of Parliament. See Morgan, 'British Encounters', 158–60; E. O. Shyllon, *Black Slaves in Britain* (London: Oxford University Press, 1974); James Oldham, 'New Light on Mansfield and Slavery', *Journal of British Studies* 27 (1988): 45–68.

63 Fryer, *Staying Power*, 72–80; Paul Edwards and James Walvin, *Black Personalities in the Era of the Slave Trade* (Baton Rouge LA: Louisiana State University Press, 1983) 31–2.

64 Ukawsaw Gronniosaw, *Wondrous Grace Display'd in the Life and Conversion of James Albert*

Ukawsaw Gronniosaw (Bath, 1770), 171. Slave and free black labour was protested against by white artisans in other towns in England and the empire as posing a threat to their livelihoods: Morgan, 'British Encounters', 191.

65 Sir John Fielding, *Extracts from such of the Penal Laws, as Particularly Relate to the Peace and Good Order of this Metropolis* (London, 1768), 144.

66 Walvin, *Blacks in Britain*, 64–5. The spiritual imperialism of such organizations as the SPCK, which had been actively converting Africans since the late seventeenth century, aided the process; C. F. Pascoe, *Two Hundred Years of the SPG* (London: London Society for the Propagation of the Gospel, 1901), 256–7.

67 *London Chronicle*, 17 February 1764; Shyllon, *Blacks in Britain*, 79–81; J. J. Hecht, *Continental and Colonial Servants*, in *Eighteenth Century England* (Northampton MA: Department of History, Smith College, 1954), 54.

68 See, e.g., the letters of the Sons of Africa in *Memoirs of Granville Sharp* (London, 1828) and those reprinted in Shyllon, *Blacks in Britain*, appendix II. For black radicals in later decades, see Peter Linebaugh, *The London Hanged: Crime and Civil Society in the Eighteenth Century* (Cambridge: Cambridge University Press, 1992), 415–16; Iain McCalman, 'Anti-Slavery and Ultra Radicalism in Early Nineteenth-century England', *Slavery and Abolition*, 7 (1986); Fryer, *Staying Power*, 214–36.

69 Henry Louis Gates, Jr, 'Writing "Race" and the Difference it Makes', in Gates, ed., *Race, Writing and Difference*, 11–15; Ferguson, *Subject to Others*, 125–33; Shyllon, *Blacks in Britain*, 169–203; Cugoano, *Thoughts and Sentiments on the Evil and Wicked Traffic of the Slavery and Commerce of the Human Species* (London, 1787), reprinted in Francis D. Adams and Barry Saunders, eds, *Three Black Writers in Eighteenth Century England* (Belmont CA: Wadsworth, 1971); Olaudah Equiano, *The Interesting Narrative of the Life of Olaudah Equiano, or Gustava Vassa, the African* (London, seventh edition, 1793).

70 See, e.g., Midgley, *Women against Slavery*.

71 The most recent and detailed examination is that by Stephen J. Braidwood, *Black Poor and White Philanthropists: London's Blacks and the Foundation of the Sierra Leone Settlement, 1786–1791* (Liverpool: Liverpool University Press, 1994).

72 Belisarius was the Roman general blinded by the Emperor Justinian and forced to wander the world as a beggar for presumed disloyalty – the classic example of the fickleness of princes. The third ship to be commissioned was named the *Vernon*.

73 Shyllon, *Black People in Britain*, 136–46; Cugoano, *Thoughts and Sentiments on the Evils of Slavery*, 139–42; *Morning Herald*, 15 December 1786, 2 January 1787, quoted in Shyllon, *Black People in Britain*, 140–1.

74 *Public Advertiser*, 1 January 1787; *Morning Post*, 22 December 1786, quoted in Shyllon, *Black People*, 142.

75 *Public Advertiser*, 3 January 1787; George, *London Life*, 116–57; James Tobin, *A Short Rejoinder to the Reverend Mr. Ramsay's Reply* (London, 1787); Winthrop Jordan, *White over Black: American Attitudes toward the Negro 1550–1812* (Chapel Hill NC: University of North Carolina Press, 1968); *Omiah's Farewell, Inscribed to the Ladies of London* (London, 1776); 'Song on the Cherokee Chiefs Inscribed to the Ladies of Great Britain' [1763], quoted in Tom Hatley, *The Dividing Paths: Cherokees and South Carolinians through the Era of Revolution* (New York: Oxford University Press, 1993), 151–2 (thanks to Nancy Shoemaker for this reference). The imbalance in the numbers of black men and women – the result of slave recruitment patterns – meant that African men frequently took white wives. See *Cobbett's Weekly Political Register*, 16 June 1804 for disparagement of such intermarriage.

76 *London Chronicle*, 19–22 October 1765, my emphasis. That blacks born in Britain or her colonies may also have been 'natives' did not seem to occur to the *Chronicle* writer, who not only thereby exposed the priority of 'race' in the national identity but also anticipated by almost 200 years the anti-immigration arguments of the British right since World War II.

77 Bhabha, 'Signs Taken for Wonders', *Location of Culture*, 108.

78 Equiano, *Interesting Narrative*, 132, 340 and *passim*; Geraldine Murphy, 'Olaudah Equiano, Accidental Tourist', *Eighteenth Century Studies* 27 (1994): 551–68; *Morning Chronicle*, 15 July

1788 (letter from the Sons of Africa to Sir William Dolben, Bart.); Linebaugh, *London Hanged*, 415. For the hybrid and 'radically nonbinary' nature of slave narratives in general and Equiano in particular, see Bhabha, 'Signs Taken for Wonders', 102–22, and Susan M. Marren, 'Between Slavery and Freedom: The Transgressive Self in Olaudah Equiano's Autobiography', *PMLA* 108 (1993): 95; for Du Bois, see Gilroy, *Black Atlantic*.

79 Quoted in Shyllon, *Blacks in Britain*, 193.

80 *Imagined Communities*, 16.

81 As argued by Colley, *Britons*, ch. 3, and Richard Helgerson, *Forms of Nationhood: the Elizabethan Writing of England* (Chicago IL: University of Chicago Press, 1993).

82 Quotation from George Lillo, *The London Merchant* (London, 1731), 3.1.11–19 – an immensely popular play in London and the provinces in this period. For the retailing of this view of empire, see Wilson, 'Empire of Virtue', 141–3.

83 See, e.g., *Gentleman's Magazine*, 28 (1758), 393; *Salisbury Journal*, 14 January 1760; *Newcastle General Magazine*, 11 (1758), 242–5.

84 Rev. Richard Brewster, *A Sermon on the Thanksgiving Day* (Newcastle, 1759); *Gentleman's Magazine*, 33 (1763), 291.

85 *Parliamentary History*, XVII (1771–74), 857–8 and *passim*; Samuel Foote, *The Nabob* (London, 1772); *Public Advertiser*, 14 March 1774, 10 July 1769, 26 March 1771; *Lancashire Magazine*, I (1763), 60–2, II (1764), 515–16; H. V. Bowen, *Revenue and Reform: the Indian Problem in British Politics* (Cambridge: Cambridge University Press, 1991).

86 *Parliamentary History*, XVII (1771–74), 567–73, 722–43; *Scots Magazine*, 34 (1772), 588; and Peter Hulme, *Colonial Encounters: Europeans and the Caribbean* (London: Methuen, 1986), ch. 6.

87 [John Hawkesworth] *An Account of the Voyages … Successively performed by Commodore Byron, Capt. Wallis, Capt. Carteret and Captain Cook*, 3 vols (London, 1773); Bernard Smith, *European Vision and the South Pacific* (New Haven CT: Yale University Press, 1985); Shyllon, *Black Slaves in Britain*, ch. 4. For the Somerset case, see note 62.

88 Public Record Office, HO 55/13/2.

89 Peter Marshall, 'Empire and Authority in Later Eighteenth Century Britain', *Journal of Imperial and Commonwealth Studies* 15 (1987): 115. The *Zong* incident of 1781, when 133 captive Africans aboard a slave ship headed for Jamaica were thrown overboard for the insurance money, added immeasurably to public shock and disillusionment. See Fryer, *Staying Power*, 127–30.

90 Edward Gibbon, *The Decline and Fall of the Roman Empire* (London, 1776-88); Society for Constitutional Information, *The Second Address to the Public* (London, 1782); see also *Newcastle Chronicle*, 19 August 1786.

91 Benjamin, *Illuminations*, 261. These past and present moments collided again in Alan Bennett's dramatic Tory panegyric to George III, *The Madness of George III* (London: Faber, 1992), which should also be located in the post-imperial crisis of national identity inaugurated by decolonization, Suez and immigration.

92 'To the ENGLISH NATION', *Norfolk Chronicle*, 10 October 1778.

93 *Parliamentary History*, XVII, 570–5, 735–6.

94 Homi Bhabha, 'Of Mimicry and Man: the Ambivalence of Colonial Discourse', *October* 28 (1984): 125–33. For contemporary recognition of and complaints about this conceptualization of Englishness, see *Gentleman's Magazine*, 25 (1765), 589–90.

8

Death on the Nile: fantasy and the literature of tourism, 1840–60

JOHN BARRELL

The mid-nineteenth century, say from the early 1830s to 1860, has been represented as a missing link in the history of Egyptology.[1] In terms of general enthusiasm and interest, however, as distinct from scholarly research, the same period is probably the high point of admiration in Europe and the United States of the culture of the Ancient Egyptians. With the decipherment of the hieroglyphics, the extraordinary age of Egyptian civilization was becoming increasingly clear, and so were the questions it raised about the chronology of world history and especially of ethnology. It was then still possible to believe that what was best in Greek civilization had been learned from Egypt. More crucially, it was still possible to believe that the religion of Ancient Egypt, in whatever vulgar forms it had been propagated to the populace at large, had been at its best moments a monotheism: the forerunner of Judaism and therefore of Christianity. It is as if the true test of a civilization was that it should be based on a monotheist religion, a test failed even by the Greeks, except in the opinion of those few who believed that they too were closet monotheists. It may seem odd, then, that so often in the tourist literature of the period, admiration of the Ancient Egyptians seems to grow at the expense of any respect for the civilization of modern Egypt. In the confrontation of Western tourists and the Arabs, the Turks, and the Nubians they encountered between Alexandria and Abu Simbel, it is not often this test that is used to judge the degree of civilization attained by the modern Egyptians; quite other criteria are used, ethnological and anthropological rather than theological.

A case in point is Harriet Martineau's *Eastern Life*, the narrative of her tour in Egypt first published in 1848. As we shall see, the book is remarkable for the liberal position it takes up in relation to the politics of Egyptology. Martineau held what to many in the mid-nineteenth century had become incompatible beliefs: that the Ancient Egyptians were black,[2] and that they had created one of the great civilizations of the world. Her account of the religion of Ancient Egypt – an account evidently directed against an Evangelical fear and contempt of 'idolatry' –

is a model for the mid-nineteenth century of how to conduct the discussion of cultural difference.[3] But what are we to make of passages such as this, a parting reflection as she takes leave of Karnac after a final, moonlit visit?

> Here was enthroned the human intellect when humanity was elsewhere scarcely emerging from chaos. And how was it now? That morning I had seen the Governor of Thebes, crouching on his haunches on the filthy shore among the dung heaps, feeding himself with his fingers among a circle of apish creatures like himself. (*Eastern Life*, 217)

Here as so often in the tourist literature I shall be talking about, a distinction between the modern and the ancient Egyptian seems to do duty also as a distinction between East and West. And it takes the form of denying, sometimes in tones of elaborate disgust, sometimes with a casualness hardly less disturbing, that the Muslim inhabitants of modern Egypt, whether Arab, Nubian, Turkish or Albanian, are human at all. This vision of the Governor of Thebes as an ape who does not hold himself upright but crouches on his haunches, who has insufficient manual dexterity to use tools and so feeds himself with his fingers, is evidently offered in terms which evoke and question the anatomical distinctions made, most notably by Blumenbach, between human beings and apes.[4] And the fact that he is represented, not as eating but as feeding himself, in a place of filth, among dung heaps, and in that offensive crouching posture, suggests that for Martineau the question about where the line is drawn, between human and animal, is calling up distinctions and confusions between the mouth and the anus, between eating and excreting. The Governor of Thebes has become an extraordinary emblem for what Freud described as the formation of judgement, expressed in the language of the oral impulse, about what belongs to the ego and what it rejects or projects as alien to itself.[5]

All the recent work on what is called colonial discourse and on the relations of the West and East has started from the binary distinction, however much it may come to be complicated, between the Western self and its exotic or oriental other, in which the other is conceived in terms of the projection of whatever in the Western psyche is an object of disgust and terror: the East as the embodiment of Western fears. Beyond that common starting point, however, this work seems to take one of two main directions, though sometimes (as in the work of Gayatri Spivak or Homi Bhabha, for instance) it may take both at once. There has been the attempt to produce an account of the relations of Western imperialism and the East in the terms of hegemony and of power; of the discourses by which the West positions itself as subject and the East as object, and of the practices by which that distinction is established as a matter of established academic or administrative fact. There has also been an attempt — I associate it particularly with Sander Gilman — to focus more closely on the operations of fantasy and projection, and to talk about that attitude of disgust towards the Other which is always a self-disgust, about the Western fear of the Oriental, including the Jew, as a fear of something inside the Western psyche, something which is imperfectly repressed or is even produced by the civilizing process.[6] As its title suggests, this will be the emphasis of my chapter too.

It is in these terms that I have become interested in the literature of tourism, and specifically of tourism in Egypt, as one of the genres in which the mid-nineteenth-century fear and loathing of the East may find its most articulate and most violent expression. The literature of tourism in Egypt is only one of several genres of Western writing in which the British, in particular, were reinventing the Western image of Egypt and the East. There was also a literature of exploration, for example – of the search for the hidden source of the Nile, eventually 'discovered' by John Hanning Speke in 1858; there was a literature of social anthropology, though the term is of course an anachronism, represented most famously by E. W. Lane; there was an expanding literature of archaeology, in which Sir John Gardner Wilkinson was the most famous name.[7] The variety of writings in which Egypt was being described and constructed in the mid-nineteenth century makes it easier here than elsewhere to attempt to define a genre of tourist literature.

I shall not spend much time on that attempt here, except to remark that although there is no clear line between these genres and what I think of as tourist literature, there is an obvious difference of emphasis. Authors like Lane and Wilkinson think of themselves as engaged to some degree or another in the practice of a science, and as obliged to attempt to write with some degree of impersonality. Whatever notions of occidental superiority are encoded in that attempted impersonality, and whatever eludes its vigilance, such writers are in a very different position from tourists, whose accounts of the country seem often to have been judged in terms of the degree of personality displayed in what are always represented as 'personal impressions' of the country. The geography of Egypt ensured that everyone made more or less the same tour, and the idiosyncratic variety of the tourist literature should probably be thought of as an essential commercial response to the sameness of the itinerary.

This is not to say that a writer like Martineau, in particular, does not aspire to provide useful knowledge of the antiquities, the ancient religion, the history, the geography and the political economy of Egypt. Other tourists, one of whom I will talk about, attempted to represent their treasure-hunting and grave-robbing as responsible archaeology. In spite of all that, however, the generic obligation of the writers of tourist literature, that they should describe the impression Egypt has made upon them, how deeply or otherwise it has imprinted itself into their personality, encourages or requires the use of a language especially hospitable to fantasy, to that virus of inferiority which seems to break out in the imaginative literature of the 1820s, which spreads so insidiously and so unchecked through Victorian writing, and which enables the unguarded utterance of sentiments such as Martineau's in her description of the Governor of Thebes.

Tourist accounts of Egypt are of special interest, too, because they are so much a part and an effect of imperialism. The growth of British tourism in Egypt after about 1840 was partly an effect of 'agreements' imposed on Egypt, largely by the British, with the aim of reversing its progress towards economic as well as political independence.[8] In particular, it was an effect of the development of the overland route to India. In 1841, the Peninsular and Oriental Steam Navigation Company was granted the concession to land at Suez; by the following year there was a regular P&O service on both sides of the isthmus; and though earlier in the century there had been travellers to Egypt whom we can think of as tourists, it was only now that Egypt began to become a convenient and fashionable tourist destination.[9] The tourists arrived in Alexandria usually in November or December, when the weather was at its most bearable and when the conditions were right for a voyage on the Nile; they travelled by canal and river to Cairo; hired their houseboat and crew; sailed and were towed directly up-river, taking advantage of the north wind and virtually ignoring the sights until they reached the second cataract; and then, turning round, they began a leisurely inspection of the monuments, beginning at Abu Simbel.

In the 1840s and 1850s dozens of narratives of tourism in Egypt were published in Britain, as well as in the United States, France and Germany. In this chapter I shall be mainly concerned with Martineau's *Eastern Life*, with Florence Nightingale's *Letters from Egypt*, privately printed in 1854, and William C. Prime's *Boat Life in Egypt and Nubia*, published in 1857.[10] Prime was a lawyer from New York City. Pressure of time will not permit me to discuss more than these, which of course I have chosen because they contain passages that enable me to make my points fairly economically; in different ways they are not at all untypical, however, of the dozen or so tours from this period which I have read so far.[11]

I want to look at just one more incident from Martineau's narrative, her last glimpse of the antiquities of Egypt, when on their return journey her party stopped to inspect the Pyramids and the Sphinx. She was disappointed by the Pyramids themselves, which were somehow less, or at any rate no more, than she expected; as for the Sphinx, at first she could not see it at all. It is only when her party has passed it by, and someone refers to the Sphinx as something they have already seen, that Martineau realizes that, unaccountably enough, she has simply missed it. I should explain that in the mid-nineteenth century little more than the head of the Sphinx was visible above the sand – though that was over 20 ft high, and very hard to miss, as Martineau herself acknowledges. The whole account of the visit turns on and returns to this moment of non-recognition: Martineau is 'utterly bewildered', as she puts it, by the incident, and cannot leave it unexplained. In fact, she writes, when her party returns to examine the Sphinx, 'I found I had seen it'; intent on looking at the Pyramids, she had taken the Sphinx only for 'a capriciously-formed rock'. 'I rather doubt,' she writes, 'whether any traveller would take the Sphinx for anything but a rock unless he was looking for it, or had his eye caught by some casual light,' though this hardly explains why she had forgotten to look for it in the first place. (*Eastern Life*, 244).

Her description of the Sphinx itself is extraordinary: it seems to carry the weight of an intense anxiety about the boundaries of Western self and Eastern other, which once again compels her to reflect upon that moment of non-recognition. 'What a monstrous idea was it from which this monster sprang! ... I feel that a stranger either does not see the Sphinx at all, or he sees it as a nightmare.'

> When we first passed it, I saw it only as a strange-looking rock; an oversight which could not have occurred in the olden time, when the head bore the royal helmet or the ram's horns. Now, I was half afraid of it. The full, serene gaze of its round face, rendered ugly by the loss of the nose, which was a very handsome feature of the old Egyptian face; – this full gaze, and the stony calm of its attitude almost turn one to stone. So lifelike, – so huge, – so monstrous, – it is really a fearful spectacle. (*Eastern Life*, 254)

The inability to *see* the Sphinx, and the terror it inspires, are both explained in terms of the lack of some identifying projection. She *would* have recognized it if the helmet or the ram's horns had been there; it would have been handsome if the nose had been there. We are positively invited, it seems, to discuss the Sphinx – a new Medusa's Head, the sign of an absence which can petrify[12] – in terms of the crudest version of an anxiety about sexual difference. For the purposes of this chapter, however, I want to suggest that it speaks just as emphatically of an anxiety about the difference between human and animal as between male and female. Each of course may involve, may be a figure for, the other, by the convention which attributes to the 'other woman', including the exotic and/or oriental woman, an 'animal' sensuality. Appropriately, perhaps, Martineau's description of the 'fearful spectacle' of the Sphinx is recalled a few chapters later, when, in Cairo, she encounters an Egyptian 'dancing girl' – a 'horrid sight', 'so hideous a creature ... I never saw', her movements just a 'disagreeable and foolish wriggle' (*Eastern Life*, 283).

The Sphinx of course is part human, part animal, and Martineau's visit to the Pyramids occurs between a discussion of the mummification of animals and a series of anecdotes about cannibalism in Egypt consequent upon the failure of the inundation. Dead animals treated as humans, dead humans treated as animals, humans behaving as animals: the boundary between the two is especially unstable in this part of Martineau's narrative. Earlier in the book, the Sphinx as idea is understood by Martineau in the conventional terms of a union of mind and body, wisdom and strength, human and animal (*Eastern Life*, 122). But when she finally encounters the Sphinx itself, it appears not as the union but as the confusion of all those binaries.

Martineau's anxiety about the humanity of the Sphinx needs to be understood within a specific historical and discursive context, ethnological and Egyptological. 'We have here,' she writes,

> a record of the Egyptian complexion, or of the Egyptians' own notion of it, as well as of the characteristic features of the race ... The face is (supposing the nose restored) much like the Berber countenance. The long, mild eye, the thick, but not protuberant lips, ... and the projecting jaw, with the intelligent, gentle expression of the whole face, are very like what one sees in Nubia at every village. (*Eastern Life*, 255)

This description, which gives clear indications of Martineau's familiarity with ethnological debate, is the last of her many declarations that she believes the Ancient Egyptians were black. In this she shows her allegiance to a number of French Enlightenment thinkers from Volney on who stressed the importance of Upper Egypt or even Ethiopia as the sources of Egyptian civilization. The most influential British ethnologist, James Cowles Prichard, had pronounced that, though their racial character was considerably modified in later ages, the Egyptians had originally been 'nearly' Negro.[13] I use the word 'negro', here and elsewhere, in its pseudo-technical sense, which refers to one of the races or families which for nineteenth-century ethnologists made up the 'Ethiopian' variety of mankind, the black Africans. The notion that the Ancient Egyptians had been black was, however, regularly denounced; most recently by Samuel George Morton, the Philadelphia craniologist, whose research – even as Martineau was writing – was giving a new scientific justification for slavery in the southern United States. Prichard himself came to accept Morton's view, and by 1848 Martineau's belief in the blackness of the Egyptians was becoming increasingly hard to sustain.[14] What was at stake, of course, was more than the identity of the Ancient Egyptians; it was the humanity of the blacks. The 'Negro race', wrote Cuvier, is marked by 'the projecting muzzle and thick lips'. The same characteristics that Martineau sees in the Sphinx are those which, according to Cuvier, 'approximate' the negro 'to the Apes'. [15]

What may be showing through, then, in Martineau's reaction to the Sphinx – the fear, the racial typing – is the anxiety caused by her belief in the blackness of the Ancient Egyptians, an anxiety no doubt especially severe at a time when that belief was generally thought to have been discredited. It is as if the strain of that belief, in opposition not only to science but to her own inner doubts about the humanity of non-European peoples, is at last finding expression, at the end of her Nile journey, at her last sight of the civilization of Ancient Egypt. The description of the Sphinx, and the description of the Governor of Thebes, may reveal the price she pays for that belief, as well as the price to be paid by the modern Egyptians. Like every tourist in Egypt I have read, but more frequently and much more inventively, Martineau represents the inhabitants of Egypt as animals: in her narrative the modern Egyptians or individuals among them are described as or associated with frogs, camels, bees, ants, beavers, sheep, birds, pigs, deer, rabbits, and apes.[16] To insist, as Martineau does, that the Ancient Egyptians were black, is to acknowledge that blacks, and *a fortiori* the modern Egyptians, are human, are like us Europeans. It may be this acknowledgement that is withheld in Martineau's original failure to recognize the Sphinx; or it may be the acknowledgement that she too is animal as well as human, or female as well as human, a sexual as well as an intellectual being. But however we understand that curious moment of non-recognition, of negation, what the Sphinx tells Martineau, and what at first she will not hear, is that she is kin with all those – Turks, Arabs, Copts, Nubians, and women of the East of whatever 'race' – with whom she also denies all kindred.

Two pages or so after William Prime's party disembarked at Alexandria, they went to inspect Pompey's pillar. 'Shall I confess it?' he writes:

> There was an Arab girl, who came from a mud village close by, ... whose face attracted more of my attention than this mysterious column, in whose shade I sat. She was tall, slender, graceful as a deer, and her face exceedingly beautiful. She was not more than fourteen. She was dressed in the style of the country; a single blue cotton shirt ... It was open from the neck to the waist, exposing the bust, and it reached but to her knees. She stood erect, with a proud uplifted head, and to my imagination she answered well for a personification of the degraded country in which I found myself. The ancient glory was there, but, clothed in the garb of poverty, she was reduced to be an outcast among the nations of the earth.
>
> As I sat on the sand and looked at her, I put out my hand to support myself, and it fell on a skull. Bones, whether of ancient or modern Egyptians I knew not then, lay scattered round.
>
> When I would have apostrophised the brown angel, she started, in affright, and vanished in a hut built of most unromantic materials, such, indeed, as lay sun-drying all around us. It was gathered in the streets, and dried in cakes, which served the purpose of fuel, and occasionally of house building. (*Boat Life*, 34–5)

The passage is a convenient anthology of many of the clichés of nineteenth-century Western attitudes to the Middle East. I am thinking in particular of the expression of simultaneous desire and disgust for the Arab woman; the habit of personifying the East itself, or individual countries of the East, as a woman who is to be seen unveiled if the true East, or the true Egypt, is to be discovered; the representation of the landscape of Egypt, especially, as a place of death.

I am quoting the passage now, though, to point out two things in particular. First, there is the description of the Egyptians as a degraded nation, which is obscurely reinforced by the skull that lies so oddly to hand. This may well be a submerged memory of, or reference to Samuel Morton's *Crania Aegyptiaca*, published in 1844, and sumptuously illustrated with hundreds of engraved Egyptian skulls, which had identified the *fallāhín* as the nearest descendants of the Ancient Egyptians, though degraded almost beyond recognition.[17] Morton's work was probably, by the mid-century, the most influential element in ethnological accounts of the Ancient Egyptians as well as of the black slaves in America, and it would almost certainly have been known, by reputation at least, by all three of the tourists I am discussing. Secondly, I want to point out once more the association between the modern inhabitants of Egypt, in this case a peasant girl, and the earth, itself associated with excrement. This 'brown angel' is said to live in a hut built at first of mud, then of dung; she 'vanishes' into it, as if entirely camouflaged by it, as if she has rejoined her natural element. It is a continuous theme of this tourist literature to associate, or rather to identify 'the sordid mud and clay of human nature and human life' – the phrase is Florence Nightingale's (*Letters*, 42) – with earth and with their habitations.

Of Asyût, Nightingale wrote that it looked like 'the sort of city the animals might have built ... a collection of mud heaps' (*Letters*, 69). The remark makes it clear that the most vulnerable element in the association between the mud of human nature and mud huts is the adjective 'human'. It is as if the belief that mankind is made of dust has given rise to a notion that a civilization is to be measured by the degree of distance a people has managed to put between itself and its earthy origins, or between its mouth and its anus. This notion is reinforced not only by the distinction made in comparative anatomy between ape and human, in terms of which is best at standing upright, but by the similar distinction, imposed after the Fall, between human and reptile.

Nightingale represents Luxor as overrun, as infested, as crawling with intrusive Arabs who are figured as reptiles. She was particularly shocked by the village which had grown up in the great temple itself. What offended her was not just the intrusion of the sordid modern into the grandeur of the past. It was also the fact that the houses of the village were built with doorways only 4 ft high. Nightingale does not pause to wonder if there might be a good reason for this design feature in a windy and sandy desert where the temperature dropped rapidly at night. She exclaims against 'the moral degradation, the voluntary debasement'

> to see human beings … choosing to crawl upon the ground like reptiles, to live in a place where they could not stand upright, when the temple roof above their heads was all they needed! … If they had been deserted, you would have thought it was the dwelling-place of some wild animal. I never before saw any of my fellow creatures degraded (thieves, bad men, women and children), but I longed to have intercourse with them, to stay with them, and make plans for them; but here, one gathered one's clothes about one, and felt as if one had trodden in a nest of reptiles … these seem voluntarily to have abdicated their privilege as men. The thieves in London, the ragged scholars in Edinburgh, are still human beings; but the horror which the misery of Egypt excites cannot be expressed, for these are beasts. (*Letters*, 104–5)

The progression by which these *falláhín* are progressively dehumanized as the passage proceeds could hardly be clearer. They begin as humans with free will, who choose to degrade themselves, to be *like* animals: 'it seemed as if they did it on purpose,' writes Nightingale, 'to be as like beasts as they could' (*Letters*, 104). By the end, emphatically, they *are* beasts; and it is the comparison and contrast between the poor of Egypt and the poor of Britain – even they are human – which finally tears the veil of humanity from the villagers of Luxor, and reveals them as inhuman, as entirely alien to Nightingale. In the essay entitled 'Vision of Temples' which concludes her volume, Nightingale images Amunoph II returning to his temple in the nineteenth century, and finding it 'full of unclean beasts and creeping things; and of the unclean things, of all the dogs, and goats, and asses, the most unclean was man; and vilest of the creeping things and most abject was man' (*Letters*, 325).

In the essay on Florence Nightingale in her book *Uneven Developments*, Mary Poovey has discussed the strategies of representation by which the working class and the colonial subject could be made available as the objects of the middle-class career nurse. 'When she displaced class,' writes Poovey, so as to transform the brute soldier into a tractable, infantilized patient, she provided a strategy that could also displace race by transforming the Indian from a dirty foreigner into a sickly child. In … England's imperial dream, conquest and colonial rule could … be rewritten as the government of love.[18]

In Nightingale's account of the temple at Luxor, however, the point of evoking the children of the poor in Britain is that they fail to provide the terms on which the foreign, colonized subject could be drawn within the pale of the human. The passage was written, of course, before Nightingale had begun her professional career, and long before her concern with the Indian hospitals. Nevertheless, it seems to demonstrate either the limits of the strategy that Poovey has described, or the resistance that had to be overcome before that strategy could develop. Throughout her tour of Egypt Nightingale is troubled by the impossibility of deciding whether the modern Egyptians are human or animal. The villages around Cairo, for example, are similarly populated with 'crawling creatures', creatures who bend and crouch and cannot walk upright. 'They do not strike one,' she says, 'as half-formed beings, who will grow up and grow more complete, but as evil degraded creatures,' evil because they have chosen their own degradation. 'Oh, if one could either forget, or believe, that the people here were one's fellow creatures, what a country this would be!' (*Letters*, 30, 32.)

That flesh is dust, and that burial is the return of dust to dust, is the organizing metaphor of Prime's *Boat Life in Egypt*. The mummified bodies which, as a result of the new market in antiquities, are now exhumed and strewn across the desert, and which collapse into dust when trodden upon or merely touched, are among the most conspicuous instances of this figure. So are the jackals which haunt the cemeteries, exhuming the corpses of the dead, eating them, and ejecting them as excrement. The figure allows the fantasy that the whole desert is composed of the decomposed bodies of 4,000 years of its oriental inhabitants, of all races, from the Ancient Egyptians to the modern Turks. The dust is scattered and mixed by the wind so that the bodies of individuals and races become horrifyingly undifferentiated; it is carried away by the river, to the sea, to unknown worlds.

Prime's account of his own excavations, and those carried out on his behalf, returns continually to this figure and the anxiety it gives rise to, an anxiety which is apparently associated with a sexual guilt. This is perhaps especially clear when he describes an encounter at Isna with 'one of the noblest specimens of feminine beauty that I remember'. The passage recapitulates the meeting with the silent and beautiful Arab girl Prime had seen at Alexandria; and as is usual in descriptions of encounters between male tourists and beautiful peasant women, the wind blows back this woman's garment to reveal 'the outlines of a perfect form, one that Praxiteles might have dreamed, one such as it is seldom permitted human eyes to see'. There follows a detailed account of her appearance, offered in the apparent belief that the invocation of Praxiteles will guarantee the purely aesthetic character of Prime's gaze. The woman returns that gaze with 'cold curiosity, and eyes devoid of interest, but dark, lustrous eyes withal, that had fire in them which might be made to flame'. She is wearing a necklace of antiques, mainly scarabs. 'I walked up to her and took hold of them. She stood like a statue, motionless, with her black eyes fixed on mine, but was silent, and allowed my examination without fear or objection.' He asks her how much she wants for the necklace: she makes no reply, but lifts up her jar, places it on her head, and walks off without looking back. Was she deaf? Prime wonders. Was she an idiot? How else could her behaviour possibly be explained? (*Boat Life*, 338–9.)

A few pages later Prime takes an elaborate revenge for his rejection, in an extended fantasy about the practice of grave-robbing, in which the association in the waking encounter, between the desire to possess the peasant woman and the desire to possess her necklace, is now refigured as the violation of a tomb by Arabs, and the robbery, rape and destruction of a mummified woman. Prime invites us to imagine a young, beautiful and (unaccountably) golden-haired woman who lived in Egypt 3,000 years ago, and whose tomb is opened by Arab grave robbers. Outraged by what is, after all, his own fantasy, Prime demands to know

> What fingers tore the coverings from her delicate arms! What rude hands were around her neck, that was once white and beautiful! What sacrilegious wretches wrested the jewelled amulet from its holy place between those breasts, once white and heaving full of love and life, and bared her limbs to the winds, and cast them out on the desert sand! (*Boat Life*, 345)

One answer to that question is clear enough: at Alexandria and elsewhere, Prime had done his own grave-robbing, which he had described in a language elaborately poeticized and eroticized: 'it was a strange sensation that of crawling into these resting-places of the dead of long ago on my hands and knees, feeling the soft and moss-like crush of the bones under me, and digging with my fingers in the dust for memorials of its life and activity' (*Boat Life*, 48). What fingers? His fingers. And the point can be made more generally: grave-robbing in the mid-nineteenth century was the main means of supplying the tourist demand for antiques, and was often carried out at the direct instigation of tourists. Prime himself encourages those he describes, wittily, as 'resurrectionists', to open tombs and to bring him the antiquities they discover.

But just as grave-robbing is represented as an Arab crime in that earlier fantasy of the violation of an Egyptian tomb, so Prime's desire to possess the Egyptian woman is fantasized as another Arab violation of a Europeanized victim, white, golden-haired. It is an unambiguously Caucasian body that is pulverized and scattered to the winds. 'I have,' he writes, on discovering that one grave he has rifled was the grave of an early Christian, 'a more than Roman veneration for the dead; and, though I felt no compunctions of conscience in scattering the dust of the Arabs … yet I did not like the opening of that quiet place in which a Christian of the early days was buried' (*Boat Life*, 52). There is an issue of boundaries at stake here: violation must be by Arabs on Westerners; only Arab bodies must be scattered to the winds. But the image and fear of decomposition that run through Prime's book make it only too clear that, at the most intimate level of the body, boundaries are impossible to secure. This is most apparent in Prime's fear that instead of being decently and separately interred in a New England burying ground, he might die and be buried in Egypt; that his own Christian dust might be mixed with the dust of all those dead Egyptians; that he would be absorbed into the terrifying masses of the Orient, lose his Western identity, and with it all individuality. He writes repeatedly of his desire to be buried

> under green sods, whereon violets may grow, and ... this vile dust of humanity may have a resurrection in roses or myrtle blossoms ... No grave in Egypt has turf on it ... I do not think I could sleep here at all. I do not think that my dust would consent to mingle with this soil. (*Boat Life*, 209–10)

> God forbid that I die here! to be laid, coffinless, three feet deep in the dry sand, and to-night disentombed by the jackals, or to-morrow by the wind. Such burial ... who would not abhor? (*Boat Life*, 277)

Sometimes, however, the fantasy works as it were in reverse: instead of dying and being dispersed in the dust, Prime's exploration and excavation of the tombs of humans and of mummified crocodiles leave him covered in dust, which enters his mouth, as if he is ingesting the oriental dead, with all the danger that involves that he will become them. The most extreme instance of his fear of dying and being buried in Egypt, among orientals – of becoming dust with their dust – is his visit to the crocodile caves at Manfalût, where, as Prime reminds us, at least one earlier explorer had died of suffocation.[19] 'I found that I was actually crawling over mummies'; the caverns 'were piled full of mummied crocodiles to the very ceiling', and among the crocodiles were the mummies of men. 'If I thought that I were to be laid in that horrible company – I would – I would – if they did lay me there I would rise up and walk from very horror and find another grave for myself' (*Boat Life*, 433). But though he avoids becoming part of the dust of the Orient, the dust of the Orient becomes part of him. After this exploration, everything tastes of mummy; there is an 'impalpable dust' of mummy in his mouth, on his moustache; on emerging from the pits, 'my complexion was dead crocodile, my odour was dead crocodile, my clothes were dead crocodile ... I was but little removed from being a dead crocodile myself' (*Boat Life*, 429–35). In eating the dust he is eating the dead of the Orient, as the jackals do; he is ingesting the Orient; he is becoming an animal, which is how he so often describes the modern Egyptians.

Alongside the notion of Egyptians as animals, or as mere dust, the terror of losing one's identity as human, as Western, among these unindividualized orientals, there are also fantasies in Prime's narrative which attempt to make Egypt a safe place. The most elaborate of these is reserved for the final pages of the book, where Prime makes an attempt to appropriate the dust of Egypt, to represent it as a hospitable medium in which to bury Christians. Egypt, he now argues, is a holy land. It is sanctified not by those who have walked the earth of Egypt – Abraham,

Jacob, Solon, Plato, Aristotle, Herodotus, Mary, even Christ – but by those who have become the earth itself. Joseph, his brethren and his sons are buried here: 'This that I hold in my hand, this grain of dust, may have been part and parcel of the clay that throbbed against the heart of Joseph …'. Not only these men, but 'their' women also are buried in Egypt: and here as elsewhere in the narrative the corpses of these women are eroticized, and they are visualized in prurient detail (some of them are blonde), lying in the arms of their dead husbands (*Boat Life*, 460–4).

The fantasy ends as a religio-imperialist dream of Christian or Judaic ownership of Egypt. At the day of judgement there will be 'no spot on all the surface of the earth where the scene will be like this'. At various occasions through the narrative, Prime has expressed a fear that 'the dust of all the earth' will suddenly be reanimated and start back into life: 'what strange, wild countenances of affright and horror would men see staring at them from the earth beneath their feet in every land!' (*Boat Life*, 142). In the final pages of the book that fear is enlisted into an optimistic vision of the last day as it will be in Egypt. The present inhabitants, 'followers of the prophet', will rise in their millions and 'start in horror' to find the land crowded with Ancient Egyptians. But among them there will be 'a few tall forms and calm faces uplifted to the heavens', and all 'will be awed to silence by the majestic appearance of the men they trampled on and despised. The very sand of the desert will spring to life. If it could but now do so! If the lips that are dust here now under my feet would but syllable words!' (*Boat Life*, 467). These are the saved; all the others will be resurrected, as if by the grave robbers, but only to perish again.

It is in the context of the anxieties I have been charting, about whether the modern inhabitants of Egypt are animals or humans, that we should situate another no less disturbing aspect of much of this tourist literature, the death wish so often directed at the modern Egyptians, which amounts to a fantasy of their extinction, a kind of imaginative mass-murder, even genocide. At Luxor Nightingale decides that 'Egypt should have no sun and no day, no human beings. It should always be seen in solitude and by night' (*Letters*, 99). At Qena she compares America with the East: in America, 'there is no Past, an ugly and prosperous Present, but such a Future!' In the East, 'there is a such a Past, no Present, and, for a Future, one can only hope for extinction!' (*Letters*, 93). At the island of Elephantine, the silence of the river is broken by the yells of 'troops of South Sea savages'. These Nubian children are a disappointment: they are 'not shiny as savages *ought* to be', and were quite without the glossiness attributed by various ethnologists to the inhabitants of the banks of the Upper Nile.[20] Instead, their 'black skins [were] all dim and grimed with sand … their naked hair plaited in rats' tails'. 'I heard some stones fall into the river,' writes Nightingale, 'and hoped it was they, and that that debased life had finished' (*Letters*, 113–14). There are occasions in Prime's narrative, too, where the strategy used to make the East safe is a kind of imaginary genocide. At Aswan, contemplating the journey over the first cataract south to Abu Simbel, he writes that if all that lies beyond here – the men, the buildings, the trees, the river – 'were blotted out of existence, swept off from the chart of the world and the page of history, who would miss any thing? Verily the world ends just here' (*Boat Life*, 253). At Cairo, too, he composes this night-time meditation on the populousness of the city.

> Two hundred thousand people were lying around me, and I asked who and what they were, and what part they formed in the grand sum of human valuation? Literally nothing. They are not worth the counting among the races of men. They are the curse of one of the fairest lands on this earth's surface. (*Boat Life*, 93)

Compared with Prime or Nightingale, Martineau is more guarded. Reflecting on a harem she visited in Cairo, she writes:

> These two hellish practices, slavery and polygamy, which, as practices, can clearly never be separated, are here connected; and in that connexion, are exalted into a double institution, whose working is such as to make one almost wish that the Nile would rise to cover the tops of the hills, and sweep away the whole abomination. (*Eastern Life*, 299)

At this point I am reminded of Freud's first example of 'negation', in his essay of that name: "'Now you'll think I mean to say something insulting, but really I've no such intention'".[21] No doubt Martineau's casual 'almost' is intended to put a strong negative to the suggestion that she really *did* desire the extinction of everyone involved in the institution of the harem – still less of all the Egyptian people, though the means by which she 'almost' desires the end of the harem would have extinguished the entire nation. At some level too, perhaps, Nightingale's and Prime's exclamations and meditations do not mean what they appear to say: though the expected extinction of degraded races was certainly established as a topic of civilized conversation in the 1850s, the modern Egyptians were not generally regarded as destined for early extinction, and I shall say more about this in a moment. I want to leave open, therefore, the possibility that Prime and Nightingale would have been unfeignedly horrified – as horrified as Martineau would have been – by a reading of the passages I have quoted from them as fantasies of mass-murder. This wishing the inhabitants of Egypt dead, it might be argued, is no more than an ill-considered hyperbole, a way of putting what is only a wish to be away from the continual affronts to a liberal conscience or the incessant demands for *baksheesh*; a wish for stillness, for space in which to contemplate the sublime of Ancient Egypt. It is a wish for a kind of contemplative *Lebensraum*, and the hyperbole should be taken simply as an index of how urgent that wish is. On the other hand, one might argue that a desire for the extinction of the modern Egyptians is indeed in the minds of all three writers, and can find expression in their writings only as a figurative, a hyperbolic expression of some more acceptable desire. If these passages are taken as hyperbole, that hyperbole may be operating here as what Freud describes as a 'symbol' of negation,[22] which frees the mind from the restrictions of repression by marking its utterances with an asterisk, as if spurious, as if not participating in the authority of the author. But it is impossible to imagine the wish for peace and silence taking the violent and uncensored form it does except in relation to a people who are not recognized as human; whose death can so casually be wished precisely because it will not be like real death, like human death. The claim that this death wish does not mean what it says can be sustained only in so far as it also means *exactly* what it says – that these people do not, *should* not, belong in the world of the human.

It is important to understand that these fantasies of the modern inhabitants of Egypt as less than human, as animals of one kind or another, and as destined, hopefully, to disappear from the face of the earth, do not all have the same weight, or rather would not all have been weighed equally by readers in Britain and the United States in the mid-nineteenth century. Historians of nineteenth-century ethnology and anthropology are familiar enough with the claim that blacks are less human than others, and with debates about the degree to which they can be humanized or made more human, especially in the writings of militant polygenists, those who denied that human beings shared a common origin and who allowed the possibility therefore that they could be classified by type or species.[23] It is perfectly clear that Nightingale in particular harbours some such notions of those she classifies as blacks. The distance, she suggests, between Europeans and Nubians is about the same as between 'men and animals' (*Letters*, 156). She has clear doubts about whether the 'Ethiopian' slaves she sees are human or not, and she does not seem to expect them to be treated as humans (*Letters*, 116).[24]

All British or American tourists on the Nile seem to have been well-enough up in ethnological science to know that at the first cataract on the Nile or thereabouts, they were entering what most ethnologists regarded as a new racial division of the globe, a new ethnic territory: behind them were Arabs, ahead of them were blacks – Barabras or Nubians, often classified as Ethiopians and identified as belonging to the same variety of mankind as those who were classified as 'negroes'.[25] These are the people that Nightingale wishes drowned at Elephantine; whom she describes, at Aswan, as not men but 'monsters' (*Letters*, 117–18); these are the people, together with all the peoples to the south of Nubia, that Prime wishes into extinction, also at Aswan. It is certainly shocking, but it is not especially surprising to find Nightingale fantasizing as she does about those she classifies as blacks, and it is still less surprising to find Prime doing so, for when he was writing there were more American than British ethnologists prepared to hint that the humanity of blacks might be in question.[26] It is odder, and in the context of this chapter it may demand more comment, that in their anxiety to distinguish themselves as Franks from these oriental others, Martineau, Nightingale and Prime should be harbouring similar fantasies about Arabs, who did not usually figure on the ethnological hit list.

'Oh, if one could either forget, or believe, that the people here were one's fellow creatures, what a country this would be!' Are the modern Egyptians white or black? Human or animal? Food or excrement? The same or different? These questions were not questions in Nightingale's mind alone: in the early and mid-nineteenth century the ethnology of the modern Egyptians was the subject of widespread uncertainty and disagreement. There was disagreement, to begin with, about whether the *fallāhín* were of the same race as the other Arab groups in Egypt. Then there was argument and uncertainty about whether the Arabs of Egypt were racially the same as the inhabitants of peninsular Arabia.[27] More urgent, however, was the question whether the Arabs and/or the modern Egyptians were of the same variety of mankind as northern Europeans. The question took two forms, philological and anatomical. Were the Semitic and the Indo-European languages unrelated? And if so were Semitic languages, as some suggested, of African origin? Were they human languages, in Schlegel's terms, or animal languages?[28] Or were the Semitic and the Indo-European languages consanguineous? And if so, should Hebrew and Arabic nevertheless be seen as stunted growths on a degraded, somehow inorganic branch of the Indo-European?[29] Were the Arabs, including the inhabitants of Lower Egypt at least, Caucasians, as Blumenbach and Cuvier and Prichard believed? Or were they black, as R. G. Latham believed? Or had they become, by conquest, polygamy and slavery, an entirely hybrid or mongrel race?[30]

More complicated still, did the modern inhabitants of Egypt put in question the very possibility of combining the conclusions of physical anthropology and of comparative philology in a unified science of ethnology? Were they anatomically Japetic and philologically Semitic? Or, still more confusing, were they fair of face and black of tongue – a white race speaking a language of Africa?[31] Writers about Egypt in the years around 1850 were confronted with all these various versions of the question 'Who are the modern Egyptians?', and with all the various answers they imply, for the science of ethnology itself, confronted with the Egyptians, collapsed into an untidy heap of borrowed opinions, hearsay evidence, prejudice and self-contradiction. There was as little agreement about their ethnic identity as there was about the ethnic identity of the Ancient Egyptians, and no doubt for the same reasons. For both peoples, ancient and modern, had been manoeuvred into occupying a borderline, a liminal, facing-both-ways position between white and black; and there was no comfort to be had either by acknowledging one's racial kinship with the Bedouin and the *fallāhín*, or by crediting a black race with the invention of algebra, chemistry and whatever else.

At about the same time as Florence Nightingale was despairing of finding the solution to this new riddle of the Sphinx, the anatomist Robert Knox – till this point famous mainly as the man who had employed the Edinburgh resurrectionists Burke and Hare to furnish him with a supply of 'fresh' corpses – was preparing for the press his notorious 'fragment' *The Races of Men*, first published in 1850. Contemplating the *fallāhín*, Knox asks, 'What race constitutes the present labourers of Egypt? No one that I know has condescended to clear up this question.' And just as Nightingale appeals by implication to the ethnologist to resolve her doubts about the humanity of the Arabs, so Knox appeals in vain to the tourist for a solution: why is it, he asks, that all the 'silly books of travels' written about Egypt had not managed to clear up this question? In the end, Knox answers it by a figurative chain of similes and substitutions which is entirely out of control and which ends, as we might expect, in a fantasy of genocide. It is not clear from Knox's excitable prose whether he decides that the *falláhín* are the same as the Copts, or like the Copts, or whether he simply confuses them with the Copts. Either way, he appears to identify the two, and he goes on to explain that the Copts are like Jews but are not 'precisely Jews' but that the Jews, when racially pure, are 'Egyptian – that is African', and are like the Copts in that both belong 'to the dark races of men', and like all the dark races are destined for 'extinction'. As if to make sure that this inevitable fate applies to all the Egyptians, of whatever supposed race, Knox announces his further belief that *all* the inhabitants of Egypt, whether Copt, Arab, Turk or negro, will prove unable to hold their ground against the twin incursions of the Saxon race and the desert. 'Thus,' he writes, 'may the whole motley population of Egypt perish.'[32] The fate which Nightingale devoutly wishes on the modern Egyptians is in Knox's view the inevitable fate that awaits so impure, so degraded, so motley and so unclassifiable a people.

It goes without saying that all forms of racism depend upon a denial of similarity as well as of difference: on a refusal to recognize the self in the other, as well as a refusal to acknowledge or to come to terms with otherness. The evident similarities between Europeans and blacks were easy to ignore, because of the evident differences between them, which could easily be made the basis of theories about the supposed physical, cultural and intellectual inferiority of blacks, an inferiority so great – it could be alleged – as to call into question the right of blacks to be thought of as humans at all, or to be treated with humanity. The extermination of native Africans, native Australians, native Americans, could be imagined in part because it was believed they could be shown to be members, if not of other species, at least of other, inferior varieties of mankind. In the case of the Arabs, however, the sciences of philology and ethnology could give no unambiguous and quasi-objective justification to the desire of the West to deny its kinship with the East. It is in the affront, I am suggesting, of that uncertainty, as unbearable in its way as the affront of absolute otherness, that we can understand the genocidal fantasy I have been pointing out; for it produces an uncertainty about the identity and even the humanity of the European, too, and so about the very grounds of similarity and difference. The failures of recognition; the fantasmatic logic which defines Arabs as black in all but colour, as it also defines Jews in just the same way; the figurative negation of the humanity of the Egyptians; the deniable genocidal fantasy by which they are wished away; the chain of comparisons and substitutions which has no reason to end and so can end only in extinction – these are all ways of wishing away that uncertainty, by wishing away the Egyptians themselves. They are forms of a final solution to the Egyptian, the Arab, the Semitic question, to the uncertainty of its answers.

I have said that tourist accounts of Egypt are of special interest because they are so much a part and an effect of imperialism. In the minds of all the tourists from Britain, especially, but from elsewhere too, the visible importance of the overland route to the future of the empire meant that they all arrived in Cairo with the same question in their minds: will the British annex Egypt, and if so, how can its annexation be justified, in terms of the process and progress of civilization? The subsequent history of Anglo-Egyptian relations suggests that the structure of feeling I have been looking at may be understood, in part, as an unofficial answer to that question. The official answer, of course, offered everywhere in this tourist literature, is very different: the inhabitants of Egypt, it is argued, the slaves, the women of the harem, the overtaxed *fallāhín,* are indeed humans – and look how they are brutalized, degraded to the level of animals, by their own masters, their own husbands, their own governors. The structure of feeling I have been tracing in this chapter should perhaps be thought of as the repressed of this official argument. I do not believe for a moment that it is simply in the service of imperialism. But it may have been as serviceable as the official argument, in enabling imperialism to be thought; in permitting a general disregard for the interests of the colonized, under cover of the claim that it is primarily in their interests that their country is to be invaded and occupied.

Notes

The F. W. Bateson Memorial Lecture, given in Oxford on 13 February 1991. From *Essays in Criticism* 41:2 (April 1991): 97–127.

1 See Martin Bernal, *Black Athena: The Afro-Asiatic Roots of Classical Civilization,* I, *The Fabrication of Ancient Greece 1785–1985* (1987), ch. 5, 'Romantic Linguistics: The Rise of India and the Fall of Egypt, 1740–1880', 224–80.
2 For Martineau's belief in the blackness of the Ancient Egyptians, see *Eastern Life, Present and Past* (1848, new edition, 1850), 60, 77, 106–7, 255, etc.
3 For examples of Martineau's discussion of Ancient Egyptian religion, see *Eastern Life,* 110–11, 124–6, 203–4, 188–98; for an account of her motives in respect of these discussions of religion, see *Harriet Martineau's Autobiography* (1877, 2 vols, reprinted 1983), 2: 278 ff.
4 See J. F. Blumenach, 'On the Natural Variety of Mankind', first edition (1755) and third edition (1795), in *The Anthropological Treatises of Johann Friedrich Blumenbach,* trans. Thomas Bendyshe (1865), 84–6, 166–71. For recent discussions of this question in early nineteenth-century ethnology, see William Stanton, *The Leopard's Spots: Scientific Attitudes toward Race in America 1815–59* (Chicago IL, 1960); Christine Bolt, *Victorian Attitudes to Race* (London and Toronto, 1971), 1–28, and Nancy Stepan, *The Idea of Race in Science: Great Britain 1800–1960* (1982), 1–46.
5 See the essay 'Negation' in *The Standard Edition of the Complete Psychological Works of Sigmund Freud,* ed. James Strachey and Anna Freud, 24 vols (1966–74), XIX: 237.
6 See Sander L. Gilman, *Difference and Pathology: Stereotypes of Sexuality, Race, and Madness* (1985), 31–5, on the image of Jews as black.
7 J. H. Speke's *Journal of the Discovery of the Source of the Nile* (Edinburgh and London, 1863), was followed in 1864 by his *What Led to the Discovery of the Source of The Nile.* Though not strictly a writer on Egypt, Speke's 'discovery' of the source of the Nile was an important moment in the history of the Western imagining of Egypt, which frequently represented the hidden source as the central 'mystery' of the country: see for example Eliot Warburton, *The Crescent and the Cross; or, Romance and Realities of Eastern Travel* (1845), 2 vols bound as one (Leipzig, 1852), I: 30–1. Lane and Wilkinson were probably the two most-read British writers on India, other than tourists, in the nineteenth century: see Edward William Lane, *An*

Account of the Manners and Customs of the Modern Egyptians, written in Egypt during the Years 1833–1835, 2 vols (1836); Sir John Gardner Wilkinson, *The Manners and Customs of the Ancient Egyptians*, 6 vols (1837–41); in part popularized in two later publications by Wilkinson, his *Modern Egypt and Thebes* (1843), which became Murray's *Handbook for Travellers in Egypt* (1847), and his *A Popular Account of the Ancient Egyptians*, 2 vols (1854).

8 See A. Abdel-Malek, *Idéologie et renaissance nationale: l'Égypte moderne*, second edition (Paris, 1969), 32–64; Afaf Lutfi al-Sayyid Marsot, *Egypt in the Reign of Muhammad Ali* (Cambridge, 1984), 196–257.

9 For a history of British tourism in Egypt, see Anthony Sattin, *Lifting the Veil: British Society in Egypt 1768–1965* (1988); for the P&O and the overland route, see 44–63.

10 Florence Nightingale, *Letters from Egypt* (printed 'for private circulation only' by A. and G. A. Spottiswoode, 1854). For an almost complete and more easily available text, see Antony Sattin (ed.), *Letters from Egypt: A Journey on the Nile 1849–50* (1987); William C. Prime, *Boat Life in Egypt and Nubia* (New York, 1857).

11 W. H. Bartlett, *The Nile Boat; or, Glimpses of the Land of Egypt* (1849, second edition, 1850); M. L. M. Carey, *Four Months in a Dahabëeh; or, a Narrative of a Winter's Cruise on the Nile* (1863); Hon. Robert Curzon, *Visits to the Monasteries of the Levant* (1849); John Gadsby, *My Wanderings: Being Travels in the East in 1846–47, 1850–51, 1852–53* (1855, 1872); Alexander Crawfurd, Lord Lindsay, *Letters on Egypt, Edom, and the Holy Land* (1838, fourth edition, 1847); Richard Monckton Milnes, *Palm Leaves* (poems) (1844); Mrs Romer, *A Pilgrimage to the Temples and Tombs of Egypt, Nubia, and Palestine, in 1845–6*, 2 vols (1846); J. A. St John, *Egypt and Nubia* (1845); Eliot Warburton, *The Crescent and the Cross*, see above, note 7.

12 See Freud's essay 'Medusa's Head', *Standard Edition* XVIII: 273–4.

13 For the Sphinx as exhibiting 'negro' features, see C.-F. Volney, *Voyage en Syrie et en Égypte pendant les années 1783, 1784, et 1785*, 2 vols (Paris, 1787), I: 74; Vivant Denon, *Travels in Upper and Lower Egypt, during the Campaign of General Bonaparte*, 2 vols (1802, reprinted in facsimile, 1986), I: 101; and James Cowles Prichard, *Researches into the Physical History of Man*, first edition (1813), 379, 384. For the belief, held in particular by Volney, Dupuis and Champollion, that the Egyptians were black, see Bernal, *Black Athena* I: 240–6. See also (among scientists who held this belief) John Frederick Blumenbach, 'Observations on some Egyptian Mummies opened in London', *Philosophical Transactions of the Royal Society of London … abridged* XVIII (1791–96, 1809), 392–402; and (among travellers) R. R. Madden, *Travels in Turkey, Egypt, Nubia, and Palestine, in 1824, 1825, 1826, and 1827*, 2 vols (1829), II: 85–95. In Britain the belief was reinforced by Prichard's argument that in the early stages of their civilization the Ancient Egyptians were black, and he enlists Blumenbach, Denon and Volney in support (James Cowles Prichard, *Physical History*, first edition, 376–88). By 1837, however, Prichard was beginning to qualify his belief in the blackness of the Ancient Egyptians: see his *Researches into the Physical History of Mankind*, third edition, 5 vols (1836–47), II (1837): 230–1, and by the time of the second edition of his *The Natural History of Man* (1845), Prichard believed that the Ancient Egyptians had been a mixed race, some black, some white (154–5), all manifesting 'tokens of relationship with the people of Africa', but all with the skull form of 'highly cultivated nations' (161). Of British ethnologists thereafter, perhaps the most tenacious of the belief that the Ancient Egyptians had been black (and had created a great civilization) is Thomas Smyth: see his *The Unity of the Human Race proved to be the Doctrine of Scripture, Reason and Science* (Edinburgh, 1851), 359–65.

14 See Samuel George Morton, *Crania Americana … to which is prefixed An Essay on the Varieties of the Human Species* (Philadelphia PA and London, 1839), 29 n.–31 n.; Samuel George Morton, *Crania Aegyptiaca; or, Observations on Egyptian Ethnography* (Philadelphia PA and London, 1844), 33–42, 65. For Prichard's attitude to Morton, see Stanton, *The Leopard's Spots*, 51; but Prichard became less sure of the blackness of the Ancient Egyptians even before the publication of the results of Morton's craniological researches; see previous note. For Morton, see *The Leopard's Spots*, especially pp. 50–1, 97, and Stephen Jay Could, *The Mismeasure of Man* (New York and London, 1981), 50–69.

15 Georges Cuvier, *Cuvier's Animal Kingdom, Arranged According to its Organisation* (1840), 50.

16 These examples of the animalization of the modern Egyptians are taken from the early pages of *Eastern Life*. The sound of 'screaming Arabs' at Alexandria is compared with 'a frog concert in a Carolina swamp' (4). The comparison of the 'willing, intelligent, and proud' horse and 'impatient', 'malignant', *'damned'* camel (5–6) is, I take it, an implied comparison of the occidental and oriental temperaments. The modern Egyptians live in huts of 'bee-hive form', which oddly 'suggest the idea of settlements of ants or beavers' (13). Some boys encountered on the Nile 'had to be flogged out of the path, like a herd of pigs' (64). The crew of Martineau's *dahabieh* sing in a minor key: nature's key, favoured by birds and sheep (22). One of the crew is referred to by Martineau as the 'Buck' (81): whether deer or rabbit is intended is as unclear as it is in the phrase 'buck nigger'. There is less of this animal imagery in Prime's *Boat Life*, but as Prime concentrates on describing the Muslim inhabitants of Egypt as dogs and pigs (see for example 281, 293, 314, 317), the insult is perhaps more deliberate. For the modern Egyptians as animals in Nightingale's *Letters*, see below, pp. 000–00.

17 Morton, *Crania Aegyptiaca* 42–3. Prime's final meditation on race, death and resurrection in Egypt, discussed below, begins with the casual observation of 'two skulls … white and ghastly in the moonlight' *(Boat Life*, 460).

18 Mary Poovey, *Uneven Developments: The Ideological Work of Gender in Mid-Victorian England* (Chicago IL, 1988), 197.

19 Prime quotes Thomas Legh's extraordinary account of his visit to the crocodile caves, where one of his Arab guides was suffocated: see Legh, *Narrative of a Journey in Egypt and the Country beyond the Cataracts* (1816, second edition, 1817), 221–39.

20 On the special glossiness of the Nubians' skin, quite different from what Nightingale found, see Denon, *Travels in Egypt*, I: 72, who becomes the authority for this fact in Prichard, *Physical History*, third edition, II: 174, and in Robert Gordon Latham, *The Natural History of the Varieties of Man* (1850), 501. Burkhardt, *Travels in Egypt by the late John Lewis Burkhardt* (1819, second edition, 1822), 199–200, explains that although the Berber of Nubia are 'very dark coloured, their skin is as fine as that of a white person', and is kept glossy by being anointed, sometimes with fresh butter, sometimes with perfumed sheep's fat. For Carlyle, like Nightingale, blacks were distinctly preferable if glossy. 'Do I then hate the Negro?' he asks himself in 1849. 'No; except when the soul is killed out of him, I decidedly like the poor Quashee; and find him a pretty kind of man. With a pennyworth of oil, you can make a handsome glossy thing of Quashee, when the soul is not killed in him!' – Thomas Carlyle, 'The Nigger Question', *English and other Critical Essays* (London and New York, 1915), 311.

21 Freud, 'Negation', *Standard Edition*, XIX: 235.

22 Freud, *Standard Edition*, XIX: 236.

23 See Michael Banton, *The Idea of Race* (1977), 27–62; Bolt, *Victorian Attitudes to Race*, 9 ff; Stanton, *The Leopard's Spots*; Stepan, *The Idea of Race in Science*, 1–46.

24 'We passed a boatful [of 'Ethiopian slaves'] yesterday, crammed together, all women, half naked. As we came back after dark, they were sitting round their fire for the night; they came out to beg of us, and, in the dusk, looked like skulls, with their white teeth; they set up a horrid laugh when we gave them nothing: our guide poked one with his stick, when *it* was sitting down, as if *it* were a frog' (*Letters*, 116, my emphasis).

25 See for example *Boat Life*, 252–3, 271; Charles Pickering, *The Races of Man; and their Geographical Distribution* (1848, new edition, 1850), 210–12.

26 See especially Stanton, *The Leopard's Spots*.

27 Many writers make no distinction at all, in racial terms, between the *fallāhín* and the (other) Arabs of Egypt. Prichard, however (*Physical History*, third edition, II: 259–61), cites Volney, who had distinguished the Arab peoples of Egypt into three varieties, the *fallāhín*, who had come to Egypt from peninsular Arabia, and were taller than both the 'Maghrabyn', originally from Mauritania, and the Bedouin; and Burkhardt, who argued that the *fallāhín* were a mixed race of peninsular Arabs and Maghrebin. Prichard also cites (IV: 594) Barron Larrey, who accepted Volney's classifications but saw no physical difference between the *fallāhín* and the Maghrebin. For Morton in *Crania Americana* (26) the *fallāhín* are a mixture of Copt and

Arab, though they still qualify as Caucasians, and are bigger (28) than the other Arabs of Egypt; in *Crania Aegyptiaca* (42) they have become a mixture of Arab stock with 'the old rural population of Egypt'. Richard Lepsius, *Letters from Egypt, Ethiopia, and the Peninsula of Sinai* (1852), trans. Leonora and Joanna B. Horner (1853, 76), distinguishes between the 'more manly' Arabs and *falláhín*, 'who have reached a low point of degradation'. Robert Knox makes a similar distinction (but confusedly) in *The Races of Men: A Philosophical Enquiry into the Influence of Race over the Destinies of Nations* (1850, 1862), 187. According to Pickering, *The Races of Man*, 257, the *falláhín* are darker than the other Arabs only because more tanned. Lane makes no racial distinction between *falláhín* and other Egyptian Arabs, but (*Manners and Customs*, I: 31) he does represent the Arabs of Egypt as racially different from the peninsular Arabs, as do Morton (*Crania Aegyptiaca*, 47) and Latham (*Varieties of Man*, 515).

28 According to Friedrich von Schlegel, 'On the Language and Philosophy of the Indians' in *The Aesthetic and Miscellaneous Works of Friedrich von Schlegel* (1848), trans. E. J. Millington, (1881), 448–51, the Sanskritic and Semitic languages were unrelated, and the former far more advanced and organic than the latter; according to Prichard (*Physical History*, third edition, IV: 547–51), the Indo-European and the Semitic were unrelated, the former being developed adventitiously, in response to unforeseen accidents and contingencies; the latter bearing the marks of a Providence which had foreseen every possible accident and contingency. According to Philip D. Curtin, *The Image of Africa: British Ideas and Action, 1780–1850* (1965), 369, R. G. Latham regarded the Semitic languages as African languages. The term 'animal languages' is Schlegel's: see Bernal, *Black Athena*, I: 231, 344.

29 The Indo-European or Sanskritic languages were regarded as related by, for example, Sir William Jones and C. J. Bunsen: see Bernal, *Black Athena*, I: 230, 255, and see C. J. Bunsen, 'On the Results of the Recent Egyptian Researches in Reference to Asiatic and African Ethnology', in *Report of the Seventeenth Meeting of the British Association for the Advancement of Science* (1848). On Hebrew and Arabic as stunted, degraded or inorganic languages see Bernal, *Black Athena*, I: 344–50; Bunsen 'On the Results', 256; Edward Said, *Orientalism* (1978, 1985), 143–5. For Prichard's defence of the Semitic languages, apparently in answer to Schlegel, see previous note.

30 See Blumenbach, 'On the Natural Variety of Mankind', 99 and n. 4; Cuvier, *Animal Kingdom*, 50 – Cuvier (52) quotes Bory St Vincent saying that Jews and Arabs are of the Japetic 'species'; see also Lawrence, *Lectures*, 477; Morton, *Crania Americana*, 25; ch. xiii in Pickering's *The Races of Man*, entitled 'The White or Arabian Race'; and Prichard, *Physical History*, third edition, I: 247 – Prichard prefers the term 'Iranian' to 'Caucasian', with whatever consequences for Western *amour-propre* in the late twentieth century. Among those who did not regard Arabs as Caucasian is Michelet, cited by Bernal, *Black Athena*, I: 341–2. Latham (*Varieties of Man*, 14, 511) regards Arabs as 'Atlantidae', of the same variety as 'negroes', and warns that 'no error is greater than to imagine that connection with the Semitic is synonymous with separation from the African stock' (511); Knox (see *The Races of Men*, 447) may have regarded them as black. In his *Natural History*, 139–40, Prichard uses a system of classification which distinguishes the 'Syro-Arabian' race from the 'Indo-European' race, which includes northern Europeans, endorsing the view quoted from the French anatomist Baron Larrey to the effect that 'the Syro-Arabian or Semitic race' was the 'model of perfection' and 'prototype of the human family'. According to Larrey, young Arabs in Egypt are 'without doubt' craniologically superior to northern Europeans. There was a widespread opinion, however, that the Arabs had an immensely complex racial history, and could not easily be assigned to any 'variety' of mankind: see for example R. G. Latham on the 'numerous complications' in the 'minute ethnology' of the Arabs (*Varieties of Man*, 515), and see his *The Ethnology of the British Colonies and Dependencies* (1851), 92; see also William Lawrence, *Lectures on Physiology, Zoology, and the Natural History of Man* (1819, 1822), 476, on the intermixture of the Caucasian and Ethiopian varieties in Africa.

31 On the difficulty of making racial classifications by language, see Bolt, *Victorian Attitudes to Race*, 13 ff.

32 Knox, *The Races of Men*, 179, 447, 456.

9

Race against time: racial discourse and Irish history

LUKE GIBBONS

He was a young Irishman … he had the silent enduring beauty of a carved ivory negro mask, with his rather full eyes, and the strong queerly-arched brows, the immobile, compressed mouth; that momentary but revealed immobility, an immobility, a timelessness which the Buddha aims at, and which negroes express sometimes without ever aiming at it; something old, old, and acquiescent in the race! Aeons of acquiescence in race destiny, instead of our individual resistance. And thus a swimming through, like rats in a dark river. (D. H. Lawrence, *Lady Chatterley's Lover*)

During the twilight of colonialism, a children's toy circulated in the 'Big Houses' of the Irish ascendancy which purported to give the 'British Empire at a Glance'.[1] It took the form of a map of the world, mounted on a wheel complete with small apertures which revealed all that was worth knowing about the most distant corners of the empire. One of the apertures gave a breakdown of each colony in terms of its 'white' and 'native' population, as if both categories were mutually exclusive. When it came to Ireland, the wheel ground to a halt for here was a colony whose subject population was both 'native' and 'white' at the same time. This was one corner of the empire, apparently, that could not be taken in at a glance.

In his analysis of colonial discourse, Homi Bhabha has written that 'colonial power produces the colonized as a fixed reality which is at once an "other" and yet entirely knowable and visible': hence 'in order to conceive of the colonial subject as the effect of power that is productive – disciplinary and "pleasurable" – one has to see the surveillance of colonial power as functioning in relation to the regime of the scopic drive'.[2] The apparent ease with which colonial discourse establishes its legitimacy derives from the paradox that it locates discrimination in a primal act of *visual* recognition – notwithstanding the fact that the visual, in this Lacanian sense of the Imaginary, obviated the very basis of difference in the first place. For this reason, it is clear that a native population which happened to be white was an affront to the very idea of the 'white man's burden', and threw into disarray some of the constitutive categories of colonial discourse. The 'otherness' and alien character of Irish experience was all the more disconcerting precisely because it did not lend itself to visible racial divisions, as is evident from Charles Kingsley's anxious ruminations on a visit to Sligo, Ireland, in 1860:

> I am haunted by the human chimpanzees I saw along that hundred miles of horrible country. I don't believe they are our fault. I believe ... that they are happier, better, more comfortably fed and lodged under our rule than they ever were. But to see white chimpanzees is dreadful; if they were black, one would not feel it so much, but their skins, except where tanned by exposure, are as white as ours.[3]

Carlyle expressed similar impatience with the resistance of the Irish to neat classifications: 'Black-lead them and put them over with the niggers' was his perfunctory solution to the Irish question.[4]

This lack of fixed boundaries, of clear racial markers, has led some commentators to conclude that there was no rational basis for the 'ancient quarrel' between Ireland and England, and that the separatist movement was fuelled simply by the wilful obscuranticism of Irish nationalism. Calling for a reappraisal of Irish colonial stereotypes, Sheridan Gilley argues that 'since an objective criterion of race like skin colour is lacking to define Saxon dislike of the Celts, there is a difficulty of definition in deciding at what point vague talk about Celtic character amounts to "racial prejudice"'.[5] So far from evincing the kind of repulsion and hatred characteristic of racism, Gilley contends that English attitudes towards the Irish were distinguished by a spirit of toleration and a willingness to accommodate Irish difference. As the *Times* put it in an editorial after the Clerkenwell prison bombing in 1867:

> This is not a quarrel of race with race, nation with nation, or people with people, but between isolation, exclusion, inhospitality and egotism, on the Irish side, and liberality, hospitality and neighbourliness on ours ... The Irish portion of this mixed community [in England] is quite as large as any that could call itself pure Saxon.[6]

Oblivious to the irony in the phrase 'Killing Home Rule with Kindness', Gilley proceeds to point out that apologists for imperial rule such as Matthew Arnold advocated a commingling of the Saxon and the Celt, and called for an infusion of Celtic blood into the enervated body politic of post-Benthamite England. This apparent magnanimity is hardly consistent with the fears about intermarriage and miscegenation which stalked the deep south in America, and as such it is an important corrective to a simplistic equation of the plight of the native Irish with that of the black population in the southern states of the United States, or in other British colonies. But while Gilley is right to emphasize that the analogy with the oppression of black people cannot be fully sustained, it does not follow that this was the only model of racism available to colonial regimes.[7] Far more important for understanding the distinctive character of Irish stereotypes was the analogy with the native Americans, or American Indians, an analogy, moreover, which had a foundation in the shared historical experience of being at the receiving end of the first systematic wave of colonial expansion. Research by historians such as D. B. Quinn and Nicholas Canny has suggested that it was Ireland – 'that famous island in the Virginian sea', as Fynes Morison called it – which helped to turn the attention of the Elizabethan settlers towards America, and many of the earliest colonizers of the New World such as Humphrey Gilbert and Walter Raleigh alternated between Ireland and Virginia or Newfoundland.[8] In this initial phase, there was far less confidence about the absorptive powers of English civilization, and Lord Mountjoy, for example, warned of the dangers of succumbing to the primitive native culture in Ireland (the fate of the previous settlers which he designates the English-Irish):

> Because the Irish and English-Irish were obstinate in Popish superstition, great care was thought fit to be taken that these new colonies should consist of such men as were most unlike to fall to the barbarous customs of the Irish, or the Popish superstition of Irish and English-Irish, so as no less cautions were to be observed for uniting them and keeping them from mixing with each other than if these new colonies were to be led to inhabit among the barbarous Indians.[9]

This type of comparison between the subject populations of both colonies established a network of affinities that was to recur in descriptions of both the Irish and the Indians. Referring to the 'booleys' or wigwams built from the bark of walnut trees and mats, Thomas Morton remarked in 1632 that 'the natives of New England are accustomed to build their houses much like the wild Irish' and this perception of a common primitive culture also extended to dress and sleeping habits. When Shane O'Neill presented himself at the court of Queen Elizabeth in 1562, decked out in a vivid saffron cloak, the historian Camden wrote that he was looked upon with as much wonderment as if he had come from 'China and America'. William Strachey frequently couched descriptions of the Indians in Irish terms, remarking of their sleeping habits that 'some lie stark naked on the ground from six to twenty in a house, as do the Irish', and observing of their fashions that 'the married women wear their hair all of a length, shaven, as the Irish, by a dish'.[10] What is important for the purposes of understanding the implicit primitivist assumptions underlying these apparently casual observations on the state of the Irish peasantry is that comparisons with the American Indians persisted well beyond the initial period of conquest. Visiting Ireland on the eve of the Famine in 1839, Gustave de Beaumont, who had travelled widely in both the old and the new worlds, wrote ominously that the state of the Irish peasant was so wretched that he did not even have the redeeming qualities of the noble savage:

> I have seen the Indian in his forests and the negro in his irons, and I believed, in pitying their plight, that I saw the lowest ebb of human misery; but I did not then know the degree of poverty to be found in Ireland. Like the Indian, the Irishman is poor and naked, but he lives in the midst of a society which enjoys luxury, honours and wealth … The Indian retains a certain independence which has its attraction

and a dignity of its own. Poverty-stricken and hungry he may be, but he is free in his desert places; and the feeling that he enjoys this liberty blunts the edge of his sufferings. But the Irishman undergoes the same deprivations without enjoying the same liberty, he is subjected to regulations: he dies of hunger. He is governed by laws; a sad condition, which combines the vices of civilization with those of primitive life. Today the Irishman enjoys neither the freedom of the savage nor the bread of servitude.[11]

There is even evidence that the comparison of the native Irish to American Indians as a justification of conquest has survived down to the present day in loyalist popular memory in Northern Ireland. As Anthony Buckley reports in his ethnographic study of Ulster Protestants:

I have heard many individuals separately state, viz. 'nobody expects that America should be given back to the Indians' (or Australia to the Aborigines). In part, this familiar statement is a plea to let bygones be bygones: 'it all happened a long time ago'. In part, however, it also contains an imperialist rhetoric that Protestants in Ireland, like white people in America, Australia and elsewhere in the British Empire, have been the bringers of Christianity and civilization.[12]

De Beaumont's sympathetic observations show that the apparently carefree lifestyle of the Indian was not without its appeal to the white sensibility: yet there is little doubt that the American Indians were also the victims of some of the gravest acts of genocide ever perpetrated by white supremacist policies, policies, moreover, which owed a considerable amount of their impetus to the initial Irish pattern of conquest.[13] In a comparison of the image of the Indian and the Black in American history, Michael Rogin has pointed out that Indians were not viewed with the kind of virulent hatred which whites reserved for blacks, but were often treated with bemused fascination and the type of paternalist affection which adults display towards children. Like the Irish, and in marked contrast to blacks, fears of mis-cegenation and interracial contact did *not* figure prominently in the white demon-ology of the Indian. In fact, all the mitigating or 'positive' features which, in Sheridan Gilley's view, extenuate the British from charges of racism with regard to Irish people, were evident in American attitudes towards the Indians, including the crucial expectation that they commingle with the whites and, in Andrew Jackson's words, 'become merged in the mass of our population'. The alternative to assimi-lation, however, was the stark prospect of annihilation: like Shakespearean drama, this particular racist scenario ended in either marriage or tragedy. As the US House Committee on Indian Affairs forecast in 1818: 'In the present state of our country one of two things seem to be necessary, either that those sons of the forest should be moralized or exterminated.'[14]

The extermination of the Indian way of life, if not the Indians themselves, was facilitated by the convenient belief that they were children of nature, 'sons of the forest', and thus were bereft of even the most meagre forms of civilization:

The Indian is hewn out of rock ... [wrote Francis Parkman] He will not learn the arts of civilization, and he and forest must perish together. The stern, unchanging features of his mind excite our admiration from their very immutability; and we look with deep interest on the fate of this irreclaimable son of the wilderness, the child who will not be weaned from the breast of his rugged mother.[15]

The Indian remained at a primitive oral stage, and had not made the transition to the symbolic order of civilization. Ironically, this was the attribute of Indian society, translated into an opposition between speech or oral tradition on the one hand, and the acquisition of writing on the other, which led to its rehabilitation by Rousseau, and indeed by a tradition of romantic primitivism in anthropology extending down to Claude Lévi-Strauss at the present day. Oral culture, in this sense, is seen as a source of plenitude and stability, of a prelapsarian innocence or communion with nature before the fall brought about by the invention of letters. The primacy of speech, the voice of experience, attests to the authenticity of a culture, presenting, as Derrida puts it, 'the image of a community immediately present to itself, without difference, a community of speech where all the members are within earshot' of one another.[16]

The problem with this form of romantic primitivism, as it presented itself to native Irish historians in the eighteenth century, was that such a state of primordial innocence offered an open invitation to conquest. The plenitude of an original, oral state of nature, as Derrida argues, is paradoxically constituted by what it lacks, in this case the absence of 'civilization': 'the unity of nature or the identity of origin is shaped and undermined by a strange difference which constitutes it by breaching it'.[17] If apologists for colonialism in the New World insisted on portraying America as virgin territory, as if its native inhabitants were simply hewn out of the rock formations which dominated the landscape, then it was decidedly in the interests of native Irish historians to deny that Ireland was ever in a state of nature, and that it was culturally inscribed from the dawn of antiquity. The difficulty with this position was that the testimony on which it was based depended to a large extent on an oral heritage, and thus had to contend with a prejudice *against* popular memory, derived ultimately from the Protestant valorization of the written word at the expense of custom and tradition. The *locus classicus* for this attack on oral culture was John Locke's argument that whereas an original text ('the attested copy of a record') bears witness to truth, in tradition *each remove weakens the force of the proof*, and the more hands the tradition has successively passed through, the less evidence and strength does it receive from them'.[18] In this schema the *written* text enjoys the status of an originating presence, and is the standard against which the inferior claims to truth of speech and tradition may be judged.

Hence the relative ease with those who opposed the enlisting of cultural nationalism in the cause of Catholic emancipation at the end of the eighteenth century could reject native pretensions to an ancient Irish civilization. According to David Hume, tradition lacked the clear-cut simplicity of scripture in that it was 'complex, contradictory and, on many occasions, doubtful'. 'Popish legends' not only led to a fragmentation of truth – 'though every one, almost, believed a part of these stories, yet no one could believe or know the whole' – but also lacked foundations, the grounds of knowledge: 'all must have acknowledged [of tradition], that no one part stood on a better foundation than the rest'.[19] Hume lost little time in extending this critique to Irish culture, arguing that tradition and popular memory were indistinguishable from credulity and superstition:

> As the rudeness and ignorance of the Irish were extreme … The ancient superstitions, the practices and observances of their fathers, mingled and polluted with many wild opinions, still maintained an unshaken empire over them, and the example alone of the English was sufficient to render the reformation odious to the prejudices of the discontented Irish … The subduing and civilizing of that country seemed to become every day more difficult and impracticable.[20]

Faced with this dismissal of what they considered their intellectual birthright, it is not surprising that Irish historians, whether of native or old English stock, took considerable pains (and an even more considerable degree of poetic licence) to argue that the ancient Irish acquired literacy and kept written records in the prehistoric era. As early as 1633, in what is perhaps the first modern history of Ireland, and the last great book to be circulated in manuscript form, Jeoffry Keating wrote that both the accuracy and the extent of the ancient 'chronicles of the Kingdom' was such that it procured for the Irish a superior esteem to the antiquities of any other nation, except the Jewish, throughout the world'.[21] By the eighteenth century, this had been transformed into an argument that the Irish, by virtue of their alleged Phoenician ancestry, actually invented letters, and introduced the alphabet to classical Greece. In 1753, in the first systematic work written by a native historian, Charles O'Conor could assert 'that our nation and language are coeval':

> the annals of the nation were, from a very early age, committed to writing. Blind tradition, or ulterior invention, could never, in ages of simplicity, and so distant from each other, concur in so many marks of authenticity.

This was part of a general counter-offensive by a new wave of nationalist historians which posited the existence of an *original* Irish civilization, rivalling Greece and Rome in its cultural attainments. If subsequent generations – indeed, epochs – have receded from the plenitude of this founding moment, then there is at least the consolation, as O'Conor puts it in characteristically Lockean terms, 'that our copy of the earliest times is pretty just to the original'.[22]

The difficulty with this argument was that it had to account for an extensive amount of mimetic shortfall to compensate for the gap between the glories of the past and the destitute condition of the mass of the Irish population in the eighteenth century. Native historians had to face Edmund Spenser's taunt, quoted with evident satisfaction by Thomas Campbell as part of a counter-offensive against native historians in 1789: 'if such "old scholars", why so unlearned still?'[23] Why, in other words, was there so little to show of the achievement of remote antiquity? The obvious answer was the destruction wrought by conquest; but to acknowledge the disruptive effect of successive invasions was to concede the discontinuous, fragmented nature of Irish history – the charge levelled at tradition by critics such as Hume. It was precisely for this reason that conservative-minded nationalists sought to impose narrative form on the amorphous mass of Irish history, discerning a totalizing design in what A. M. Sullivan was later to refer to as 'the Story of Ireland'. As Charles Gavan Duffy expressed it in the 1840s: 'The history of Ireland abounded in noble lessons, and had the unity and purpose of an epic poem.'[24]

This provided a cue for *race* to enter the proceedings, securing the image of an embattled people surviving intact and maintaining unity in the face of 2,000 years of upheaval, invasion and oppression. The concept of race also helped to explain the persistence of continuity in the midst of change and, even more to the point, the racial notion of an original native purity allowed nationalists to cite the effects of conquest to explain away some of the less desirable aspects of Irish life, attributing them to the slave's propensity to mimic the vices of his master. As Douglas Hyde expressed it in his lecture on 'The Necessity for De-Anglicizing Ireland', one of the founding texts of the Literary Revival:

> The Irish race is at present in a most anomalous position, imitating England and yet apparently hating it. How can it produce anything good in literature, art, or institutions as long as it is actuated by motives so contradictory? Besides, I believe it is our Gaelic past which, though the Irish race does not recognize it just at present, is really at the bottom of the Irish heart, and prevents us becoming citizens of the Empire.[25]

In the hands of less astute propagandists, race became a scouring agent, removing from the Irish people all the impurities acquired from contamination by the 'Saxon foe'. In an unabashed tirade entitled *The Celt above the Saxon*, published at the turn of the century, Fr C. J. Herlihy sought to restore Ireland's reputation as an island of saints, scholars and sobriety:

> How many Englishmen ever reflect that England is responsible for [the] intemperance of the Irish? Our Celtic ancestors were a very temperate people before the English landed on their shores. In the time of St Patrick drunkenness was unknown amongst them. In all his writings the great apostle does not even refer once to Irish intemperance. It was only after they lost their independence that this vice broke out among the Irish; and when we take into consideration all that they suffered from English tyranny during the last seven hundred years, can we be astonished that they turned to drink?[26]

For Gilley this would exemplify the ambivalence and essentially contested nature of Irish colonial stereotypes, for here is clearly a case of attributing an English provenance to a trait of national character that was, unfortunately, home-grown: 'behind the English conception of the Irish', concludes Gilley, 'lies the Irish idea of the Irishman', as if colonial rule had no role at all to play in fabricating the self-images of the Irish.[27] What Gilley conveniently overlooks, however, is that the process is a two-way (albeit unequal) transaction, and that many of the concepts requisitioned by nationalist propagandists in defence of Irish culture are, in fact, an extension of colonialism, rather than a repudiation of it. The racial concept of an Irish national character is a case in point: the mimicry of English life castigated by Douglas Hyde may have extended down to the concept of 'the Irish race' which he posited to counteract alien influences. The 'Celt', and by implication the Celtic Revival, owed as much to the benevolent colonialism of Matthew Arnold as it did to the inner recesses of the hidden Ireland, and the facility with which Gilley construes the Arnoldian stereotype as benign – in fact, as not a stereotype at all – explains how it could be taken to heart by Irish Revivalists. The racial mode is, moreover, the version of Irish nationalism which has passed into general academic circulation in recent years through the 'revisionist' writings of Conor Cruise O'Brien and F. S. L. Lyons (among others) – largely, one suspects, because it redefines even resistance within the colonial frame and thus neutralizes the very idea of anti-colonial discourse.[28]

Yet not all the concepts of Irishness which emerged under the aegis of cultural nationalism were dependent on racial modes of identity. Indeed, it is worth noting that while moderate, anti-republican politicians such as Arthur Griffith voiced some of the most bigoted expressions of nationalism (to the point of condoning black slavery, for instance), others associated with militant republicanism rejected racial concepts out of hand on account of their exclusivity and simplistic approach to historical change.[29] In his posthumous work *Literature in Ireland* (published after his execution as one of the leaders of the 1916 Rising), the poet and critic Thomas MacDonagh took issue with the Arnoldian idea of 'the Celtic Note' on the grounds that it carried with it unacceptable racial undertones:

> I have little sympathy [he wrote] with the criticism that marks off subtle qualities in literature as altogether racial, that refuses to admit natural exceptions in such a naturally exceptional thing as high literature, attributing only the central body to the national genius, the marginal portions to this alien strain or that.[30]

MacDonagh's thinking on this point was greatly influenced by the outstanding translator and scholar Dr George Sigerson (to whom, in fact, he dedicated his book). In a series of works beginning as early as 1868, Sigerson sought to remove the racial epithet 'Celtic' entirely from the cultural canon, arguing that Irishness incorporated the residue of several cultural or 'racial' strains, as befitted a country exposed to successive waves of invasion and internal strife over the centuries.[31] This carried with it the implication that history did not run in a straight line from the Milesians to the Celtic Revival, but was closer to an alluvial deposit, secreting an unstable, porous version of Irish identity. As David Hume rightly observed, the lack of secure foundations prevented the most dynamic strands in Irish nationalism from succumbing to 'fixed dogmas and principles'.[32]

The construction of a continuous, unaltered tradition, stretching back to remote antiquity, can be seen, in fact, as precisely a colonial imposition, an attempt to emulate in an Irish context the Burkean model of the English constitution based on a theory of community and the inherited wisdom of the ages. The past can be eulogized when it is truly dead and gone and when even revolution leads to social stability, but these comforting sentiments were not so easily transferable to a country such as Ireland in which history was still a matter of unfinished business. As a commentator in *The Nation* newspaper put it, writing at the height of the Famine in 1847, England's reassuring image of a common, unified past – a society in which 'history knits together all ranks and sects' – is strangely at odds with the uneven, fractured course of Irish history:

> There are bright spots in our history; but of how few is the story common! and the contemplation of it, *as a whole*, does not tend to harmony, unless the conviction of past error produces wisdom for the future. We have no institution or idea that has been produced by all. We must look to the present or future for the foundations of concord and nationality.[33]

There was nothing organic about Irish history, despite the best attempts of the editors of *The Nation* to make it 'racy of the soil'.

Hence in the case of the Ossian controversy that raged in the latter half of the eighteenth century, it was precisely Macpherson's claim to faithfully reproduce the originals, to be in perfect communion with the past, which aroused the suspicions of his most perceptive Irish critics. Notwithstanding his emphasis elsewhere that 'many volumes of well-authenticated records have escaped the ravages of time and of foreign spoils' the antiquarian Joseph Cooper Walker's comments on Oisin show that he had no illusion about the preservative power of either texts or traditions:

> Only a few fragments of his works, and those much mutilated and ill-authenticated, have come down to us. Indeed, had his productions reached us in a state of original perfection, our best Irish scholars would have found much difficulty in translating them; for there are many passages, in Irish poems of the fifth and sixth centuries, which seem at present, and *probably ever will remain*, inexplicable. Yet, we are told, that the poems of Oisin are recited and sung, at this day, by ignorant Scottish hinds, though the characters of the language, in which they were composed, are as unintelligible to the modern Scots, as the hieroglyphics of the Egyptians.[34]

The impossibility of gaining direct access to the past is not because it is sealed off, as in a time capsule, but because it is part of an unresolved historical process which engulfs the present. It is lived history that prevents the kind of omniscient narration envisaged by Locke which sees texts as transparent windows on the past. The romantic nostalgia for Ossian, and its vogue in the metropolitan centre, was not unrelated to the fact that after the battle of Culloden, and the elimination of the Jacobite threat, it was relatively safe to rake over the embers of the Scottish past.[35] But such an option was not available in Ireland: the past was not simply part of recorded history but *remembered* history, an open-ended narrative which was not safely interred in *texts* (as Hume would have it) but continued to haunt contemporary political struggles. As Donal McCartney has written with reference to the constant invocation of key historical events such as the 1641 rebellion and the 1691 Treaty of Limerick, in the campaign that led to Catholic emancipation in 1829:

> With our eyes on the 1829 act, we may say that a single topic from Irish history kept constantly before an organized people and forced upon the intentions of parliament, had tremendous influence in altering the law of the United Kingdom. The treaty argument [of Limerick, 1691], which passed out of the written page and penetrated the walls of parliament, was more than the mere spearhead of the emancipation struggle. For, like 1641, the interpretations of 1691 never passed into history, inasmuch as they never passed out of politics.[36]

Texts, in other words, were not simply *about* history: they were *part of* history, fragments of a past that still awaited completion.

In his essay on '*Ulysses* in History', Fredric Jameson cites Roland Barthes in support of his observation that under the impact of modernity, the gap between meaning and existence, the representation and the real, has widened:

> The pure and simple 'presentation' of the 'real', the naked account of 'what is' (or what has been), thus proves to resist meaning; such resistance reconfirms the great mythic opposition between the vécu [that is, the experiential or what the existentialists called 'lived experience'] and the intelligible ... as though, by some de jure exclusion, what lives is structurally incapable of carrying a meaning – and vice versa.[37]

Reality has become dislocated from structures of signification, and takes the form of the random impression, the passing moment or the descent into the contingency of the detail. Yet, as David Frisby writes:

> modernity as a distinctive mode of experiencing (social) reality involves seeing society and the social relations within it as (temporally) transitory and (spatially) fleeting then this implies, conversely, that traditional, *permanent* structures are now absent from human experiences.[38]

As to the source of these 'traditional, permanent structures', Nietzsche, for one, had no doubt where it lay: in history, or more accurately in historicism, precisely that view of the past which looks to tradition to confer a permanent structure on experience.[39] If we turn to Ireland, however, it will be seen that it is history itself which is irrevocably scarred with the traces of contingency. The fall from grace brought about by writing, the violent wrenching of tradition by the advent of the text, was present in Irish history from the very outset. In the novels of Walter Scott, or even in the Ossianic poems, the invocation of the past often had a therapeutic effect, the distance in time affording a common ground and a sense of stability which ensured that history was kept firmly in its place. This is the complacent historicism to which Nietzsche objected so strenuously. But in Ireland the recourse to history was the problem. As a writer in the appropriately entitled *The Voice of the Nation* expressed in 1844:

> In other countries the past is the neutral ground of the scholar and the antiquary; with us it is the battlefield.[40]

Irish culture did not have to await modernity to undergo the effects of fragmentation – the cult of the fragment was itself the stuff from which history was made. The sense of disintegration and 'unconditional presentness' (Simmel) which exerted such a fascination for writers from Baudelaire to Benjamin was pre-eminently spatial, the result of a new topology of social relations in the metropolis. In Ireland it was bound up with *temporality*, as the endless preoccupation with ruins and ancient manuscripts in cultural nationalism made all too evident. In main-stream romanticism (if such a generalization may be permitted), ruins represented the triumph of natural forces over human endeavour, and if at one level this was a process of destruction, at another level it was redeemed as a higher totalizing moment, in the form of a transhistorical communion with nature. For Georg Simmel, the nature-encrusted ruin was of a piece with the organicist conception of history which came so easily to countries in control of their own destinies:

> The charm of a ruin resides in the fact that it presents a work of man while giving the impression of being a work of nature … The upward thrust, the erection of the building, was the result of human will, while its present appearance results from the mechanical force of nature, whose power of decay draws things downwards … Nature has used man's work of art as the material for its own creation, just as art had previously taken nature as its raw material.[41]

In Ireland, by contrast, as David Lloyd has shown, ruins were the result of a clash not between nature and culture, but between several opposing cultures, the debris of a history of invasions. In a state of seditious reverie, the United Irishman William Drennan meditated on the round tower of Glendalough, Co. Wicklow, which he saw as 'raising its head above the surrounding fragments, as if moralizing on the ruins of the country, and the wreck of legislative independence'.[42] Or as the narrator of James Clarence Mangan's lament on the ruins of the abbey at Timoleague has it:

> – Tempest and Time – the drifting sands –
> The lightning and the rains – the seas that sweep around
> These hills in winter-nights, have awfully crowned –
> The work of unpious hands! …
> Where wert thou, Justice, in that hour?
> Where was thy smiting sword? What had good men done
> That thou shouldst lamely see them trampled on
> By brutal England's power?[43]

The conviction that it was history in its refractory Irish variant which led to the shredding of experience formed the basis of one of the most powerful contemporary critiques of James Joyce, that formulated in Wyndham Lewis's *Time and Western Man*. Lewis was impatient enough with the accumulation of detail in naturalistic fiction as language sought to catch up with the proliferation of sense-data unleashed by modernity. But in Joyce, even this took a turn for the worse, for in his obsession with place and the relations between objects his writing dispenses with the graphic clarity that is necessary to fix the contours of, and impart solidity to, the objects in our environment:

> The local colour, or locally coloured material, that was scraped together into a big variegated heap to make *Ulysses*, is – doctrinally even more than in fact – the material of the Past … As a careful, even meticulous craftsman, with a long training of doctrinaire naturalism, the detail – the time detail as much as anything else – assumes an exaggerated importance for him … The painful preoccupation with the *exact* place of things in a room, for instance, could be mildly matched in his writing. The *things themselves* by which he is surrounded lose, for the hysterical subject, their importance, or even meaning. Their *position* absorbs all the attention of his mind.[44]

If Joyce's language dissolved the objective world into subjective experience, then that at least would have the consolation of stabilizing the subject, of consolidating the ego of the narrator, the author and, indeed, the reader. But this is not what happens: the torrent of Joyce's prose carries all before it, leaving no room for a transcendental essence on either side: at the level of brute reality, or the ineffable realm of the sovereign self. 'No one who looks *at* it,' Lewis writes, 'will ever want to look *behind* it,' and he continues, with reference to the persistence of history in related, aberrant forms of modernism:

> You lose not only the clearness of outline, the static beauty of the things you commonly apprehend; you also lose the clearness of outline of your own individuality which apprehends them … 'you' become the series of your temporal repetitions; you are no longer a centralized self, but a spun-out, strung along series … you are a *history*: there must be no Present for you. You are an historical object, since your mental or time-life has been as it were objectified. The valuable advantages of being a 'subject' will perhaps scarcely be understood by the race of *historical objects* that may be expected to ensue.[45]

Joyce's use of language – in *Ulysses* at any rate – bears an inescapable resemblance to the fractured course of oral tradition which drew the fire of Lockean inspired critics of native Irish history in the eighteenth century. It is akin to the language of *rumour,* as analysed by Gayatri Chakravorty Spivak, that is to say, to a form of spoken utterance which carries back into its innermost structure the effects of spacing and rupturing which, according to Derrida, characterize written texts.[46] Rumour or tradition, in this sense, is not available to the detached reader or spectator but only to the active – one is tempted to say the *committed* – participant in social communication. Yet if it presupposes a face-to-face setting, it cannot be taken at face value for, unlike the phonocentric voice, it does not carry with it its own authenticity. As Spivak writes:

> Rumour evokes comradeship because it belongs to every 'reader' or 'transmitter'. No one is its origin or source. Thus rumour is not error but primordially (originarily) errant, always in circulation with no assignable source. This illegitimacy makes it accessible to insurgency.[47]

The amorphousness which Barthes attributes to existence, to the surplus or excess of the real which constantly eludes signification, is here the hallmark of language itself, and it is this above all which threatens the imperious eye of Wyndham Lewis:

'whatever I, for my part, say, can be traced back to an organ; but in my case it is *the eye*. It is in the service of the thing of vision that my ideas are mobilized.'[48] The problem with Joyce, however, was that *'He thought in words,* not images', and this forfeited any chance of stabilizing the flux of events by discerning the organic totality of experience:[49]

> Where a multitude of little details or some obvious idiosyncrasy are concerned, he may be said to be observant; but the secret of an *entire* organism escapes him …[50]

As Fredric Jameson has stated, 'the visual, the spatially visible, the image is … the final form of the commodity itself, the ultimate terminus of reification', and yet, as he goes on to note, one of the minor but astonishing triumphs of Joyce's prose is that he succeeds in inserting even a sandwich-board man – the ultimate in both visual and human reification – back into a network of social relations: 'Everything seemingly material and solid in Dublin itself can presumably be dissolved back into the underlying reality of human relations and human praxis.'[51]

Jameson's and Lewis's insistence on the unremitting temporality of Joyce's writing contrasts starkly with Franco Moretti's attempt to annex Joyce for the metropolitan centre, and to disenfranchise him of both his Irishness and his profound engagement with history:

> *Ulysses* is indeed static [writes Moretti], and in its world nothing – absolutely nothing – is great. But this is not due to any technical or ideal shortcoming on Joyce's part, but rather to his subjection to English society: for Joyce, it is certainly the only society imaginable … (whatever has emerged from the studies that interpreted Joyce on the basis of Ireland?)[52]

Whatever about Moretti, Wyndham Lewis, for one, had no illusions about Joyce's Irishness, and it is difficult not to suspect that underneath the elaborate tracery of his critique of Joyce lay a colonial frustration with a form of cultural difference which offered intense resistance to what Homi Bhabha, following Freud, terms the scopic drive – or what an Irish dramatist has called 'the artillery of the eye'. In an extraordinary appendix to his study of Shakespeare, *The Lion and the Fox*, Lewis launched a sustained assault on those critics such as Renan, Lord Morley and Matthew Arnold who claimed that Shakespeare owed his genius to the Celtic strain in his personality. This was too much to take. Lewis heaped abuse on the exponents of this heresy and sought, in the process, to demolish the very foundations of the Celtic claim to be a separate race. Interestingly, these foundations, in his estimation, had solely to do with *visual* characteristics, and their absence, for Lewis, was sufficient proof there was no difference at all between the Irish and the English. In a remarkable passage, he writes of his response to the funeral of Terence McSwiney, the Lord Mayor of Cork, whose death by hunger strike in 1920 proved a turning point in the Irish war of independence:

> During the martyrdom of the Lord Mayor of Cork I had several opportunities of seeing considerable numbers of irish people [Lewis refused to capitalize adjectives referring to nationality] demonstrating among the London crowds. I was never

able to distinguish which were Irish and which were English, however. They looked to me exactly the same. With the best will in the world to discriminate the orderly groups of demonstrators from the orderly groups of spectators, and to satisfy the romantic proprieties on such an occasion, my eyes refused to effect the necessary separation, that the principle of 'celtism' demanded, into chalk and cheese. I should have supposed that they were a lot of romantic english-people pretending to be irish people, and demonstrating with the assistance of a few priests and pipers, if it had not been that they all looked extremely depressed, and english-people when they are giving romance the rein are always very elated.[53]

There is a certain macabre irony in Lewis's persistence in adhering to an 'epidermal schema' (to cite Homi Bhabha's phrase), to visible bodily differences, in a context in which the dematerialization of the body through hunger striking is itself a means of affording political resistance. Lewis's dogged refusal to register the traumatic reverberations of McSwiney's funeral at anything other than a visual level is, in effect, an attempt to reduce it to *spectacle*. As such, it is consistent with his desire to remove all traces of history from the colonial experience, for it was precisely spectacle, in its collective modern variant, which sought to step outside history, transforming it into a set of horizontal, spatial relations.[54] As if to pre-empt this erasure of history, the nationalist response to McSwiney's funeral inserted history back into spectacle, seeing it as a means, in Benjamin's terms, of blasting open the centuries-old continuum of British rule in Ireland. As the anonymous writer of a contemporary pamphlet on the hunger strike wrote:

> A prominent man, occupying an eminent position, holding the chief office in one of the most important cities in his country, offers himself as a *spectacle* to the world that it may behold in him *a living document* of the secular injustice of England … The crisis has come … with a swiftness that is without parallel in our time. Old solutions are discarded. The new wine is bursting in old bottles … There may be other factors in the accomplishment of this astounding conversion, brought about as it has been in a space of time that is, compared to the slow march of events in history, phenomenally short. These other factors it will be for the historians to rehearse when the whole drama is unfolded.[55]

Lewis may have been indifferent to the impact of McSwiney's funeral but it devastated Irish public opinion to such an extent that even James Joyce was forced to break his silence on the war of independence, penning a scurrilous broadside against the English authorities. The difference between Irishness and Englishness escaped Lewis's notice, but it was all too plain to those Irish people who identified with the colonial administration in their own country. After all, it was the Unionist Provost of Trinity College, Dublin, J. P. Mahaffy, who remarked:

> James Joyce is a living argument in favour of my contention that it was a mistake to establish a separate university for the aborigines of this island – for the corner-boys who spit in the Liffey.[56]

Notes

From the *Oxford Literary Review*, 13: 1–2 (1991), 95–117.

1 This educational aid, along with other amusing board games such as 'Trading with the Colonies', can be inspected at Strokestown Park House, Co. Roscommon, Ireland. I am grateful to the administrator of the house, Luke Dodd, for drawing my attention to these relics of 'old decency'.

2 Homi K. Bhabha 'Difference, Discrimination and the Discourse of Colonialism', in *The Politics of Theory* (Colchester: University of Essex, 1983), 199, 203–4. Revised versions of the essay appear in *Screen* 24:6 (1983), and in Frances Barker *et al.*, eds, *Literature, Politics and Theory: Papers from the Essex Conference, 1976–84* (London: Methuen, 1986).

3 *Charles Kingsley: His Letters and Memories of his Life*, ed. Frances E. Kingsley, III (London: Macmillan, 1901), 111 (cited in G. J. Watson, *Irish Identity and the Literary Revival* (London: Croom Helm, 1989), 17).

4 Cited in Francis Hackett, *Ireland: A Study in Nationalism* (New York: B. W. Huebsch, 1919), 227.

5 Sheridan Gilley, 'English Attitudes to the Irish in England, 1780–1900', in C. Holmes, ed., *Immigrants and Minorities in British Society* (London: Croom Helm, 1978), 91. Gilley's work has been conscripted into the front rank of contemporary polemical exchanges over anti-Irish racism. As the historian Roy Foster expresses it: 'Innocent and sometimes naively hilarious works of piety about the Fenians or Young Irelanders, written by amateur historians on the British left, fall into a much cruder category [of propaganda]. They are joined by the half-baked "sociologists" employed on profitably never-ending research into "anti-Irish racism", determined to prove what they have already decided to be the case. Historians like Sheridan Gilley may have scrupulously and sympathetically explored the definitions of historical "racism" and rejected them for the Irish but this matters [little] to such zealots'. Roy Foster, '"We are all Revisionists now"', *Irish Review*, 1 (1986), 3.

6 *The Times*, 17 December 1867 (cited in Gilley, 'English Attitudes', 96). These sentiments are endorsed by Gilley: 'When the Irish conformed to English values they were quietly accepted in England. But that is surely the point: it was the Irish rejection of English values, which – rather than race – aroused English dislike of them' (93). What this argument overlooks is the extent to which those who failed to conform to English values were not only deemed to be outside English civilization, but to be beyond 'the pale of humanity', in Goldwyn Smith's felicitous phrase.

7 Gilley's criticism is directed mainly at works such as Lewis Curtis's influential study *Apes and Angels: The Irishman in Victorian Caricature* (Newton Abbot: David & Charles, 1971).

8 See Nicholas Canny, *The Elizabethan Conquest of Ireland: A Pattern Established* (Hassocks: Harvester Press, 1976): 'Events in Ireland, 1565–76, have a significance in the general history of colonization that transcends English and Irish history. The involvement of men in Irish colonization who afterwards ventured to the New World suggests that their years in Ireland was a period of apprenticeship' (p. 15). See also D. B. Quinn's pioneering work, *The Elizabethans and the Irish* (Ithaca NY: Cornell University Press, 1966), and K. R. Andrews, N. Canny and P. E. H. Hair, eds, *The Westward Enterprise: English Activities in Ireland, the Atlantic and America 1480–1650* (Detroit MI: Wayne State University Press, 1979).

9 Cited in Quinn, *The Elizabethans*, 119. Mountjoy's statement was a response to a modest proposal that the entire native population of Ireland be transported to the Plantations of America.

10 Quinn, *The Elizabethans*, 25, 153, 24.

11 Nicholas Mansergh, *The Irish Question 1840–1921* (London: Unwin University Books, 1965), 23.

12 Anthony Buckley, '"We're Trying to Find our Identity": Uses of History among Ulster Protestants', in Elizabeth Tonkin, Marijon McDonald and Malcolm Chapman, eds, *History and Ethnicity*, ASA Monograph 27 (London: Routledge, 1989) 187.

13 According to Canny: 'We find the colonists in Virginia using the same pretexts for the extermination of the Amerindians as their counterparts used in the 1560s and 1570s for the slaughter of segments of the native Irish population ... no determined effort was ever made to reform the Irish, but rather, at the least pretext – generally resistance to the English – they were dismissed as a 'wicked and faythles peopoll' and put to the sword. This formula was repeated in the treatment of Indians in the New World' (160).

14 Michael Rogin, 'Liberal Society and the Indian Question' in *Ronald Reagan the Movie and other Episodes in Political Demonology* (Berkeley CA: University of California Press, 1987), 153

15 Rogin, 'Liberal Society', 142.

16 Jacques Derrida, *Of Grammatology*, trans. Gayatri Chakravorty Spivak, (Baltimore MD: Johns Hopkins University Press, 1977), 136.

17 Derrida, *Of Grammatology*, 198.

18 John Locke, *An Essay Concerning Human Understanding* II (London: Dent, 1974), 258. For a useful exposition of Locke's theory of history, see Ian Haywood, *The Making of History* (Rutherford NJ: Fairleigh Dickinson University Press, 1986).

19 David Hume, 'The Natural History of Religion', in *Hume on Religion*, ed. Richard Wollheim (London: Fontana, 1968), 79–80.

20 David Hume, *A History of England*, new edition V (London, 1796), pp. 397–8.

21 Jeoffry Keating, *The General History of Ireland*, trans. Dermod O'Connor (Dublin, 1841), 53. Keating's history was composed in Irish and was first translated by O'Connor in 1723.

22 Charles O'Conor, *Dissertations on the History of Ireland* (1753), third edition (Dublin, 1812), 78, ix, 77.

23 Thomas Campbell, *Strictures on the Ecclesiastical and Literary History of Ireland* (Dublin, 1789), 9.

24 Charles Gavan Duffy, *Young Ireland: A Fragment of Irish History, 1840–1850* (London, 1880), 44 (cited in David Lloyd, *Nationalism and Minor Literature: James Clarence Mangan and the Emergence of Irish Cultural Nationalism* (Berkeley CA: University of California Press, 1987), 68). It is interesting that the title of Duffy's book – 'Fragment' – belies the seamless unity he sought to impose on Irish history.

25 Douglas Hyde, 'The Necessity for De-anglicizing Ireland', in *The Revival of Irish Literature* (London, 1894), 121.

26 Rev. C. J. Herlihy, *The Celt above the Saxon* (Boston MA: Angel Guardian Press, 1904), 171.

27 Gilley, 'English Attitudes', 81.

28 Conor Cruise O'Brien, *States of Ireland* (London: Hutchinson, 1972); F. S. L. Lyons, *Culture and Anarchy in Ireland 1890–1939* (Oxford: Oxford University Press, 1979).

29 See Griffith's virulent defence of slavery in 'Preface to the 1913 Edition' of John Mitchel's *Jail Journal*, reprinted, with critical introduction by Thomas Flanagan (Dublin: University Press of Ireland, 1982), 370–1.

30 Thomas MacDonagh, *Literature in Ireland* (Dublin: Talbot Press, 1919), 57.

31 George Sigerson, *Modern Ireland* (London, 1868); *Bards of the Gael and Gall* (London: Unwin, 1925), first published in 1897. I have dealt with MacDonagh and Sigerson at greater length in the sections which I have edited in vols II and III of *The Field Day Anthology of Irish Writing*, ed. Seamus Deane (London: Faber, 1991).

32 Hume, 'The Natural History of Religion', 80.

33 'The Individuality of a Native Literature', *The Nation*, 21 August 1847, 731 (cited in Lloyd, *Nationalism and Minor Literature*, 72).

34 Joseph Cooper Walker, *Historical Memoirs of the Irish Bards* (1786), second edition, I (Dublin, 1818), 55.

35 For the Jacobite background of Ossian, see Albert Boime, *Art in an Age of Revolution 1750–1800* (Chicago IL: University of Chicago Press, 1987), 218–27.

36 Donal Mac[*sic*]Cartney, 'The Writing of History in Ireland, 1800–30', in *Irish Historical Studies*, 10 (1957), 359. For an extended discussion of the differences between Irish and English conceptions of history, see Oliver MacDonagh, *States of Mind: A Study of Anglo-Irish Conflict 1780–1980* (London: Allen & Unwin, 1983), ch. 1.

37 Fredric Jameson, '*Ulysses* in History', in W. J. McCormack and Alistair Stead, eds, *James Joyce and Modern Literature* (London: Routledge & Kegan Paul, 1982), 129.

38 David Frisby, *Fragments of Modernity* (London: Polity Press, 1985), 45.

39 For Nietzsche's aversion to historicism, see Frisby, 32ff.

40 *The Voice of the Nation: A Manual of Nationality*, by the writers of *The Nation* newspaper (Dublin, 1844), 156.

41 Georg Simmel, 'Die Ruine', in *Zur Philosophie der Kunst* (Potsdam, 1922) 127–88 (cited in Louis Hawes, *Presences of Nature: British Landscape 1780–1830*, New Haven CT: Yale Center for British Art, 1982).

42 William Drennan, *Glendalloch and other Poems* (Belfast, 1859), 279.

43 'Lament over the Ruins of the Abbey of Teach Molaga', in *Poems of James Clarence Mangan*, ed. D. J. O'Donoghue (Dublin: O'Donoghue, 1903), 26–7. For a detailed and perceptive reading of this poem, see Lloyd, *Nationalism and Minor Literature*, 90 ff.

44 Wyndham Lewis, *Time and Western Man* (London: Chatto & Windus, 1927), 99–100, 106–7.

45 *Ibid.*, 109, 175, 181.

46 This is not to contradict Derrida's insistence that all speech carries with it the disruptive effects of writing: the point is, rather, that models of speech in societies which dominated Western thought operated, as Spivak puts it, 'on an implicit phonocentrism, the presupposition that speech is the immediate expression of the self'. The argument here is that the same powerful cultures were not so willing to grant this self-validating phonocentrism to the speech of subaltern cultures. It is precisely, therefore, the phonocentric presuppositions of dominant cultures, particularly in their imperial or colonial manifestations, which are thrown into disarray by subaltern modes of communication such as rumour. See the section on 'Rumour' in Gayatri Chakravorty Spivak, 'Subaltern Studies: Deconstructing Historiography' in *In Other Worlds: Essays in Cultural Politics* (New York: Methuen, 1987), 211–15, as well as Jameson's remarks on gossip as a means of 'dereification' ('*Ulysses* in History', 135).

47 Spivak, 'Subaltern Studies', 213. Spivak remarks in the course of her discussion that in certain cases, e.g. the codes of law, written texts operate on an implicit phonocentrism, a description that would seem to apply to the valorization of scripture and *written texts* in Locke's and Hume's approaches to religion and history.

48 Lewis, *Time and Western Man*, 7–8.

49 *Ibid.*, 122 (quoting from his own book, *The Art of Being Ruled*, ch. vi, part xii).

50 *Ibid.*, 118.

51 Jameson, '*Ulysses* in History', 135–6.

52 Franco Moretti, 'The Long Goodbye: *Ulysses* and the End of Liberal Capitalism', in *Signs Taken for Wonders* (London: Verso, 1983), 189–90.

53 Wyndham Lewis, *The Lion and the Fox* (London: Grant Richards, 1927), 322.

54 See Guy Debord, *Society of the Spectacle* (Rebel Press, AIM Publications, 1987), paras 158, 162: 'The spectacle, as the present social organization of the paralysis of history and memory, of the abandonment of history built on the foundation of historical time, is the *false consciousness of time* ... *thus spatial alienation*, the society that radically separates the subject from the activity it takes from him, separates him first of all from his own time'.

55 *The Ethics of Hunger Striking*, by a Catholic priest (London: Sands, 1920), 14–15.

56 Watson, *Irish Identity*, 28.

10

Uncovering the *zenana*: visions of Indian womanhood in Englishwomen's writings, 1813–1940

JANAKI NAIR

> Here as there [in England] the end object is not merely personal comfort but the formation of a home – that unit of civilisation where father and children, master and servant, employer and employed can learn their several duties … When all is said and done also, herein lies the natural outlet for most of the talent peculiar to women … An Indian household can no more be governed peacefully, without dignity and prestige, than an Indian Empire. (F. A. Steel and G. Gardiner, *The Complete Indian Cook and Housekeeper*)

The growth of feminism in the past two decades and the emergence of women's history as a field have produced a desire not only to establish that women too have a history, but also that they took part in the well known moments of human history.[1] A relentless search for new areas of enquiry into women's pasts has left few stones unturned. If attempts have been made to recover the role that women played in revolutionary moments of human history, some liberal feminist historians have also asserted a place for women in other domains traditionally held 'masculine', such as imperialism.[2] The nostalgia for the Raj, whose multiple cultural productions mark an acknowledgement of the end of empire and arises from the complexities of postcolonial race relations in Britain, has amply prepared the ground for an easier recovery of the roles of Englishwomen in India in support of such a contention.[3] As a result, colonialists' writings, a long critiqued source in nationalist or Marxist scholarship, have, in certain feminist intellectual practices, retained a kind of credibility they had lost elsewhere.

In this chapter, I will propose an alternative scheme for the reading of Englishwomen's writings on India, not in order to establish the 'correctness of the representation nor its fidelity to some great original'[4] but to locate them within the production of colonial discourse on India.[5] Within such a 'discourse analysis', my emphasis will be on plotting the multiple, and apparently ambiguous, ideological purposes that were served by the various representations of Indian women engendered in these writings on the Indian *zenana*.[6] Such ideological functions revealed the primary economic role that India played as Britain's colony but must also be revealed in terms of 'the exigencies of domestic – that is European – and colonialist politics and culture'.[7] The 'family' and the 'empire' were not the homologous structures that Steel and Gardiner suggest they were: the idealized family as represented in the writings I examine below served as a means not only to critique the colonized but emerged as a response to the 'threats' to the English family posed by the women's movement. The correspondence of these representations of Indian women with English feminist discourse of the period must also be traced. Implicit in this analysis, too, is a critique of some of the most recent instances of the recuperation of Englishwomen's roles in India.

Englishwomen were rare in India during the period of the East India Company, especially in the seventeenth and eighteenth centuries. By the time direct governance was assumed in 1857, and as larger areas of the Indian map came under British rule, there was a gradual shift in the control of intercourse between English men and Indians, and the colonial regime actively began discouraging officials from marrying indigenous women.[8] The separate and superior nature of the master race began to be emphasized, a separateness that could not be established without replicating the English home, which, therefore, necessitated the presence of Englishwomen. By their very sense of leisure, made possible by retinues of Indian servants, these women could communicate an ambience of gentility. They could also, and even more importantly, provide the sexual services that had been met by Indians in the past.[9] This also helped maintain the 'purity of the race'. By the middle of the nineteenth century, following the opening of the Suez Canal, which considerably shortened the passage to India, regular 'cargoes' of British women were offloaded from 'fishing fleets' at Bombay, terms entirely in keeping with India's role as supplier of raw materials for Britain.

There could obviously be no simple transference of life-in-Britain to colonial India. Apart from the physical impossibilities of such an enterprise, Englishwomen became part of a complex grid of power, constantly reconstituted, which blurred more familiar distinctions. To begin with, there was the need to assert 'femininity', in order to buttress the masculine nature of the colonial project. The British, deeply disturbed by the 'androgyny' of Indian men, had to stifle any sign of weakness in order to make their rule plausible; the admission of a native patriarchal order would only empower the colonized male. Thus, by characterizing the entire Indian race as feminine – that is, weak – colonial ideology put (British) patriarchy in the service of imperialism. Especially after the revolt of 1857, which made the Indians appear far more treacherous to the colonial regime, the public assertion of English femininity had undeniable advantages in accentuating the 'dubious masculinity' of Indian men.[10]

The repeated assertion of what was properly female as opposed to male not only ignored cultural difference but implied an acceptance by Englishwomen of their inferior role as the female (colonized) Other.[11] Englishwomen's perceptions of the violation of the codes of 'nature' were innumerable. Fanny Parks, wife of a customs collector, finally saw a *zenana* after four years in India and was disappointed it was not as 'lady-like' as a gathering of Englishwomen.[12] Even the martial races were no exception to the 'feminization'; Helen MacKenzie, wife of an army officer in the north-west, wrote that Hasan Khan nursed his sickly wife, dressed, and even gossiped like a woman![13] Mary Carpenter, a no-nonsense educationist who was invited by the Government of India to propose a scheme for female education, recorded with dismay that 'the sight of women employed as ordinary labourers – as porters toiling under heavy burdens – is most repulsive ... the degrading employments they are compelled to undertake seems to destroy the sense of feminine propriety.'[14] Worse yet, she said, were the feminine tasks that men performed, washing, needlework and 'numberless light tasks',[15] all of which rendered Indian women unfit to perform the duties of nature. It was their public and willing acceptance of their role as breeders for race and nation that Englishwomen would uphold before the Indians.

The importance of racial difference in India overwhelmed class divisions: the ruling race had to seal the ranks, distasteful as it was to a number of the men and women of the colonial regime. All the British in India were, thus, committed to live in 'a manner well above the station from which they had sprung in England'.[16] This in turn meant the erasure of class differences between Indians: even high-class women of the *zenanas* of Nawabs and other noblemen failed to meet the critical standards of Emily Eden.[17]

Although their roles were severely circumscribed, the wilful leisure to which Englishwomen were condemned had its uses, serving by itself to emphasize the separate spheres of male and female colonialists. When they began recording in writing or painting the shocks of their first encounter with the 'frontiers' of civilization, this leisure was turned to a more active purpose. Neither writing nor painting was an activity that Englishmen in India had ignored or belittled in the past. If anything, the compulsions of empire required that the unfamiliar be reduced to 'an accepted grid for filtering through the Orient into Western consciousness',[18] to be 'preserved, contained, studied, admired, detested, pitied, mourned'.[19]

To some extent, Englishwomen continued the project of 'verbally depopulating landscapes'. But there were some areas that Englishmen had been unable to penetrate (and here the copulative metaphor is intended) such as the dark, enclosed spaces of the *zenana* or women's quarters. Pamela Hinkson, who visited India in the late 1930s, remarked that the 'home behind that curtain [the *zenana*] is an unknown world even to the British official of long experience and deep sympathy'.[20] The private domain of the *zenana*, which Indian men had so jealously guarded, comprised an absence in the constitution of colonial discourse. By its very unknowability, it was a seat of sedition and intrigue,[21] as much as it was a site of ambiguous sexuality.[22]

The principal space, then, from which Englishwomen could produce new 'knowledge' of the colonized was the *zenana*, to which they gained privileged access by virtue of being the same sex. In the course of the late nineteenth and early twentieth centuries, the *zenana* was brought before the public/colonial gaze, in itself 'representing' (in the sense of speaking for) Indian womanhood. This increased visibility was made possible in a variety of writings, some of which retained a separate textual space (corresponding to the *zenana*) for Indian women.[23]

The *zenana* was confined to certain classes and regions: the upper and middle classes of north, north-western, and eastern India,[24] or where Moghul influence had been most direct and sustained. There were large areas of India, and of course, other classes where women were far more 'visible', and their exclusion from this representation of Indian womanhood – or somewhat selective inclusion – is of interest to us here. Such 'inclusions' and 'exclusions' were crucial in the attempt to restore 'order' in the field of shifting political and cultural forces, both in India and in England. It is to some of these forces that I shall briefly turn below.

Britain's economic interests in India were quite transparent, though the colonial regime strenuously presented a variety of non-economic reasons for governance.[25] From the early nineteenth to the mid-nineteenth century, British policy was marked by a desire to reform, reform almost without limit and with enthusiasm. These efforts, epitomized in the policies of Lord William Bentinck, Governor General from 1828 to 1935, were influenced to a large extent by the twin ideas of evangelism and utilitarianism.[26] James Mill was intoxicated by the possibilities of compensating India for the misgovernment of the past and saw India as a *tabula rasa* on which the British inscription would remain for ever. This was what fuelled the moral certitude of Macaulay's infamous Minute on Education (1835) by which India would be transformed into a Christian, English-speaking country, free of idolatry.[27]

By the middle of the century and especially after the Mutiny of 1857 (or the First Indian War of Independence) the reformist impulse faded, and India gradually became the hope of reactionaries since it 'attracted the person who was disturbed by the growing democratisation of English life' (although in India, too, the period was marked by slow and moderate reform). By the late nineteenth and early twentieth centuries, when Macaulay's brown *sahibs* had invaded the upper echelons of the Indian Civil Service and had to be excluded by various other strategies, the colonial regime had to adopt a new rhetoric and explain its mission as one of keeping peace and order, 'an admission that England had abandoned her interest in giving India anything more than this'.[28]

The shifts in India's role as a colony are, however, inadequate to establish the context in which Englishwomen's writings on Indian women were produced. The emerging politics and culture of Britain, challenges to the British state, especially after 1880, and how these challenges were met, contained, and overcome become crucial to our analysis, especially of how the 'knowledge' of Indian women was deployed in the the emerging discourse of feminism and its critics. It is with this stereoscopic vision that I discuss successive representations of the *zenana* in the writing of Englishwomen on India.

This approach marks a difference from and is a critique of certain liberal feminist approaches to the role of Englishwomen. At a time when Third World women are writing their own histories, and the homogeneous 'Woman' as a subject of history is being undone, such intellectual practices appear as First World efforts to reinstate the colonized subject. In some cases, this has been done through producing as objects of investigation the history of Third World women and their testimony. But there has also been a search for 'active' women of the First World: the additive strategy of this enterprise, that is, to multiply the instances of female presence in history, presumes the existence of a unified 'Woman' subject and is often inattentive to the manner in which the history of the colonial period is being narrativized. The very critical voice that such historiography purports to raise here drowns out other critical voices, for example, critiques of colonialism itself. Part of this unified approach to women's history implies a celebration of women's roles, even when they belonged and contributed to the dominant, usually male, discourse. Thus Pat Barr's assessment of Englishwomen's roles in the Victorian period establishes that they, too, as wives of Viceroys, military officers, and civil officials, fulfilled the arduous task of building an empire.[29] The task of bringing 'Western-style order out of Eastern-style chaos', if only by dispensing the daily rations to the 'cunning' servants of the colonial household, was thus the Englishwoman's as well as the Englishman's task.[30] Recounting Englishwomen's contributions, she hopes, will render less 'masculine' the Kiplingesque attributes of imperialism.[31]

The reluctance to engage with the intersecting discourses of race, class, and gender, which persists in more recent work, obscures the location of English-women within structures of power that engendered a 'knowledge' of India and Indian womanhood.[32] 'I have tried to right the balance, tell a small part of the women's story of India, the *private view of heart and mind*', Marian Fowler claims in a book published in 1987.[33] Fowler privileges this 'private' vision as fleshing out more fully the Raj pageant.[34] By simply maintaining their 'private lives' in the midst of their husbands' public activities, Fowler claims that these women performed a 'civilising, humanising' mission.

In contrast to Fowler's celebration of the private sphere, Mary Ann Lind focuses on the 'compassionate memsahibs' active in the public spheres of charity and education who displayed 'a more realistic and balanced view of Indian life than traditional memsahibs since they were involved in and committed to Indian affairs'. Here too, the additive impulse triumphs over an analysis that explains the causes for and limits of the shifts in Englishwomen's roles.[35] But the clearest disregard for critiques of the colonial experience comes in Margaret Macmillan's *Women of the Raj*, in which she declares, 'whether it [the Raj] would have been better or worse, women were there and their story is a part of the Raj's history too.'[36] Unlike Lind, Macmillan does not suggest that the colonial woman's role was anything other than 'raising little empire builders of the future'[37] but claims that Englishwomen's roles went unhonoured and unsung, even though it is to their credit that they 'could so often love their servants and be loved in return'.[38] There is little in these recent works to distinguish them from the 'essentialized feminine' view of the women of the Raj in K. K. Dyson's *A Various Universe*,[39] a distinctly neocolonial and non-feminist work.

If the liberal feminist recovery of the roles of Englishwomen in India is undertaken in order to suggest that the colonial enterprise was not entirely 'masculine', there is irony in the repeated assertions of the essentially feminine roles fulfilled since they were always overwhelmed by and subordinated to the patriarchal/imperialist order. Such women as Honoria Lawrence tried not to be an obstacle to her husband's career by uncomplainingly enduring childbirth in difficult places.[40] Even a woman horrified by 'the severe oppression of their sex in India' such as Annette Ackroyd, founder of the first working women's college in London (1854), gave up all ambitions of pioneering schemes for women's education in India to become the dutiful wife of Henry Beveridge, a civil servant.[41] Indeed, as this text will indicate, even some women who were critics of patriarchy at home and of the empire itself unwittingly resorted to the formulations of earlier writers in their visions of Indian womanhood.

Such writings as I have examined above intervene to reconstitute what is continually being politically and economically dismantled. Gender was a constitutive element of colonial discourse but always 'overdetermined'[42] by the ideology of race, which in the Indian context also conferred a superior class position on the English *vis-à-vis* the Indian. The copious literary productions of colonial women were themselves a sign of the intersecting discourses of race and class, continually rearticulated throughout the colonial period, but a sign whose meanings can only be unpacked within the discourse of colonialism. This implies mapping the ideological functions served by such production, not in a reductive sense but in order to perceive what is stable and persistent beneath the proliferation of meanings. The writings of colonial women, parading under the rubric of ethnography, whether in diaries, journals, or travel writing, were profoundly ideological; they require a symptomatic reading, an analysis of what was said but also left unsaid since 'we always find at the edge of the text the language of ideology, momentarily hidden but eloquent by its very absence'.[43]

The earliest of the writings that I have examined in this chapter was written in 1813. The other writings extend over the period until 1940 and range from the journals of wives of Raj officials, camp notes of missionaries, and diaries of Vicereines. There were also Englishwomen who came to India for the specific purpose of generating 'information' on aspects of Indian womanhood, such as Mary Carpenter and Mary Frances Billington. I have also chosen to look at the writings of three women (of Irish descent) who formed an active part of the nationalist challenge in India. The texts that I have chosen represent only a small part of a sizeable genre: my criterion for the choice of these particular texts has been the attention each has paid to the position of Indian women.[44] I have, in this analysis, excluded the entire genre of fiction.[45] For a valuable additional dimension, I have also used the recent reprint of the series *The Englishwoman's Review of Social and*

Industrial Questions, one of the oldest women's journals, in which some of the colonial women's writings found an airing.[46]

In the following analysis of Englishwomen's writings, I have abandoned a unidirectional, chronological narrative in favour of a thematic discussion of the writings not only to emphasize the ambiguities in such representations but equally to emphasize that which is persistent in the ordering of the social reality of the *zenana*, and to grasp the apparent 'contradictoriness' of these Englishwomen's writings. The dates in parentheses, therefore, serve only as markers of the periods of the texts chosen for each section.

The *zenana* as site of reform/change (1813–74)

As early as 1813, Maria Graham had hoped that there would be a few more examples of English Christian women in India to prove the virtues of enlightenment and reason.[47] Science had not yet entered the confines of the *zenana*, 'where nature and superstition reigned supreme'; during the cholera epidemic of 1833 in north India, Fanny Parks found an unhealthy propitiation of goddesses to stave off the disease.[48] In spite of the East India Company's commitment not to meddle with the social customs and religious practices of India, the benefits of converting the mothers and educators of young Indians were undeniable and could even result in the transcendence of the only two states to which all Indians were condemned: 'a state of violent action and excitement and one of perfect repose'.[49] Whereas missionaries had had some success in converting Indian men, the liberating influence of Christianity could not spread through the continent until the 'female influence in preventing conversion' was undermined; 'there is little hope for Christianity in India,' said A.U., 'till the women can be reached, and if only the wives and mothers could be won, the greatest obstacles to progress and the religion would at once be swept away.'[50]

However, Christianity alone could not ensure the liberation of women from the oppressive conditions in which they lived. As A.U. claimed, 'native women are so accustomed to a life of inferiority and seclusion that even Christianity does not at once restore them to their true position.'[51] As we have already seen, the legislative arm of the colonial regime had done its share of trying to protect women *from Indian men* with the abolition of *sati* in 1829 and the widow remarriage Act of 1857. But legislation was rendered meaningless by the low educational levels of women. By the 1860s, the *zenana* as a site for conversion gradually yielded place to the notion of the *zenana* as a site of education, after which the undoubted virtues of Christianity would be easily recognised.[52] The new notion of the *zenana* as a site for educational reform paralleled the development of British interest in universal education as a form of social control in the late 1860s and 1870s; the earlier notion that people were born into original sin was replaced by a concept of 'original ignorance'.[53] As Colin Mackenzie claimed before his (Indian) troops in the Punjab, 'we educate our women that they may be good wives and mothers, for a man can hardly be a good man without a good mother'; clearly, women in England could no

longer be trusted 'naturally' to become good mothers and wives.[54] Mary Carpenter
was the epitome of unflagging enthusiasm for the possibilities of female education.
Indeed, she observed, 'under good female instruction, Hindoo girls are quite equal
to their English sisters'.[55] Echoing the domesticating/homogenizing aspirations of
the British ruling class (since the discipline afforded by a school system would
reduce the threat of dangerous deviants), Carpenter said that 'education must coax
the middle and upper classes out of the walls in which they are immured', an act
which would simultaneously restrain the lower classes in India, hitherto deprived of
the 'refining influences' of the secluded upper classes.[56] This dangerous isolation
was also useful in explaining the unacceptable 'freedom' other groups of women
encountered. Thus, Mrs Mitchell expressed the same hope of a refining influence
in her description of the Todas, a tribe of south India, whose women enjoyed an
openness and freedom admirable in Eastern women and who yet lacked the
'decency' 'femininity' and 'self restraint' of the upper classes.[57] However, she warned,
this had to be a gradual process; the dangers of premature introduction of women
to general society were already evident. It was through education of women in the
zenana that gradual change could be accomplished and Indians could be convinced
of the virtues of colonialism, since, Mitchell claimed, 'it seems so hard for them to
believe that the only reason [for the British presence] is to try to do them good.'[58]
Education, and especially of women, was the catalyst that would urge India along the
continuum of 'progress', for what the *zenana* was made to represent as a reformable
space was the reminder of a dim past, one that England had long superseded.

The *zenana* as symbol of the collective past (1850–95)

An unshakable faith in progress enabled the vision of the Indian *zenana* as a symbol
of a collective past, one from which Englishwomen could easily distinguish themselves. The *Englishwoman's Review*, the first British periodical devoted to women's
issues and the longest lived and most inclusive journal of its time,[59] regularly gave a
fair amount of space to the position of women in various parts of the empire and the
world. Mary Carpenter's researches on India received a wide audience in their
rewritten versions,[60] and the books by other visitors to the subcontinent were
regularly reviewed. The 'Englishwoman was a very superior article,'[61] Emily Eden had
claimed many years earlier, and this was something of which not only to be proud but
grateful. A.U. asked Englishwomen not to shrink in horror from the unenviable
situation of Indian women, but instead

> before you blame them, free denizens of happy English homes, thank god for the
> long ages of liberty of thought and action that have made it simply impossible for
> you to comprehend their bondage.[62]

Indian *zenanas* were those cavernous depths of 'idolatry and superstition' that
the blinding light of reason had not yet reached. The appeal for the education of
women in India, the *Englishwoman's Review* claimed, corresponded exactly to an

earlier need expressed in England, which had been adequately met.[63] By characterizing the Indian woman as a primitive ancestor, the women's movement was provided with an opportunity to count its blessings rather than advancing its critique of the English situation. Carpenter commented on the 'vivid contrast' between woman in England and 'her painful seclusion in this country'[64] while A.U. spoke of the *zenana* as 'historyless' and as containing beings who 'had no knowledge of the grand past or the busy present or the eternal future' more than a fond hope for the indefinite continuance of British colonialism.[65] But the signs of progress were everywhere, Mackenzie remarked, citing a teacher who said, 'the difference between the children of her pupils and those of uneducated mothers is very marked, not only in knowledge but in civilisation, in moral habits and the observance of decency.'[66]

A similar vision of progress informed discussions of medical facilities for women in India. The Marchioness of Dufferin, Vicereine from 1884 to 1888, received wide publicity for starting a fund for supplying female medical aid to the women of India.[67] 'Few people know the dreadful cruelties perpetrated by the Dhais [Indian midwives],' said Lady Dufferin, again insisting that their methods were primitive.[68] At the time of Lady Dufferin's benevolent acts in India, we may recall, the 'medicalization' of the woman's body was proceeding in England; whereas midwifery had earlier been seen as essential for the practice of medicine, by the middle of the nineteenth century it was viewed as wholly 'unscientific'. Midwives were gradually elbowed out of an increasingly specialized profession presided over by male doctors.[69] Therefore, it was only a matter of time before education and increased medical attention for the women of India would enable a steady 'progress towards Western ways and customs', one that Frances Billington, in 1895, was willing to testify was well under way.[70]

The foremost sign of the primitive quality of the lives of Indians was 'a plurality of wives',[71] which had destroyed everything resembling domestic and family ties.[72] Yet this condemnation of the *zenana* as a polygamous, 'primitive' institution was not without its ironies. In the southern states of Cochin, Travancore, and Malabar, Mitchell found other marital practices that were equally distasteful. Of her encounters with barebreasted Nair and Shanar women (who, in their very 'nakedness,' were an invitation to reform) she records 'a strange country [where] husbands seem only to be appendages'.[73] The Marimakkathayam or matrilineal tradition of the Nairs revealed the obverse of the situation of the *zenana*, an empowering of women which disrupted tidy notions of patriarchal power to which England had become accustomed. 'In this sense,' she continued, 'one has to fight here not for woman's rights but for man's. I am afraid this state of things points to a very loose morality.'[74] Such a contradiction in the essentialist conception of Indian womanhood, derived from the overarching importance given to *zenanas*, was, thereby, suppressed under the normalizing rubric of patriarchy as superior and evolved, a stage ahead of (primitive) matriliny. What, then, was the *zenana*? It was not quite patriarchal, since patriarchy, but of the English kind alone, ensured the continuity of race and preservation of imperial order.

There is also a trace here of 'social purity' issues that marked the agitation for the repeal of the Contagious Diseases Acts in England (1869–86) by asserting the morality of monogamous female and male sexuality.[75] Perhaps the emergence of a more active female heterosexuality in the British women's movement prompted Billington, who visited India just ten years after Mitchell, to revise the latter's position to the claim that 'Nayars had the most civilised marriage system in the world.'[76] However, Carpenter, Mitchell, and Billington all shared the belief in progress, especially since, as Mitchell claimed, 'a glimmering of light has penetrated the darkness of these homes; they see their bonds.'[77] By splitting off the position of women in the colonies from the context of colonialism itself, which structured inequalities between Englishwomen in Britain and Indians, these Englishwomen took steps towards homogenizing the history of 'Woman'.

Zenana as the symbol of female power (1880–1915)

In the 1880s and 1890s, just as Britain's position in the world economy was clearly in decline, the state was faced with formidable domestic challenges not only from democratic forces such as the labour movement and the women's movement but even from the Tory (Orangeist) rebellion in Northern Ireland.[78] The feminist movement, organized initially as a campaign to repeal the Contagious Diseases Acts[79] and to expand educational opportunities, broadened to encompass the women's suffrage movement and developed a much wider conception of women's emancipation.[80] Notwithstanding the primarily 'social purity' (and separate sphere) content of the CD campaigns, and the ultrapatriotic anti-union conservatism of Evangelene and Christabel Pankhurst,[81] the women of Britain had seized the initiative in entering the public domain of politics. By their alliances with the growing socialist and labour movement, women, too, joined the ranks of the dangerous classes. Threatened internationally by the growing economic import-ance of Germany and the United States, the beleagured British state was forced into a realignment of its political forces. In such a context, the representation of the *zenana* as a site of power-in-femininity added strength to anti-feminist reaction.

A reinterpretation of earlier formulations on the *zenana* was most explicit in the triptych of texts by Billington, Steel, and Diver, although several other writings also expressed similar sentiments.[82] Billington's journalistic mission took her across the entire country and brought her in contact with the widest range of Indian women of all the authors whose writings I have examined. At the Girideh coal mines, she found women working underground to be a perfect contrast to the women of English mining towns, whom she described with alliterative fury as 'swearing, drunken, degraded disgraces'; the most remarkable point about the Girideh women was their 'perfect gentleness and modesty', 'general quiet, good order, discipline, and respect'.[83] The Indian family could not be dismissed as it had earlier been because it cultivated such 'praiseworthy domestic ideals' as the devoted care of husband and children. She admitted that to 'speak of womanhood in the

East as satisfied in the present conditions in life is always sufficient to send those of a certain school of thought into something like a frenzy', but she could not suppress the fact that the 'zenana possessed a prestige and dignity' that were preferable to the 'lot of Europeanised excresences' many sought to graft on to India.[84]

In 1905, Flora Annie Steel found few happier households than Indian ones, where women upheld a standard of morality far higher than in England.[85] Steel's message verged on the profoundly anti-feminist: the 'stability afforded by the Indian household was incomparable, the highest in the world'.[86] She readily admitted that this was made possible by the acceptance of an ideal quite different from the one being fashioned in the West, of a 'human being who is not the equal of man, who cannot be so, since the man and woman together make the perfect human being to whose guardianship is entrusted the immortality of race'.[87] This is a fore-taste of the eugenicist movement of the early decades of the twentieth century.[88] There were definite threats to the reproduction of the 'master race', from the Divorce Act of 1857, the increased use of contraceptives, and the development of new female sexuality delinked from marriage and reproduction.[89] Young, vigorous, rapidly growing economies like Germany and the United States made the falling birth rate a serious cause for alarm.

However, we could also read Steel's plea as reflecting more closely an interest in defending a kind of 'separate sphere' feminism, rather than anti-feminism. This provided a dignified, public role for woman that did not transgress the 'natural' disabilities of her sex. The representation of the *zenana* as powerful provided a case for linking power with femininity, with the 'primal natural power of her sex', without posing any challenge to the patriarchal household. The Indian woman established her chastity as an undeniably important *fact* and, by doing so, recog-nized the 'supreme importance of her own position'.[90] Far from being a 'melancholy place of moping and anaemic martyrs',[91] the *zenana* was a place where women enjoyed 'self-possession and dignity'.[92]

The constant reference to alarming changes in Britain was most direct in Maud Diver's account of Indian womanhood. Diver, no critic of colonialism or racism, nevertheless chose to say:

> The advanced woman of the west is apt to conclude over hastily that the narrow hidden life of her eastern sister with its lack of freedom, its limited scope for self-development and individual action, must need constitute her a mere lay figure, a being wholly incapable of influencing the larger issues of life, whereas a more intimate knowledge of facts would reveal to her the truth that from the same hidden corner, and by the *natural primal power of her sex*, the eastern woman moulds the national character far more effectively than she could hope to do from the platform or the hustings.[93]

The pioneers of the women's movement in England, Diver claimed, wrongly rejected femininity as weakness, so that the 'old world flower of gentleness' ran the risk of being trampled out of the feminine character, an unnecessary loss. In the East, narrow though her sphere may be, the Indian 'Queen' presided over her 'kingdom' – 'The Inside – a place of peace or of petty persecution'.[94] 'Feminine India,' Hinkson remarked many years later, 'wisely does not discard that femininity when she takes to affairs and politics.'[95]

The *zenana*, then, was the seat of 'primal natural feminine power', but what did this power imply? The contradictions that marked the nationalist discourse on social reform were portentous. Even as Behramji Malabari and M. G. Ranade were vigorously campaigning to raise the age of consent to twelve years, in the tradition of Ram Mohun Roy and K. C. Sen, they met a formidable opponent in B. G. Tilak. In 1895, Tilak drove the National Social Conference from the Congress *pandal* (awning), where it had always met since 1887, and, thereby, expressed a growing anger at the interference of the colonial regime in social questions, overreaching itself in transgressing the sacred site of the Hindu home.[96] Could the Indian nationalists be *retaining* the *zenana* (as an uncolonized space) at a time when the mark of the British Raj was everywhere? Could it, in other words, be developed as a site of resistance?

The *zenana* as the site of resistance to 'civilization' (1900–40)

There was a profound ambiguity in the image of the *zenana* as a centre of female power. By stressing such power in a place that had long been dismissed as powerless and demonstrating only the urgency of change, Englishwomen successfully displaced the responsibility of the Raj for its stupendous failures and shifted it to the Indians themselves. The earlier reformist impulses had all but evaporated by the end of the nineteenth century and the continued exploitation of India as a field for capital investment was difficult to sheath in any 'civilizing' rhetoric.[97] Macaulay's Indian gentleman had begun embarrassing the colonial regime by seeking greater representation in government (the Indian National Congress first met in 1885) and by writing devastating critiques of the size and scale of the 'drain of wealth'.[98] Crippling famines in 1876–77 that recurred in the 1890s, the proliferation of peasant and tribal unrest,[99] the drop of Indian *per capita* income (by Britain's own admission) to an all-time low of £2 (Rs 30),[100] culminated at a time when the colony at its doorstep (Ireland) was agitating for Home Rule.[101] But the failures of the British in India could at least in part be pinned on the immutable strongholds of Indian society, which were impervious to any British effort. An obvious location of such immutability was the *zenana*. 'It was not the man, that reputed tyrant, who most effectually barred the way to progress,' said Diver. 'It is the gentle, invisible, woman whose reserve of obstinacy, all the wild horses in the Empire would fail to move.'[102] This was the unreasonable, illogical space that resisted colonization and, thus, civilization; 'it is therefore within the zenana that women must first be freed'.[103] The Indian woman, more than the men of the country, 'voluntarily follow an unpractical, uncomfortable, and unworldly-wise course of literal obedience to some idealistic concept', said Stratford in 1922.[104]

When pressure on the Raj was mounting in the turbulent years of 1928–29, with protests by peasants, workers, women, and even businessmen marking the prelude to the massive Civil Disobedience of 1930–31, the Simon Commission remarked in its report:

> No one with any knowledge of India would be disposed to underrate the power its women wield within the confines of the household. The danger is that, unless the influence is illumined with knowledge … its weight may be cast against the forces of progress.[105]

This uncolonized space could subvert the project of civilization, but its continued existence also provided ample reason to deny the Indian people the responsibility of independence.[106] There was an early indication that such a strategy could be successfully pursued. It was through an invocation of this uncolonized space that Annette Beveridge (*née* Ackroyd) had led the vociferous opposition to the Ilbert Bill in 1883. This Bill, which was a feeble attempt by Lord Ripon (Governor General, 1880–84) to expand the circle of collaborators in India by allowing Indian judges to preside over cases in which English people were involved, aroused Englishwomen in India to political action (which I have mentioned above). Such a concession could not be granted to Indians unless they exposed themselves more fully to the colonizing project. Beveridge's letter to *The Englishman*, a British-owned daily, in Calcutta bears quotation at length:

> It is not pride of race which dictates this feeling which is the outcome of something deeper: it is the pride of womanhood. This is a form of respect which we are not ready to abrogate in order to give such advantages to others as are offered by Mr Ilbert's bill to its beneficiaries … In this discussion … the ignorant and neglected women of India rise up from their enslavement in evidence against their masters. They testify to the justice of the resentment which English women feel at Mr Ilbert's proposal to subject 'civilised' woman to the jurisdiction of men who have done little to redeem the women of their own races and whose social ideas are still on the outer verge of civilisation.[107]

This extraordinary delusion of the solidarity of women (English and Indian) against the oppression by men (that is, the Indian man of the English woman) concealed the actual complicity of English men and women in India. It appears as if the subtext of female solidarity, across race and class, could disrupt the seamless surface of imperialist discourse, but, in fact, such solidarity was invoked only to affirm the patriarchal/colonial order. In its report on the Ilbert Bill agitation, the *Englishwoman's Review* chose a similar route out of the inevitable squaring up with the politics of race in the empire by a refusal to 'discuss the merits or demerits of Mr Ilbert's Bill' and by choosing instead to applaud the occasion it provided Englishwomen in India to prove 'an interest in politics'.[108] (In the final section below, I will discuss the significance of this remark for the expanding 'opportunities' of Englishwomen in India.)

The fear that the *zenana* could, in nationalist discourse, take on 'positive' attributes as a site of resistance was not entirely misplaced. The writings of three

British women with nationalist sympathies anticipated the emergence of a 'separate' but powerful strand in nationalist politics. Margaret Noble, who, as the disciple of Swami Vivekananda assumed the name of Sister Nivedita, wrote consistently from 1898 to 1911 of Indian life and was widely acknowledged in reviews in India, Britain, and America.[109] Rejecting the Eastern–Western dichotomy, as well as the medieval–modern one for women, she divided human society into communities dominated by the 'civic' and communities divided by the 'family' ideal.[110] The Indian woman, fully empowered by her (natural primal) position in the family, could make the transition to the wider 'civic' world quite easily since the family was only a cellular form of society. The 'nation' now became the 'home' to which Indian women owed a duty of nurturing and caring.[111] 'Let every Indian woman incarnate for us the whole spirit of the mother and the culture and protection of the homeland, Bhumia Devi,' Noble said. Woman alone represented that unbroken continuity with a precolonial past through her residence in that uncolonized space, the *zenana*. Through her very domesticity, extended now beyond the 'stones' and 'walls' of her home to include 'land and people', the Indian woman was a repository of resistance'.[112]

Woman power was not, after all, alien to Indian women, said Annie Besant, for Shakti was the true power of Deva, and 'in the representatives of Shakti will be the certain triumph of India in the nation and the Indian home'.[113] She claimed to have tapped the reservoirs of 'heroism, endurance and self-sacrifice of the feminine nature' in the Home Rule movement.[114] Separate, therefore equal, the public domain was now made safe for the entry of women in the national movement through the characterization of nation as home and woman as mother.

Margaret Cousins, writing in 1940, testified to the true genius of M. K. Gandhi in harnessing this new 'mass' of Indian people:

> the revered leader Gandhiji was sufficient guarantee to the women of the righteousness of whatever new actions had to be taken by women in national life.[115]

Cousins made an earnest plea that 'Indian women express the needs of the "mother-half" of humanity' since the present world order needed 'the creative and conserving qualities of women'.[116] Her recognition of the economic importance of housework, the need for woman's control of her own sexuality, and for extended legal rights, all of which were radical ideas for her time, could not, however, overcome the characterization of *satyagraha* as eminently suited to the 'feminine character' whose 'whole nature and function is to create and not to destroy'.[117] Even in the writings of nationalist sympathizers, we now see, the final reliance was on the 'primal', natural power of woman's biology, a power which could be summoned at will at particular historical junctures.

The *zenana* as uncolonized space – prolongation of the colonial project (1860–1940)

When even the illusion of permanence of the Raj had vanished, the rendering of the *zenana* as an uncolonized space was deployed to yet another advantage. The stubborn unchanging *zenana*, a trope of ultimate, irreducible difference, provided a site for the prolongation of the colonial project, which, given the circumstances, would never be accomplished. The *Englishwoman's Review* had seized upon this rendering with great enthusiasm and to the advantage of its readers: India could become a theatre for the expanding energies of the Englishwoman. It periodically advertised positions in India for the educated women of Britain.[118] In 1881, it had even suggested that the segregation of women in India was a useful 'prejudice' since it provided Englishwomen doctors and lawyers an opportunity to exercise their newly won skills, an opportunity largely denied them in Britain.[119] Diver had already championed India as a place that could deflect some of the (dangerous) energies of Englishwomen. 'In this age of restless, nervous energy, a brave woman in search of work worth doing might do worse than devote her power to the service of India's stricken millions.'[120] By the time of the Sex Disqualification Act of 1919, which allowed Englishwomen the right to enter the civil service in various parts of the empire, single women were being increasingly employed in India.[121]

However, the futility of the effort in the colonies should be remembered, for small battles could be waged and won (a school started, a hospital run, a Bill passed), but weighed against the twin tyrannies of 'custom and tradition', said Maud Diver, 'the innovations of a decade are as dust in the balance.'[122] Norah Hamilton even pointed to unintended (read wasteful) uses to which skills bestowed by the British on Indians were put, that is, in nationalist agitation.[123] Hinkson also complained of the hopelessness of the task of education since 'a failed BA reads newspapers to the illiterates rather than preaching the evils of suttee'.[124] But this recognition of futility did not serve as a deterrent: Englishwomen were urged to share the arduous, 'fruitless' tasks of governing the empire. The real price of empire was not paid by the indigenous people, who suffered the destruction of handicrafts, extraction of impossibly high revenues, blatantly racist judicial and legal systems, as well as incomplete capitalist development, to list a few of the exorbitant costs that India paid. The real price was being paid, Diver revealed, by the self-sacrificing men and women of England, so that 'India's gradual movement towards mental and national awakening is the net result of countless seemingly futile, individual struggles, of daily battles, against heat, dust and cholera and that insidious inertia of soul and body that is the moral microbe of the East.'[125] By thus shifting the burden of empire on to individual men and women, Diver successfully effaced the structures of power that were in place and trivialized the price paid by the colony. All of these problems, with the possible exception of cholera, were incurable and, therefore, made the colonial enterprise in India all the more admirable and allowed it to stretch indefinitely into the future. By stubbornly refusing colonization, India invited redoubled effort.

Even worse than their refusal to transform themselves – that is, willingly surrender to the process of colonization – was the ingratitude of Indian women, Hinkson felt in 1938–39. Given the incomparable challenges faced by the British in governing India,[126] the reluctance of an 'ardent Congress lady' to praise British rule was unacceptable, so it was a rather triumphant Hinkson who forced her to admit that the British had abolished 'suttee' for which act 'alone I felt that their rule of India was justified'.[127] At last, the very fatalism of which colonial discourse had been so intolerant now proved itself useful as an explanation of unmistakable failure.

I have shown that the literary productions of Englishwomen in India, far from being random and marginal glosses or scattered observations of exotica, fulfilled a number of ideological functions as a part of colonial discourse. Indian women, in these writings, inhabited the very limits of society, the shadowy margins, now keeping out chaos and disorder, now embodying it. This 'knowledge' about Indian womanhood provided alibis to deflect growing criticism of British rule in India and formed part of the efforts to contain the disruptive forces that threatened liberalism in Britain. For Englishwomen themselves, positioned in a context where their power yielded new 'knowledge', the potential for developing any critique of their own subordinate status was thwarted. By making 'visible' the woman of the colonies, they could successfully make 'invisible' their own colonization by Englishmen, who had appropriated their capacities for the reproduction of colonial order. Their own housewifization, enabled by the subordination of men and women in the colonies, paralleled the housewifization that was occurring in England.[128]

There were a few flashes in these women's perceptions that could have formed the basis for questioning their own status. Billington's radical revision of earlier views of the Nair family and Fanny Parks's admission that the Rule of Law, supposedly democratic in England, condemned married Englishwomen to 'eternal sati'[129] never gained enough importance to challenge the dominant colonial discourse. In even the writings of critics of empire and patriarchy, earlier characterizations of the *zenana* were far from obscured. The dark private world of the *zenana* provided some of the Englishwomen discussed with the satisfaction of belonging to the dominant race, and, therefore, to the superior class, a privilege won by the fore-closure of the troubling 'woman's' question. By assuming the mantle of housewife in the public world of empire, the Englishwoman performed the crucial task of fulfilling Steel's and Gardiner's prescriptions for the maintenance of order between 'father and children, master and servant, employer and employed', or the main-tenance of that trinity of patriarchy, imperialism, and capitalism.

Notes

From the *Journal of Women's History*, 2II (spring 1990), 8–34. This chapter bears traces of the critical voices of Cissie Fairchilds, Rajeshwari Mohan, Rosemary Hennessy, and Madhava Prasad. Several others have patiently borne its other incarnations. I remain solely responsible for the arguments.

1 In this sense, the optimism expressed by Joan Scott that historians are no longer satisfied with these two approaches may be a bit premature. See 'Gender as a Category of Historical Analysis', in *American Historical Review*, 91 (December 1986): 1053–75.

2 Such an intention probably underlay the inclusion at the American Historical Association convention (Cinncinnati, December 1988) of a session entitled 'Women in masculine domains', under which rubric the role of women miners and of women in imperialism was highlighted.

3 The term Raj refers to the period of British rule in India, that is, 1757 to 1947.

4 Edward Said, *Orientalism* (New York, Vintage Editions, 1979), 21.

5 I employ the term 'discourse' in the sense developed by Michel Foucault in *The Archaeology of Knowledge* (New York: Pantheon Books, 1972). Following Foucault, discourse is taken not as a group of signs (and, therefore, as reducible to language) but as 'practices that systematically form the objects of which they speak' (49). In this article, discourse analysis permits plotting the 'identity and persistence of themes' (in the simultaneous or successive emergence of concepts, even their incompatibility) (35).

6 The *zenana* refers to the separate women's quarters in certain Hindu and Muslim homes, usually in north India. This text, however, argues that it came to represent far more than a 'geographical space' within households to Englishwomen in India.

7 A. R. Jan Mohommed, 'The Economy of the Manichean Allegory in Colonial Writing: The Function of Colonial Difference in Colonial Literature', in *'Race', Writing and Difference*, ed. Henry L. Gates (Chicago IL: University of Chicago Press, 1987), 78–106, esp. 81.

8 Margaret Macmillan, *Women of the Raj* (New York: Thames & Hudson, 1988), 110.

9 Not all Englishmen were allowed this expensive privilege of importing Englishwomen. A small number of English subalterns were allowed to marry; for the others, who were thought to lack the moral and intellectual resources required for continence, supervised prostitution was arranged near the cantonments. Kenneth Ballhatchet discusses the complex politics of such arrangements in *Race, Sex and Class under the Raj: Imperial Attitudes and Policies and their Critics, 1793–1905* (New York: St Martin's Press, 1980).

10 Ashis Nandy, in *The Intimate Enemy: Loss and Recovery of the Self under Colonialism* (Delhi: Oxford University Press, 1983), analyses the profound psychological impact of colonialism on both colonizer and colonized. Francis Hutchins cites the case of John Beames, a Punjab officer who incurred the wrath of John Lawrence, Governor of the Punjab, for having brought a piano with him. See *The Illusion of Permanence: British Imperialism in India* (Princeton NJ: Princeton University Press, 1967), 44.

11 Joan Liddle and Rama Joshi make a similar point in 'Gender and Imperialism in British India', *Economic and Political Weekly*, 20 (26 October 1985): WS 72–8.

12 Fanny Parks, *Wanderings of a Pilgrim in Search of the Picturesque* (Karachi: Oxford University Press, 1975), 59.

13 Helen Mackenzie, *Life in the Mission, the Camp and the Zenanai, or, Six Years in India*, 3 vols (London: Bentley, 1853), II, 204.

14 Mary Carpenter, *Six Months in India*, 2 vols (London: Longman, 1868), I, 80.

15 *Ibid.*, I, 80.

16 Hutchins, *Illusion of Permanence*, 107. This had a useful corollary in England itself. The increasing use of the metaphor of 'colony' for the place where the labouring and dangerous classes of England resided was no coincidence. The dark continent was the East End of London, to be 'discovered', 'governed' and 'contained'. See George Sims' 'How the Poor Live', in *Into Unknown England, 1866–1913: Selections from the Social Explorers*, ed. Peter Keating (Manchester: Manchester University Press, 1978), 237. Lord Curzon, Viceroy of India from 1898 to 1905, was astonished to discover that some lower-class enlisted soldiers in India, whom he observed bathing, were the same colour as he. Hutchins, *Illusion of Permanence*, 133.

17 Emily Eden, *Up the Country: Letters Written to her Sister from the Upper Provinces of India* (London: Curzon Press, 1978), 237.

18 Said, *Orientalism*, 6.

19 Mary Louise Pratt, 'Scratches on the Face of the Country, or, What Mr Barrow saw in the Land of the Bushmen', in Gates, *'Race', Writing, and Difference*, 138–62, esp. 145. The outstanding example of the encyclopaedic proportions of this enterprise was Francis Buchanan's work. Buchanan was invited by Lord Wellesley to investigate the newly acquired dominions of Mysore, Malabar and Canara following the defeat of Tipu Sultan in the Fourth Mysore War (1799). His work was so well admired that he was invited to perform a similar task for provinces of Bengal in 1809.

20 Pamela Hinkson, *Indian Harvest* (London: Collins, 1941), 260.

21 Parks, *Wanderings of a Pilgrim in Search of the Picturesque*, 39.

22 The English conviction of Indian immorality/uncontrolled sexuality was based on three empirical certainties, child marriage, polygamy, and worship of the 'phallus' all of which retained their mystery in the *zenana*.

23 See, for example, chapters on women in Mortimer Menpes, *India*, text by Flora Annie Steel (London: Adam & Charles Black, 1905); 'A.U.', *Overland, Inland and Upland: A Lady's Notes of Personal Observation and Adventure*, micrographic edition (Calcutta: Stamp Digest, 1984); Barbara Wingfield Stratford, *India and the English* (London: Jonathan Cape, 1922); and Hinkson, *Indian Harvest*.

24 Some contradictory evidence for contemporary South Asia has been suggested by Hannah Papanek in 'Purdah: Separate Worlds and Symbolic Shelter,' in *Separate Worlds*, ed. Hannah Papanek and Gail Minault (Delhi, Chanakya Publications, 1982), 3–53, esp. 42–3.

25 India successively served three major purposes in the British Empire: first as a supplier of manufactures; second as a supplier of raw materials and consumer of British manufactures; and finally as a field for the export of British capital and a strategic military outpost, especially after the First World War.

26 That such reform did not necessarily mark an 'improvement' or even an understanding of the complexities of the existing situation is argued by Lata Mani in 'Production of an Official Discourse on Sati in early Nineteenth-century Bengal', *Economic* and *Political Weekly* 21 (26 April 1986): WS 32–40.

27 Hutchins, *Illusion of Permanence*, viii. The minute primarily met the colonial need for a cheap pool of Indian labour to staff the imperial machine.

28 *Ibid.*, 187.

29 Pat Barr, *The Memsahibs: The Women of Victorian India* (London: Secker & Warburg, 1976), introduction.

30 See especially the manual by Flora Annie Steel and G. Gardiner, *The Complete Indian Cook and Housekeeper* (London: Heinemann, 1902).

31 Barr, *The Memsahibs*, 197.

32 After all, the very act of writing, especially after the printing press became widespread, 'was taken to be the visible sign of reason, which was valorised above all other human characteristics'. H. L. Gates, 'Writing, "Race" and the Difference it Makes', in *'Race', Writing and Difference*, especially 8.

33 Marian Fowler, *Below the Peacock Fan: First Ladies of the Raj* (Penguin, 1987), 5 (emphasis mine).

34 Even when Emily Eden, sister of Lord Auckland, Governor General of India 1836–42, declared, 'I cannot abide India, and that is the truth,' Fowler chooses to remember her as possessed of a 'serious empathy and awareness of India's unique pulse' (*ibid.*, 62).

35 Mary Ann Lind, *The Compassionate Memsahibs: Welfare Activities of British Women in India, 1900–1947* (New York: Greenwood Press, 1988), 4. Six of the 15 women she studies did not mention 'the Raj [*sic*], Indian politics, or Gandhi' in a period of heightened nationalist activity when women played a crucial role (*ibid.*, 107. However, see Geraldine Forbes, 'From Purdah to Politics: The Social Feminism of the All-India Women's Organisations', 219–61, and Gail Minault's 'Pudah Politics: The Role of Muslim women in Indian Nationalism, 1911–24', 245–61, in *Separate Worlds*. See also Forbes's 'The Politics of Respectability: Indian Women and the Indian National Congress', in *The Indian National Congress: Centenary, Highlights*, ed. D. A. Low (Delhi: Oxford University Press, 1988), 54–97.

36 Macmillan, *Women of the Raj*, 15.

37 *Ibid.*, 14.

38 *Ibid.*, 236.

39 Ketaki Kushari Dyson, A *Various Universe: A Study of the Journals and Memoirs of British Men and Women in the Indian Subcontinent, 1765–1856* (Delhi: Oxford University Press, 1978).

40 Barr, *The Memsahibs*, 66.

41 *Ibid.*, 163.

42 'Overdetermined' is used here in the Althusserian sense to suggest that gender is often inseparable from considerations of race and class, 'determining but also determined by the various levels and instances of the social formation it animates'. (Louis Althusser, *For Marx*, London: New Left Books, 1977), 101.

43 Pierre Macherey, *A Theory of Literary Production* (London: Routledge & Kegan Paul, 1978), 60.

44 They are (in order of year of writing): Maria Graham, *Journal of a Residence in India* (Edinburgh: Constable, 1813); Fanny Parks, *Wanderings of a Pilgrim in Search of the Picturesque*; Emily Eden, *Up the Country: Letters Written to her Sister from the Upper Provinces of India*; Helen Colin Mackenzie, *Life in the Mission, the Camp, and the Zenana, or, Six Years in India*; Mary Carpenter, *Six Months in India*; A.U., *Overland, Inland and Upland*; Marchioness of Dufferin and Alva, *Our Viceregal Life in India: Selections from my Journal, 1884–1888* (London: J. Murray, 1890); Mrs Murray Mitchell, *In Southern India: A Visit to some of the Chief Mission Stations in the Madras Presidency* (London: 1885); Mary Frances Billington, *Woman in India*, second edition (Delhi: Sri Satguru Publications, 1987); Flora Annie Steele, text for *India*; with G. Gardiner, *The Complete Indian Cook and Housekeeper*; Maud Diver, *The Englishwoman in India* (London, 1909); Norah Rowan Hamilton, *Through Wonderful India and Beyond* (London, 1915); Yvonne Fitzroy, *Courts and Camps in India: Impressions of Viceregal tours, 1921–24* (London, 1926); Barbara Wingfield Stratford, *India and the English*; Margaret Noble, *The Complete Works of Sister Nivedita*, 5 vols (Calcutta: Ramkrishna Sarada Mission, 1967); Annie Besant, *The India that Shall Be* (Madras: Theosophical Publishing House, 1940); *India: Bound or free?* (London: G. Putnam's Sons, 1926); Margaret Cousins, *Indian Womanhood Today* (Allahabad: Kitabistan, 1941); and Pamela Hinkson, *Indian Harvest*.

45 See, however, Rosemary Hennessy and Rajeshwari Mohan, 'The Construction of Woman in three popular Texts of Empire: towards a Critique of Materialist Feminism,' *Textual Practice* (forthcoming).

46 *The Englishwoman's Review of Social and Industrial Questions*, facsimile reprint, 1868–1910, advisory editors Janet Horowitz Murray and Myra Stark (New York: Garland Publishing, 1980).

47 Graham, *Journal of a Residence in India*, 115.

48 Parks, *Wanderings of a Pilgrim in Search of the Picturesque*, 281.

49 Mackenzie, *Life in the Mission, the Camp, and the Zenana*, I, 189.

50 A.U., *Overland, Inland and Upland*, 142. Mrs Murray Mitchell, touring the south in the early 1880s, voiced the same optimism.

51 A.U., *Overland, Inland and Upland*, 237.

52 Carpenter, *Six Months in India*, I, 76.

53 In *The Feminists: Women's Emancipation Movements in Europe America and Australasia, 1840–1920* (London: Croom Helm, 1977), Richard Evans says that the Royal Commission report of 1858 recommended the establishment of a national system of girls' secondary schools to educate middle-class girls in the new and complex tasks of household management. Charles Woods' *Educational Despatch* in 1854 made suggestions for universal education in India and prominently featured female education.

54 Mackenzie, *Life in the Mission*, I, 243.

55 Carpenter, *Six Months in India*, I, 107.

56 *Ibid.*, I, 85, 188. Gareth Stedman Jones, in *Outcast London: A Study in the Relationship between Classes in Victorian Society* (New York: Pantheon, 1984) notes the prevalence of similar

attitudes among London reformers towards poorer sections. See especially 'The Deformation of the Gift.'

57 Mitchell, *In Southern India*, 365.

58 *Ibid.*, 5.

59 See *ER*, introduction to index, ed. Jane H. Murray and Anna K. Clark (1985).

60 *ER* (1866–67): 316; (1868): 472; (1871): 85; (1876): 366; (1880): 107. Back in England, Mary Carpenter founded the India Association, which produced a journal aimed at educating fellow Britons about the condition of women in Britain's largest dominion. See *ER* (1871): 85.

61 Eden, *Up the Country*, 132.

62 A.U., *Overland, Inland and Upland*, 129.

63 *ER* (1890): 58

64 Carpenter, *Six Months in India*, 1, 230.

65 A.U., *Overland, Inland and Upland*, 124.

66 Mackenzie, *Life in the Mission*, 3, 321.

67 *ER* (1889): 146.

68 *ER* (1891): 139.

69 Patricia Branca, *Silent Sisterhood: Middle Class Women in the Victorian Home* (Pittsburgh PA: Carnegie Mellon University Press, 1975), 63.

70 Billington, *Woman in India*, 1–12.

71 Parks, *Wanderings of a Pilgrim in Search of the Picturesque*, 390.

72 Mackenzie, *Life in the Mission*, 307.

73 Mitchell, *In Southern India*, 244.

74 *Ibid.*, 198.

75 Judith Walkowitz, *Prostitution and Victorian Society: Women Class, and the State* (New York and Cambridge: Cambridge University Press, 1980). Her excellent analysis of the CD campaigns could have been enriched by a discussion of the prior institution of such forms of sexual control in the cantonments of India, and the controversies that surrounded their repeated abolition and restitution in the presidencies throughout the nineteenth century. See Ballhatchet's *Race, Sex and Class under the Raj*.

76 Billington, *Woman in India*, 80, 112–15.

77 Mikhell, *In Southern India*, 53.

78 The economic decline between 1870 and 1914 is widely acknowledged, though the causes are debated. See Paul Warwick's 'Did Britain Change? An Inquiry into the Causes of National Decline', *Journal of Contemporary History*, 20 (1985): 99–133. Warwick does not deal with the political challenges as they are dealt with in *Crisis in the British State, 1880–1930*, ed. Mary Langan and Bill Schwarz (London: Hutchinson, in association with the Centre for Contemporary Cultural Studies, 1985). Tom Nairn, similarly, develops the notion of crisis as posed by Irish nationalism and the working class in the period but neglects feminist challenges. See *The Break-up of Britain: Crisis and Neo-nationalism*, second edition (London: NLB, 1981). See also G. S. Jones, *Outcast London*, for perceptions and responses to the labouring poor in this period.

79 Walkowitz, *Prostitution and Victorian Society*, 1.

80 Susan Kingsley Kent, *Sex and Suffrage in Britain, 1860–1914* (Princeton NJ: Princeton University Press, 1987). 'The vote became both the symbol of the sexually free autonomous woman and the means by which the goals of a feminist culture were to be obtained.'

81 Martin Durham outlines the heterogeneity of the women's movement in this period in 'Suffrage and After: Feminism in the Early Twentieth Century', in Langan and Schwarz, *Crisis in The British State*, 179–91, esp. 185. See also Walkowitz, 'Male Vice and Feminist Virtue: Feminism and the Politics of Prostitution in Nineteenth Century Britain', *Past and Present*, 13 (spring 1982): 79–93.

82 Billington was a journalist with the *Daily Graphic* and was assigned to investigate the position of women in India. Flora Annie Steel and Maud Diver were the wives of civil servants in the Punjab who spent long years in India and produced a number of novels on the Raj. Their writings received wide publicity in England; *The Complete Indian Housekeeper and*

Cook completed ten editions. Barr, *The Memsahibs*, 153.

83 Billington, *Women in India*, 155.

84 *Ibid.*, 176. Billington's observations of working-class women revealed an opposition to Lancashire industrialists who were clamouring for factory reform in India at that time to reduce competition from cheap Indian cloth. Low wages were not only adequate in India, she argued, but were a mark of the higher quality of life in India compared with the indignities of working-class life in Britain.

85 Steel, *India*, 165.

86 *Ibid.*, 166.

87 *Ibid.*, 157.

88 See Jane Lewis, *Women in England, 1810–1950: Sexual Division and Social Change*, Brighton: Wheatsheaf Books, 1984): 98–9, and Jeffrey Weeks, *Sex, Politics and Society: The Regulation of Sexuality since 1800* (London: Longman, 1981) 128–38.

89 Lewis, *Women in England*, 75–141; Frank Mort, 'Purity, Feminism and the State: Sexuality and Moral Politics, 1880–1914,' in Langan and Schwarz, *Crisis in the British State*, 209–25, esp. 222.

90 Steel, *India*, 159.

91 Stratford, *India and the English*, 119.

92 Hamilton, *Through Wonderful India and Beyond*, 258.

93 Diver, *Englishwoman in India*, 100–1 (emphasis mine).

94 *Ibid.*, 168.

95 Hinkson, *Indian Harvest*, 73.

96 That this was at a time when the Hindu community in UP was actively campaigning for legislation against cow slaughter was but one of the many ambiguities that marked nationalist politics. See Gyan Pandey, 'Rallying Round the Cow: Sectarian Strife in the Bhojpuri Region, 1888–1917,' in *Subaltern Studies* (New Delhi: Oxford University Press, 1983), II, 60–129.

97 Through an interlocking system of export-import banks, managing agencies, and shipping companies, all of which were British-owned, the benefits of external trade accrued entirely to British capital. India was the first of oriental countries to feel the impact of industrialization, yet it was never allowed to complete the transition to industrialization.

98 See Bipan Chandra, *The Rise and Growth of Economic Nationalism* (New Delhi: People's Publishing House, 1982) for an analysis of the critiques of moderate nationalists in this period.

99 See Ranajit Guha's *Elementary Aspects of Peasant Insurgency* (New Delhi: Oxford University Press, 1983) for an analysis of peasant and tribal movements at the time.

100 See Amiya Bagchi's *Private Investment in India, 1900–1939* (Cambridge: Cambridge University Press, 1972) for the economic condition of India in 1900.

101 Stuart Hall and Bill Schwarz, 'State and Society, 1880–1930', in *Crisis in the British State*, 7–32, esp. 29.

102 Diver, *The Englishwoman in India*, 120.

103 Hamilton, *Through Wonderful India and Beyond*, 259.

104 Stratford, *India and the English*, 122.

105 As quoted in Pamela Hinkson, *Indian Harvest*, 256.

106 Margaret Cousins referred to this strategy of the British many years later in *Indian Womanhood Today*, 85. See also Liddle and Joshi, 'Gender and Imperialism in British India'.

107 Barr, *The Memsahibs*, 186.

108 *ER* (1883): 202–4.

109 See the editor's preface to *The Complete Works of Sister Nivedita* and chronological table in each volume.

110 Noble, 'The Present Position of Women', in *Complete Works* (1968) IV, 238.

111 *Ibid.*, 369.

112 Noble, 'The Web of Indian Life,' in *Complete Works* (1967) II, 68.

113 Besant, 'Women in India' (1917) in *The India That Shall Be* (Madras: Theosophical Publishing House, 1940), 254.

114 Besant, *India Bound or Free?*, 183.

115 Cousins, *Indian Womanhood Today*, 68. The 'separate sphere' feminism of Gandhi was anticipated in the 1905 Congress call during the Swadeshi movement for women to keep the 'hearths cold' to protest at the partition of Bengal. Gandhi's spectacular success was in drawing women into the national movement (as he did the peasant masses) while keeping mass activity strictly pegged to safe levels. The symbolic shelter that he offered women in the public domain of politics enabled the easier acceptance of women in public life throughout the nationalist period and in the decades after independence.

116 *Ibid.*, 184.

117 *Ibid.*, 198–9.

118 *ER* (1867): 319; (1868): 482; (1877): 278–9; (1881): 515–16; (1885): 146; (1889): 146; (1890): 327–30.

119 *ER* (1881): 515–16.

120 Diver, *The Englishwoman in India*, 104.

121 Lind, *Compassionate Memsahibs*, 19.

122 Diver, *The Englishwoman in India*, 96–7. This remark was prompted by her assessment that the impact of Lady Dufferin's fund for female medical services in India was decidedly poor.

123 Hamilton, *Through Wonderful India and Beyond*, 259.

124 Hinkson, *Indian Harvest*, 258.

125 Diver, *The Englishwoman in India*, 128–9 (emphasis mine).

126 Hinkson, *Indian Harvest*, 97.

127 *Ibid.*, 320.

128 Maria Mies, *Patriarchy and Accumulation on a World Scale: Women in the International Division of Labour* (London: Zed Books, 1987), 106.

129 Parks, *Wanderings of a Pilgrim in Search of the Picturesque*, 420.

11

Sex, citizenship, and the nation in World War II Britain

SONYA O. ROSE

During World War II, there was widespread public apprehension about the declining morals of girls and young women in British cities and towns. Social workers, probation officers, and police worried about the young girls who were said to hang around bus and train terminals on the lookout for soldiers. High-level officials of government deliberated on what could be done about the women who reportedly 'accosted' soldiers on the streets of cities and towns. And in various districts of the country, there was talk about young women whose behaviour was threatening to populate the country with illegitimate babies, some of whom could well be black.

There have been, of course, periodic upsurges of public concern about immorality on the part of women and girls. The closing decades of the nineteenth century, for example, witnessed heightened public apprehension about prostitution and the sexual vulnerabilities of girls and young women.[1] So-called 'white slavery' – the national and international traffic in women, especially girls – preoccupied social purity groups and the media in pre-war London.[2] Early in World War I, 'khaki fever' was said to afflict girls who openly associated with men in uniform.[3] Flappers and 'dope girls' peopled media portrayals of transgressive female sexuality during the inter-war period.[4]

Such incidents of rampant unease may best be understood as episodes in a relatively continuous public discourse about sexuality and especially about appropriate norms of female sexuality.[5] What distinguishes these episodes are the particular events or circumstances that trigger heightened and extensive fascination with and commentary about the sexual activities of women and girls, and the rhetoric and cultural imagery that simultaneously portray these activities as indicative of sweeping moral transgressions and link them to more general preoccupations and debates.

Scholars have traditionally thought about moral discourses in two ways: as statements of the sacred rules that dictate behaviour and as the evaluative and normative categories that organize perception and action.[6] In a fruitful shift of emphasis, philosopher Richard Rorty suggests that morality is 'the voice of ourselves as members of a community, speakers of a common language'.[7] This shift of emphasis focuses attention on the connections between morality and collective identities. Morality, Rorty proposes, is a matter of 'we-intentions,' and the core meaning of 'immoral action' is 'the sort of thing *we* don't do … If done by one of us, or if done repeatedly by one of us, that person ceases to be one of us.'[8] This way of thinking about morality suggests that there may likely be an outpouring of moral discourse in periods when the issue of community identity has become especially significant, times when questions about the nature and extent of community or national solidarity become highly charged, and when the bases of unity are seen to be fragmented.[9] Moral discourse becomes especially intensified, I am suggesting, when perceptions of difference and the diversity within nations or communities become problematic. War is just such a time.

War exaggerates the significance of the nation as a source and object of identity. War is an especially critical juncture, since people in a nation-state are called on to unify in defence of their supposedly common 'way of life.' During wartime, propagandists manipulate patriotic sentiment to stimulate loyalty and sacrifice; they focus public attention on questions such as who 'we' are and what it is that 'we' stand for. It is a time when physical bodies and the social body – the national body – are threatened on a variety of fronts. War, especially total war, transforms the everyday in unparalleled ways, as women and men face various new and untested opportunities with unforeseen consequences. Thus war's liberating potential threatens the very unity that the nation is imagined to represent. Under such conditions, and in a society with a long history of constructing female sexuality and the pursuit of pleasure as dangerous, women who were perceived to be seeking out sexual adventures might well be defined as subversive.

In this chapter, I shall first examine how, in the context of wartime Britain, race and national difference exacerbated public concern about the romantic and pleasure-seeking activities of women and girls. My exploration of the dynamics of racial ideology leads me to suggest that anxiety about interracial sexuality significantly amplified concern about female sexual propriety. Then, to analyse further how women's transgressive behaviours were given meaning in public discussion, I explore the symbolic links between the commentary about women's sexuality and popular discourses of national identity and ideals of citizenship. I suggest that expressions of anxiety about women's sexual morality were framed by constructions of national identity and the ideals of citizenship elaborated in a variety of sites of cultural production.

As war became increasingly imminent in 1939, the National Council of Women and representatives of various moral welfare and social purity organizations began to express their concern about young girls hanging around military encampments. During World War I, as Philippa Levine has detailed, their predecessors had advocated hiring women to control the women and girls who were seen consorting with soldiers.[10] These groups, led by the National Council of Women, which took as one of its special missions the promotion of women's unique capacities for police work, continued to advocate the hiring of women police in the inter-war period. With the onset of World War II, they stepped up their campaign, lobbying the Home Office to pressure local constabularies to hire policewomen who would deal with the women and girls whose behaviour they deemed questionable.[11] While the Home Office made funds available for the purpose of adding women as auxiliary police personnel, it exerted no pressure on the constabularies. Local women's groups, such as the Women's Citizens' Association of Preston, campaigned to persuade their chief constables and the watch committee to hire women police.[12] But at least in Preston and possibly in other communities as well, they were not successful until or after the autumn of 1942.[13]

Beginning in late 1942, a greater proportion of the public commented on and denounced the romantic escapades of women and girls, intensifying both official and unofficial scrutiny of their behaviour. Participants included not only social purity and moral welfare workers and the National Council of Women but private citizens, social workers and probation officers, clergymen, a variety of national and local government officials, the military, and the press. Newspapers in geographically dispersed rural and urban districts increased widespread anxiety by printing lurid headlines, feature articles, a proliferation of letters to the editor, and editorials that dissected the causes and consequences of teenage girls 'running wild' or going out 'for a good time'.[14] Routine reports often went into excruciating detail describing their 'indiscretions,' fuelling the panic by exciting both outrage and prurient attention.[15]

Media attention thus both documented and contributed to public anxiety about girls and young women. Initially, it coincided with the government's first nationwide educational media campaign to curb the spread of venereal disease. By 1941, rates of syphilis had increased 13 per cent among males and 63 per cent among females.[16] In October 1942, the ban on radio broadcasts dealing with such matters was lifted, and the government's chief medical officer spoke on the air about the perils of venereal disease. The Ministry of Information followed with an extensive poster campaign, and Parliament debated and enacted an anti-venereal disease control measure, Regulation 33B. This stipulated that if a person was identified as the source of venereal disease by at least two informants, he or she was legally required to undergo treatment or would be arrested and forced to undergo treatment. Opposed by those who thought it would do nothing to prevent venereal disease, Regulation 33B was vilified by Church and social purity groups as a stimulus to vice and by feminists who feared its enforcement would target women but not men. Both the VD educational campaign and the debate over 33B contributed to making sex a subject of extensive public discussion.

But, more significant, the public commentary about the behaviour of women and girls was stimulated by the growing presence of American GIs in British towns and cities. The Americans began arriving in late 1942, and the numbers of Americans on British soil began to grow rapidly during that year and early in 1943.[17] By D-Day, there were around a million American soldiers in Britain. They were most often the ones who appeared in reports as the objects of desire of these young women, and it was their presence that triggered the widespread perception that a wave of 'moral laxity' was engulfing the country. The Americans, however, did not cause a dramatic change in young women's sexual behaviours to the extent that the public uproar suggested. What had changed was that they, rather than local British men and boys, became the objects of women's desires. The arrival of these foreign troops made visible what might have occurred with much less comment had there not been a war.[18] The fact that they were not British and that they often represented themselves as coming to Britain's rescue undoubtedly threatened national pride. Their associations with British women also potentially could undermine the morale of British soldiers fighting overseas. Additionally, the presence of the Americans added the issue of race to apprehensions that wartime conditions were causing women and girls to lose self-control and were putting the moral fabric of the nation in jeopardy.

Public criticism of Americans in general, however, was discouraged if not overtly censored by the government. Especially in the first year of the American presence, the British press rarely published articles about friction with the GIs or criticism about their behaviour.[19] Even when the war was ending, the British-American Liaison Board, which dealt with relations between GIs and British civilians, discussed a pamphlet of cartoons by a British resident of Exeter, 'More Gum Chum', depicting American soldiers and British women. The committee maintained that its 'contents were calculated to do harm' because the 'morale of the troops and relations with Americans were bound up with it.'[20] As a consequence, Clarence Stilling, the author, was 'encouraged' not to publish or try to sell any more of the pamphlets.[21] Such sensitivity combined with a historically enduring sexual double standard shielded American men from being held responsible for the presumed breakdown of moral standards of women and girls.

White American soldiers were generally portrayed by the press as playing no sexual role other than being associated with the girls.[22] For instance, the front page of a Leicester newspaper carried the headline, '"Model Daughter" Became Infatuated.' The case was described as 'A tragedy due to wartime infatuation'. The seventeen-year-old girl had been accused of stealing clothing worth £6.

> Counsel said she had been a model daughter … and a regular attender of Salvation Army meetings until she became infatuated with two American soldiers last August. Eventually, instead of coming home, she took the first step that led to her ruin. They went to a public house and afterwards to the soldiers' camp, and slept the night in an air raid shelter. When the soldiers were transferred, the girl stole a bicycle and followed them.[23]

In this report, and in others like it, the silence about the white soldiers represented them as being the source of apparently irresistible temptation; thus descriptions of their behaviour were unnecessary for the story to make sense. One exception to this general pattern is a story in the *Luton News*, which suggested that the (white) American soldiers' gifts and money explained why British women were attracted to them. The article reported on a court case involving two young women ages nineteen and sixteen who were described as wearing new shoes and gloves given to them by the Americans, and 'one admitted receiving £6 from soldiers'.[24] But the rhetorical strategy in all of these accounts focused full attention on the figure of the wayward girl.[25]

The outrage over young women's morals intensified when the soldiers with whom they associated were black. In the press, virtually the only identifying feature ever supplied about American soldiers was race, and that was usually given only when the soldiers were black. The issue of race, generally, was a topic that generated extreme discomfort on the part of British government officials. Earlier, prior to the US entry into the war, the British government had requested that Negro troops be barred from working or serving on the West Indian bases that the British had leased to the Americans.[26] Also, the Royal Air Force had rejected on the grounds of race an American black pilot who had applied to serve as a ferry pilot guiding planes between Montreal and Great Britain, although subsequently the RAF's requirement that 'all applicants must be of the white race' was dropped.[27] Qualified African-Americans had also been denied employment with the British Purchasing Commission in Washington; a black doctor from New York, who had volunteered to come to Britain to help because of the widely publicized shortage of physicians in London during the Blitz, was rejected by the Ministry of Health. While the British military services during the war suspended the requirement that people who enlisted and received commissions must prove they were of European descent, they made it clear that this was 'for the duration only' and resisted making any statements about what would happen after the war.[28] These instances suggest that many government officials certainly favoured racial exclusivity even prior to the American forces' actual arrival.

Their apprehensiveness about the problems they imagined would arise if non-whites were integrated into the home-front war effort mounted, however, when it became clear that the Americans intended to move large numbers of black troops into the country.[29] They anticipated that the presence of black American soldiers would create problems of both diplomacy and social control.[30]

The Foreign Office was concerned that long-term diplomatic ties between the United States and Britain would be damaged if situations resulted that rankled the Americans. The Foreign Office, in fact, hoped to use the American presence as a way to strengthen these ties, and to instil in the Americans a positive opinion and appreciation for the British.[31] Although there were voices in the Foreign Office that cautioned against alienating those Americans with more progressive views on race, as well as those concerned about offending the southerners, the War Office wanted the government to issue instructions encouraging the British to accommodate American segregationist attitudes and practices.[32]

The Colonial Office, however, was extremely apprehensive that, whatever stance the British took on the presence of black Americans on British soil, it should not intensify colonial disaffection with British rule. The Colonial Office worried especially that if the British appeared to sanction or participate in overtly racist practices, such behaviour would exacerbate anti-British sentiment on the part of colonial elites. As sociologist Kenneth Little wrote in a memorandum to the Colonial Office:

> As you yourself know, these representatives of the British colonials over here have been made very uneasy, and justifiably so in my opinion, at the prospects of American methods of Segregation, etc. being copied here as well as reinforcing existing colour bar mechanisms. What the ordinary statesman or politician apparently does not realize is that news of such events and 'incidents' flies very quickly these days, and particularly at a time like the present when coloured people everywhere are almost morbidly alive to anything over here which savours of discrimination.[33]

For officials, then, hosting large numbers of American blacks was very complex indeed. Additionally, the Colonial Office had to cope with the problem that continued throughout the war of white Americans subjecting black British subjects to Jim Crow practices.[34]

Such incidents began soon after Americans arrived on British soil. The Colonial Office almost immediately began receiving numerous complaints about the 'threatening attitude of American troops' to black Britons and colonials.[35] By January 1943, there were reports from Liverpool and Manchester about a 'steady deterioration in the relationship between white soldiers and our own Colonial People'.[36] The Colonial Office was told of the 'tremendous bitterness amongst (West Indian) technicians by these attacks.' And as Learie Constantine, renowned and popular former Trinidadian cricketer, employed as a welfare officer by the Ministry of Labour in Liverpool, put it, 'I have lived in this country for a long time and claim many friends amongst the white population, and I shiver to think that I am liable to attack by these men if I am seen in the company of my friends.'[37] Subsequently, Constantine was denied a room at a London hotel on the grounds of race by a manager who claimed that the presence of blacks bothered American officers staying at the hotel. Constantine successfully sued the hotel for damages.[38] In another incident, he officially protested to the Ministry of Labour and National Service in May 1944 about his treatment at a London pub by two white Americans. Constantine bitterly suggested in his letter that neither the Colonial Office nor any other branch of government seemed willing to confront the Americans about their treatment of black Britons.[39]

British responses consisted mainly of the equivalent of 'hand wringing'. The problems created by American racist behaviour toward black British subjects resident in the metropole were handled by powerless, though well-meaning and hard-working, officials in the newly formed Colonial Welfare section of the Ministry.[40]

For many segments of the civilian British population, however, as well as ordinary British soldiers, the presence of black Americans was a source of fascination. In spite of the reports of a 'colour bar' operating in Britain prior to the arrival of the Americans, white American soldiers' open hostility toward black Americans provided many Britons with a way to enhance their own sense of national pride by contrasting white American racist practices with what they believed to be British racial tolerance.[41] These varied responses by white Britons to the issue of race suggests that the highly unstable meanings of the category of 'black' or 'coloured' – a category in Britain that included peoples from the Indian subcontinent, the loose subcategory of 'Arabs', West Indians, and Africans from a host of British colonies – were further destabilized by the American presence. Black Americans were often favourably contrasted by British civilians to white Americans, and were seen as more polite and better mannered than their white compatriots. African-American soldiers, however, became racial 'others' when it came to sexual relations with white British women.

Fears of both interracial marriage and sex between men of colour and white women had a long cultural history in Britain. As Ann Laura Stoler's work on nineteenth-century European colonialism has suggested, the policing of interracial sexuality to maintain 'racial purity' is intimately bound up with constructing and maintaining white supremacy.[42] While her work explicitly deals with maintaining the boundaries of empire, the empire 'came home' during World War I when non-white colonial troops were stationed in Britain. They were closely guarded while on leave and not allowed to participate in the victory celebrations held in London. Their being attended by white female nursing staff in hospitals that treated wounded soldiers in Britain aroused considerable controversy as well.[43] During the inter-war period, the Cardiff chief constable argued for the desirability of anti-miscegenation legislation as had recently been passed in South Africa to secure the 'welfare' of the British.[44] Paul Rich has suggested in his discussion of inter-war racial ideology that '"welfare" … was assumed to accrue from implicit racial separation and the prohibition on inter-racial marriage and sexual contact'.[45]

As in World War I, numerous non-white colonials were present in the metropole during the 1940s, in addition to the approximately 7,000 permanent non-white residents in the port cities.[46] Unlike World War I, there were no non-white colonial regiments or battalions stationed in Great Britain except for very short periods of time, although there were non-white colonials in the country who had enlisted in the military.[47] More than 10,000 men and a small number of women from the West Indies were volunteers in the armed services. Almost all of the men were in the RAF; most were from Jamaica, with lesser numbers from Trinidad, British Guiana, and other Caribbean islands; the women enlisted in the Auxiliary Territorial Service (ATS).[48] Additionally, during the war, approximately 700 Indians were brought for training and then sent back to India to boost production of munitions. There were around 1,000 skilled technicians and trainees brought from the West Indies for employment in ordnance factories, and about the same number of men from British Honduras were brought to work in the forests of Scotland.⁴⁹

Bringing West Indians to the country to work was important not just to the Ministry of Labour and National Service, desperate for manpower, but also to the Colonial Office, which saw such schemes as colonial development projects and as a way to reinforce or foster positive West Indian views of the British. To achieve the latter end, the Ministry of Labour and National Service and the Colonial Office arranged for local hospitality to be offered. In the town of Bolton, where there was an ordnance factory, this included 'informal dances' and having 'ladies interested in the Colonial problem to accompany the coloured men to theatres and dances'.⁵⁰ A report about the town suggested that the West Indians' association with white British women did not 'appear to give rise to really serious problems in Bolton'. The report writer, indicating he was surprised, offered as possible explanations the small number of black men in Bolton and the fact that the community already included a few black professional men.⁵¹

This seemingly benign attitude toward interracial heterosexual associations applied as well to the British Hondurans in Scotland when they first arrived, although it did not last.⁵² In August 1942, Harold Macmillan, Parliamentary Under-secretary of State for the Colonies, received a complaint from the Duke of Buccleuch about the British Honduran unit:

> The people in the neighbourhood were encouraged to be friendly to them and the girls have interpreted this rather widely ... I ... learned that there have been a number of marriages and births, and much intercourse is allowed, even in the Camp itself ... Personally, I dislike this mixture of colour and regret that it should be allowed with no discouragement. There are already sufficient births of foreign extraction in the country without the additional complication of colour ... I feel that unsophisticated country girls should be discouraged from marrying these black men from Equatorial America.⁵³

Macmillan ordered an inquiry and responded to the duke, reassuring him that there was no evidence that the British Hondurans had abused the social hospitality given by local residents, although several women of 'an undesirable type' from Edinburgh had gained access to one of the camps, which prompted immediate police action.⁵⁴

Not to be quieted, the duke characterized Macmillan's response as having a 'not unexpectedly official tone which puts the matter in a more favourable light than is factual ... I think it can be admitted that loose relations between black men of totally different standards, both moral and material, and our simple country girls has unpleasant features, and that improper intercourse with decent young women should be strongly discouraged.'⁵⁵

The duke also sent a private letter to Sir Samuel Strange Steel of the Ministry of Supply to alert him to the problems involving the British Hondurans. The Ministry of Supply, which had jurisdiction over the foresters, also became involved in monitoring the situation.⁵⁶ Its officials took a dire view of what they saw as the 'increasingly difficult' problem of sexual relations between British Honduran men and white British women.[57] In addition to relations with women of 'an undesirable type', the idea that the British Hondurans were associating with farmers' daughters and with white wives of British soldiers was of particular concern.[58] Eventually, the Ministry of Supply insisted that the British Honduran units be repatriated, claiming that there was no longer any need for their labour.[59]

Sexual relations, whether actual or potential, between white British women and men of colour in World War II appeared especially disturbing to many Britons, for they jeopardized Britons' sense of themselves as white. The spectre of 'half-caste' babies threatened to blur the racial lineaments of white British national identity and make the new black presence a permanent 'social problem' rather than a temporary wartime inconvenience or one limited to the colonies and to a few port areas in the metropole.[60] As Laura Tabili's work has shown, policies to limit the size and duration of the black presence in Britain had a venerable if unsuccessful history.[61]

Popular and official reactions to British women's associations with American soldiers clearly were transformed by race. The racial inflection of the construction of the problem is illustrated by an extensive article detailing the behaviour of young women and black men in the *Huddersfield Daily Examiner* in the summer of 1943.[62] The report, which initiated an extensive series of letters to the editor, contained considerable details of the writer's investigative reporting and included depictions with clear erotic overtones.[63]

> Two of the officers suddenly flashed their torches into the road. There stood a negro and a girl with their arms round each other. Titters and subdued American voices came from the other side of the road where the lorries were drawn up. Girls were inside one of the lorries with the men. As the engine was being started the girls got out. The lorry moved slowly away and in the darkness of the night a female voice cried out, 'Goodnight, my darkie boy. I'll see you at eight tomorrow night.' The girl and one of her friends then walked a few yards and joined men who were going by another lorry. Men's and women's voices came from neighbouring doorways. Once when an officer flashed his lamp I saw two negroes and two girls in fond embraces.[64]

The problem of British women and girls' immoral behaviour in their associations with Americans was redefined here as a problem of interracial sex.

While white American soldiers ('Americans') were represented as a 'presence' tempting girls along the 'road to ruin' – which the white British young women were supposed to resist – the positioning of black soldiers ('coloured Americans') in public discussions was somewhat different. The Huddersfield reporter made it clear that the race of the soldiers was absolutely critical to the problem of young women's sexual morality, and that restricting the access black men had to white British women might well be necessary: 'some people who wish a certain course to be adopted … are perhaps attaching blame to those who, if not altogether blame-less, are victims of circumstances which might even be too much for some white men similarly situated.'[65] The statement hinting that black men were less capable of self-control than white men drew on long-standing ideas that unbridled sexuality and lack of self-control were racial traits that made non-whites both morally inferior and more childlike than whites – ideas that legitimated the subordination of black men to white control.[66]

Racial ideology led not only to differing symbolic representations of the issue, it also shaped the deployment by British officials of various techniques of surveillance and control.[67] Primarily, these efforts were aimed at the girls and young women, not the African-American soldiers. While the presence of black soldiers was constructed as a generic problem, racial identification in news reports often was used to suggest that the girls who associated with 'coloured Americans' were especially immoral or degraded. The race of the men with whom young white British women and girls were consorting affected the *extent* to which the behaviour of these young women and girls was seen to be immoral. Interracial sex, in other words, was understood as a kind of sexual perversion. Howard Tyrer, head of the Public Morality Council, made this association when reminiscing about his twenty-six years of vice surveillance activities in London. He described the patrons of a club in Soho as consisting of 'women in male attire, effeminate men and coloured men accompanied by white women'.[68] The reports of interracial sex in World War II, then, magnified further the apprehension about women's sexual morality that had been provoked by wartime conditions and the presence of large numbers of foreign troops on British soil. White British women and girls were not only having illicit sex, but many were having it with black men.

But what are we to make of this anxiety over female sexuality? What was so threatening about young women's associations with soldiers black and white, and why weren't these associations seen simply as wartime romantic flings or, like the American black presence, a temporary problem that would pass once the war was over? These questions may best be approached by investigating the idioms and metaphors that expressed apprehension about female sexuality. Examining the language used to articulate the nature of the problem posed by the behaviour of women and girls helps us to understand why their morals became an intense focus of public discussion. It exposes the larger cultural context that both contributed to and was informed by discussions about them. In what follows, I suggest that images of pleasure-seeking women disturbed the developing definition of the nation in British public culture and contrasted with the definition of 'good citizenship' central to those new understandings of national identity.

Public officials responsible for civilian morale, participants in discussions about Britain's post-war future, as well as artists and writers (especially those under the tutelage of the Ministry of Information), portrayed the nation as composed of self-sacrificing, relentlessly cheerful, and brave people who had heroically withstood the Blitz and were stalwart as they coped with the material deprivations of a war economy.[69] As a brief guide to Britain for the arriving GIs observed, ordinary Britons had shown amazing strength during the Blitz. Expressing how the nation was being imagined in Britain at the time but using terms that would resonate with Americans, the pamphlet declared, 'A nation doesn't come through that, if it doesn't have plain, common guts. The British are tough, strong people, and good allies.'[70]

Britain was depicted by numerous social commentators as engaging in a war being fought by and for a country imagined as a unified land of 'ordinary people'. It was a nation whose identifying virtues emerged along with what Angus Calder has called 'the myth of the Blitz' – one in which the '"people," improvising bravely and brilliantly', had fought off the German Luftwaffe and had withstood its fire.[71] A *Picture Post* photograph of May 1941, for example, portrayed 'The Man the Nazis are Trying to Rattle: a British Citizen of 1941'. It shows a working-class man wearing a cap and overcoat sifting through rubble. The caption declares, 'He is the English city dweller. His home is the Nazi bombers' target. His few poor possessions, bought with the savings of years, are their military objective. And when a bomb falls, and makes of his home a shapeless heap of bricks, he calmly salvages what he can and starts afresh.'[72] The mythical notion that the British of all classes remained stalwart in the face of nightly bombings, in other words, was actively being created as it contributed to the redefinition of the nation.

J. B. Priestley's radio broadcast following the evacuation of British troops from Dunkirk a year prior to the Blitz and George Orwell's famous essay on patriotism both captured and helped to articulate the meanings of the nation being elaborated during the war. Priestley suggested that Dunkirk was 'very English … in the way in which, when apparently all was lost, so much was gloriously retrieved'.[73] Unlike the Germans, he proudly declared, 'the English' [Priestley said he really meant 'British'] are able to create an 'epic of gallantry' from what starts as a 'miserable blunder'.[74] As Calder has argued persuasively, the idea that the British traditionally have rescued victory from the jaws of defeat is clearly mythological.[75] Priestley proposed that what was so 'characteristically English' about this particular epic

> was the part played in the difficult and dangerous embarkation – not by the warships, magnificent though they were – but by the little pleasure-steamers. We've known them and laughed at them, these fussy little steamers, all our lives. We have watched them load and unload their crowds of holiday passengers – the gents full of high spirits and bottled beer, the ladies eating pork pies, the children sticky with peppermint rock. Sometimes they only went as far as the next seaside resort. But the boldest of them might manage a Channel crossing, to let everybody have a glimpse of Boulogne.[76]

Priestley used language that coded these little 'boats' as working-class. By focusing on the 'little pleasure-steamers' and depicting them in working-class cultural images, Priestley conjured up the heroism of the ordinary people of Britain in a narrative not unlike the children's story 'The Little Engine that Could'.

George Orwell also depicted the nation as comprised of ordinary people when he wrote,

We are a nation of flower-lovers, but also a nation of stamp-collectors, pigeon-fanciers, amateur carpenters, coupon-snippers, darts-players, crossword-puzzle fans. All the culture that is most truly native centres round things which even when they are communal are not official – the pub, the football match, the back garden, the fireside and the 'nice cup of tea'.[77]

Implicitly contrasting the British with the Germans, Orwell used this characterization of Britons in their private lives to make the point that these ordinary, pub-going, and flower-loving people were not innately drawn to nationalism or to participating in affairs of state.[78] Portraying the British people as characterized by diversity rather than a 'mass mentality', he also remarked on the deep class divisions in this 'land of snobbery and privilege, ruled largely by the old and silly. But in any calculation about it one has got to take into account its emotional unity, the tendency of nearly all its inhabitants to feel alike and act together in moments of supreme crisis.'[79] In spite of its diversity and these divisions, Britain, he maintained, is like a family that 'closes ranks' upon the approach of an enemy. Thus Orwell depicted Britain as composed of people not innately given to heroic public deeds but who, despite deep class divisions and their heterogeneous pastimes, were able to put aside their differences and their individual interests to defend the nation.[80] In other words, Orwell portrayed the nation as a *unified* if not homogeneous community. These portraits of national unity suggested that those who best represented Britain at war were not exceptional individuals but rather were everyday, ordinary people; those who were 'doing their bit.'

This same spirit of everyday sacrifice by ordinary people was portrayed in *Diary for Timothy*, the Humphrey Jennings documentary made in the closing months of the war, which focused on baby Timothy, born 3 September 1944, the war's fifth anniversary. The baby signified the future, and the script recorded, for his benefit, the sacrifices that were being made on his behalf and pictured a Britain on the verge of peace. It depicted the national mood as represented by Peter, a pilot convalescing in a hospital after having been wounded during D-Day; Geronwy, a coal miner injured in a mining accident; Alan, a gentleman farmer who reclaimed portions of his land to grow food for the war effort; and Bill, an engine driver who has united them all by carrying munitions, coal, and food. Michael Redgrave, the narrator, tells Timothy, 'All these people are fighting for you.'[81]

These portraits of the nation by Orwell, Priestley, and Jennings were among many that portrayed the nation as a unified community of ordinary people contributing to the war effort. This vision of World War II British patriotism prefigured Benedict Anderson's pathbreaking definition of the nation 'imagined as a *community* … as a deep, horizontal comradeship'.[82] But what of those whose behaviour suggested that they were not 'doing their bit'? How do images of sexually active, pleasure-seeking young women and girls fit with a nation being characterized as unified around self-sacrifice?

It is characteristic of nation-defining projects that they elide difference and mask divisions to create a common, overarching identity for the subjects of a nation-state.[83] Yet, as Mary Poovey has suggested, 'the process by which individuals or groups embrace the "nation" as the most meaningful context for self-definition necessarily involves temporarily marginalizing other rubrics that could also provide a sense of identity. If these identities cannot be submerged into the national community, they are excluded, and become a potent contrast against which the nation defines itself.'[84] Thus the solidarity that supposedly binds the national community has been depicted in numerous societies by nationalist rhetoric and policy that celebrate versions of race, class, and ethnic homogeneity and promulgate norms of sexual purity and particular ideals of gender difference.

Recent scholarship has illuminated the significance of gender and the importance of sexual morality to defining and maintaining national boundaries, and to distinguishing which individuals are fit to claim the rights and carry out the responsibilities of citizenship.[85] As Anne McClintock has proposed, 'All nations depend on powerful constructions of gender. Despite many nationalists' ideological investment in the idea of popular *unity*, nations have historically amounted to the sanctioned institutionalization of gender *difference*.'[86] A number of scholars have shown that, while women have been excluded from being full citizens of the nation-state, and have been depicted in political theory from the ancient world through the Enlightenment as unworthy or inappropriate to assume the rights and obligations of citizenship, images of women have often symbolized the nation.[87] Furthermore, the status of women has been a central theme in nationalist discourses.[88] Yet most scholars have argued that nations are constructed as fraternities and are characterized by male bonds, largely because of the significance of war (that most gendered of activities in which states engage) to their development.[89] Women have generally been included within the nation in their role as mothers – as reproducers of the race, rather than as political participants in civil society.[90]

Additionally, numerous scholars have suggested that sexual morality has been crucial to delineating the boundaries of the nation. In his provocative work on nationalism and sexuality, George Mosse has argued that the control of sexual desire, deeply constitutive of bourgeois notions of respectability, was integral to developing nationalisms.[91] And Ann Laura Stoler has written,

> Discourses of sexuality do more than define the distinctions of the bourgeois self; in identifying marginal members of the body politic, they have mapped the moral parameters of European nations. These deeply sedimented discourses on sexual morality could redraw the 'interior frontiers' of national communities, frontiers that were secured through – and sometimes in collision with – the boundaries of race.[92]

This literature suggests, then, that sexual propriety and control often have been central to nation building. And so it was in Britain during World War II.

Two major themes characterized the nation during the war and were implicit in the passages by Priestley and Orwell quoted above.[93] The first was the nation as a brave and quietly (rather than bombastically) heroic people. The second was a nation of quintessentially reasonable citizens who willingly and with good humour sacrificed their private and personal interests and desires for the collective good. These combined narrative devices figured the nation as both maternal and masculine. This was also the sense of the nation captured by Jennings in *Diary for Timothy*. The film celebrated masculine sacrifice with its focus on four male characters, while Timothy's mother, the only female figure of note in the film, exemplified the maternal. Priestley, for his part, articulated a masculine and maternal sensibility in his depiction of how the little pleasure steamers put aside their frivolous feminine ways in the service of the nation.

> They were usually paddle steamers, making a great deal more fuss with all their churning than they made speed; and they weren't proud, for they let you see their works going round. They liked to call themselves 'Queens' and 'Belles' ... But they were called out of that world ... Yes, these 'Brighton Belles' and 'Brighton Queens' left that innocent foolish world of theirs – to sail into the inferno, to defy bombs, shells, magnetic mines, torpedoes, machine-gun fire – to rescue our soldiers.[94]

This was a nation that could not incorporate within it pleasure-seeking, fun-loving, and sexually expressive women and girls. The women and girls who could not or would not put aside their 'foolish world' to rescue the nation were being constructed as anti-citizens – in contrast to those who were self-sacrificing.

The term 'moral laxity' was repeated over and over again in letters, editorials, and official documents. As the Bishop of Norwich put it in his proclamation 'Moral Laxity', 'nothing is more alarming than the decay of personal standards of sexual morality ... nothing threatens more the future of our race. When men and women grow loose in personal morality they endanger their own eternal salvation and they endanger too the England of to-morrow.'[95] The bishop chastised the 'women and especially young girls in town and village alike' for their 'casual acquaintances' with soldiers, warning, 'We are in danger of our national character rotting at the root.'[96] 'Moral laxity' was a phrase that connoted weakness and a lack of will, and the prelate figured it as a threat to Britishness.

The women and young girls who were perceived to be straying from convention, and were overtly seeking entertainment and pleasure, were given the ironic label of 'good-time girls' or 'good timers'. These terms were omnipresent in the language of moral alarm and were used to describe women who were irresponsible – who failed to consider their commitments to others.[97]

'Good-time girls' often were associated with venereal disease in official documents as well as in public discussion. Blame for VD often was placed on the so-called 'amateur prostitute' as it had been in World War I.[98] While the debates and discussions were focused on disease control, and anxiety about the spread of VD was heightened to a large extent because of the potential impact on Britain's relations with Allied forces, the problem was understood in moral terms to be caused by 'good-time girls' who were described as 'out of control' and 'irresponsible'. At a meeting of the Joint Committee on Venereal Disease, at which representatives of both the Canadian and US military were present along with delegates from the War Office, the Ministry of Health, the Home Office, and the Metropolitan Police, the representative of the Metropolitan Police argued that the greatest source of infection 'was to be found among young, irresponsible "good time" girls and young women', rather than among the regular 'professional type'.[99] At another meeting, the committee expressed the shared belief that the most dangerous sources of infection were 'good-time girls' who were 'in search of excitement' and young persons 'who have no moral background and who are out of control'.[100] Fears about the rising rates of venereal disease contributed to the larger discourse about the 'moral laxity' of women and girls, while the language of moral outrage concerning the behaviour of women and girls shaped official as well as popular discussion about the medical problem.[101]

In addition to being an epithet to describe the behaviour of girls and young unmarried women, and evoking apprehensions about VD, 'good-time girl' also was used to describe irresponsible married women and mothers. Government officials and social welfare agencies were as concerned about them as about the single women. They anticipated the problems of morale that would occur if married women pursued extramarital relationships.[102] Additionally, social service agencies increasingly had to deal with cases of married women bearing children fathered by men other than their husbands.[103]

Open public discussion in newspapers about married women and mothers, however, rarely if ever dealt directly with these issues. Rather, disapprobation of adult women was framed in the language of irresponsible, pleasure-seeking behaviour and child neglect. For example, the *Leicester Evening Mail* featured a report in the summer of 1943 with the headline 'City Woman Out for "Good Time" Neglects Child.' A young mother whose husband was away in the services was sent to prison for three months for neglecting her two-year-old. A probation officer said that 'the woman's one desire seemed to be to have a good time', and the report went on to state that the court had learned from neighbours that men visited her at various times of night. The police inspector who made the arrest described observing a soldier entering the house around midnight and later hearing 'voices and the distinct drawl of an American'.[104]

Geoffrey Field has persuasively argued that such concerns about the behaviour of mothers and apprehension about family life were directed specifically at the working class.[105] The rhetoric about 'good-time girls' drew on a long-standing implicit association between working-class women and promiscuity or prostitution. During the inter-war period, with changing understandings of female sexuality and a growing emphasis on sex as an expression of marital love, the term 'gold-digger' came into common parlance, referring to women who accepted gifts for sex or who married out of their class for the sake of money. As Judy Giles has suggested, the term had both gender and class connotations.[106] Thus anxieties about irresponsible women drew on and were, at least in part, framed within the context of a newly recharged apprehensiveness about working-class family life on the part of bourgeois and elite moralizers. Clearly, police surveillance and action as well as programmes and policy considerations by social welfare organizations targeted working-class women and girls.

L. Boyd, who participated in the exchange of letters to the editor in Leicester about the behaviour of young women, however, altered the class meanings of the language of moral outrage to make a statement about class privilege. She wrote: 'many in the middle class are doing little … We all know the type – those who sit back and watch others work, playing bridge to excess and having as comfortable a time as possible. These good-timers should be rooted out and sent to dirty their dainty fingers in war factories.'[107] As this letter suggests, the gendered language of irresponsible pleasure-seeking and selfishness was polyvalent. While it often resonated with a discredited working-class morality, it could also be used by working-class women to critique privileged women for not contributing to the war effort. Thus, while the objects of moral purity rhetoric might well have been working-class girls and women, it was framed in a universal language that could take on different class inflections. Moral purity rhetoric, then, echoed the construction of the national 'we' as a society in which class was less important than virtuous behaviour in defining the members of the national community.

One strand of the construction of 'good-time girls' harkened back to the late 1920s 'flapper' panic that coincided with anxiety about the possibility of extending the suffrage to young women and arose in the aftermath of World War I.[108] The 1920s witnessed an unprecedented explosion of writings about 'the contemporary young female', writings that blurred rather than emphasized class distinctions, especially in a shared 'motif of the young female as androgyne'.[109] Furthermore, the persistent discussion about population decline both during the inter-war period and throughout the war, which especially fixed on middle-class and elite family size, often decried the selfishness of such bourgeois women and married couples who put their own material desires and selfish pleasures above their responsibilities for reproducing the next generation of fit Britons.[110] The wartime discussion about young women's morality, therefore, fashioned a class-neutral, normative female moral subject who would exhibit both sexual restraint and social responsibility. This was a female whose behaviour would reinforce rather than disturb the myth of a heroic Britain emerging victoriously from the throes of war due to the efforts and sacrifices of the 'ordinary people'.

In the morality tales published in newspapers and in the depictions by social purity organizations, social workers, and clergy, the characters of those women and girls wearing bright make-up, drinking in pubs, and on or in the arms of soldiers were implicitly being contrasted with the virtues of self-restraint, moral fortitude, and cheerful altruism that were being touted as characterizing the British people in this time of adversity. This was made explicit in a War Office memo that expressed concern about the 'depressing effect on those British women who are working hard, sacrificing much and cheerfully embracing austerity, when they see so many young women allowed to evade their National Responsibilities, wasting money on drink, trafficking in clothing coupons, getting more than their share of smart clothes,

encouraging the black market and escaping Income Tax'.[111] The Liverpool Youth
Organizations Committee annual report for 1944 contrasted the heroism, endurance, and cheerfulness that the British displayed at Dunkirk, Arnhem, and during
the Battle of Britain with the 'lamentable outbreak of hooliganism, theft, sexual
immorality and various forms of anti-social behaviour that make social welfare
workers wonder for a moment whether all their labours have not been in vain'.[112]

The persistent expressions of concern about sexual morality were peppered with
key references to the importance of 'good citizenship'. For example, a Mrs Foster,
who spoke for the Association for Moral and Social Hygiene, called on the
government to 'make it known that all who engage in sexual promiscuity might not
only be responsible for spreading V.D., but were lacking in good citizenship'.[113] A
report on venereal diseases by the Medical Advisory Committee of Scotland
maintained that 'to eradicate venereal diseases completely from civilized communities will require ... a high standard of enlightened citizenship'.[114] Urging legal
measures to deal with the problem of 'safeguarding young girls who cheerfully risk
wrecking their lives', an editorial in the *Leicester Evening Mail* said that public
conscience should be aroused, and more needed to be done by parents 'that will
ensure their [young girls] attaining a standard of decent citizenship'.[115] The repeated
references to 'citizenship' warrant attention. Why was there such an emphasis on
the citizenship of young women and girls during the 1940s?

    In the first place, universal suffrage had been granted only eleven years prior to
the start of the war. The 1918 Representation of the People Act had granted virtual
universal manhood suffrage, but it restricted the women's vote by age. This
restriction entrusted the vote to women likely to be mature wives and mothers, not
to young and possibly frivolous single women. In 1928, women under the age of
thirty were given the right to vote in national elections on the same basis as men.
The 1928 Act was called 'the flapper vote', signifying that the flapper, symbol of the
modern young woman, depicted as both androgynous and libidinous, could now
vote.[116] Resistance to women's participation in politics persisted during the inter-
war period. Women were slow to be adopted as candidates for the House of
Commons. And they were excluded from the House of Lords until the late 1950s.
In the debate over that issue, the Earl of Glasgow claimed that women 'are not ...
suited to politics ... They are often moved by their hearts more than they are by
their heads.'[117] Discussion in the 1930s and 1940s about education for citizenship,
therefore, responded in part to apprehension that those who were newly
enfranchised could not be trusted with the political rights of citizenship without
instruction and control.

    A second reason that citizenship was an important discursive focus during the
war concerned the particular meanings of what it meant to be a 'good citizen' in a
people's war. Citizenship is a term denoting the relationship between individuals
and the nation as well as between individuals and the state – a term that has broadly
symbolic as well as more narrowly juridical meanings. In addition to describing the

formal rights and duties of membership, it can have multiple and contested meanings.

All modern states recognize certain persons as belonging to the nation as citizens and define as aliens those who are not specifically included in the category. Formally, those who are included as citizens are accorded certain rights and have designated obligations. Rules of membership and the specification of rights and duties constitute the juridical aspects of citizenship.[118] But citizenship is also a moral category – one that delimits how persons should conduct themselves as members of the national community. And this was how it was being used in the rhetoric about female sexuality during the war. 'Good citizenship' was the mid-twentieth-century version of the much older notion of 'civic virtue'. 'Virtue' signified the capacity of persons to participate in the polity because they were capable of self-discipline and could be trusted to put aside their private interests for the public good.

The idiom of citizenship in World War II discussions in Britain referred to the obligations that national subjects have to their communities, and it envisioned citizens as active contributors to a democratic society. The ideal of the citizen who actively expresses a 'public spirit' was being articulated in a variety of very different discursive arenas in the 1940s and was especially consonant with the image of the nation as a unified community whose members elevated the common good over their personal desires and interests.[119] The notion of 'public-spiritedness' or what is now called 'active citizenship' could have various meanings, including the volun-tarist ideal that has been reappropriated of late by Conservatives who touted it as antithetical to the supposedly 'passive citizen' created by the welfare state – an ideal of citizenship resonating with liberal political thought.[120]

The ideal of citizenship that was emerging during the war, however, bore a decided family resemblance to notions of citizenship in the tradition of civic republicanism or civic humanism rather than of liberal individualism. Drawn from classical republicanism, the ideals of civic republicanism made their way into British thought from the classical world of Greece and Rome, via development by Machiavelli, then James Harrington, John Milton, and other seventeenth-century radicals.[121] Plebeian radicals of the late eighteenth and early nineteenth centuries, influenced by Thomas Paine's *Rights of Man*, modified republican thought, making it more egalitarian.[122] Some of the ideals of civic republicanism were incorporated in British idealist thought of the late nineteenth and early twentieth centuries.[123] The New Liberalism of this same period had also incorporated and revitalized political symbols and issues that were akin to those in republican and communitarian thought, including the importance of citizenship, communal responsibility, and social welfare.[124]

In the past, civic republicanism had emphasized property as the basis for citizenship. Landed property was believed to enable individuals to exercise their political judgement independently. Independence was thus the key to virtue. But only men could own land and be independent legal subjects. While this is not the place to chart the changing historical meanings of the concept of 'virtue', it is important to note that in the era of universal suffrage and in the hands of those on the left who particularly promoted ideas about active citizenship and the common good, it assumed a more egalitarian and democratic cast. Nonetheless, 'good citizenship' and the older meanings of 'virtue' both were defined in opposition to 'passion'. Self-control would enable political persons to rule their passions, subordinating their private concerns and appetites to the public good.

Ideals of republicanism, expressed in contemporary language, worked particularly well in the late 1930s and 1940s as a way of articulating a vision of the nation and its patriotic citizenry that contrasted with fascism. The tradition of civic republicanism emphasizes both the notion of a common good that is prior to or takes precedence over individual desires and interests *and* the idea that it is only by the active involvement of citizens in the affairs of the community that individual liberty can be preserved in the face of tyranny.

During the 1940s, the principles of republican citizenship were not only being constructed in relation to the wartime nation, they were fostered and elaborated in the exploding public discussion about reconstruction that actively imagined the kind of society that could be built after the war. Architects, town and city planners, educational reformers, and advocates of expanding the state's social provision attempted to imagine how the country could be rebuilt and its institutions reformed to foster the continuation of that community spirit and sense of active citizenship so widely depicted as characterizing the British at war. While the rhetorics of planning and architecture, for example, were multi-vocal with varying degrees of emphasis on rationality, orderliness, particular aesthetic values, and differing social values, a major theme in these literatures was constructing *communities* – places of sociability that would maximize the spirit of citizenship.[125] Planner-architect C. B. Purdom, for example, articulated the values of civic republicanism in his discussion of what ought to be the right size for a city:

> The mass-mind makes democracy impossible, for it disintegrates human personality … If civilization has any object it must be to prevent the existence of the mass-mind, which is its greatest danger. Human values are realized in personalities, who take responsibility and are capable of self-government. To develop personalities is the highest function of civic existence. Education, economic and political responsibility, co-operation in the conduct of affairs, and, above all, personal knowledge of other people through which criticism can be brought to bear upon social affairs, are the means through which personality is developed and citizenship raised to a high level.[126]

Purdom further suggested, 'A new architecture is needed for the cities of tomorrow, not that of the aggressive le Corbusier school, but an architecture that has a true community spirit.'[127] A. Trystan Edwards, advocating the plan for building 'A Hundred New Towns' (proposed in the mid-1930s), maintained that one kind of 'vulgarity in architecture' is when 'buildings show bad manners' by expressing 'unsociability'.[128] The eminent architect Ralph Tubbs, remarking on his sketch for a town centre, maintained that it should be the 'architectural interpretation of the fact that we are, each of us, in the words of John Donne, "involved in Mankinde"'.[129]

One of the most elaborate plans to maximize community spirit and to minimize an ethos of individualism and self-oriented behaviour was the Reilly Plan, published in *Picture Post* in 1944. Lawrence Wolfe, who promoted the plan, touted it as 'community planning *not* suburb planning'. The Reilly Plan addressed the problem of designing a small community to stimulate a co-operative spirit among its residents that would nurture the wartime collective spirit in the post-war future. To do this, Wolfe suggested, it was necessary to 'create conditions under which the selfish impulses of our selfish fellow-men will quite naturally manifest themselves in a way that constitutes co-operation'.[130] Wolfe tied the issue of sexual morality to the nature of community provision and spirit.[131] To cure the proclivities of young people from engaging in sexual immorality and juvenile delinquency, he argued, communities need to provide 'sufficient legitimate occupation for their hands as well as their minds'.[132] More generally, when the idiom of citizenship was deployed in discussions of sexual morality during the war, it referred to the question of how to fashion responsible, self-disciplined, and self-denying subjects who would be capable of actively participating in a democratic society.

Young people especially (and particularly young women) were the objects of the exhortations expressed in the language of citizenship. The YWCA's newsletter, whose intended audience was teenage girls, carried a regularly appearing special section, 'News for Citizens'. A surprising range of topics was considered by the editors as inspiring good citizenship. The column in December 1941 urged young women doing war work to 'Join Your Trade Union', proclaiming, 'We British have great democratic traditions of which we can justly be proud; for it was *our* country which was the pioneer in organising trade unions and co-operatives.' The remainder of the article was devoted to the importance of being a patriotic unionist, working for the future.[133]

Issues of 'News for Citizens' in 1943 informed readers about the content of the government's White Paper on education and the importance of the Beveridge Report, which set out plans for the creation of Britain's welfare state.[134] While these topics generally encouraged a political civic awareness in young people, the June 1943 'News for Citizens' column dealt with sex education. It encouraged readers to think of sex as 'the creative energy and, rightly directed, it exists for marriage: marriage exists for the family, the family for the Church and the Church for God'. The article then proceeded to detail the 'wrong attitude' toward sex as 'any action or thought that may cheapen sex or use it lightly and carelessly … It is only too easy to slip into this, especially in war-time.' It went on to ask rhetorically how this happens to respectable and well-meaning girls.

> A pretty girl has a nice time dancing with someone she has just met. She becomes a little alarmed at his 'freshness'. Her conscience warns her that it is time to stop. However, the Devil is in on this too, and he whispers that, after all, she is not a kid and everyone else seems to like this sort of thing, anyway. So she gives in … and

there may be several sad endings to the story … [T]he real bitterness is in fact that 'having a good time', as it is so wrongly called, affects the whole community.[135]

The YWCA treatise on sexuality made use of the wartime language of community spirit to associate sex and citizenship. It suggests the importance of self-control and self-discipline to the 'ethic of responsibility' that was key to the symbolic meaning of citizenship in wartime discourse.

Youth groups and organizations were seen as routes to educating young people for citizenship. Welfare workers, educators, and government officials campaigned actively to have teenagers participate in youth organizations and in the newly established Youth Service. The idea that organized leisure activities and clubs for youth instilled a sense of duty and commitment to self-discipline and responsible behaviour increasingly became an article of faith during the inter-war period.[136] During World War I, the Girl Guides was started, partly in response to the 'epidemic' of 'khaki fever' that was thought to be sweeping the country.[137] During World War II, participation in youth groups was seen as a preventive and cure for 'moral laxity', as well as a vehicle for citizenship training. Youth workers referred to morally recalcitrant teenagers as 'unclubbable'.[138]

In December 1941, young people of sixteen or seventeen were required to register with local education authorities. As the White Paper *Youth Registration in 1942* declared, 'The purpose of the registration was to enable Local Education Authorities to make contact with all young people of the ages concerned and to encourage them to find the best way of fitting themselves to do their duty as citizens and of assisting the present national effort.'[139] The main purpose was to reach 'those who had left school and who were no longer under educational supervision and discipline'. The young registrants were asked to list the clubs and organizations to which they belonged. If they were 'non-participating' they were 'invited to an interview' where they would be urged to join. The idea was to encourage young people to make good use of organized leisure activities rather than spending their time in unsupervised activities such as 'hanging about' or going to the cinema and dance halls.[140] The emphasis of youth organizations was teaching young people to use their leisure time properly and 'to make the right choices'.[141] In other words, the youth movement, as it was called, was created to fashion self-disciplined and responsible moral subjects.[142] The World War II obsession with the morality of girls and young women in Britain was thus articulated in terms that constructed moral subjects as responsible citizens. How are we to understand this particular articulation?

It is useful to consider again the tradition of civic republicanism that was echoed in wartime reimaginings of the nation and citizenship. This tradition, as I have suggested, emphasizes both the ideal of 'active citizenship' and the notion that a common good exists 'prior to and independent of individual desires and interests'.[143] As Chantal Mouffe has argued, civic republicanism is antithetical to pluralism (and to true democracy) when it is mobilized for a kind of communitarian vision that emphasizes a particular notion of the common good and shared moral values.[144] Mouffe's analysis of the problems with civic republicanism suggests that while in World War II it required what Raphael Samuel called 'a secular altruism', it also, as he suggested, 'stigmatized anyone who stepped out of line as "antisocial"'.[145]

One way to understand the apparent relationship between sexual morality and citizenship is to see it as growing out of the elevation of particular notions of the common good over expressions of individual desire. But why were expressions of individual sexual desire, particularly by women, so threatening? What made sex itself such an issue? Republicanism historically, most notably in the hands of Machiavelli and Jean-Jacques Rousseau, has constructed the citizen in opposition to the feminine, and to women seen to be sexual predators by nature and suscept-ible to uncontrollable desire.[146]

Iris Young's ideas about the centrality of 'impartial reason' to the concept of virtue in civic republicanism help to make sense of why sexual desire, especially by women and by racially subordinated men, poses such a threat to citizenship in the modern era. She suggests that 'impartial civilized reason' is crucial to the concept of republican virtue that enables citizens to rise above passion and desire to work toward the common good.[147] An impartial point of view is arrived at, Young argues, 'by abstracting from the particularity of the person in situation. This requires abstracting from the particularity of bodily being, its needs and inclinations, and from the feelings that attach to the experienced particularity of things and events.'[148] Thus, in modern thought, reason stands opposed to desire and affectivity. Young writes,

> By assuming that reason stands opposed to desire, affectivity and the body, the civic public must exclude bodily and affective aspects of human existence. In practice this assumption forces homogeneity upon the civic public, excluding from the public those individuals that do not fit the model of the rational citizen capable of transcending body and sentiment. This exclusion has a twofold basis: the tendency to oppose reason and desire, and the association of these traits with kinds of persons.[149]

As Genevieve Lloyd has argued, in philosophical thought, the 'metaphor of maleness is deeply embedded in philosophical articulations of ideas and ideals of reason. It had been constitutive of ways of thinking of reason which have deep repercussions in ways of thinking of ourselves as male or female.'[150]

In Western societies, European men have been associated with reason while women and racialized men have been associated with the body and desire.[151] Young brilliantly observes,

> Modern normative reason and its political expression in the idea of the civic public, then, attain unity and coherence through the expulsion and confinement of everything that would threaten to invade the polity with differentiation: the specificity of women's bodies and desire, differences of race and culture, the variability and heterogeneity of needs, the goals and desires of individuals, the ambiguity and changeability of feeling.[152]

The association of reason with European maleness and its contrast with body and desire are ideas that have been deeply embedded in Western political culture. These ideas are articulated and rearticulated historically, and they take on new contemporary resonances and meanings. But I am arguing that they are fundamental to understanding the historically recurring discursive association between female sexual morality and social and political order.

If the nation was being imagined as a unified community of people capable of putting the national interest above their own needs and desires, then fun-loving, sexually expressive women and girls threatened that sense of unity that was imagined to be the essence of Britishness in wartime. This was a maternal and masculine nation, one exemplifying not only heroic self-sacrifice but also 'impartial reason', which defined itself against the feminine.[153] The discourses of moral purity thus figured duty and sexuality, bravery and pleasure, and sacrifice and desire as oppositional human characteristics.

Although narratives about the moral laxity of 'good-time girls' and the various techniques of social control employed to police women's behaviour aimed both to construct moral citizens and to limit their association with soldiers, ironically they also advertised the adventures and pleasures of wartime life. Moreover, neither the rhetoric of moral purity nor the efforts to police young women's behaviour were uncontested. Occasional letters to the editors of newspapers ridiculed the moral purity advocates as being old-fashioned or simply old and having forgotten what it was like to be young. Others defended Britain's youth or simply rejected the outrage as overblown. Still others maintained that it was necessary for hardworking young people to have time for themselves and to have fun.

Many of the young women and girls continued to seek pleasure and adventure with soldiers throughout the war. Enmeshed in a popular culture that linked sex and love and valorized romance, they resisted a definition of citizenship that excluded carnal pleasure and passionate desire. The following front-page story appeared in the *Sunday Pictorial* at the end of August 1945:

> The scene was Bristol, most English of all English cities. The time was 2 A.M. yesterday. The actors were a mob of screaming girls aged between 17 and 25.

The cause of the 'hysteria' according to the report was that four companies of 'American Negro soldiers in the city were leaving for home'.

> The girls besieged the barracks where the soldiers were and began singing, 'Don't Fence Me In.' This was too much for the coloured men who began to break down the barbed wire. In a few minutes hundreds of girls and U.S. soldiers were kissing and embracing.[154]

While the obsessive expressions of concern with the moral behaviour of women and girls continued throughout the war to construct moral subjects as responsible citizens who would refrain from such behaviour, many young women drew their moral lessons from other sources. The cautionary morality tales that were published in newspapers across the country suggest more about a fantasy of moral purity linked to a utopian longing for a new Britain whose citizens would be responsible community participants than about the romantic fantasies and sexual desires of the young women who were their primary objects.

In constructing this national fantasy, the rhetorics of moral disapprobation depicted some women and girls as antithetical to the nation, especially those women whose amorous escapades were so perverse as to jeopardize the nation's racial homogeneity. It simultaneously incorporated virtuous women and all men as comrades in struggle. Although class differentiated which women were made the targets of overt policies of social control, public expressions of apprehension about women and girls who frolicked with soldiers constituted a normalizing discourse that had as its goal the making of female moral citizens appropriate to fighting a 'people's war' and building a 'new Britain' when it was over. Femaleness and public expressions of sexuality by women and girls, or what might be termed 'libidinal femininity', in other words, characterized an 'internal other' against which the nation was defining itself. The construction of pleasure-seeking women as villainous and contemptuous 'anti-citizens' was part and parcel of the process by which the nation was imagined as a 'deep horizontal comradeship' of virtuous citizens.

Notes

From the *American Historical Review*, 103:4 (October 1998), 1147–75. The second and third sections of the chapter make use of and further develop portions of my 'Girls and GIs: Race, Sex, and Diplomacy in Second World War Britain,' *International History Review* 19 (February 1997): 146–60. A number of my colleagues have given helpful comments on various drafts of this chapter. They include Julia Adams, Geoff Eley, Susan Grayzel, Leslie Hall, Susan Kingsley Kent, Philippa Levine, William G. Rosenberg, David Scobey, Carroll Smith-Rosenberg, Dror Wahrman, and Angela Woollacott. Versions were presented at a number of different venues, including the annual meeting of the American Historical Association, Atlanta GA, 1996; Berkshire Conference, Chapel Hill NC, 1996; Social Science History Association Meeting, New Orleans LA, 1996; Center for European Studies at Harvard, 1997; and University of Portsmouth Seminar in Social History, 1997. The questions and comments made by members of the audience at each of these presentations helped to guide subsequent revisions. Finally, anonymous reviewers for the *American Historical Review* gave constructive and often challenging comments.

1 See Judith R. Walkowitz, *Prostitution and Victorian Society: Women, Class, and the State* (Cambridge, 1980); Walkowitz, *City of Dreadful Delight: Narratives of Sexual Danger in Late Victorian London* (Chicago, 1992); Edward J. Bristow, *Vice and Vigilance: Purity Movements in Britain since 1700* (Dublin, 1977).

2 Jeffrey Weeks, *Sex, Politics and Society: The Regulation of Sexuality since 1800* (London, 1981), 86–92; Paul Ferris, *Sex and the British: A Twentieth-Century History* (London, 1993); Bristow, *Vice and Vigilance*.

3 Angela Woollacott, '"Khaki Fever" and its Control: Gender, Class, Age and Sexual Morality on the British Home Front in the First World War', *Journal of Contemporary History* 29 (April 1994): 325–47. For an extensive cultural analysis of contested gender relations in World War I, see Susan Grayzel, *Women's Identities at War: The Cultural Politics of Gender in Britain and France, 1914–1919* (Ph.D. dissertation, University of California, Berkeley, 1994).

4 See Billie Melman, *Women and the Popular Imagination in the Twenties: Flappers and Nymphs* (London, 1988); Marek Kohn, *Dope Girls: The Birth of the British Drug Underground* (London, 1992).

5   Simon Watney, *Policing Desire: Pornography, AIDS, and the Media*, second edition (Minneapolis MN, 1989).
6   See, for example, Arthur Stinchcombe, 'The Deep Structure of Moral Categories', in Jeffrey C. Alexander, ed., *Durkheimian Sociology: Cultural Studies* (Cambridge, 1988), 68–9.
7   Richard Rorty, *Contingency, Irony, and Solidarity* (Cambridge, 1989), 59.
8   Rorty, *Contingency, Irony, and Solidarity*, 59.
9   In her study of the politics of censorship, Nicola Beisel suggests something similar when she argues that the 'cultural power' of moral appeals stems in part from how they 'construct group and individual identities'. See Beisel, 'Morals versus Art: Censorship, the Politics of Interpretation, and the Victorian Nude', *American Sociological Review* 58 (April 1993): 148.
10 Philippa Levine, '"Walking the Streets in a Way No Decent Woman Should": Women Police in World War I', *Journal of Modern History* 66 (March 1994): 34–78. Also see Lucy Bland, 'In the Name of Protection: The Policing of Women in the First World War', in Julia Brophy and Carol Smart, eds, *Women-in-Law: Explorations in Law, Family and Sexuality* (London, 1985); and Woollacott, '"Khaki Fever" and its Control'.
11 Church of England Moral Welfare Council, *Quarterly Leaflet* 5 (February 1940): 3; *Quarterly Leaflet* 6 (July 1940): 4. In February 1939, the National Council of Women sent a deputation to the Home Office to ask that they enlist women as special police constables, a request that was refused. Memo to Mrs E. Wood, 25 September 1942, Box 3, National Council of Women Papers, Police Federation, Surbiton, Surrey.
12 Women Police Sectional Committee Minutes, December 1941, National Council of Women Papers, Miscellaneous Documents, Police Federation, Surbiton.
13 Rose, 'Girls and GIs', 146–60.
14 See, for example, *Daily Herald* (23 March 1943): 5; *Chard and Ilminster News* (13 February 1943): 4; *Bath and Wiltshire Chronicle and Herald* (1 July 1943): 8; *Leicester Evening Mail* (16 January 1943): 3; *Liverpool Daily Post* (2 July 1943): 4.
15 The work of Judith Walkowitz demonstrates the role of the media in fashioning audiences for sexual scandal and discourses of sexual danger; *City of Dreadful Delight*. On the role of contemporary media in focusing public attention on issues of sexual morality, see Watney, *Policing Desire*.
16 Cate Haste, *Rules of Desire: Sex in Britain, World War I to the Present* (London, 1992), 133; Arthur Salusbury MacNalty and W. Franklin Mellor, *Medical Services in War* (London, 1968), 331.
17 For works devoted to the American presence in Britain during World War II, see David Reynolds, *Rich Relations: The American Occupation of Britain, 1942–1945* (New York, 1995); Juliet Gardiner, *'Over Here': The GIs in Wartime Britain* (London, 1992); Graham Smith, *When Jim Crow Met John Bull: Black American Soldiers in World War II Britain* (New York, 1988). For a more extensive discussion of the issues produced by the interaction of American men and British women than presented here, see Rose, 'Girls and GIs', 146–60.
18 See, for example, the description by Stephen Humphries of 'larking about between the sexes' by adolescents in the years prior to the war. *Hooligans or Rebels? An Oral History of Working-Class Childhood and Youth, 1889–1939* (Oxford, 1981), 135–40. For a description of the interaction of inter-war Preston youth, see Derek Thompson, 'Courtship and Marriage between the Wars', *Oral History* 3 (April 1975): 42–3. David Reynolds also suggests that wartime behaviour was not radically different; *Rich Relations*, 276. Constance Nathanson suggests that when immoral behaviour becomes highly visible, its meaning changes. What was once understood to be aberrant behaviour on the part of individuals becomes identified as a public problem. *Dangerous Passage: The Social Control of Sexuality in Women's Adolescence* (Philadelphia PA, 1991), ch. 1.
19 Reynolds, *Rich Relations*, 184.
20 Minutes of the nineteenth meeting of the British-American Liaison Board (hereafter, BALB), 30 January 1945, FO, 371/44625, Public Record Office (hereafter, PRO), Kew, London. The BALB was composed of representatives of the American Embassy, the Ministry of Information, the US Army, the Foreign Office, and the War Office and was

established in the winter of 1944.

21 Twenty-third meeting of the BALB, 22 March 1945, FO 371/44625, PRO, Kew. From the perspective of today, the cartoons seem harmless. One of them, for example, depicted a popular joke in Britain at the time. It showed a young British soldier coming upon a GI embracing a woman, with the caption reading 'Mother?!' Clarence Stilling, 'More Gum Chum', typescript (n.d.), Devon Record Office, Exeter.

22 The analysis that follows stems from my reading of accounts in various newspapers, including the *Norfolk News and Weekly Press* between 7 February 1942, and 25 June 1944; *Huddersfield Daily Examiner*, 20 September 1943 to 4 October 1943 (when the editor called a halt to the correspondence on the association of British girls with black American soldiers); *Chard and Ilminster News*, January 1943 through May 1944; *Bath and Wiltshire Chronicle and Herald* between January 1943 and June 1944; *Leicester Evening Mail* between January 1943 and May 1945.

23 *Leicester Evening Mail* (19 January 1943): 1.

24 *Luton News* (20 January 1944): 3.

25 Examining the relationship of American soldiers and women as portrayed in Australian women's letters and diaries, Marilyn Lake notes a similar objectification of American men. See Lake, 'The Desire for a Yank: Sexual Relations between Australian Women and American Servicemen during World War II', *Journal of the History of Sexuality* 2 (November 1992): 621–33. In both Australian women's representations of American men and in the reports about the involvement of British women with American men, the women were depicted as the active subjects. What differentiates them is that the women in Lake's account portrayed themselves as actively desiring subjects, while British women were portrayed by others as acting on immoral desires. Also see Marilyn Lake, 'Female Desires: The Meaning of World War II', *Australian Historical Studies* 24 (October 1990): 267–84.

26 Smith, *When Jim Crow Met John Bull*, 29.

27 *Ibid.*, 29–30.

28 See David Margesson, War Office, to Lord Walter Moyne, Colonial Office, 11 February 1941, CO 968/37/12, PRO, Kew. Reply, Moyne to Margesson, 11 March 1941, CO 968/37/12, PRO, Kew; 'Colour Bar in the Armed Forces', memo signed by J. A. Calder, 10 November 1941, CO 968/38/10, PRO, Kew; War Office to C. H. Thornley, Colonial Office, 2 December 1941, CO 968/38/10, PRO, Kew.

29 See, for example, Regional Commissioner's Report for Region 10, January 1943, HO 199/426, PRO, Kew: 'The problem of the negro troops remains, and whilst many of the anticipated difficulties have not yet manifested themselves on the scale expected, I hope that further drafts coming into the country will not include negro troops'. For other analyses, see Smith, *When Jim Crow Met John Bull*; Reynolds, *Rich Relations*, 216–37, 302–24. Also see Cynthia Enloe, *Bananas, Beaches and Bases: Making Feminist Sense of International Politics* (Berkeley, CA, 1989), 67–71.

30 Smith, *When Jim Crow Met John Bull*, 39–40.

31 For a discussion, see Reynolds, *Rich Relations*, 164–82.

32 War Office draft paper, 8 September 1942, CO 876/14, PRO, Kew.

33 Kenneth Little, 'Treatment of Colour Prejudice in Britain', to J. L. Keith, Colonial Office, n.d. [probably late September or early October 1942], CO 875/19/14, PRO, Kew.

34 On overt hostility to black Britons, see Regional Commissioner's Report for Region No. 10, FO 371/34123, January 1943; J. L. Keith's minute about a letter concerning the 'alleged threatening attitude of American troops to coloured persons in this country', CO 876/14, 30 June 1942, Sir Charles Jeffries's memo to Gent and Keith, 1 August 1942, on white American troops ousting British Honduran soldiers from a Scottish rest house, CO 876/14; 'Welfare of Colonial People in the U.K.: Relations with American Forces in the U.K.', n.d. [probably January 1943], CO 876/15, PRO, Kew.

35 See, for example, J. L. Keith, Minute, re letter from Professor Gilbert to Audrey Richards, 30 June 1942, CO 876/14, PRO, Kew.

36 'Welfare of Colonial People in the U.K'.

37 Memo, Learie Constantine to Arnold Watson, Regional Controller, Registration Office, Manchester, n.d. [early January 1943], CO 876/15, PRO, Kew.

38 Peter Fryer, *Staying Power: The History of Black People in Britain* (London, 1984), 365–6; John Flint, 'Scandal at the Bristol Hotel: Some Thoughts on Racial Discrimination in Britain and West Africa and its Relationship to the Planning of Decolonisation', *Journal of Imperial and Commonwealth History* 12 (May 1983): 75–6.

39 Extract from Constantine to Ministry of Labour and National Service, Liverpool Welfare Office, 8 May 1944, LAB 26/55, PRO, Kew.

40 For a discussion of other incidents of racism involving West Indians, see Ben Bousenquet and Colin Douglas, *West Indian Women at War* (London, 1991), chs 7, 9.

41 See, for example, League of Coloured Peoples, *News Letter* (April 1940): 3, (September 1940): 100–1; (March 1941): 133. Also see Ernest Marke, *In Troubled Waters: Memoirs of my Seventy Years in England* (1975; reprinted, London, 1986); Learie Constantine, *Colour Bar* (London, 1954). For an excellent analysis of the imposition of racial discrimination in the maritime industry, see Laura Tabili, *'We Ask for British Justice': Workers and Racial Difference in Late Imperial Britain* (Ithaca NY, 1994).

42 See Ann L. Stoler, 'Making Empire Respectable: The Politics of Race and Sexual Morality in Twentieth-Century Colonial Cultures', *American Ethnologist* 16 (November 1989): 634–60; Stoler, 'Rethinking Colonial Categories: European Communities and the Boundaries of Rule', *Comparative Studies in Society and History* 13 (May 1992): 134–61.

43 Philippa Levine, 'Battle Colours: Race, Sex and Colonial Soldiery in World War One', unpublished manuscript. On the treatment of Indian troops in Britain during the war, see Rozina Visram, *Ayahs, Lascars and Princes: Indians in Britain, 1700–1947* (London, 1986), 122–39. On West Indians, see Fryer, *Staying Power*, 294–7.

44 As reported in Paul Rich, *Race and Empire in British Politics* (Cambridge, 1986), 127–8.

45 Rich, *Race and Empire in British Politics*, 128.

46 Ian Spencer, 'World War Two and the Making of Multiracial Britain', in Pat Kirkham and David Thoms, eds., *War Culture: Social Change and Changing Experience in World War Two Britain* (London, 1995), 209.

47 The War Office steadfastly refused throughout the war to allow West Indian regiments to be raised in spite of the desires of the West Indians and the Colonial Office. There were regiments of Africans and Indians, but they were rarely in Great Britain and only then for brief periods of training.

48 Spencer, 'World War Two and the Making of Multiracial Britain', 212.

49 *Ibid.*

50 Colonel Matthews, Memo to J. L. Keith, Welfare Section of the Colonial Office, 'Visit to West Indian Technicians in Bolton', 15 November 1943, CO 876/48, PRO, Kew.

51 Matthews to Keith, CO 876/48, PRO, Kew.

52 A report on their welfare in January 1941 indicated that the 'men seem to have found many friends amongst the local inhabitants; they visit the neighbouring villages and towns and are well received … dances are given and attended'. Report on Health, Welfare, etc. of British Honduras unit, 5 January 1941, CO 876/41, PRO, Kew. For a study of the British Honduran Forestry Unit, see Marika Sherwood, *The British Honduran Forestry Unit in Scotland 1941–43* (London, 1982). I thank Anna Davin for telling me about this booklet.

53 Duke of Buccleuch, Drumlanrig Castle, Thornhill, Dumfries-shire, to Colonial Office, 10 August 1942, CO 876/41, PRO, Kew.

54 See Harold Macmillan to J. L. Keith, 13 August 1942; Macmillan to Buccleuch, 13 August 1942; and draft of Macmillan to Buccleuch, 31 August 1942, CO 876/41, PRO, Kew.

55 Buccleuch to Macmillan, 30 September 1942, CO 876/41, PRO, Kew.

56 Memo from official (illegible signature) to J. L. Keith, Colonial Office, 21 August 1942, AVIA 22/1239, PRO, Kew.

57 T. Fitzgerald, Home Timber Production, to W. H. Ekins, Ministry of Supply, 2 December 1942, AVIA 22/1239, PRO, Kew.

58 Report of meeting of representatives of Ministry of Supply and the Department of Home

Timber Production, 30 January 1943, AVIA 22/1349, PRO, Kew.

59 See report of Ivor G. Cummings to J. L. Keith, 3 September 1943; and telegraphed memo, Colonial Secretary to Governor of British Honduras, 9 September 1943, CO 876/42, PRO, Kew.

60 For approximate numbers of blacks living in communities in Britain in 1942, see survey by Colonial Office, fall 1942. The largest concentrations were in Cardiff and Liverpool (approximately 2,000 in each); there were approximately 1,000 in London and 1,000 in South Shields. CO 876/14, PRO, Kew.

61 Tabili, *'We Ask for British Justice'*.

62 *Huddersfield Daily Examiner* (10 July 1943): 3.

63 The correspondence lasted two weeks and ended with a notice to correspondents that, although the newspaper had received a number of further letters about 'Girls Who Prey on Negroes', the editor decided that the question had been 'sufficiently ventilated, and the correspondence must be regarded as closed'. *Huddersfield Daily Examiner* (4 October 1943): 3. This series of letters has been reprinted, in part, and discussed by Elbert L. Harris, 'Social Activities of the Negro Soldier in England', *Negro History Bulletin* 11 (April 1948): 15.

64 *Huddersfield Daily Examiner* (4 October 1943): 3.

65 *Ibid*.

66 These racialized depictions of unbridled sexuality had been applied earlier to the Irish and also to the British poor. See Mary Poovey, 'Curing the "Social Body" in 1832: James Phillips Kay and the Irish in Manchester', *Gender and History* 5 (summer 1993): 196–211.

67 For discussions of official responses, see Smith, *When Jim Crow Met John Bull*, 177–8, 192–6; Reynolds, *Rich Relations*, 224–30; Rose, 'Girls and GIs', 148–60.

68 *Sunday Chronicle* (2 March 1941): 4.

69 For a discussion of the significance and centrality of these depictions of British national character and behaviour both during the war and afterward, see Angus Calder, *The Myth of the Blitz* (London, 1991).

70 War and Navy Departments, *A Short Guide to Great Britain* (Washington DC, 1942, 1944), 5.

71 Calder, *Myth of the Blitz*, 125.

72 *Picture Post*, 3 May 1941, in *Picture Post 1938–50* (London, 1984), 89.

73 J. B. Priestley, Broadcast from 5 June 1940, in Priestley, *Postscripts* (London, 1940), 2.

74 *Ibid*.

75 Calder, *Myth of the Blitz*, ch. 1.

76 Priestley, *Postscripts*, 2–3.

77 George Orwell, *The Lion and the Unicorn: Socialism and the English Genius* (London, 1941), 15.

78 For a discussion of Orwell, and other left-leaning commentators who idealize the heterogeneity of the 'English', see Miles Taylor, 'Patriotism, History and the Left in Twentieth-Century Britain', *Historical Journal* 33 (September 1990): 980–3.

79 Orwell, *The Lion and the Unicorn*, 33.

80 Simon Featherstone argues provocatively that the myth of unity despite diversity articulated in World War II literature is a central component of the literary construction of 'nation as pastoral', which exposes division as it seeks to deny it. Featherstone, 'The Nation as Pastoral in British Literature of the Second World War', *Journal of European Studies* 16 (summer 1986): 155–68.

81 Humphrey Jennings, *Diary for Timothy*, Crown Film Unit, 1945.

82 Benedict Anderson, *Imagined Communities: Reflections on the Origin and Spread of Nationalism*, revised edition (London, 1991), 7.

83 As Renata Salecl has put it, psychologically the nation is 'the fantasy structure through which society perceives itself as a homogeneous entity'. Salecl, 'The Fantasy Structure of Nationalist Discourse', *Praxis International* 13 (October 1993): 217. Or, as Katherine Verdery has written, the nation is an ideological construct; it does 'ideological work'. Verdery, 'Whither "Nation" and "Nationalism"?' *Daedalus* 122 (summer 1993): 39.

84 Poovey, 'Curing the "Social Body" in 1832', 196.

85 For a useful discussion of the links between 'women, the state and ethnic/national processes',

see Floya Anthias and Nira Yuval-Davis, 'Introduction', *Woman – Nation – State*, ed. Yuval-Davis and Anthias (London, 1989), 1–15.

86 Anne McClintock, *Imperial Leather: Race, Gender and Sexuality in the Colonial Conquest* (New York, 1995), 353.

87 For the contested use of feminine allegorical symbols during the French revolution, see Lynn Hunt, *Politics, Culture, and Class in the French Revolution* (Berkeley CA, 1984), esp. 60–2, 90–4; Joan Landes, 'Representing the Body Politic: The Paradox of Gender and the Graphic Politics of the French Revolution', in Sara E. Melzer and Leslie W. Rabine, eds, *Rebel Daughters: Women and the French Revolution* (New York, 1992), 15–37. On the transformation of female symbols of the nation to suit nationalist purposes, see George L. Mosse, *Nationalism and Sexuality: Middle-Class Morality and Sexual Norms in Modern Europe* (Madison WI, 1985), ch. 5, and McClintock, *Imperial Leather*, 352.

88 See, for example, Deniz Kandiyoti, 'Women and the Turkish State: Political Actors or Symbolic Pawns?' in Yuval-Davis and Anthias, *Woman – Nation – State*, 126–49; Kandiyoti, 'From Empire to Nation State: Transformations of the Woman Question in Turkey', in Susan Jay Kleinberg, ed., *Retrieving Women's History: Changing Perceptions of the Role of Women in Politics and Society* (Oxford, 1988), 219–40.

89 Mosse, *Nationalism and Sexuality*, 91; Andrew Parker *et al.*, 'Introduction', in Parker *et al.*, eds, *Nationalisms and Sexualities* (London, 1992), 6–7; McClintock, *Imperial Leather*, 352–3.

90 For a pathbreaking work on this issue for England, see Anna Davin, 'Imperialism and Motherhood', *History Workshop* 5 (spring 1978): 9–65. For Russia, see Elizabeth Waters, 'The Modernisation of Russian Motherhood, 1917–1937', *Feminist Review* 33 (autumn 1989): 3–18. On republican motherhood and the French revolution, see Joan B. Landes, *Women and the Public Sphere in the Age of the French Revolution* (Ithaca NY, 1988). On republican motherhood in the United States, see Linda K. Kerber, 'The Republican Mother: Women and the Enlightenment – An American Perspective', *American Quarterly* 28 (1976): 187–205. On the centrality of women as mothers, but not as wives or citizens, to the making of the Irish republic, see Sarah Benton, 'Women Disarmed: The Militarization of Politics in Ireland 1913–23', *Feminist Review* 50 (summer 1995): 148–72.

91 Mosse, *Nationalism and Sexuality*.

92 Ann Laura Stoler, *Race and the Education of Desire: Foucault's History of Sexuality and the Colonial Order of Things* (Durham NC, 1995), 7.

93 There were other themes that constituted the imagined community. For example, Simon Featherstone has pointed to the significance of rural life in wartime literature. 'Nation as Pastoral', 155–68. And Geoffrey Fields has pointed to the social patriotism, the 'new "structure of feeling"' that 'emerged, one that fused bitter memories of the inter-war past, hostility to the traditional class structure, and expectations of social change. The new vocabulary was both unifying and levelling'. See Fields, 'Social Patriotism and the British Working Class', *International Labor and Working-Class History* 42 (fall 1992): 20–39.

94 Priestley, *Postscripts*, 3.

95 *Norfolk News and Weekly Press* (9 October 1943): 4. The Reverend A. Lynch, Rector of Desford, similarly asked, 'What kind of a Britain can be made out of this debauchery?' *Leicester Evening Mail* (1 February 1944): 5.

96 *Norfolk News and Weekly Press* (9 October 1943): 4.

97 On the links between a medical discourse of responsibility, national health, and the behaviour of women, see Lucy Bland and Frank Mort, 'Look out for the "Good Time" Girl: Dangerous Sexualities as a Threat to National Health', in Bill Schwarz, ed., *Formations of Nation and People* (London, 1985), 131–51.

98 Woollacott, '"Khaki Fever" and its Control'; Bland, 'In the Name of Protection'; Frank Mort, *Dangerous Sexualities: Medico-moral Politics in England since 1830* (London, 1987).

99 Minutes of the Joint Committee on Venereal Disease, second meeting, 10 July 1943, MH 55/2325, PRO, Kew.

100 Minutes of the Joint Committee on Venereal Disease, third meeting, 1 October 1943, MH 55/2325, PRO, Kew.

101 It was, in Frank Mort's terms, a medico-moral discourse. See Mort, *Dangerous Sexualities*. US representatives, in contrast to British commentators on the question of venereal disease, blamed British prostitutes and wanted the British government to enact laws or change police procedures so that prostitutes would be swept off the streets – something the British government refused to do. See Reynolds, *Rich Relations*, ch. 13.

102 'Morale Report', February–May 1942; 'Draft Morale Report', May–July 1942; 'Morale Report' 'August–October 1942; 'Morale Reports', August–October 1943; 'Morale Report', November 1943–January 1944, all in War Office files, WO 32 15772, PRO, Kew.

103 Lettice Fisher, *Twenty-one Years and After, 1918–1946* (London, 1946); National Council for the Unmarried Woman and her Child, *23rd Report* (July 1941–September 1942): 15–16; *24th Report* (October 1942–1943): 8; *26th Report* (October 1944–April 1946): 4.

104 *Leicester Evening Mail* (7 July 1943): 5.

105 Geoffrey Field, 'Perspectives on the Working-Class Family in Wartime Britain, 1939–1945', *International Labor and Working-Class History* 38 (fall 1990): 3–28.

106 Judy Giles, '"Playing Hard to Get": Working-Class Women, Sexuality and Respectability in Britain, 1918–40', *Women's History Review* 1 (spring 1992): 247.

107 *Leicester Evening Mail* (8 July 1943): 3.

108 Melman, *Women and the Popular Imagination*.

109 *Ibid.*, 149.

110 On pro-natalism, see Denise Riley, '"The Free Mothers": Pronatalism and Working Women in Industry at the End of the Last War in Britain', *History Workshop* 11 (spring 1981): 59–118.

111 This document concerned prostitution, but it uses some of the same language, including the term 'moral laxity', to describe how Americans must view Britain when they see prostitution flourishing in the country. See 'Accosting in City Streets', Memo, Colonel Rowe, War Office, to Foreign Office, 2 February 1943, FO 371/34124, PRO, Kew.

112 Liverpool Youth Organizations Committee, Annual Report, in Liverpool Council of Social Services Annual Report for 1944, p. 10.

113 'Loose Morals: Blame Men as Well as Girls', *Leicester Evening Mail* (10 July 1943): 4.

114 Medical Advisory Committee (Scotland), *Report on Venereal Diseases*, Cmd. 6518 (Edinburgh, 1944), 8.

115 *Leicester Evening Mail* (27 October 1943): 3.

116 Melman, *Women and the Popular Imagination*, 149.

117 As quoted in Brian Harrison, *Separate Spheres: The Opposition to Women's Suffrage in Britain* (London, 1978), 235.

118 For an important analysis of how nationhood influenced citizenship as a formal institution or as a juridical relationship in France and Germany, see Roger Brubaker, *Citizenship and Nationhood in France and Germany* (Cambridge MA, 1992), esp. ch. 1 and his discussion of citizenship as an instrument and an object of social closure – as defining the rules of inclusion and exclusion of membership in the nation.

119 For a discussion of the active citizen taken up by the British Left that emerged in response to war, see Taylor, 'Patriotism', 980–83. This view of citizenship, which certainly was populist and fitted neatly with a collectivist spirit, was not limited only to the Left. For a general discussion of citizenship as it was understood in World War II, see David Morgan and Mary Evans, *The Battle for Britain: Citizenship and Ideology in the Second World War* (London, 1993). For a discussion of working-class patriotism that drew on the heroism of the Blitz, see Field, 'Social Patriotism and the British Working Class'.

120 For a discussion of current Conservative ideas about 'active citizenship', see Michael Ignatieff, 'Citizenship and Moral Narcissism', in *Citizenship*, ed. Geoff Andrews (London, 1991), 26–36, Morgan and Evans, *Battle for Britain*, ch. 7. On voluntarism during the period, see William Beveridge, *Voluntary Action: A Report on Methods of Social Advance* (London, 1948). For a discussion of voluntarism during the first half of the twentieth century, see Geoffrey Finlayson, 'A Moving Frontier: Voluntarism and the State in British Social Welfare 1911–1949', *Twentieth Century British History* 1 (April 1990): 183–206. Also see Jose

Harris's discussion of British idealism, 'Political Thought and the Welfare State 1870–1940', *Past and Present* 135 (1992): 116–41; and Andrew Vincent and Raymond Plant, *Philosophy, Politics and Citizenship: The Life and Thought of the British Idealists* (Oxford, 1984).

121 There is a huge literature on civic republicanism. For discussions of particular aspects of these ideas, see Steve Pincus, 'Neither Machiavellian Moment nor Possessive Individualism: Commercial Society and the Defenders of the English Commonwealth', *American Historical Review* 103 (June 1998): 705–36; Quentin Skinner, 'On Justice, the Common Good and the Priority of Liberty', in *Dimensions of Radical Democracy: Pluralism, Citizenship, Community*, ed. Chantal Mouffe (London, 1992), 211–24; J. G. A. Pocock, *The Machiavellian Moment: Florentine Political Thought and the Atlantic Republican Tradition* (Princeton NJ, 1975); Pocock, 'Virtue and Commerce in the Eighteenth Century', *Journal of Interdisciplinary History* 3 (spring 1972): 119–34; Adrian Oldfield, *Citizenship and Community: Civic Republicanism and the Modern World* (London, 1990); Hanna Pitkin, *Fortune is a Woman: Gender and Politics in the Thought of Niccolo Machiavelli* (Berkeley CA, 1984).

122 For a discussion, see Anna Clark, *The Struggle for the Breeches: Gender and the Making of the British Working Class* (Berkeley CA, 1995), 142–6, 264–5.

123 Vincent and Plant, *Philosophy, Politics and Citizenship*, esp. ch. 9.

124 For discussions of New Liberalism, see Michael Freeden, *The New Liberalism: An Ideology of Social Reform* (Oxford, 1978); Peter Weiler, *The New Liberalism: Liberal Social Theory in Great Britain 1889–1914* (New York, 1982), Stefan Collini, *Liberalism and Sociology: L. T. Hobhouse and Political Argument in England, 1880–1914* (Cambridge, 1979). The lineage of many of the ideas espoused during the late 1930s and 1940s about social reform, the creation of ethical institutions, the importance of community and the common good undergirding the premises of the welfare state can be traced to the New Liberalism of L. T. Hobhouse and J. A. Hobson. Yet the rhetoric of citizenship and the nation during the war was framed by the classic republican notion that 'good citizenship' was embodied in the capacity of (rational) persons to put aside their individual interests for the public good.

125 Morgan and Evans suggest that in contrast to the pre-war years, when the idea of planning had been resisted by advocates of *laissez-faire*, in the context of the political and social climate of World War II it reached its apotheosis. See *Battle for Britain*, 32. On planning during the war, see John Stevenson, 'Planners' Moon? The Second World War and the Planning Movement', in Harold L. Smith, ed., *War and Social Change: British Society in the Second World War* (Manchester, 1986), 58–77.

126 C. B. Purdom, *Britain's Cities Tomorrow: Notes for Everyman on a Great Theme* (London, 1942), 24.

127 *Ibid.*, 27–8.

128 A. Trystan Edwards, *A Hundred New Towns?* (London, 1944), 26.

129 Ralph Tubbs, *The Englishman Builds* (Harmondsworth, 1945), 57.

130 Lawrence Wolfe, *The Reilly Plan – A New Way of Life* (London, 1945), 35–6. Rather than seeing 'the spirit of the Blitz' as inherent in 'British Character', he argued it was a product of 'external circumstances'; 42.

131 *Ibid.*, 56–78.

132 *Ibid.*, 63.

133 YWCA, 'News for Citizens', *Blue Triangle*, December 1941.

134 On the Beveridge Report, see YWCA, 'News for Citizens', *Blue Triangle*, March 1943; 'Education for Tomorrow', in 'News for Citizens', *Blue Triangle*, December 1943.

135 YWCA, 'News for Citizens', *Blue Triangle*, June 1943.

136 See, for example, 'The Purpose and Content of Youth Service: Report of Youth Advisory Council to Minister of Education in 1943' (London, 1945), 10.

137 Richard A. Voeltz, 'The Antidote to "Khaki Fever"? The Expansion of the British Girl Guides during the First World War', *Journal of Contemporary History* 27 (October 1992): 627–38.

138 'Adolescence and Sex Problems', Report of Sheffield Probation Officer, 1945, Reports of Principal Probation Officers, HO 45/20730, PRO Kew.

139 *Youth Registration in 1942*, HMSO, Cmd. 6446, May 1943: 2.

140 The primary objects of the White Paper discussion were the approximately 50 per cent of boys and the two-thirds to three-quarters of girls who were 'unattached'.

141 See 'Purpose and Content of the Youth Service'; and 'The Youth Services after the War: Report of Youth Advisory Council to the Board of Education' (London, 1943).

142 As Mariana Valverde has suggested, discourses of moral purity in general construct moral subjects. See Valverde, 'The Rhetoric of Reform: Tropes and the Moral Subject', *International Journal of the Sociology of Law* 18 (February 1990): 61–73; Valverde, *The Age of Light, Soap, and Water: Moral Reform in English Canada, 1885–1925* (Toronto, 1991).

143 Chantal Mouffe, 'Feminism, Citizenship and Radical Democratic Politics', in Judith Butler and Joan W. Scott, eds, *Feminists Theorize the Political* (New York, 1992), 377.

144 Mouffe, 'Feminism, Citizenship and Radical Democratic Politics', 378. Also see her analysis comparing liberal citizenship and civic republican citizenship: 'Democratic Citizenship and the Political Community', in Mouffe, *Dimensions of Radical Democracy*, 225–39.

145 Raphael Samuel, 'Introduction: Exciting to be English', in Samuel, ed., *Patriotism: The Making and Unmaking of British National Identity* I (London, 1989), xxi.

146 On Machiavelli, see Pitkin, *Fortune is a Woman*, Part 3; on Rousseau, see Carole Pateman, "The Disorder of Women': Women, Love, and the Sense of Justice', in Pateman, *The Disorder of Women: Democracy, Feminism and Political Theory* (Stanford CA, 1989), 17–32.

147 Iris Young, 'The Ideal of Impartiality and the Civic Public: Some Implications of Feminist Critiques of Moral and Political Theory', in Seyla Benhabib and Drucilla Cornell, eds, *Feminism as Critique: On the Politics of Gender* (Oxford, 1987), 67.

148 Young, 'The Ideal of Impartiality', 62.

149 Iris Marion Young, 'The Ideal of Impartiality and the Civic Public', in Young, *Justice and the Politics of Difference* (Princeton NJ, 1990), 109.

150 Genevieve Lloyd, *Man of Reason: 'Male' and 'Female' in Western Philosophy*, second edition (Minneapolis MN, 1993), viii.

151 Young, 'The Ideal of Impartiality', 110–11.

152 *Ibid.*, 111.

153 For an analysis of the revolutionary period in American history that suggests very similar processes, see Carroll Smith-Rosenberg, 'Beyond Roles, Beyond Spheres: Thinking about Gender in the Early Republic', *William and Mary Quarterly*, third series, 46 (June 1989): 623–31.

154 *Sunday Pictorial* (26 August 1945): 1.

PART III
The empire and its others 'away'

12

Real men hunt buffalo: masculinity, race and class in British fur traders' narratives

ELIZABETH VIBERT

British fur traders arrived in the Plateau region of north-western North America early in the nineteenth century to find the indigenous peoples living in an 'unhallowed wilderness', supporting themselves by fishing, hunting, and gathering – living, as one trader phrased it and all presumed, in a 'rude state of nature'. In their writings from the region the traders ranked Plateau societies, casting those they identified as 'fishing tribes' as indolent, improvident, and suffering periodic starvation. Those described as hunters, by contrast, were cast as brave, industrious, stoic – in a word, manly. In this chapter I probe the gendered nature of traders' representations of 'the Indian buffalo hunter'. The aim is to expose the cultural logic by which this hunter was constructed and became the standard-bearer of manly Indianness.[1] Integral to the project is the illumination of the process by which middle-class British masculinity, in its fur trade variant, was constructed as the norm and elevated above Indian manhood.[2] This was not a simple feat, even in the realm of narrative. The masculinity of the traders was never secure, defined as it was in a local context of gender, race and class conflict and resistance.

The rude state in which Plateau peoples were said to dwell was not new to these early nineteenth-century observers. The British had been encountering 'natives' abroad for centuries, inscribing them as savages both noble and ignoble.[3] Fur traders produced their own voluminous, and in many ways distinctive, cultural commentaries. The ideological baggage they carried with them from their British and colonial homes functioned as a kind of co-ordinating grid in the travellers' encounters with 'the Indian'. The outline of the grid was defined by an imagination which was white, male, middle-class and British.

While inherited discourses were influential, they were not intractable. A large part of the project of analysing traders' narratives is to assess how their cultural knowledge was produced, reproduced, and reordered in the North American Plateau in the period 1807 to 1846.[4] Cultural meanings were surely open to inventive refashioning. The traders' purpose was to carry on a profitable, and therefore peaceable, trade with indigenous peoples; many lived for years in this 'Indian country' (if generally behind insulating walls) and married indigenous women. They were surely subject to that 'jarring of meanings and values' which one cultural theorist so convincingly portrays as the consequence of inhabiting the liminal spaces of interacting cultures. The images that arose were shifting and contradictory, vacillating between what was already 'known' about the Indian and what was in need of anxious repeating.[5] With these observations in mind, I will place the traders not only in the context of their own shifting ideological heritage but also in their fluid North American setting.

The unpacking of trader narratives is of more than merely academic interest. As the earliest 'ethnographic' records of the indigenous societies of northern North America, traders' accounts have been extensively, and far too often uncritically, mined for data. The construction of these texts demands analysis.[6] In addition, the narratives present an early rendering of 'the Indian' which proved to be extraordinarily potent and enduring. So powerful was the image of the buffalo-hunting Indian that by the late nineteenth century, he had displaced his eastern woodland cousins (Hiawatha, Pocahontas, and their vaguely Algonquian kin) as *the* Indian of the Euro-American imagination. In casting the buffalo hunter as the quintessential manly Indian, traders' narratives anticipated generations of popular iconography.[7]

In casting Plateau buffalo hunters as industrious and praiseworthy, traders' narratives also departed from what is often taken to be a basic theme of the colonial encounter, the representation of indigenous hunters as wasteful, lazy, and far from manly. By the eighteenth century the hunting way of life was clearly associated with a backward social state: witness its position as the most rudimentary phase in Adam Smith's four-stage theory of social development. In settler commentaries from the eastern woodlands of North America at this time, hunters – indigenous or white – were frequently condemned as indolent and improvident. Fur trader narratives from farther west rarely praised Indian hunters. David Thompson expressed a general view in his 1785 account of subarctic hunter-gatherers. In the regions to the south and west of Hudson Bay, a relatively mild climate and abundance of game assured the hunters of a 'manly appearance', Thompson wrote. But they could not tolerate hard labour, a weakness Europeans frequently ascribed to the natives of the colonies. The hunters' very choice of activity was evidence of their degeneracy. These lazy people would rather rove for six hours over rough terrain 'than work one hour with the pick axe and spade'. Thompson concluded that 'naturally [the Indians] are not industrious'.[8]

Similar commentaries may be found in many other colonial settings in the late eighteenth and early nineteenth centuries. However, the most harshly condemning images of wasteful, cruel, and unmanly hunters gained ascendancy only as colonizer and colonized came into intense competition for access to wildlife, other resources, and land.[9] Earlier travellers' impressions of indigenous hunters were more mixed; still, hunters' perceived indolence was a common theme. To take just one example, in the early period of white exploration in interior southern Africa, game constituted an essential resource for expansionist Europeans. British travellers in the Cape interior relied heavily on Khoikhoi hunters, in particular, for subsistence. Such dependence led to at least a grudging acknowledgement of native skills, and at best a measured admiration.[10] Yet 'indolence' and 'idleness' were frequently called upon to describe the Khoikhoi way of life. Interestingly, Afrikaners (Boers) were described in much the same terms. As one student of African colonial literatures has put it, the mobile hunting and mixed subsistence patterns of both white Afrikaners and black Africans were regarded as a rejection of British ethics of discipline and labour: 'the fruits of the earth are enjoyed as they drop into the hand, [and] work is avoided as an evil.'[11] As a growing British presence brought the Cape Colony into the international capitalist economy, local animal resources began to be studied for science and hunted for sport. By the 1820s, the increasing tendency to view the Cape as hunting estate had led to a hardening of discourse about indigenous hunters; now, as well as indolent, they were described as wanton, cruel, or cowardly.[12] In North America a similar hardening came when the fur trade gave way to settlement and 'roving' hunters became an obstacle to those who sought to pre-empt their lands.

Fur traders' glowing accounts of Plateau buffalo hunters, which quite explicitly depicted them as industrious, appear all the more exceptional against this background. This positive view was restricted to buffalo hunting, however; the neighbouring 'fishing tribes' were 'indolent and lazy to an extreme'. As I have argued elsewhere, the traits of the fishers were defined quite clearly *in contrast to* those of the buffalo hunters.[13]

In much of North America the fur trade preceded settlement by several decades (and longer in the east). At base the fur trade entailed the exchange of European manufactures for furs and hides produced by indigenous peoples. The traders whose writings concern us here were the men on the ground in the extractive industry on which Canada and much of the northern United States were founded. Beginning in the late 1500s, the fur trade brought French, British, Dutch, Spanish, Russian and other mercantile interests to the continent. Beaver pelts were the principal inducement, for the felt demanded by the European clothing and hatting industries.[14] After a long history of imperial and commercial jockeying for power, by the early nineteenth century the fur trade of British North America was presided over by arch-rival enterprises, the London-based Hudson's Bay Company and the Montreal-based, Scots-dominated North West Company. The NWC, having established itself west of the Rocky Mountains ahead of its rival, was able to monopolize the trade of the Plateau and the larger Columbia district until economic pressures forced the companies to amalgamate in 1821.[15] Until the early 1840s, the Hudson's Bay Company remained the only effective non-native presence in the region; in that decade growing numbers of American settlers and missionaries began to arrive over the Oregon Trail.

In the context of the Plateau fur trade, 'British' included men of Scots, English, Welsh and Irish background. The traders' personal histories prior to joining the North West and Hudson's Bay companies are generally not well known. The interaction of class and ethnicity created a distinctive and taut hierarchy in the North West Company which persisted in the Plateau region throughout the period under study. Promising Scots and Englishmen and their colonial counterparts were recruited in their teens to the rank of clerk, their advancement all but assured by the patronage of a real or fictive kin member in the position of senior officer.[16] Many of these young clerks appear to have come from tenant farming or trades families. The fur trade offered these men opportunities which simply were not available at home. Not only could the thrifty among them put aside sufficient funds to return to Britain or the eastern colonies much wealthier than when they had left; within fur trade society itself, they achieved a social rank far beyond that from which most had come. They cultivated this status with some finesse. Those of other ethnic backgrounds, principally French Canadians, peripheral Scots,[17] *métis* (literally 'mixed', the offspring of traders and their country wives), Aboriginals, and Hawaiians, faced less attractive prospects. They entered the North West Company as boatmen and labourers, the 'servants' of the trade. Upward mobility was the exception for these men.

Members of the officer class, the clerks included, styled themselves the 'gentlemen' of the trade. The most immediate referent for this self-identification was 'the men', the company servants; but there were many others against whom the gentlemen defined themselves. Rituals to mark off their exclusive social space were highly formalized. Dining arrangements, for instance, spoke to class, ethnic, and gender hierarchies. Gentlemen and servants dined separately, and local Indians were rarely found at either mess table. By the early nineteenth century, however, virtually all the traders had Aboriginal or *métis* wives. The women ate after the men.[18]

Alexander Ross described the dining practices of the North Westers with a touch of irony. 'You take your seat,' Ross wrote, 'as a Chinese Mandarine [*sic*] would take his dress, according to your rank'. Even the common beverage was class-specific: there were three grades of China leaf tea, and as many of sugar. Such boundary-defining exercises were widespread and officially sanctioned. In a policy directive of 1822, the governing council of the reorganized HBC decreed that the 'line of distinction' between gentlemen and servants needed highlighting. To this end, a prohibition was issued on guides and interpreters dining with the officers. These men were in the upper ranks of the servant class, but they also tended to be French Canadian or native. Their occasional presence in the gentlemen's hall had apparently become a threat.[19]

Recent research indicates that the early nineteenth century was a period of hardening social distinctions throughout fur trade society. For instance, whereas in the eighteenth century tradesmen (the 'labour aristocracy' of the fur trade) and common labourers had generally lived together in barracks-style accommodation at HBC posts, by the early 1800s tradesmen and labourers were housed in separate buildings. Similarly, married and unmarried men were segregated. And whereas senior and junior officers had often shared a single officers' bastion, senior officers now enjoyed detached residences.[20] The advent of private family dwellings for the elite of the fur trade echoes developments in middle-class housing in Britain at the time. As Leonore Davidoff and Catherine Hall have shown, acquisition of a comfortable private home was the 'utmost ambition' of middle-class families by the turn of the nineteenth century. Not only was the home a symbol of status, proof that one had arrived; it was a sanctuary from external pressures.[21] Surely it performed this function in fur trade country, where added to the class and gender pressures of daily working life were those of an alien environment, alien peoples, and perceived threats to the civilized, white order.

The gentlemen traders' attempts to draw boundaries around themselves in order to secure their particular brand of masculine identity were not entirely successful. The refuge that they sought to construct was rooted in a cultural and political setting shot through with the antagonisms of class, gender and ethnicity. And there was a profound ambivalence at the heart of the project. Virtually every officer in the Columbia, and most servants, had Aboriginal or *métis* wives. Throughout fur trade country Indian women had from the early years been taken as wives 'by the custom of the country'. As *métis* daughters of these liaisons became numerous, they displaced Indian women. Their upbringing in fur trade communities and their tutelage at their fathers' knees were believed to have fitted them perfectly for the role of wife and servant of the trade. Indian or *métis*, these women were important to their husbands for economic and diplomatic purposes and for the 'many tender ties' which softened life at the posts. As George Barnston, a long-time Columbia trader, observed, as long as there was love 'within doors ... many a bitter blast may be borne from without'.[22]

Ultimately, though, marriages to women of the country came to be seen as a threat to the traders' gentlemanly self-fashioning. The arrival of missionaries in the territories east of the Rockies in the 1810s, and the introduction by the 1830s of British women to the fur trade scene, led to attacks on the morality and social acceptability of country unions. High-ranking company officers were first to follow the missionaries' admonitions to avoid mixed-race marriages, which one man of the cloth described as 'the snare which has ruined many of our countrymen'.[23] With this new model of racial and social etiquette in place, it was no longer seemly for men of the officer class to take indigenous wives. By the 1830s, the racial hierarchies encoded in traditional fur trade practice – hierarchies which had seen *métis* women displace Aboriginal women, and which had given rise to occasional epithets such as 'his bit of brown' – erupted into full view. The possession of an imported British wife became a key marker of proper fur trade manhood.[24]

The man personally responsible for the introduction of white 'ladies' to fur trade society was the Hudson's Bay Company's overseas governor, George Simpson. His return from England in 1830 with his young bride, Frances, prompted instant imitation by a number of officers.[25] Simpson, a proud Highland Scot with solid London connections, cut a very manly figure. He was precise in defining the qualities expected of his officers: 'zeal', 'hard work', 'firmness' and 'restraint' were pet phrases. Simpson's own zeal is legendary. He was a tirelessly competitive man, who earned both notoriety and reverence among fellow traders for his habit of pushing his canoe brigades to eighteen-hour days as he travelled about the region under his control, all the while clad in top hat and dress coat. On his first trip up the Columbia river in 1825, Simpson noted the 'hard marching' of his canoes, and boasted that their pace 'beats anything of the kind hitherto known in the Columbia'.[26]

Simpson prided himself on striking the right balance between 'firmness' and 'restraint'. These traits marked his handling of business matters (he arrived in the Columbia Department bent on 'oeconomy' and the reduction of 'wasteful extravagance') and his perception of how best to manage both company servants and Indians.[27] John McLoughlin, chief of Columbia operations, set out the accepted practice. The 'proper management' of the Indians entailed treating them with 'apparent openness and confidence' (restraint) while maintaining their respect (firmness).[28] Hence the juxtaposition of pipe-smoking and gift-giving ceremonies at the trade posts with fortifications, well armed brigades, and the perpetual readiness to use force.

Contemporary notions of the manly behaviour befitting fur trade gentlemen are spelled out in the officers' narratives and form a strong undercurrent in their commentaries on indigenous men. For example, in the midst of a passage praising the clean and handsome dress of Plateau hunters, John Work drew attention to a lapse:

> The young, and especially the males … occupy no inconsiderable portion of the morning decorating themselves[;] in point of time, and the degree of pains taken to ornament their hair, paint their faces &c they may compete with the more accomplished fops in the civilised world.[29]

The resonance with early nineteenth-century, middle-class notions of respectable manhood is striking. For the new man of enterprise such affectations were a waste of time, and invoked the decadence of an idle and self-absorbed aristocracy. The alternative model implied here would seem to be one of serious manhood, modesty, and self-restraint. The emergence of this new man in Britain, in an era of burgeoning urban capitalism and ascendant Evangelical religion, has been convincingly portrayed by Davidoff and Hall. Masculinity was redefined in terms of a harsh work ethic, independent enterprise, piety, sobriety, and dedication to family.[30] This model of manhood had more significance, perhaps, for the traders' self-image than for their imaginings of buffalo hunters. However, the two are closely intertwined. While the texts considered here are explicitly about manly buffalo hunters, implicitly they are about white, middle-class men.

Simpson's own model points to the paradoxes that marked fur trade manhood in this period. Simpson was very much the sober man of business yet he also sought to prove his worth in more physical pursuits. His pride in the success of his canoes drew on a sporting code more closely associated with the gentry, the very social class whose notions of masculinity the middle class in this era so vigorously rejected. Perhaps fur trade country provided an irresistible arena for such physical tests of manhood. Certainly, buffalo hunters provided an irresistible challenge to British men.

Trader commentary on Plateau hunters was a transparently masculine discourse. The masculinity that traders imagined the buffalo hunters to possess was complex, conceived as it was in the encounter with cultural difference. These hunters were at once brave and martial, savage and technologically backward. Difference was defined in trader narratives in cultural terms, as a matter of 'customs', 'manners' and 'habits' rather than organic or biological difference. The formal questionnaire on 'Natural History' which the London Committee of the Hudson's Bay Company began circulating to its trade posts in the mid-1820s, for instance, asked after the Indians' 'habits', usual occupations' and practices.[31] In keeping with dominant eighteenth- and early nineteenth-century assumptions about the universal brother-hood of man and the perfectibility of the 'backward' races, British traders believed in the potential of the Indian for improvement. The doctrine of perfectibility was, however, a double-edged sword: encoded within it were both equality and difference. If Indian hunters were potentially just like British men, even the most noteworthy of them were not there yet. Assumptions of essential difference – or, more accurately, essential inferiority – frequently rose to the surface in trader narratives.

All this attention to the symbolism in traders' texts is not meant to downplay the material logic; the trade itself shaped traders' perceptions of the manly and the good. The furs and hides produced by Plateau buffalo hunters, particularly the Salish Flathead and Kutenai, were critical to the profits of the trading companies in the Columbia Department. Between 1825 and the late 1840s, the only period for which reliable records exist, the trade district which included outposts in Salish and Kutenai territories produced, on average, 52 per cent of total fur returns from the Columbia Interior (about 18 per cent of fur returns for the entire region west of the Rockies). The buffalo hunts of these peoples were also vital to Columbia operations, providing leather for pack cords, portable hide lodges, and horse gear, as well as welcome infusions of fresh and dried meat for the local posts and travel food. Material concerns loomed large, then, in the traders' valorization of the buffalo hunters. But there was far more than instrumental logic to this imagery.

The principal distinguishing feature of the Plateau buffalo hunt, as traders depicted it, was the premium it placed on bravery. As the Salish chief known as Cartier told David Thompson, 'when [we] go to hunt the Bison, we also prepare for war'.[32] Hunting by Plateau groups in the parklands of the Rocky Mountains and the Plains to the east brought them into pitched competition with their long-standing Plains foes, the members of the Blackfoot Confederacy. Traders based in the Plateau favoured local hunters in these confrontations, not least because the Blackfoot had so resolutely resisted traders' attempts to penetrate their territory *en route* to the Plateau in the opening years of the nineteenth century.

Traders endowed the buffalo hunting of Plateau groups with a lofty moral significance. In his ethnographic summary of these peoples, Ross Cox emphasized that those qualities which 'ranked among the virtues' were most conspicuous among the buffalo hunters. He singled out the Salish and Upper Kutenai for special praise:

> Their bravery is pre-eminent; a love of truth they think necessary to a warrior's character. They are too proud to be dishonest, too candid to be cunning. Their many avocations leave them no leisure for gambling; and their strict subordination, joined to the necessity of exerting all their energies against the common enemy, prevents them from quarrelling.[33]

Burdened as it is by Cox's taste for purple prose, the passage captures well the perceived nobility of these hunters. What are the implications of the form of masculinity affirmed here for men of Cox's station? The answer is not readily gleaned from his narrative. Cox does on occasion admit to insecurity in the presence of armed Indian warriors. But it seems that he aspired to a rather different model of manhood. In another passage he depicts himself 'hunting, fishing, fowling, horse-racing', enjoying the classic sporting pursuits of the man of leisure.[34] Cox's social aspirations were consistent with his design to make his book attractive to a British travel literature audience, many of whom would have been members of the leisured classes. His buffalo hunter presents an alternative image of manhood. Here is the noble savage in all his glory: brave to a fault, proud, morally upright, diligent, and warlike.

Warrior imagery pervades traders' accounts.[35] The Plateau hunters' exploits against the Blackfoot were rendered in gripping detail in a number of the narratives. Thompson's account made very explicit the link between buffalo hunting and war. By 1811, three years after their first trade of muskets from the North West Company, the Salish and Kutenai had regained much of the buffalo territory they had long claimed as their own. The following summer, a massed war party of about 350 Salish, Kutenai, Kalispel, Spokane, and others set off to extend their hunting territory on to lands claimed by the Piegan, members of the Blackfoot Confederacy. Thompson was impressed with the sentiments expressed in the council that preceded the battle. Although they would prefer peace, it could not be relied upon in present circumstances, so the Plateau hunters would go to war. Chief Cartier urged the warriors, in Thompson's rendition, to 'show ourselves to be men, and make ourselves respected'.[36]

At the appointed time in August, when the buffalo bulls were in best condition for the kill, the Plateau party proceeded to the Plains:

> The hunting was carried on with cautious boldness into the lands of their enemies, this insult brought on a battle ... [the Piegan] advanced singing and dancing, the Saleesh saw the time was come to bring their whole force into line ... they also sung and danced their wild war dance; the Peegans [sic] advanced to within about one hundred and fifty yards, the song and the dance ceased, the wild war yell was given, and the rush forward; it was gallantly met, several were slain on each side,

and three times as many wounded, and with difficulty the Peegans carried off their dead and wounded and they accounted themselves defeated.[37]

In Thompson's eyes, the Salish and their allies had indeed shown themselves to be men. What began as courageous hunting soon developed into its natural extension, war. Here two of the most enduring and powerful images of idealized masculinity in the European tradition, the hunter and the warrior, form a potent combination.

Thompson's account betrays the tensions and ambiguities inherent in the valorizing of indigenous buffalo hunters. The traits which define their exceptional masculinity are the very traits which mark them as Indian, and therefore inferior to their British observers. The boundary between the heroic culture of hunter-warrior and savage nature is a brittle one in trader discourse. What starts as a display of masculine bravery ends in a display of the primitive natural world – the 'wild war dance' and the 'wild war yell' – played out in the enmity of two savage peoples. The account reveals just how close the noble savage is to his ignoble *alter ego*, how quickly the brave hunter can become the murderous brute. Governor Simpson slipped into similarly essentialist assumptions. On one occasion he extolled the Kutenai as fine hunters; on another, he scorned them as treacherous barbarians bent on plunder.[38] The buffalo hunter might be manly and noble but he was, still, representative of a savage race. The tensions inherent in this hunter-warrior imagery ran very deep.

Quite apart from the warfare it entailed, the buffalo hunt was seen as requiring courage of another sort. The buffalo itself epitomized savage nature in this region. Buffalo herds presented an awesome spectacle. Alexander Ross reported seeing one herd that numbered at least ten thousand. With his customary flourish, and with the Victorian adventure reader in mind, he asserted that there was no animal more fierce than a buffalo bull in the rutting season: 'Neither the polar bear nor the Bengal tiger surpass that animal in ferocity.' Ross's allusion to other British colonial possessions places his work squarely in the tradition of the imperial adventure tale, which was just coming into full flower at the time his narratives were published.[39]

According to traders' accounts, when not mortally wounded the buffalo was known to turn on its hunter. It fairly defied man to kill it. Yet so savage was this beast that, in Thompson's words, it was 'never pitied'. Ross recounted how a badly wounded animal propped itself on its front legs and stared him down until he and his colleagues had pumped ten balls into its mass. Even then, they kept their distance, 'for such is their agility of body, their quickness of eye, and so hideous are the looks of the beast, that we dared not for some time approach him'.[40] In this instance Ross himself donned the mantle of heroic hunter. In doing so, Ross may well have been influenced by the model of manhood presented by Indian hunters. Cultural theorist Homi Bhabha observes that representation of cultural others always involves an ambiguous process of projection and introjection, of condemnation and desire.[41] In casting himself in the role of manly buffalo hunter pitted against the West's most savage foe, Ross is momentarily united with the Indian hunter of his imagination.

But again this imagery is complex. In his big-game hunting exploits, Ross has another point of identification which lies closer to his own ethnic home. Generations of more privileged men in Britain had routinely sought to prove their manhood and their social status in the pursuit of this most excellent sport. By the early nineteenth century the hunting cult of the British upper classes was being extended to the colonies, and to men who in Britain might have had no claim to gentility. By the time Ross published his Plateau narratives at mid-century, growing numbers of British traders, army officers, colonial administrators and others were testing their masculine mettle against the big game of Africa, India, and to a lesser extent North America. 'Shooting madness' was an increasingly common affliction which Ross could be sure his readers would appreciate. The emerging class, national and gender connotations of big-game hunting go some way toward explaining Ross's proud portrayal of his encounter with a buffalo and his invocation of Bengal tigers and polar bears.

A central feature of Victorian hunting discourse was its preoccupation with the masculinity of *British* hunters. In pointing up the exceptional manliness of white sportsmen, Victorian hunting ideology tended to emphasize the cowardliness and wastefulness of indigenous hunters. The pattern is clearly revealed in the narratives of British sport hunters in Africa and India in the mid- and late-nineteenth century.[42] Ross sought to cast his lot with these imperial hunters, but he stopped short of representing indigenous hunters as inferior. This peculiarity of trader accounts may have arisen because the men were operating in a very different political-economic context than later, imperial hunters. Fur traders were in the advance guard of colonialism. They did not compete with Aboriginal people for land and resources; rather, they were dependent on them for access to those resources. Not until the fur trade gave way to the settlement frontier would material competition lead to a hardening of colonial discourse and a systematic refiguring of the Indian hunter as wasteful brute.[43]

The buffalo hunt, with its dual challenge of Plains enemies and savage beasts, represented the supreme test of the courage and fortitude of manly Indian hunters. In facing such challenges, Plateau hunters distinguished themselves yet again through their successful application of the tools of European technology. Here, too, the tensions implicit in making these hunters into heroes come to the surface. By Cox's account, Salish hunters had been brave even before they acquired firearms from the traders. They had yearly marched to the buffalo plains with nothing to oppose the Blackfoot 'but arrows and their own undaunted bravery'. This bravery had the whisper of a fatal flaw. The Salish were frequently routed by their better-armed foes, but despite their losses appeared unable to restrain themselves. What was at the root of this destructive obsession? It was the love of the hunt, what Cox called their 'unconquerable hereditary attachment' to the chase.[44] The Salish were brave – braver, perhaps, than Cox could ever hope to be – but that bravery was itself a mark of their Indianness. Their desire to hunt was unreasonable, an expression of primitive nature. As is so often the case in such colonial discourses, in the midst of a passage praising the virtues of the Indian comes a forceful – perhaps an anxious – reminder of his difference.

Thompson recalled the joy of Salish elders in 1810 at seeing the 'alacrity' with which the younger men went off to the Plains with their new guns. A dogged proponent of European technology, Thompson reasoned that, without guns, the Salish would have been 'pitiful', 'defenceless', forced to operate in the Plains 'by stealth'. Stealth, in his view, was the mode of cowards; real men would 'hunt boldly and try a battle'.[45] The image of these hunters as possessors of new, progressive power over the forces of nature and human foes is most pronounced in Thompson's writings. His devotion to the theme is not surprising, given his personal commitment to the technologies of the day. During his twenty-six years in fur trade country, Thompson's principal interest was exploration, scientific survey, and observation; he produced a series of remarkably accurate maps of the vast area between Hudson Bay and the Pacific Ocean, south to the Columbia river. Thompson's activities are in many ways emblematic of his culture's increasing confidence in the capacity of humans to delve into and master the secrets of the natural world. His views on the salutary effects of firearms were registered in his account of improvements in Salish and Kutenai hunting. He was convinced that guns allowed these hunters greater technical mastery. Their flint-headed arrows 'broke against the Shield of tough Bison hide … their only aim was the face; these [bows and arrows] they were now to exchange for Guns, Ammunition and Iron headed arrows', the better to face both beasts and men.[46] Thompson's optimism about the superiority of firearms for buffalo hunting was overstated. His views might have moderated had he stayed in the Columbia beyond 1812, and seen that bow and arrow remained in wide use long after guns became available.[47]

Implicit in all this discussion of bravery in the face of beastly foes and technology in the service of men is a whole set of European ideas about the human capacity to dominate nature. Contemporary discourse on the subject, and on the relationship between the state of a society and its physical environment, is too complex to rehearse here.[48] By the measures of the day, Plateau peoples dwelt in the state of nature, the rudimentary 'hunter' stage. It would require a rash leap of logic to suggest that British traders equated the killing of buffalo by Indian hunters with the perceived domination of nature by European culture. But a critical aspect of the presumed relationship between humans and their environment was its mutability. Progress out of the rude state of nature was possible, indeed many would say inevitable. In the minds of the traders, the first imperative of that progress was mastery of the tools of a superior technology. The native skills of the buffalo hunters enabled them to master those tools and to extend their authority over nature.

The perception that buffalo hunters were rendered more manly and more powerful by the possession of firearms at once reinforced and checked their imagined masculinity. Many traders remarked that those they defined as hunters (in contrast to 'fishermen') were better equipped to cope with the demands of this new and powerful European technology. Writing of the Salish and Kutenai,

Thompson noted that their long practice at hunting deer from horseback made them adept with bow and arrow and prepared them well for the change to muskets. Another trader made a similar observation about the Cayuse, remarking that their experience as hunters gave them a 'singular dexterity'. Interestingly, Thompson described the skill of the Plateau hunters as superior to that of their Plains foes.[49] This observation probably says more about traders' biases against the Blackfoot than it does about relative hunting abilities.

In an intriguing inversion of such reasoning, the gun also served as a marker of the native hunters' inferiority. Whether the hunters were heroic or 'pitiful' before the gun, they were all rendered dependent on the traders for its benefits. The narratives speak volumes about the confidence this advantage bestowed. In his first winter in the Plateau (1811), Ross found his musket to be of profound practical and symbolic benefit. It gave him a sense of security in the face of a wolf attack, an event which he recalled had terrified the Indians. The gun also afforded a symbolic dominance over the Indians, who, according to Ross, were awed by this technology. After killing a wolf at a distance he claimed to be five arrow shots, the trader enthused that 'nothing but [the Indians'] wonder could exceed their admiration of this effect of firearms'. Ye-whell-come-tetsa, a prominent Okanagan leader, appears in the narrative thanking Ross for his assistance and proclaiming 'we have nothing to fear … I shall always love the whites'.[50] Manly as the hunter-warriors might be, they were in the end representatives of a primitive race. Their manliness was always constrained, in trader discourse, by the assertion that they lacked certain attributes which only the British traders could supply.

This rhetorical strategy had the added benefit, of course, of securing the traders' masculinity. The 'warrior' nature of Plateau hunters at times posed a serious threat to the traders, who had to live safely among these people if they were to succeed in their venture and retain their own manly identities. Ross penned what must be the most self-conscious assertion of imperial masculine hegemony in the whole of the Plateau record. Recounting the 1818 building of Fort Walla Walla, a strategic post on the Columbia river, Ross mustered his considerable narrative skills. A formidable structure was needed to protect traders and to tame the 'many war-like tribes that infest the country'. Fort Walla Walla was the only North West Company post protected by a double wall; Indian traders were admitted through the outer wall and had to conduct trade through a small aperture in the inner one, which shielded the company dwellings and storehouse. The whole was surrounded by six-metre palisades and fortified towers, and defended with cannons and muskets. Ross's enthusiasm at the building of the fort exposes the symbolic function of such a structure for the traders.[51] Dubbed 'the Gibraltar of the Columbia', it kept 'savagery' at bay:

> as if by enchantment, the savage disposition of the Indians was either soothed or awed, a stronghold had arisen in the desert, while the British banner floating over it proudly proclaimed the mistress of a vast territory; it was an example of British energy and enterprise, of civilization over barbarism.[52]

The imperial discourse is loud and clear, and surely tailored to Ross's intended Victorian readership. Britannia prevails over a race which may be martial and powerful, but is at base savage. The remark that the Indians are perhaps 'soothed' by this assertion of British power even hints that they are aware of their own inferiority. The masculine discourse is embedded in and inseparable from the imperial.[53] The warlike tribes are subdued by the appearance of this hulking fortress, and British traders have proved their worth, both as traders and as men. They have prevailed over the threat from these potential enemies, and exhibited their manliness in the very act of erecting the fort. It stands as a symbol of their 'energy and enterprise', ultimate masculine virtues in the idioms of early nineteenth-century capitalism and the fur trade alike.

As it turned out, control over these groups was elusive. Ross soon resumed complaining about the 'insolence' and 'independence' of the people around Walla Walla, and his successors voiced similar sentiments.[54] But the historical accuracy or inaccuracy of Ross's account is not the point. The gap between his initial, confident assumption of British male authority and his later accounts of continued challenges to that authority speaks to the gap that probably will always exist between imagined and lived masculine identities. Ross anxiously hoped that British traders would prevail over Indian hunters in this desert 'wilderness'. The reality, it seems, was continual challenges to British manhood, continual contests between variant expressions of masculine identity. Still, Ross's writings reveal the gendered nature of traders' relationships with indigenous men and the ways in which the traders' discourse was constituted through hierarchies of gender, class and race.

Notes

From *Gender and History*, 8:1 (April 1996), 4–21. My thanks to the Hudson's Bay Company Archives, Winnipeg, Canada, for permission to quote from its collection. I am grateful to Terence Ranger, Megan Vaughan, Glyndwr Williams, Keith McClelland, and two anonymous reviewers for suggestive comments on an earlier version of this chapter. I especially thank Todd Hatfield and Lynne Marks for their careful criticism and support.

1 The quotations are from Alexander Henry's 'Journal', in *New Light on the Early History of the Greater Northwest ... II, Alexander Henry's Journal*, ed. Elliott Coues (Ross and Haines, Minneapolis MN, 1897), p. 707. The terms 'Indian', 'hunter', and 'fisherman' are used here as categories employed by the traders. 'Indian' refers throughout to the discursive Indian, the indigenous male (for traders wrote mainly about men) inscribed in trader narratives. On the rhetorical displacement of indigenous peoples implicit in the use of the label 'Indian', see Carroll Smith-Rosenberg, 'Captured Subjects/Savage Others: Violently Engendering the New American', *Gender and History*, 5 (1993), pp. 177–95. The terms 'hunter' and 'fisherman' set up artificial categories. The seasonal rounds of all Plateau societies were far more complex, and based on a more diverse range of gathered, hunted, and fished resources, than such labels imply. Women's production was critical to the subsistence base. See Elizabeth Vibert, 'Traders' Tales: British Fur Traders' Narratives of Cultural Encounters in the Plateau, 1807–1846' (Oxford University D.Phil. dissertation, 1993; revised and forthcoming, University of Oklahoma Press, 1996).

2 This chapter focuses on relationships between British trader and Plateau hunter masculinities. Traders' relationships with Plateau femininities are explored in Vibert,

Traders' Tales, ch. 3. Differences of national identity among traders were eroded in the North American fur trade, where men's identities and interests came into line with the agendas of British-run overseas trading companies. Men of 'gentleman' or officer rank became an 'imagined community', collaborating across divisive boundaries and internal hierarchies. Benedict Anderson's notion of 'horizontal comradeship' seems especially appropriate in this context; see his *Imagined Communities: Reflections on the Origins and Spread of Nationalism* (Verso, New York, 1983).

3 For discussions of the complexity and ambivalence of European attitudes toward the indigenous peoples of the Americas, see Hugh Honour, *The New Golden Land: European Images of America from the Discoveries to the Present Time* (Pantheon Books, New York, 1975); Tzvetan Todorov, *The Conquest of America: The Question of the Other* (Harper & Row, New York, 1984); Robert Berkhofer, *The White Man's Indian* (Vintage, New York, 1978); Mary Louise Pratt, *Imperial Eyes: Travel Writing and Transculturation* (Routledge, London, 1992); Anthony Pagden, *The Fall of Natural Man: The American Indian and the Origins of Comparative Ethnology* (Cambridge University Press, Cambridge, 1986); Fredi Chiapelli (ed.) *First Images of America: The Impact of the New World on the Old*, 2 vols (University of California Press, Berkeley CA, 1976); P. J. Marshall and Glyndwr Williams, *The Great Map of Mankind: Perceptions of New Worlds in the Age of Enlightenment* (Harvard University Press, Cambridge MA, 1982); Antonello Gerbi, *The Dispute of the New World: The History of a Polemic, 1750–1900* (University of Pittsburg Press, Pittsburgh PA, 1973).

4 These dates mark, respectively, the entry of North West Company traders into the Plateau region and the establishment of the international boundary between US and British North American possessions west of the Rockies. By 1846 political events and swelling numbers of settlers were pointing to the demise of the fur trade in the region.

5 Homi Bhabha, *The Location of Culture* (Routledge, London, 1994), p. 162.

6 These days, traders' writings are routinely pillaged for information about Aboriginal land use patterns by those involved in land-claims cases before the British Columbia and federal courts. In a controversial decision, Chief Justice Allan McEachern of the BC Supreme Court, finding against the Gitksan and Wet'suwet'en plaintiffs, privileged traders' accounts as 'fact' while dismissing Aboriginal elders' oral histories as 'cultural belief'. There are as yet very few studies of the social construction of fur traders' narratives. The best recent analysis, on a limited theme, is Mary Black-Rogers, 'Varieties of "Starving": Semantics and Survival in the Subarctic Fur Trade', *Ethnohistory*, 33 (1986), pp. 353–83. It should be noted that most, though not all, of the writings under scrutiny here were prepared specifically for publication; this shaped their production in particular ways, and distinguished them from daily fieldnotes, journals, letters, and annual post reports. See Ian MacLaren, 'Exploration/Travel Literature and the Evolution of the Author', *International Journal of Canadian Studies*, 5 (1992), pp. 39–67. For broader discussion of the implicit demands imposed on authors and publishers by travel literature audiences, see Paul Carter, *The Road to Botany Bay: Landscape and History* (University of Chicago Press, Chicago IL, 1987); Pratt, *Imperial Eyes*; Billie Melman, *Women's Orients: English Women and the Middle East, 1718–1918: Sexuality, Religion and Work* (University of Michigan Press, Ann Arbor MI, 1992); Stephen Greenblatt, *Marvellous Possessions: The Wonder of the New World* (University of Chicago Press, Chicago IL, 1991); Germaine Warkentin, 'Introduction', in *Canadian Exploration Literature: An Anthology*, ed. Germaine Warkentin (Oxford University Press, Toronto and Oxford, 1993), pp. ix–xxi.

7 On the process whereby the buffalo-hunting Indian became *the* Indian of popular imagination, see Rayna Green, 'The Tribe Called Wannabee: Playing Indian in America and Europe', *Folklore*, 99 (1988), pp. 30–43, and John Ewers, 'The Emergence of the Plains Indian as the Symbol of the North American Indian', *Annual Report of the Smithsonian Institution* (1964), pp. 531–55.

8 David Thompson, 'Narrative', in David Thompson's *Narrative of his Explorations in Western America, 1784–1812*, ed. J. B. Tyrrell (Champlain Society, Toronto, 1916), p. 80.

9 See John MacKenzie, *The Empire of Nature: Hunting, Conservation and British Imperialism*

(Manchester University Press, Manchester, 1988); Mahesh Rangarajan, 'Hunting and Conservation in India' (Oxford University D.Phil. dissertation, 1992); William Beinart, 'Empire, Hunting and Ecological Change in Southern and Central Africa', *Past and Present*, 128 (1990), pp. 162–86; E. R Thompson, *Whigs and Hunters: The Origin of the Black Act* (Allen Lane, London, 1977). On hunting in North America, see R. M. Ballantyne, especially *The Buffalo Runners: A Tale of the Red River Plains* (Nisbet, London, 1891) and *Away in the Wilderness* (Nisbet, London, n.d.).

10 MacKenzie, *Empire of Nature*, pp. 86–95; Beinart, 'Empire, Hunting', pp. 163, 167, 174; Richard Grove, 'Scottish Missionaries, Evangelical Discourses, and the Origins of Conservation Thinking', *Journal of Southern African Studies*, 15 (1989), pp. 163-87.

11 J. M. Coetzee, *White Writings: On the Culture of Letters in South Africa* (Yale University Press, New Haven CT, 1988), p. 32.

12 MacKenzie, *Empire of Nature*, p. 95; Beinart, 'Empire, Hunting', p. 163.

13 Hudson's Bay Company Archives D.3/1, fos 61–2. All HBC documents, housed at the Provincial Archives of Manitoba, Winnipeg, are denoted hereafter by the prefix HBCA. For a more nuanced account of perceptions of Plateau fishing groups, see Vibert, *Traders' Tales*, chs 3–4.

14 For accessible overviews of the North American fur trade see Glyndwr Williams, 'The Hudson's Bay Company and the Fur Trade, 1670–1870', special issue of *The Beaver*, 314 (1983); E. E. Rich, *The Fur Trade and the Northwest to 1857* (McClelland & Stewart, Toronto, 1967). For an international perspective, see Eric Wolf, *Europe and the People without History* (University of California Press, Berkeley CA, 1982), ch. 6.

15 The NWC faced fierce competition from the American Fur Company in the period 1811–13; otherwise, it had the land-based fur trade of the region to itself. The Plateau, or 'Columbia Interior' in fur trade parlance, comprised the interior reaches of the Columbia Department. This latter name applied to the entire administrative district west of the Rocky Mountains: present-day British Columbia, Washington State, and portions of Oregon, Idaho, and Montana.

16 The best treatments of fur trade social history remain Jennifer S. H. Brown, *Strangers in Blood: Fur Trade Company Families in Indian Country* (University of British Columbia Press, Vancouver, 1980), and Sylvia Van Kirk, *'Many Tender Ties': Women in Fur-Trade Society, 1670–1870* (Watson & Dwyer, Winnipeg, 1980). While most NWC officers were Scots, those whose writings are canvassed here were more diverse: Thompson was of Welsh parentage; Cox and Work were Irish.

17 The Orkneys and Hebrides were popular recruiting grounds for 'stout' and 'serious' young men with few economic alternatives. They were never figured as Scots by their superiors, although they were less 'other' than French Canadian, *métis*, Aboriginal or Hawaiian men. Given the relatively favourable discourse about Orcadians, they could be said to have functioned as what Spivak calls 'self-consolidating' others. Gayatri Spivak, *In Other Worlds: Essays in Cultural Politics* (Methuen, London, 1987).

18 After a long period of institutional resistance and counter-resistance by company employees, by the nineteenth century unions made in the custom of the country were sanctioned by 'immemorial custom' as proper marriages. HBCA B.223/b/21 fos 4–12.

19 Ross Cox, *The Columbia Rivers, or, Scenes and Adventures …*, ed. E. I. Stewart and J. R. Stewart (London, 1831; reprinted University of Oklahoma Press, Norman OK, 1957) pp. 230, 360; Alexander Ross, *Fur Hunters of the Far West*, ed. K. A. Spaulding (London, 1855; reprinted University of Oklahoma Press, Norman OK, 1956), pp. 7–10, 19–20; R. Harvey Fleming (ed.), *Minutes of Council, Northern Department of Rupert Land, 1821–31* (Champlain Society, Toronto, 1940), pp. 25–6; HBCA B.233/b/4 fo. 31.

20 See Michael Payne, 'Daily Life on Western Hudson Bay 1714–1870: A Social History of York Factory and Churchill' (Carleton University Ph.D. dissertation, 1989), pp. 389–90. A similar pattern developed in the Plateau; see, for example, Cox, *The Columbia Rivers*, p. 230.

21 Leonore Davidoff and Catherine Hall, *Family Fortunes: Men and Women of the English Middle Class, 1780–1850* (University of Chicago Press, Chicago IL, 1987), pp. 17, 357 and ch. 8.

22 Quoted in Van Kirk, *'Many Tender Ties'*, p. 136.

23 Rev. William Cockran, quoted in Van Kirk, *'Many Tender Ties'*, p. 172.

24 On the shifting processes of racial and class ranking associated with Aboriginal, *métis* and British women in fur trade society, see Van Kirk, *'Many Tender Ties'*, and Brown, *Strangers in Blood*.

25 Some traders privately denounced the callousness with which Simpson had treated his country wife, Margaret Taylor, and remained committed to their own wives and families. See Van Kirk, *'Many Tender Ties'*, and Christine Welsh, 'Voices of the Grandmothers: Reclaiming a *Métis* Heritage', *Canadian Literature*, 131 (1991), pp. 15–25.

26 George Simpson, 'Journal 1824–25', in *Fur Trade and Empire: George Simpson's Journal … 1824–25*, ed. Frederick Merk (1931; reprinted Harvard University Press, Cambridge MA, 1968), p. 140; HBCA D.3/1 fo. 102.

27 HBCA D.3/1 fo. 24.

28 These are persistent themes in fur trade records. See HBCA B.223/b/30 fo. 49, McLoughlin to the Governor and Committee, 15 November 1843; E. E. Rich (ed.), *The Letters of John McLoughlin* I, p. 48; HBCA D.5/6 fos 173–4.

29 HBCA B.45/e/2 fo. 5.

30 Davidoff and Hall, *Family Fortunes*, pp. 108–18.

31 HBCA, PP 1828–1, 'Queries Connected with the Natural History of the Honorable Hudson's Bay Company's Territories'.

32 Thompson, 'Narrative', p. 533.

33 Cox, *The Columbia Rivers*, pp. 264, 267.

34 *Ibid.*, pp. 93–4, 215.

35 *Ibid.*, p. 81; Ross, *Fur Hunters*, p. 200; HBCA B.69/a/1 fo. 3. For similar observations see Alexander Ross, *Adventures of the First Settlers on the Oregon or Columbia River* (London, 1849; reprinted Lakeside Press, Chicago IL, 1923), pp. 243, 268; John Work, 'Journal No. 4', fo. 166, original in British Columbia Archives and Records Service, Victoria BC.

36 Thompson, 'Narrative', pp. 548–52.

37 *Ibid.*

38 HBCA D.3/1 fo. 11; HBCA D.3/2 fo. 93.

39 Ross, *Fur Hunters*, pp. 243, 283. Although his service in the Plateau ended in the mid-1820s, Ross's two Plateau narratives were not published until 1849 and 1855.

40 Ross, *Fur Hunters*, pp. 243, 283; Thompson, 'Narrative', p. 432.

41 Bhabha, *The Location of Culture*, chs 3–4.

42 MacKenzie, *Empire of Nature*.

43 An expansion of this argument can be found in Vibert, *Traders' Tales*, ch. 7.

44 HBCA B.69/a/1 fos 3, 6; Cox, *The Columbia Rivers*, p. 134; HBCA B.45/e/3 fos 12–13.

45 Thompson, 'Narrative', pp. 411, 420, 424.

46 *Ibid.*, pp. 411, 463.

47 Vibert, *Traders' Tales*, chs 4 and 6.

48 See Ludmilla Jordanova, 'Earth Science and Environmental Medicine: The Synthesis of the Late Enlightenment', in *Images of the Earth: Essays in the History of the Environmental Sciences* (British Society for the History of Science, Chalfont St Giles, 1979), and Jordanova, *Sexual Visions: Images of Gender in Science and Medicine* (Harvester Wheatsheaf, Hemel Hempstead, 1989); Richard Grove, *Conservation and Colonial Expansion* (forthcoming, Cambridge University Press, Cambridge); Marshall and Williams, *The Great Map of Mankind*.

49 Thompson, 'Narrative', pp. 411, 420, 424, 463, 549; Philip Rollins (ed.), 'Journey of Mr. Hunt and his Companions …', in *The Discovery of the Oregon Trail* (Edward Eberstadt, New York, 1935), p. 303.

50 Ross, *Fur Hunters*, pp. 48–52, 114.

51 His enthusiasm apparently got the better of him. Archaeological evidence indicates that the fort was rather smaller than Ross recalled. See Theodore Stern, *Chiefs and Chief Traders: Indian Relations at Fort Nez Percés, 1818–1855* (Oregon State University Press, Portland OR, 1993), ch. 1.

52 Ross, *Fur Hunters*, pp. 119–20, 144–6.

53 For recent studies analysing nineteenth-century British imperialism as a profound historical expression of British masculinity, see Graham Dawson, 'The Blond Bedouin: Lawrence of Arabia, Imperial Adventure, and the Imagining of English-British Masculinity', and other essays in *Manful Assertions: Masculinities in Britain since 1800*, ed. Michael Roper and John Tosh (Routledge, London and New York, 1991); Catherine Hall, *White, Male and Middle Class: Explorations in Feminism and History* (Polity and Routledge, London and New York, 1992); J. A. Mangan and James Walvin (eds), *Manliness and Morality: Middle-Class Masculinity in Britain and America, 1800–1940* (Manchester University Press, Manchester, 1987); Lynne Segal, *Slow Motion: Changing Masculinities, Changing Men* (Virago, London, 1990), esp. ch. 7; Mrinalini Sinha, 'Gender and Imperialism: Colonial Policy and the Ideology of Moral Imperialism in Late Nineteenth-Century Bengal', in *Changing Men: New Directions in Research on Men and Masculinity*, ed. Michael S. Kimmel (Sage, London, 1987). Also suggestive are Helen Callaway, *Gender, Culture and Empire: European Women in Colonial Nigeria* (University of Illinois Press, Urbana IL, 1987); Chandra Talpade Mohanty, 'Introduction: Cartographies of Struggle', in *Third World Women and the Politics of Feminism*, ed. Chandra Talpade Mohanty, Ann Russo and Lourdes Torres (Indiana University Press, Bloomington and Indianapolis IN, 1991).

54 Ross, *Fur Hunters*, pp. 154–5; HBCA B.146/a/1,2; HBCA B.223/b/11fo. 49.

13

Colonial conversions: difference, hierarchy, and history in early twentieth-century evangelical propaganda

NICHOLAS THOMAS

Colonial discourse, sometimes referred to in the singular, seems unmanageably vast and heterogeneous, for it must encompass not only the broad field of colonialism's relations and representations which constitutes or arises from the business of official rule, including administrative reports and censuses, but also the works of metropolitan literature and other forms of high culture which deploy images of the exotic or the primitive, paintings of unfamiliar landscapes, tourist guides, anthropological studies, and Oriental fabric designs. Colonial discourse includes chinoiserie, *Kim*, the Victoria and Albert Museum, Camus's Algerian stories, Frans Post, and *Indiana Jones*, as well as the *Vital Statistics of the Native Population for the Year 1887* and the annual reports from wherever. But if all of these texts, edifices, images, and artefacts are rightly seen to be constituted within, or at least influenced by, the relations of imperialism, how can one break up and particularize this colonial culture while sustaining a sense of its global character and development? How are different periods and projects most effectively brought into view?

Hierarchy and incorporation

In his discussion of the constitution of European anthropological ideas, Johannes Fabian proposes that premodern and modern conceptions of space and time are quite different and that the transition to the latter entailed a fundamental shift in approaches to the status of other peoples:

> Enlightenment thought marks a break with an essentially medieval, Christian (or Judeo-Christian) vision of Time. That break was one from a conception of time/ space in terms of a history of salvation to one that ultimately resulted in the secularization of Time as natural history ... the pagan was always *already* marked for salvation, the savage is *not yet* ready for civilization ... one [model] consists of concentric circles of proximity to a center in real space and mythical Time, symbolized by the cities of Jerusalem and Rome. The other is constructed as a

system of coordinates (emanating of course also from a real center – the western metropolis) in which given societies of all times and places may be plotted in terms of relative distance from the present.[1]

Evolutionary thought must equate a variety of other peoples with certain stages in the history and prehistory of the centre. Although premodern thought postulated that various barbarians and infidels were inferior and different, something singular and very powerful in the evolutionary spatialization of time consigned distinct groups, such as Hottentots, to particular historical stages. In premodern discourse the canonical native was the heathen or pagan, who was primarily understood as a candidate for salvation; subsequently the canonical savage became the exemplar of another race situated on a certain rung of the ladder. In some cases, where mutability and relative temporal proximity were presupposed, a particular race might be situated only at a few generations' remove from the civilized reference point. This might be consistent with an incorporative or integrationist orientation like that characteristic of premodern discourse. In other cases, and perhaps more commonly, the advancement of subject populations was taken as an extremely long-term affair. As Lord Milner maintained, 'the white man must rule, because he is elevated by many, many steps above the black man; steps which it will take the latter centuries to climb, and which it is quite possible that the vast bulk of the black population may never be able to climb at all'.[2] Temporal gaps that might be notionally overcome in the continuum of evolution were therefore, for all present purposes, stabilized and rendered absolute through a fixed hierarchy.[3]

Many studies of European representations of non-Western peoples and the associated notions of national or racial difference have operated through periodization in the manner typified by Fabian's argument: particular stereotypes, such as the ignoble savage, or doctrines like evolutionism have been linked with particular times and shown to succeed one another. Often such histories have been careful and nuanced,[4] but this chapter aims to develop a complementary perspective on constructions of others that emphasizes the differing interests of particular sorts of colonizers, taking that term in its broadest sense, and their associated genres of representation. It appears that the approaches to difference and ways of perceiving natives prevalent among classes of European intruders, such as explorers, missionaries, officials, and planters, may persist across epochs but conflict sharply with the images presupposed and purveyed by differently situated contemporaries. I thus address the differences of location and perspective rather than period and follow a number of writers in emphasizing the need to move away from monolithic notions of colonialism and to examine the 'tensions of empire', not merely in the sense of the surface conflicts arising from divergent interests but also with regard to the underlying ambiguities and contradictions of colonial projects.[5] This also implies a shift of focus from the extensively reviewed images and stereotypes of the other to an interest in the relations and circulations of difference on colonial peripheries and through various understandings of the civilizing process.[6]

Fabian argues that although some modern regimes may appear incorporative, they are 'founded on distancing and separation'.[7] It is clear, however, that certain administrations were far more preoccupied with maintaining racial separateness and coherent domains of native custom than others: in some contexts the horror of miscegenation was extreme, but assimilation was positively favoured elsewhere.[8] Without exploring official colonialism further here, I suggest that the propaganda discourse, especially the interventionist practice, of some early twentieth-century evangelical missions amounts to a significant exception to Fabian's characterization of modern colonialism and is in fact quite consistent with his discussion that the premodern approach to otherness would persist in discourses which were not secularized. Although, I suggest, the evangelical culture has a relation of alterity that is quite distinctive, the missions clearly shared a great deal with secular colonizers at another level. Thus, there was the complex deployment of shared metaphors and 'common ground' in texts arising from distinct interests and practical projects that were in tension if not mutually contradictory.[9]

Travellers' attitudes toward Pacific Islanders

This chapter focuses not only on visual and textual propaganda associated with the Methodist mission in the western Solomon Islands in the early part of the twentieth century[10] but also on making apparent the peculiarity of these constructions by briefly discussing imagery typical of the vast number of non-missionary Pacific travel books published around the same time. Little commentary needs to be added to Frank Burnett's 'Tahitian Beauty' (Plate 13.7).[11] The Polynesians depicted in his book, *Wanderings with a Camera in Southern Seas*, are mostly undressed women. As a commentator on colonial African postcards has noted, this work amounts to 'an anthology of bosoms'.[12] The women, called 'Belles' and 'Woodland Nymphs', are unambiguously sexualized: the images often effect partial disclosure by positioning the subjects away from the camera or shrouding them in exotic foliage, thus suggesting an enticing, half hidden but nevertheless accessible space. Burnett's mixture of uncredited studio portraits and his own distinctly less professional photographs thus reinforced an image with its origins in the early explorers' accounts of promiscuity in Tahiti and Hawaii and perpetuated up to the present in scholarly as well as travel writing, tourist culture, and popular films (like most versions of the *Bounty*).

The people of the western Pacific, categorized as Melanesians, were represented differently, but this representation was again based on imagery that emerged early in the history of European exploration and contact. Melanesians were seen as members of a Negro race distinct from the lighter-skinned Polynesians and were thought to be less advanced in every respect. One key marker of their savage state, which was ranked below the barbarism of the Polynesians, was the socially degraded condition of the women, who were also often said to be physically ugly.[13] These constructions were conspicuous in another photographer-traveller's book, Frank Hurley's *Pearls and Savages*. Hurley represented himself to the public as an explorer and adventurer, and his presentations of remote and lost worlds through the book, films, slide shows, and lecture tours were enormously popular in Australia and the United States. He described a longhouse from which he stole some artefacts in the following terms:

> Everything was inexpressibly crude and primitive. We had entered the Stygian homes of prehistoric swamp-dwellers living by the shores of a primeval sea ... Skulls, human bits, and tit-bits filled our bone-bag, while axes, knives and fabrics were substituted. Surely, indeed, Father Christmas had visited the house! Iron and steel replaced bone and stone, and a million years was bridged in a day![14]

This imagination accords precisely with Fabian's description of the temporalization of space. The hyperbole of extreme savagery – adumbrated elsewhere in speculation about the customs associated with headhunting – was mirrored in the absolute character of temporal distancing. For Hurley, the Papuans were not, like Lafitau's Iroquois, survivors from some distinct stage of antiquity or prehistory but rather reflections of a positively primeval condition at the very margins of human existence; and their humanity was in fact placed in doubt: women smeared with clay in accord with mortuary observances were 'so filthy and hideous it is difficult to believe them human'.[15]

At the most general level, this racist misogyny informed the colonizing projects of the time: Hurley demonstrated that there were tracts of land to be opened up and never countenanced the idea that the inhabitants of such places as the Papuan gulf were to be acknowledged as landowners or otherwise reckoned with. Of course, Hurley's work did not directly legitimize or inform any particular extension of European control or settlement, and the radical alterity and evolutionary distance he evokes are perhaps best understood as a project of self-glorification. The explorer was more of an explorer if he underwent danger, penetrated the unknown, met the inexpressible, and like Professor Challenger in Conan Doyle's *The Lost World*, found the dawn of man and prehistory in the jungle's depths.

Such was one current in early twentieth-century popular representation. At the same time, though, many of my grandparents' and parents' generation in Australia, New Zealand, Britain, and elsewhere learnt about the South Seas through presentations of slides or films at churches, in the lectures by missionaries on furlough, popular magazines, children's books, and missionary memoirs that presented detailed information of an ethnographic type, horror stories of pagan customs, heroic tales of missionary martyrdom, and accounts of the elevation of indigenous peoples once converted. The importance of these constructions of the other thus arises partly because they constituted not merely a private archive but a set of published images and texts which conveyed ideas about a place and a social process – namely the story of conversion – to a mass audience.

The mission examined here was established in the western Solomon Islands in 1902 by the Australian branch of the Methodist Church, which had inherited various south Pacific fields from the London-based Wesleyan Methodist Missionary Society.[16] On the islands of New Georgia, Vella Lavella, and Choiseul, the mission's opponents were not only initially recalcitrant heathen islanders; Catholics and Seventh Day Adventists also had interests in the region, the latter to such an extent that they were referred to as 'pests', 'freaks', and 'parasites' in private correspondence.[17] The Methodists' representations were thus not motivated exclusively by the projects of knowing the other and representing a certain relation of alterity but arose as well from the mission's competitive interest in justifying its specific programme and orientation.

The fact that much of the material[18] is visual compounds the question of the ambiguity of missionary discourse mentioned above.[19] Although strictly linguistic texts may be meaningfully slippery and ambiguous, they do tend to express moral constructions and attitudes in an accessible and explicit way; at least it often seems possible to contrast a certain specificity in the evaluation of the subject represented with the open and unclear character of much photography. A missionary portrait of a heathen Melanesian chief who had a reputation as a organizer of headhunting raids might be expected to be far less ambiguous than this (see Plate 13.2). The camera's relatively close position reveals the subject's individuality and slightly puzzled but confident and intelligent expression. The caption informs us that the man, Mia Bule, is not just any chief but the 'Chief of Munda, Solomon Islands'. The localization singularizes the character while the attribution of authority within the indigenous system reinforces the image of a reflective man of stature. The surrounding text makes no reference to activities epitomizing savagery, such as raiding, so viewers at the time of publication might have made a primarily positive evaluation of the man, even though his traditional style of dress could convey no suggestion that he was a Christian native.

Images of houses and structures associated with pre-Christian religion are often also open to a variety of attitudes. Their representation, as well as such items as shrines, thus seems to invite a relatively neutral curiosity of a quasi-ethnographic kind, rather than adjudication. Sometimes the associated text amplifies rather than diminishes the ambivalence of perception, if the caption is either non-existent or bland, such as 'A New Ireland House'. This is even more so when the photographs are disconnected from any narrative or report on mission activities in a specific area. The ritual site on the cover of the Australasian Methodist Missionary Society's *Review* (see Plate 13.3) might have been described elsewhere as 'a shrine for devil worship' or presented in a distinctly threatening manner, but the framing and typeface appear to aestheticize rather than distance the idol as an object of revulsion, thus resulting in a discontinuity between the images and those texts functioning literally or metaphorically as captions.

The master caption: the before and after story

One central feature of mission discourse, the narrative of conversion, contrasts former savagery with a subsequently elevated and purified Christian state. This is not just a matter of religious change but of wider social transformation. The characterization of indigenous society as barbaric thus depends on general social markers, such as the low status of women[20] and their treatment as beasts of burden, and on practices directly associated with heathen religion:

> All the filthy and degrading customs associated with idol-worship obtained. Sorcery and witchcraft flourished … None died a natural death; all sickness was attributed to witchcraft; and the most revolting and horrible cruelty was practised to extort confessions from the unfortunate women charged with the offence.[21]

Narratives concerning particular mission fields[22] tended to dramatize one or two key practices with which the state of savagery or heathenism was identified: cannibalism and widow-strangling in Fiji or *sati* (in India). In the western Solomons, headhunting was rendered emblematic, as it was in some official literature and in traveller's accounts; but the manner in which this form of violence related to the characterization of a savage race differed crucially between these genres. Although staged photographs of warfare or cannibalism among Pacific islanders are common (Plate 13.8), such practices are generally set at a temporal distance in missionary collections. The viewer is not supposed to be titillated by the actuality of these horrific practices but instead interested in the work to abolish them. The missionary representation thus entails temporal marking and tends to convey a narrative of barbarism as past rather than as an immediate and persisting condition, which is often signalled by the presence of indigenous weapons in photographs of persons who are obviously converted inhabitants of a Christian order. Clubs, hatchets, and shields – intricately made and thus open to being aestheticized – are rendered as curios or specimens of native craft. But their inclusion (as in Plates 13.1 and 13.13) is obviously not a matter of simple ornamentation. What stands out is that these things are no longer used: their context of use has been abolished. Such articles are now instead the picturesque products of ingenuity, and more significantly, the tokens of a former order.[23] Their inclusion in a picture condenses into a synchronic image a larger story of rebirth conveyed more fully in the film *The Transformed Isle.* The long opening sequence representing a head-hunting raid explicitly offers a fictional reconstruction of horrific events supposedly typical of the time before the missionary arrived.

In a contribution to a centennial review of Methodist work in the Pacific, John Francis Goldie, the head of the Solomons mission, drew predictably on the before and after story mentioned above. He alluded to the horrors of the past, and contrasted them with 'brighter, happier days', rhetorically asking, 'Was it worth while?'[24] However, he distinguished the former state of the Solomons from that of certain other Pacific natives:

> One navigator, who visited the group many years ago, avers that the natives of New Georgia 'were the most treacherous and bloodthirsty race in the Western Pacific' and that 'human flesh formed their chief article of diet'. This may have been true fifty years ago, but I much doubt the latter part of the statement. The people of the New Georgia group were cannibals, but not in the same sense as the Fijians, who loved human flesh as an article of diet. Those who have taken part in these cannibal

feasts tell me that in connexion with human sacrifices and great religious festivals human flesh was partaken of, but few liked it; to many it was so obnoxious it made them ill. The New Georgians were crafty and cruel; but they were also remarkably clever and intelligent.[25]

The last qualification makes it clear that the point of the passage is not ethnological discrimination but the separation of the subjects of conversion from the most extreme expression of barbarism. If savages are quintessentially and irreducibly savage, the project of converting them to Christianity and introducing civilization is both hopeless and worthless. The prospect of failure would be matched by the undeserving character of the barbarians, which is why mission discourse must at once emphasize savagery yet signal the essential humanity of the islanders to be evangelized. For writers such as Goldie, it was important to be able to differentiate one's own people from some other 'real savages' at a convenient geographic remove and to suggest ambiguity by qualifying the image of barbarism with depictions of other dimensions of indigenous life. Of course, the missionaries who worked in Fiji also had to qualify and distance a state of absolute savagery, which they did, not through reference to another group which could be said to be more barbaric still than the Fijian warriors but by complicating and partially undoing that stereotype. In a very successful publication from the earlier Methodist mission in Fiji, Thomas Williams placed considerable overt emphasis upon what he saw as the peculiarly contradictory nature of Fijians. A chapter in his book on the manners and customs of warfare described massacres, cannibalism, and horrific physical violence, but this was followed by material on agriculture and crafts emphasizing the natives' skill and industry. The inconsistency was not simply present, as in *The Transformed Isle*, but was marked as a point of depictive rupture:

> It is pleasing to turn from the horrible scenes of barbarous war, to the gentler and more profitable occupations of peace ... At this point there is observable one of the strange and almost anomalous blendings of opposite traits in the Fijian character. Side by side with the wildest savageism, we find among the natives of this group an attention to agriculture, and a variety of cultivated produce, not to be found among any other of the numerous islands of the western Pacific.[26]

This was followed by a forty-page appreciation of horticulture and a variety of native arts. What is important, then, is not the mixture of positive and negative elements in the portrayal of the other, which may be true of liberal or reflective accounts in any genre, but that this ambivalence is rhetorically central, a necessary predicate for the history of conversion. The film has a parallel interest in the production of various types of artefacts[27] among other aspects of the creativity and humanity of the Solomons people, who are seen engaged in ordinary work, playing, travelling in canoes, and fishing. This is the other side of the mode of constructing savagery on the basis of particular forms of barbaric practice: missionaries did not suggest that in some sense part of the racial constitution of the Vella Lavellan or the Fijian was essentially savage, a cannibal at heart. The humanity of Solomon

Islanders was in parts: some parts were condemned to the past, while others were drawn into creating a new Christian Islander.

Because the depiction of artefacts is part of a project to convey a rounded, though obviously selective, image of native life, objects are often represented in association with people, rather than as stable and symmetrical arrays in the manner of ethnologists or official publications. The point is not to display the weapons and implements of some bounded tribe or ethnic group, making a social geography visible for the state (as in Plate 13.13), but to prompt reactions of sympathy and empathy to coexist with those of horror and revulsion. Common human appreciation of artistry is clearest in the film, in which the maker of the tortoiseshell ornament holds it up for his own regard as well as that of the audience.

The story of children

A few photographs which include both white and black children (such as Plate 13.1) most directly express the natives' humanity. The remarkable 'Study in Black and White', published as a postcard, differentiates the white girl, shown fully clothed, with a hat, from her two native friends, who are only wearing loincloths. Because all three appear to be barefoot, holding hands, and in the same basic group, the photograph seems to convey that they are all on the same level and in some sense have the same potential. This impression is strengthened by the fact that the picture shows only three children of more or less the same age and size. A similar message emerges from some larger, differentiated groups; but because these contain hierarchical differences based on age, the suggestions of friendship, voluntary association, and equality, are submerged. It is, of course, difficult to see the picture in the way that a purchaser of the postcard in 1910 would have, but – to put the proposition negatively – nothing in the image implies that the boys are in any way unsuitable playmates for the girl or that there is anything disturbing in the conjunction. The conclusion that the photograph essentially equates the three children represented in human worth seems inescapable.

Children carry a specific burden in the before and after narrative which dominates the understanding of change in a particular mission field. Another sympathetic photograph (Plate 13.12) of a small boy appeared in the magazine (on a children's page) with the following text:

> This picture is a photograph of a little boy born in a heathen land – the Solomon Islands. Until ten years ago, no missionary had been to the part where this boy's home is, and the people there were dark and cruel and wicked. But to-day, hundreds of them know all about Jesus, and many of them love Him. This little boy is now in one of our Mission Schools, and he, with scores of other children, is being taught the way of truth and purity. But there are thousands upon thousands of children in the islands of the Pacific still in the heathen darkness. Their homes are full of evil, their lot is very sad, for they are surrounded by wicked people. We want *you* to help to make known to them the joys of the Christian faith.[28]

These stronger statements about native life before conversion have tensions and contradictions with the more positive side of native life shown, for instance, at length in the film *The Transformed Isle*. The above passage attempts to negotiate the disjunction between the imagining of native humanity and the evil nature of the past by focusing upon children, who seem to be naturally innocent: under heathenism they might live among the wicked, in 'homes full of evil', but it is not suggested that they are wicked themselves or even degraded. Rather 'their lot is very sad' because of surrounding circumstances. The projected child reader is invited to identify with these thousands of children who happen to inhabit the heathen darkness. The category of children is stretched beyond any particular culture, and the plight of those who (as it were contingently) live with 'wicked people' is stressed. If the social circumstances change, these children can grow up being no less Christian than any others.

In an important sense the before and after story is thus generationally staged, a theme expressed with considerable redundancy. It is emphasized at many points that every school student is 'the son of a head-hunter';[29] the image even provides the title for R. C. Nicholson's biography of Daniel Bula, a prominent native teacher, *The Son of a Savage*.[30] Older people (and particularly young adults) are frequently assimilated into the category of children growing out of heathenism because all are referred to as 'mission boys' or 'girls', irrespective of age. A Roviana preacher, Boaz Suga, who was probably in his twenties, is described as 'a Solomon Island boy … once a heathen … now a happy Christian lad'.[31] The odd conjuncture of the temporal structure and the negative imagery of savagery is encapsulated in lines quoted by Goldie in order to stress the need for a broad civilizing project: 'We are not dealing with people of the older civilizations of India and China, but "Your new-caught sullen peoples / Half devil and half child."'[32]

This tendency to regard indigenous people as infantile also, of course, contained a statement about the missionaries' relationship with them. This was clearly manifested in the various photographs in which the combination of the indigenous people and the missionaries or their wives (Plates 13.5–6) convey the hierarchy and order of a family group. In this context, the sharp contrast between this discourse and those which use sexual difference to understand racial difference is most apparent. Much of the other colonial discourse sees the difference between the civilized man and the savage as clear and irreducible as that between man and woman, grounding both kinds of physical difference in nature. If one takes on the attributes or environment of the other, if a process of conversion is initiated, the result can only be repugnant or dangerous, as in Kurtz's insanity or the threatening parody of the native who is a 'bad imitation' of a European.[33] The notion that types are essentially stable in their differences and that any admixture, hybridization, or conversion cannot lead to any good is also present in more benevolent discourses, manifested for instance in the notion that ill-health and depopulation arise partly from the natives' inability to make sensible or correct use of European clothes. In a highly instructive work entitled *The Essential Kafir*, Dudley Kidd notes that

13.1 'A study in black and white' (Crown Studios postcard, c. 1908)

13.2 Mia Bule, Chief of Munda, Solomon Islands, taken c. 1904–05 (from the *Australasian Methodist Missionary Review*, 4 August 1909)

13.3 Cover, *Missionary Review* (4 May 1903)

13.4 Decorated cover of Henry Stanley's *In Darkest Africa* (London, Sampson Low, 1890)

13.5 J. F. Goldie and some school boys (Crown Studios postcard, c. 1908)

13.6 Mrs Goldie and school girls (*Australasian Methodist Missionary Review*, 4 November 1907)

13.7 'Tahitian Beauty', from Frank Burnett's *Through Polynesia and Papua* (London, Francis Griffiths, 1911)

13.8 'The banquet', staged photograph by Thomas Andrew, c. 1894

13.9 'At work', mission plantation, Rubiana (Crown Studios postcard, c. 1908)

13.10 Road through mission plantation, Rubiana (Crown Studios postcard, c. 1908)

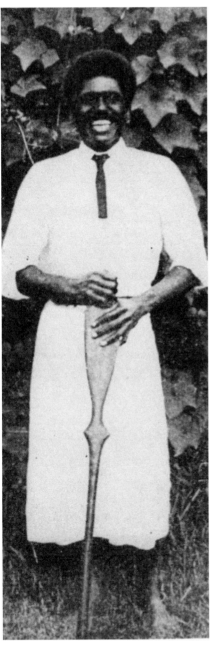

13.11 Boaz Suga, with canoe paddle (*Australasian Methodist Missionary Review*, 4 April 1912)

13.12 A mission boy, Soloman Islands (*Australasian Methodist Missionary Review*, 4 April 1912)

13.13 New Caledonians (Duffy Studios, Noumea)

An educated native will try to make himself white; but we should be able to prevent that calamity. After all, the feat is impossible. No man in his senses would suggest that we should give our daughters to black men; no one would wish to have them sitting at our tables as a regular thing; no one would care to take a native into partnership. It is a thousand pities that we cannot banish all European clothing from native territories, and allow the Kafirs to evolve naturally, and form a society of their own, just as the Malays have been doing in Cape Town. Such a plan would be better for both black and white.[34]

The discourse of racial types very frequently operated through gender imagery: Asiatics and particularly Hindoos were effete or effeminate; Polynesians were canonically women of the kind that Frank Burnett imagined, and Polynesian men were passive, idle, and languorous; Melanesians, on the other hand, were cannibal warriors with clubs and axes, men of the kind displayed with their artefacts in the fixed ensemble of the New Caledonians.[35] Their race and sex were both biologically fixed; the evangelical project of incorporation, on the other hand, was powerfully captured in the familial metaphor. Although merchants or the state might envisage passive and luxuriant countries which can be uncovered and acted upon or islands occupied by wild headhunters who must be pacified and emasculated, the mission postulates neither masculinity nor femininity but infancy, a protosocial condition from which Christian manhood and womanhood are imagined to emerge.

Shared metaphors and familial practice

The tropes of missionary propaganda may thus be contrasted sharply with the essentialist understanding of racial types that in the domain of policy was epitomized by the British codification of native custom notionally sustained as a separate domain through indirect rule and colour bar regulations. It follows that the missionary project is less distinct from the stereotypic French assimilationist approach, which Michael Crowder suggests combined 'a fundamental acceptance of [the Africans'] potential human equality [and] a total dismissal of African culture as of any value'.[36] Although the content of what Africans lacked, and hence what the civilizing mission supplied, was quite different in official assimilationist and missionary imaginations, the form of difference and presumptions about the history following from it are similar. The indigenous condition is postulated above all in the absence and lack of enlightenment, rather than through positive markers thought to be characteristic of a particular stage of social development. In practice, of course, both missionary and official colonial interventions had to take existing institutions and relations into account, and Christian or republican ethics of underlying human equality are likely always to have been placed in the background by hierarchizing practices or submerged by more specific ethnological discourses about the nature of particular societies and peoples. Although missionary propaganda is a distinct genre produced and circulated through visual media and publications that made a series of assumptions about their constituency, individual missionaries, especially from the mid-nineteenth century on, often wrote for geographical and anthropological audiences as well and were thus authors whose practical reactions and actions in the field reflected a diverse range of assumptions and influences.[37]

This brings into focus a necessary qualification and elaboration of the argument developed thus far. I have argued that infantilization is a crucial feature of missionary culture, but it is apparent that such constructions of indigenous peoples as children or as immature have great generality. To refer merely to the approximate contemporaries of the missionaries discussed here, Dudley Kidd observed that 'one would no more think of giving the native a vote on European matters than one would think of giving fourth-form boys at school a vote in the management of lessons'.[38] Neatly encompassing a series of unsocialized others, the administrator M. V. Portman said that he 'often likened [the Andamanese] to English country schoolboys of the labouring classes'.[39] Somewhat earlier, Stanley not only posed as an adult in relation to the black child (see Plate 13.4) but also appropriated the canonical Christian trope: in his titles, Africa was not only 'dark' but 'darkest', and the text at the bottom of the spine illustrated here reads, 'Let there be light.'[40] In evoking the half-infancy of the savage, Goldie was after all quoting not a theorist of missions but Kipling's famous poem, 'The White Man's Burden'.

The distinctiveness of evangelical colonialism arises not from the terms or metaphors of its propaganda, if these are taken in isolation, but from narratives in which these tropes have specific meanings and from practices which were inflected, at least, by the terms of missionary rhetoric. In one sense evangelical missions in both Africa and the Pacific apparently had entirely different objectives to Stanley's expedition, but it is also true more specifically that missionary work employed and enacted the notions of infantilization and quasi-familial hierarchy in a far more thorough way than any other colonial project. The construction of difference in terms of a familial relation was not a static condition but articulated with an attempt to implement social change on the colonial periphery in a particular way. In several sequences of the film, and in the literature in general, there is a great emphasis upon schooling and more generally upon the novel creation of a social order. It is as if these children are being brought up and socialized for the first time.

The mission, much more than 'a house in the bush', is a whole structure of institutions which reorganizes work and social life, creating order to some extent. The postcard images in Plates 13.9–10 reflect this. The postcard showing 'Road through Mission Plantation, Rubiana' constructs the image symmetrically (Plate 13.10), while the group photographs convey various kinds of domestic and institutional order, with a particular emphasis upon the islanders at work, such as the hard labour of clearing a new plantation and 'Discharging Timber for Mission House at Vella Lavella'. These images are linked with the doctrine of the industrial mission that seems to have become the dominant view of how missions should be run among the Australasian Methodists in the early twentieth century. (This approach had its antecedents in Moravian missions and earlier in the Nonconformist societies of the nineteenth century, including the Wesleyan Methodist Mission from which the Australasian Methodist Church inherited the Pacific circuits. Moffat and Livingstone, among others, had closely identified the civilizing process and the promotion of commerce.[41]) Goldie argued in a 1916 article that in other, unnamed missions, natives were allegedly Christians in name but lazy and dishonest in behaviour; therefore, a broad approach to morality, work, and commerce was called for.

> Is the Christianity we ask ['these savage islanders'] to accept merely a creed, and the nominal membership of a human society called the Church, or is it a new vision, new aspirations, and a new power to will and to do – in other words, a new life? ... all Missionary workers will agree that the real *objective* in Mission work is certainly not the successful running of a commercial undertaking, however profitable, or merely the turning out of carpenters and boat-builders, however skilful. The chief business of the Missionary is not to make boats and plantations but to make men – Christian men. Not to build houses, but to build character.[42]

Despite the androcentric language, it should be added that this programme definitely included women; and great emphasis was placed especially on sewing and garment making, which was directly linked to conversion because those who attended church necessarily did so attired in fabric skirts and blouses or sarongs, rather than in heathen dress.[43] These activities were moreover regularized: rather than being conducted individually or with friends at home in the interstices of a working day, mats and other such articles were prepared by groups working around the mission station during regular hours. *The Transformed Isle* presents the industrial mission in considerable detail. The segment is signalled by an explicit reference and the claim that 'a healthy vigorous young life is springing up because they are taught that there is no such thing as a lazy Christian';[44] we then see the roads, much as they appear in the postcards; a substantial wharf built by mission labour, and the activity of cutting copra (which had developed earlier in response to the demand of traders and remains one of the most important forms of petty commodity production in the Pacific).

The statements made through the film and photographs about this process of social growth and transformation do not relate merely to the before and after story, the story of the horrors of the past, and the happiness of the Christian present. They also make claims about the mission's role in the civilizing process. The mission, in fact, is identified as the sole author of positive social change in the islands, a point about which Goldie was quite explicit:

> They are making model villages and improving the conditions under which they live. They are learning how to utilize their idle lands, and are making plantations of food and coco-nuts. We began this work amongst a purely savage people in May 1902. No track had been blazed, and we were the pioneers. We have not laboured in vain.[45]

But so far as commercially oriented native industry is concerned, many groups in the western Solomons had extensive experience of casual trading with ships before 1850, and in the second half of the nineteenth century more systematic relationships with white resident traders developed, usually involving the pro- duction of copra and ivory nuts; barter of ordinary food for guns and various other articles; and the collecting of bêche-de-mer, pearlshell, and tortoiseshell. The plantations represented in the Methodist photographs *circa* 1910 were by no means the only ones then operated in the region.[46] More significantly, given its pro- minence in mission rhetoric, the notion that the mission put an end to headhunting is totally misleading: this in fact resulted entirely from the work of the government, which had virtually pacified all the tribes of what became the Western Province several years before the mission entered the area.

Although the government's activities are invisible in *The Transformed Isle*, white traders do appear and are represented exclusively as criminal exploiters of the natives. The film creates a sub-narrative around incidents supposedly typical of recruiting for the Pacific islander labour trade (mainly to Queensland canefields) and reflects a much wider controversy between those engaged in the trade and their liberal opponents, principally the missions and bodies such as the Anti-Slavery Society (whose correspondents in the islands were nearly all missionaries). The critics used the term blackbirding and insisted that recruiting usually amounted to nothing other than kidnapping. The film shows us gullible islanders being lured on to a vessel's deck by unattractive thuggish-looking traders proffering strings of trinkets and hatchets. Despite their ignorance the natives, wary and hesitant, are neverthe- less enticed on board and below decks. After a certain number have gone below, the treacherous Europeans smartly bolt the hatch and chase the others overboard, using rifle fire to drive away the substantial crowd borne in canoes: 'The brutal kidnappers weigh anchor and make for the open sea with their human freight.'[47] This scenario is rather out of place in the western Solomons, where the number of Melanesians who were ever indentured was miniscule. In any case it ignores the point that once the trade had been going on for a few years, returned labourers were telling stories at home; and indigenous men thus almost always understood what sort of work they would be engaging in on what terms and had various reasons for voluntarily participating. Cases of kidnapping certainly occurred but were not typical of a system that entailed thousands of recruits and lasted for decades.[48]

Although the larger inequalities of these relationships are quite inescapable, it is apparent that the missionary view seizes upon victimization by certain whites and ignores the active and collaborative character of the indigenous peoples' role in these exploitative relations. This is not surprising, given the construction of natives as children, but underspecifies the motivation of the image. The characterization of white traders in exclusively negative terms is curious, for in practice these missionaries got on moderately well with most other white residents, but this is simply the correlate of the mission's attempt to construct itself as the only civilizing agent in the heathen land. The missionaries' industry derives purely from their endeavours in a place that was savage to start with. It is implied that there are no other plantations than the industrial mission's but since it can hardly be pretended that there had been absolutely no other contact between Solomon Islanders and whites, this is represented as purely destructive.

Not only was the mission as an entity the key actor in a larger historical drama, but individual missionaries were presented not merely as adult parents who cared for and naturally supervised their native children but also as singularly transcendent and historically empowered figures in a different way. The head of the mission, John Frances Goldie, is seen in two intriguing pictures with a group of 'mission boys' in one case (Plate 13.5) and what is evidently a school class in another. Everyone looks directly into the camera – except him. Perhaps Goldie merely had a personal aversion to watching the photographer, but the results convey a kind of wider engagement with and wider vision of the world which is not limited to the immediate circumstances.[49] This implication is particularly strong in the picture of the school group, because we see a globe through the window directly behind and above the missionary.[50]

The social process of conversion and the development of a new Christian society in the native land is thus represented as a dyadic affair: the missionaries on one side show the light and provide guidance, while on the other the natives respond to the dawn and happily learn and work within the new order. The immediate reasons for this rather extravagant distortion of the actual situation are transparent. The mission had a constituency, so it needed to advertise its work, needed to raise funds, needed to convey satisfaction to those who had already made donations, and – not least – needed to engage in rivalry with other denominations, such as the Seventh Day Adventists. The emphasis on the industrial nature of the mission was significant in the context of inter-mission competition because it could be claimed, perhaps accurately, that certain denominations did little more than secure nominal adherence.

At the same time there is clearly more to the project than differentiation for the purposes of advertisement. It is quite crucial to the whole structure of this discourse that the mission was not simply a religious instrument but rather a total social fact. The mission created an entire social geography of stations and circuits, which in some cases reflected indigenous political divisions or trade routes but gave even these entirely new functions. It sought to impose a new temporal regime of work, leisure, celebration, and worship; and through education it offered a new global and local history marked by the life of Wesley, the foundation of the mission society, the opening of Pacific mission fields, major events of conversion, and the commemoration of martyrs. The mission produced not just a population of Christians but a people engaged in periodic plantation work who were notionally subject to rigorous behavioural codes and who had notionally brought their social and domestic habits into conformity with Christian norms. Within this effort, ideas of the location and transformation of familial life are projected in a number of ways which are not entirely consistent; in one context native existence may be deplorably non-familial; elsewhere indigenous families are shown to be imperfect but in the process of change; and in other cases, and particularly in the materials I have presented here, actual indigenous families seem almost dissolved within the mission station, which takes the form of a sort of macrofamilial institution. The white missionaries are parents to native boys and girls, who are instructed and brought up not in specifically religious or technical training but in the whole field of practical, recreational, and spiritual living. The notion that the mission thus encompassed indigenous life was clearly to some extent a fantasy, but it is true that in many instances boarding schools and orphanages were created which did in fact give missionaries an enormous amount of control over children;[51] and it is also the case that individual missionaries or missionary wives often formed close attachments with converts, especially privileged converts such as mission teachers, which the whites understood in familial terms.[52] Needless to say, the indigenous views of these friendships are usually not accessible; most of the available recollections bearing on the question were compiled or edited by missionaries and are thus constrained in a predictable manner.[53]

Incorporation and difference

In this case, the attitude in missionary rhetoric toward savage peoples conforms with Fabian's depiction of premodern alterity: the canonical other is not the primitive man or woman understood as an exemplar of a race that can be characterized in an essentialist manner but the heathen or pagan marked fundamentally by his or her lack of Christianity, a lack that can be remedied. The dominant movement of colonial history in this imagination is not the establishment of a fixed hierarchical relationship but a process of conversion that abstracts infants from the social milieux of savages and socializes them under the guidance of white missionaries.[54]

Though the case considered here has its own peculiarity, it permits certain general claims to be made about evangelical discourse. In the eighteenth as well as the nineteenth and twentieth centuries, missionary propaganda never displayed much interest in the project of differentiating and ranking various native populations – Hottentots and Kaffirs, Melanesians, and Polynesians – that so preoccupied ethnology and the secular discourses of evolutionism. Although the missionaries no doubt regarded Australian Aborigines and tribal peoples elsewhere as baser or more degraded than the heathens of Asiatic civilizations, the fundamental premise of the missionaries' efforts was an ethic of potential human equality in Christendom, which was particularly conspicuous in missions directing their efforts among slaves or other oppressed peoples. This is manifest for instance in a Moravian painting of 'The First Fruits' (by Johann Valentin Haidt, painted in 1747). The assembly of converts included a Persian, an Eskimo, a Hottentot, and various others, who were notionally named and baptized individuals, not exemplars of races.[55] Similarly and more immediately, the Methodists' interest in children was replicated in many publications of the same period from the Religious Tract Society and other bodies

dealing with India, Africa, east Asia and elsewhere. There are broad similarities in
ideas between all of these endeavours, but these are perhaps less significant than the
recurrent conflicts between colonizing projects. Just as the Methodists in the
Solomons were extraordinarily hostile to the white traders and labour recruiters,
the Boers saw the Moravians (in the late eighteenth century) and the London
Missionary Society (in the nineteenth) as entirely subversive forces that aimed to
transform the native world in a revolutionary manner that would deprive them of
their labour force:

> the Boers firmly believed that the LMS harbored the 'Utopian idea of laying the
> foundation, under their own special priestly guidance, of a model kingdom of
> regenerated natives'. Not Moffat nor Philip nor Livingstone, for all the clarity with
> which they envisaged an Eden of the Spirit, could have better phrased the charter
> for their civilizing colonialism.[56]

The point is not that there was some intrinsic missionary hostility toward slave
ownership or colonial servitude: the Moravians' attitude in the West Indies was
somewhat equivocal, and Moravian settlers in North Carolina were in fact slave
owners. If one is seeking an elementary structure of colonial discourse, it is not to
be found at the level of a particular idea or metaphor but rather in the contradictory
character of the colonial objectives of distancing, hierarchizing, and incorporating:
It is problematic to assimilate the other through the disavowal of hierarchy while
implicitly sustaining the inequality that all colonialism presupposes. Hierarchizing
and assimilating colonialisms are, on the surface, radically opposed; and this contradiction emerges practically in the struggles between missionaries and those whose
models of colonization presuppose essential difference and fixed relations of
dominance. But these models also each have internal contradictions, partly arising
from the fact that each operation presupposes something of the other. The analysis
here has not explored the full range of problems but does suggest that the
missionaries had to confront a contradiction between the desirability of postulating
human equality in certain contexts and their will to control the process of
conversion and the localized theocracies that were occasionally effectively established. By imagining that others were part of a family, the mission was able to
reconcile common humanity and hierarchy in a manner that was as natural and
intelligible in the short term as it was insecure in the long term: after all, children
grow up. That is also why this metaphor was part of the common ground of
colonial discourse yet also a resource to be valorized in a specific way in evangelical
propaganda.

Although this inclusiveness and ambiguous egalitarianism might be attributed
to missionary discourse in general, some features of the Methodist representation,
such as the preoccupation with industry, are obviously not characteristic of all
evangelical bodies or all periods. Some missions, such as Seventh Day Adventists,
made health and medical work central and presented the missionary as the healer of
diseased and degraded native bodies.[57] In other cases, as in the early nineteenth-

century London Missionary Society accounts of Polynesia and India, idolatry was the hallmark of heathenism, and the destruction of idols conveniently marked conversion. The implications of these figures of difference and forms of change were clearly different but shared a key feature with the case discussed: savagery was a contingent state of heathenism, illness, or adherence to false doctrine, not an immutable character of a distinct kind of human being. The content and emphases of particular forms of missionary propaganda are thus variable; more important, the Methodist mission in the Solomons was peculiarly situated in relation to other forms of colonialism. Though the islands had been made a British protectorate, administrative intervention was very limited; the combination of indigenous disinclination to engage in migrant labour and the fact that white settlement and expropriation were very limited made the mission a consequential player with much greater scope for implementing its projects than was possible in most other colonized areas, in which capitalists and the colonial state had a much higher profile. In comparison with the experience in Asia, where evangelists were mostly ineffective and marginal, missionaries gained acquiescence and compliance from the people; in Africa, conversion of course took place on a large scale on much of that continent, but missionaries there also had to confront and contest settler states and huge proletarianizing forces, such as the South African mines. From the perspective of these global patterns, the case of the Solomons seems marginal and idiosyncratic, but this very peculiarity enabled the mission to express itself more comprehensively – to understand the 'transformed isle' as the outcome of its own work – even if the missionaries themselves inevitably overestimated the real effect of the missionary project.

It seems important, in conclusion, to briefly consider a range of questions that seem to be entirely separate but ought not to be excluded or silenced. This analysis has confined itself to the frame of European discourse and has attempted to delineate what is specific about one kind of colonial representation. I have argued that the distinctiveness of missionary discourse corresponded with something distinct about interventionist missionary practice but have not attempted a broader analysis of the workings of missionary influence or the dynamics of indigenous response, accommodation, and resistance. It is obviously not always possible to present both sides of colonial history, and it is surely important to imagine not two but a plurality of hegemonic and counterhegemonic perspectives among colonizers and colonized; it would also seem important to recover the views of, say, Solomon Islanders at the time of missionary intrusion, rather than to take modern oral history to speak for the pagans whose Christian descendants, like the succession of hostile and benevolent Europeans, now regard their ancestors as the other. The partial perspective of this sort of discussion must avoid recapitulating one central assumption of the discourses that it criticizes: that indigenous and colonized peoples are primarily passive recipients of Western impositions, rather than agents empowered to represent things in different terms and in some cases turn them to their own purposes. Hence, what I have analysed does not specify what Christianity was or became for Solomon Islanders; it does not specify that what was given was the same as what was received; and although Goldie does seem to have been understood paternalistically as a big man by his Roviana boys,[58] the hierarchical relations that the mission imagined were not necessarily those that the western Solomons people were prepared to collaborate with. More significant, Methodism, and to a varying extent other forms of Pacific Christianity, has now been appropriated by Pacific Islanders and in Fiji is interwoven with the chiefly hierarchy and traditionalist nationalism.[59] In the western Solomons, a substantial section of the Methodist population on New Georgia was captured in the early 1960s by the Christian Fellowship Church, an independent local charismatic sect led by the 'Holy Father', a man who claimed to be Goldie's true successor.

Although these developments cannot be explored here, the discourse that I have described was imposed by the Europeans upon themselves. It was contingently related and practically mediated as a real imposition upon Solomon Islanders, and even when the restructuring of indigenous sociality was most effectively conducted, it never encompassed indigenous consciousness or indigenous understandings of colonial change. Hence, these representations did not dictate the terms of Pacific Islanders' resistance, even though they later supplied them with resources that aided various kinds of accommodation and struggle.

Although this is thus a partial and incomplete analysis, I would affirm the importance and value of studies which restrict themselves to the European side of colonial culture; after all, the varieties of colonial discourse which are present in popular culture and scholarship and which continue to condition our ways of thinking owe a good deal to their religious and secular antecedents. Do we not persist in seeing other societies primarily in terms of what they lack – that they are less developed? And are not the conversions of newly industrialized countries marked by a certain hesitancy and fallibility that demand nurture and guidance? Does not research on practical and applied development often embody a kind of assimilationism, seeking to give peripheral economies, if not pagan souls, the same cast as our own? I am not suggesting that an echo of conformity with the enduring structures of imperialism makes anthropological or economic consultants into insincere conspirators who seek ultimately to subordinate rather than elevate those whose future they can influence; but I have also never doubted that John Francis Goldie was, in his own way, a good and sincere man.

Notes

From *Comparative Studies in Society and History* 34 (1992), 366–95. I thank the staff of the Mitchell Library for their assistance, and the State Library of New South Wales for permission to reproduce the photographs, which, with the exceptions of Plates 13.4 and 13.7, are from the pictorial collections of the Mitchell Library. The Australian Religious Films Society kindly provided me with a videotape of *The Transformed Isle*. Earlier versions of this chapter were presented at seminars at the Humanities Research Centre and the Department of Anthropology at the Australian National University, and the Tisch School of the Arts at New York University.

For discussion of this material and related matters, I thank Harriet Guest, Chris Pinney, Rosemary Wiss, Ranajit Guha, David MacDougall, Jeremy Beckett, and especially Margaret Jolly; without her encouragement, and the example of her own work on missions and colonialism, the chapter would not have been written.

1 Johannes Fabian, *Time and the Other: How Anthropology Makes its Object* (New York: Columbia University Press, 1983), 26. See also Bernard McGrane, *Beyond Anthropology: Society and the Other* (New York: Columbia University Press, 1989), 68 f.

2 *The Milner Papers: South Africa 1899–1905*, ed. Cecil Headlam (London: Cassell, 1933), II, 467.

3 For more extensive discussion, see my *Colonialism's Culture* (Cambridge: Polity Press, forthcoming), ch. 4.

4 See particularly Bernard Smith, *European Vision and the South Pacific*, second edition (New Haven CT: Yale University Press, 1985).

5 See John L. Comaroff, 'Images of Empire, Contests of Conscience; Models of Colonial Domination in South Africa', *American Ethnologist*, 16:4 (1989), 661–85, especially 662; Ann L. Stoler, 'Rethinking Colonial Categories: European Communities and the Boundaries of Rule', *Comparative Studies in Society and History*, 31:1 (1989), 134–61, especially 135–6; see also Jean and John Comaroff, 'Through the Looking-glass: Colonial Encounters of the First Kind', *Journal of Historical Sociology*, 1:1 (1988), 6–32; Frederick Cooper and Ann L. Stoler, 'Tensions of Empire: Colonial Control and Visions of Rule', *American Ethnologist*, 16:4 (1989), 609–21; Nicholas Thomas, 'Colonialism as Culture', *Age Monthly Review*, 9:9 (1989/ 90), 30–2, and *Entangled Objects: Exchange, Material Culture and Colonialism in the Pacific* (Cambridge MA: Harvard University Press, 1991), ch. 4, which examines the divergent projects of various explorers, traders, missionaries and officials through the prism of their interest in collecting indigenous artefacts.

6 Cf. Homi K. Bhabha, 'The Other Question: Difference, Discrimination and the Discourse of Colonialism', in *Literature, Politics and Theory*, ed. Francis Barker, Peter Hulme, Margaret Iversen, and Diana Loxley (London: Methuen, 1986), 152.

7 *Ibid.* Here I do not dispute the value of Fabian's general claim for the critique of anthropology in which he engages. The lucid character of its formulation makes it a helpful departure point for the present analysis.

8 For a clear statement of the familiar contrast between British and French approaches, see Michael Crowder, *Senegal: A Study of French Assimilation Policy*, revised edition (London: Methuen, 1967), especially 1–8.

9 This is the theme of a separate work of Fabian's, 'Religious and Secular Colonization: Common Ground', *History and Anthropology*, 4:2 (1990), 339–55.

10 The general topics of Christianity and gender in the Pacific are explored in a number of books, including Margaret Jolly and Martha Macintyre, eds, *Family and Gender in the Pacific: Domestic Contradictions and the Colonial Impact* (Cambridge: Cambridge University Press, 1989); the culture and social origins of the nineteenth-century Protestant missions are discussed by Niel Gunson in *Messengers of Grace* (Melbourne: Oxford University Press, 1978), but there is no comparable overview for the period after 1860.

11 From *Through Polynesia and Papua: Wanderings* with *a Camera in the South Seas* (London: Francis Griffiths, 1911), facing p. 17. Although Burnett claimed to have taken most of the photographs in the book, it is likely that some of those of Tahitians, including that reproduced here, were taken by a professional studio photographer, which partly explains their conformity with standard poses.

12 Raymond Corbey, 'Alterity: The Colonial Nude', *Critique of Anthropology*, 8:3 (1988), 81.

13 On the origin and development of these ideas, see N. Thomas, 'The Force of Ethnology: Origins and Significance of the Melanesia/Polynesia Division', *Current Anthropology*, 30:1 (1989), 27–41, 211–13; for a detailed examination of the early reactions to a particular Melanesian population, see Margaret Jolly, '"Ill-natured Comparisons": European Perceptions of ni-Vanuatu from Cook's Second Voyage', *History and Anthropology* (forthcoming).

14 Frank Hurley, *Pearls and Savages* (New York: Putnam, 1923), 379.

15 *Ibid.*, caption to plate facing p. 352.

16 The WMMS was established in 1813 and was active in India and South Africa, among other places. Its South Pacific missions were taken over by the Australian Wesleyan Methodist Missionary Society in 1855 (Gunson, *Messengers of Grace*, 17).

17 J. F. Goldie, head of the Solomons mission, to J. G. Wheen, general secretary of the Australasian Methodist Missionary Society, 2 January, 18 July 1920, Methodist Overseas Mission collection, Mitchell Library, Sydney, box 554.

18 The photographs were mostly taken between 1907 and 1909; others during the First World War. Photographs from the western Solomons, along with many pictures of other Pacific islanders (and their houses and artefacts) appeared in the *Australasian Methodist Missionary Review* (hereafter, *AMMR* – also simply called the *Missionary Review* at certain times), sometimes in conjunction with reports from the mission field (as it was in the agricultural-cum-military metaphor), but often out of context (a New Ireland or Solomons picture might appear in the middle of an article about India). The forty-minute film, *The Transformed Isle*, was made under the direction of R. C. Nicholson, the missionary based on Vella Lavella from 1907 (also the author of *The Son of a Savage*, London: Epworth Press, 1924, the only book which emerged from the Solomons mission in this early period). Some of the footage was evidently shot during that year, but, curiously, the film does not seem to have been put together in its final version until 1917 or 1918. An earlier version of this chapter included more extended discussion of the film, but I have since located a number of other early missionary films from the Pacific.

19 This is clearly not the place to review photographic theory but it will be apparent that I agree with John Tagg that '*every* photograph is the result of specific and, in every sense, significant distortions which render its relation to any prior reality deeply problematic' (*The Burden of Representation*, London: Macmillan, 1988, 2) and cannot entertain the assertion of realism put forward by Roland Barthes in *Camera Lucida* (London: Cape, 1982). I also accept that the ambiguity of photographs and the multiplicity of possible readings make claims about what photographs convey or express problematic, but the readings here depend more upon contrasts between types of colonial photographs than an implicit claim that my responses to images are the same as those of the consumers of missionary propaganda. In so far as propositions of the latter type are unavoidable, the interpretations arise from readings in the discourses of the period.

20 Cf. Nicholas Thomas, 'Complementarity and History: Misrecognizing Gender in the Pacific', *Oceania.* 57:4 (1987), 261–70.

21 John Francis Goldie, 'The Solomon Islands', in *A Century in the Pacific*, ed. James Colwell (Sydney: Methodist Book Room, 1915), 563. It is interesting that witches in the mission accounts are always female, as other reports from the area make it clear that they could be of either sex.

22 Both the agricultural and military connotations were often elaborated upon. The symbolic importance of the latter is especially explicit in a much earlier text, John Williams's *Missionary Enterprises in the South Sea Islands* (London: John Snow, 1838).

23 See *AMMR*, 4 April 1912, for another example. The point is explicit in the caption to a later photograph in a Seventh Day Adventist periodical of a western Solomons man 'holding in one hand the Bible, and in the other some relics of heathen worship and customs' (*Australasian Record*, 1 October 1956) and a vignette of a 'Group of rejected war weapons' at the end of a nineteenth-century memoir (William Gill, *Gems from the Coral Lands; or, Incidents of Contrast between Savage and Christian Life in the South Sea Island*, London: Yates & Alexander, n.d. [*c.* 1875], 344). Pictures of abandoned sites of heathen worship obviously have a similar function (as in Plate 13.3).

24 Goldie, 'The Solomon Islands', 573, 574.

25 *Ibid.*, 563.

26 Thomas Williams, *Fiji and the Fijians* (London: Alexander Heylin, 1858),1, 60.

27 The extremely intricate tortoiseshell breast and forehead ornaments are upheld as 'marvels of patience and design' (*The Transformed Isle*, 28:35).

28 *AMMR*, 4 April 1912.

29 Goldie, 'The Solomon Islands', 573.

30 London, 1924. The central structure of this narrative form may be further illustrated from Goldie's overview of the mission's history. He began with a conversation between himself and a notorious old warrior chief, Gumi, who 'became one of [his] earliest friends' ('The Solomon Islands', 562). As befits the then-and-now structure, they talked about a headhunting raid ('Some of them … jumped into the water … But we took 200 heads back to Roviana!'). One of the perpetrators is thus now a reflective old man, a domesticated heathen, but the story is completed by Goldie drawing us into the present: 'It is nearly ten years since the old chief told me this story. As I pen these words his son is sitting at my elbow typing the translation of Mark's Gospel. Leaning over his shoulder, I read in his own language, "All things are possible to him that believeth"' (*ibid.*, 563).

31 *AMMR*, 4 April 1912.

32 Goldie, 'Industrial Training in our Pacific Missions', *AMMR*, 4 July 1916, 2, quoting Kipling, 'The White Man's Burden' (see *Rudyard Kipling's Verse – Definitive Edition*, London: Hodder & Stoughton, 1940 and reprints, 323–4).

33 Cf. N. Thomas, 'Sanitation and Seeing: The Creation of State Power in Early Colonial Fiji', *Comparative Studies in Society and History*, 32:1 (1990), 156.

34 Dudley Kidd, *The Essential Kafir* (London: Adam & Charles Black, 1904), 406.

35 On late eighteenth-century representations of Indians and Polynesians, see Harriet Guest, 'The Great Distinction: Figures of the Exotic in the Work of William Hodges', *Oxford Art Journal*, 12:2 (1989), 36–58; for the development of views of Melanesians, Margaret Jolly's '"Ill-natured Comparisons"'.

36 Crowder, *Senegal*, 2.

37 It is clear for instance that much of Livingstone's writing needs to be interpreted within the framework of exploratory rather than missionary literature: *Missionary Travels and Researches in South Africa* was in fact dedicated to Murchison, then president of the Royal Geographical Society. Although observations characteristic of missionary writings are certainly not absent, these are less conspicuous than objectivist descriptions of places visited, notes on natural phenomena, and disquisition on topics, such as the divisions of southern African tribes (David Livingstone, *Missionary Travels and Researches in Southern Africa*, London: John Murray, 1857, 201–2). The fact that the book was published by Murray, rather than one of the usual presses associated with the London Missionary Society, such as John Snow, or the Religious Tract Society, is telling in itself, but the book's main orientation is also reflected in the frontispiece depicting Livingstone's discovery of Victoria Falls; frontispieces of other mission works were often portraits of prominent converts (see, for example, T. Williams, *Fiji and the Fijians* (London: Heylin, 1858); J. Williams, *A Narrative of Missionary Enterprises in the South Sea Islands* (London: Snow, 1837); and William Ellis, *A History of Madagascar* [London: Fisher, *c.* 1838]).

38 Kidd, *The Essential Kafir*, 407.

39 M. V. Portman, *A History of our Relations with the Andamanese* (Calcutta: Government Printer, 1899), I, 33.

40 Henry M. Stanley, *In Darkest Africa, or, The Quest, Rescue and Retreat of Emin, Governor of Equatoria* (London: Sampson Low, 1890). The actual text is a blow-by-blow narrative of the military venture that contains relatively little extended observation upon indigenous life (but see vol. II, 354 ff).

41 Livingstone, *Missionary Travels and Researches*, 28: 'The laws which still prevent free commercial intercourse among the civilized nations seem to be nothing else but the remains of our own heathenism. My observations on this subject make me extremely desirous to promote the preparation of the raw materials of European manufactures in Africa, for by that means we may not only put a stop to the slave-trade, but introduce the negro family into the body corporate of nations, no one member of which can suffer without the others suffering with it … neither civilization nor Christianity can be promoted alone. In fact, they are inseparable.' For further discussion of Livingstone and Robert Moffat, see Jean and John

Comaroff, *Of Revelation and Revolution* (Chicago IL: University of Chicago Press, 1991).

42 Goldie, 'Industrial Training in our Pacific Missions', 2–3.

43 For parallels with the Presbyterian mission in southern Vanuatu (then the New Hebrides), see Margaret Jolly, '"To save the Girls for Brighter and Better Lives": Presbyterian Missionaries and Women in the South of Vanuatu, 1848–1870', *Journal of Pacific History*, 26 (1941), 127–48. As is shown in the film (35:20–36:14), there were also classes given in mat weaving by the wives of teachers – in this case a Tongan woman. The importance of dress was such that in Fiji the idiom in oral tradition for adopting Christianity is 'taking the *sulu*' (a sarong-style piece of fabric worn around the waist by men and to cover the breasts by women). In a number of these cases it was the local people rather than the missionaries who made the abandonment of local for introduced clothing a necessary element and marker of conversion.

44 *The Transformed Isle*, 82:38.

45 Goldie, 'The Solomon Islands', 584.

46 Judith A. Bennett, *Wealth of the Solomons: A History of a Pacific Archipelago* (Honolulu: University of Hawaii Press, 1987), chs 2–4, *passim*.

47 *The Transformed Isle*, 14:04–16:30. A second sequence (16:30–19:25) relates a parallel story. In this case the whites land and attempt to entice young women with similar trinkets. 'Intuition caused their victims to remain aloof' (17:29), but a trader seizes his chance, grabs one of the women by the arm, and drags her into one of two waiting boats. They row rapidly out into the bay, shooting numerous warriors who pursue them into the surf. This elaboration of the kidnapping theme thus emphasizes the base sexuality and immorality of these other white men. The mission's construction stipulates that sexual relationships between foreign men and islander women took the general form of kidnapping and rape. It can be argued instead that women may have actively wished to engage either in casual sexual contact with whites or form longer-term relations with them. Comparatively stable relations with native wives do not figure in the mission depiction but were by no means uncommon (Bennett, *Wealth of the Solomons*, 69–72, 179–81). In so far as women entered into such liaisons and *de facto* marriages voluntarily, their diverse motives must usually have included an interest in acquiring foreign manufactured articles. Although the absence of evidence for women's perspectives obviously constrains any understanding of these early twentieth-century relations, there is thus evidence that their involvement had a basis other than mere coercion.

48 This issue has been debated extensively in Pacific history. See, for a general discussion, Clive Moore, *Kanaka: a History of Melanesian Mackay* (Port Moresby: Institute for Papua New Guinea Studies/University of Papua New Guinea Press, 1985), and Margaret Jolly, 'The Forgotten Women: A History of Male Migrant Labour and Gender Relations in Vanuatu', *Oceania*, 58:2 (1987), 119–39.

49 There are parallels in nineteenth-century photography in the contrast between the bourgeois subject of a *carte de visite* portrait, who reflectively looks away from the camera but not toward an object which can be seen and whose vision is hence not contained by the image or act of photography, and on the other hand the official photos of those such as criminals, who appear either in profile or looking directly at the camera (or both). In the latter case the subordination of the individual to the state, in the person of the police photographer, is manifest (cf. Tagg, *The Burden of Representation*, 35–6 and ch. 3).

50 The same notion that the missionary mediates and introduces a broader world to the innocent and childlike islanders is expressed in a more realistic and comic manner in *The Transformed Isle* (21:20–2:14). Shortly after the Missionary (Nicholson) arrives on Vella Lavella, his native cook boy puts an array of bottles and jars on his eating table, mistaking such things as Vaseline and kerosene for food. Through sign language the inedible/undrinkable nature of the substances is demonstrated. The humour turns upon native ignorance but establishes at the same time Nicholson's knowledge of a broader world and its products, and the narrative is constitutive in the sense that this difference is one of the key elements of the social relationship between the missionary and his flock.

51 The practical workings of the project to 'rescue children' or 'gain control of the means of

social reproduction' are discussed by Michael Young, in 'Suffer the Children: Wesleyans in the D'Entrecasteaux', in *Family and Gender in the Pacific*, ed. Margaret Jolly and Martha Macintyre, 108–34.

52 Cf. Margaret Jolly, 'To save the Girls for Brighter and Better Lives'.

53 See for instance, George G. Carter, *Tie Varane: Stories about People of Courage from the Solomon Islands* (Rabaul/Auckland: Unichurch Publishing, 1981), which includes interesting if constrained life histories of a number of local teachers.

54 This is strictly an observation about the way in which difference was envisaged; I do not, of course, suggest any historical continuity with medieval or Renaissance colonial practice. Sharp contrasts might be drawn between the functioning of Spanish colonization in the New World, in which force and coercion were continuously conspicuous, and nineteenth- and twentieth-century colonial regimes which depended upon far more elaborate regimes of education, welfare, and persuasion (compare, for example, Nathan Wachtel, *The Vision of the Vanquished*, Hassocks: Harvester Press, 1977, with Timothy Mitchell, *Colonising Egypt*, Cambridge: Cambridge University Press, 1988). The distinct character of nineteenth-century Protestant missionary activity is itself an index of this change that seeks a kind of wilful inner rebirth on the part of the colonized individual and the colonized nation, a relation of hegemony and compliance rather than brute dominance. The transformation is perhaps analogous to the shift from punishment to discipline postulated by Foucault, but no simple characterizations could be made of national variants of colonial practice over the epochs. Despite the broad differences, early forms of colonialism obviously entailed programmes of socialization and relations of collaboration, while violence has hardly been absent from modern imperialism.

55 Hugh Honour, *Slaves and Liberators*, vol. 4, pt I, of *The Image of the Black in Western Art* (Houston TX: Menil Foundation/Cambridge MA: Harvard University Press, 1989), plate 21 and pp. 59–60.

56 John Comaroff. 'Images of Empire', 678, quoting George W. Stow, *The Native Races of South Africa* (London: Swan Sonnenschein, 1905), 268. On the Moravians and Boers, see for instance John Barrow, *Travels in the Interior of Africa by Mungo Park, and in Southern Africa by John Barrow* (Glasgow: A. Napier, 1815), 452–5.

57 See for instance the Seventh Day Adventist magazine, *Appeal for Missions* (copies from 1926–30 are held in the Australian National Library, Canberra); the covers of most issues show a white missionary doctor attending to injured or afflicted Melanesians. Such attention is also conspicuous in the film *Cannibals and Christians of the South Seas* (*c.* 1929), which deals with the work of Seventh Day Adventists in Papua (in the National Film and Sound Archive, Canberra ACT).

58 Frances Harwood. 'Intercultural Communication in the Western Solomons: The Methodist Mission and the Emergence of the Christian Fellowship Church', in James A. Boutilier, Daniel T. Hughes, and Sharon W. Tiffany, eds, *Mission, Church, and Sect in Oceania* (Lanham MD: University Press of America, 1978). 241; this article provides an overview of the CFC's breakaway.

59 Martha Kaplan, 'Christianity, People of the Land, and Chiefs in Fiji', in John Barker, ed., *The Ethnography of Christianity in the Pacific* (Lanham MD: University Press of America, 1990).

14

'Cocky' Hahn and the 'Black Venus': the making of a Native Commissioner in South West Africa, 1915–46

PATRICIA HAYES

This study draws upon research into processes of state construction in the mandated territory of South West Africa (present-day Namibia) from 1915. Unlike central and southern South West Africa (SWA), the so-called Police Zone which had been affected by German colonial efforts to dominate and dispossess since 1884, the northern areas of the territory faced colonization for the first time. The most populous region which straddled the northern SWA border with Angola was called Ovamboland, 'Ovambo' being the generic name given to a cluster of kingdoms and polities located in this floodplain area (see Map 14.1). Germany had not attempted to occupy this region, for the eastern kingdoms of Ondonga and Oukwanyama were well armed and powerful. But during the First World War the Union of South Africa had defeated Germany in SWA, and South Africa proceeded to send officials to occupy Ovamboland. At the same time, a Portuguese army effected military control over the northern Ovambo area located in Angola. Thus, in Ovamboland, the year 1915 represented a radical break with the autonomy of the past.[1]

The new political and structural features in Ovamboland – colonial occupation, the demarcation of a boundary between Angola and SWA, and the development of a system of colonial overrule – raise questions about the mapping and remapping of power between the colonizers and the African societies undergoing colonization. This study will be confined to those areas of Ovamboland which came under the control of South Africa, an unusual colonial power since it had achieved a degree of autonomy from Britain with the Act of Union in 1910 but was still a semi-colony.

Recent scholarship has argued that these processes of state construction in Namibia were profoundly gendered, involving 'alliances' between colonial officials and African men to prevent the mobility of women and to ensure the labour migration of younger men.[2] This chapter shifts the focus to explore how gendered meanings were constructed through colonial violence, administration and ethno-

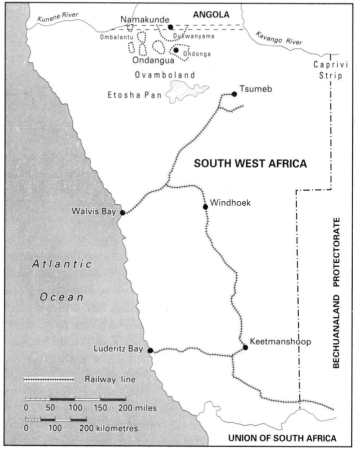

Figure 14.1 South West Africa (Namibia), 1915–17

graphy. How, for example, was the promotion of male labour migration and the fixing of women in a subsistence rurality linked to the physical force employed to displace centralized royal power in Ovambo polities? How was 'indirect rule' established under colonialism, and what were its gender politics? How do these processes connect with colonial representations of the Ovambo, their stereotyping and objectification as 'Ovambo' men and women, and how do Ovambo self-representations and historical (re)constructions differ from colonial ones? These questions arise from the convergence of two different worlds: Ovamboland, pre-modern though deeply affected by merchant capitalism; and South Africa, an expanding sub-imperial power with modernizing pretensions. What sorts of gendered politics and relations emerged on this new colonial frontier?

Central to all these questions is the figure of the Native Commissioner of Ovamboland, who served for three decades in a region encompassing roughly half of the population of SWA: Carl Hugo Linsingen Hahn, dubbed 'Cocky' Hahn by whites but known universally to the Ovambo as 'Shongola' (the whip). Hahn played a crucial, mediating role in constructing the colonial state in Ovamboland and in constructing 'the Ovambo' for consumption by officials and wider audiences. Hahn wrote ethnographic texts on 'the Ovambo', and for thirty-two years he authored the administrative reports on Ovamboland from which present-day historians, anthropologists and researchers of customary law must garner *their* knowledge. Given SWA's unusual circumstances as a mandated territory, with South Africa accountable first to the League of Nations and later (briefly) to the United Nations, the roles assumed by Hahn take on very important dimensions.

Collecting and compiling a coherent body of knowledge on the Ovambo was integral to South African efforts to construct a colonial state in northern Namibia. Hahn's was the most authoritative voice in these intellectual and administrative initiatives. This study will show the highly ambivalent means by which Hahn's voice became that of the expert and explore its powerful legacy. This expanding voice incorporated selective Ovambo viewpoints that were in fact extremely conservative and increasingly contested during his career and long afterwards, culminating in militant rejections of Hahn's version of history by many *oshiWambo*-speakers in the liberation struggle some decades later.

This chapter focuses on a moment when the ambivalence lying at the heart of Hahn's project was briefly laid bare and then subsequently smoothed over. The Native Commissioner's name was raised in a set of legal investigations in the 1920s, which took the form of an Official Complaints Enquiry prompted by the allegations of a junior officer based in Ovamboland. Here we find evidence that Hahn used violence in his dealings with the Ovambo at the same time as he gathered information about them, and that he did not confine these power dynamics to his interactions with men but extended them to women as well.

In effect, this study focuses on the *préterrain* of Hahn's ethnographic production. The *préterrain* has been described as 'the local milieu from which the ethnographer departs'.[3] Hahn was the type of non-academic ethnographer who embarked upon practical 'administrative anthropology' which often fed the academic but which more immediately serviced and shaped colonial administration.[4] Conceptually, it is helpful here to draw on the expanded and more politicized definition of the term *préterrain* developed by Pels.[5] Here the emphasis is on breaking down the process through which ethnographic writing emerges as a product. Pels points to the stages by which the ethnographer becomes immersed, first in local *milieux*, and then in the politics of the 'ethnographic occasion' in which material is garnered, both of which are profoundly revealing but which are glossed over as the final product is written up, usually removed in space and time from the site of research. In Pels's definition, the *préterrain* refers to the power relationships in which the ethnographer is caught up, which include both indigenous relationships and those brought in by the colonizers.[6] I should like to tease this out still further, to emphasize firstly that we are dealing with a gendered Ovambo *préterrain* and secondly that violence was an intimate part of the landscape in which the ethnographer Hahn was moving, just as it was an intimate part of his own past. It is to the formation of Cocky Hahn, South African official in Namibia, that we now turn.

Hahn came from a family with a long and prominent association with SWA. His grandfather was Hugo Hahn, amongst the first Rhenish missionaries from Germany to enter the territory in 1842 and the first Protestant missionary to visit Ovamboland. The family had gravitated towards the Cape, where Hahn's father served as the Lutheran minister in Paarl. Hahn's maternal grandfather, Baron von Linsingen, had died in dramatic and romantic circumstances in one of the Eastern Cape frontier wars.[7]

Hahn was born in 1886 and raised in the Cape, where he attended Paarl Boys' High School. The school in Paarl took pride in imparting 'discipline of body and mind', and later claimed to have always given absolute equality to English- and Dutch- (later Afrikaans-) speaking students.[8] Physicality was an integral feature of Paarl Boys' High; indeed, this was a spiritual home of both sport and flogging.[9] Such influences suggest a great deal about 'becoming a man' at that time.[10] This ethos had some similarities with the 'Muscular Christianity' that emerged in English public schools from the 1830s, which was designed to inculcate a sense of 'discipline, service and authority'[11] and included paternalistic overtones of male responsibility towards the 'weaker sex' and the 'weaker races'.[12] The starting point was the disciplining of the body, which through sport could be 'by turns orderly and extraordinary, competent and excellent' but which also offered a sublimation of the sexual energies and the simultaneous encouragement and discipline of violence.[13]

Hahn developed considerable sporting prowess, especially in rugby.[14] After leaving school to take up work in the Transvaal, including bank employment in Johannesburg and a spell as a mine compound manager, Hahn enjoyed a flourishing rugby career. He played for Pirates Rugby Football Club and was selected as wing for the Springboks in their three Test matches against England in 1910. In one of these Test games, in the same year that the Act of Union made South Africa a nation, Hahn scored a try for his country.[15] Right up to the end of his life, Hahn's rugby skills were recalled by his admirers,[16] and they became inextricable from sympathetic representations of his brutality.

In the culturally mixed context in which he was raised, speaking German at home, Cape Dutch at the school in Paarl, and English in broader Cape society, Hahn seems to have been flawlessly trilingual, but as an adult identified most strongly with an 'English' culture. The process by which this anglicization took place is not entirely clear, but neither Hahn nor his siblings had any problem with offering their services to the Union government and to Britain against Germany in both world wars. In the inter-war years his pungent criticisms of German nationalism in SWA were well known. In 1926 he married Alcye Fogarty, daughter of the Anglican Bishop of Damaraland. And Hahn most attached himself to the small but elite coterie of English-speaking administrators in SWA.[17]

Hahn joined the Imperial Light Horse when South Africa enter the First

14.1 'Cocky' Hahn with Ndapona, the mother of Mandume ya Ndemufayo, and her attendant in Oukwanayama, c. 1915–21

World War.[18] He first went north in 1915 as part of Pritchard's expedition to Ovamboland following the German surrender to General Botha. Judged to be 'skilful in handling Africans',[19] Hahn then served as Intelligence Officer to Charles Manning, the Resident Commissioner, and was crucial in gathering information and mustering the support of Kwanyama headmen against their king, Mandume ya Ndemufayo, between 1915 and 1917. He participated in the military action against Mandume in 1917.[20] In 1920, when Manning transferred to Windhoek and became Chief Native Commissioner, Hahn became Native Commissioner of Ovamboland and remained in that post until 1946. He then served one year on the Public Service Commission in Windhoek, and retired to his farm in Grootfontein where he died in 1948.[21]

As part of his mediation of the Ovambo to the outside world, Hahn represented SWA at a 1937 meeting of the Mandates Commission of the League of Nations in Geneva. In 1942 Hahn accompanied Lawrence, the South African Minister of Justice, to the League of Nations to advise on the 'treatment of natives' in the territory, and he performed the same service for Smuts at the UN Conference in New York in 1946, at a time of intensifying international criticism of South Africa's handling of the mandate.[22] Hahn's attraction to South African politicians was his exceptional image as an enlightened administrator, successfully controlling 100,000 Ovambo under his brand of indirect rule and preserving their tribal ways to boot. This view of Hahn appeared to be validated internationally. Lord Harlech reportedly described Hahn, after an official visit to address Ovambo leaders during

14.2 'Cocky' Hahn in Ondangua, Ovamboland, c. 1915–21

World War II, as 'one of the ablest Native administrators in the whole of Africa'.[23]

Beyond the accolades of administrative colleagues, the man attained legendary proportions. Hahn embodied the popular romance of the 'Lords of the Last Frontier'.[24] His personal attributes appealed to a wide white southern African audience. Because of his location in the north, rugby anecdotes were superseded by hunting exploits which 'required all the most virile attributes of the imperial male'.[25] It was not only his sporting prowess, vigour and air of command that fed the imagination of Hahn's admirers; it was also the location of the handsome former Springbok player in the remotest wilds of 'Old Africa'. Ovamboland's distance from the South African metropole was an important factor in the cultural elaboration and romanticization of Cocky Hahn, and it offered a new cultural frontier for South African masculinity. South Africa had perpetuated the old division in SWA between the Police Zone, characterized by a settler-state type *modus operandi*, and 'the north', where 'Native Administration' now operated and where whites needed permits to enter. Hahn's place on this northern periphery, distant even from SWA's capital, Windhoek, allowed him to exercise enormous independence as Native Commissioner. This autonomy reinforced Hahn's voice as mediator of the Ovambo to the outside world as much as it did his authority, which in turn facilitated the smooth functioning and positive public image of what he later came to term 'indirect control'.

Indirect rule has been described as 'that hybrid compound of formal bureaucratic power above and of orderly and cooperative traditional power below'.[26] This concept of local government in Africa was originally developed in Nigeria and then formally applied in British colonies elsewhere, notably Tanganyika. From the outset in Ovamboland, the South African administration had taken what seemed the most practical and economical route, and sought to rule indirectly through the embodiments of African power: those kings, headmen and sub-headmen who already held position in Ovambo polities. Lugard's book on the 'dual mandate',[27] which Hahn assimilated in the late 1920s, provided the Native Commissioner with a language through which practice could be crystallized into policy and the *de facto* situation elevated into principle.

The very success of what came to be formulated as the Ovamboland model of indirect rule owed much to the pre-existence of centralized and stratified social organizations. In order to work effectively, indirect rule needed 'tribes' and hierarchical political structures. In many areas, one or both of these had to be created. Ombalantu, a decentralized clutch of kin-based groupings in western Ovamboland, was a case in point.[28] Indirect rule, as it became more systematized in British tropical Africa and in northern SWA, was designed to prevent or at least control social breakdown. The point was 'to develop the native on lines which will not Westernize and turn him into a bad imitation of a European', and to consolidate 'tribal organisation' which would in turn preserve 'the African atmosphere, the African mind, the whole foundations of his race'.[29]

One of the problems inherent in systems of indirect rule (or the forerunners of these systems) was that colonial officials wanted to appropriate to themselves the awe in which subjects held their chiefs, yet found the most awe-inspiring chiefs inconvenient allies.[30] In Ovamboland this led to the removal of two kings, Mandume ya Ndemufayo in Oukwanyama in 1917, and Iipumbu ya Shilongo in Uukwambi in 1932, and their replacement by councils of headmen. In both these cases of severe tampering with political systems, Hahn was directly involved. Despite this fact, much was made officially of Hahn's skill in preserving the Ovambo in their 'raw tribal state'.

Hahn made high claims for the special features of Ovambo history. He took particular pains to dwell on their historical longevity, asserting that the Zulu were 'newcomers' compared with the Ovambo, who were 'the oldest settled people in Southern Africa'.[31] An Ovambo identity was served up for outside consumption, most literally so in the case of the Ovambo homestead constructed in Windhoek under Hahn's co-ordination for the 1936 trade fair exhibition. In Ovamboland itself, the large homestead of the co-operative Kwanyama headman, Nehemia, at Omhedi was the tourist or ethnographic destination for many a white visitor.[32] A relatively homogenous 'traditional' identity was presented in these show-places; Ovamboland's isolation and Hahn's lengthy period as Native Commissioner lent it credibility to most outsiders.

In Hahn's view, the mechanisms of social and ideological control by Ovambo ruling groups, while making life at times hidebound for the subordinate, were healthy and admirable. Hahn argued that where westernizing influence was least apparent, 'the natives are virile, well-ordered and progressive'. The term 'virile', which Hahn frequently applied both to Africans and to animals in the Etosha Game Reserve, implied the opposite of domestication and arose from his belief in letting 'nature' run its course.[33] Hahn doubtless also drew from his pre-war exposure to mine compound discourses on the problems posed by the 'detribalized' or 'dressed natives'. There was an instrumentality to these opinions, as Hahn frankly admitted: 'The "raw" native is also generally preferred at labour centres.'[34]

The encouragement of migrant labour was of course the primary purpose of native administration in Ovamboland, and this was the only contact the Ovambo were allowed with the outside world. It was hoped (unrealistically, as it would prove) to prevent 'detribalization' by keeping labour contracts short. No commercial traders were permitted into the area from 1915, and animal disease control ensured that the Ovambo had no access to markets elsewhere in the territory.[35] As a result, agriculture remained of the subsistence rather than the peasant order, and women's labour remained crucial in cultivation. Women who attempted to go south and escape this role were summarily punished if caught, usually being handed over to their headman for a beating.[36] Women's mobility was seen as highly threatening to the 'traditional' order, which highlights the fact that African women were designated not only as the bearers of agriculture but also as the bearers of culture. Such thinking was not simply imposed from above. It was reinforced through temporary alliances between officials and conservative male elders and leaders, who in their turn drew selectively on African cultural precedents concerning gender norms.[37]

Hahn as a matter of course also defended polygyny. In his view numerous wives in a homestead ensured plenty; the headman Nehemia's thirteen wives in Omhedi were a case in point. Hahn pointed disparagingly to the relative poverty of monogamous Christian homesteads in Ondonga, the historical core area of mission work in Ovamboland.

Official anxiety over rapid Christianization was inevitable, and showed itself in the slowness with which the administration opened up the region to new mission denominations and the stringent conditions imposed on all mission work, including that of the Finnish mission which had been in Ovamboland since 1870. Tensions came to a head in the 1930s. While missions typically argued that the administration was backward in facilitating education and training, that 'Natives are most useful to the Europeans as raw labour, and they must be encouraged to "stay put'",[38] Hahn typically complained that the large-scale Christianization and education of the Ndonga by the Finnish mission in particular had made it 'an uphill fight to get Christianised natives to regard themselves as tribal natives'.[39] This had 'practically destroyed the authority of the chiefs and headmen; so much so that little tribal discipline is left and it becomes more obvious that the tribe is retrogressing'.[40] 'Retrogression' in this case was accompanied by a very unsatisfactory Ndonga labour migration rate, particularly compared with the numbers of migrants from Oukwanyama. Hahn ominously raised the spectre of social unrest: 'The Union Government is today tasting the bitter fruit of past mistakes in allowing the breaking up of native areas and tribal organisation'.[41]

Nowhere was the division over tribal 'integrity' between Hahn and Ovambo traditionalists on the one side, and missions and Christian subjects on the other, more obvious than over the *efundula*, the female initiation rite. These often massive ceremonies occurred every few years in all areas, and ritualized the passage of young women into full maturity after which they were entitled to marry. Rigorous physical endurance sessions were undergone to test both stamina and illicit pregnancy, but fertility was a major emphasis in the overall ritual. The Finnish Missionary Society complained that Hahn glamorized *efundula* by having its dances performed for his official visitors. As for what took place during *efundula*, the Finns insisted that no decent person could even speak of it.[42] In the less reserved Anglican view, the whole *efondula* ritual was tainted because of its 'phallic flavour'.[43] Hahn brushed this prudery aside and argued that the main objective of the missionaries was 'to have the "efundula", the most important of all Ovambo rites, smashed up and wiped out'.[44]

It is easy to see how Hahn's creation of a body of ethnographic knowledge provided him with ammunition against missionaries. He frequently responded to their criticisms concerning administrative reinforcement of local power structures with the rejoinder that their knowledge of the putative Ovambo mentality was faulty. Hahn sought to show that he enjoyed the monopoly of expertise amongst white people.

Hahn was by no means unique among colonial administrators in having a reputation for expertise on 'the customs' and history of the Africans he governed. But neither was he unique among administrators in combining this with an apparent readiness to resort to force.[45] When I first researched Hahn, I thought that the whiff of brutality that clung to him and emerges from much oral history was prominent in his early years as an official, and that intellectual attainments came later in life. He engaged in academic exchanges with noted anthropologists such as Winifred Hoernlé, co-published the important ethnography, *The Native Tribes of South West Africa*, with Vedder and Fourie, and conducted a distinguished international correspondence in which from the late 1920s he elaborated his conception of indirect rule in Ovamboland.[46]

The initial question, then, was to explain the apparent transition from unthinking to thinking man. On closer reading, however, it was not as simple or as chronological as it had initially seemed. Within the first few years of his arrival in Ovamboland, Hahn was eliciting information from his father in Paarl, sending him to consult German mission ethnographic accounts of the Ovambo and their rituals and political institutions.[47] The date of publication of *Native Tribes* is also revealing: 1928, only three years after a Staff Complaints Enquiry in which he is depicted as particularly brutal by the complainant, a junior officer. Hahn therefore had a curiosity and a desire to know from the very outset. Far from being in transition from physical to mental exertion, as it were, Hahn integrated both throughout his career in Ovamboland. As one official admirer euphemistically expresses it, Hahn always combined 'both brains and pluck'.[48]

The simultaneity of the exercise of power through physical force and the exercise of power through the production and dissemination of ethnographic knowledge concerning the Ovambo is the anchoring argument in this chapter. Africanists have become increasingly concerned recently with the more abstract forms of exercising power, and at times with their own sinister role in reproducing this phenomenon.[49] While this concern is well placed, it has gone so far that historiography now faces two dangers. The first is that the decrease in emphasis on questions of enforcement, the quotidian practice from which violence (both systemic and contingent) is not excluded, means that power associated with modernity is given precedence. For example, 'the African' is constructed as an object of knowledge around which systems and practices are elaborated that are intrinsic to colonial power. But forms of power associated with pre-modern regimes, which act through repression and prohibition, which act on the body,[50] are de-signified in some of the new historiographies. The second danger that we run here is of overlooking the consequences for those among the colonized whose bodies were at the receiving end of violence, 'de-traumatizing' their history.[51]

Questions need to be asked concerning the origins of violent practices, the wider aetiologies of violence in both white and African histories, and how these are constructed and portrayed. The effects on both perpetrators and victims also need scrutiny, and should be related to issues of domination, control and resistance. We should not assume, moreover, that colonial violence in Ovamboland was simply functional. Studies of violence elsewhere have argued that it goes beyond 'the search for profits, the need to contract labour'. What must be taken into account are those 'inextricably construed long-standing cultural logics of meaning – structures of feeling – whose basis lies in a symbolic world and not in one of rationalism'.[52]

Popular white literature and favourable official discourses surrounding Hahn are challenged by oral accounts of Ovambo subjects and by the detailed set of enquiries following an official complaint against Hahn in the 1920s. An initial complaint lodged in 1923 against Hahn had been dismissed, but when related accusations were made against a fellow officer, Harold Eedes, by the postmaster in the nearby town of Tsumeb in 1925, both cases were thrown open for full investigation. The ensuing

Ovamboland Enquiry constituted a counterpoint in colonial discourse. In itself, it represented some of the conflicts within coloniality at a time in the early 1920s when there was still a degree of space to question the practices of senior officers. In this brief moment before the consolidation of South African colonialism in Namibia, dissensions amongst those in the administration could become public transcripts.[53]

The main enquiry against Hahn was brought on the complaint of an aggrieved junior officer, a clerk serving in Ovamboland between 1921 and 1923. Percival Chaplin was an Englishman in his early forties who had been sent out to South Africa late in 1914. He was deployed in the mechanized transport service and occupied several clerical posts upon leaving the military.[54] Personal differences between himself and Hahn abounded, and it was plain these existed between other officers too. Anglicized he might have been, but Hahn 'had no time for an Englishman born in England'.[55] It seems that the cultural production of an 'Englishman' in the Union of South Africa, imitative though it was in some respects, was quite specific to this colonial periphery and probably appealed to an earlier and more manly imperial age.[56]

While Chaplin had apparently worked competently in Native Affairs in Windhoek,[57] criticisms of his service record elsewhere were dragged out during the enquiry. These highlighted much that was antithetical to the ideals of masculinity held amongst white southern Africans at the time. The magistrate at Okahandja described Chaplin as 'very childish and weak', 'neurotic' and 'out of his element here', while Manning judged him to be 'peculiar' and 'particularly unsuitable for camp and veld life'.[58] His poor hunting and riding skills were widely deplored. Hahn revealed his own means of surviving the isolation of Ovamboland when he put Chaplin's discontentedness down to the fact that he 'had no hobbies except playing a mandolin and never used to do any reading'.[59] Chaplin was no sportsman, being rather inclined to 'brooding' instead. He was not physically vigorous, having received a bayonet wound in war service which still troubled him and in a sense feminized him. As Chaplin explained: 'Whenever I sat down anywhere I had to fold my handkerchief into a knob and sit on it. I was not always fit as my wound would sometimes bleed and when I was in this condition I could not ride.'[60] He also claimed that a blow to the head from a tree whilst driving through thick bush during the Ovamboland Expedition in 1917, not to mention the odd fever and the worry caused by the enquiry, contributed to the ruin of his health.[61] He alleged that he had been mistreated by the administration, being passed over for positions because he did not belong to the necessary patronage networks. Chaplin seems to have had something of a persecution complex, and was not always consistent in the statements he made. A less heroic figure and a greater contrast to the confident and manly Cocky Hahn would have been difficult to find.

In several sets of documents, we hear accusations of illegal trading activities and hunting by Hahn and his predecessors, and Hahn's explanation of relevant procedures and how they had been misinterpreted; we hear allegations of beatings administered on the orders of or personally by Hahn, resorting to kicking when his

14.3 'Hahn and his spoil', a giraffe he had slain during a hunting trip in Angola whose legality was questioned by the Ovamboland inquiry

fists grew tired, and his admission of one case where whipping took place but denial of any other occasion on which he used force; we hear of a disturbing assault by Hahn on an Ovambo woman, and Hahn's categorical rejection that any such incident ever took place.[62]

This bald summary of the different voices emerging from the Ovamboland enquiry demonstrates that emotions were riding high. As Hahn was officially exonerated of trading for profit, of gratuitous beatings and the assault on the woman, merely taken to task for not keeping proper records of his transactions in goods with chiefs,[63] one may ask, what is the point of exploring the accusations against him? It is impossible to verify whether Hahn abused the Ovambo woman, whether he beat men as frequently as some witnesses testified, or even whether he preferred tinkering with machinery to writing reports in his office, as the complainant alleged.[64] Verification would be desirable in all these cases, but it is not the point. It is what the report raises as issues, what was deemed to be officially and publicly acceptable and unacceptable in the northern administration, what dissident colonial discourse emerges and how it is dealt with, that is so suggestive here.

The issue of trading dominated the first investigation in 1923 and also occupies most of the pages of the enquiry proceedings in 1925. Rumours had become rife that Hahn and others were trading for profit with the Ovambo, which was strictly against official policy in the north. Timber was allegedly brought in illegally from Angola, and goods sold to Portuguese officers on the border. Chaplin reported another officer's estimate that Hahn made £5,000 to £6,000 over and above his salary by selling goods over a period of years to the Ovambo.[65] Manning too was accused of having pocketed proceeds from such trade in his time as Resident Commissioner. In their defence, both Manning and Hahn argued that it was government policy in Ovamboland to 'increase the wants of the natives' in the absence of trading stores in the north beyond Tsumeb. Their activities came under this official rubric and were argued to be necessary, given the commercial vacuum. Thus goods such as clothing and horses were said to be passed on to headmen and kings at cost price, through the offices of the Native Commissioner.[66] Hahn also handled King Martin of Ondonga's savings for the purchase of a motor-car. It was acknowledged that blankets were often purchased and then exchanged with Ovambo for 'curios', as most people had little use for cash at this time. This unusual public transcript provides a revealing glimpse of how colonial officials created alliances with Ovambo headmen and kings and cemented them with objects of exchange, and documents one very important way leading officials, especially Hahn, controlled the north.

Both investigations of 1923 and 1925 cleared Hahn and Manning of all charges of illegal trading. The enquiry moved on to a range of less serious accusations, including illegal hunting in Angola and failure properly to record the death of government horses. Hahn pointed out that his official counterparts in Angola had invited him to hunt while a distinguished guest visited Ovamboland, and the hunting question was dropped. But the problems of his record-keeping were taken more seriously, to the extent that he was ordered to adopt more rigorous methods in future.[67] This was the only area in which the Native Commissioner received any rebuke.

The Ovamboland enquiry of 1925 brought in a set of charges which had not been raised in 1923 and related to flogging and mistreatment of 'natives'. This subject produced widely divergent testimonies, which fell either into the category of violence represented by Chaplin or the category of officially sanctioned enforcement represented by Hahn. Chaplin presented a vivid picture of Hahn's use of force, both calculated and seemingly random. He described one case in Namakunde in Oukwanyama where Hahn ordered a Kwanyama man to be held down by his hands and feet and made the 'police boy' flog him. Chaplin also alleged that when Hahn grew tired of beating, he used to resort to kicking.[68]

The response that emerged was an official admission of the limited use of floggings, but only in the unstable, post-confrontational conditions of 1915–17. Hahn acknowledged the administration of floggings to Kwanyama 'troublemakers' immediately after Mandume's demise and to bandits in Ombalantu in western Ovamboland.[69] The Native Commissioner argued that floggings had been administered in Oukwanyama because after Mandume's death it was 'a most difficult matter for one official new to the work to keep the balance and affairs in order'. He stated that he had had to dissuade headmen who advocated more severe punishments, which were 'very drastic indeed'. He argued that 'caning' was never administered except after an open trial in which headmen were present and approved the sentence. He alleged that since 1921–22 he had succeeded in prevailing on these headmen to abolish all corporal punishment.[70]

This admission of regulated and sanctioned violence is very revealing in the context of colonial occupation. The Ovambo region constituted a strong exception to the trend elsewhere in SWA to do away with flogging completely, to build a case for South African humaneness and superiority to the German system, in which flogging was very widespread. The Germans had endorsed flogging practices by settlers in the Police Zone, who were allowed the right to 'parental chastisement'. The apogee of the South African arguments against the brutality of German rule was the Blue Book of 1918,[71] which included photographs of flogging atrocities. Tony Emmett argues that in the years of martial law until 1920, South Africa had to prove to the League of Nations that it was a better colonizer than Germany in order to win the mandatory award.[72] Thus, just as floggings were commencing in Ovamboland, which was being occupied for the first time, floggings were ceasing in the centre and south. Flogging in fact resumed in certain parts of SWA,[73] being by far the cheapest and least 'inconvenient' form of punishment, but acknowledgement of its practice after 1917 virtually disappeared from official records in Ovamboland.

An important measuring stick for South African officers in Ovamboland was the conduct of their counterparts across the border in Angola. Portuguese soldiers were said to be brutal and undisciplined; they and officials openly cohabited with black women;[74] they were ill-supplied from their regional centres and at times depended on the South Africans for medicine and supplies. There was a very high turnover of senior officials. Any sign of sliding down to Portuguese standards, particularly regarding inter-racial sexual relations, was stiffly and officially rebuked. For example, a South African soldier who served with Manning found himself transferred from Ovamboland when he began a liaison with an Ndonga woman and fathered her child.[75]

South Africans prided themselves on being much less violent than the Portuguese. There were certainly differences between them, but these should be seen in their respective contexts. For example, while Manning and Hahn inflicted floggings on the Kwanyama after Mandume's death in 1917, General Pereira de Eça had inflicted hangings after the Portuguese conquest of northern Oukwanyama in 1915 as part of the imposition of martial law in southern Angola.[76] Moreover, South African claims to being more enlightened with regard to forced labour should be treated with caution. On both sides of the border road-building was undertaken by unpaid and reluctant Ovambo men.[77]

Ovamboland in 1915 had just emerged from a high phase of merchant capitalism through trade mainly in guns and cattle, but now on the SWA side was connected to the capitalist economy in a very restricted way, through labour migration to the south. Forms of control were often symbolic and physical, signalling a pre-modern ethos. For example, the show of unity between Hahn and Kwanyama headmen after the death of Mandume was achieved through floggings of 'radicals', with all parties present at the spectacle. This ritualized sharing of authority represented a displacement to a new central power far away, mediated through the bodies of young Kwanyama men undergoing this punishment. Power was now dispersed from king to headmen, some of whom had been victimized by Mandume for tugging centrifugally at the core of the precolonial kingship.[78] The display cemented the bond between the administration represented by Hahn and the headmen. New colonial nuances accompanied this gendered and generational form of disciplining the young men who had been Mandume's fighters and were now expected to insert their bodies into the channels of the migrant labour system.

Chaplin's testimony covering the early 1920s, however, depicted violence which spilled over from any regulated framework constructed by officials. It is not necessary to labour the point concerning whether Hahn admitted instances of gratuitous brutality; he may have denied this in 1925, but he did not always do so during the twenty-one years that remained to him as Native Commissioner. The report of a meeting which followed disturbances at the jubilee celebration in 1936 in the Windhoek location, for instance, tells us that 'Major Hahn, who was present, had stated that in his sphere of work he would have used the sjambok [rhino-hide whip] on any natives who behaved as the location natives did on that day'.[79] Furthermore, references are sprinkled through oral history regarding Hahn's beatings of Ovambo men, particularly at road and other construction sites.

Most white literature and forms of discourse had ways of representing Hahn's violence that rendered it less disturbing by projecting it in sporting terms. For example, an incident during the 1915–16 famine is embellished in literary form in Negley Farson's popular and suggestively entitled account *Behind God's Back*. Hahn is said to have rugby-tackled young men and laid about him with a *sjambok* in the case of queue-jumpers during famine relief distribution. This account states that the approving Ovambo audience, in gratitude for Hahn's forceful and protective action, bestowed on him the name 'Shongola'.[80]

Sporting metaphors abounded in colonial discourses in Africa.[81] In Hahn's case, the rugby metaphor projected humour on to brutality, distancing those observers who shared his cultural background from the trauma of actuality, defusing the impact of violence for white onlookers and later writers who packaged these incidents in sporting terms. Hahn's jaunty nickname among whites, bestowed on him at least as early as his Springbok days, would also have helped to reduce the distance between him and his audience[82] and increased the distance between such white audiences and the Africans who suffered him.

A specific case of unregulated or gratuitous violence against an Ovambo woman is related in the 1925 enquiry report. The woman in question was given no name. In front of at least two witnesses, so Chaplin alleged, Hahn came up behind this woman as she was on her hands and knees smearing polish on the *stoep* (veranda) of the residence. She was probably wearing the *omihanga*, the short leather apron which, apart from ropes of beads around the hips, constituted the dress of most Ovambo women at that time. One officer described her as being 'without clothes'. Hahn came up from behind and kicked the woman straight 'in her private parts'.[83] According to Chaplin, 'Hahn took a running kick at the girl'.[84] The conjunction of the sporting metaphor and brutality appears to have been too disturbing to be humorous in this case. Chaplin reported that his fellow officer Anderson, who witnessed the scene, said it was 'disgraceful' of Hahn.[85] In his rebuttal of the accusation of kicking this woman 'between her legs', Hahn stated that the whole incident had been fabricated.[86]

It is impossible to ascertain whether the incident occurred. When the enquiry made its conclusions known, it was not even mentioned. Instead, Chaplin was found to have behaved improperly, making accusations that were motivated by malice rather than public duty, and his allegations (except for certain instances of Hahn's bureaucratic ineptitude) were judged to be unfounded.[87] Chaplin stood alone in the gravity of the accusations made; he argued that other officers shared his complaints but chose to say nothing to impugn Hahn in the enquiry. Judging from the verdict that Chaplin's conduct was 'improper and unbecoming', bringing accusations against Hahn would have seriously damaged officers' careers.[88]

Since a variety of evidence corroborates that Hahn did personally use physical violence against Ovambo, it is not inconceivable that he may have abused an Ovambo woman in this way. While no oral accounts by women have been elicited which relate to assaults of this kind, evidence of gendered violence – let alone sexual violence – is notoriously difficult to gather. Whatever the case, the episode involving the assault on the woman stands in this chapter as a symbol and a pivot around which to pose a variety of questions about Hahn, about the socio-cultural system that produced him, about the administration in the north, and about the documentation this administration has produced and on which we rely for historical research. It tells us a tremendous amount about constructions of gender and race.

The incident involving the woman occupies remarkably little space in the report of the enquiry. It emerges in the late stages of Chaplin's final testimony, and he stated that he had only just remembered it in the course of presenting his final case against Hahn.[89] This in itself could be seen as compelling evidence of a colonial ethos in which African women were so unimportant that their mistreatment could be forgotten or repressed almost completely. It calls to mind the argument made about sexual violence more generally in history, that frequently all that we are left with in sifting through the material is 'a conspicuous absence: a configuration where sexual violence against women is an origin of social relations and narratives in which the event itself is subsequently elided'.[90] I have argued elsewhere that the apparent invisibility of women in Ovamboland is largely a product of androcentric attitudes and archives, and that 'the often silent and hidden operations of gender … are nonetheless present and defining forces' in these societies.[91] In this instance, the highly visible and vocal Hahn came into contact with what was usually invisible, and we are left with an inkling of how that invisibility was reproduced, both through the action which would make any woman keep her distance and through the official attempts to dismiss the episode.

But Chaplin did remember its occurrence; and instead of dismissing him as no more than the victim of his own illusions and the possessor of an unreliable memory, as the magistrate conducting the enquiry opined, there could be another type of explanation for him personally inserting the incident at a particular point in his testimony. A simple but effective argument has been advanced by Halbwachs, to the effect that memory is collective, that the social collectivity shapes the way human beings remember.[92] What may well have prompted Chaplin to remember the case of Hahn's abuse against the woman was the combative public position in which he found himself during the enquiry. Once he recalled the incident, he returned to it again and again. He had little else to lose.

While her existence was not quite lost to memory, the woman described in the enquiry never had any name. It is her anonymity and inaudibility coupled with the nature of her transient visibility, which has prompted the title 'Black Venus' in this chapter. There is no documented mention of a 'Black Venus' or 'Hottentot Venus', as the phenomenon is more popularly known in southern Africa, by any of the officials serving in Ovamboland. This is purely an authorial intervention. But it is taking no liberty to call this anonymous woman the Black Venus, for the archive shows that Cocky Hahn was familiar with this form of representing women. Indeed, in the midst of his photograph collection is a postcard showing a naked woman in the Kalahari, posed for the camera to show the extent of her 'Bushman' steatopygeia. The postcard dates from the 1930s, when Nazi activities in SWA emerged, for this figure has a swastika engraved on one buttock.[93]

The image of the 'Hottentot Venus' was a trope that was very thick on the ground in the Cape where Hahn was raised. From highbrow publications such as Galton's to well advertised exhibitions, newspapers and popular magazines, this celebrated marker of racial and sexual difference had been in very wide circulation for a very long time.[94] The name became synonymous with Saartjie Baartman, the Khoi woman who travelled to Europe in the early nineteenth century to be exhibited by her keeper and then later pathologized by the French scientist, Cuvier.[95] But Saartjie Baartman was only the most famous of numerous women who were thus objectified. In South Africa itself, an ongoing process of producing images and knowledge on the subject during and well beyond Hahn's lifetime fed into the development of human and social sciences in academic institutions.[96]

European ideas about African women focused on their supposedly excessive sexuality. Buttocks and private parts (particularly of Khoisan women) were repre-sented as unusual and were made the subject of both scientific enquiry and, as Carmel Schrire puts it, 'covert pornography'.[97] Like other categories of women marked out as different, if not freakish, the ironic negation or inversion of the classical connotation of 'Venus' leaves us with a painful juxtaposition. The values loaded into the term 'Black' (or 'Hottentot') and the values loaded into 'Venus' are diametrically opposed, constituting a paradox at the very heart of things. Because of her race, the Black Venus is objectified and denigrated, and should not be desired. But because of her gender, she also stands to be sexualized by men. Hahn was surely conscious of these ironies when he referred to those Ovambo women he photographed as 'dusky belles'.[98]

Representation aside, the text of the enquiry presents a very immediate Black Venus: the pseudo-scientific detachment of a Cuvier is not what we are dealing with here. Hahn was in the field, where the Ovambo numbered over a hundred thousand and white men probably twelve. Though there were white women working on several mission stations, the first decade of administration in Ovamboland saw no white woman gracing any official residence and Hahn himself was not yet married. The Ovambo woman's body and sexuality, made vulnerable by the combination of 'traditional' clothing and the posture of servitude while polishing the *stoep* of the colonial residence, were visible and available to a man raised in the Victorian Cape in a missionary household, and who had rounded out his life to date in the masculine worlds of boys' school, mine, bank, army and administration.[99] His repertoire of behaviour was indeed limited.

The concept of a Black Venus is used here to go beyond historical fascination with the 'production of knowledge' and the textual objectification of African females and to show the link between representation and physical violence. This Black Venus should remind historians that Africans were not only having knowledge about them produced, they were being assaulted. In Namibian history, as elsewhere, violence has been gendered and at times sexualized. The statement from a study of Cuvier and the Venus Hottentot, that '[w]e should no longer be surprised to find Africa represented by the genitalia of its women',[100] should be lifted out of its purely representational paradigm to embrace the corporeal. Cocky Hahn was confronted with the immediate embodiment of the tribal Ovambo woman and we should not be surprised that she was the object of physical abuse.

Most of the African staff working in the official quarters in Ondangwa came from outside Ovamboland. A southern woman called Frederica was in charge of housekeeping, and she recruited local women to work in the domestic quarters and kitchens of the officials. At times old clothes were passed on to domestic workers,[101] but it would appear that in this case, and maybe in others, women still carried out their duties in 'tribal' gear. Unlike the elaborate 'domestication' of women performing tasks for whites in the Belgian African case analysed by Nancy Rose Hunt,[102] the woman in the text was in a dangerous limbo between the wild/tribal and the domestic. She represented feminized 'raw labour', transposed suddenly into a white masculine space. This kicking incident shows that the intellectual Hahn was also a physical Hahn acculturated to violence against blacks. On this frontier it was a short step from the violence of representation to the violence of action. There was a direct connection between the ethnographic images of the African woman with which Hahn was familiar, whose defining feature was her buttocks, and the opportunity for abuse that was presented to him by the 'unclothed' woman labouring on the *stoep*.

14.4 'Efandula dancing', photograph taken by 'Cocky' Hahn, Ovamboland, n.d.

Both the treatment meted out to this woman and the representation of her 'social skin'[103] had a bearing on everything else going on in newly colonized Ovamboland. Hahn was a vocal supporter of the *efondula* and attended its ceremonies regularly, where numbers of young women would be in various stages of dress marking their change in status, none of which missionaries would have deemed decent. Hahn is recalled by female oral informants as attending the ceremonies and taking many photographs of the dancing.[104] The woman in the text was 'without clothes' on the *stoep* of the Residence. Hahn was at odds with missionaries who were trying to clothe and Christianize the Ovambo: 'As soon as a native is christianized he thinks he must wear European clothes ... In his natural state he manufactures his garments from the produce of the country ... he need not be ashamed to appear everywhere in them; and above all he retains his caste.'[105] One of the implications of Hahn's project to maintain 'tribal health' in Ovamboland was that he sought to maintain rituals which kept the bulk of the tribe 'unclothed'.

One way of regarding nakedness in such contexts is through its associations with innocence. Looked at through the lens of the white administrator with a 'European' and Christian outlook, such a view would have infantilized Africans and placed them in a continuum of civilization below the acquisition of 'knowledge' and 'shame', with connotations of backwardness and weakness. This may have fitted in with the educational background of men such as Hahn, coming from schools which sought to imbue some sense of paternalistic responsibility towards the 'weaker races'. Moreover, corporal punishment such as flogging would have appeared in the light of 'parental' chastisement. The trouble with this argument, however, is that the concept of paternalism implies the eventual development of the 'child'. In this respect, missionaries in Ovamboland were far more paternalistic than Hahn because they sought to influence and Christianize the Ovambo in their own mould. Hahn was an agent of reification rather than of progress.

Anthropologists have rightly described nakedness as a more complex trope, suggesting darkness, disorder and pollution to missionaries and proclaiming 'savagery' more generally. A more convincing way to approach Hahn's assault on the Ovambo woman and gratuitous beating of other people in Ovamboland is to recall Michael Taussig's comment from his study of genocide in the Putumayo rubber forests, that 'it is not the jungle but the sentiments men project into it that is decisive in filling their hearts with savagery'.[106] Unlike missionaries who sought to take the Ovambo out of their culture, Hahn in some ways tried to step into Ovambo culture. He reportedly dressed himself in the leather apparel worn by Kwanyama men when he attended *efondula*,[107] a refashioning of himself which could be read as an appropriation, to deepen his knowledge of 'the native' through participation. It is also possible to argue that in doing so he took on some of the 'savagery' imputed to the Ovambo. Such propensities certainly need much further examination than can be given here,[108] but we should note that Hahn also set careful limits on how far he stepped into Ovambo-ness. For example, despite being fluent in the two main languages of eastern Ovamboland he always took care to conduct official business through an interpreter. White people who romanticized Hahn might have referred to him as 'a real live Ovambo' or the 'Super-Ovambo',[109] but the Ovambo themselves were highly conscious of the ways he maintained distance and kept them in their place. In sum, the notion of paternalism cannot encompass the complexity of a Native Commissioner whose own brother-in-law Cope, the labour recruiter based in Ondangwa, dubbed Hahn 'the Paramount Chief'.[110]

There are other questions besides whether Hahn saw innocence or savagery in the nakedness of the 'tribal' Ovambo. We can, after all, only speculate as to the influences at work. The most crucial point here is that Hahn vigorously worked to keep the Ovambo cut off from outside influences and trade, without radios[111] and 'without clothes'. Arguably it was in this condition that people could be more easily controlled and more easily abused.

This violence had implications far beyond its functionality in enforcing dominance and hierarchy, especially in its excessiveness. Allen Feldman argues that violence acts to bifurcate the self of the other.[112] Literature on the effects of violence suggests that one of the outstanding symptoms is for the subject affected simply to vacate space, especially the space where the violence might have occurred.[113] This displacement may last until those affected by violence can reconstruct a world for themselves, be it through the counter-violence of cult movements in Mozambique suggested in the work of Ken Wilson[114] or the sacrifice of the body through hunger striking by IRA prisoners in Northern Ireland described by Feldman. These turn violence back on to the perpetrators, and no small part of the process is the production of a wholly different cultural construction of violence from that of the aggressors. Integral to the process of this reconstruction is the narration and recasting of events through oral history. Oral history has the capacity to recreate subjectivity after the process of objectification and domination. Feldman goes so far as to say that 'in oral history, the body fragmented is reassembled, and this act, the weaving of a new body through language, as much as any act of violence, testifies to the emergence of political agency'.[115] We should be asking not only 'what history does to the body but what subjects do with what history has done to the body'.[116] There may well be the outward appearance of submission but the inward development of politicization and attitudes of resistance.

The Ovambo created and reproduced histories orally that showed the impact of colonization over time but also signalled forms of integrity which were resistant to colonial force and cultural manipulation. Hahn exercised power on a variety of levels in Ovamboland, but the figure of Shongola himself has been incorporated, blamed and processed in sites where the Ovambo have relied on their own forms of knowledge.

This was shown in an entirely different set of court hearings from those conducted in the 1920s. At the height of nationalist struggle against South African colonialism, the name of the late Native Commissioner in Ovamboland came up once again in court. The years 1973–74 saw South Africa attempt to enforce full-blown apartheid policies in Namibia, which met with widespread resistance. Masses of striking contract workers returned to Ovamboland and elections which were intended to establish a bantustan government were boycotted.[117] In the midst of this ferment, public floggings had been staged. Many Ovambo who were perceived to be opponents of the South African regime and its 'tribal' system in the north (founded by Hahn) were beaten with the *epokolo,* a lethal whip made from the central rib of the *makalani* palm tree. Others were sent away to prison. In an attempt to end the public humiliation of respected teachers, leaders and nurses being stripped and flogged in the open, an urgent application was brought in court by Church figures sympathetic to the nationalist movement, SWAPO. The South African authorities argued that the floggings were legitimate because they were traditional and were being administered by the new bantustan power based on precolonial custom. But the victims and their supporters refused to accept what they saw as an invented tradition. Instead, affidavits were submitted which argued that the flogging system originated not with their forebears, but with 'Shongola'.[118]

During the two decades following the Ovamboland enquiry's official exoneration of Cocky Hahn, his career as Native Commissioner flourished. This period roughly coincided with the greater consolidation of South African rule in SWA and the decreasing likelihood, especially in the north, that colonial practices might be called into question from within. Likewise Hahn's personal life settled into a new phase in 1927 with his marriage to Alcye Fogarty, the tomboyish daughter of the Anglican Bishop of Damaraland.[119] They had one son and occupied the Residency in Ondangwa as a family. The Ovamboland enquiry became no more than a bad memory, part of a troubling *préterrain* whose ambiguities could now fade in the light of Hahn's growing fame as an administrator and the stabilization of his domestic life. He broadened his intellectual interests to include botany, zoology and game conservation, and continued his amateur photography. His visual representations of public occasions, especially in his favourite region, Oukwanyama, projected a consensus over indirect rule and were considered so persuasive that they were regularly included in the official *Annual Reports to the League of Nations*.[120]

The questions raised by the Ovamboland enquiry remain crucial to Namibian historiography and to an understanding of the processes of state construction in Ovamboland from 1915. That these processes were connected to projections of white male identity must be obvious. But the most important point made in this chapter is that colonial power worked simultaneously through the production of knowledge and the exercise of physical force, and both were gendered to the core. The smooth image of Hahn and 'native' administration in the first decades of South African rule is disrupted, which broadens the possibilities for those other histories which arise from individual and collective memory in Ovamboland.

Some questions of course will never be answered. There remains tremendous difficulty in understanding exactly what happened to the Ovambo woman whose presence erupts and then disappears from the text of the enquiry, and why she appeared and vanished from the historical record. Her suffering prefigures the fate of many more women in the war zone that Ovamboland became in the 1970s and 1980s. And can resistance strategies, including those nationalist historical reconstructions which critique the colonial system inaugurated by Hahn, ever address the wrongs arising from gender?[121]

Notes

From *Gender and History*, 8:3 (November 1996), 364–92. Thanks are due to many colleagues and friends who offered insights, references and inspiration in the writing of this chapter, to those who attended presentations of earlier drafts in Boston, Basel and the Western Cape, and to *Gender and History*'s editors and anonymous readers. I am indebted to the South African Museum (Cape Town), and the Basler Afrika Bibliographien (Switzerland) for the photographs; the views expressed about them are my own.

1 A full account of the simultaneous colonization by South Africa and Portugal in Ovamboland can be found in Patricia Hayes, 'A History of the Ovambo of Namibia, *c.* 1880–1930' (Ph.D. thesis, Cambridge University, 1992).

2 See Jeremy Silvester, Patricia Hayes and Marion Wallace, 'Introduction', in *Trees Never Meet': Mobility and Containment in Namibia, 1915–1946*, ed. Patricia Hayes, Jeremy Silvester, Marion Wallace, Wolfram Hartmann with Ben Fuller (Windhoek, 1996 forthcoming); also Marion Wallace, '"A Person is Never Angry for Nothing": Women, Venereal Disease and Windhoek'; Patricia Hayes, '"The Famine of the Dams": Gender, Labour and Politics in Colonial Ovamboland, 1929–1930', and Meredith McKittrick, 'Generational Struggles and Social Mobility in Ovambo Communities, 1915–1954', all in *Trees Never Meet'*.

3 Peter Pels, 'The Construction of Ethnographic Occasions in Late Colonial Uluguru', *History and Anthropology*, 8 (1994), p. 322.

4 Peter Pels and Oscar Salemink, 'Introduction: Five Theses on Ethnography as Colonial Practice', *History and Anthropology*, 8 (1994), pp. 1–34, especially p. 4.

5 Pels, 'The Construction of Ethnographic Occasions', p. 322.

6 *Ibid*.

7 Cape Archives Depot, A2048 Vol. 13 MS 12/986, Hugo Hahn, biographical notes and drafts 'Baron von Linsingen', n.d.

8 Paarl Boys' High School, *Hoër Jongenskool Paarl Eeufees* (Paarl, 1968).

9 Patrick Harries, personal communication, July 1994.

10 This phrase is borrowed from Paul Monette's suggestive autobiographical work on the development of male identity, *Becoming a Man* (London, 1994).

11 Toby Miller, 'A Short History of the Penis', *Social Text*, 43 (1995), p. 4.

12 Patrick Harries, personal communication.

13 Miller, 'Short History of the Penis', pp. 1–2, 4.

14 Paarl Boys' High School, *Hoër Jongenskool*.

15 Teddy Schnapps, A *Statistical History of Springbok Rugby: Players, Tours and Matches* (Johannesburg, 1989), pp. 39, 170.

16 See obituaries in the *Cape Times* and *Cape Argus*, 28 September 1948.

17 On the rivalries and cliques among white settlers and officials in this period of Namibia's history, see *'Trees Never Meet'*, ed. Hayes *et al.*, Introduction.

18 Hayes, 'History of the Ovambo', pp. 291–2.

19 Eric Rosenthal, *Southern African Dictionary of National Biography* (London and New York, 1966), p. 155.

20 Excellent primary sources on this episode include Union of South Africa, *Report on the Conduct of the Ovakuanyama Chief Mandume and on the Military Operations conducted against him in Ovamboland* (Cape Town, 1917); National Archives of Namibia (NAN), A450, Vol. 23, Intelligence Diary, Ovamboland Expeditionary Force, 1916–1917; and Hayes, 'History of the Ovambo', vol. 2, Interview with Vilho Kaulinge, Ondobe, 30 September 1989, pp. 27–86.

21 NAN, NAO 1 1/2 v 1, C. H. L. Hahn, 1919–36.

22 Nissan Davis, '"Shongola": Cocky Hahn, "The Whip"', *South West Africa Annual*, 1977, p. 33; see NAN, A450 Vol. 15 8/1–8/5 for Hahn's record of these proceedings.

23 Cited in Davis, '"Shongola"', p. 33. For details of Harlech's and Hailey's tours to Ovamboland in the 1940s, see NAN, NAO 27, 22/1, Tours to Ovamboland: itinerary Lord Harlech; itinerary Lord Hailey.

24 Lawrence G. Green, *Lords of the Last Frontier* (Cape Town, 1952).

25 John M. MacKenzie, 'The Imperial Pioneer and Hunter and the British Masculine Stereotype in Late Victorian and Edwardian Times', in *Manliness and Morality: Middle-Class Masculinity in Britain and America 1800–1940*, ed. J. A. Mangan and James Walvin (Manchester, 1987), p. 179.

26 Gwyn Prins, 'The Battle for Control of the Camera in Late Nineteenth Century Western Zambia', *African Affairs*, 89 (1990), p. 97.

27 Lord Lugard, *The Dual Mandate in British Tropical Africa* (London, 1922).

28 Hayes, 'History of the Ovambo', pp. 245–50, and McKittrick, 'Generational Struggles and Social Mobility', in *'Trees Never Meet'*, ed. Hayes *et al.*

29 John Iliffe, *A Modern History of Tanganyika* (Cambridge, 1979), p. 321, citing the Tanganyikan administrator, David Cameron.

30 Steven Feierman, *Peasant Intellectuals. Anthropology and History in Tanzania* (Madison WI, 1990), p. 153.

31 Green, *Lords of the Last Frontier*, p. 234.

32 See Negley Farson, *Behind God's Back* (London, 1941), pp. 91–101, Green, *Lords of the Last Frontier*, p. 238; NAN, NAO 27, 22/1, Tours to Ovamboland, itinerary General Holcomb 1946; itinerary Lord Hailey 1946; itinerary Lord Harlech 1944.

33 On Hahn's theories concerning 'balance' in nature, see NAN, NAO Vol. 39 33/1, NC

Ovamboland – Secretary SWA, 15 February 1938.

34 NAN, NAO Vol. 13 6/2/5 v 1, NC Ovamboland – Secretary SWA, 11 January 1935; Vol. 13 6/3/1, NC Ovamboland – Secretary SWA, 28 July 1936. On 'dressed natives' and the influence of mining discourses on Native Affairs, see Randall M. Packard, 'The "Healthy Reserve" and the "Dressed Native": Discourses of Black Health and the Language of Legitimation in South Africa', *American Ethnologist*, 16 (1989), pp. 686–703.

35 One store run by the mining concerns was opened in Ondonga from the mid-1920s.

36 For analysis of the contradictions inherent in allowing men to migrate while attempting to maintain a 'tribal' system, see McKittrick, 'Generational Struggles and Social Mobility' in *Trees Never Meet*, ed. Hayes *et al.* Attempts to control the movement of women from Ovamboland are covered in Hayes, '"Famine of the Dams"', also in *Trees Never Meet*.

37 See the Introduction and articles by Hayes, Wallace and McKittrick in *Trees Never Meet*, ed. Hayes *et al.*

38 Bishop Tobias, *Ovamboland Mission Quarterly Paper*, July 1935.

39 NAN, NAO Vol. 13 6/4/1 v 1, NC Ovamboland – Secretary SWA, 16 March 1936.

40 NAN, NAO Vol. 13 6/2/5, NC Ovamboland – Secretary SWA, 27 August 1935.

41 NAN, NAO Vol. 13 6/4/1 v 1, NC Ovamboland – Secretary SWA, 16 March 1936.

42 NAN, NAO Vol. 11 6/1/1, Kivinen – Secretary SWA, 8 March 1937.

43 NAN, NAO Vol. 13 6/3/1, NC Ovamboland – Secretary SWA, 28 July 1936.

44 NAN, A450, C. H. L. Hahn papers, Vol. 4, Minute No. 32/5, Hahn, 17 April 1947.

45 A similar case is broached in Hilary Sapire, 'Apartheid's "Testing Ground": Urban "Native Policy" and African Politics in Brakpan, South Africa, 1943–1948', *Journal of African History*, 35 (1994), pp. 99–123.

46 C. H. L. Hahn, L. Fourie and H. Vedder, *The Native Tribes of South West Africa* (Cape Town, 1928). The Medical Officer of the territory, Louis Fourie, solicited and edited this and other writings by Hahn for the League of Nations and local publications such as the *Journal of the South West Africa Scientific Society*. NAN, A450, personal correspondence, Fourie to Hahn, 27 April 1928.

47 NAN, A2048, Vol. 13, Carl Hugo Hahn – C. H. L. Hahn, 15 June 1919.

48 Farson, *Behind God's Back*, p. 99.

49 For one example of such interrogation, see Robert Gordon, *The Bushman Myth: The Making of a Namibian Underclass* (Boulder CO, 1992), pp. 216–20.

50 An analysis of such processes in the production of medical knowledge about Africans can be found in Megan Vaughan, *Curing their Ills: Colonial Power and African Medicine* (Cambridge, 1991), esp. pp. 8–12. Material from Namibia suggests that the view of Engels and Marks that *violence directe* was the exception rather than the rule (at least in the British Empire) is not quite correct; see Dagmar Engels and Shula Marks (eds), *Contesting Colonial Hegemony: State and Society in Africa and India* (London and New York, 1994), esp. Introduction.

51 Luise White, 'Vampire Priests of Central Africa: African Debates about Labour and Religion in Colonial Northern Zambia', *Comparative Studies in Society and History*, 1993, p. 756, citing Hayden White, 'Historical Text as Literary Artifact', in *Tropics of Discourse: Essays in Cultural Criticism* (Baltimore MD, 1978), pp. 86–7.

52 Michael Taussig, 'Culture of Terror – Space of Death: Roger Casement's Putumayo Report and the Explanation of Torture', *Comparative Studies in Society and History*, 26 (1984), p. 483.

53 See James C. Scott, *Domination and the Arts of Resistance: Hidden Transcripts* (New Haven CT and London, 1990), pp. 55–6. This periodization of the consolidation of South African rule is argued in *Trees Never Meet*, ed. Hayes *et al.*, Introduction.

54 Percival Cameron Chaplin was born in Colchester, Essex, in 1880. NAN, SWAA 1893, 406/4/103.

55 NAN, SWAA 2/19/3, Complaints against Ovamboland Officials, Exhibits: P. Chaplin, 'My Experiences in the South West Africa Administration', n.d. (*c.* 1923–25).

56 See MacKenzie, 'The Imperial Pioneer and Hunter', and Allen Warren, 'Popular Manliness: Baden Powell, Scouting and the Development of the Manly Character', both in *Manliness and Morality*, ed. Mangan and Walvin, pp. 176–98 and 199–219.

57 NAN, NAW 7/1919/10, Officer in Charge, Native Affairs, Windhoek – P. Chaplin, Clerk in Charge, Location Office, Windhoek, 26 February 1919.

58 NAN, SWAA 2/19/3, Ovamboland Enquiry, Manning to Secretary SWA, 27 November 1923.

59 NAN, SWAA 2/19/3, Ovamboland Enquiry, Hahn statement, Ondonga, 26 October 1923.

60 NAN, SWAA 2/19/3, Ovamboland Enquiry, Proceedings, p. 17. The notion that this wound feminized Chaplin is influenced by recent scholarship on male sexuality in prisons and mine compounds in southern Africa; see for example Zackie Achmat, '"Apostles of Civilised Vice": "Immoral Practices" and "Unnatural Vice" in South African Prisons and Compounds, 1890–1920', *Social Dynamics*, 19 (1993), pp. 92–110.

61 NAN, SWAA 2/19/3, Complaints against Ovamboland Officials, Exhibits: P. Chaplin, 'My Experiences in the South West Africa Administration', n.d (*c.* 1923–25).

62 NAN, SWAA 2/19/3, Ovamboland Enquiry, Proceedings, p. 138.

63 NAN, SWAA 2/19/3, Ovamboland Enquiry, Scott – Administrator SWA, 15 September 1925.

64 NAN, SWAA 2/19/3, Ovamboland Enquiry, Proceedings, p. 9.

65 *Ibid.*

66 NAN, SWAA 2/19/3, Ovamboland Enquiry, Proceedings, pp. 99–105 and 126–7.

67 NAN, SWAA 2/19/3, Ovamboland Enquiry, Scott – Administrator SWA, 15 September 1925.

68 NAN, SWAA 2/19/3, Ovamboland Enquiry, Proceedings, pp. 1–24.

69 NAN, SWAA 2/19/3, Ovamboland Enquiry, Proceedings, p. 137.

70 NAN, SWAA 2/19/3, Ovamboland Enquiry, Proceedings, pp. 137–8.

71 Union of South Africa, *Report on the Natives of South West Africa and their Treatment by Germany*, Command Paper 9146 (Pretoria, 1918).

72 Anthony Brian Emmett, 'Popular Resistance in Namibia', in *Namibia 1884–1984: Readings on History and Society*, ed. Brian Wood (London, 1988), pp. 224–58. See also David Killingray, 'The "Rod of Empire": The Debate over Corporal Punishment in the British African Colonial Forces, 1888–1946', *Journal of African History*, 35 (1994), pp. 201–16.

73 Reference to flogging in Windhoek can be found in NAN, MWI 36/1/37 Vol. 10, Advisory Board Minutes.

74 NAN, RCO 10/1916/1 v 1, Fairlie, Memorandum, Omatemba, *c.* 1916.

75 NAN, RCO 1/1916/11, RC Ovamboland – Secretary Protectorate, 14 November 1916. A subtext to the Ovamboland Enquiry was the affidavit submitted to Hahn's lawyers in Windhoek in 1925, which stated that Chaplin had spread rumours concerning Hahn's sexual activities with Ovambo women but that these were unfounded. NAN, A450 Vol. 1, W. Eedes affidavit, 13 October 1925.

76 NAN, A 233, William Chapman Memoirs Vol. 2, p. 83.

77 Interviews with Titus Iita, Ombalantu, 3 November 1989; Simpson Ndatipo, Nakayale, 3 November 1989; and Petrus Amutenya, Ongandjera, 28 September 1989,

78 Patricia Hayes, 'Order Out of Chaos: Mandume Ya Ndemufayo and Oral History', *Journal of Southern African Studies*, 19 (1993), pp. 89–113.

79 NAN, MWI 36/1/37 v 13, Deputation to the Administration of Hereros Resident in the Location on 12 June 1936.

80 Farson, *Behind God's Back*, p. 99; also in Davis, '"Shongola"', p. 33. The official interpreter, Booi, also refers to this incident in NAN, SWAA 2/19/3, Ovamboland Enquiry, Proceedings, pp. 70–1.

81 One of the numerous examples can be found in Elizabeth Schmidt, *Peasants, Traders, and Wives: Shona Women in the History of Zimbabwe, 1870–1939* (London, 1992), p. 77.

82 See Albert Grundlingh, 'Playing for Power: Rugby: Afrikaner Nationalism and Masculinity in South Africa', in *Beyond the Tryline: Rugby and South African Society*, ed. Albert Grundlingh, André Odendaal and Burridge Spies (Johannesburg, 1995), pp. 106–35. The German name 'Hahn' translates as 'cock' or 'rooster'; it was common in South Africa for nicknames to be ironic derivatives of such surnames.

83 NAN, SWAA 2/19/3, Ovemboland Enquiry, Proceedings, p. 113.

84 NAN, SWAA 2/19/3, Ovamboland Enquiry, Proceedings, p. 109.

85 NAN, SWAA 2/19/3, Ovamboland Enquiry, Proceedings, p. 113.

86 NAN, SWAA 2/19/3, Ovamboland Enquiry, Proceedings, p. 138.

87 NAN, SWAA 2/19/3, Magistrate Scott – Administrator SWA, 15 September 1925.

88 *Ibid*. The only other figure to bring an accusation against Ovamboland officers, Postmaster Downey in Tsumeb, was charged with misconduct. NAN, SWAA 2/19/4, Ovamboland Enquiry, G. W. Downey, November 1925–March 1926.

89 NAN, SWAA 2/19/3, Ovamboland Enquiry, Proceedings, p. 109. Chaplin blamed his previous lapse of memory of this incident on the 'worry and injustice' he had received at the hands of the SWA administration over a long period of time.

90 Lynn A. Higgins and Brenda R. Silver (eds) *Rape and Representation* (New York, 1991), pp. 2–3.

91 Hayes, '"Famine of the Dams"', in *'Trees Never Meet'*, ed. Hayes *et al.*, citing Joan Scott, *Gender and the Politics of History* (New York, 1988) p. 27.

92 Maurice Halbwachs, *On Collective Memory*, ed. and trans. Lewis A. Coser (Chicago IL, 1992), esp. p. 23.

93 NAN, A450. See photograph collection, boxes P1–P4. It is unclear whether the swastika was placed on this postcard for pro- or anti-Nazi purposes, probably the latter.

94 The plenitude of this image in print comes out strikingly from the exhibition of historical representations of the Khoisan mounted in Cape Town, entitled 'Miscast: Negotiating Khoisan History and Material Culture' (South African National Gallery, 13 April–15 September 1996, curated by Pippa Skotnes). See Francis Galton, *Narrative of an Exploration in Tropical South Africa, being an Account of a Visit to Damaraland in 1851* (third edition, London, 1890), p. 54. The longevity of this fascination is discussed in Carmel Schrire, 'Native Views of Western Eyes', in *Miscast: Negotiating the Presence of the Bushmen*, ed. Pippa Skotnes (Cape Town, 1996), p. 350.

95 On Cuvier and the Venus Hottentot, see Sander Gilman, 'Black Bodies, White Bodies: Toward an Iconography of Female Sexuality in Late Nineteenth Century Art, Medicine and Literature', *Critical Inquiry*, 1985, pp. 204–42. Griqua communities in the northern Cape have requested the return of her remains from the Musée de l'Homme in Paris for honourable reburial; see 'Forum on Khoisan History and Material Culture', South African National Gallery, 14 April 1996, and testimonies submitted to the Truth and Reconciliation Commission hearings, South Africa, April–May 1996.

96 See Raymond A. Dart, 'The Physical Character of the Bushman', *Bantu Studies*, 11 (1937), pp. 219–26; Phillip V. Tobias, 'Bushmen of the Kalahari', *Man*, 36 (1957), pp. 33–40. (Thanks to Ciraj Rassool for these connected references.) For Hahn's correspondence with Hoernlé at the University of the Witwatersrand in Johannesburg and his receipt of lecture notes on Bantu Studies from that institution, see NAN, A450.

97 Schrire, 'Native Views of Western Eyes', pp. 343–54.

98 NAN, NAO 1, 1/2 v 2, NC Ovamboland – Clarke, 1 April 1937.

99 Hahn was not yet married; he shared quarters in Ovamboland with other male officers.

100 John Comaroff and Jean Comaroff, *Of Revelation and Revolution: Christianity, Colonialism, and Consciousness in South Africa* I (Chicago IL, 1991), p. 123.

101 NAN, SWAA 2/19/3, Ovamboland Enquiry, Proceedings, pp. 88–9.

102 Nancy Rose Hunt, 'Domesticity and Colonialism in Belgian Africa: Usumbura's Foyer Social, 1946–1960', *Signs*, 15 (1990), pp. 447–74.

103 Terence S. Turner, 'The Social Skin', in *Not Work Alone*, ed J. Cherfas and R. Lewin (London, 1980).

104 Interviews with Helena Shihutuka, Oshatotwa, 28 June 1994, and Albertina Hipulenga ya Hamukoto, Onekwaya, 26 June 1994

105 NAN, NAO Vol. 19, Annual Report 1937, pp. 19–20.

106 Taussig, 'Culture of Terror – Space of Death', p. 483.

107 Interviews with Helena Shihutuka, Oshatotwa, 28 June 1994, and Albertina Hipulenga ya

Hamukoto, Onekwaya, 26 June 1994.

108 Carolyn Hamilton's study of Theophilus Shepstone and the Zulu suggests that the receptivity of certain white men to African forms of power explains their performance of power and even in some cases the perpetration of violence; see Carolyn Hamilton, 'Authoring Shaka: Models, Metaphors and Historiography' (Ph.D. dissertation, Johns Hopkins University, 1993), chs 5–6.

109 When preparing for his overseas trip in 1937, Administrator Clarke wrote to Hahn: 'The Marquis' [Theodoli] idea, if I remember correctly, was that you were a "real live Ovambo" and you must be prepared to satisfy Mlle Dannevig's thirst for the real article.' This was with reference to presenting materials on Ovamboland to members of the Permanent Mandates Commission. NAN, NAO 1/2 v 2, Clarke to Hahn, 8 February 1937. See also Davis, '"Shongola"', p. 33.

110 Jeremy Silvester provided this information from the files of the South West Africa Administration in the National Archives of Namibia in 1994.

111 Nancy Robson, personal communication, Odibo, September 1994.

112 Allen Feldman, *Formations of Violence: The Narrative of the Body and Political Terror in Northern Ireland* (Chicago IL, 1991).

113 See for example E. M. Ellis, B. M. Atkeson and K. S. Calhoun, 'An Assessment of Long-term Reaction to Rape', *Journal of Abnormal Psychology*, 90 (1981), pp. 263–6.

114 Ken Wilson, 'Cults of Violence and Counter-violence in Mozambique', *Journal of Southern African Studies*, 18 (1992), pp. 527–83.

115 Feldman, *Formations of Violence*, p. 10.

116 *Ibid*, p. 177.

117 See Richard Moorsom, 'Underdevelopment, Contract Labour and Worker Consciousness in Namibia, 1915–72', *Journal of Southern African Studies*, 4 (1977), pp. 52–87; and Richard Moorsom, 'Labour Consciousness and the 1971–72 Contract Workers' Strike in Namibia', *Development and Change*, 10 (1979), pp. 205–31.

118 The political disturbances, floggings and legal cases in Ovamboland were widely covered in the Namibian and South African press at the time. For a summary and a statement by the Lutheran Bishop Leonard Auala on Hahn's responsibility, see *The Observer*, 7 April 1974. See also David Soggott, *Namibia: The Violent Heritage* (London, 1986); Soggott was one of the lawyers employed to seek an injunction against the flogging.

119 'A Wilderness Wedding', *Windhoek Advertiser*, 26 February 1927.

120 These photographs have been analysed in the exhibition by Patricia Hayes, Jeremy Silvester and Wolfram Hartmann, 'The Colonising Camera: Photographs in the Making of Namibian History, 1915–1946', exhibited at the University of Cape Town in May 1995, Yale University in January–February 1996, and various venues in Namibia between 1994 and 1996.

121 Ovamboland became the main theatre of guerrilla warfare in the struggle against South African rule launched by the South West Africa People's Organisation (SWAPO). For the impact of warfare on women in the region, see Soggott, *Violent Heritage*; Tessa Cleaver and Marion Wallace, *Namibia: Women at War* (London, 1990); Colin Leys and John S. Saul (eds) *Namibia's Liberation Struggle: The Two-edged Sword* (London, 1995); Panduleni Kali and Ndamona Kali, 'SWAPO's Prisons in Angola', *Searchlight South Africa*, 4, February 1990; Paul Trewhela, 'Women and SWAPO: Institutionalised Rape in SWAPO's Prisons', *Searchlight South Africa*, 11, October 1993, pp. 23–9; and Siegfried Groth, *Namibia – the Wall of Silence* (Wuppertal, 1995).

PART IV
Legacies of empire

15

Not just (any) *body* can be a citizen: the politics of law, sexuality and postcoloniality in Trinidad and Tobago and the Bahamas

M. JACQUI ALEXANDER

I am an outlaw in my country of birth: a national; but not a citizen. Born in Trinidad and Tobago on the cusp of anti-colonial nationalist movements there, I was taught that once we pledged our lives to the new nation, 'every creed and race [had] an equal place'. I was taught to believe 'Massa Day Done', that there would be an imminent end to foreign domination. Subsequent governments have not only eclipsed these promises, they have revised the very terms of citizenship to exclude me. No longer equal, I can be brought up on charges of 'serious indecency' under the Sexual Offences Act of 1986, and if convicted, serve a prison term of five years. In the Bahamas, I can be found guilty of the *crime* of lesbianism and imprisoned for twenty years. In the United States of North America where I now live, I must constantly keep in my possession the immigrant (green) card given me by the American state, marking me 'legal' resident alien; non-national; non-citizen. If I traverse any of the borders of twenty-two states even *with* green card in hand, I may be convicted of crimes variously defined as 'lewd unnatural; lascivious conduct; deviate sexual intercourse; gross indecency; buggery or crimes against nature'.[1]

Why has the state marked these sexual inscriptions on my body? Why has the state focused such a repressive and regressive gaze on me and people like me? These are some of the questions I seek to understand in this chapter. I wish to use this moment to look back at the state, to reverse, subvert and ultimately demystify that gaze by taking apart these racialized legislative gestures that have naturalized heterosexuality by criminalizing lesbian and other forms of non-procreative sex. It is crucial for us as feminists to understand the ways in which the state deploys power in this domain and the kinds of symbolic boundaries it draws around sexual difference, for these are the very boundaries around which its power coheres.[2] Indeed, 'homosexual' difference is indispensable to the creation of the putative heterosexual norm. Located, then, within the very oppositional movements which the state has outlawed, I look back as part of the ongoing and complicated process of decolonization and reconstruction of the self, a project which has been seriously disrupted in most 'postcolonial' nation states.

I want to suggest a way of thinking about state nationalism and its sexualization of particular bodies in Trinidad and Tobago and the Bahamas in order to determine whether such bodies are offered up, as it were, in an internal struggle for legitimation in which these postcolonial states are currently engulfed. What kinds of reassurances do these bodies provide, and for whom? The state's authority to rule is currently under siege; the ideological moorings of nationalism have been dislodged, partly because of major international political economic incursions that have in turn provoked an internal crisis of authority. I argue that in this context criminalization functions as a technology of control, and much like other technologies of control becomes an important site for the production and reproduction of state power.[3]

Although policing the sexual (stigmatizing and outlawing several kinds of non-procreative sex, particularly lesbian and gay sex and prostitution) has something to do with sex, it is also more than sex. Embedded here are powerful signifiers about appropriate sexuality, about the kind of sexuality that presumably imperils the nation and about the kind of sexuality that promotes citizenship. Not just (any) *body* can be a citizen any more, for *some* bodies have been marked by the state as non-procreative, in pursuit of sex only for pleasure, a sex that is non-productive of babies and of no economic gain. Having refused the heterosexual imperative of citizenship, *these* bodies, according to the state, pose a profound threat to the very survival of the nation. Thus, I argue that as the state moves to reconfigure the nation it simultaneously resuscitates the nation as hetero*sexual*.

Yet, the focus on state power is not to imply rationality or even internal coherence. In fact, what is evident in the legislation and in other contextual gestures surrounding it are paradoxical and contradictory ways in which the state exerts its will to power. Seemingly emancipatory practices such as legal 'protections' of women's interests or provisions which constrain violent domestic patriarchy are crafted in the same frame that disciplines and punishes people with HIV infection, and women who exercise erotic autonomy. In addition, the state moves to police the sexual and reinscribe inherited and more recently constructed meanings of masculinity and femininity, while simultaneously mediating a political economy of desire in tourism that relies upon the sexualization and commodification of women's bodies. Further, the nationalist state mediates the massive entry of transnational capital within national borders, but blames sexual decadence (lesbian and gay sex and prostitution) for the dissolution of the nation. It may no longer be possible to understand the state purely within the boundaries of the nation because these global processes are rapidly transforming the ways that nations constitute and imagine themselves. This is why methodologically I foreground the economic and political processes of transnationalization to better examine the processes of sexualization undertaken in the legal text. The role of the imperial in transforming the national is therefore crucial.

These paradoxes raise some perplexing questions for feminist theorizing and for oppositional movements. Clearly feminist mobilizations have been successful in wresting certain concessions from the state and in inaugurating vigorous public discussion about sexualized violence. They have also challenged the state on its meaning and definitions of crisis. Yet feminists are also caught in the paradoxical discursive parameters set up by the state and end up helping to devise and monitor the state's mechanisms that surveille criminalized women. On what basis, then, would solidarity work among different women be possible? Further, when one examines the effects of these transformations, it becomes clear that some areas of patriarchy have been challenged while others have been resolidified. Citizenship, for instance, continues to be premised within heterosexuality and principally within heteromasculinity. In the absence of visible lesbian and gay movements, can feminist political struggles radically transform these historically repressive structures? How can women inscribe their own interests within fundamentally masculinist organizations?[4]

I shall begin by reading the ways in which the heterosexual is naturalized in the legal text in order to isolate its importance to the state. In the section that follows, I analyse the ways in which naturalized heterosexuality shapes the definitions of respectability, Black masculinity and nationalism. We come full circle, then, as I argue that the effects of political economic international processes provoke a legitimation crisis for the state which moves to restore its legitimacy by recouping heterosexuality through legislation. I end by suggesting that the process of decolonization, which the nationalist state had claimed as its own, has been seriously disrupted and I draw out the implications for oppositional movements and analyses.

Naturalizing heterosexuality as law

In 1986, the Parliament of the Republic of Trinidad and Tobago scripted and passed the Sexual Offences Act: 'An Act to Repeal and Replace the Laws of the Country relating to Sexual Crimes, to the Procuration, Abduction and Prostitution of Persons and to Kindred Offences.' This gesture of consolidation was, in the words of law commissioners, an attempt 'to bring all laws dealing with sexual offences under one heading'. It was the first time the postcolonial state confronted earlier colonial practices which policed and scripted 'native' sexuality to help consolidate the myth of imperial authority.

Many of the thirty-five provisions of the legislation, then, had prior lives, and were being reconsolidated under a different schedule of punishments. Prohibitions regarding sexual violence within the family (incest), and against women who exchanged sex for money (prostitutes) and those who aided them (brothel-keepers), or those who exploited them (pimps) had long been established in the emendations to the Offences against the Person Acts, that one-sided pivot of British jurisprudence. In keeping with its allegiance to hegemonic masculinity, the script upheld a prior provision that defined anal intercourse between men as buggery, outlawed it, and affixed a penalty of ten years' imprisonment, if convicted. It moved, in addition, to criminalize new areas of sexual activity. Established were prohibitions against employers who took sexual advantage of their minor employees at the workplace, and against men who had sex with fourteen-to-sixteen-year-old girls, who would now be guilty of a statutory offence. For the first time, a category called rape within marriage was established and criminalized: 'Any "husband" who had forceful intercourse with his "wife" without her consent' could be convicted and imprisoned for fifteen years under a new offence called sexual assault; and sex between women became punishable by five years under a new offence called '"serious indecency", if committed on or towards a person sixteen years or more'.

Three years later, the parliament of the Bahamas scripted and passed its own version of the Sexual Offences Act, cited as the 'Sexual Offences and Domestic Violence Act of 1989', *its* gesture of consolidation, formulated by law commissioners 'as an attempt to provide one comprehensive piece of legislation setting out sexual offences which are indictable', seeking, in its words, 'to make better provision in respect of the rights in the occupation of the matrimonial home'. As in the case of Trinidad and Tobago, it was the first attempt to impose a veiled sexual order on the chaotic legacy of colonialism. The commission had hoped to deal not only with this chaos, but also with the disruptions and violence of conjugal relations by reasserting the primacy of the matrimonial home and the rights of '*any* person' residing therein.

Its thirty-one provisions bore a close resemblance to those of Trinidad and Tobago in terms of the injunctions, prohibitions and schedule of punishments against prostitution, incest, and sexual harassment and assault in the workplace. It too, conflated buggery, bestiality and criminality: 'If any two persons are guilty of the crime of buggery – an unnatural crime, or if any person is guilty of unnatural connection with any animal, every such person is guilty of an offence and liable to imprisonment for twenty years.' This definition resembles the first civil injunction against sodomy that was legislated in 1533 in Henry VIII's parliament.[5] In its injunction against sex between women, it abandoned the coyness of the Trinidad legislature in favour of an explicit approach that pronounced, criminalized and penalized a sexual activity in one single gesture: 'Any female who has sexual intercourse with another female, whether with or without the consent of that female, is guilty of the offence of lesbianism and is liable to imprisonment for twenty years.' Similarly, under restrictive stipulations that were an exact replication of those in Trinidad, it moved to criminalize violent marital sex, but fell short of calling it rape. The legislation asserted: 'Any person who has sexual intercourse with his spouse without the consent of the spouse is guilty of the offence of sexual assault and liable to imprisonment for fifteen years.' The law also moved to imprison (for five years) anyone with HIV infection who had consensual sex without disclosing their HIV status.

Its new provision, relating to domestic violence, made it possible for *any* party in the marriage to apply to the Supreme Court for an injunction that would restrain the other party from molestation and from using violence in the matrimonial home. What is remarkable about this Act that calls itself a Domestic Violence Act is that nowhere is there a definition of domestic violence. Rather the majority of the provisions focus upon the disposition of private property and on the minute distinctions among 'dwelling, estate, apartment', etc. These were not the terms on which the women's movement in the Bahamas had pushed for the criminalization of domestic violence. Over a five-year period women held public rallies, campaigned door to door and gained more than 10,000 signatures and the knowledge from women's experiences of physical and sexual violence against themselves and their daughters. It would seem, then, that even in the face of violent disruptions in marriage, conjugal heterosexuality is most concerned with the patrilineal transfer of private property.

Legislative gestures fix conjugal heterosexuality in several ways. Generally, they collapse identities into sexual bodies which, in the particular case of lesbian and gay people, serves to reinforce a fiction about promiscuity: that sex is all of what we do and consequently the slippage, it is all of who we are. Yet lesbian and gay sex, the 'perverted', the 'unnatural' are all indispensable to the formulation of the 'natural', the conjugal, the heterosexual. This dialectic must be made visible, for there is no absolute set of commonly understood or accepted principles called the 'natural' which can be invoked definitionally except as they relate to what is labelled 'unnatural'. Here is a remarkably circular definition of sexual intercourse that was attached as a supplementary note to the Trinidad and Tobago Act:

> [The Clauses] do not necessarily define 'sexual intercourse' but give a characteristic of it. 'Sexual intercourse' means natural sexual intercourse in the clauses relating to rape and other offences of sexual intercourse with women, whereas the clause concerned with buggery relates to unnatural sexual intercourse.

Heterosexual sex, even while dysfunctional (as in rape in marriage, domestic violence and incest), assumes the power of natural law only in relation to sex which is defined in negation to it (what natural sexual intercourse is not) and in those instances where desire presumably becomes so corrupt that it expresses itself as bestiality. In other words, heterosexual practices carry the weight of the natural only in relational terms and ultimately, one might argue, only in its power to designate as unnatural those practices which disrupt marriage and certain dominant notions of conjugal family. Beyond that, sexual intercourse remains necessarily, remarkably unclarified.

Conjugal heterosexuality is frozen within a very specific and narrow set of class relations between 'husband' and 'wife' in 'marriage', narrow because the majority of heterosexual relationships are in fact organized outside of this domain. Even while the Bahamian legislation might appear to address violence in all 'domestic' domains, its skewed emphasis on private property immediately renders it class-specific. For working-class women who do not own property and are beaten by the men with whom they live, this legislation offers no protection. And even for middle-class and upper middle-class women who are beaten by their husbands and might own property, the problem they face is how to disentangle the web of well connected social relationships that protect *their* middle-class and upper middle-class husbands from being prosecuted as criminals. For most women who stand outside of the legal definitions of 'parties to a marriage', they can make no claims for relief from the state. Thus, domestic violence works as a proxy for class and facilitates the reallocation of private property in disruptive conjugal marriage.

Both pieces of legislation systematically conflate violent hetero*sexual* domination, such as rape and incest, with same-sex relations, thereby establishing a continuum of criminality among same-*sex* rape, domestic violence, adultery, fornication and dishonesty. On this continuum the psyche of homosexuality becomes the psyche of criminality. By criminalizing perverted heterosexual sex, the legislation aims to expunge criminal elements from the heterosexual so that it could return to its originary and superior moral position. However, homosexuality, inherently perverse, could only be cleansed by reverting to heterosexuality. And still, not all heterosexualities are permissible: not the prostitute with an irresponsible, 'non-productive' sexuality, and not young women whom the state defines as girls requiring its protection.

Outside the boundaries of the legislation, yet informing it, state managers generated a simultaneous discourse invoking nostalgia for a Bahamas and Trinidad and Tobago when there were ostensibly no lesbians, gay men and people with AIDS. In this move, heterosexuality becomes coterminus with and gives birth to the nation. Its antithesis can unravel the nation. The state has eroticized the dissolution of the nation, producing apocalyptic (mythic) visions of dread disease and destruction (paralleled in the destruction of Sodom and Gomorrah) brought about by prostitution and the practice of lesbian and gay sex. Yet, it simultaneously enacts the dissolution of the nation through a series of political-economic gestures (adherence to the narratives and practices of modernization through allegiance to multinational capital, tourism, etc.) that it ideologically recodes as natural, even supernatural, as the salvation of the people. In this equation, tourism, foreign multinational capital production and imperialism are as integral and as necessary to the natural order as heterosexuality. But before examining these twin processes of sexualization and internationalization more closely, one would have to understand why conjugal heterosexuality is so important for nationalist state managers and the role it plays in constituting respectable masculinity. We would have to understand the sexual inheritances of nationalism as well as the new meanings of masculinity and femininity the nationalist state has invented.

State nationalism and respectability, Black masculinity come to power 1962, 1972

Women, and all signs of the feminine, are by definition always already anti-national.[6]

It would be difficult to map the minute and nuanced ways in which colonial hegemonic definitions of masculinity and femininity insinuated themselves throughout the variety of political, economic, social and cultural structures in history. We can, however, frame these definitions by examining what Kobena Mercer and Isaac Julien have called the 'hegemonic repertoire of images' which have been forged through the histories of slavery and colonization in order to identify the sexual inheritances of Black nationalism as well as its own inventions.[7] I am not suggesting that ideologies simply get foisted on to people,[8] for there is always an ongoing struggle to redefine power. What is crucial for my argument, however, is the intransigence of dominance and, in this instance, the continuities and discontinuities between the practices of the colonial and the 'postcolonial' around those very images.

In the repertoire of images that developed during the organization of slave-plantation economy and in the consolidation of imperial rule, the English gentleman was given primacy. In Trinidad and Tobago white militarized masculinity had to concede the right to rule to the civilian who would displace the importance of war and the more visible signs of policing and terror. Similarly in the Bahamas, the pirate, the rogue and the wrecker (white predatory masculinity) were engaged in a protracted struggle with the English gentleman for cultural and economic authority until the latter was installed as representative of the Crown in 1718. It marked the triumph of respectability and honour over the boorish, the disreputable.[9]

Colonial rule simultaneously involved racializing and sexualizing the population, which also meant naturalizing whiteness. There could really be no psycho-social codices of sexuality that were not simultaneously raced. In general terms, these codices functioned as mythic meta-systems fixing polarities, contradictions and fictions while masked as truth about character. 'Laws for the governing of Negroes, Mulattoes and Indians'[10] made it possible for white masculinity to stand outside the law. As the invisible subject of the law, he was neither prosecuted nor persecuted within it. Since it was lawful to reinforce the ontological paradox of slave as chattel, Elizabethan statutes of rape operated to legitimize violent colonial masculinity which was never called rape, yet criminalized black masculinity for rape. This would solidify the cult of true womanhood and its correlates, the white madonna (untouchable) and the Black whore (promiscuous).

Here too, identities were collapsed into bodies. Black bodies, the economic pivot of slave-plantation economy, were sexualized. Black women's bodies evidenced an unruly sexuality, untamed and wild. Black male sexuality was to be feared as the hypersexualized stalker. These dominant constructions worked to erase indigenous

(Lucayan, Carib and Arawak) sexualities. Indentured Indian femininity (in Trinidad and Tobago) was formulated as dread and desire, mysteriously wanton, inviting death and destruction, although it could also be domesticated. Indian manliness was unrestrained, violent and androgynous, the latter construction drawn from Britain's colonial experience in India. Free coloured women, who outnumbered Black women in the Bahamas, and their counterparts in Trinidad and Tobago who were believed anxious to 'acquire property and wealth by inheriting land for the natural white fathers', were also sexualized, but positioned as potential mates.[11] Even with these differences in the construction of 'native' sexualities, however, colonized sexualities were essentially subordinated sexualities.

It would indeed require a complicated set of cognitive and ideological reversals for the British to turn the savage into the civilized, to turn those believed incapable of rule into reliable rulers. Herein lies the significance of socialization into British norms, British manners, British parliamentary modes of governance; into conjugal marriage and the 'science' of domesticity. This would operate in effect as social-ization into respectability which George Mosse argues emerged in Europe at the end of the eighteenth century with the beginnings of modern nationalism. He argues that respectability emerged in alliance with sexuality and helped to shape middle-class beliefs about the body, sexual (mis)conduct, normality and abnorm-ality, about virility and manly bearing. The control over sexuality evidenced in the triumph of the nuclear family was vital to respectability.[12] Whereas in Europe these processes were indigenous to the formation of the middle class, in the Caribbean it was imported through imperialism. The Black middle class would be schooled in the definitions of morality, civility and respectable citizenship in the metropolis, in the company of the British, while 'women of reduced means' and the working class would be trained at 'home'. Specialized training schools like the Dundas Civic Centre in the Bahamas were established at the turn of this century to prepare cooks, general maids and hotel workers; and the Trinidad and Tobago Home Industries and Women's Self-help Organization and the Oleander Club of the Bahamas would train Black women in housewifery, cooking, sewing and knitting.[13]

It was the elites of the middle class who established the nationalist parties which later became part of the state apparatus. They mobilized consensus for nation building, moulded psychic expectations about citizenship and therefore consolid-ated their own internal power on the ideals of sovereignty, self-determination and autonomy from foreign mandates. Ostensibly this was a neutered invocation to citizenship; yet it is in the creation of the women's wing of these parties and in their organization of 'culture' that one begins to detect a gendered call to patriotic duty. Women were to fiercely defend the nation by protecting their honour, by guarding the nuclear, conjugal family, 'the fundamental institution of the society', by guarding 'culture' defined as the transmission of a fixed set of proper values to the children of the nation, and by mobilizing on the party's behalf into the far reaches of the country. She was expected to represent and uphold a respectable femininity and, in so doing, displace the figure of the white madonna. Patriotic duty for men, on the other hand, consisted in rendering public service to the country, and in adopting the mores of respectability. Thus, we can identify a certain trajectory in the establishment of nationalism which is grounded in notions of respectability, which like eighteenth-century European nationalism came to rely heavily upon sexual gestures that involved the *symbolic* triumph of the nuclear family over the extended family and other family forms.

In order to demonstrate that it had 'graduated from all schools of constitutional, economic and social philosophies',[14] and that it could comport itself with 'discipline, dignity and decorum, with the eyes of the world upon us',[15] Black nationalist masculinity needed to demonstrate that it was now capable of ruling, which is to say, it needed to demonstrate moral rectitude, particularly on questions of paternity. This required distancing itself from irresponsible Black working-class masculinity that spawned the 'bastard', the 'illegitimate', and that thus had to be criminalized for irresponsible fatherhood by the British. It also required distancing itself from, while simultaneously attempting to control, Black working-class femininity that ostensibly harboured a profligate sexuality: the 'Jezebel' and the whore who was not completely socialized into housewifery, but whose labour would be mobilized to help consolidate popular nationalism. Of significance is the fact that Black nationalist masculinity could aspire toward imperial masculinity and, if loyal enough, complicitous enough, could be knighted,[16] although it could never be enthroned. It could never become king.

If, as Toni Morrison has suggested, rescue and indebtedness sometimes sediment as part of the psychic residue of the process of colonization, then respect-ability might well function as debt payment for rescue from incivility and from savagery.[17] But a rescued masculinity is simultaneously an injured masculinity; a masculinity that does not emerge from the inherited conditions of class and race privilege. And it is injured in a space most vulnerable to colonial constructions of incivility. At one time subordinated, that masculinity now has to be earned, and then appropriately conferred. Acting through this psychic residue, Black mascu-linity continues the policing of sexualized bodies, drawing out the colonial fiction of locating subjectivity in the body (as a way of denying it), as if the colonial masters were still looking on, as if to convey legitimate claims to being civilized. Not having dismantled the underlying presuppositions of British law, Black nationalist men, now with some modicum of control over the state apparatus, continue to preside over and administer the same fictions.

To the extent that the sexual offences legislation polices non-procreative, 'non-productive' sex, especially in relationship to women, the neutered invocation to citizenship becomes transparent. In fact we can read state practices as attempts to propagate fictions of feminine identity, to reconfigure women's desire and subjectivity and to link the terms of the nation's survival to women's sexual organs. This is what Geraldine Heng calls, in the specific case of Singapore, 'the development of a sexualised, separate species of nationalism, a nationalism gener-ated from the productive source of the womb'. To understand it in Heng's terms, the indictment of prostitutes and lesbians inscribes 'a tacit recognition that feminine reproductive sexuality refuses, and in refusing registers a suspicion of that sexuality as non-economic, in pursuit of its own pleasure, sexuality for its own sake, unproductive of babies, unproductive of social and economic efficiency'.[18] It registers a suspicion of an unruly sexuality, omnipotent and omniscient enough to subvert the economic imperatives of the nation's interests. From the point of view of the state, it is a sexuality that has to be disciplined and regulated in order that it might become economically productive.

State claims of a non-productive femininity are deceptive in a number of different ways. Both the People's National Movement (PNM) of Trinidad and Tobago and the Progressive Liberal Party (PLP) of the Bahamas could not have consolidated their power or secured support for popular nationalism without women's labour, women who ironically would later have to struggle for citizenship. Yet, once installed, state nationalism came to stand in an authorial relationship to women's interests and women's agency. The claim also works to mask women's labour in other areas of the economy, particularly in the tourist sector where women are the majority of a proletarianized and superexploited workforce. Capital accumulations from sex tourism and prostitution have been hidden, but given what we know about tourism and postcolonialism in South East Asia, it would be most plausible to assume that for the Bahamas in particular, there would be substantial (although now unacknowledged) accumulation from prostitutes' labour.[19] Further, women's unpaid labour compensates for the state's refusal to expand the social wage and for the disjunctures brought about by the adoption of structural adjustment programmes. It is to these questions I turn in the following section.

(Inter)national boundaries and strategies of legitimation

I wish to foreground the effects of international political economic processes in provoking the legitimacy crisis nationalist states are currently confronting, and argue that the sexual is pivotal in state orchestration of a new internal struggle whose contours are different now than they were at the moment of flag independence. In an almost ideal-typical sense, the nation had come to be shaped by what it had opposed.[20] Public opposition to the British had provided powerful ideological fodder for independence. We had all suffered colonial injustice together, and it was out of that experience of collective suffering that a collective vision of sovereignty could be built. Since 'independence', the state has colluded in adopting strategies that have locked these nations into a world economic and political system, the effect of which is re-colonization. The internal effects of internationalization blur the boundaries of the nation; they do not constitute anything unique any more. Further, the reproduction of private accumulation by members of the indigenous bourgeoisie has been stifled,[21] local patronage networks have been disrupted and people's material and communal lives have dramatically deteriorated. Paradoxically, these same states simultaneously preside over the transfer of substantial profits to metropolitan countries. All of these effects replicate the racialized colonial pattern of poverty, private ownership and lack of access to resources. These are the very grounds on which oppositional movements have challenged the state; it is the reason that its moral claim to leadership is unravelling.

But this is not how state managers see the crisis. Both in Trinidad and Tobago and the Bahamas they sound the danger of cultural contamination from the 'West' which they depict simultaneously as sexual intemperance, the importation of AIDS and the importation of feminism (read lesbianism). The Bahamian state has invoked an impending population crisis, positioned Haitian communities as 'immigrants', 'refugees' and repositories of crime. It has vindicated its use of military and police force to expel Haitians from the nation's borders by claiming that they are no longer legitimate citizens, they imperil the nation. There are other strategies as well, ranging from policing oppositional movements and subtle, yet coercive ideological violence where Bahamian people, for instance, believe that the ballot is not a secret ballot and fear reprisals from the state. Individual state managers develop a patronage system to build their own authority in their own political interests, not necessarily consolidating support for nationalism, but for themselves and for their political parties.

State nationalism in Trinidad and Tobago and the Bahamas has neither reformulated nor transformed the fundamental premises upon which economic and material exchange is based. Its secular adherence to a linear definition of 'development' and progress has continued to imagine an (il)logic of a movement from 'tradition' to 'modernity' in which industrialization presumably serves as the motor for economic success. The contemporary version of development now called structural adjustment finds expression in a powerful, yet unequal alliance among foreign multinational lending agencies such as the International Monetary Fund (IMF), the World Bank, United States Agency for International Development (USAID), the American state and neo-colonial regimes. Their aim is to impose a set of lending arrangements that would ostensibly reduce the foreign debt through a combination of economic measures to accelerate foreign investment, boost foreign-exchange earnings through export, and reduce government deficits through cuts in spending.[22] In particular, the programmes have been organized to reduce local consumption by devaluing currency, increasing personal taxes and reducing wages. The economy becomes privatized through state subsidies to private vendors, lowering taxes and providing tax holidays for foreign multinational corporations, expanding investments in tourism, dismantling state-owned enterprises, and curtailing the scope of state bureaucratic power by reducing the workforce and reducing the social wage – those expenditures for a range of social services for which the state had previously assumed some responsibility.

Although the Bahamas has not formalized 'structural adjustment' programmes (SAP), the continued subordination of its economy to the political and economic imperatives of the United States of North America has resulted in an economic infrastructure that bears all the marks of a country that has actually adopted structural adjustment. The most dramatic shift is evident in the displacement of capital and labour forces from agrarian production to service which now employs more than 50 per cent of the workforce, massive increases in the size of the food import bill (people are no longer able to feed themselves), the consolidation of foreign transnational capital in the tourist industry (hotels, airlines, services and tour operators, international finance capital, real estate), and the expansion of offshore companies.

But perhaps the most significant and dramatic effect of SAP is that it has exacerbated the triple processes of proletarianization, superexploitation and feminization of the work force which began in the mid-1960s. By proletarianization I am referring not only to the influx, or even the magnitude of industrial capital, or the making of a gendered, racialized working class, but perhaps more importantly to the access that capital has in exploiting and even expelling relatively large percentages of the work force. What makes this impact so profound for the nation in both Trinidad and Tobago and the Bahamas is the small size of the work force.[23] In the Bahamas industrial capital has access to a sizeable portion of the work force. More than 65 per cent of the working population is employed in service, with women comprising more than 73 per cent of all workers, performing jobs such as housekeepers, cooks, maids, cleaners and laundresses. Two-thirds of these women earn incomes of $7,000 annually. Of the total workforce 22 per cent have never been employed. Women's unemployment, which has always been higher than men's, is 13 per cent, and that of men is 11.7 per cent and steadily increasing.[24]

In Trinidad and Tobago, the process of proletarianization which began in the 1970s has had different, yet similar effects. Private capital employs roughly the same amount of the work force as the state, 36 per cent and 38 per cent respectively. Areas such as construction, the impetus for proletarianization in the 1970s, have experienced severe retrenchment. This is particularly affecting women, whose rate of unemployment in that sector is now 73 per cent, compared to the national average of 46 per cent.[25] Like the Bahamas, there has been a significant growth in the service sector, but it has come from self-employment and within the state bureaucracy, where women work as clerical workers, nurses, teachers and maids. State retrenchments under IMF restrictions have increased women's unemployment. The overall unemployment rate in Trinidad and Tobago is 19 per cent; women's unemployment rate is 23 per cent.

Gendered superexploitation can best be assessed by the gap between workers' real wages and the profit which capital accrues and never returns to the work force. Overall, the rate of return from the United States' investment in the Caribbean is considerably higher (31 per cent to 14.3 per cent) than the returns generated from investments in other parts of the world.[26] In the Bahamas, almost three-fourths of households (74 per cent) live on an annual income of $10,000. Of these households, almost all (82 per cent) are headed by women, at least half of whom are employed in the tourist industry. In contrast, earnings from tourism contributed 61 per cent of the total export earnings of the Bahamian state.[27] The limitations of tourism as a national economic strategy are immediately apparent with the recognition that 81 cents of every tourist dollar spent in the Bahamas finds its way back to the United States.[28]

In the space between foreign- and state-controlled export has arisen a substantial informal economy that operates at different levels. Some elements of it are masculinized, particularly those in the drug trade that are linked to tourism. This marks another incursion on state control because people can make quick money and improve their standard of living. Drug lords can command authority and develop a horizontal patronage system that rivals that of state managers, while simultaneously remaining outside the arm of state regulation. In fact, state managers have had to deal with an erosion of their own credibility because of their complicity in the drug trade – one of the many faces of the underside of respectability.[29] Not labelled an illegal activity by the state, the feminized informal economy is involved in trade and marketing, relying on kinship, long-established peer networks and communal ties. Much like farmers' co-operatives, these networks provide for people's everyday needs.

It is difficult to imagine that these massive economic disjunctures with corresponding deterioration in the quality of people's daily lives, precipitated by SAP, would not provoke a major political crisis for the state. Emerging within this crisis are serious contestations to the state's right to rule. The question is how do these movements frame their opposition to the state? Even with the importance of material struggles in people's lives, one of the more crucial elements uniting these varied constituencies is the urgency to move beyond questions of survival to, as Joan French has argued, 'creating, building community, deepening the understanding of oneself and of others, developing local, regional, and international structures for communication and participation'.[30] The focus of the challenges, therefore, is to transform the nature and definition of development from profit and exploitation to holistic, participatory models, the maps of which are still being worked out.[31] Not surprisingly, the most sustained, organized challenges have originated within non-governmental organizations, a loose affiliation of groups of trade unions, Churches and grass-roots organizations. Farmers' co-operatives not only challenge the state with a model of collective agricultural production, very dissimilar to the corporate profit model, but also, under difficult conditions, they are doing what the state has refused to do: feed the population. A regional feminist movement in the Caribbean as a whole and specific movements in both countries have developed some of the most sustained critiques of the devastating effects of structural adjustment as state violence. They have argued that unemployment has destroyed the identity of the male 'provider', resulting in increased violence against women for which they hold the state accountable.

State nationalism, globalization and privatization

State-supported globalization of capital is crucial not only because of the internal political effects I outlined earlier, but also because these international processes help to refigure definitions of masculinity and femininity and simultaneously undermine the ideological bases upon which the state organizes, separates and draws from the 'public' and 'private' domains. International practices dovetail with state ideologies about masculinity and femininity, and in particular with ideological constructions of women's work. The most significant retrenchment with the adoption of SAP has taken place in those sectors which have been historically coded as women's work: health, clinic and hospital service, caring for the sick and elderly, social services and education. As women continue their work in the home and their work in the private or public service sector, they work, in addition, to care for the sick and elderly, and to continue the education of their children without state subsidies. The state relies upon and operates within these dominant constructions of a servile femininity, perennially willing and able to serve, a femininity that can automatically fill the gaps left by the state. Quite the opposite of a 'non-productive' femininity drawn in the legislation, these are women doing work, and ironically, state work.

International ideological registers are significant in another important regard that has to do with the presumed disjuncture between the 'public' and 'private' spheres. In one sense, one of the effects of a privatized state is that it becomes somewhat insulated from 'public' demands; what was 'public' responsibility is now shifted elsewhere, in this case on to women, who compensate for retrenchment in both spheres. But there is also a paradoxical collapse of this dichotomy, for the state is now relying upon the private – private capital and private households – to consolidate its own quest for economic and political power. We know that the household has been an important ideological instrument for the state. It has been indispensable in the creation of the 'public' against which it can be positioned. Because it has been an important space where a particular kind of hierarchical, patriarchal power has resided, the state must move to rehabilitate this sphere by specifically recoding women's experience of domestic violence and rape within it, and generally, by disallowing any household space for lesbians. Yet state economic practices are contributing to the demise of the 'male breadwinner' especially in working-class and working-poor households which are the ones hardest hit by SAP, and in a racialized context are actually intervening to fix racial polarities as well.

We can now return to one of the central paradoxes this chapter raises, that of the nationalist state legislating against certain sexualities while relying upon women's sexualized body and a political economy of desire in private capital accumulation. Tourism is the arena in which the moves to privatize the economy through foreign investment, imperial constructions of masculinity and femininity and state constructions of sexualized woman all intersect.

The significance of tourism is that it foregrounds sexual pleasure as a commodity, based in the sexualization of land (through the old imperial trope woman-as-nation) and people. The sinister drama finds expression in commercial advertising and the production of certain fetishes that get signified as 'culture'. Bahama Mama (there is no Bahama Papa) is a buxom, caricatured, hypersensual-ized figure that can be bought in the Bahamas; she can also be consumed as 'hot and spicy sausage' at any 'Nice and Easy' convenient store in the United States. Tourists upon their return home can continue to be intoxicated by the Bahamas, order Bloody Mary along with Bahama Mama, alterity as instrument of pleasure. European fantasies of colonial conquest, the exotic, the erotic, the dark, the primitive, of danger, dread and desire all converge here on virgin beaches and are traced back through the contours of imperial geography.

How does one prepare citizens for self-determination and for dependence on its antithesis, tourism, the practice of servility and serviceability, the production of maids, washers, cooks? Black women who must braid white women's hair in the market as they flirt with Blackness, for African styles can only be adopted far away from home. Difference is exotically and fleetingly adopted. These are a complicated set of psycho-sexual gestures converging in this (hetero)sexual play ground; this arena which Caribbean state managers see as the economy of the future; where Black masculinity manages phantasmic constructions of Black femininity, satisfying white European desire for restless adventure, satisfying white European longing for what is 'rare and intangible'.[32]

Mobilizing heterosexuality: postcolonial states and practices of decolonization

My analysis suggests that the archetypal source of state legitimation is anchored in the heterosexual family, the form of family crucial in the state's view to the founding of the nation. This consolidation of domesticity in the very process of nation-building is the sphere in which a certain kind of instrumental legitimation is housed. There is an evident relationship among monogamous heterosexuality (organic representation of sexuality) nationhood and citizenship. Although presum-ably universal and falling on *every* body, we have seen that it is not just *every* and *any* body, for *some* bodies are not productive enough for the nation. The erosion of heterosexual conjugal monogamy is a perennial source of worry for state managers and so it is invoked and deployed particularly at moments when it is threatened with extinction. Nothing should threaten this sphere; not the single woman, the lesbian, the gay man, the prostitute, the person who is HIV-infected. The state must simultaneously infiltrate this domain in order to recoup its original claim to it. It must continue to legislate its existence.

To whom do state managers believe they have access in mobilizing discourses around conservative, homophobic registers? Do they believe that a large number of citizens can be mobilized in its defence? Clearly, this mobilization serves to reassure different constituencies which historically have been important anchoring points for the state, but have currently lost political ground with feminist critiques of patriarchy. It serves to reassure men, for they are the archetypal citizen, conservative elements and religious constituencies in a context in which the religious provides important explanations for daily life, and in the case of the Bahamas, the potential tourist who presumably would not encounter diseased black bodies during his travels. With the globalization of specific definitions of morality, the state believes itself able to conform to the international, and in its view to widely accepted and respectable definitions of morality. Even with efforts to reinvoke patriarchal modes of behaviour and patterns of thinking that are familiar and secure, these nationalist states have not been able to solve their legitimation crisis.

Part of the difficulty we face as feminists doing this kind of analysis, and ironically one of the reasons the state can at least be partially successful in mobilizing heterosexuality, is the persistence of the belief in naturalized heterosexuality, the belief that it lies outside of the sphere of political and economic influence and therefore state influence. In the absence of any visible lesbian and gay movements in the Caribbean, state managers believe they can rely upon heterosexuality even more heavily. Our analyses and mobilizations of the naturalization of heterosexuality have perhaps lagged behind analyses of naturalization in other areas, like women's work, for example. We face a challenge to traverse inherited analytic boundaries that have kept us within discrete and narrow formulations. Radical lesbian and gay movements in metropolitan countries which have demystified heterosexuality must now take on board analyses of colonization and imperialism, for the effects of these processes loop back to the centre from which they originated. These movements in metropolitan countries need to work assiduously, however, not to reproduce practices of imperialism. If feminists have analysed the masculinization of the state, it is imperative that we also analyse the heterosexualization of the state, for these are twin processes. The urgency of a research and political agenda that continues to make the processes of heterosexualization transparent, tying them to both national and international social interests, cannot, therefore, be overstated. If sexualization and internationalization have been linked in the strategies of domination, *we* must link them in our strategies for liberation, although admittedly along different registers.[33] It might help to reduce the impulse to conflate capitalism with democracy and the more pervasive feminist theorizing of liberal *democratic* advanced capitalist states.

More work needs to be done in disentangling the state from the nation and in figuring out differing interests. If indeed our political mobilizations are located between the spaces of state and nation, even state and party, we would need to be clearer about our allegiances and the political bases of solidarity. The analysis should help point to the political responsibility feminists inside the state apparatus have to those on the outside. At the same time, we cannot diminish the intensity of our demands to make the state more accountable.

It is both analytically, and therefore politically necessary to disentangle the processes of decolonization and nation-building. In a real sense, the work of decolonization (the dismantling of the economic, political, psychic and sexual knowledges and practices that accompanied the first 500 years of conquest) has been disrupted, especially in light of the map I have drawn of these new sexualized strategies of recolonization and the commodification of alienated sexual desire in tourism within nation states that are infiltrated by corporate globalization politics. The work of decolonization consists as well in the decolonization of the body. Women's bodies have been ideologically dismembered within different discourses: the juridical; profit maximization; religious; and the popular.

How do we, in our alternative movements, construct a collectively imagined future that takes account of these dismemberments, fractures, migrations, exiles and displacements that have been part of these processes of domination? How do we construct home when home is not immediately understood nor instinctively accessible? Our challenge within oppositional movements is to invent home in different spaces that cross geography. We cannot afford to let the international be one-sidedly pernicious.

Notes

From the *Feminist Review*, 48 (autumn 1994), 6–23. Projects like the one I have undertaken could only survive in an 'intellectual neighbourhood' (the phrase is Toni Morrison's). I am especially thankful to my neighbours Chandra Talpade Mohanty, Linda Carty, Honor Ford Smith, Jinny Chalmers and Mab Segrest for their keen insights, support and friendship. I also wish to thank David Trottman, Angela Robertson and the members of the *Feminist Review* Collective.

1 Ruthann Robson, *Lesbian (Out)law: Survival under the Rule of Law* (Ithaca NY: Firebrand, 1992), p. 58.
2 Stuart Hall, paper presented at conference 'Race Matters: Black Americans, US Terrain', Princeton University, 1994.
3 Geraldine Heng and Devan (1992).
4 Luce Irigaray, *This Sex which is not One* (New York: Cornell University Press, 1985).
5 Ed Cohen, 'Legislating the Norm: from Sodomy to gross Indecency', *South Atalantic Quarterly*, 88:1 (1989), 181-218.
   Geraldine Heng (1992).
7 Kobenu Mercer and Isaac Julien, 'Race, Sexual Politics and Black Masculinity: a Dossier', in Rowena Chapman and Jonathan Rutherford, eds, *Male Order: Unwrapping Masculinity* (London: Lawrence & Wishart, 1988), pp. 132-5.
8 Michael Burawoy, *Manufacturing Consent: Changes in the Labor Process under Monopoly Capitalism* (Chicago IL: University of Chicago Press, 1982).
9 Gail Saunders, *Slavery in the Bahamas* (Nassau: Nassau Guardian, 1985), p. 2.
10 Saunders, *Slavery in the Bahamas*, p. 8; Elea Goveia, 'The West Indian Slave Laws of the Eighteenth Century' (Mona: University of the West Indies, 1970).
11 Saunders, *Slavery in the Bahamas*, pp. 18, 19; Lorna McDaniel, 'Madame Phillip-O: Reading the Returns of an Eighteenth Century "Free Mulatto Woman" of Grenada' (unpublished MS, 1986).
12 George L. Mosse, *Nationalism and Sexuality: Middle-class Morality and Sexual Norms in modern Europe* (Madison WI: University of Wisconsin Press), pp. 2-10.
13 Saunders, *Slavery in the Bahamas*; Rhoda Reddock, 'Women, Labour and Struggle in Twentieth Century Trinidad and Tobago, 1898-1960' (Ph.D. dissertation, Amsterdam, 1984), p. 245.

14 Hon. L. O. Pindling, 'Speech at the Opening Session of the Bahamas Independence Conference' (London: HMSO, 1972).

15 Eric Williams, 'We are independent', in Paul K. Sutton, ed., *Forged from the Love of Liberty: Selected Speeches of Dr Eric Williams* (Port of Spain: Longman Caribbean, 1962).

16 Michael Craton, *A History of the Bahamas* (Canada: San Salvador, 1986).

17 Toni Morrison, ed., *Race-ing Justice, En-gendering Power: Essays on Anita Hill, Clarence Thomas, and the Construction of Social Reality* (New York: Pantheon, 1992).

18 Heng and Devan (1992), pp. 343-64.

19 Thanh-Dam Truong, *Sex, Money and Morality* (London: Zed Press, 1990), pp. 158-91.

20 Benedict Anderson, *Imagined Communities: Reflections on the Origin and Spread of Nationalism* (London: Verso, 1983).

21 Peter Gibbon, *Population and Poverty in the Changing Ideology of the World Bank*, PROP Publications series 2 (Stockholm: PROP, 1992).

22 Kathy McAfee, *Storm Signals: Structural Adjustment and Development Alternatives in the Caribbean* (Boston MA: South End Press, 1991), pp. 67-9.

23 Jane Rothenberg and Amy Wishner, 'Focus on Trinidad', *NACLA* (July–August 1978), 16-29.

24 Department of Statistics, *A Collection of Statistics on Women in the Bahamas, 1979-85* (Bahamas: Department of Statistics, 1987); *Labour Force and the Household Income Report, 1989* (Bahamas: Department of Statistics, 1991).

25 Ralph Henry and Gwendolyn Williams, 'Structural Adjustment and Gender in Trinidad and Tobago' in Selwyn Ryan, ed., *Social and Occupational Stratification in Contemporary Trinidad and Tobago* (Jamaica: ISER, 1991), p. 315.

26 Tom Barry *et al.*, *The other Side of Paradise: Foreign Control in the Caribbean* (New York: Grove, 1984), p. 19.

27 Jeffrey A. Rosensweig, 'Elasticities of Substitution in Caribbean Tourism', *Journal of Development Economics* 29:2 (1988), 89-100.

28 Barry *et al.*, *The other Side of Paradise*.

29 Smith, Gomez and Willes (1984).

30 McAfee, *Storm Signals*, p. 188.

31 Antrobus, in *ibid.*, p. 187.

32 bell hooks, *Black Looks: Race and Representation* (Boston MA: South End Press, 1992), pp. 21-39.

33 Cherrie Moraga, *Loving in the War Years* (Boston MA: South End Press, 1983).

Index